PHILIP'S

STREET ATLAS
Glasgow
and West Central Scotland

First published in 1995 by

Philip's, a division of
Octopus Publishing Group Ltd
2–4 Heron Quays, London E14 4JP

Second colour edition 2002
Second impression with revisions 2003

ISBN 0-540-08277 5 (spiral)

© Philip's 2003

 Ordnance Survey®

This product includes mapping data licensed from Ordnance Survey® with the permission of the Controller of Her Majesty's Stationery Office. © Crown copyright 2003. All rights reserved. Licence number 100011710.

Printed and bound in Spain
by Cayfosa-Quebecor

Contents

Digital Data

The exceptionally high-quality mapping found in this atlas is available as digital data in TIFF format, which is easily convertible to other bitmapped (raster) image formats.

The index is also available in digital form as a standard database table. It contains all the details found in the printed index together with the National Grid reference for the map square in which each entry is named.

For further information and to discuss your requirements, please contact Philip's on 020 7644 6932 or james.mann@philips-maps.co.uk

Key to map symbols

(22a)	**Motorway** with junction number
	Primary route – dual/single carriageway
	A road – dual/single carriageway
	B road – dual/single carriageway
	Minor road – dual/single carriageway
	Other minor road – dual/single carriageway
	Tunnel, covered road
	Road under construction
	Pedestrianised area
DY7	**Postcode boundaries**
	County and unitary authority boundaries
	Railway, railway under construction
	Tramway, tramway under construction
	Miniature railway
	Rural track, private road or narrow road in urban area
	Gate or obstruction to traffic (restrictions may not apply at all times or to all vehicles)
	Path, bridleway, byway open to all traffic, road used as a public path
58 / 230 / 241	**Adjoining page indicators**
	The map area within the pink band is shown at a larger scale on the page indicated by the red block and arrow

Acad	**Academy**	Mkt	**Market**
Allot Gdns	**Allotments**	Meml	**Memorial**
Cemy	**Cemetery**	Mon	**Monument**
C Ctr	**Civic Centre**	Mus	**Museum**
CH	**Club House**	Obsy	**Observatory**
Coll	**College**	Pal	**Royal Palace**
Crem	**Crematorium**	PH	**Public House**
Ent	**Enterprise**	Recn Gd	**Recreation Ground**
Ex H	**Exhibition Hall**	Resr	**Reservoir**
Ind Est	**Industrial Estate**	Ret Pk	**Retail Park**
IRB Sta	**Inshore Rescue Boat Station**	Sch	**School**
		Sh Ctr	**Shopping Centre**
Inst	**Institute**	TH	**Town Hall/House**
Ct	**Law Court**	Trad Est	**Trading Estate**
L Ctr	**Leisure Centre**	Univ	**University**
LC	**Level Crossing**	Wks	**Works**
Liby	**Library**	YH	**Youth Hostel**

Walsall	**Railway station**
	Private railway station
South Shields	**Metro station**
	Tram stop, tram stop under construction
	Bus, coach station
	Ambulance station
	Coastguard station
	Fire station
	Police station
	Accident and Emergency entrance to hospital
H	**Hospital**
+	**Place of worship**
i	**Information Centre** (open all year)
P	**Parking**
P&R	**Park and Ride**
PO	**Post Office**
X	**Camping site**
	Caravan site
	Picnic site
Prim Sch	**Important buildings, schools, colleges, universities and hospitals**
River Medway	**Water name**
	River, stream
	Lock, weir
	Water
	Tidal water
	Woods
	Built up area
Church	**Non-Roman antiquity**
ROMAN FORT	**Roman antiquity**

■ The small numbers around the edges of the maps identify the 1 kilometre National Grid lines

■ The dark grey border on the inside edge of some pages indicates that the mapping does not continue onto the adjacent page

The scale of the maps on the pages numbered in blue is 5.52 cm to 1 km • 3½ inches to 1 mile • 1: 18103	0 ¼ ½ ¾ 1 mile 0 250 m 500 m 750 m 1 kilometre
The scale of the maps on pages numbered in red is 11.04 cm to 1 km • 7 inches to 1 mile • 1: 9051.4	0 220 yards 440 yards 660 yards ½ mile 0 125 m 250 m 375 m ½ kilometre

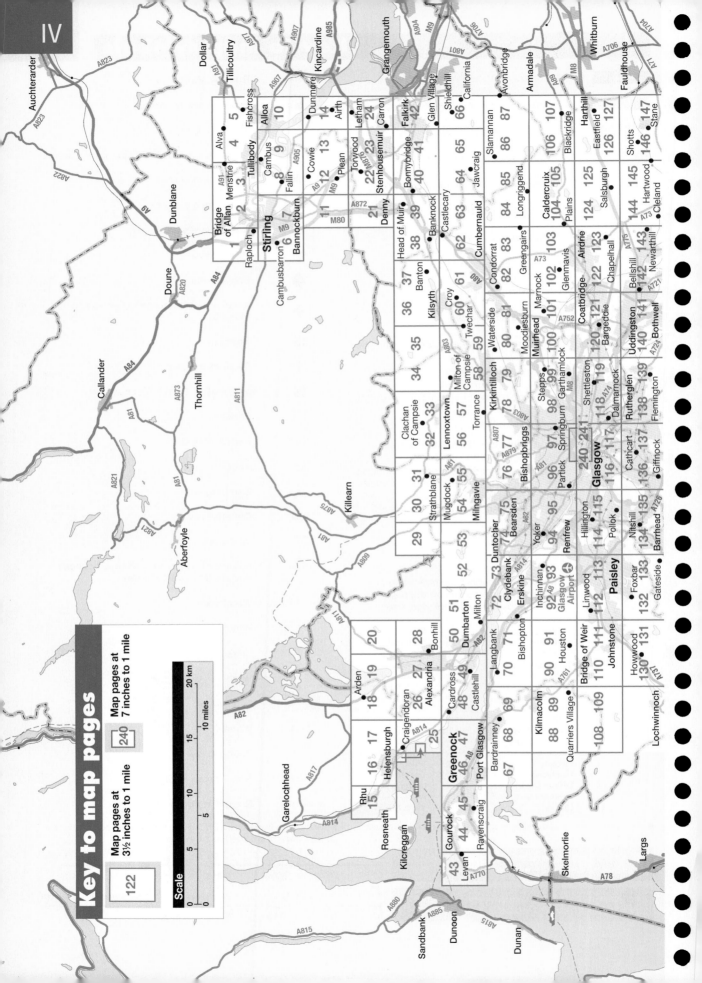

IV

Key to map pages

| 122 | Map pages at 3½ inches to 1 mile |
| 240 | Map pages at 7 inches to 1 mile |

Scale

0 — 5 — 10 — 15 — 20 km

0 — 5 — 10 miles

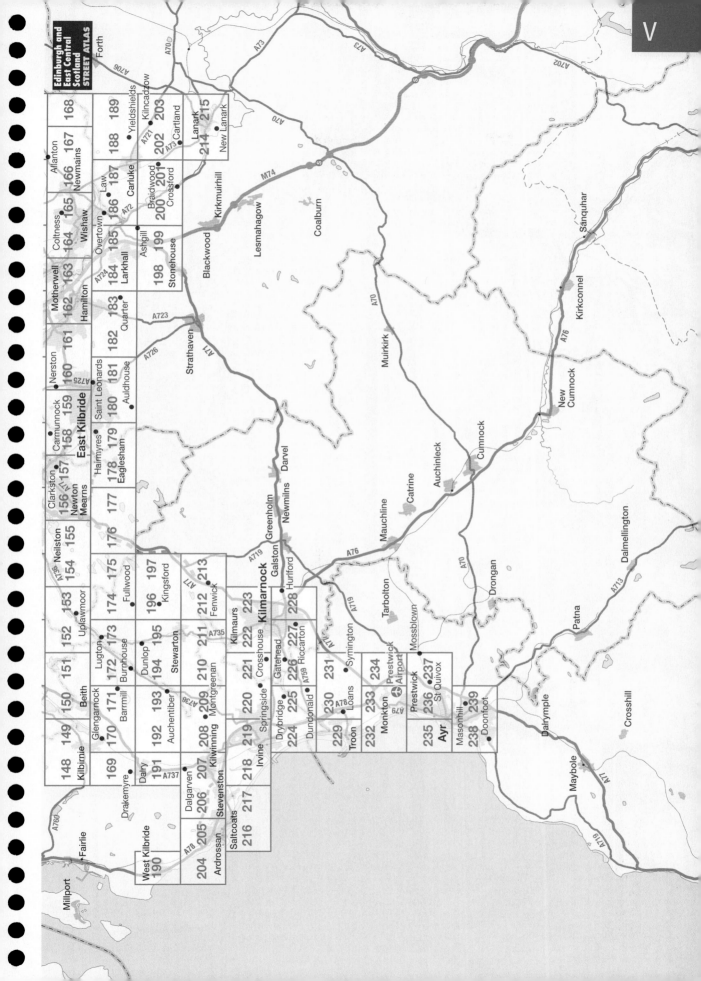

Edinburgh and East Central Scotland STREET ATLAS

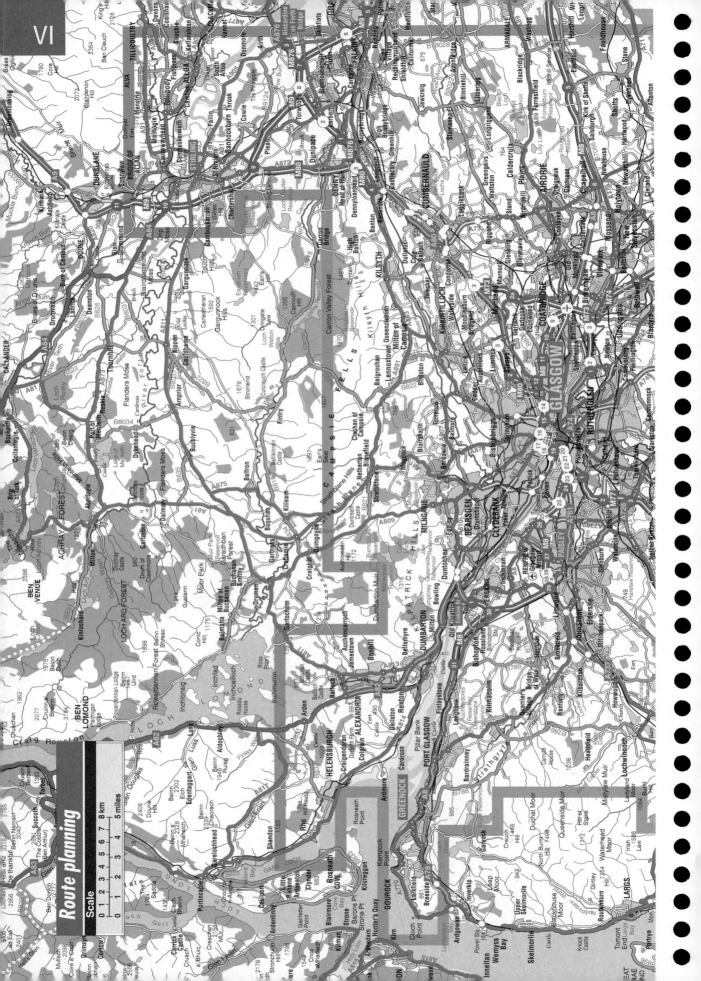

Route planning

Scale

| 0 1 2 3 4 5 6 7 8 km |
| 0 1 2 3 4 5 miles |

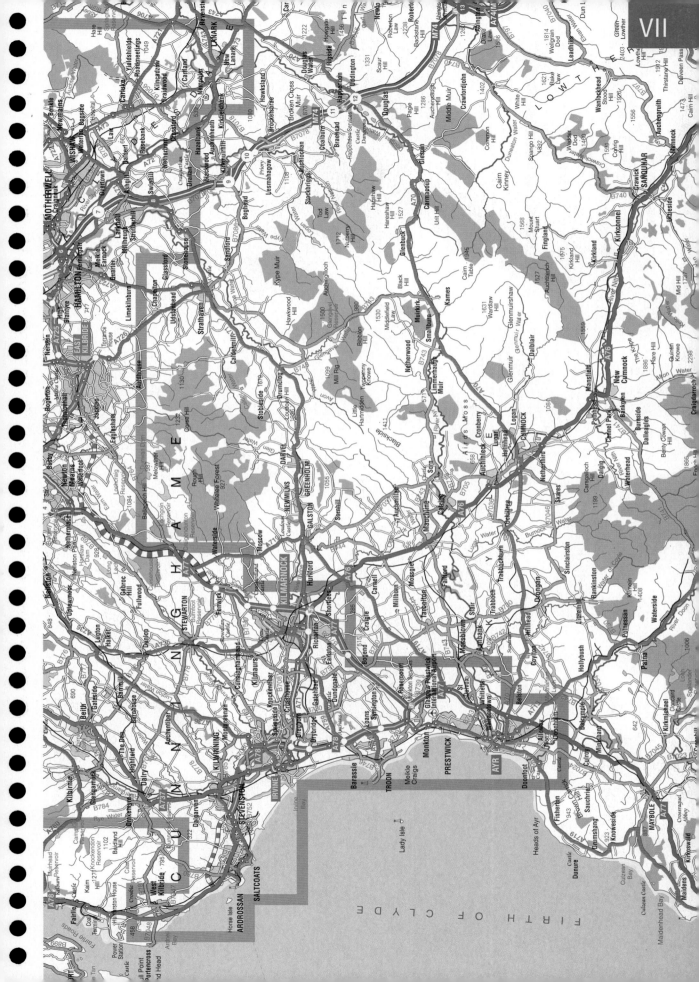

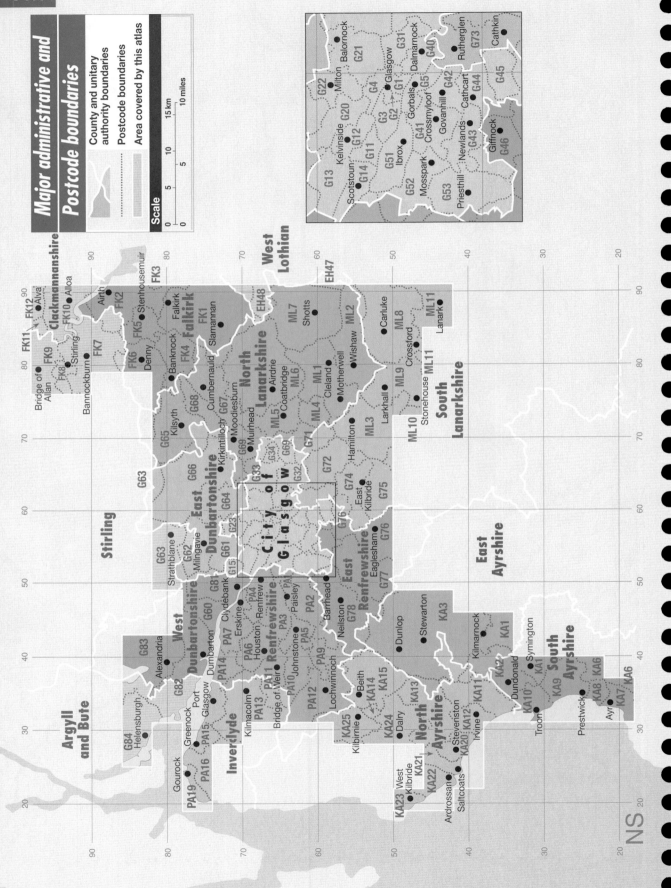

Major administrative and Postcode boundaries

County and unitary authority boundaries

Postcode boundaries

Area covered by this atlas

Scale

0 5 10 15 km
0 5 10 miles

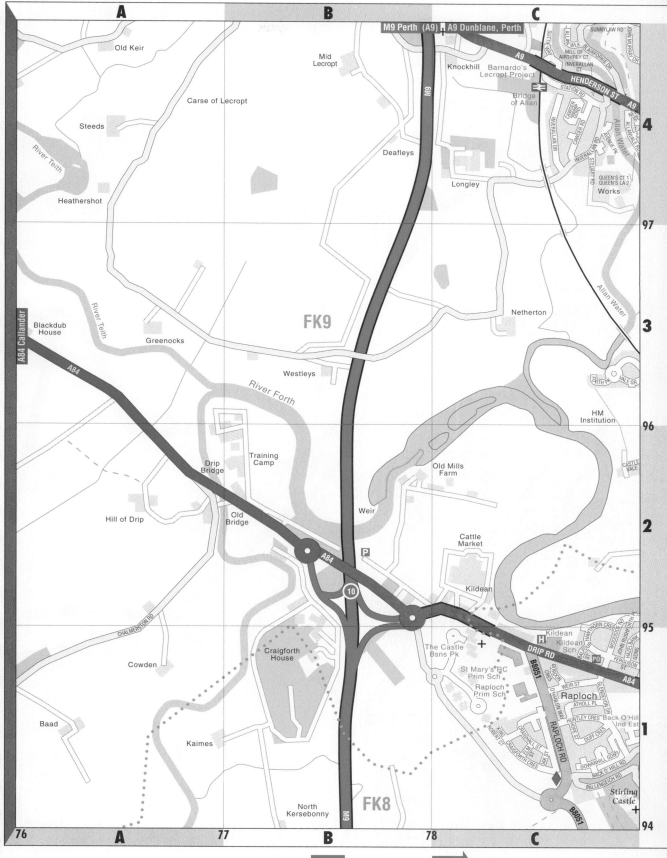

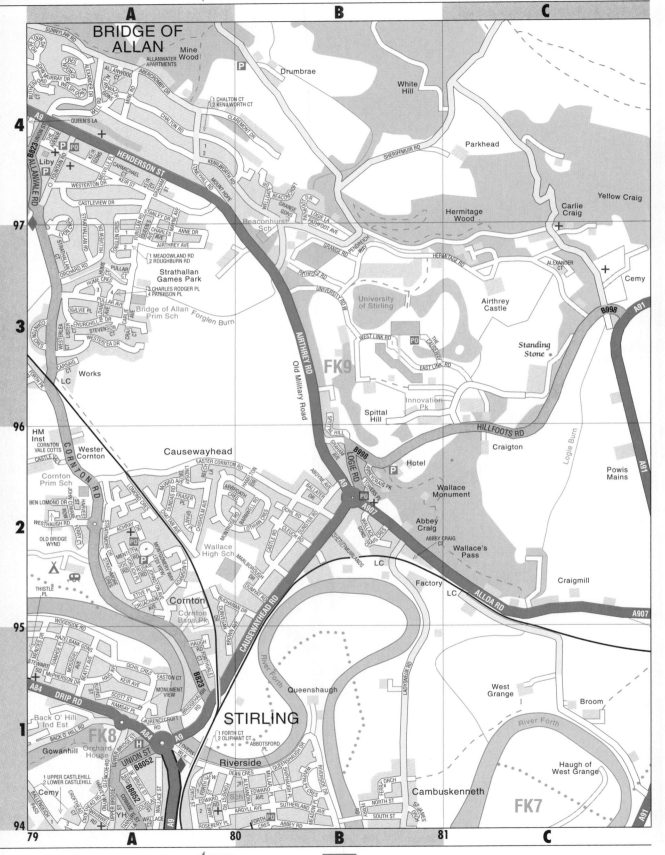

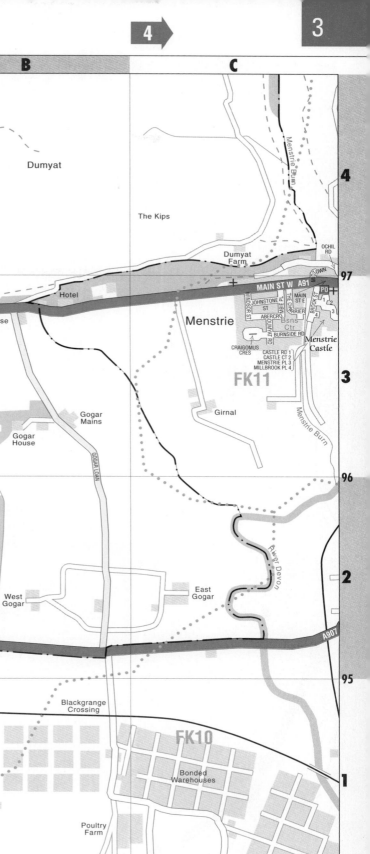

A   B   C

Dumyat

Castle
Law

Ewe Lairs

The Kips

Craig Gullies

Menstrie Burn

Dumyat
Farm

OCHIL
RD

The Blair

97

Hotel

MAIN ST W A91

P

Cotkerse

Blairlogie

JOHNSTONE PL
ST

WINDSOR ST

THE CHARRIER

MAIN
ST E

BROOK ST

Menstrie

ABERCR

Bsns
Ctr

BURNSIDE RD

CRAIGOMUS
CRES

CASTLE RD 1
CASTLE CT 2
MENSTRIE PL 3
MILLBROOK PL 4

Menstrie
Castle

PO

1
2

3

DUMYAT RD

Logie
Villa

Blair
Mains

FK9

FK11

3

Girnal

Menstrie Burn

Gogar
Mains

MANOR LOAN

Gogar
House

GOGAR LOAN

Powis Burn

96

Powis
House

River Devon

Manor

East
Gogar

2

West
Gogar

Manor
Powis

A907

ALLOA RD

MANOR POWIS
COTTS

Manor
Steps

95

A91

Manorneuk

LC

Blackgrange
Crossing

River Forth

FK10

FK7

Bonded
Warehouses

1

Lower
Taylorton

Poultry
Farm

Garvel

Midtown

94

82   A   83   B   84   C

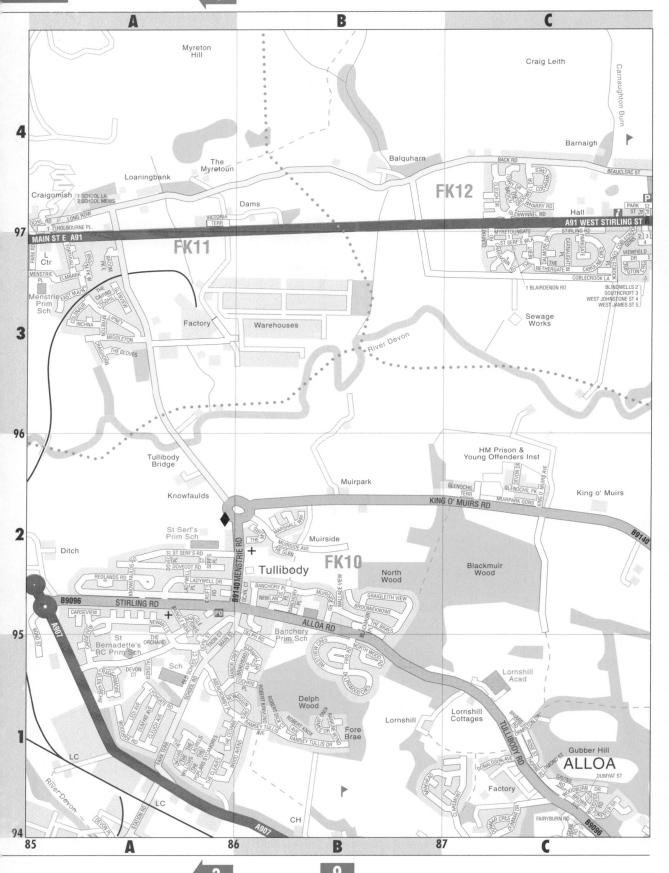

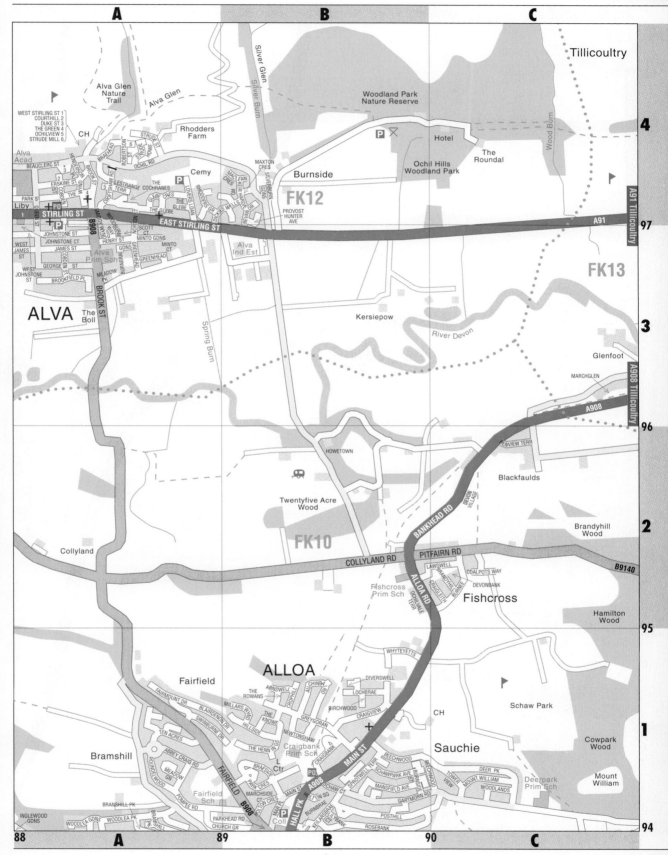

Tillicoultry

Alva Glen Nature Trail

Alva Glen

Silver Glen

Silver Burn

Woodland Park Nature Reserve

Wood Burn

WEST STIRLING ST 1
COURTHILL 2
DUKE ST 3
THE GREEN 4
OCHILVIEW 5
STRUDE MILL 6

CH

Rhodders Farm

P

Hotel

The Roundal

Alva Acad

BEAUCLERC ST

Cemy

MAXTON CRES

Burnside

Ochil Hills Woodland Park

FK12

4

A91 Tillicoultry

PARK ST

Liby

STIRLING ST

P

EAST STIRLING ST

PROVOST HUNTER AVE

A91

97

WEST JAMES ST

JOHNSTONE ST
JOHNSTONE CT
JAMES ST

Alva Ind Est

FK13

WEST JOHNSTONE ST

GEORGE ST

BROOKFIELD PL

Alva Prim Sch

GREENHEAD

B908

ALVA

The Boll

BROOK ST

Kersiepow

River Devon

Glenfoot

A908 Tillicoultry

Spring Burn

MARCHGLEN

3

96

A908

Collyland

HOWETOWN

BEAVIEW TERR

Blackfaulds

Brandyhill Wood

Twentyfive Acre Wood

FK10

BANKHEAD RD

DEVON VILLAGE

2

B9140

Collyland

COLLYLAND RD

PITFAIRN RD

LAWSWELL

COALPOTS WAY

DEVONBANK

Hamilton Wood

Fishcross Prim Sch

ALLOA RD

OCHILVALE TERR

BRANDYTHLL

CRAIGLEITH

BURKE

Fishcross

95

Fairfield

ALLOA

FAIRMOUNT DR

THE ROWANS

ARNSWELL

CHIPHILL

AUCHINBAE

DIVERSWELL

WHYTEYETTS

CH

Schaw Park

Cowpark Wood

BLAIRDENON DR

MILLARS WYND

THE KNOWE

HILLSIDE

GREYGORAN

BIRCHWOOD

LOCHBRAE

CRAIGVIEW

1

SWINBURNE DR

NEWTONSHAW

TEN ACRES

ABBEY CRAIG RD

MEADOW GN

RUNREE WOOD

Bramshill

THE HENN

Craigbank Prim Sch

Ctr

CRAIGBANK

PO

MAIN ST

BEECHWOOD

SCHAWPARK AVE

BEECHWOOD

DEER PK

TOWER VIEW

MOUNT WILLIAM

Sauchie

Deerpark Prim Sch

Mount William

FAIRFIELD

BRASIDE

PARK CRES

MARCHSIDE

GLEN CRES

SPROTTWELL TERR

MANSFIELD AVE

WOODLANDS

BRANSHILL PK

INGLEWOOD GDNS

WOODLEA GDNS

WOODLEA PK

B908

Fairfield Sch

POMPEE RD

PARKHEAD RD

CHURCH GR

P

Coll

HALL PK

A908

SCHAW CT

HOLTON SQ

BURNBRAE

KELLARSBRAE

BANK

POSTHILL

GARTMORN RD

ROSEBANK

94

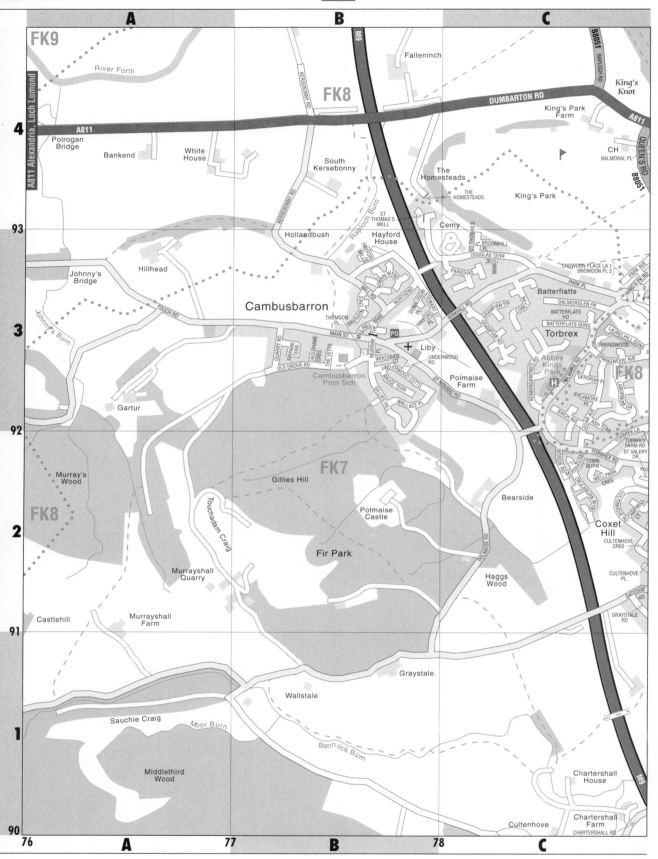

FK9

River Forth

FK8

M9

Falleninch

B8051

RAPLOCH RD

King's Knot

DUMBARTON RD

King's Park Farm

A811

4

A811

Polrogan Bridge

Bankend

White House

South Kersebonny

The Homesteads

CH BALMORAL PL

QUEEN'S RD

B8051

A811 Alexandria, Loch Lomond

THE HOMESTEADS

King's Park

KERSEBONNY RD

KERSEBONNY RD

Hollandbush

ST THOMAS'S WELL

Hayford House

Cemy

ST THOMAS'S

SNOWDON PLACE LA 1
SNOWDON PL 2

PARK AVE

93

BROOMHILL
LPL

Raploch Burn

Douglas Terr

Batterflatts

BATTERFLATS
GDNS

KING'S PK RD

Johnny's Bridge

Hillhead

PARK PL

BATTERFLATS HO

DALMORGLEN PK

PARKDYKE

Torbrex

LAURELHILL GDNS

SPRINGWOOD

FK8

Cambusbarron

THOMSON PL

MILL RD

GRIESON

MILL HILL PL

THE BRAE

BOBBIN WYND

NORTHEND

DONALDSON PL

STEWART ST

HAYFORD PL

BIRKHILL RD

GRAMPIAN RD

CONY PL

GRAMPIAN RD

BATTERFLATS HQ

SPRINGWOOD AVE

TOUCH RD

3

Johnny's Burn

MAIN ST

MURRAY PL

PO

Liby

UNDERWOOD RD

Abbey Kings Park

KENNINGKNOWES RD

KILDEAN RD

DERORAN PL

LABURNAM GR

FK8

QUARRY RD

ARPARK TERR

OLD DROVE RD

CAULDHAME CRES

THE YETTS

WOODSIDE CT

UNDERWOOD COTTS

ST NINIANS RD

Polmaise Farm

H

SYCAMORE PL

CEDAR AVE

BIRCH AVE

ASH TERR

Gartur

Cambusbarron Prim Sch

BRUCE TERR

WALLACE PL

GILLIES HILL

TORBREX LA

TORBREX FARM RD

ST VALERY DR

92

Murray's Wood

Gillies Hill

FK7

Bearside

WYNDE RD

TOWN BURN

MOSSHOLLS

CRICKETON WYND

TORBREX RD

TOWN BURN

WELLPARK CRES

Coxet Hill

CULTENHOVE CRES

CAMPBELL CT

FK8

Touchadam Craig

Polmaise Castle

POLMAISE RD

CULTENHOVE PL

GATESIDE RD

2

Murrayshall Quarry

Fir Park

Haggs Wood

GRAYSTALE RD

Castlehill

Murrayshall Farm

91

Graystale

Wallstale

Sauchie Craig

Moor Burn

1

Bannock Burn

M9

Middlethird Wood

Chartershall House

90

Cultenhove

Chartershall Farm

CHARTERSHALL RD

76 A 77 B 78 C

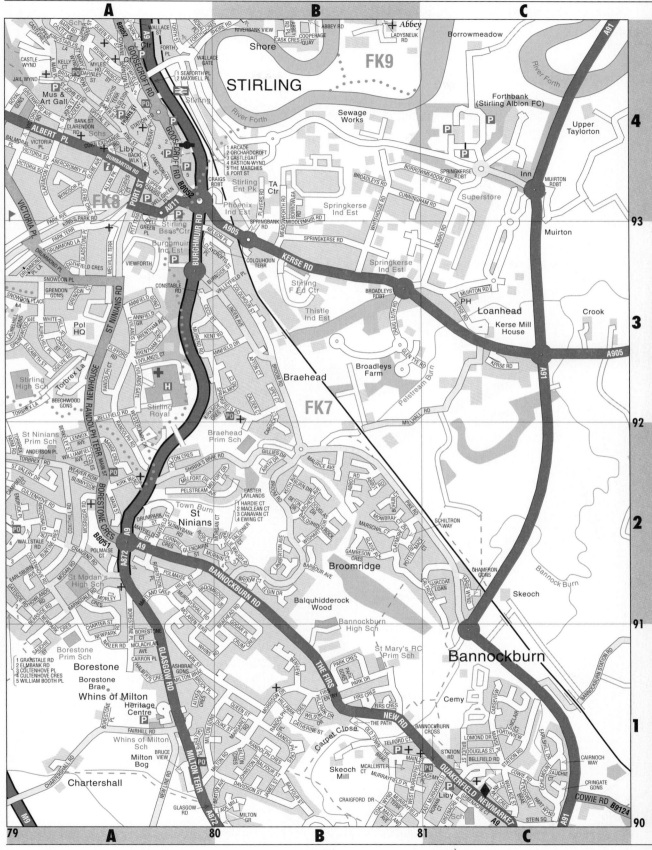

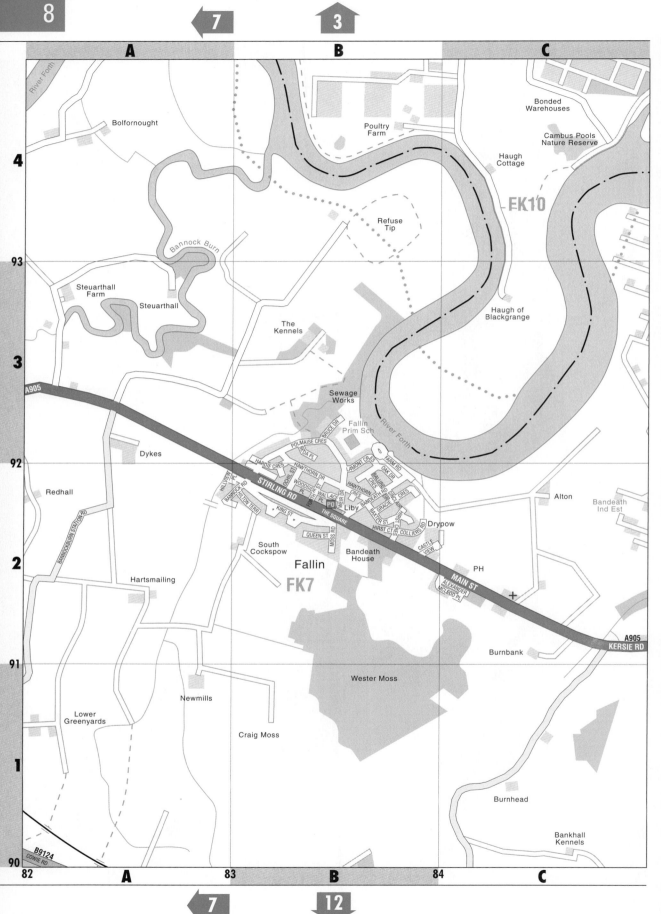

A B C

River Forth

Bolfornought

Poultry Farm

Bonded Warehouses

Cambus Pools Nature Reserve

Haugh Cottage

4

FK10

Bannock Burn

Refuse Tip

93

Steuarthall Farm

Steuarthall

The Kennels

Haugh of Blackgrange

3

A905

Sewage Works

River Forth

Fallin Prim Sch

Dykes

BRUCE DR

POLMAISE CRES

REDA PL

92

Redhall

HARDIE CRES

HAWTHORN DR

LAMONT CRES

OCH...

WOODSIDE PL

HAWTHORN CRES

FARM RD

OAK DR

BALURE CRES

BANDEATH RD

Alton

Bandeath Ind Est

HILLVIEW

BANNOCK RD

CHILTON TERR

STIRLING RD

FORTH PL

WEIR DR

WALLACE PL

PO

KING ST

THE SQUARE

Liby

GRACIE CRES

BAXTER ST

HIRST CRES

FIRST CRES

COLLIERS RD

CASTLE VIEW

Drypow

QUEEN ST

MOSS RD

South Cockspow

Bandeath House

2

Hartsmailing

Fallin

FK7

MAIN ST

PH

ALEXANDER McLEOD PL

+

A905

KERSIE RD

Burnbank

91

Newmills

Wester Moss

Lower Greenyards

Craig Moss

1

Burnhead

B9124
COWIE RD

Bankhall Kennels

90

82 A 83 B 84 C

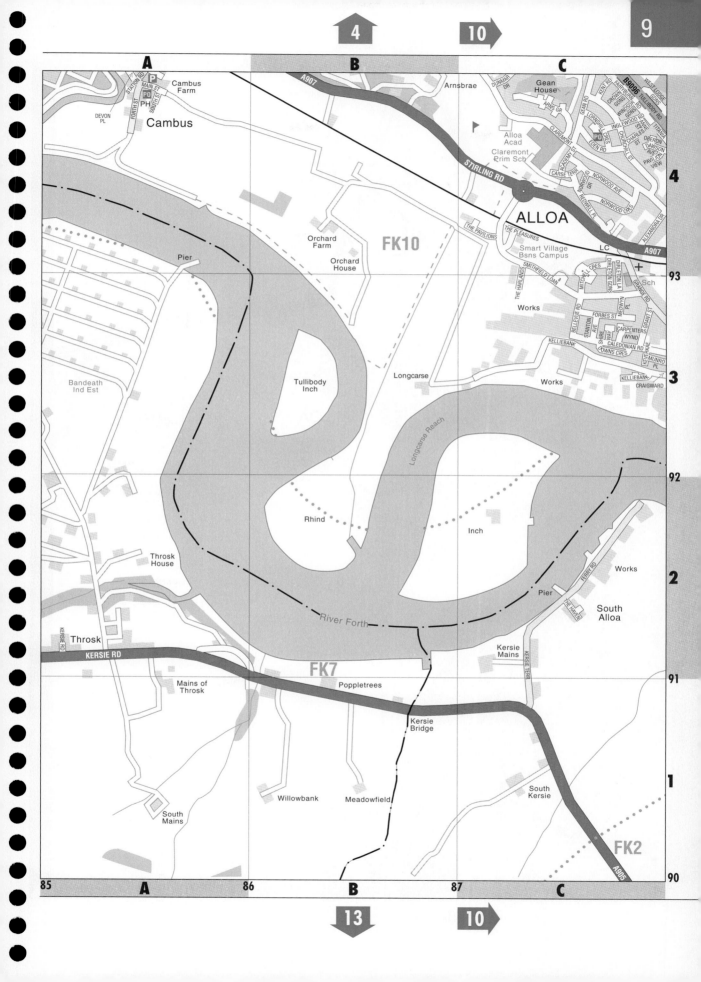

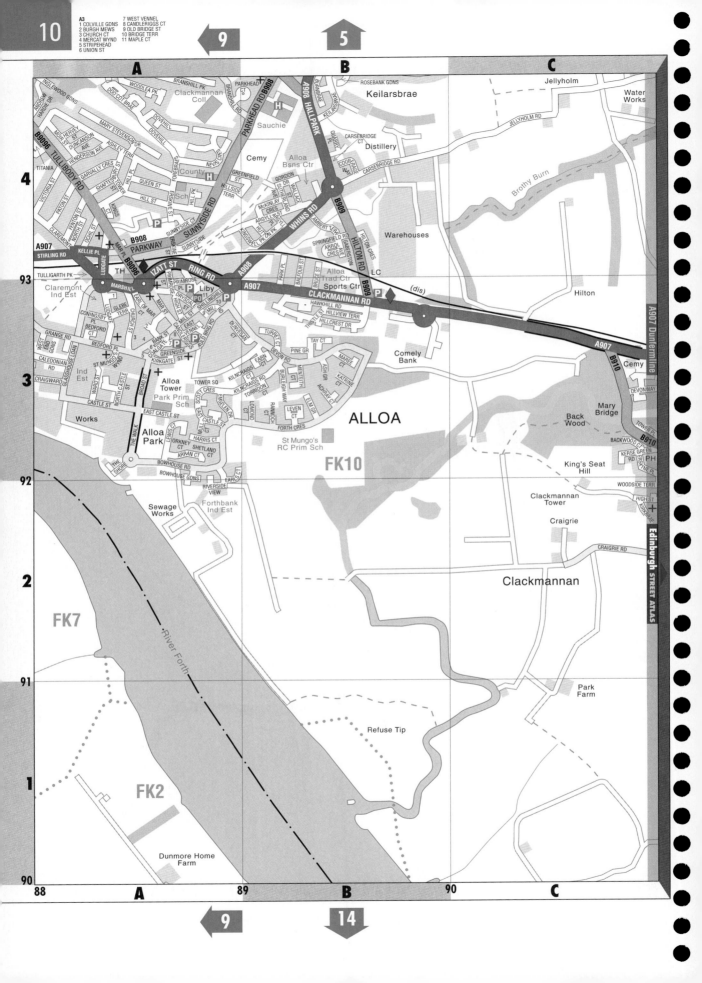

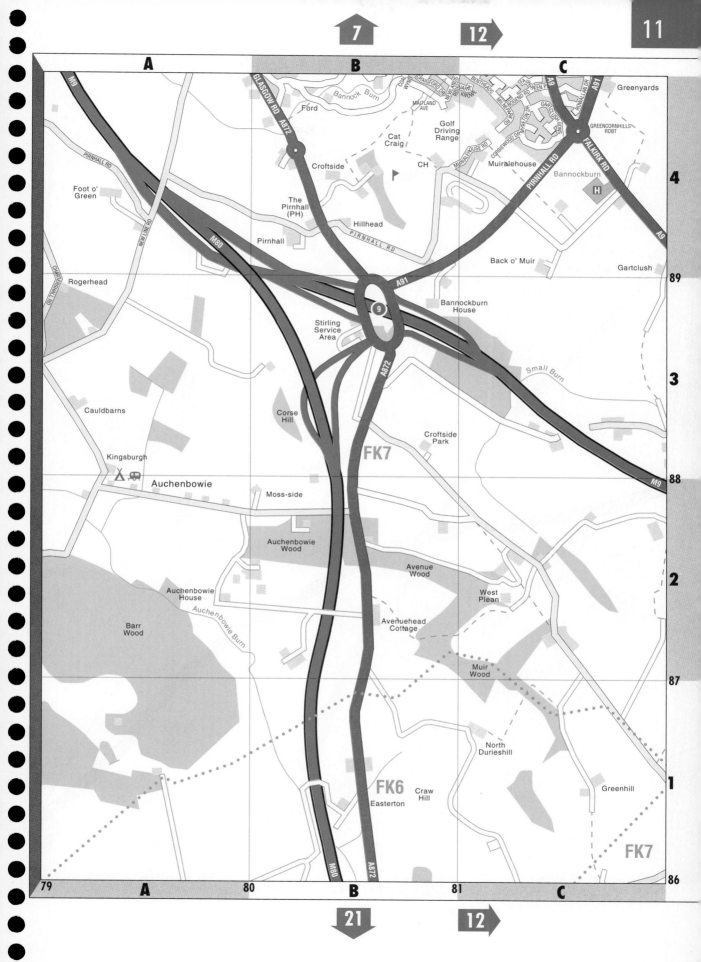

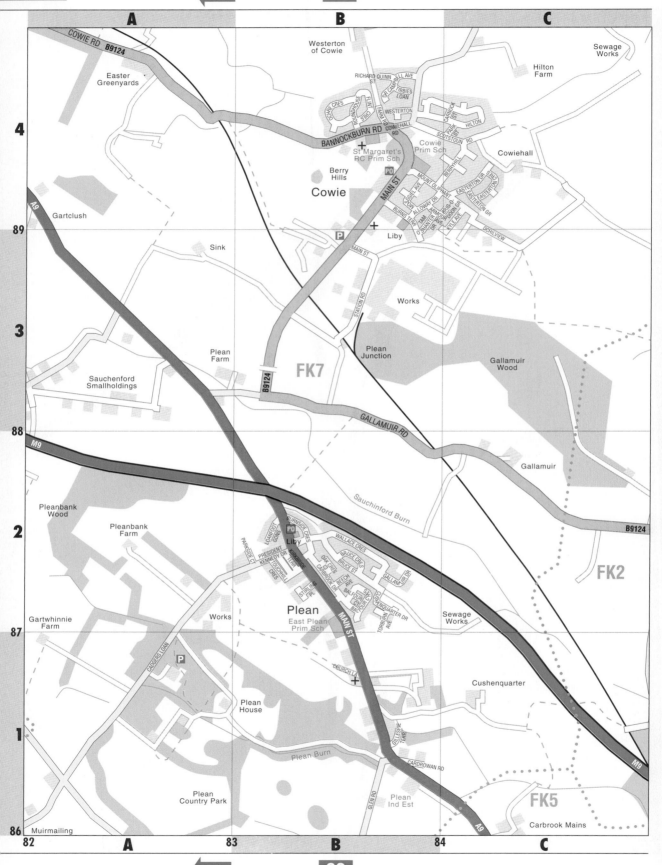

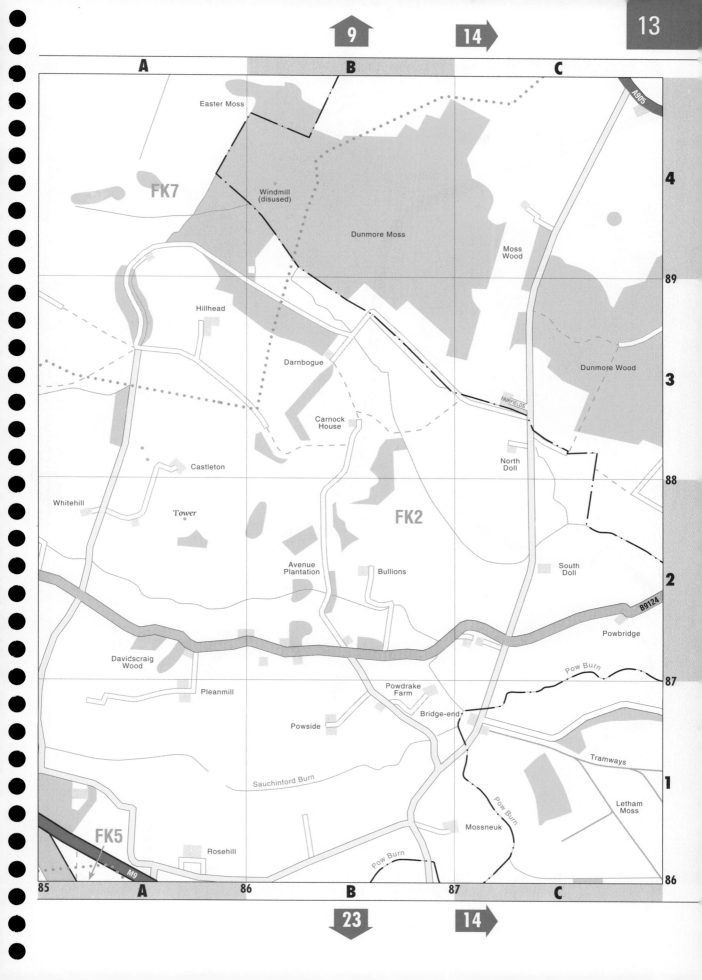

A   **B**   **C**

A905

Inch of Ferryton

Pyetrees Cottages

Loanside

4

Dunmore

ST ANDREW'S DR

FK10

Dunmore Park Farm

Dunmore Park

River Forth

89

Hill of Dunmore

Tower

The Pineapple

3

Dunmore Wood

B9124

SHERLAW GDNS

NORTH GREEN DR

North Greens

CRAWFORD SQ

BANKS VIEW

88

GRAHAM TERR

FK2

WETHERBY RD

SHORE RD

PAUL DR

THE WILDERNESS

GRAHAM TERR

SEA VIEW

Westfield

Dougalshill Farm

Sch

P.O.

Eastfield Farm

B9124

KIRKWAY

DOWER PL

MAIN ST

HIGH ST

S. JOHNSTONE CRES

2

Airth

FORRESTER PL

SOUTH LINN PL

GREEN RD

Hill of Airth

Airth Mains

CASTLE DR

KENNEDY WAY

CASTLE AVE

87

BRUCE GATE

CASTLE VIEW

Airth Castle

Pow Burn

Linkfield Farm

1

Letham Moss

Tramway

Waterslap

Tramway

Tramway

LETHAM TERRS

A905

Bowtrees

A876

SOUTH APPROACH RD

86

88   **A**   89   **B**   90   **C**

Edinburgh STREET ATLAS

A876 Kincardine Bridge,Grangemouth

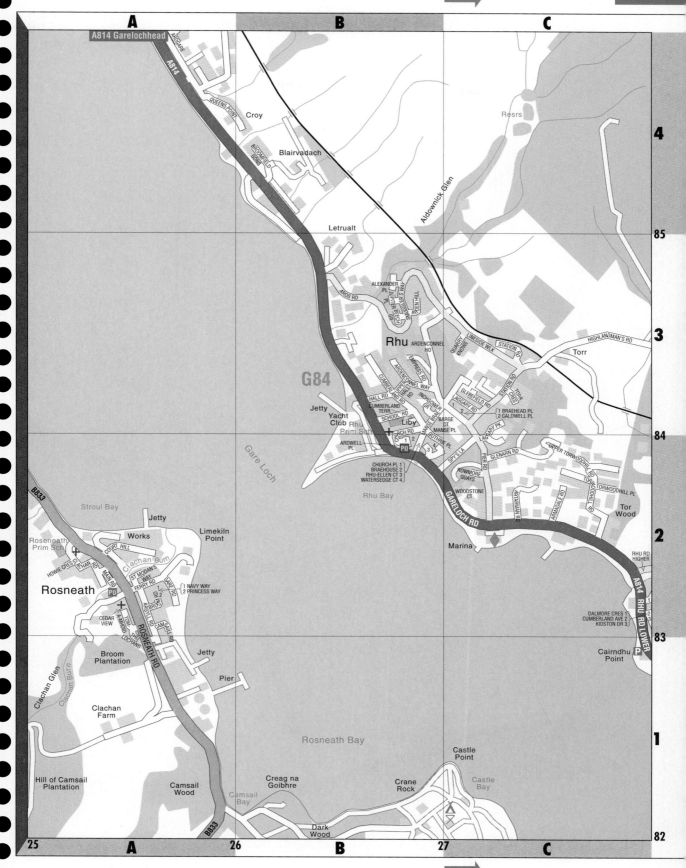

A   B   C

A814 Garelochhead

A814

ARDGARE

QUEENS POINT

Croy

BROOMFIELD GDNS

Blairvadach

Aldownick Glen

Resrs

4

Letrualt

85

AROS RD

ALEXANDER PL

JUPITER BEECH GDN

SWINTONS WAY

ABEN HILL

Rhu

ARDENCONNEL HO

LINESIDE WLK

QUARRY KNOWE

STATION RD

Torr

HIGHLANDMAN'S RD

3

G84

EMPRESS RD

ARDENCONNEL WAY

CUMBERLAND RD

INCHGOWER GR

HALL RD

GLEBFIELD RD

TORR CRES

STATION RD

1 BRAEHEAD PL
2 CALDWELL PL

Jetty

Yacht Club

CUMBERLAND TERR

SCHOOL RD

Rhu Prim Sch

SCH RD

MANSE BRAE

BARGE CT

MANSE PL

LAGGARY RD

LAGGARY PK

PIER RD

GLENARN RD

UPPER TORWOODHILL RD

TORWOODHILL RD

TORWOODHILL PL

84

Gare Loch

Liby

ARDWELL PL

GUTHRIE PL

SPY'S LA

Po

CHURCH PL 1
BRAEHOUSE 2
RHU-ELLEN CT 3
WATERSEDGE CT 4

ROWMORE QUAYS

ARTARMAN RD

ARMADALE RD

Tor Wood

2

Rhu Bay

WOODSTONE CT

GARELOCH RD

Marina

RHU RD HIGHER

A814 RHU RD LOWER

Stroul Bay

Jetty

Works

Limekiln Point

DALMORE CRES 1
CUMBERLAND AVE 2
KIDSTON DR 3

Roseneath Prim Sch

COURT HILL

Clachan Burn

HOWIE CRES

CHAN PL

ST MODAN'S WAY

FERRY RD

GARE RD

1 NAVY WAY
2 PRINCESS WAY

Rosneath

PO

MAIN RD

ARGYLL RD

CAMSAIL RD

P

Cairndhu Point

83

CEDAR VIEW

TEMP

A'CHROID

THE LOCHANS

ROSNEATH RD

Broom Plantation

Jetty

Clachan Glen

Clachan Burn

Pier

Clachan Farm

1

Rosneath Bay

Castle Point

Hill of Camsail Plantation

Camsail Wood

Camsail Bay

Creag na Goibhre

Dark Wood

Crane Rock

Castle Bay

B833

82

25   A   26   B   27   C

A   B   C

4

85

3

84

2

83

1

82

Green Burn

Drumford
Wood

Highlandman's
Wood

Highlandman's Road

Milligs Burn

Reservoir

Ardencaple
Wood

Ardencaple
Farm

G84

Blackhill
Plantation

Reservoirs

LUSS RD

B832

Duchess
Wood

Glennan Burn

The
Hill House

GLENAN RD

MACLEOD DR

PATTERSON CRES

DUCHESS DR

KENNEDY DR

URQUHART
PL

WEST DHUHILL DR

HILLVIEW DR

BLACKHILL DR

GILLESPIE DR

GLEN DR

WEST DHUHILL DR

UPPER COLQUHOUN ST

WEST DOUGLAS DR

SINCLAIR LA

MACLACHLAN
PL

DHUHILL DR E

DUNCAN RD

SINCLAIR DR

HOWFORD DR

ABERCROMBY CRES

McEWAN DR

DALMORE CRES

DALMORE CRES

KATHLEEN PK

DUCHESS PK

ROWALLAN

EDWARD DR

BARCLAY DR

WEST LENNOX DR

WEST ROSSDHU
DR

MUNRO DR W

WEST ABERCROMBY

KILBRIDE DR

DIXON RD

MUNRO DR E

WEST ROSSDHU

BAIN CRES

LEVER RD

EAST LENNOX DR

BOSTON DR

SANNOX PL

MACHRIE DR

EMPRESS

FRAZER AVE

MRS'S LN

STRATHCLYDE
CT

UPPER SUTHERLAND ST 1
LOWER SUTHERLAND CRES 2

QUEEN ST

Lomond
Jun Sch

Helensburgh
Upper

EAST ROSSDHU DR

ST ANDREWS

ABERCROMBY ST

CORRIE PL

CH

RHU ROAD HIGHER

Castle
Wood

CUMBERLAND AVE

HOOD
CT

HYLAND CT

BANNACHRA DR

UPPER SUTHERLAND CRES

STAFFORD ST W

MILLIG ST

CAMPBELL ST

Lomond
Sch

JOHN ST

STAFFORD ST E

DRUMDOON

GOLFHILL DR

LAMLASH
PL

PINNMILL
PL

SHISKINE
PL

ARDENCAPLE DR

CASTLE LOCHT DR

KIDSTON DR

ARDENCAPLE QUAD

SUTHERLAND

SUFFOLK ST

GLASGOW ST

WEST MONTROSE ST

JOHN STREET LA

Liby

LARCHFIELD

COLQUHOUN ST

Parklands
Sch

VICTORIA RD

PRINCE ALBERT
TERR

ALBERT ST

ALBERT ST

KILDONAN DR

PLADDA ST

LOCHRANZA DR

Sch

P

RHU RD LOWER

CAIRNDHU GDNS

BAIRD AVE

COULPORT

COURTRAI
AVE

SUTHERLAND

WEST KING ST

WILLIAM ST

ARGYLE ST W

GLENAN
GDNS

JAMES ST

WAVERLEY
CT

COLQ

Hermitage
Prim Sch

BIRCH
COTTS

ST MICHAEL

CHARLOTTE ST

UPPER
GLENFINLAS

HAVELOCK ST

Sch
TOWNHEAD
RD

MALCOLM

HAVELOCK PL

MAUSLAN PL

KING'S RD

BEN BOUIE DR

STRATHCLYDE PL 1
MACAULAY PL 2
COVE PL 3
ROSENEATH DR 4

FERNIEGAIR AVE

5 BONAR LAW AVE
6 CAMSAIL AVE
7 SUTHERLAND PL
8 WESTBORNE GDNS

WEST PRINCES ST

WEST CLYDE ST

LORNE ST

GRANT ST

ARGYLE ST E

LOMOND ST

EAST MONTROSE ST

GEORGE ST

KING'S CRES

ADELAIDE

ST

KING ST E

GRANVILLE ST

Victoria

OLD LUSS RD

JOHNSTON

HELENSBURGH

PRINCESS CT 1
SCOTT CT 2
COLQUHOUN SQ 3

Swimming
Pool

Pier

TOWER
PL

MAITLAND
CT

B832

MAITLAND ST

EAST PRINCES ST

CLYDE ST E

GRANT ST

COLQUHOUN ST

GEORGE ST

GLENFINLAS ST

Helensburgh
Central

P

PO

A814

JERRY BELL'S ST

MOSSEND
AVE

SOUTH KING ST

MOSSEND
PL

GARRAWAY PL 1
STUCKLECKIE RD 2
ATHOLE ST 3
WILLIAMSON DR 4

H

HANOVER ST 1
ROSEDALE GDNS 2
MILLERSLEA GDNS 3

Cemy

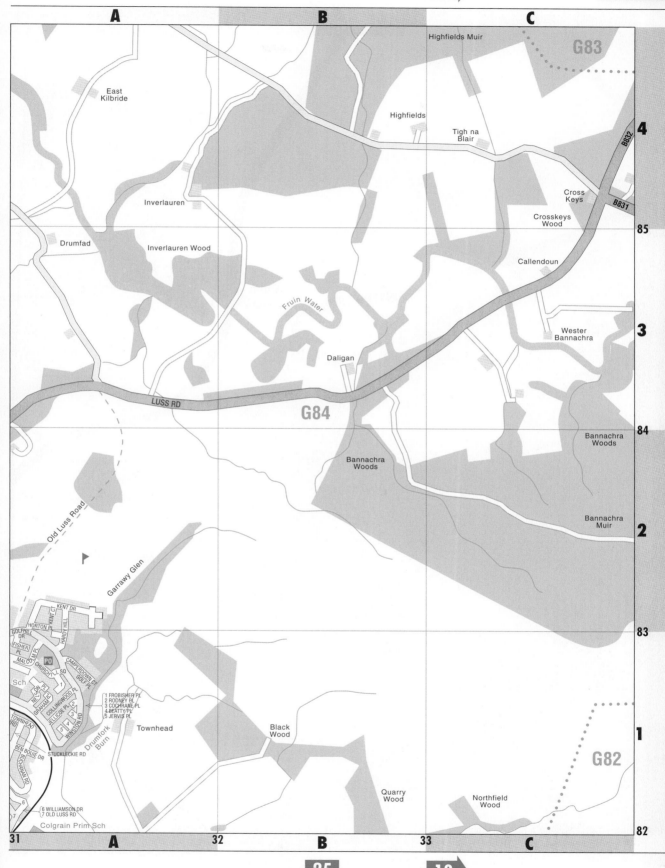

A   B   C

Highfields Muir

G83

East Kilbride

Highfields

Tigh na Blair

B832

4

Inverlauren

Cross Keys

B831

Crosskeys Wood

85

Drumfad

Inverlauren Wood

Callendoun

Fruin Water

Wester Bannachra

3

Daligan

LUSS RD

G84

84

Old Luss Road

Bannachra Woods

Bannachra Woods

Garrawy Glen

Bannachra Muir

2

KENT DR

HORTON PL

GOLFHILL DR

FISHER PL

MALCOLM PL

HARDY HILL

PO

CAMPERDOWN CT

GOLF PL

CHURCH SQ

83

Sch

COLLINGWOOD PL

JELLICOE PL

WINSTON RD

1 FROBISHER PL
2 RODNEY PL
3 COCHRANE PL
4 BEATTY PL
5 JERVIS PL

TOWNHEAD RD

Townhead

Black Wood

DRUMFORK BURN

STUCKLECKIE RD

BEN BOUIE DR

BUCHANAN RD

1

G82

6

7

6 WILLIAMSON DR
7 OLD LUSS RD

Quarry Wood

Northfield Wood

Colgrain Prim Sch

82

31   A   32   B   33   C

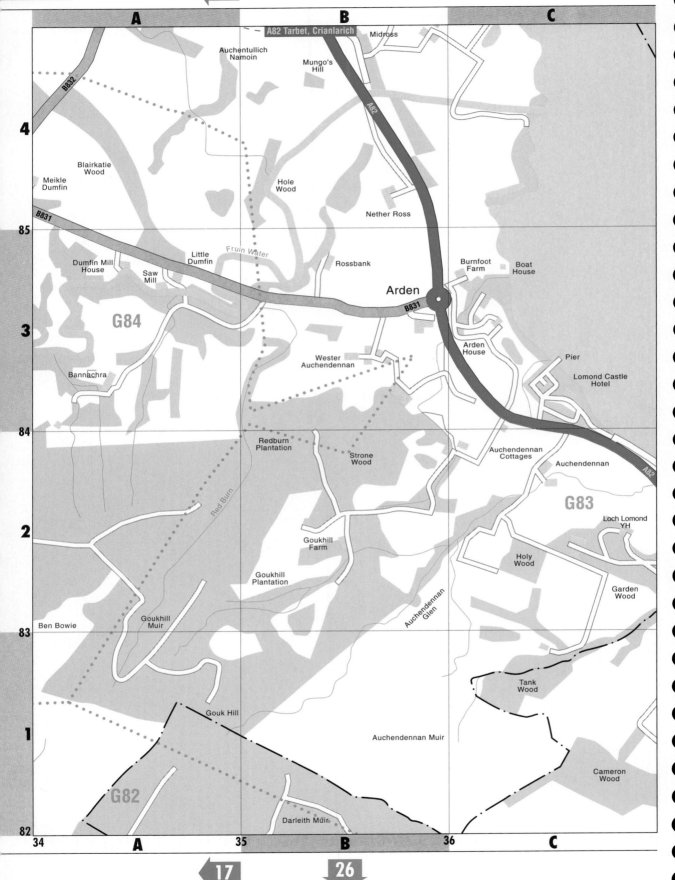

A82 Tarbet, Crianlarich

B   C

A

Midross

Auchentullich
Namoin

Mungo's
Hill

A82

4

Meikle
Dumfin

Blairkatie
Wood

Hole
Wood

Nether Ross

85

B831

Fruin Water

Dumfin Mill
House

Little
Dumfin

Rossbank

Burnfoot
Farm

Boat
House

Saw
Mill

Arden

B831

G84

Arden
House

Pier

Lomond Castle
Hotel

Bannachra

Wester
Auchendennan

84

Redburn
Plantation

Strone
Wood

Auchendennan
Cottages

Auchendennan

Red Burn

G83

Goukhill
Farm

Holy
Wood

Loch Lomond
YH

2

Goukhill
Plantation

Garden
Wood

Ben Bowie

Goukhill
Muir

83

Auchendennan
Glen

Tank
Wood

Gouk Hill

1

Auchendennan Muir

Cameron
Wood

G82

Darleith Muir

82

34   A   35   B   36   C

A B C

Knockour Wood

Lorn

4

Knockour Hill

Black Roundel

85

Boat Houses

Boturich Castle

3

Whinny Hill

Meikle Boturich

G83

84

Burn of Balloch

Ledrishmore Wood

Loch Lomond

Over Balloch

2

Horsehouse Wood

Stable Wood

Duck Bay

Cameron Bay

Cameron House (Hotel)

83

Balloch Castle

Cameron House Farm

Balloch Castle Country Park

Ledrishbeg

INCHFAD RD

CREINCH DR

1 McLEAN CRES
2 HARAN RD
3 SHANDON CRES
4 SHANDON BRAE
5 DUMBAIN RD
6 HALDANE TERR

1

Balloch Pier

Moss o' Balloch Plantations

Balloch

Lomond Shores

Gateway Ctr (Nat Pk Visitor Ctr)

River Leven

PIER RD

OLD LUSS RD

A82

A811

82

19

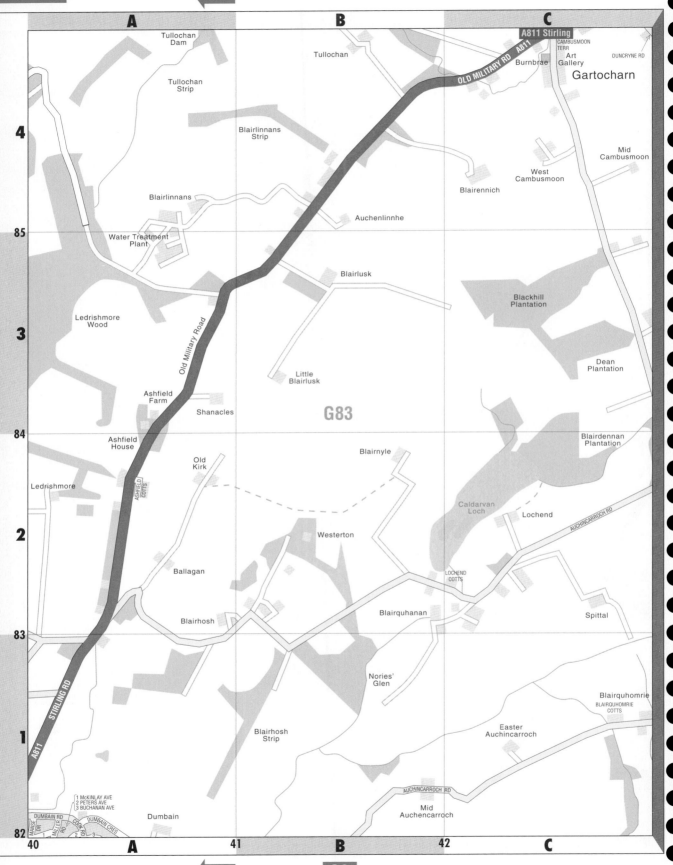

Tullochan Dam

Tullochan Strip

Tullochan

A811 Stirling

OLD MILITARY RD A811

Burnbrae

CAMBUSMOON TERR

Art Gallery

DUNCRYNE RD

Gartocharn

Blairlinnans Strip

4

Mid Cambusmoon

West Cambusmoon

Blairlinnans

Blairennich

85

Auchenlinnhe

Water Treatment Plant

Blairlusk

Blackhill Plantation

Ledrishmore Wood

Old Military Road

3

Dean Plantation

Little Blairlusk

Ashfield Farm

Shanacles

G83

84

Ashfield House

Old Kirk

Blairnyle

Blairdennan Plantation

Ledrishmore

ASHFIELD COTTS

Caldarvan Loch

Lochend

AUCHINCARROCH RD

2

Westerton

Ballagan

LOCHEND COTTS

Blairhosh

Blairquhanan

Spittal

83

Nories' Glen

Blairquhomrie

BLAIRQUHOMRIE COTTS

Blairhosh Strip

1

Easter Auchincarroch

STIRLING RD

A811

1 McKINLAY AVE
2 PETERS AVE
3 BUCHANAN AVE

AUCHINCARROCH RD

MANSE DR

DUMBAIN RD

MILLER RD

COOK RD

DUMBAIN CRES

Dumbain

Mid Auchencarroch

82

40

A

41

B

42

C

19
28

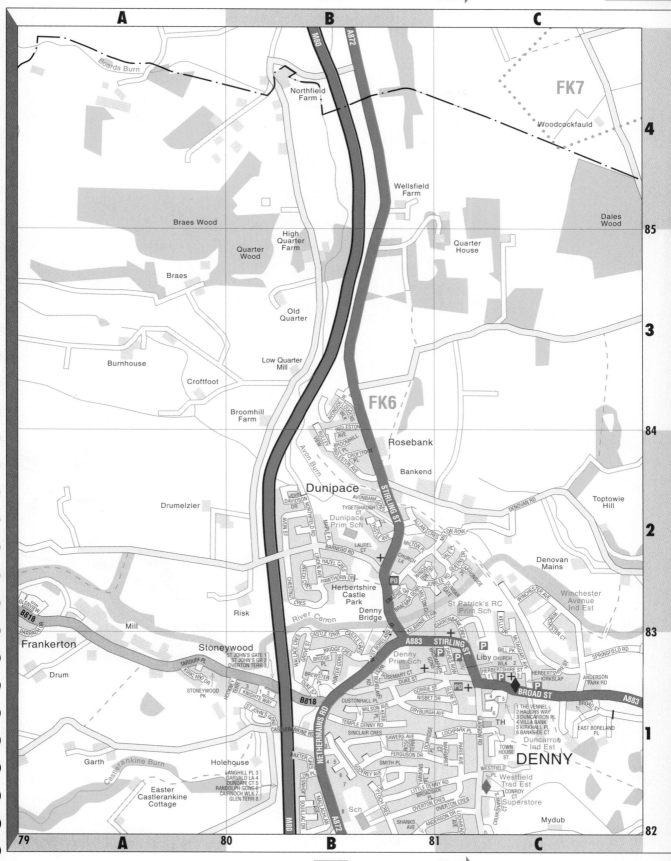

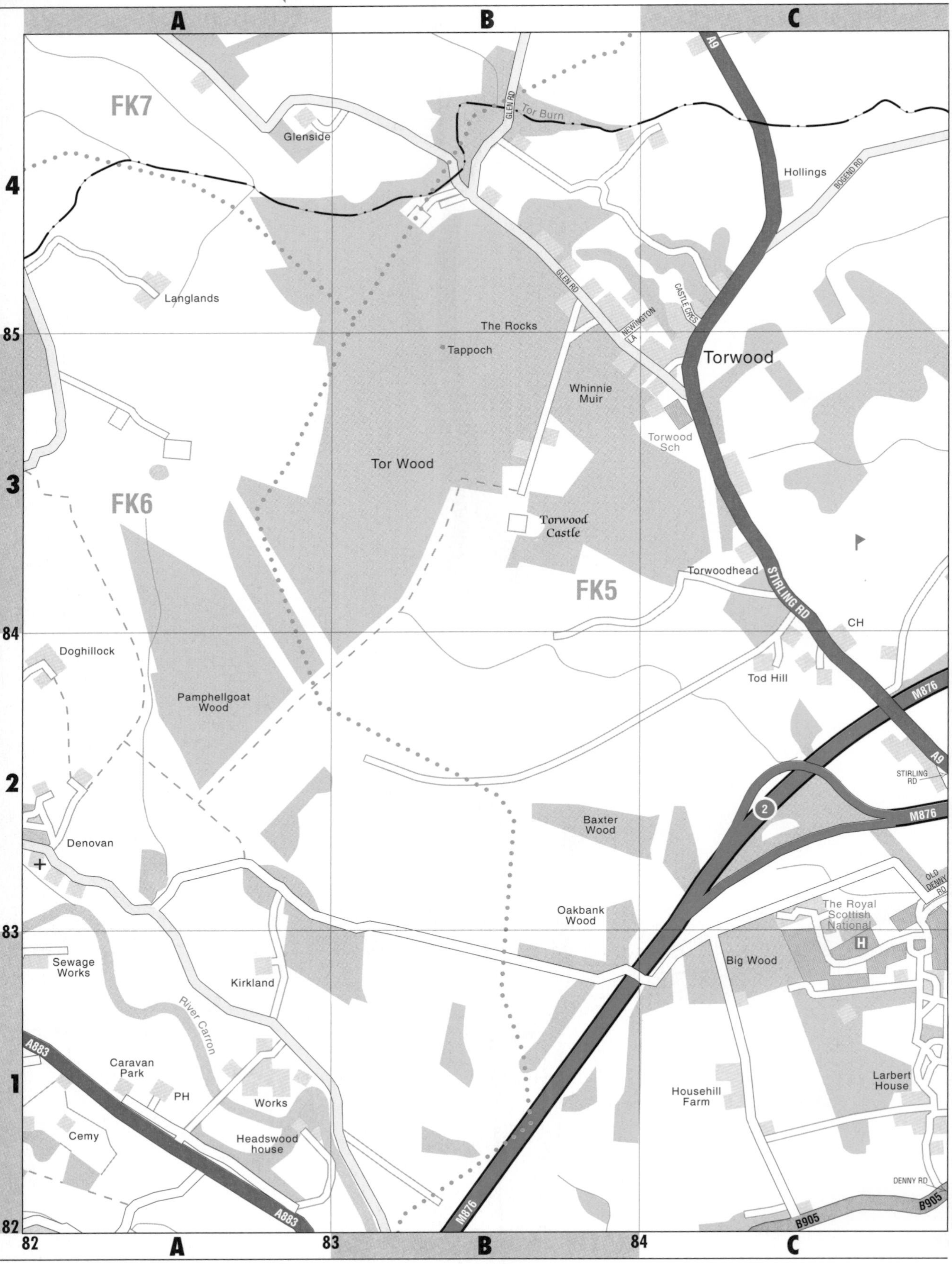

A **B** **C**

FK7

Glenside

GLEN RD

Tor Burn

A9

Hollings

BOGENDRO

4

Langlands

The Rocks

GLEN RD

NEWINGTON LA

CASTLE CRES

Torwood

85

Tappoch

Whinnie Muir

Torwood Sch

Tor Wood

3

FK6

Torwood Castle

FK5

Torwoodhead

STIRLING RD

CH

84

Doghillock

Tod Hill

M876

Pamphellgoat Wood

A9

STIRLING RD

2

Denovan

2

M876

Baxter Wood

The Royal Scottish National

OLD DENNY RD

Oakbank Wood

H

83

Sewage Works

Kirkland

Big Wood

River Carron

A883

Caravan Park

PH

Works

Household Farm

Larbert House

1

Cemy

Headswood house

DENNY RD

M876

A883

B905

B905

82

82 **A** 83 **B** 84 **C**

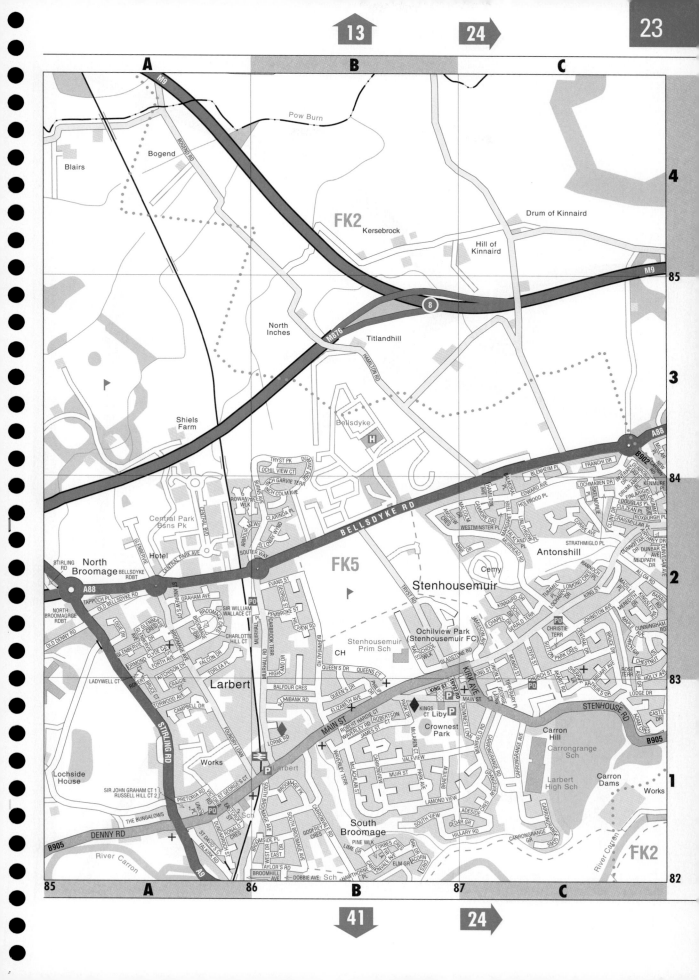

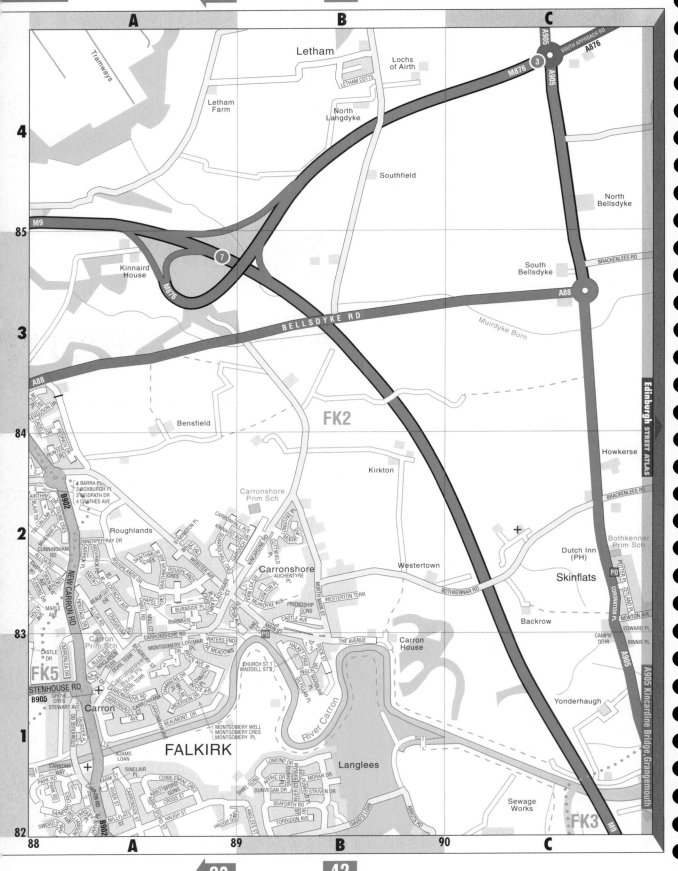

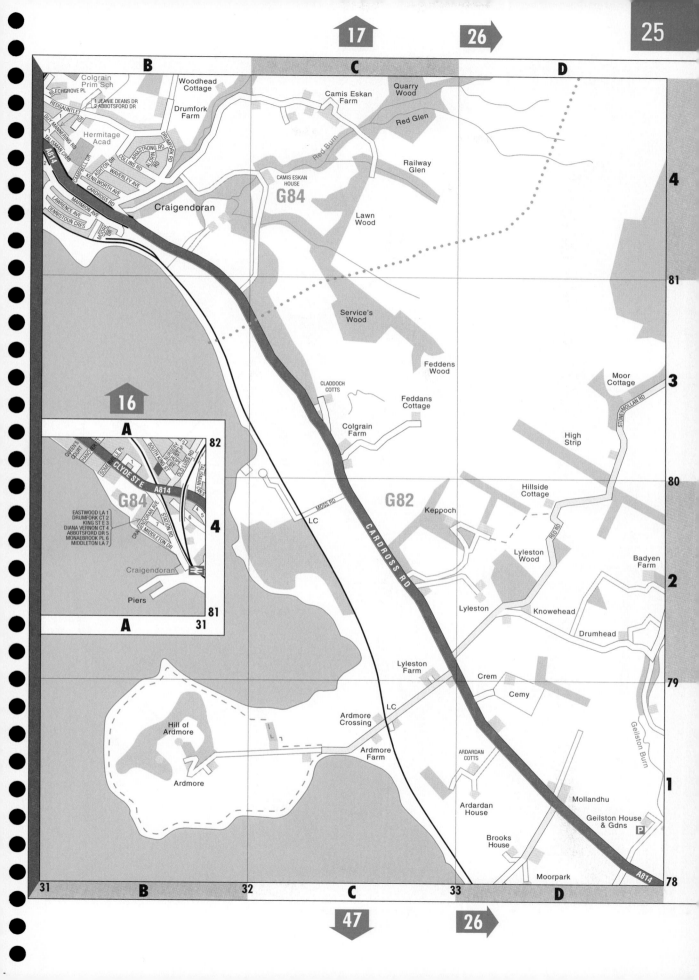

A | B | C

4

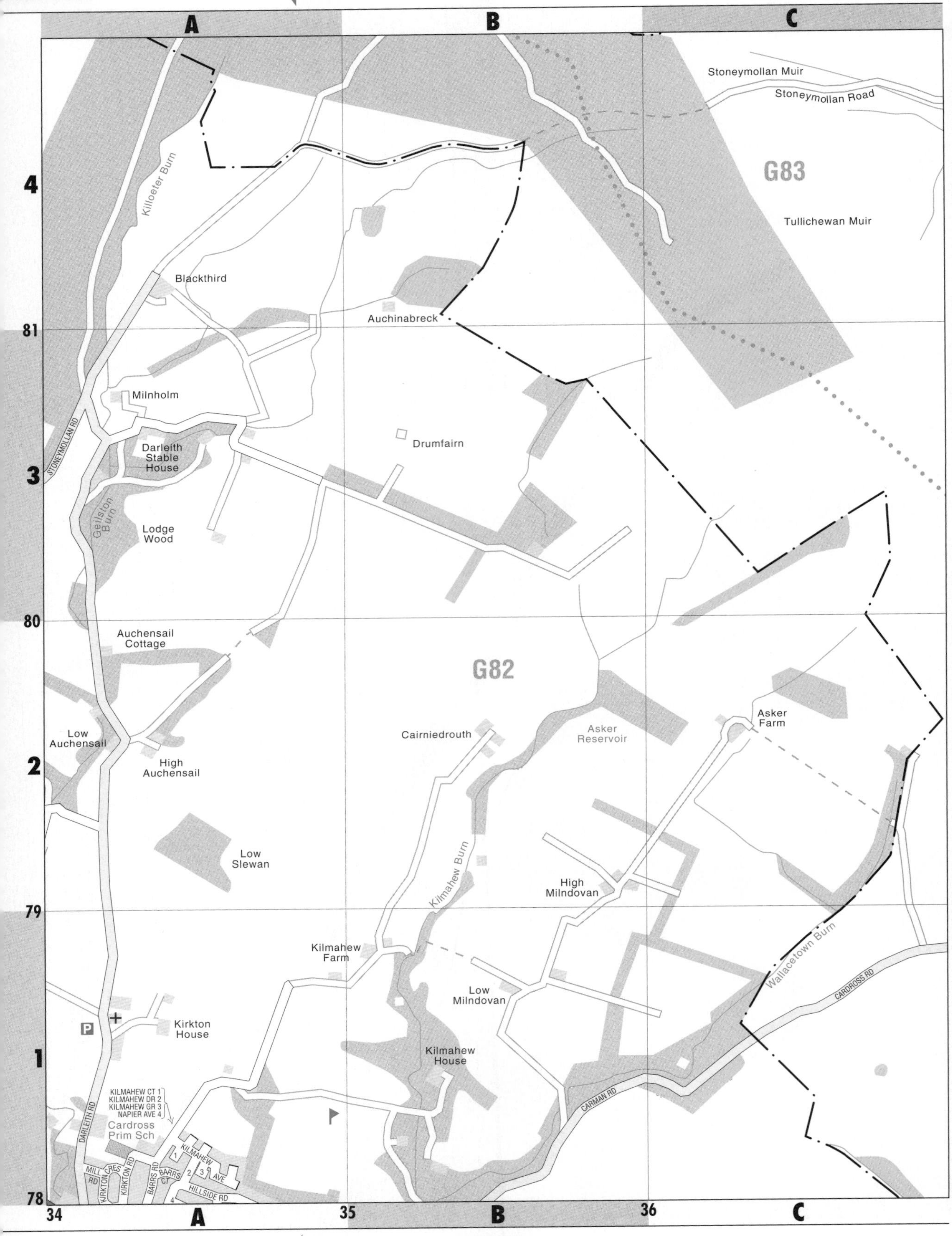

Stoneymollan Muir
Stoneymollan Road

G83

Tullichewan Muir

Killoeter Burn

Blackthird

81

Auchinabreck

Milnholm

Darleith
Stable
House

Drumfairn

3

Gellston Burn

Lodge
Wood

STONEYMOLLAN RD

80

Auchensail
Cottage

G82

Asker
Reservoir

Asker
Farm

Low
Auchensail

Cairniedrouth

2

High
Auchensail

Low
Slewan

Kilmahew Burn

High
Milndovan

79

Kilmahew
Farm

Low
Milndovan

Wallacetown Burn

CARDROSS RD

P
Kirkton
House

Kilmahew
House

1

KILMAHEW CT 1
KILMAHEW DR 2
KILMAHEW GR 3
NAPIER AVE 4

CARMAN RD

Cardross Prim Sch

DARLEITH RD

KILMAHEW AVE

MILL RD
KIRKTON RD
KIRKTON RD
BARRS RD
BARRS CT
HILLSIDE RD

78

34 | A | 35 | B | 36 | C

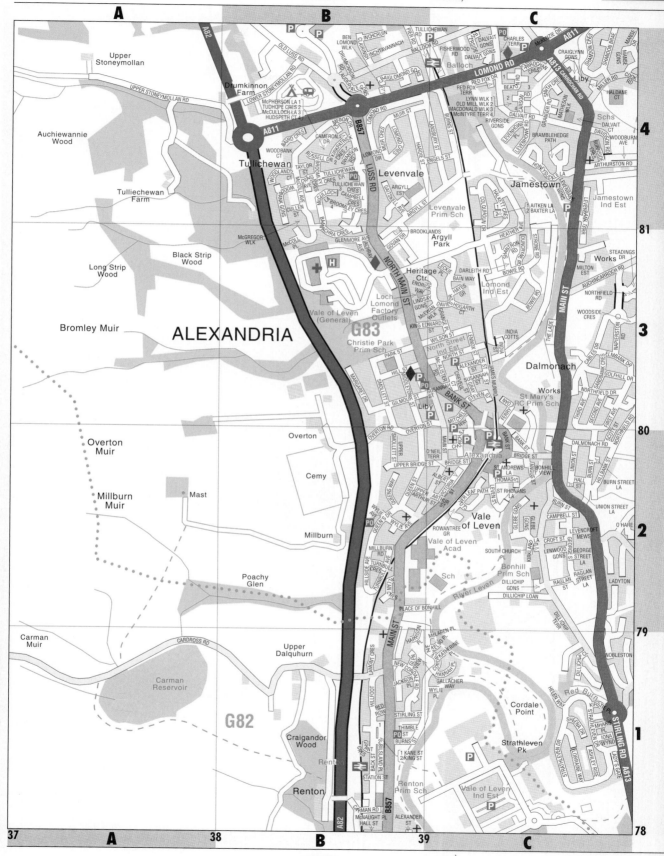

27
20

A **B** **C**

West Auchencarroch

Auchincarroch Hill

Auchincarroch Muir

Ring Farm

4

Mill of Haldane
1 MANSE DR
2 SHEARER QUADRANT
3 SIMPSON QUADRANT
4 LINDSAY QUADRANT
5 LOMOND GATE

BROOKE AVE
McGREGOR QUAD
PETERS AVE
BARTON AVE
MILLER ST
McINNES ST
BROWN ST
ROY YOUNG AVE
DUMBAIN CRES
TALBOT RD
COOK RD
MARTIN AVE
McFARLANE RD
BUCHANAN AVE
GLEN AVE
STEELE CRES
CARMONA DR
STEELE WLK
WOODBURN AVE
ARTHURSTON RD

AUCHINCARROCH RD

Blairvault Burn

Redcraig

81

Woodside

Woodside Cres

STERLINGS DR
NORTHFIELD RD

3

GOLFHILL DR

Pappert Hill

G83

CH

80

Northfield Cottage

Nobleston Wood

Hazel Glen

2

O'HARE
PAPPERT

Bonhill

Auchenreoch Muir

PO
Liby Sch
P

Sch

BRAEHEAD
BRAEHEAD

79

NOBLESTON AVE
REDBURN

Highdykes Prim Sch

Murroch Burn

Glendonachy

Auchenreoch

BEECHWOOD DR

Highdykes

1

Beech Wood

MURROCH CRES

Murroch Glen

Auchenreoch Glen

Spouts Burn

BROOMHILL CRES

STIRLING RD

Mains

Broomhill Wood

G82

A813

78
40 **41** **42**
A **B** **C**

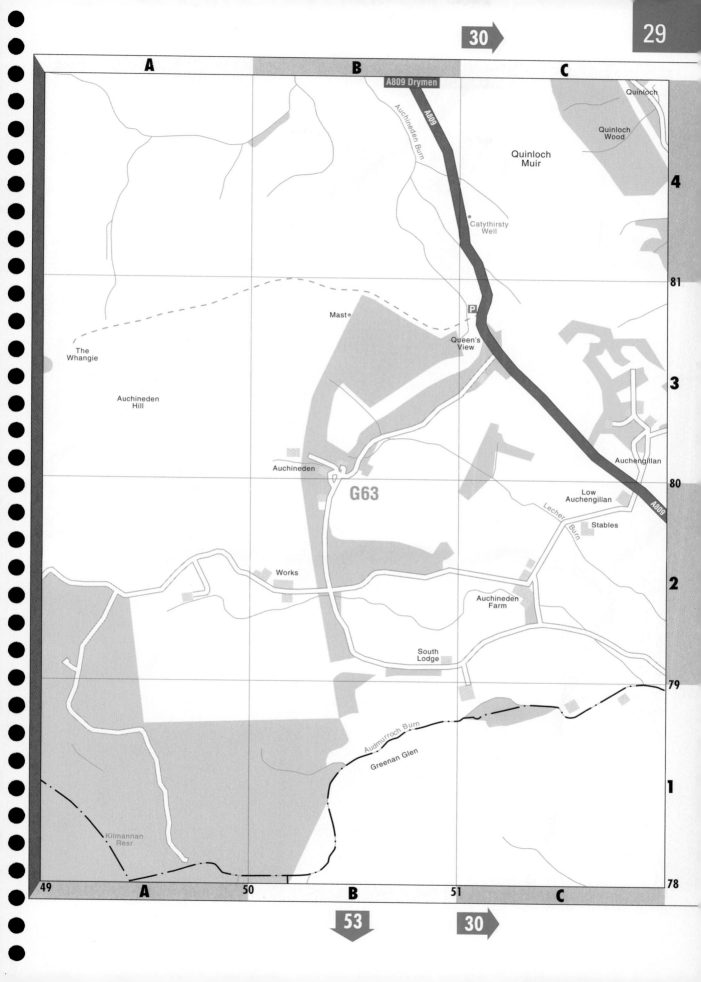

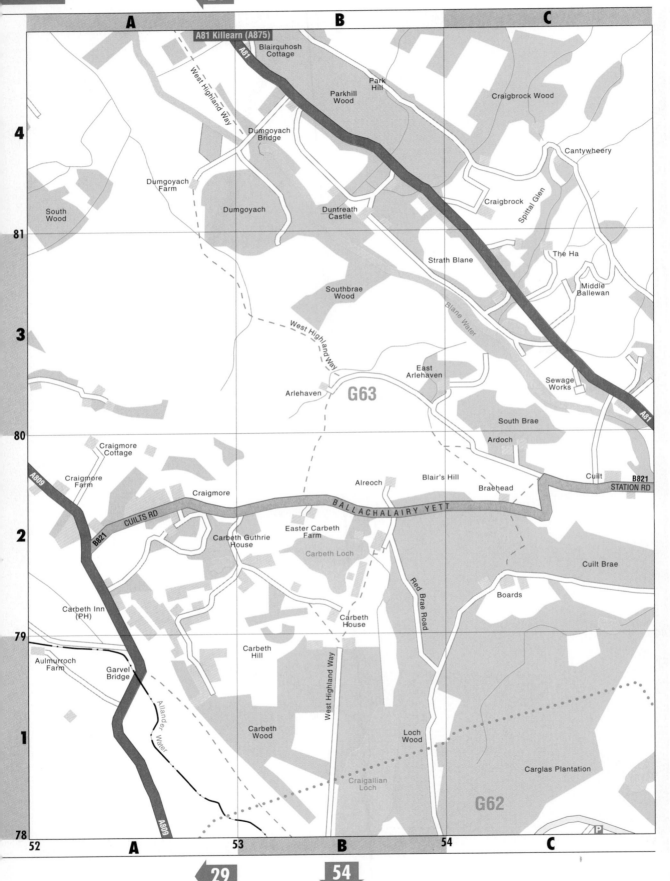

A81 Killearn (A875)

A

B

C

Blairquhosh
Cottage

West Highland Way

Park
Hill

Craigbrock Wood

Parkhill
Wood

Cantywheery

4

Dumgoyach
Bridge

Craigbrock

Spittal Glen

Dumgoyach
Farm

Dumgoyach

Duntreath
Castle

South
Wood

The Ha

81

Strath Blane

Middle
Ballewan

Southbrae
Wood

Blane Water

3

West Highland Way

East
Arlehaven

Arlehaven

G63

Sewage
Works

A81

South Brae

80

Ardoch

Craigmore
Cottage

Cuilt

B821

Craigmore
Farm

Craigmore

Alreoch

Blair's Hill

Braehead

STATION RD

A809

BALLACHALAIRY YETT

CUILTS RD

2

Easter Carbeth
Farm

Cuilt Brae

B821

Carbeth Guthrie
House

Carbeth Loch

Red Brae Road

Boards

Carbeth Inn
(PH)

Carbeth
House

79

Carbeth
Hill

Aulmurroch
Farm

Garvel
Bridge

West Highland Way

Allander Water

1

Carbeth
Wood

Loch
Wood

Carglas Plantation

Craigallian
Loch

G62

A809

P

78

52

A

53

B

54

C

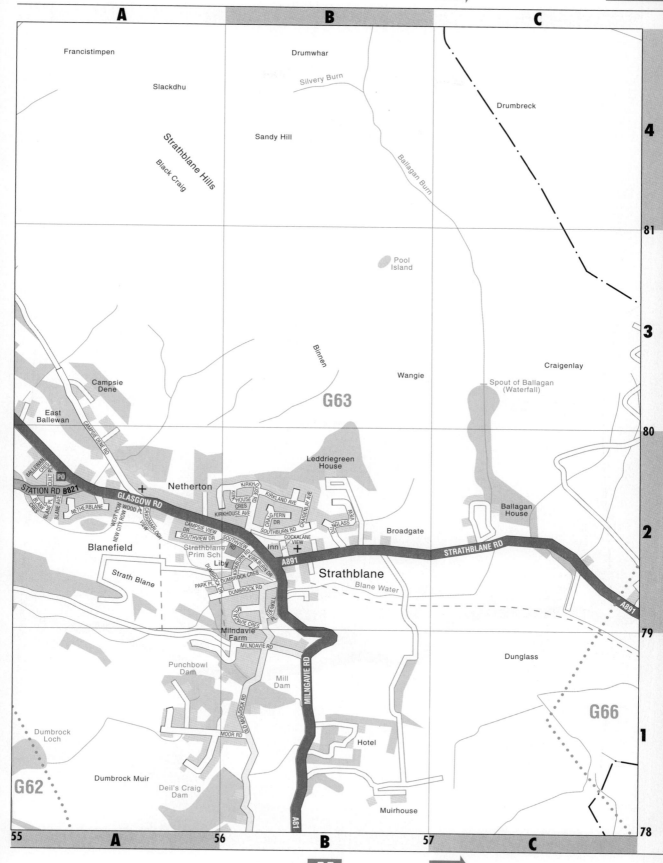

31

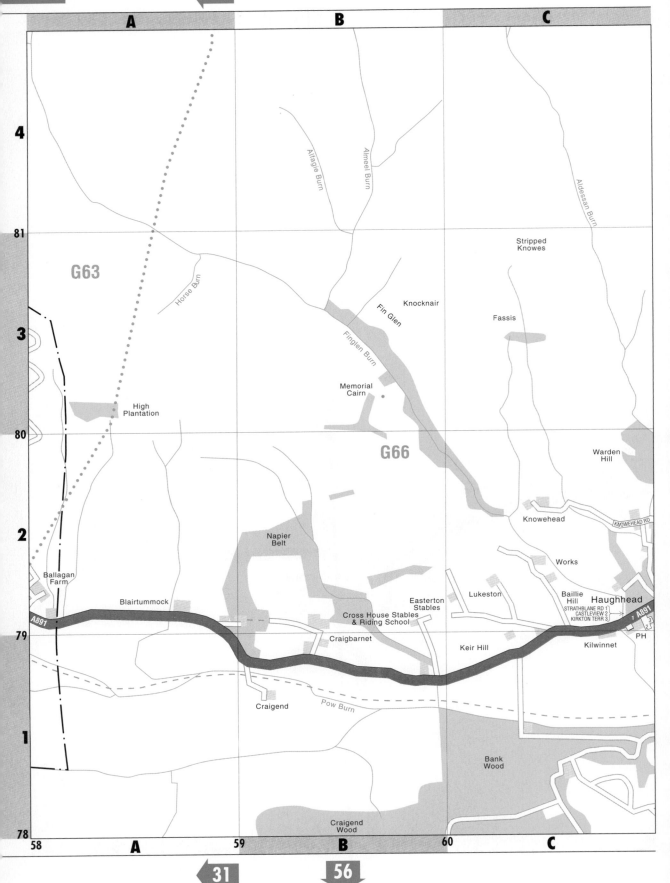

A B C

4

81

G63

Altagie Burn

Almeel Burn

Aldessan Burn

Stripped
Knowes

Knocknair

Fin Glen

Fassis

Horse Burn

Finglen Burn

3

Memorial
Cairn

High
Plantation

80

G66

Warden
Hill

Napier
Belt

Knowehead

KNOWEHEAD RD

2

Works

Ballagan
Farm

Easterton
Stables

Lukeston

Baillie
Hill

Haughhead

Blairtummock

Cross House Stables
& Riding School

STRATHBLANE RD 1
CASTLEVIEW 2
KIRKTON TERR 3

A891

A891

79

Craigbarnet

Keir Hill

Kilwinnet

PH

Craigend

Pow Burn

1

Bank
Wood

78

58 A 59 B 60 C

Craigend
Wood

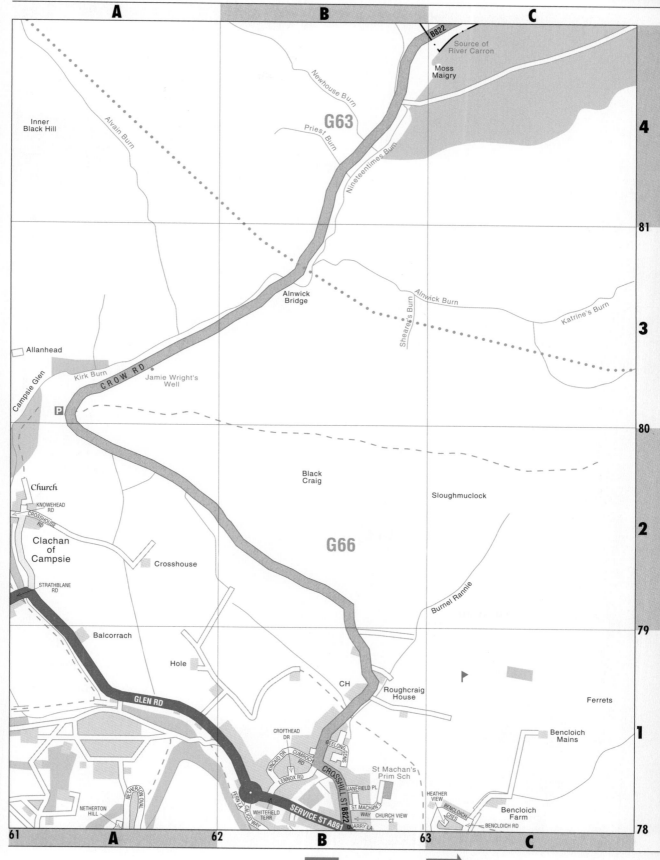

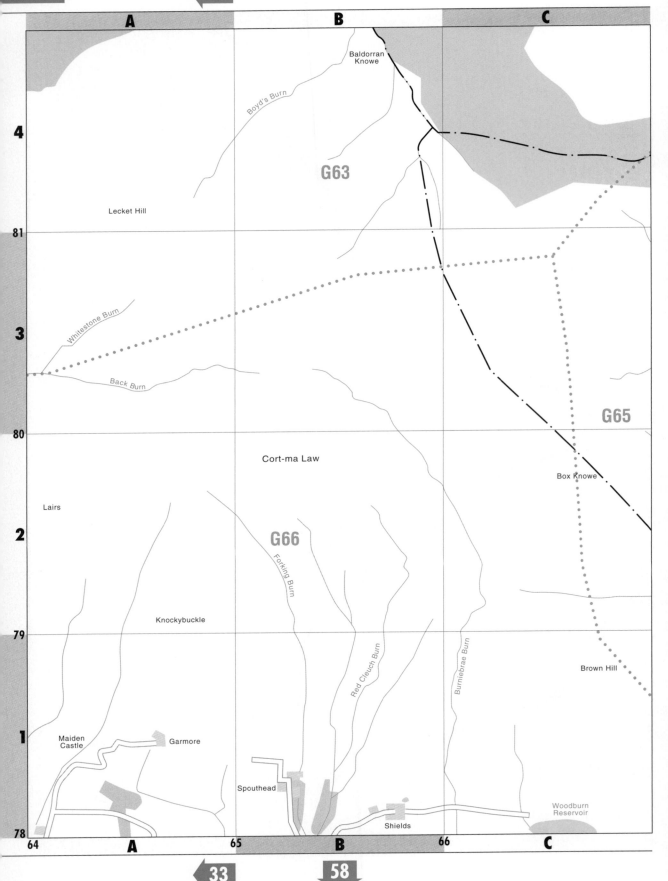

A   B   C

Baldorran
Knowe

Boyd's Burn

G63

4

Lecket Hill

81

Whitestone Burn

3

Back Burn

G65

80

Cort-ma Law

Box Knowe

Lairs

2

G66

Forking Burn

Knockybuckle

79

Red Cleuch Burn

Burniebrae Burn

Brown Hill

1

Maiden
Castle   Garmore

Spouthead

Woodburn
Reservoir

Shields

78
64   65   66
A   B   C

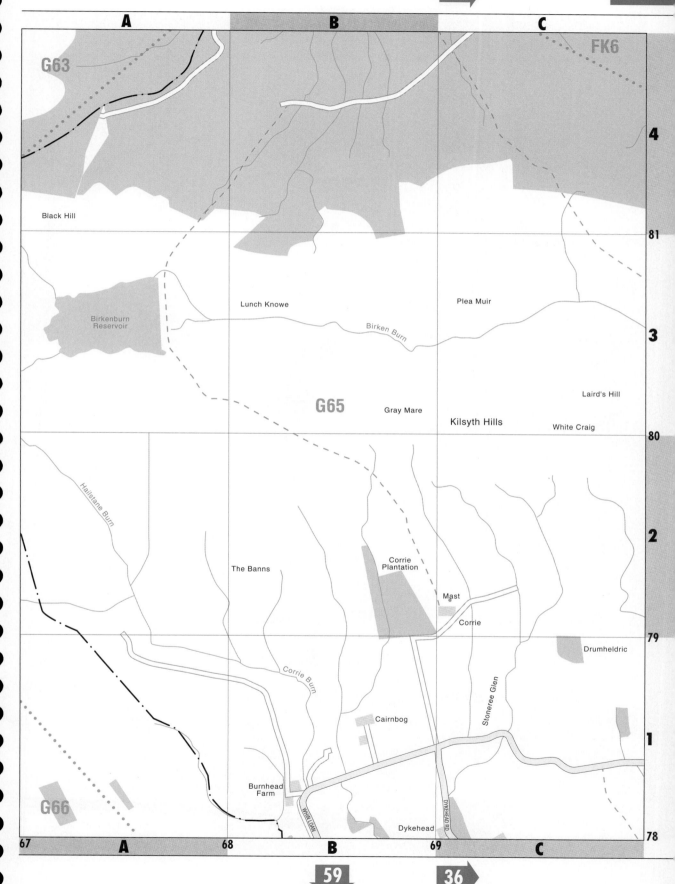

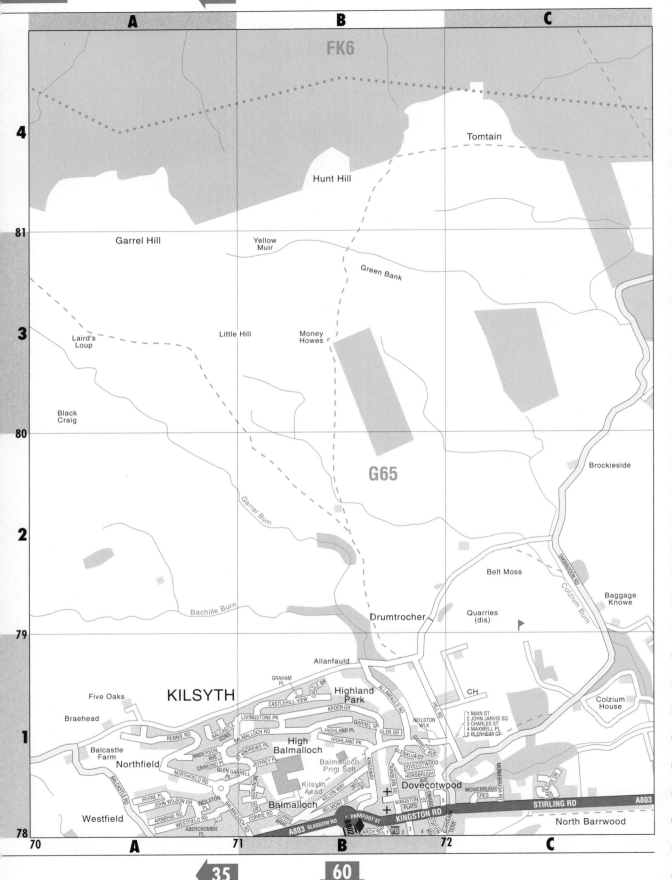

A   B   C

FK6

Tomtain

Hunt Hill

4

81

Garrel Hill

Yellow
Muir

Green Bank

Laird's
Loup

Little Hill

Money
Howes

3

Black
Craig

80

G65

Brockieside

Garrel Burn

2

Belt Moss

Colzium Burn

Baggage
Knowe

Bachille Burn

Drumtrocher

Quarries
(dis)

79

Allanfauld

CH

Colzium
House

Five Oaks

KILSYTH

Highland
Park

Braehead

GRAHAM
PL

CASTLE GR

CASTLEHILL VIEW

ARDEN GR

Garrel Gr

GLEN GR

ALLANFAULD RD

NEILSTON
WLK

1 MAIN ST
2 JOHN JARVIS SQ
3 CHARLES ST
4 MAXWELL PL
5 BLENHEIM CT

LIVINGSTONE PK

RENNIE RD

BALCASTLE
GDNS

HIGHLAND PL

HIGHLAND PK

HILL RD

1

Balcastle
Farm

ANDERSON
AVE

ST ANDREWS PL

BALMALLOCH RD

High
Balmalloch

GARRELL AVE

Northfield

CRIMOND PL

JEFFREY PL

Balmalloch
Prim Sch

GLENALVA CT

DOVECOTWOOD

MONIEBRUGH
CRES

MONIEBRUGH RD

GLEN GARRELL
PL

NORTHFIELD RD

KINGSWAY

HORSBRUGH
AVE

Dovecotwood

LADESIDE DR

MONTROSE GDNS

KELVIN WAY

GLEN

Kilsyth
Acad

Balmalloch

IRVINE PL

JOHN WILSON DR

NEILSTON
PL

BELMONT ST

KINGSTON
FLATS

PARKBURN RD

KINGSTON RD

EDWARD AVE

BURNBRAE
TERR

Westfield

ARNBRAE RD

WESTFIELD RD

ABERCROMBIE
PL

CORRIE RD

CORRIE
BRAE

BALMALLOCH RD

PARKFOOT ST

ARCH WAY

PO

A803 GLASGOW RD

B802

KINGSTON RD

STIRLING RD

A803

North Barrwood

BALCASTLE RD

78

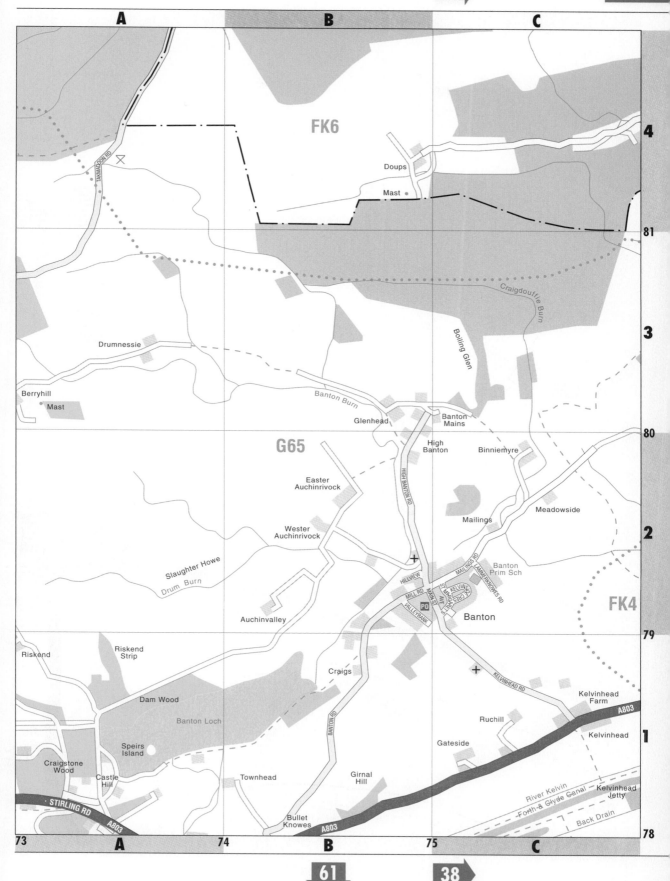

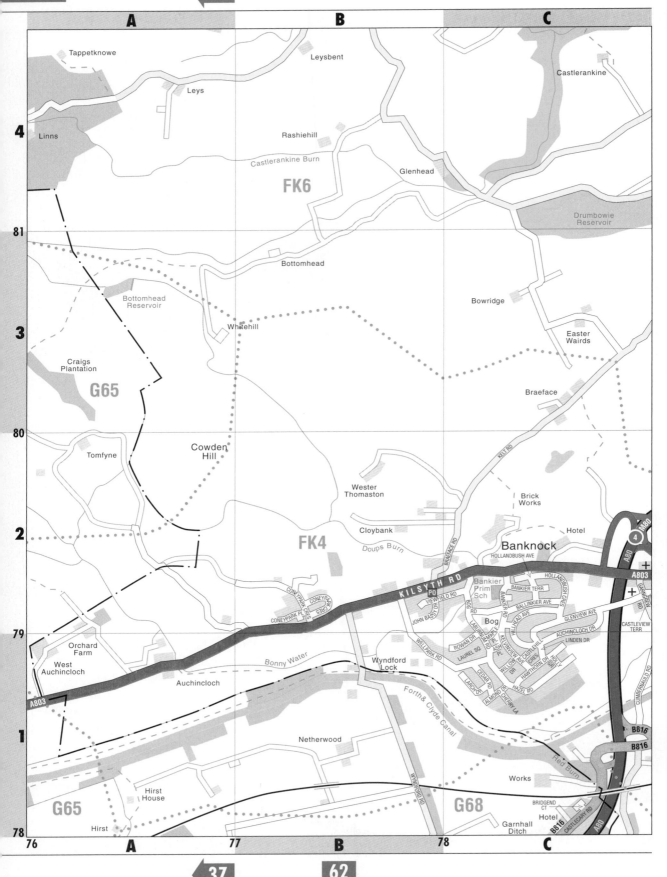

A B C

4

Tappetknowe

Leysbent

Castlerankine

Leys

Linns

Rashiehill

Castlerankine Burn

Glenhead

FK6

81

Drumbowie
Reservoir

Bottomhead

Bottomhead
Reservoir

Bowridge

3

Whitehill

Easter
Wairds

Craigs
Plantation

G65

Braeface

80

Tomfyne

Cowden
Hill

Wester
Thomaston

Brick
Works

KELL RD

2

Cloybank

Hotel

FK4

Doups Burn

Banknock

HOLLANDBUSH AVE

A80

M80

4

+

A803

Bankier
Prim
Sch

HOLLANDBUSH CRES

Bankier Terr

BRAEFACE RD

K I L S Y T H   R D

PO

VIEWFIELD RD

BANKIER PL

BALLINKIER AVE

GLENMEW RD

CONEYPARK CRES

CONEYPARK PL CRES

JOHN BASSY DR

BOG RD

Bog

HILLHEAD AVE

GLENVIEW AVE

AUCHINCLOCH DR

LINDEN DR

CASTLEVIEW
TERR

CUMBERNAULD RD

79

Orchard
Farm

WELLPARK RD

LABURNUM RD

ROWAN DR

LAUREL SQ

ASH PL

KELVINVIEW AVE

WILLOW DR

CASTLEHILL

HAWTHORN DR

AUCHINCLOCH

West
Auchincloch

Bonny Water

Wyndford
Lock

CEDAR RD

LARCH DR

ALMOND DR

HAZEL RD

CHERRY LA

Forth & Clyde Canal

B816

B816

A803

1

Netherwood

Red Burn

WYNDFORD RD

Works

G68

78

Hirst
House

BRIDGEND
CT

Hotel

B816

CASTLECARY RD

A80

G65

Hirst

Garnhall
Ditch

78

76

A

77

B

78

C

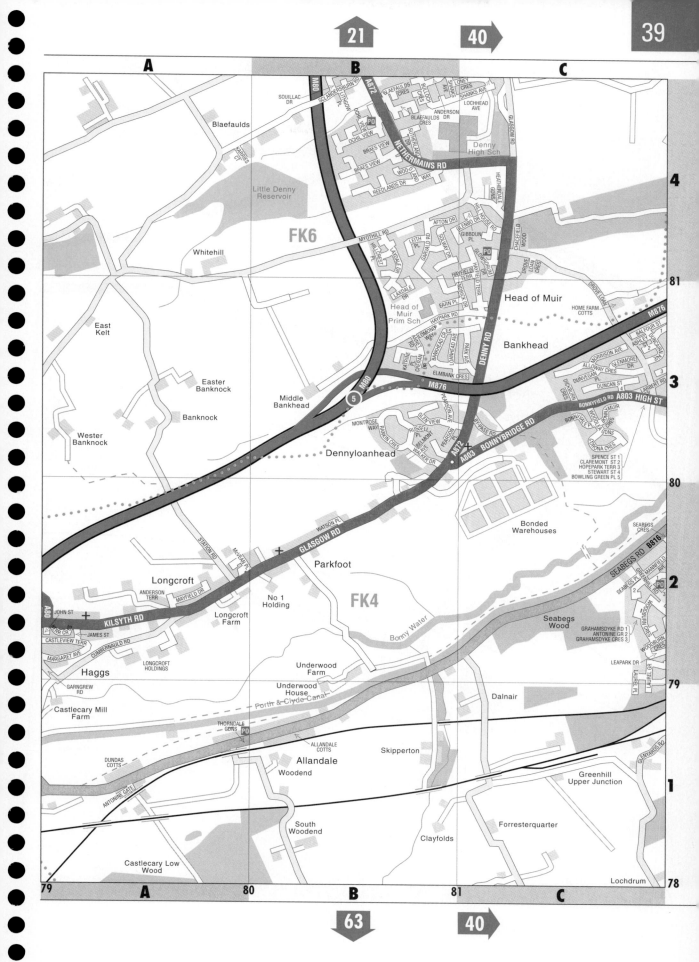

39
22

A   B   C

Cuthelton

FK6

FK5

Chacefield Wood

Cemy

Nursery

Hills of Dunipace

4

B905

B905

M876

A883

A883

B905

CHECKBAR RDBT

River Carron

Bogton

CH

FAIRWAYS PL

NORWOOD CT

Sewage Works

Wester Carmuirs

Works

81

M876

PRIMROSE ST

NORWOOD PL

ROSE ST

DRUMMOND PL

FERGUSON GR

ROBERT BRUCE AVE

BALFOUR ST

SPENCE ST

SKENE ST

URE CRES

CHACEFIELD ST

WHEATLANDS AVE

LARBERT RD

HIGHLAND DYKES CRES

HIGHLAND DYKES DR

BONNYVIEW GDNS

GREENFIELD ST

Bonnybridge Prim Sch

THORNTON AVE

THORNTON AVE

GATESIDE AVE

Bonny Water

A803

WEST CARMUIRS LOAN

A803

COWAN ST

CHAPELPARK TERR

MARGARET DR

PEATHILL RD

FAIRFIELD AVE

WELLPARK TERR

DUNURE CRES

FORTH DR

WADE RD

THORNTON AVE

ANDERS ST

CAMDEN HILL GDNS

BARLEYHILL

PRINCESS ST

PATTISON PL

FALKIRK RD

Park

Bonnybridge

H

Rowan Tree Burn

3

A803

HIGH ST

MAIN ST

BRIDGE ST

MOUNT BARTHOLOMEW

Bonnybridge

P P

Cowden Hill

Liby

HUNTER RD

FOUNDRY RD

BONNYSIDE RD

Bonnyside Farm

Forth and Clyde Canal

80

SEABEGS RD

B816

MURNIN RD

SEABEGS CRES

MANNFIELD AVE

Murnin Road Ind Est

Canal Bank Ind Est

Antonine Prim Sch

BROOMHILL RD

Bonnybridge Ind Est

PARK ST

PARK ST STH

REILLY GDNS

WAVERLEY CRES

MILLAR PL

CHURCH ST

LOCHINVAR PL

Chattan Ind Est

FK4

ANTONINE WALL

Rough Castle ROMAN FORT

FK1

Works

P

B816

2

GRAHAMSDYKE RD

ROMAN RD

ATRIUM WAY

St Joseph's RC Prim Sch

Milnquarter

1 GRAHAMSDYKE CRES
2 WOODBURN DR
3 BANTON PL
4 LAURELBANK AVE

REILLY RD

HILLVIEW RD

NEW RD

BROOMSIDE RD

BONNYHILL RD

Works

High Bonnybridge

79

GLENYARDS RD

LEAPARK DR

LAUREL GR

GREENHILL RD

Greenhill

Margreta

Bonnyhill Farm

Howierig

1

FK1

Drum Farm

Drum Wood

Greenrig

78

82   A   83   B   84   C

A　B　C

BROOMHILL AVE
Lochlands
JONES AVE
LADESIDE PRIM SCH
CARRONVALE HOUSE
DOBBIE AVE
BEECH CRES
CHARLES ST
CALLENDER DR
WOODSIDE GR
CARRONVALE RD
FALKIRK RD
FALKIRK RD
TAIT DR
LADE
South Broomage
River Carron
FK5
Lochlands Ind Est
River Carron
Mill
STIRLING RD
P
Dorrator
Longdales
Mungal Farm
Crem
Cauldhame
A883
River Carron
FK2
Cemy
CH
CENTURION WAY
MACADAM PLACE
P
81
A803
GLASGOW RD
Works
Camelon
REDBRAE RD
P
P
P
ABERCROMBIE ST
AITKEN GDNS
MERCHISTON RD
KILNS PL
P
A9
ELIZABETH CRES
ST GILES WAY
ST GILES SQ
MARINER DR
CARMUIRS DR
ROSSVAIL SCH
WILSON GDNS
WALL ST
WATLING ST
WATLING AVE
BROWN ST
HAMILTON DR
SIMPSON ST
NAPIER ST
WATT ST
DORRATOR RD
FLEMING ST
ARBUTHNOT ST
SUNNYSIDE RD
COTTAGE CRES
PROSPECT ST
TOPHILL ENTRY
ARNOTHILL CT 1
ARNOTHILL LA 2
Easter Carmuirs Prim Sch
CARMUIRS AVE
Camelon
ROMAN DR
BAIRD ST
SCH
MAIN ST
GORDON PL
IRVING ST
Ed Ctr
C1
3
Carmuirs
KEIRHILL ST
GLENCAIRN ST
OCHILTREE TERR
CLARINDA AVE
MOSSGIEL ST
MARINER ST
WILSON DR
ANTOINE DR
ROSS GDNS
GLENFUIR ST
CARMUIRS ST
CARMUIRS AVE
FAIRLIE AVE
FAIRLIE DR
STARK AVE
UNION GDNS
THE HEDGES
PARK VIEW CT
DORRATOR CT
BURNSIDE TERR
COLLINGWOOD CT
ROSEBANK
ROSEBANK AVE
SPRINGFIELD
QUEEN'S CRES
MAGGIE WOODS LOAN
A803 CAMELON RD
B816
Falkirk Wheel
P
FAIRLIE GDNS
LOCK SIXTEEN
Forth and Clyde Canal
PORTDOWNIE
CANAL ST
GLENFUIR RD
B8080
STRACHAN ST
BEGG DR
BLINKBONNY RD
FORDYCE GDNS
RALEIGH
GRENVILLE CT
FRÖBISHER AVE
QUEENS RD
HOWARD ST
80
Tamfourhill
TAMFOURHILL AVE
Tamfourhill Ind Est
WHITEGATES PL
SLAMANNAN
NURSERY RD
HAWTHORN CT
Falkirk High Sch
WESTBURN AVE
Bantaskin
DERWENT AVE
CONWAY
SHW
MAYFIELD MEWS
H
Falkirk & District Coll
B8080
TAMFOURHILL RD
BONNYHILL RD
ROWAN CRES
LIME RD
HOWIE'S PL
KILBRENNAN DR
BRODICK PL
MACHRIE CT
CUMBRAE DR
KINTYRE PL
KILMORY CT
CORRIE PL
CARRICK
ARRAN TERR
SUMMERFORD
SUMMERFORD RD
Bantaskin Prim Sch
BANTASKINE RD
BANTASKINE DR
WINDSOR RD
WINDSOR AVE
WINDSOR GDNS
OSBORNE GDNS
GARTCOWS RD
P
2
B816
MARYFIELD PL
DALMAR PL
CARRADALE AVE
FK1
SUMMERFORD GDNS
Summerford
Union Canal
GREENBANK PL
P
BANTASKINE GDNS
BALMORAL ST
BANTASKINE ST
BALMORAL DR
HIGHWORTH
1
FALKIRK
Tamfourhill Wood
Greenbank
GREENBANK RD
Greenbank Farm
Mon
GREENHORN'S WELL CRES 1
GREENHORN'S WELL DR 2
GREENHORN'S WELL AVE 3
Bantaskine Estate
MYRETON WAY
GARTCOWS DR 1
GARTCOWS GDNS 2
GARTCOWS CRES 3
79
Canada Wood
P
THOMSON CRES
DUMYAT DR
CRAIGHORN DR
DRUMMOND PL
LOCHGREEN RD
SUNNYLAW
BLAIRDENON
KINGSEAT PL
DUMYAT DR
SLAMANNAN RD
B803
Princes Park
BRAIGLEITH AVE
LENDRICK AVE
SKYTHORN WAY 1
GLENTYE GDNS 2
MELLOCK GDNS 3
HILLCREST RD
STYLES PL
MCGHEE PL
NICHOLSON
TREAD DR
PARKVIEW AVE
GLENVIEW DR
Greenrig Strip
THORNDENE CT 1
SEAFIELD CT 2
CRAIGBURN CT 3
FORTHVIEW CT 4
NEWHOUSE DR
GRAEME PL
DE KILBEAN DR
MITCHELL PL
GARRY CRES
GLENGARRY
1
Craigburn Wood
LIONTHORN RD
ABBOTS MOSS DR
JAMES CROFT DR
Fox Covert
CLANRANALD PL 5
FARQUHARSON WAY 6
KEPPOCK PL 7
MACPHERSON PL 8
MCKENZIE PL 9
MACINTOSH PL 10
Craigieburn
Seafield
Glen Burn
B803
78

85　A　86　B　87　C

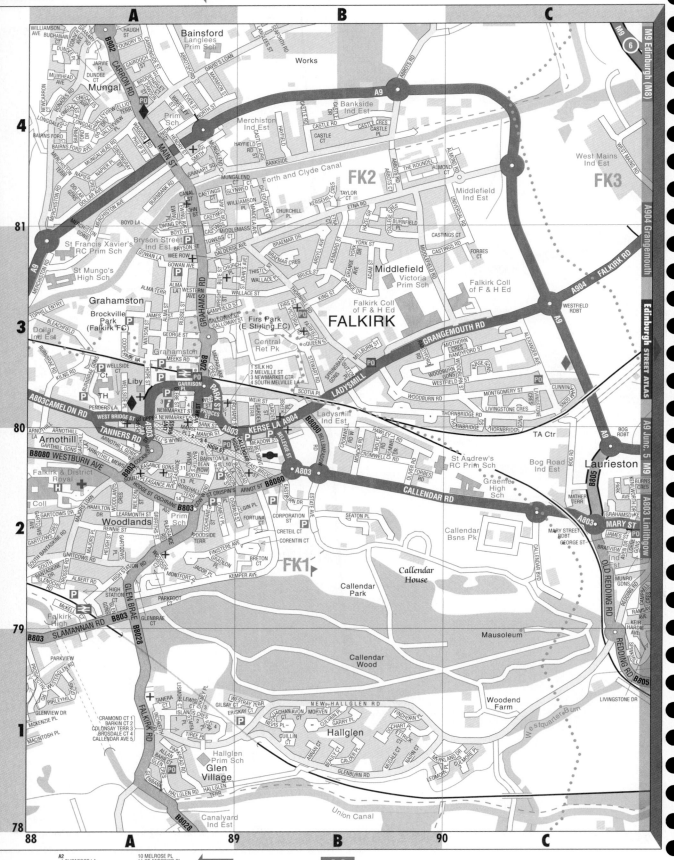

A2
1 BURNFOOT LA
2 KIRK WYND
3 TOLBOOTH ST
4 WOOER ST
5 Callendar Square Sh Ctr
6 ARNOTHILL BANK
7 Howgate Sh Ctr
8 KINGS CT
9 MISSION LA
10 MELROSE PL
11 ST ANDREWS PL
12 PLEASANCE SQ
13 PLEASANCE CT
14 ST MODANS CT
15 COMELY PARK TERR

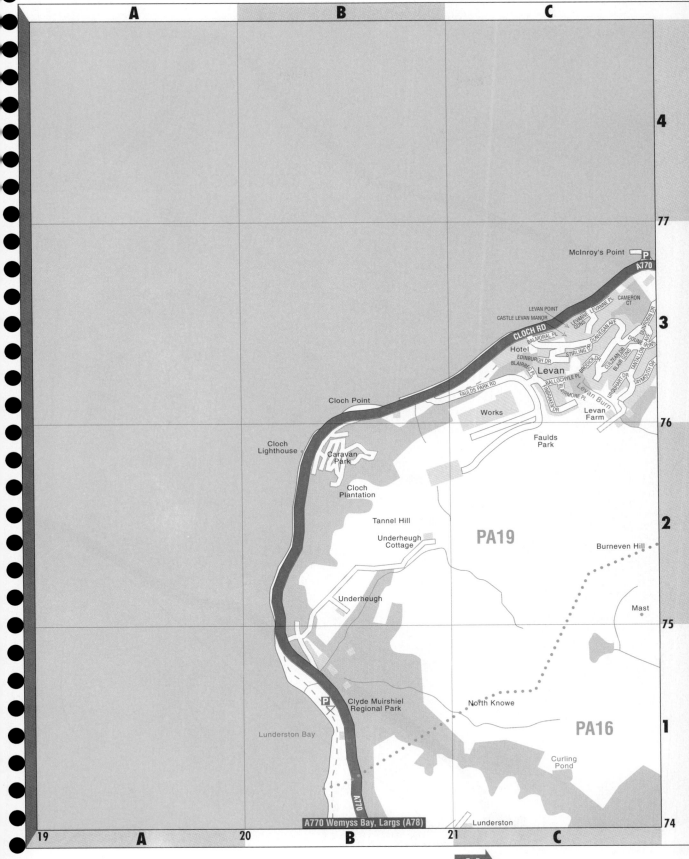

A   B   C

4

77

McInroy's Point P

A770

CAMERON CT

Levan Point
CASTLE LEVAN MANOR
CLOCH RD
BALMORAL PL
Hotel
EDINBURGH DR
BLAIRBEG PL
LEVANNE GDNS LEVANNE PL
DUNVEGAN AVE
DUNFOBOIL DR
STIRLING PL DINWOCK DR
CULZEAN DR
BLAIR GDNS
DOUNE AVE
DOUNE GDNS
TRAYMOUTH DR
TANTALLON DR
URQUHART DR

3

Levan
BALLOCHYLE PL
FINBRACKEN DR
Levan Burn
FINMORE PL

Cloch Point

FAULDS PARK RD

Works

Levan
Farm

76

Cloch
Lighthouse

Caravan
Park

Faulds
Park

Cloch
Plantation

Tannel Hill

Underheugh
Cottage

PA19

Burneven Hill

2

75

Underheugh

Mast

Clyde Muirshiel
Regional Park

North Knowe

PA16

1

Lunderston Bay

Curling
Pond

A770

Lunderston

74

19   20   21

A   B   C

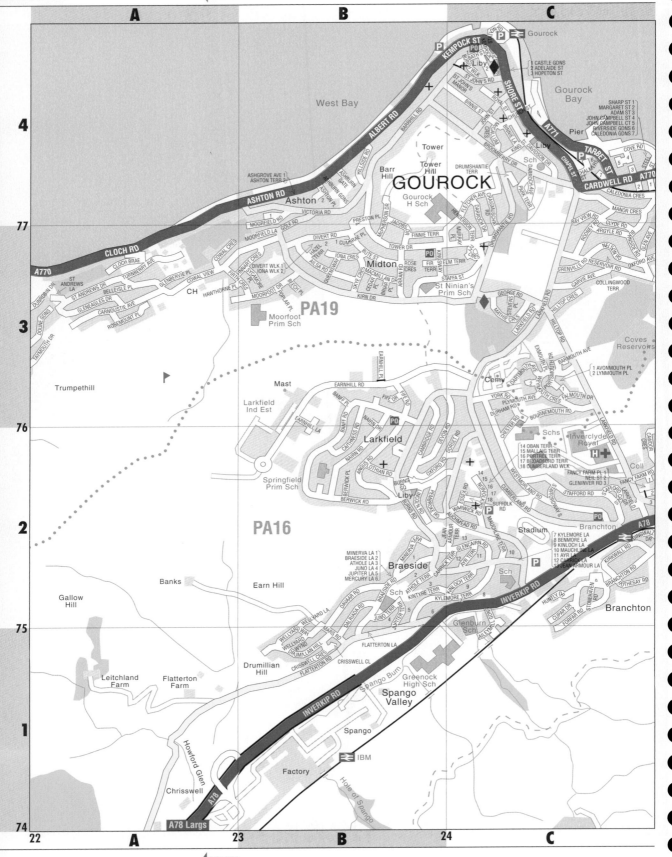

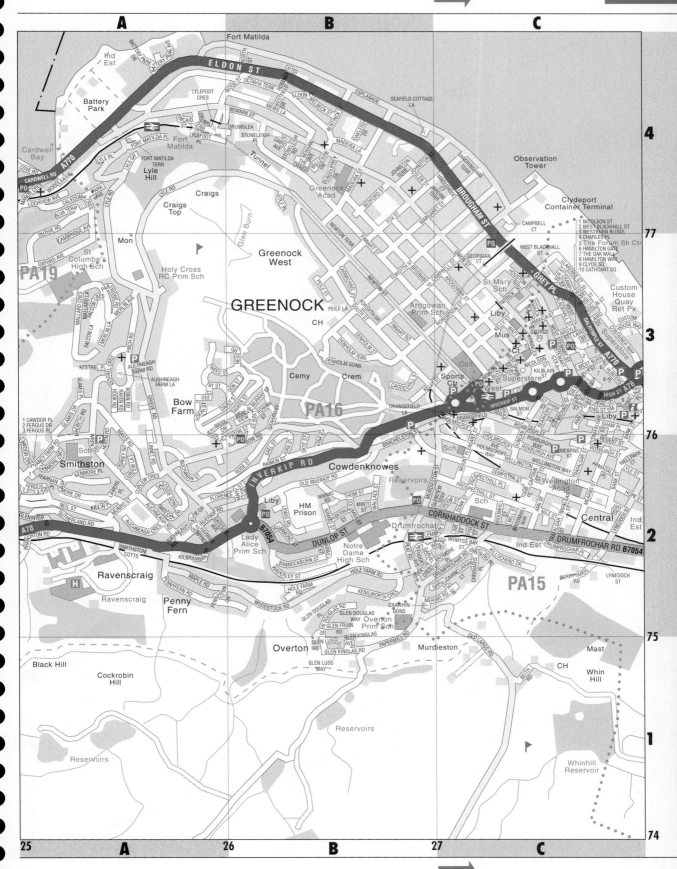

45

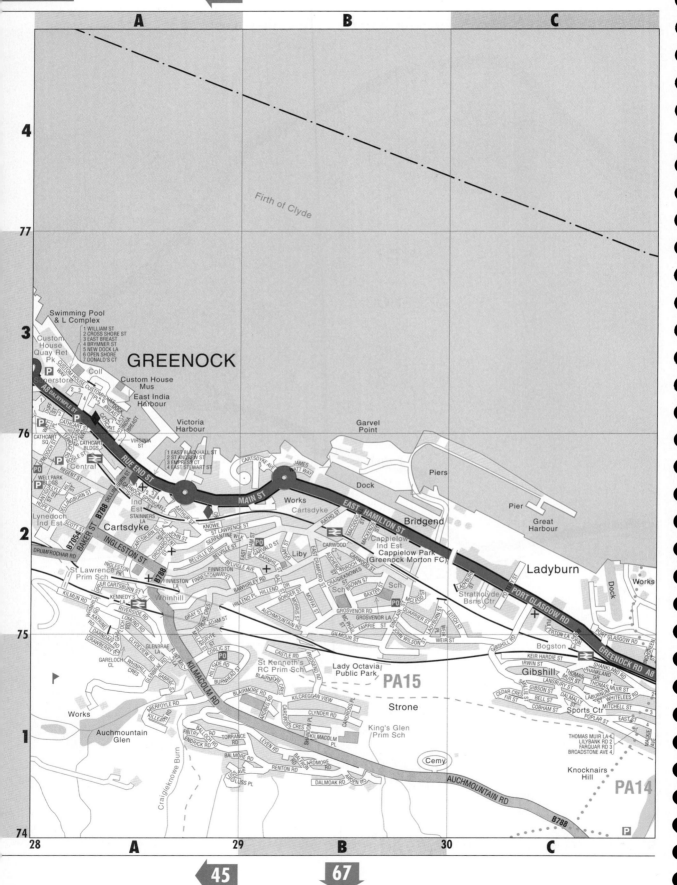

GREENOCK

1 WILLIAM ST
2 CROSS SHORE ST
3 EAST BREAST
4 BRYMNER ST
5 NEW DOCK LA
6 OPEN SHORE
7 DONALD'S CT

Swimming Pool
& L Complex

Custom
House
Quay Ret
Pk

Superstore

Custom House
Mus

East India
Harbour

Victoria
Harbour

Garvel
Point

Firth of Clyde

Coll

Cathcart
Sq

Cathcart
Bldgs

Central

Wellpark
Bldgs

Cartsdyke

1 EAST BLACKHALL ST
2 ST ANDREW ST
3 EMPRESS CT
4 EAST STEWART ST

RUE END ST

MAIN ST

Works

Cartsdyke

EAST HAMILTON ST

Dock

Bridgend

Piers

Pier

Great
Harbour

Dock

Works

Ladyburn

St Lawrence
Prim Sch

Ind
Est

Cartsdyke

Whinhill

Liby

Cappielow
Ind Est

Cappielow Park
(Greenock Morton FC)

Strathclyde
Bsns Ctr

PORT GLASGOW RD

GREENOCK RD A8

Sch

Sch

Bogston

Gibshill

Keir Hardie St
Irwin St

Sports Ctr

KILMACOLM RD

St Kenneth's
RC Prim Sch

Lady Octavia
Public Park

PA15

Strone

King's Glen
Prim Sch

Cemy

AUCHMOUNTAIN RD

Knocknairs
Hill

PA14

THOMAS MUIR LA 1
LILYBANK RD 2
FARQUAR RD 3
BROADSTONE AVE 4

Works

Auchmountain
Glen

Craigieknowe Burn

B788

45   67

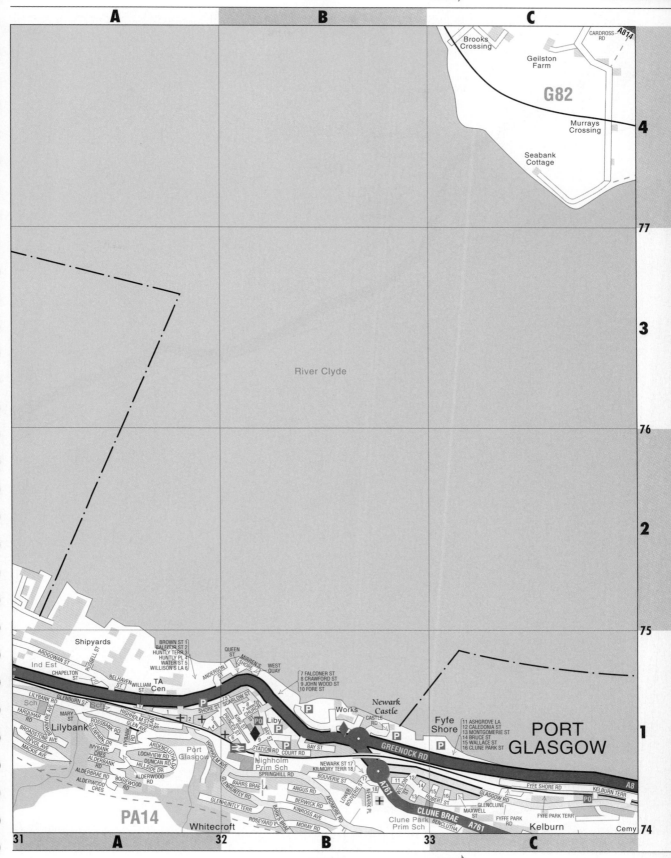

47
26

A
B
C
4
77
3
76
2
75
1
74
34
35
36
A814
KIRKTON CRES
KIRKTON RD
DARLEITH RD
BARRS TERR
BARRS CRES
BARRS RD
HILLSIDE RD
FAIR WAY
MUIREND RD
RIVER VIEW CRES
HILLSIDE RD
NAPIER AVE
NAPIER CT
Geilston
CARDROSS RD
RICHIE AVE
SMITHY CT
SMITHY RD
REAY AVE
DICK QUAD
PARK GR
PARK TERR
Cardross
CHURCH AVE
CEDARWOOD CT
PO
MAIN RD
Liby
STATION RD
GEILSTON PK
CH
LC
Cardross
CEDAR GR
PEEL ST
BURNFOOT
GRAHAM CRES
BAINFIELD RD
MITCHELL DR
FERRY RD
Moore's Bridge
Bloomhill
CARMAN RD
Wallaceton
G82
Walton
Craigend
Ardoch Farm
Westerhill
Ardoch
Caravan Site
Lea Farm
Ardoch
A814
River Clyde
Woodhall
A8
GREENOCK RD
KELBURN TERR
Cemy
GLASGOW RD
HEGGIES AVE
WOODHALL TERR
A8
Finlaystone Point
Parklea
PA14

47
69

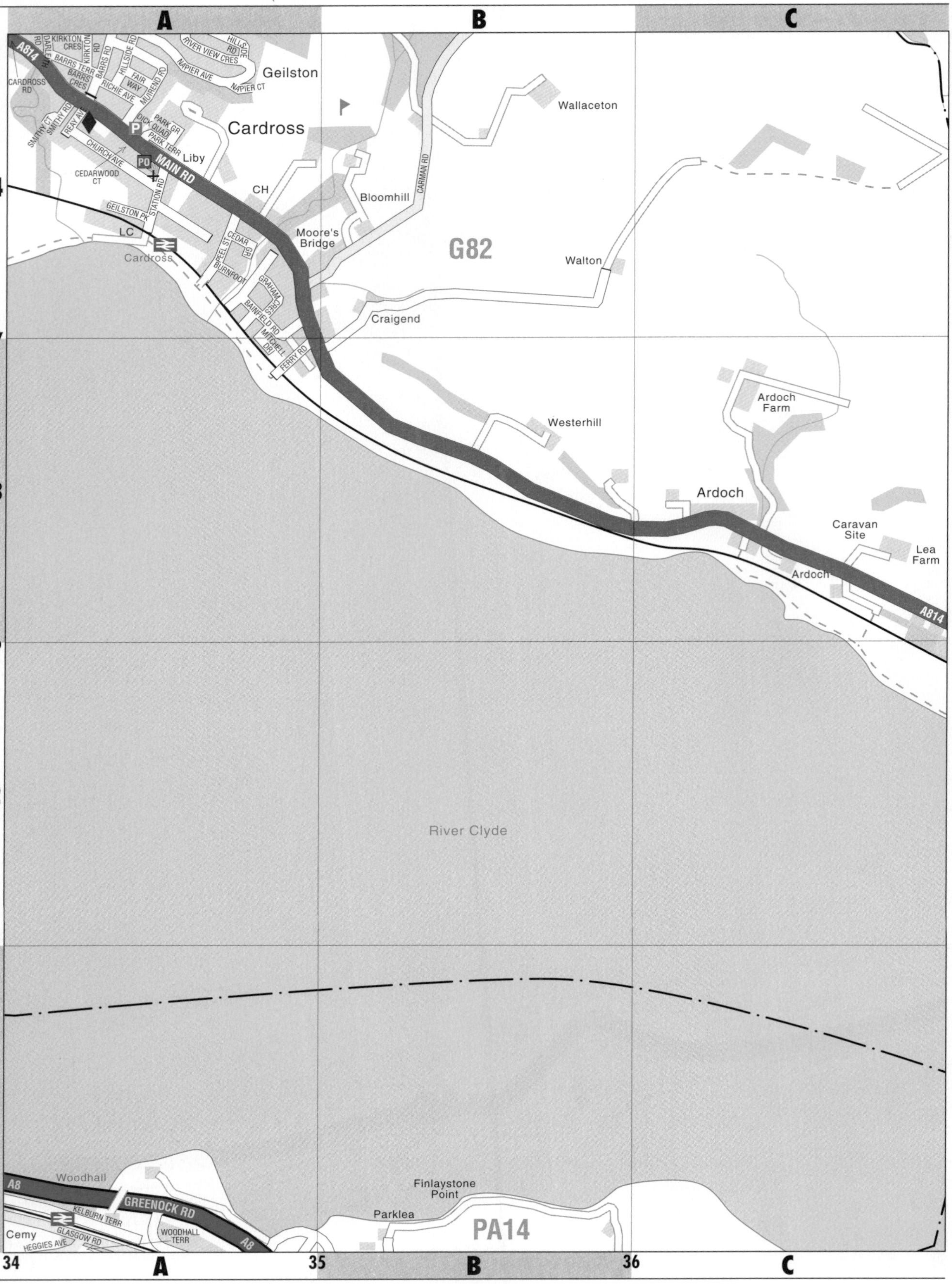

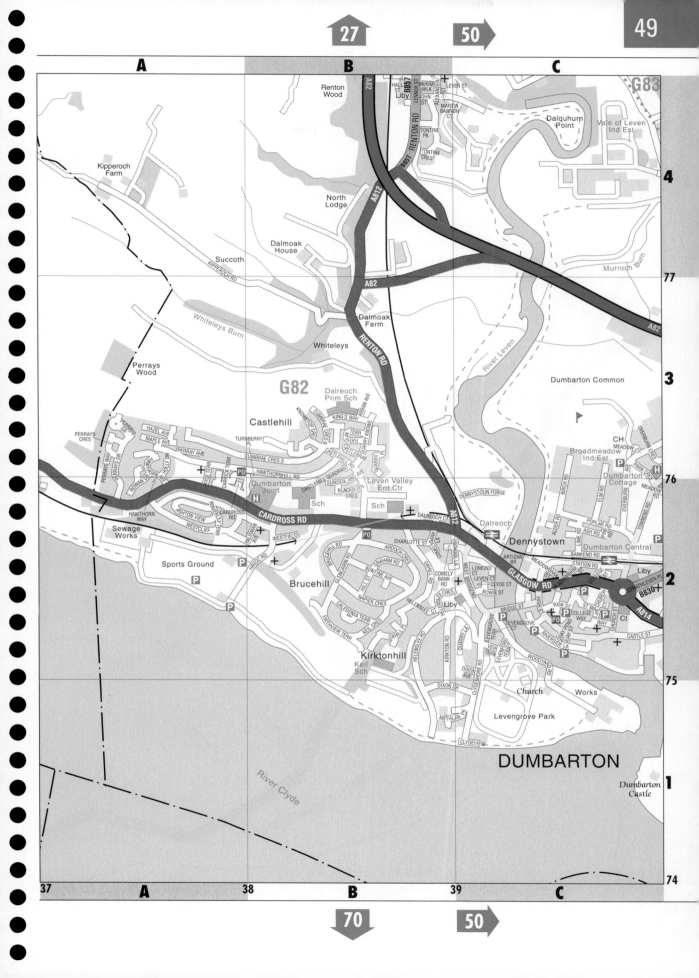

49 28

A   B   C

G83

Murroch Burn

Murroch

Square Wood

Black Wood

4

A813

STIRLING RD

Barr Wood

Maryland

77

Bellsmyre Cottage

Bellsmyre

St Peter's RC Prim Sch

BELLSMYRE AVE
LANGLANDS TERR
MCKENZIE AVE
TAY PL
ALLAN PL
LOANINGHEAD DR
BARWOOD HILL
LONG CRAGS VIEW
MARYLAND RD
BRACKENHURST ST
MURROCH AVE
AUCHENREOCH AVE
AITKENBAR DR
STONYFLATT AVE
GLASGOW RD

Garshake Burn

Water Works

Garshake

Garshake Reservoir

A82

3

A813

OVERBURN AVE
STRATHCLYDE RD
OVERBURN CRES
GOOSEHOLM RD
GOOSEHOLM DR
DOVEHOLM
BARLOAN CRES
CHAPELTON AVE
CHAPELTON ST
BARTON PL
MANSWOOD DR

St Andrew's Brae
OXFORD DR
ST ANDREW'S BRAE
AITKENBAR CIRC
BRAESIDE DR
BROOMHILL DR
STONYFLATT RD
WHITECROOK
PENNIECROFT AVE
AITKENBAR PRIM SCH

B830

Cemy

PINEWOOD CT
WHITEFORD PL
HILLFOOT TERR
GARSHAKE AVE
GARSHAKE RD
GARSHAKE
MCFARLANE
MACPHIE RD

Garshake

Spardie Linn

Overtoun Estate

Overtoun Burn

76

Townend Sch

MEADOW RD
POINDFAULD TERR
WILLIAMSON ST
ALEXANDER ST
COLQUHOUN ST
GIBSON ST
OVERWOOD GR
ROUND RIDING RD
NETHERBOG AVE
KILPATRICK VIEW
DUMBUCK AVE

Hamilton St
HARTFIELD GDNS
LATTA ST

Silverton
Dumbarton Acad Sch

BONHILL RD
B830

BOGHEAD RD
MILLER ST
BOGHEAD RD
OVERWOOD DR
MILLBURN RD
CROSSLET AVE
WHITE AVE
CROSSLET

BROWN AVE

POL HQ

CROSSLET
ARGYLL AVE
ARGYLL AVE
STUART DR
FRASER AVE
CAMPBELL TERR
CAMPBELL DR
CAMPBELL DR

DUMBARTON

Barwood Hill

Barnhill

Tom's Seat

2

1 BANKEND RD
2 STRATHLEVEN PL
BROOMFAULD GDNS

Superstores

HARTFIELD CT

DOUGLAS ST
CROSSLET RD
CROSSLET PL
MILLBURN CRES
DUMBIE AVE

MURRAY PL
OVERTLAND
CAMPBELL DR

Crosslet

MacEWAN'S WELL
Gruggies Burn

G82

Loch Bowie

Middleton

A814

Dumbarton East

PARK ST
PARK AVE
SILVERTONHILL LA
SILVERTON AVE
OVERTOUN AVE
SNIDDLE RD

Silvertonhill La

ALCLUTHA AVE
DUMBRITTON RD
STROWAN'S RD
STROWAN RD
GREENHEAD RD
GELLS HADRANT
HIGH MAINS AVE
FOURTH AVE
GLENPATH
BARNHILL RD
HUNTER'S AVE

STIRLING RD

Northwood

Dumbowie

75

Superstores

Mus
CASTLE ST
LEVEN ST
LENNOX
WALLACE ST
VICTORIA ST
BRUCE ST
BUCHANAN ST

Knoxland Prim Sch

CASTLEGREEN LA
CASTLEGREEN ST
CASTLEGREEN
EASTFIELD CRES

GREENHEAD GDNS
GREENHEAD AVE
DUMBUCK CRES
GELS AVE
SECOND AVE
THIRD AVE
FIRST AVE

Milton House

MILTON BRAE

Football Ground

CASTLE RD

KNOXLAND SQ
PIONEER PK
KNOXLAND ST 1
BURNSIDE PL 2
BURNSIDE RD 3
EASTFIELD PL 4

CASTLEGREEN GDNS

CATRINE AVE
MARY FISHER CRES
BERENICE PL
OTAGO PL
CUTTY SARK PL

GLASGOW RD

OAKTREE GDNS

Hotel

1

Dumbuck

Milton

LENNOX RD
HILL VIEW
COLQUHOUN RD
MILTON CT
MILTON HILL
Milton Prim Sch
PO

CRANNOG CT
CRANNOG RD

DUMBARTON RD

MILLERSLEA
WHYTE CNR

A814

A82

Works

River Clyde

74

40   A   41   B   42   C

49 71

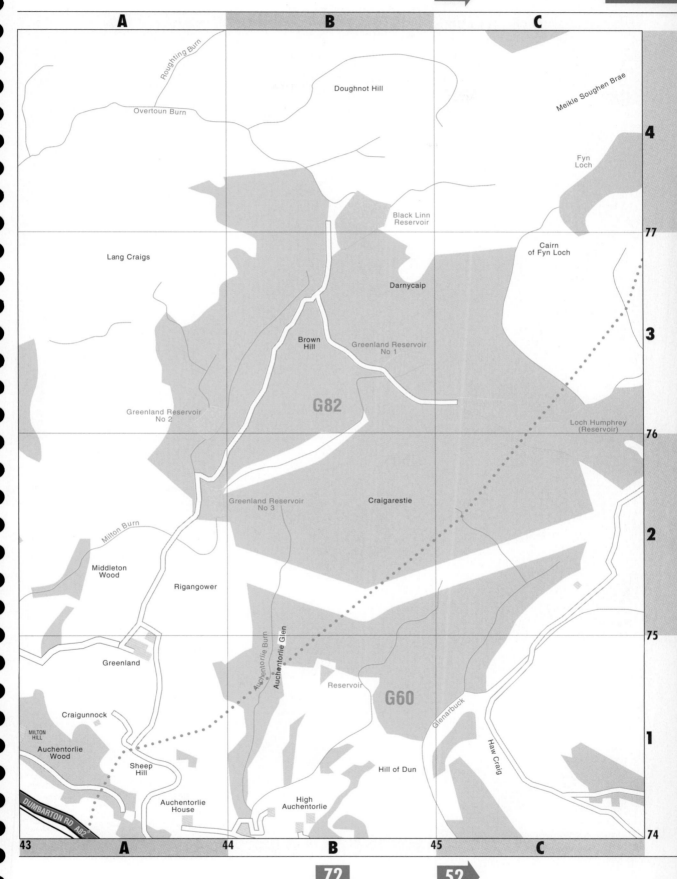

A   B   C

Roughting Burn

Overtoun Burn

Doughnot Hill

Meikle Soughen Brae

4

Fyn Loch

Black Linn Reservoir

77

Lang Craigs

Cairn of Fyn Loch

Darnycaip

3

Brown Hill

Greenland Reservoir No 1

G82

Greenland Reservoir No 2

Loch Humphrey (Reservoir)

76

Greenland Reservoir No 3

Craigarestie

Milton Burn

2

Middleton Wood

Rigangower

75

Greenland

Auchentorlie Burn

Auchentorlie Glen

Reservoir

G60

Glenarbuck

Craigunnock

MILTON HILL

Auchentorlie Wood

Sheep Hill

Hill of Dun

Haw Craig

1

Auchentorlie House

DUMBARTON RD A82

High Auchentorlie

74

43   A   44   B   45   C

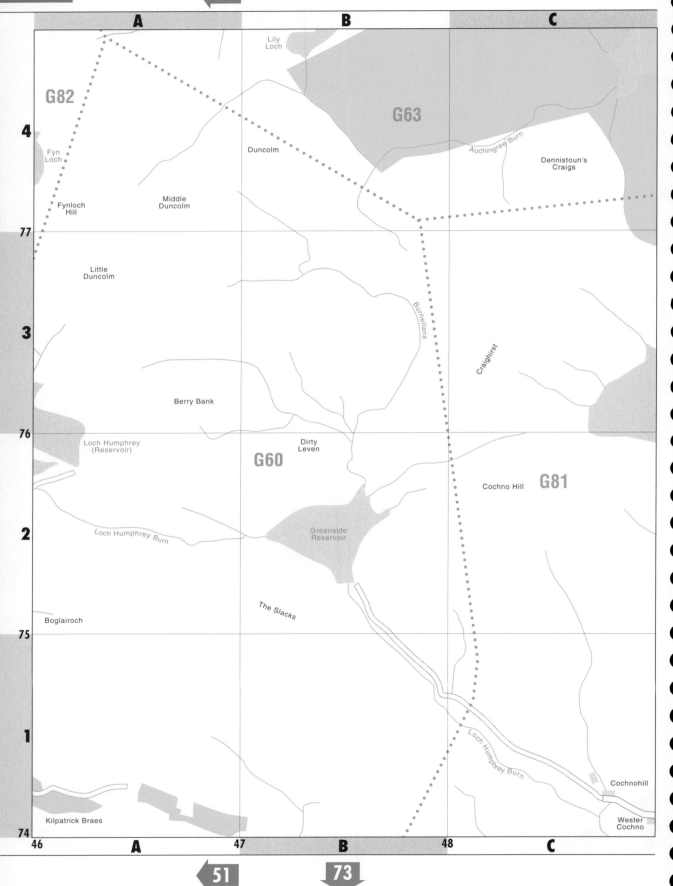

51

A   **B**   **C**

G82

Lily
Loch

G63

4

Duncolm

Auchingree Burn

Dennistoun's
Craigs

Fyn
Loch

Fynloch
Hill

Middle
Duncolm

77

Little
Duncolm

Burnellans

Craighirst

3

Berry Bank

76

Loch Humphrey
(Reservoir)

Dirty
Leven

G60

Cochno Hill

G81

Loch Humphrey Burn

Greenside
Reservoir

2

The Slacks

Boglairoch

75

Loch Humphrey Burn

1

Cochnohill

Kilpatrick Braes

Wester
Cochno

74

46   **A**   47   **B**   48   **C**

51

73

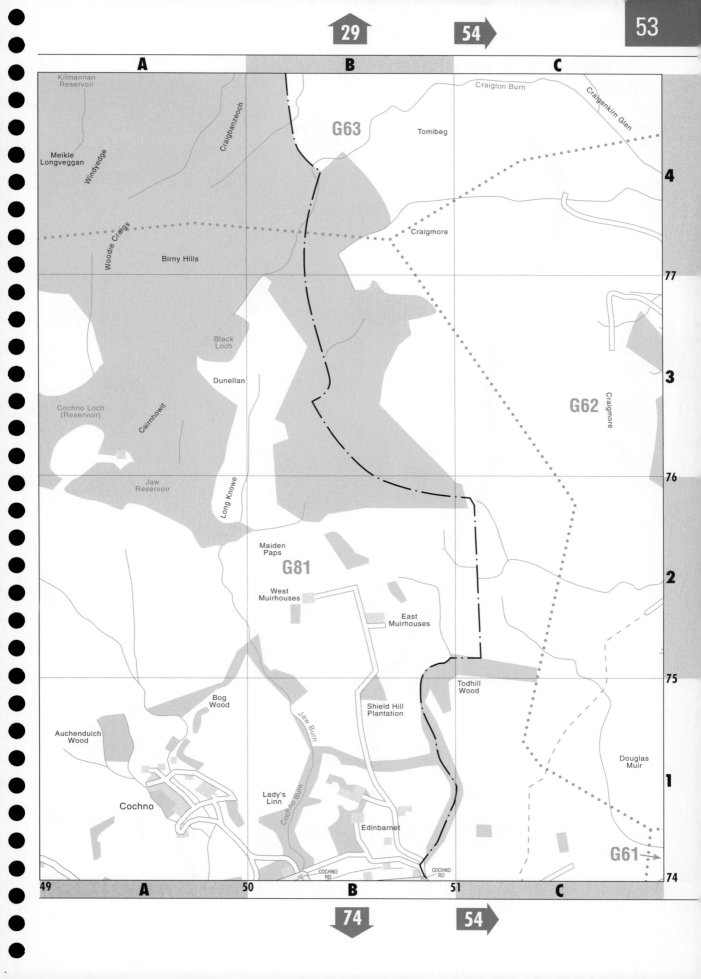

G63

A809

CH

4

G62

77

Craigton Burn

Craigallian Bridge

West Highland Way

Allander Water

Mugdock Wood

High Craigton

Shank Burn

Mount Zion

3

CH

Carneddans Wood

Low Craigton

Craigton Cotts

Laighpark

Wks

76

Field Wood

Braval

Craigton Village

CARNEDDANS RD

THE LOAN

2

Tambowie

Little Balvie

Douglas Acad

CRAIGTON RD

McGrigor RD

Crawford RD

Stable RD

Bleach Field

Cloberfield

Blackwood RD

Birrell

James Watt RD

Watt PL

Dunlop PL

Cloberfield Gdns

Clober Farm LA

Cloberhill RD

North Dumgoyne AVE

Clochbar Gdns

CH

Ardlui Gdns

Achray PL

Kilmannan Gdns

Dungoyne

Fallloch RD

Catter Gdns

Carnock Gdns

Endrick Gdns

Cawder RD

Hilton RD

Craigbo Dr W

Kelvin RD

Lye SQ

Craigton Gdns

Tambowie AVE

75

Dumoil PL

Dunglan RD

Drumbeg Terr

Ballagan PL

Graham Dr

Garbeth RD

Balvie AVE

Dumgoyne AVE

Dumburn Cres

Balviebank

Craigdhu Burn

Crossburn

Auldmurroch Dr 1

Craighead Dr 2

Douglas Muir RD

Craigbo RD

Drumbrock RD

Castle Mains RD

Kirvel PL

Kirbie PL

Garbel RD

Anerlees Cres

Kirk ST

Clober Prim Sch

Craigielea Cres

Ashburn RD

Carbeth Rd

Carrick AVE

Tambowie Cres

North Campbell AVE

Ferguson AVE

1

Douglas Muir

Dalnair RD

Calderstream PL

Cairnlea RD

Hunter PL

Ashburn Gdns

Oakburn AVE

Dumgoyne Sch Gdns

Craigdow

Craigdhu RD

B8050

G61

Craighead Knowe

Mains Plantation

Old Mains Farm

Chestnut LA

B8050

Brea

Drimshannan Dr

Crossbank AVE

Braehead AVE

Vivian AVE

South Mains RD

Prestonfield

74

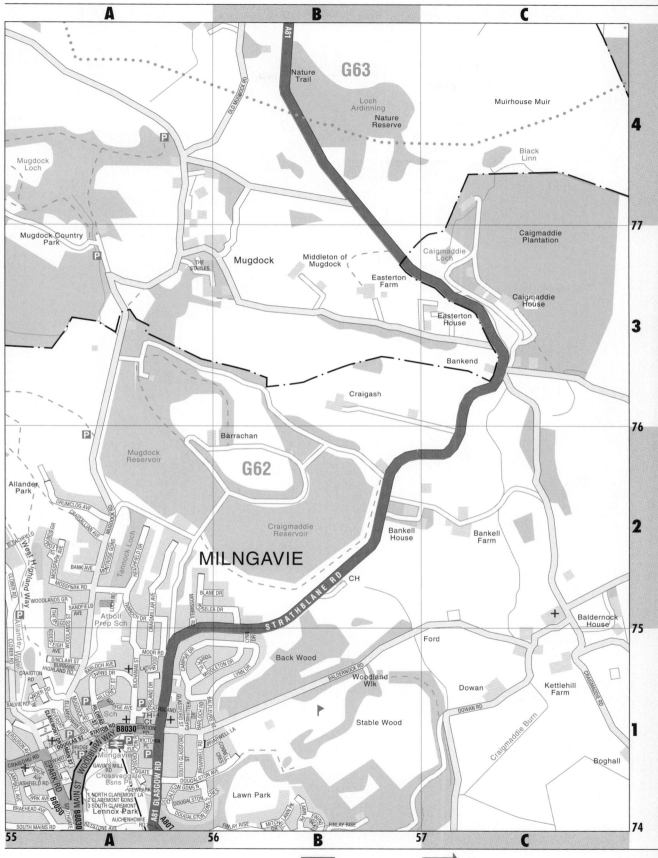

A   B   C

Pattie's Bughts

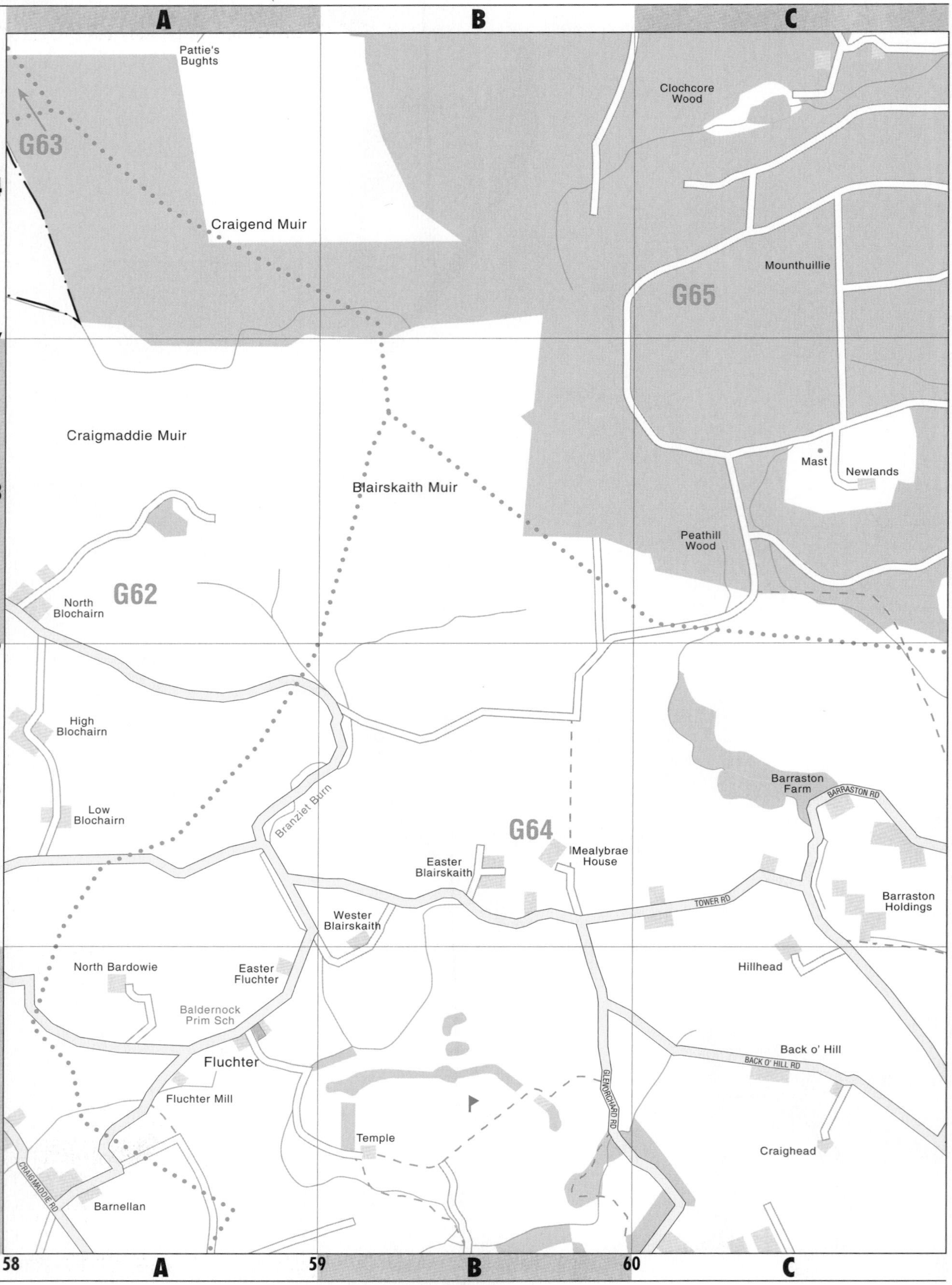

Clochcore Wood

G63

Craigend Muir

Mounthuillie

G65

4

77

Craigmaddie Muir

Mast   Newlands

Blairskaith Muir

3

Peathill Wood

North Blochairn

G62

76

High Blochairn

Barraston Farm

BARRASTON RD

Low Blochairn

Branziet Burn

G64

Mealybrae House

Barraston Holdings

2

Easter Blairskaith

TOWER RD

Wester Blairskaith

75

North Bardowie

Easter Fluchter

Hillhead

Baldernock Prim Sch

Back o' Hill

BACK O' HILL RD

Fluchter

GLENORCHARD RD

1

Fluchter Mill

Temple

Craighead

CRAIGMADDIE RD

Barnellan

74

58   A   59   B   60   C

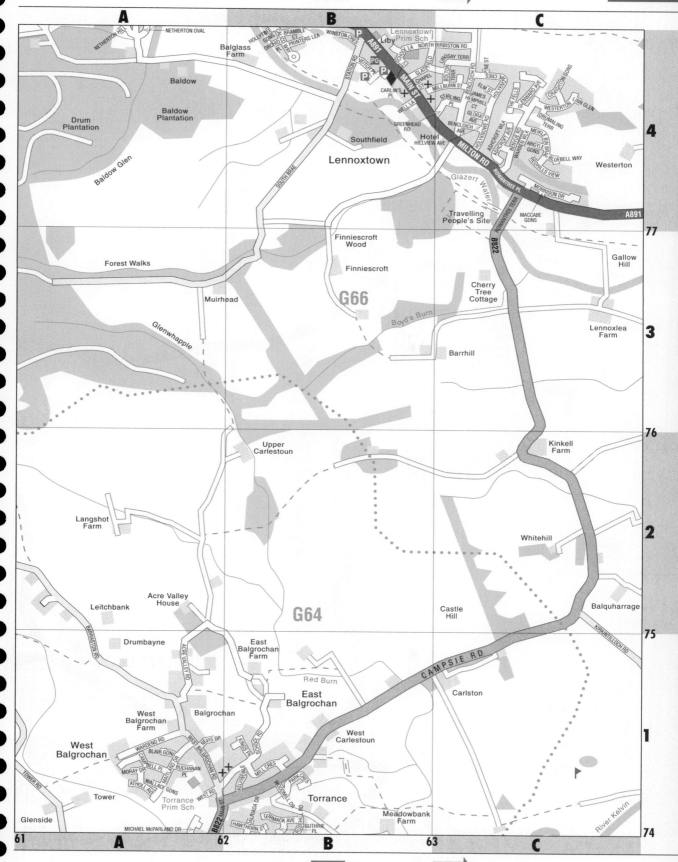

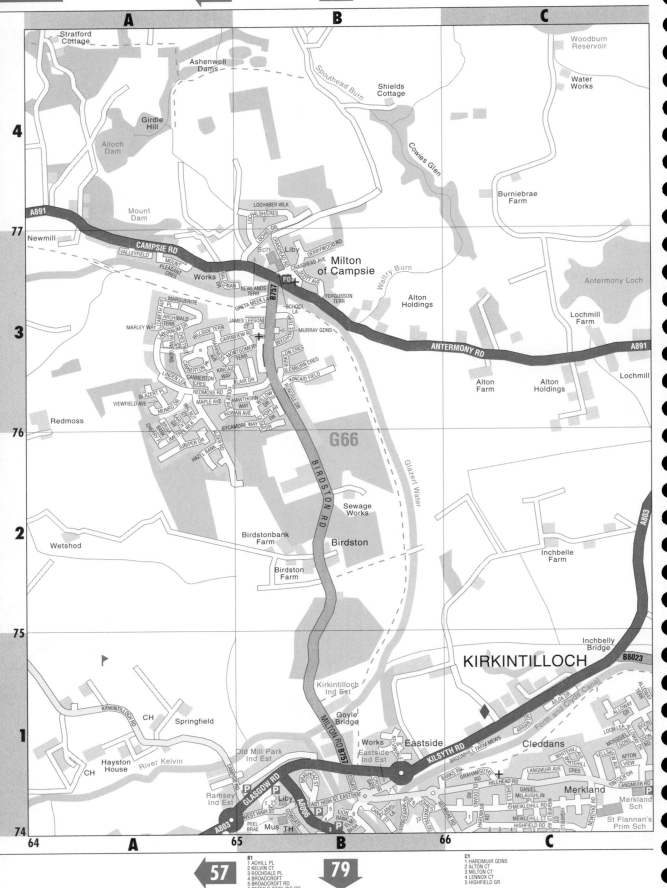

A   B   C

Stratford Cottage

Woodburn Reservoir

Ashenwell Dams

Shields Cottage

Water Works

Girdle Hill

4

Alloch Dam

Cowies Glen

Burniebrae Farm

Mount Dam

Antermony Loch

A891

77

Newmill

CAMPSIE RD

LOCHABER WLK
HALSH CRES
LOCHIE DR
CRAIGHEAD RD
Sch
Liby

DERRYWOOD RD

Milton of Campsie

Waltry Burn

Lochmill Farm

Valleyfield

MOUNT PLEASANT CRES

Works

BALDERNAN DR

NEWLANDS TERR
GRETA MEEK LA

B757

P.O.
CRAIGHEAD RD
SCOTT AVE

SCHOOL LA

FERGUSSON TERR

Alton Holdings

Lochmill

MARGUERITE PL
ELIZABETH AVE
ARCHIBALD TERR
LABURNUM DR
CHESTNUT

JAMES LEESON CT

PETER TERR

MURRAY GDNS

A891

ANTERMONY RD

MARLEY WAY
HILLSIDE TERR
IRVINE GDNS
HARKNESS

CAIRNVIEW RD

BEECH TERR

3

LINDEN LEA
CANNERTON CRES
CANNERTON CRES
MONTGOMERY TERR
KINCAID WAY
BLAIR DR
HOLLY DR
RINDELL DR
GLENBURN CRES
LOCKERBIE CRES
KINCAID FIELD

Alton Farm

Alton Holdings

Lochmill

GLAZERT PL
VIEWFIELD AVE
MUNRO DR
WALNUT
LARCH
HAWTHORN WAY
WILLOW DR
POPLAR DR

REDMOSS RD
MAPLE AVE
ROWAN AVE

Redmoss

CHERRY PL
BRIAR BANK
LIME TREE WLK
ALDER RD
JUNIPER DR
SYCAMORE WAY
CEDAR DR

HAZEL BANK

76

G66

Glazert Water

Wetshod

BIRDSTON RD

Sewage Works

2

Birdstonbank Farm

Birdston

Inchbelle Farm

Birdston Farm

A803

75

Inchbelly Bridge

B8023

KIRKINTILLOCH

Kirkintilloch Ind Est

KIRKINTILLOCH RD

CH

Springfield

MILTON RD

Goyle Bridge

B757

Forth and Clyde Canal

AILSA DR

ALLOWAY TERR
ALLOWAY GR
LOCH LEA
MOSSGIEL GDNS

1

Hayston House

River Kelvin

CH

Old Mill Park Ind Est

Works

Eastside

KILSYTH RD

Eastside Ind Est

Broomhill Farm Mews

Cleddans

AFTON VIEW
FINTOCK DR
LANGMUIR AVE

Merkland

Merkland Sch

Ramsey Ind Est

GLASGOW RD

CAMPSIE RD

A803

Liby

P

BRAEHEAD ST

A806

P

EAST HIGH ST EASTSIDE
LION ST
CROSS GATE
RENVILLE

BANKS RD
GRAHAMSDYKE RD
HILLHEAD RD

DANIEL McLAUGHLIN

LANGMUIR AVE

KELLS PL

St Flannan's Prim Sch

WEST HIGH ST
PEEL BRAE

COWGATE
Mus
TH

P

LOGIEGARBH
CANAL ST
BAIN ST

CANAL LA
WATERLOO

SHELLS RD
MEIKLEHILL CT
MEIKLEHILL RD

HIGHFIELD
HIGHFIELD AVE
HIGHFIELD RD

74

A   B   C

64   65   66

B1
1 ACHILL PL
2 KELVIN CT
3 ROCHDALE PL
4 BROADCROFT
5 BROADCROFT RD
6 PETER D.STIRLING RD
7 HOPKIN'S BRAE
8 WATERLOO GDNS

C1
1 HARDMUIR GDNS
2 ALTON CT
3 MILTON CT
4 LENNOX CT
5 HIGHFIELD GR

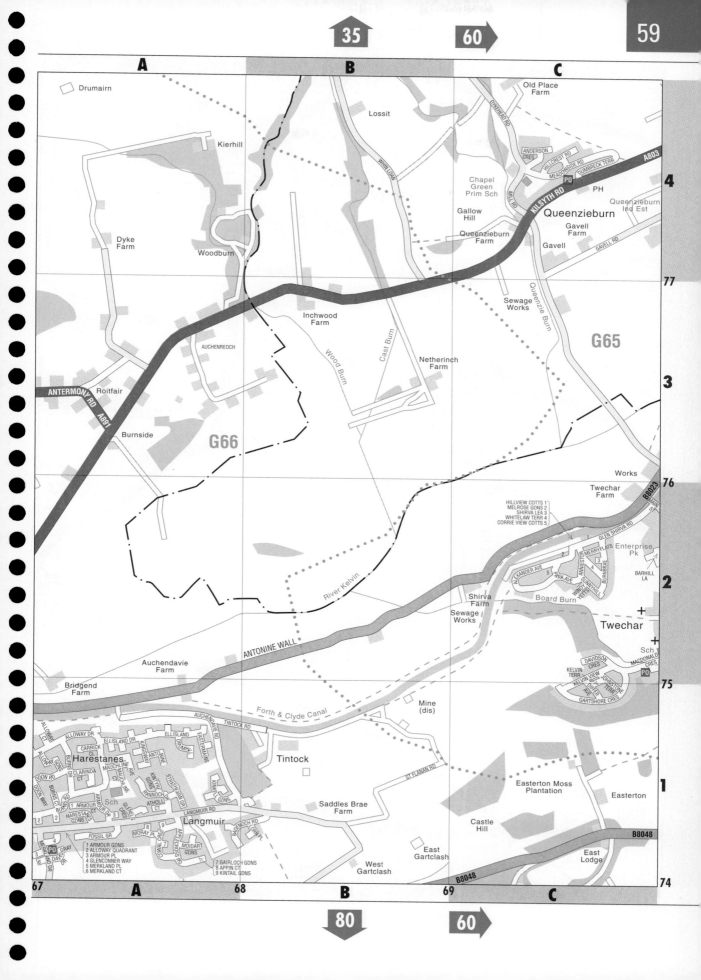

A   B   C

Drumairn

Old Place
Farm

Lossit

Kierhill

DYKEHEAD RD

A803

ANDERSON
CRES

HILLCREST RD
MEADOWSIDE RD
DUMBRECK TERR

MILL RD

KILSYTH RD

4

Chapel
Green
Prim Sch

PO

PH

Dyke
Farm

Gallow
Hill

Queenzieburn

Queenzieburn
Ind Est

Woodburn

Queenzieburn
Farm

Gavell
Farm

Gavell

GAVELL RD

Inchwood
Farm

Sewage
Works

77

AUCHENREOCH

Queenzie Burn

G65

Wood Burn

Cast Burn

Netherinch
Farm

3

ANTERMONY RD

Roitfair

A891

Burnside

G66

Works

Twechar
Farm

76

B8023

HILLVIEW COTTS 1
MELROSE GDNS 2
SHIRVA LEA 3
WHITELAW TERR 4
CORRIE VIEW COTTS 5

GLEN SHIRVA RD

MAIN ST

Enterprise
Pk

MERRYFLATS

ANNISTON

WINDYYETTS

BURNBRAE

BARHILL
LA

ALEXANDER AVE

PARK AVE

SUNNYHILL

River Kelvin

Shirva
Farm

Board Burn

2

Twechar

Sewage
Works

Sch

MACDONALD
CRES

DAVIDSON
CRES

KELVIN
TERR

JOHNSTONE
TERR

PO

Auchendavie
Farm

ANTONINE WALL

KELVIN VIEW

DIFFER
AVE

GARTSHORE CRES

75

Bridgend
Farm

Forth & Clyde Canal

Mine
(dis)

Easterton Moss
Plantation

Easterton

1

ALLOWAY
CT

ALLOWAY DR

ELLISLAND DR

KIRKSMAN

ANTONINE

ELLISLAND
DRUMHL

AUCHENDAVIE RD

TINTOCK RD

EASTERMAINS

Tintock

ST FLANAN RD

CARRICK
CL

CLARINDA
CT

MAUCHLINE AVE

KILTYRE

STRATHERD GR

KINNEL
GDNS

ALLOWAY

BURNS DR

DOON RD

MAUCHLINE

RANNOCH

KILTYRE
GDNS

KINNEL
GDNS

Harestanes

Sch

1 ARMOUR GDNS

ARMOUR DR

GLENELG
CRES

ATHOLL
CT

LANGMUIR RD

BADENOCH RD

DRIN PL

Saddles Brae
Farm

DOON WAY

BURNS CT

ARMOUR
CT

2

HARESTANES
GDNS

2

8

MORAY PL

COWAL CRES

9

APPLECROSS RD

MOIDART
GDNS

Langmuir

Castle
Hill

PO
GRAY

DAVD
DR

MERKLAND CT

FOSSIL GR

1 ARMOUR GDNS
2 ALLOWAY QUADRANT
3 ARMOUR PL
4 GLENCONNER WAY
5 MERKLAND PL
6 MERKLAND CT

7 GAIRLOCH GDNS
8 APPIN CT
9 KINTAIL GDNS

West
Gartclash

East
Gartclash

East
Lodge

B8048

B8048

74

A   B   C

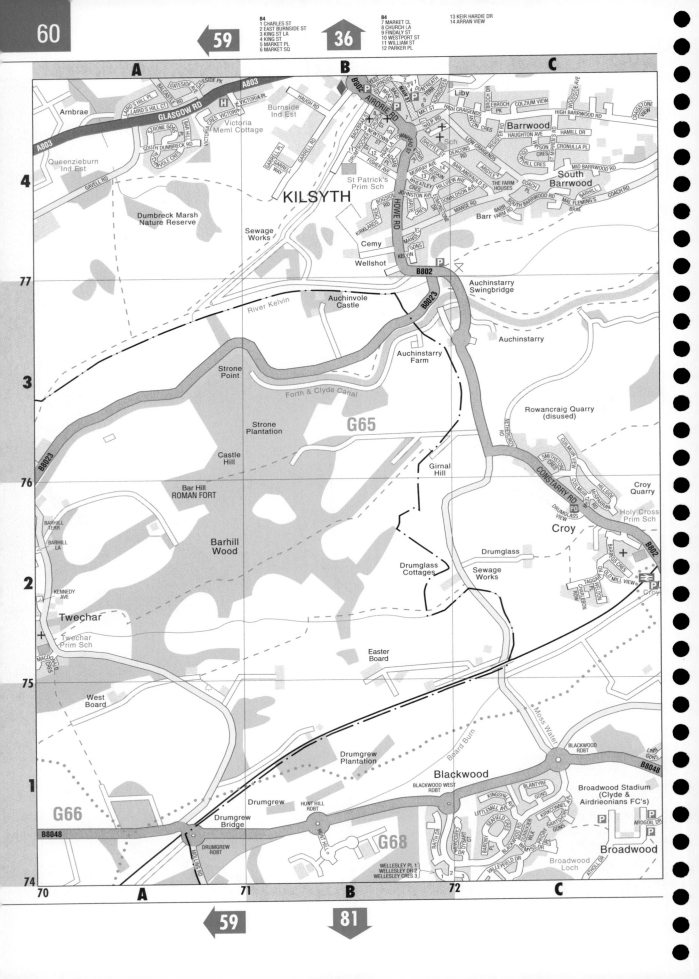

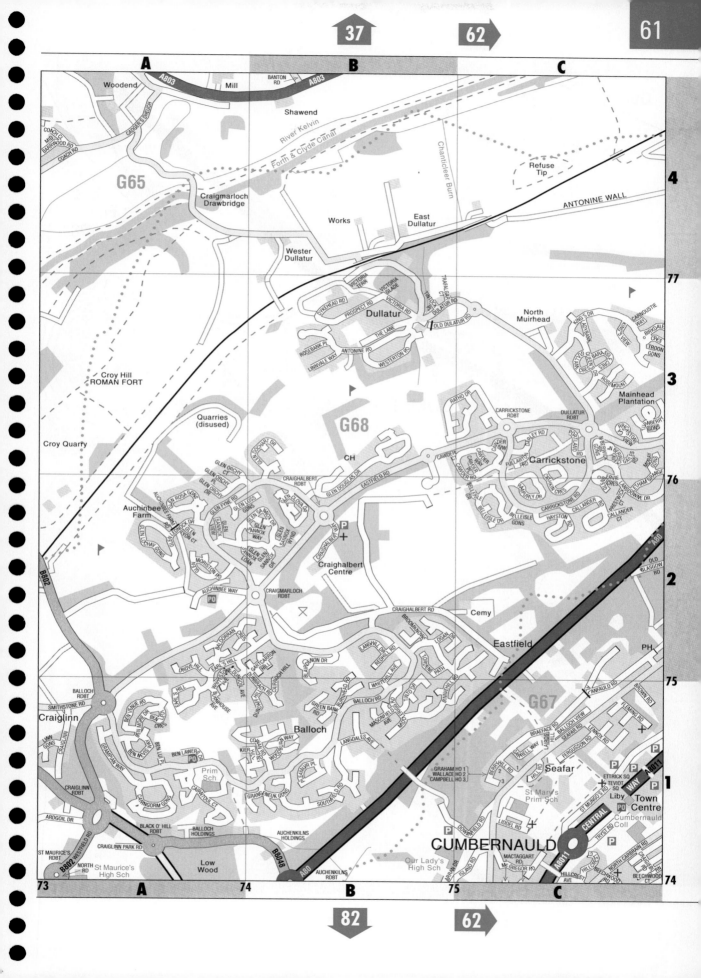

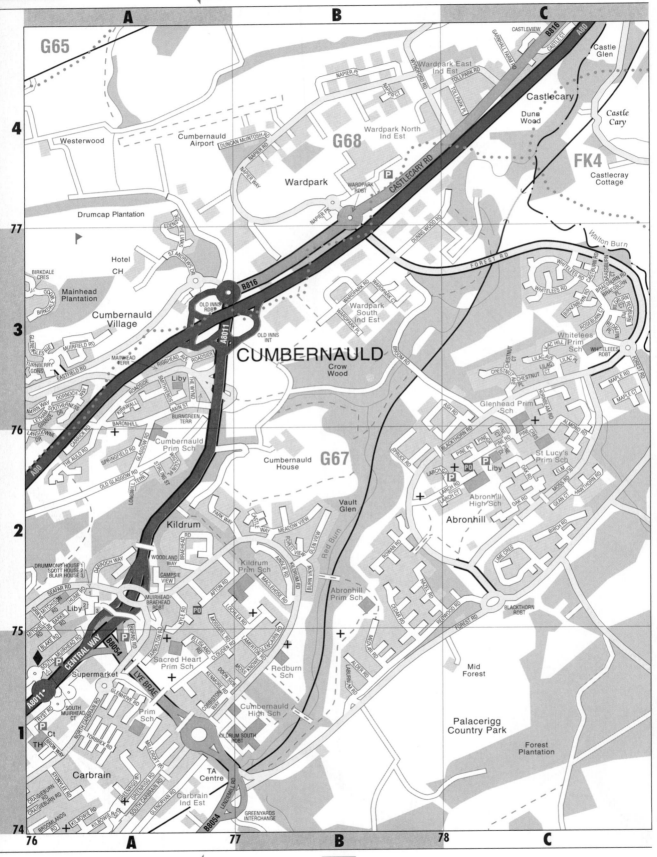

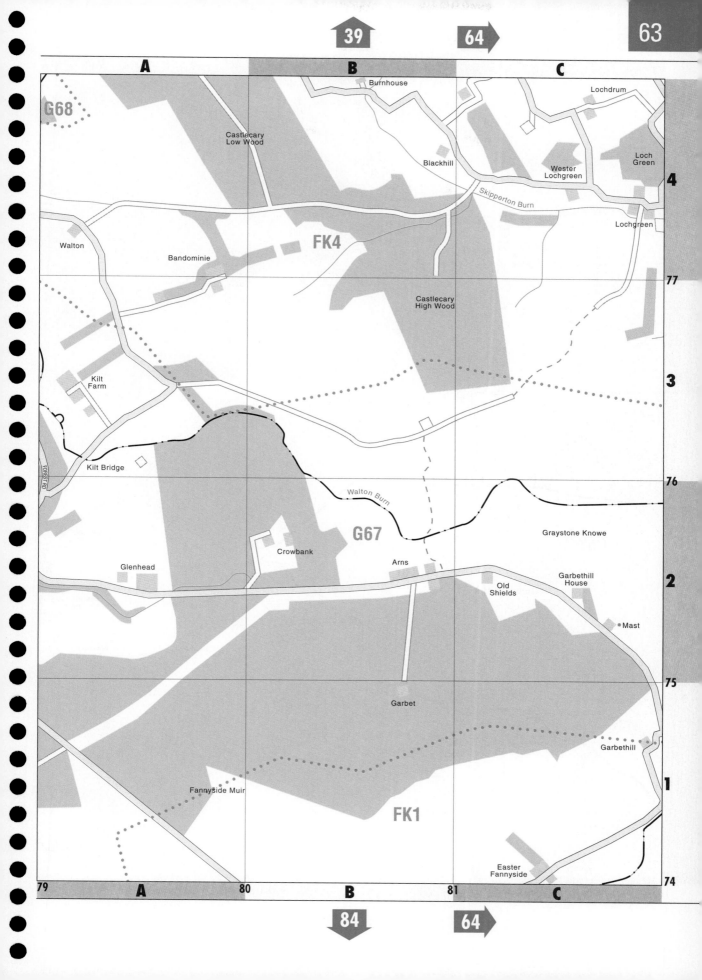

A
B
C

Drum Wood

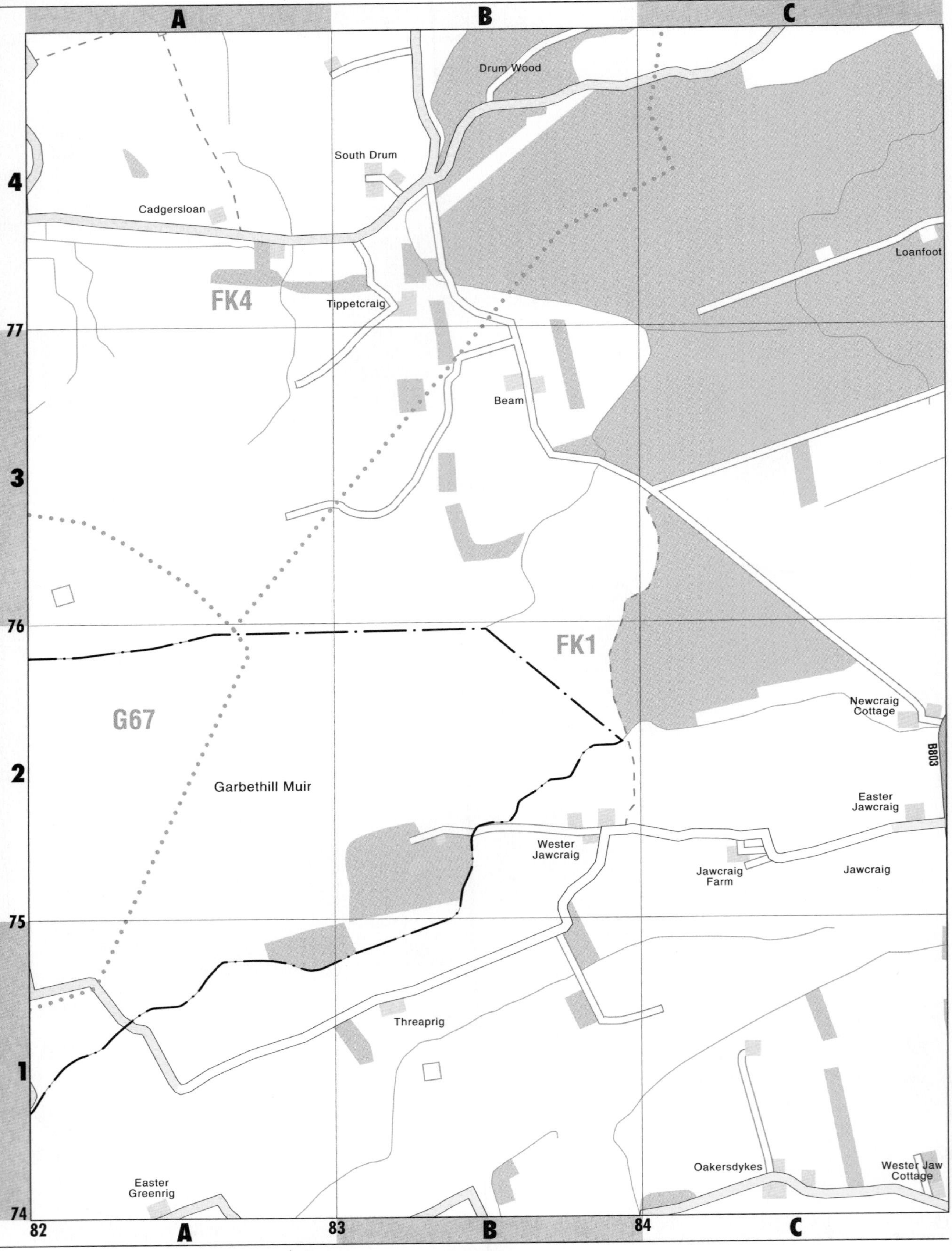

4

South Drum

Cadgersloan

FK4

Tippetcraig

77

Beam

3

76

FK1

G67

Newcraig
Cottage

Garbethill Muir

2

Easter
Jawcraig

Wester
Jawcraig

Jawcraig
Farm

Jawcraig

75

Threaprig

1

Oakersdykes

Wester Jaw
Cottage

Easter
Greenrig

74

Loanfoot

B803

82
A
83
B
84
C

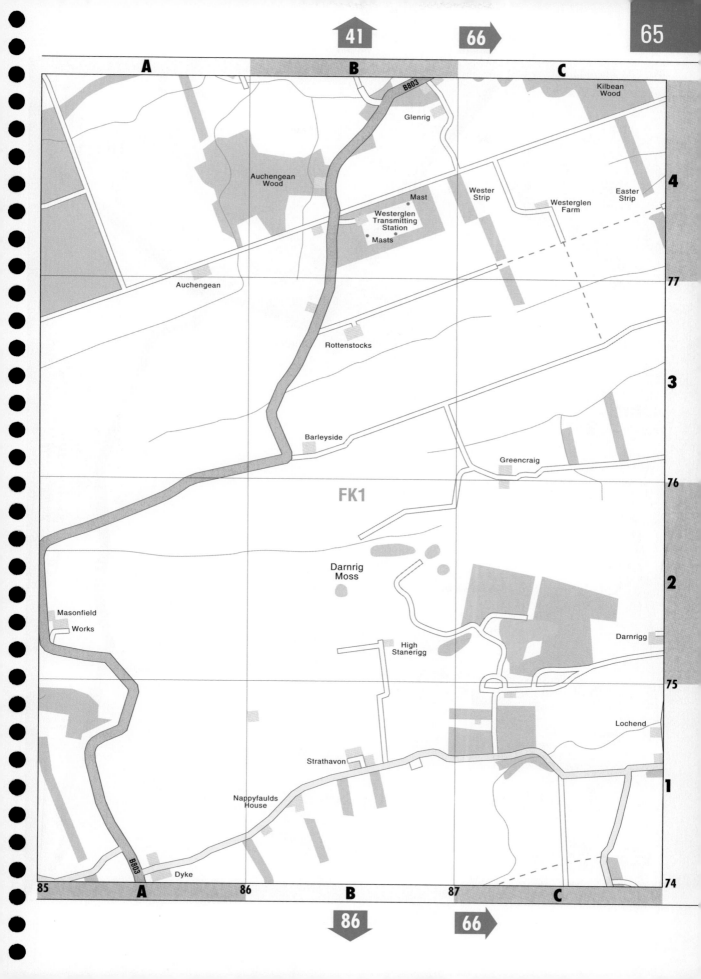

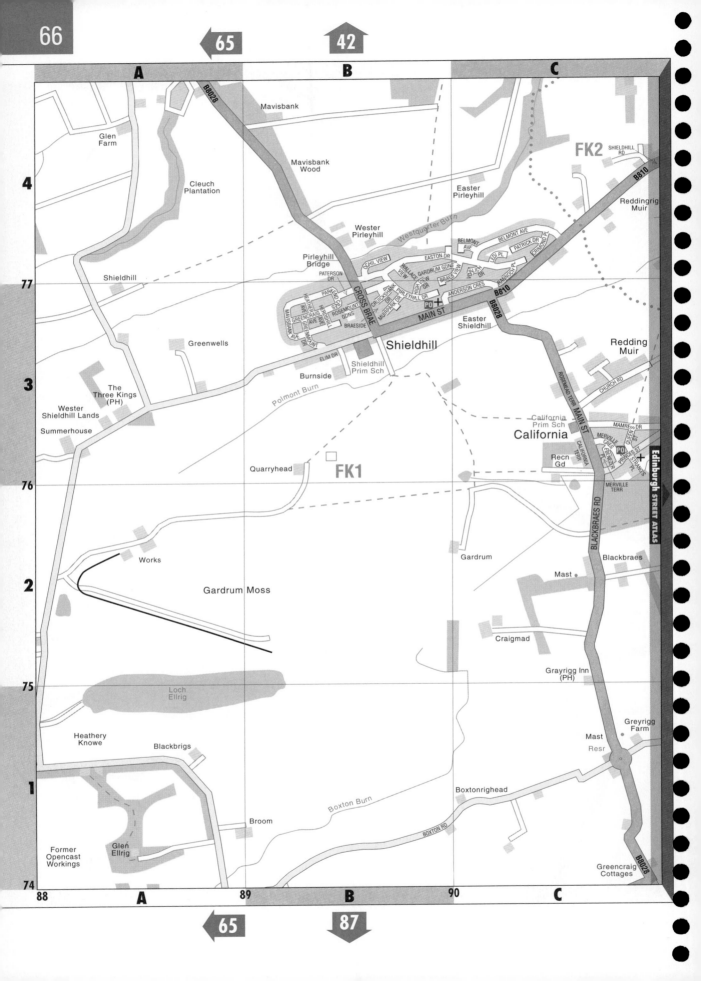

Glen Farm

Cleuch Plantation

Mavisbank

Mavisbank Wood

FK2

SHIELDHILL RD

B810

Easter Pirleyhill

Reddingrig Muir

Westerquarter Burn

Wester Pirleyhill

BELMONT AVE

BELMONT AVE

PATRICK DR

ARMAND PL

Pirleyhill Bridge

EASTON DR

SHIL VIEW

LEDI PL

VORLICH DR

Shieldhill

GARDRUM GDNS

WALLACE VIEW

HIGH VIEW

BRAES VIEW

RHANNOCH PL

PATERSON DR

PARK RD

CRUCKSHANK DR

PIRLEYHILL DR

ANDERSON CRES

B810

4

77

B8028

HEATHER AVE

GREENMOUNT

HERONSHILL

GREENCRAIG AVE

MAVISBANK AVE

ROSEMOUNT GDNS

BRAESIDE

CROSS BRAE

MUIRPARK DR

PO

MAIN ST

B8028

Easter Shieldhill

Redding Muir

Greenwells

ELIM DR

Shieldhill Prim Sch

Shieldhill

CHURCH RD

3

The Three Kings (PH)

Burnside

Polmont Burn

ROSEBANK TERR

California Prim Sch

MAIN ST

MAMRES DR

QUEENS ST

Wester Shieldhill Lands

California

MERVILLE CRES

EBENEZER PL

PRINCES ST

STRANGS

Summerhouse

California Prim Sch

CALIFORNIA TERR

PO

Edinburgh STREET ATLAS

Recn Gd

MERVILLE TERR

Quarryhead

FK1

76

BLACKBRAES RD

Gardrum

Blackbraes

Works

Mast

2

Gardrum Moss

Craigmad

Grayrigg Inn (PH)

75

Loch Ellrig

Greyrigg Farm

Heathery Knowe

Blackbrigs

Mast

Resr

1

Boxtonrighead

Broom

Boxton Burn

Former Opencast Workings

Glen Ellrig

BOXTON RD

B8028

Greencraig Cottages

74

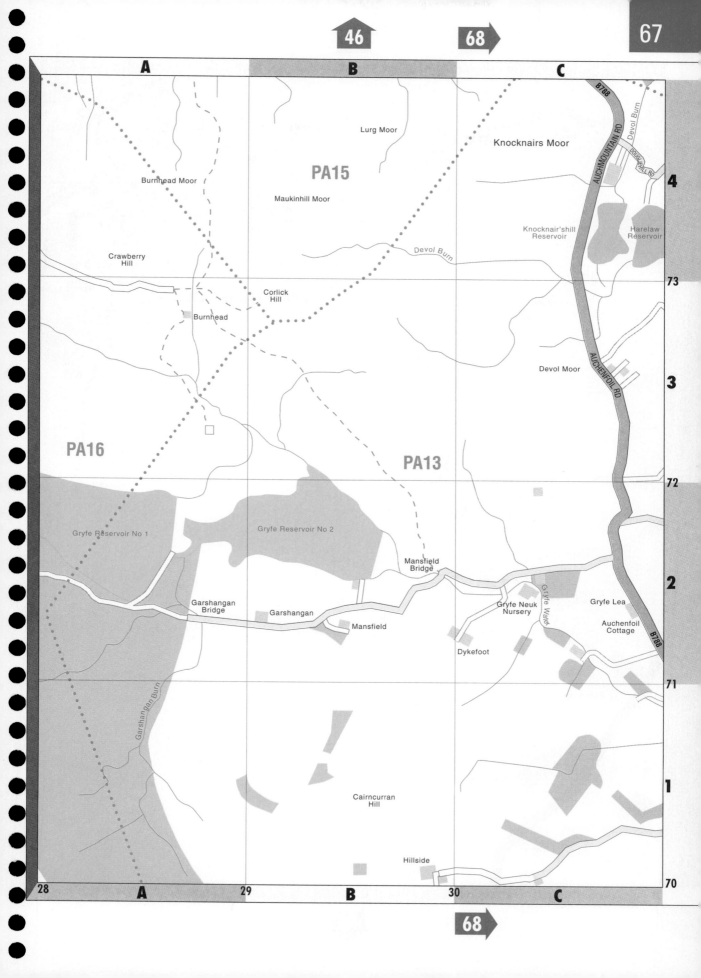

46

68

A   B   C

Lurg Moor

Knocknairs Moor

PA15

Burnhead Moor

Maukinhill Moor

Knocknair'shill
Reservoir

Harelaw
Reservoir

4

Devol Burn

Crawberry
Hill

73

Corlick
Hill

Burnhead

Devol Moor

3

PA16

PA13

72

Gryfe Reservoir No 1

Gryfe Reservoir No 2

Mansfield
Bridge

2

Garshangan
Bridge

Garshangan

Gryfe Neuk
Nursery

Gryfe Lea

Mansfield

Auchenfoil
Cottage

Dykefoot

71

Garshangan Burn

Cairncurran
Hill

1

Hillside

70

28   A   29   B   30   C

68

67
47

A   **B**   **C**

CLUNE BRAE
+A761
PH Cemy
HEGGIES AVE
HIGH CARNEGIE RD
PARKHILL AVE
BROOKFIELD RD
KILMACOLM RD
WESTFIELD
NORTHFIELD AVE

MORAY RD
SELKIRK RD
ARDMORE RD
CARDROSS AVE
CLYDEVIEW RD
BENVIEW AVE
BRAEHEAD
BRIDGEND AVE
MID AVE
BURNSIDE AVE

DOUGLIEHILL TERR
DOUGLIEHILL PL
BURNHEAD LA
BURNHEAD RD
GARELOCH LA
GARELOCH RD
Schs
WEST RD
BRIDGEND RD
SOUTH RD

West Dougliehill
DOUGLIEHILL RD

BARR'S BRAE
AUCHENFOIL RD
AUCHENFOIL LA
Ind Est
MUIRSHIEL LA
Boglestone
P

Dougliehill Reservoir

East Dougliehill
BURNBANK TERR
MILLBURN RD
MILLBANK RD
GOLF RD
HARPA AV
MOORFIELD AV
MUIRDYKES AVE
LANGSIDE TERR
MERRYLEE AVE
DUBBS RD
GARELOCH RD
Port Glasgow Ind Est
BARSCUBE AVE
CROSSHILL PL
GRYFE RD
SOUTHFIELD AVE
KILMACOLM RD
Hotel
OAKBANK RD

4

P
CH
Devol
GLENSIDE RD
FENEUK RD
GLENBRAE RD
AUCHENLECK RD
AUCHENLECK LA
LEVERSTON AVE
MONKTON PL
P
Liby
+

Harelaw Reservoir
Mid Auchinleck
MALLAIG RD
MELROSE RD
MOIDART RD
MINARD RD
MUSSAR RD
EAST CRAWFORD
EAST BARMOSS AVE
EAST MOSS RD
Schs

PA14 ▶

73

Devol Moor
PORT GLASGOW
High Auchenleck
MONTROSE RD
MILTON RD
MAYBOLE RD
METHIL RD
MARKINCH RD
TEVIOT RD
WOODSIDE RD
SLAEMUIR
SIDLAW AVE
PENTLAND AVE
CULLINS VIEW
MAXWELLTON
Bardrainney
MARLOCH AVE
SLAEMUIR GDNS

Harelaw

3

Cunston Cottage
CROSSHILL RD

72

Auchentiber
West Kilbride

2

Auchentiber Bridge
PA13
Pennytersal

Priestside Farm

B788

71

Auchenfoyle
High Mathernock
Mathernock Bridge
Gryfeside
Strathgryfe

Gryfe Water

Horsecraigs

1

Cauldside
Blacksholm Bridge
Strathgryfe

Faulds
B788

70

31   **A**   32   **B**   33   **C**

67
88

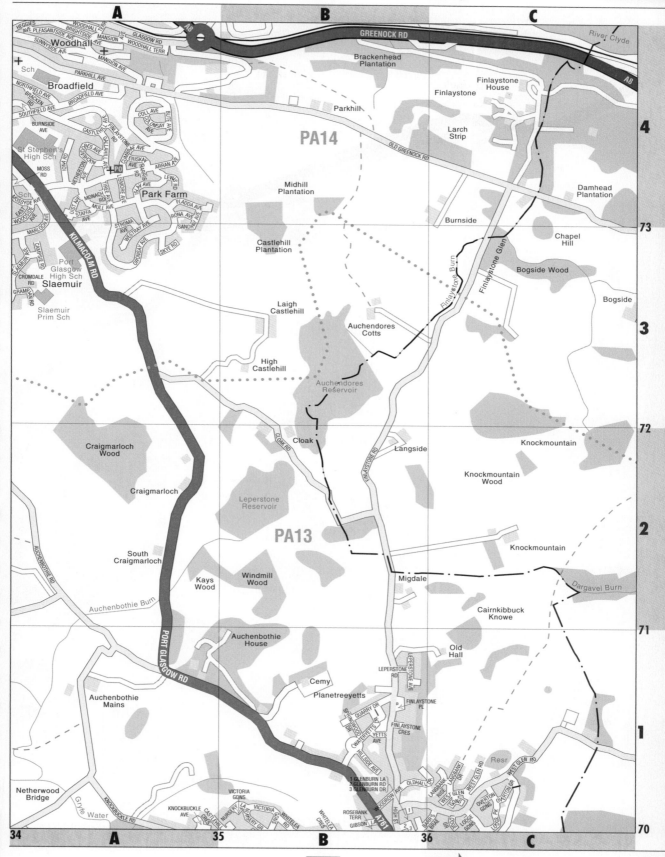

A
B
C

Woodhall
HEGGIES AVE
PLEASANTSIDE AVE
BRIGHTSIDE AVE
WOODHALL AVE
MANSION AVE
GLASGOW RD
WOODHALL TERR
Sch
Broadfield
PARKHILL AVE
NORTHFIELD AVE
BROADFIELD AVE
SOUTHFIELD AVE
BRACKEN RD
CASTLEHILL
BURNSIDE AVE
St Stephen's High Sch
MOSS RD
Sch
MOSSYDE AVE
EAST AVE
WOODSIDE AVE
MARLOCH AVE
SLAEMUIR AVE
CAMPSIE RD
CROMDALE RD
GRAMP
Port Glasgow High Sch
Slaemuir
Slaemuir Prim Sch
METHERTON AVE
MOORE AVE
LISMORE AVE
GIGHA LHILL AVE
TIREE AVE
MONACH AVE
UIST AVE
STAFFA AVE
MULL AVE
STROMA AVE
WESTRAY AVE
PLADDA AVE
RONA AVE
ORONSAY AVE
SKYE RD
SANDY
CASTLEHILL
FINLAYSTONE AVE
ERISKAY AVE
HARRIS AVE
ARRAN AVE
LEWS AVE
COLL AVE
COLONSAY AVE
BUTE AVE
PO
Park Farm
SUNNYSIDE AVE
MANSION AVE

GREENOCK RD
A8
Brackenhead Plantation
River Clyde
A8

Finlaystone
Finlaystone House
Parkhill
Larch Strip
PA14
OLD GREENOCK RD
Damhead Plantation
Midhill Plantation
Burnside
73
Castlehill Plantation
Chapel Hill
Finlaystone Burn
Finlaystone Glen
Bogside Wood
4

KILMACOLM RD
Laigh Castlehill
Auchendores Cotts
Bogside
3
High Castlehill
Auchendores Reservoir
Craigmarloch Wood
CLOAK RD
Cloak
Langside
Knockmountain
72
Craigmarloch
Knockmountain Wood
Leperstone Reservoir
PA13
FINLAYSTONE RD
2
South Craigmarloch
Kays Wood
Windmill Wood
Knockmountain
AUCHENBOTHIE RD
Migdale
Dargavel Burn
Auchenbothie Burn
Cairnkibbuck Knowe
71
PORT GLASGOW RD
Auchenbothie House
Old Hall
Auchenbothie Mains
Cemy
Planetreeyetts
LEPERSTONE RD
LEPERSTONE AVE
Finlaystone PL
Finlaystone Cres
QUARRY DR
SPRINGWOOD DR
WATERYETTS DR
YETTS AVE
1
Netherwood Bridge
HILLSIDE AVE
1 GLENBURN LA
2 GLENBURN RD
3 GLENBURN DR
WOODROW AVE
OLDHALL DR
LANGBANK RISE
LANGBANK
WEST GLEN RD
GLEN MAV
RESR
WEST GLEN RD
KNOCKBUCKLE RD
Gryfe Water
KNOCKBUCKLE AVE
VICTORIA GDNS
NURSERY LA
INSERT GR
CASTLEHILL CRES
VICTORIA GDNS
WHITELEA RD
WHITELEA CRES
ROSEBANK TERR
GIBSON
A761
HIGH ST
BAIRD'S BRAE
SCOTT ST
LODGE GDNS
OVERTON GDNS
LODGE PK
OVERTON DR
70

34
A
35
B
36
C

69
49

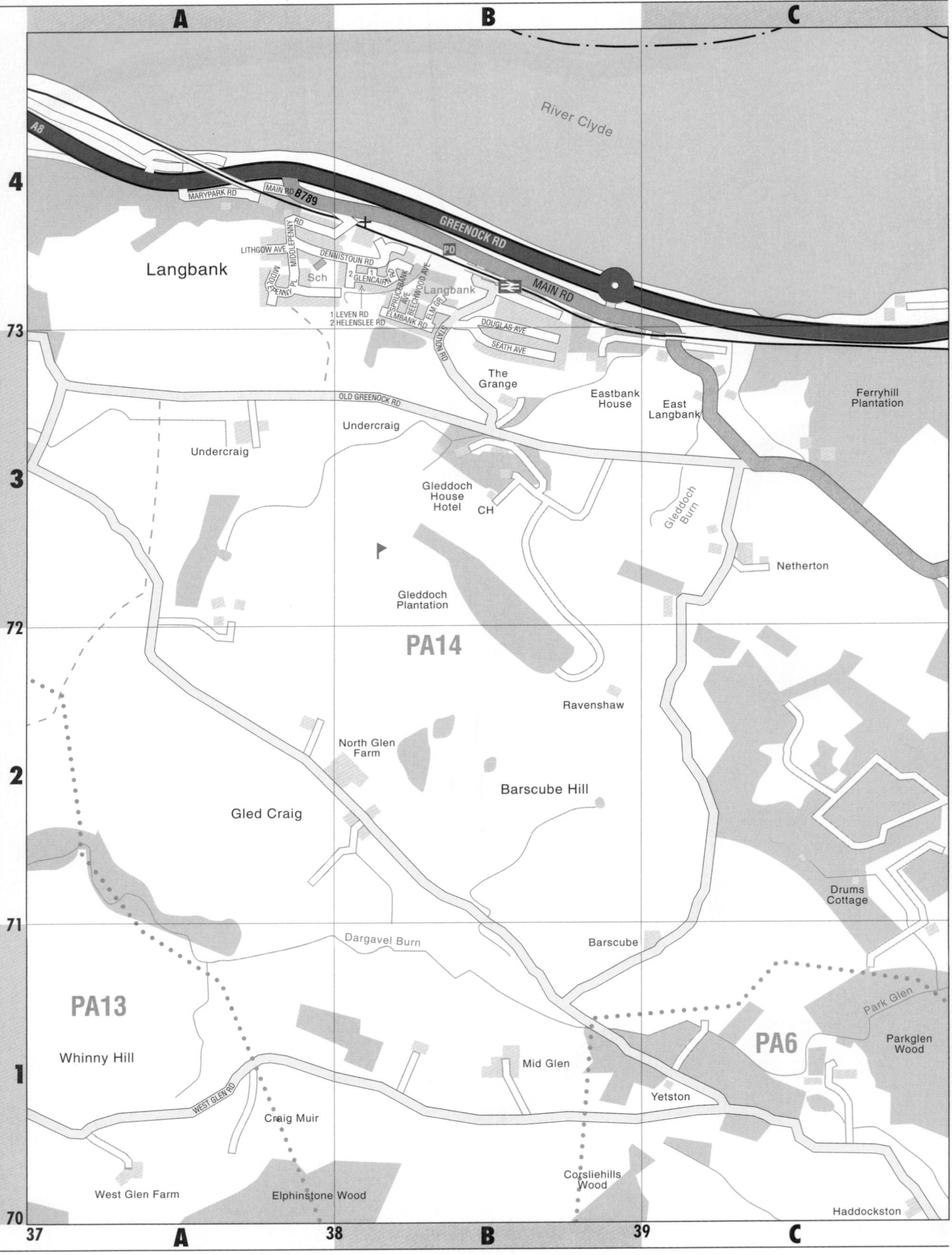

A

B

C

River Clyde

A8

MARYPARK RD

MAIN RD **B789**

GREENOCK RD

4

LITHGOW AVE

DENNISTOUN RD

ANNE PENNY RD

MIDTOUN PL

MIDTOUN CRENNY PL

Langbank

Sch

2 GLENCAIRN

1

SOUTHCRAIG AVE

BEECHWOOD AVE

ELMBANK RD

ELM GR

Langbank

PO

MAIN RD

1 LEVEN RD
2 HELENSLEE RD

MIDTOUN RD

DOUGLAS AVE

SEATH AVE

73

The
Grange

Eastbank
House

East
Langbank

Ferryhill
Plantation

OLD GREENOCK RD

Undercraig

Undercraig

Gleddoch
House
Hotel

CH

Gleddoch
Burn

3

Netherton

Gleddoch
Plantation

72

PA14

Ravenshaw

North Glen
Farm

Barscube Hill

2

Gled Craig

Drums
Cottage

71

Dargavel Burn

Barscube

PA13

Park Glen

Parkglen
Wood

PA6

Whinny Hill

Mid Glen

Yetston

1

WEST GLEN RD

Craig Muir

Corsliehills
Wood

Haddockston

West Glen Farm

Elphinstone Wood

70

37

A

38

B

39

C

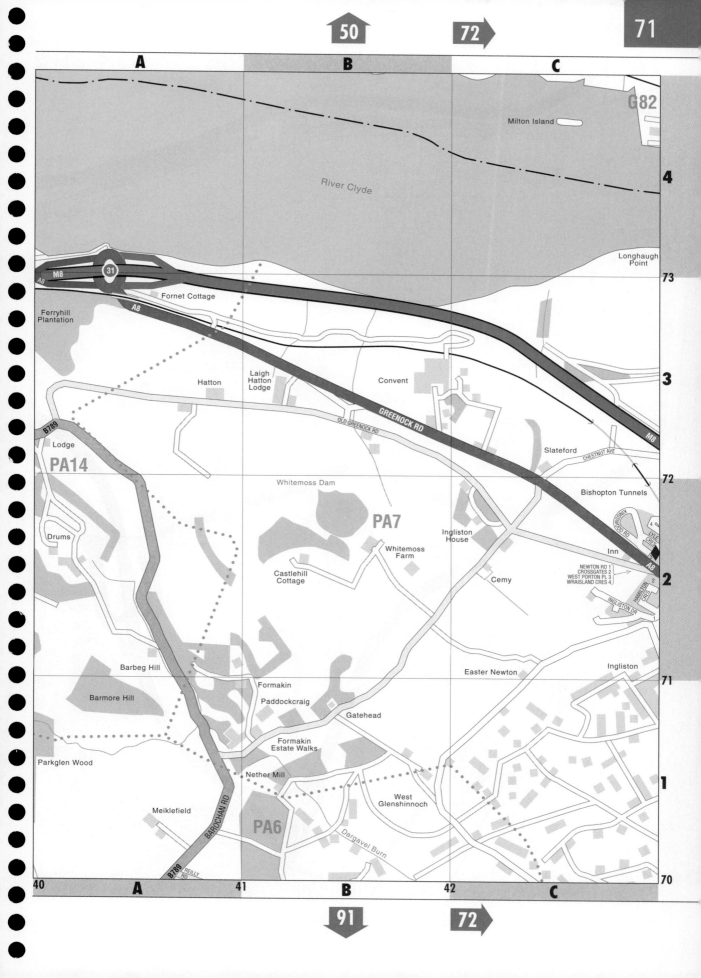

A
B
C

G82

Milton Island

River Clyde

Longhaugh
Point

4

M8
31
A8

73

Fornet Cottage

Ferryhill
Plantation

A8

Laigh
Hatton
Lodge

Hatton

Convent

3

OLD GREENOCK RD

GREENOCK RD

M8

B789

Lodge

Slateford

CHESTNUT AVE

PA14

72

Whitemoss Dam

Bishopton Tunnels

PA7

Drums

Ingliston
House

Inn

Whitemoss
Farm

LYLE
CRES

4

NEWTON RD 1
CROSSGATES 2
WEST PORTON PL 3
WRAISLAND CRES 4

A8

2

Castlehill
Cottage

Cemy

2

HAMILTON
CRES

INGLISTON DR

1

Barbeg Hill

Easter Newton

Ingliston

71

Formakin

Barmore Hill

Paddockcraig

BAROCHAN RD

Gatehead

Parkglen Wood

Formakin
Estate Walks

1

Nether Mill

West
Glenshinnoch

Meiklefield

PA6

B789

REILLY
RD

Dargavel Burn

70

40
A
41
B
42
C

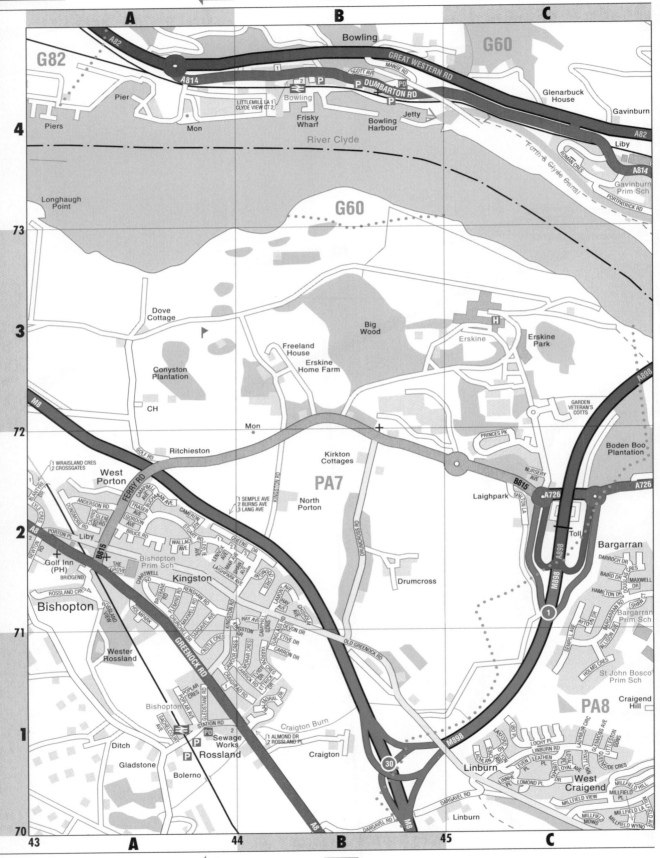

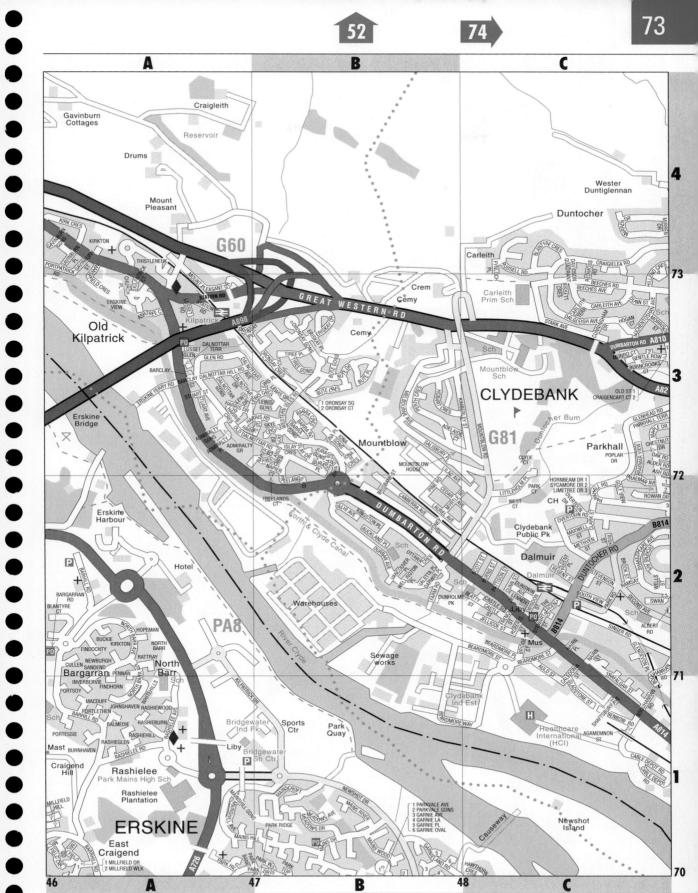

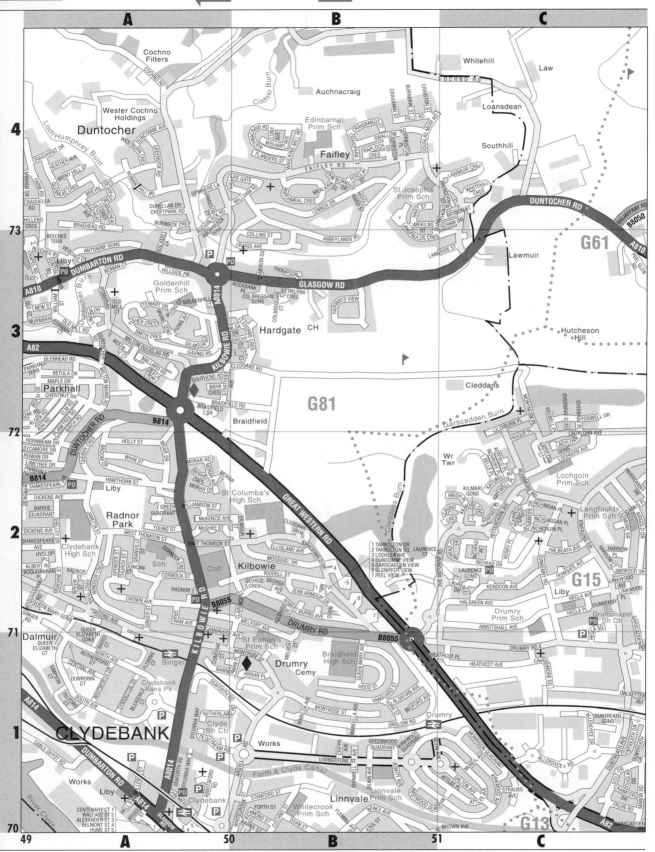

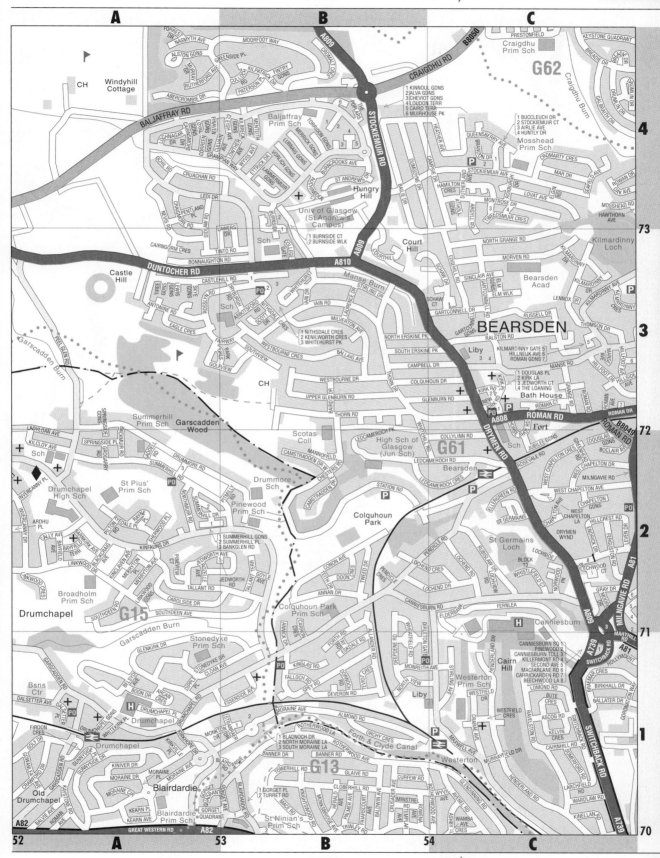

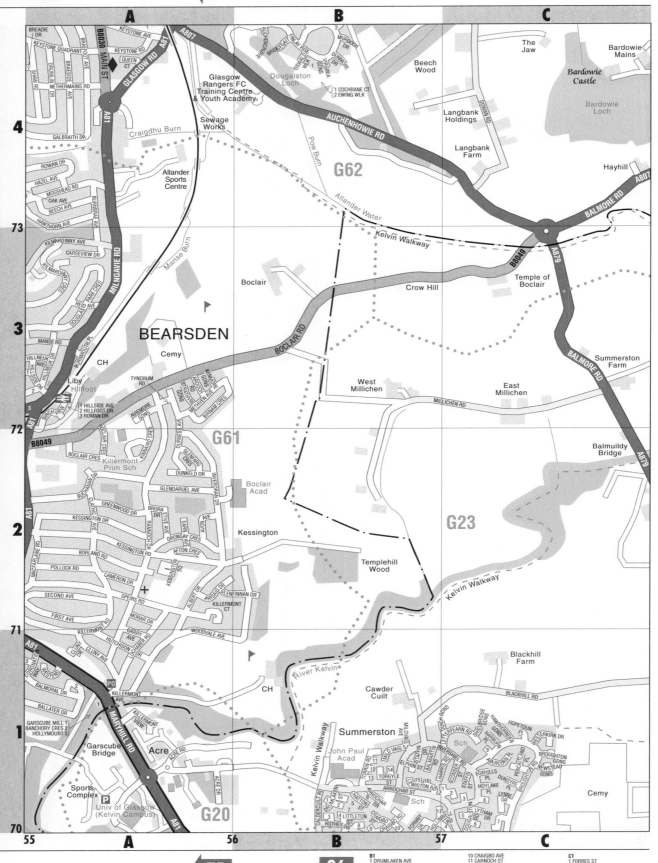

B1
1 DRUMLAKEN AVE
2 DRUMLAKEN CT
3 ROTHES PL
4 LITTLETON DR
5 DRUMLAKEN PL
6 ARROCHAR PATH
7 DRUMLAKEN PATH
8 MULLARDOCH ST
9 CRAIGBO DR
10 CRAIGBO AVE
11 CARNOCH ST
12 ARDESSIE ST
13 GEARY ST
14 CARBOST ST
15 LEWISTON DR
16 LEWISTON PL
17 GLENBERVIE PL

C1
1 FORRES ST
2 TOLSTA ST
3 GALLAN AVE
4 LINDRICK DR
5 WENTWORTH DR
6 MUIRFIELD CRES
7 CROSSFORD DR
8 CROSSPOINT DR
9 NEWCASTLETON DR

56
78

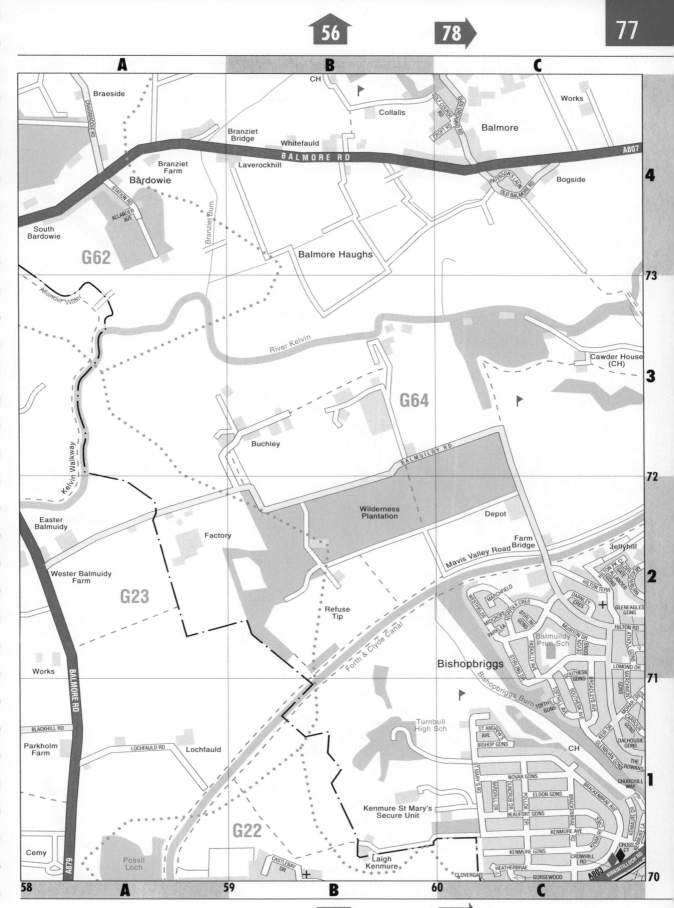

97
78

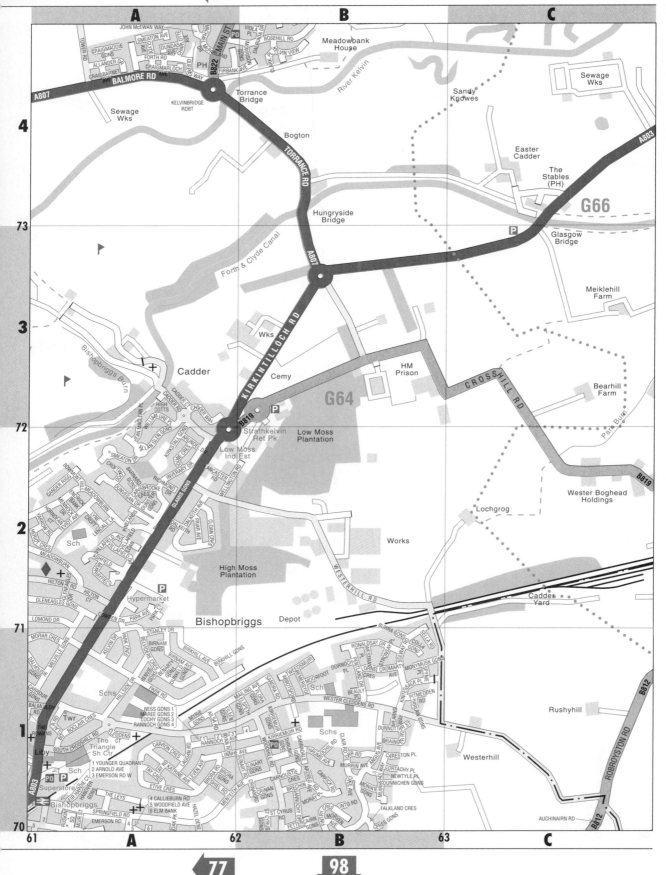

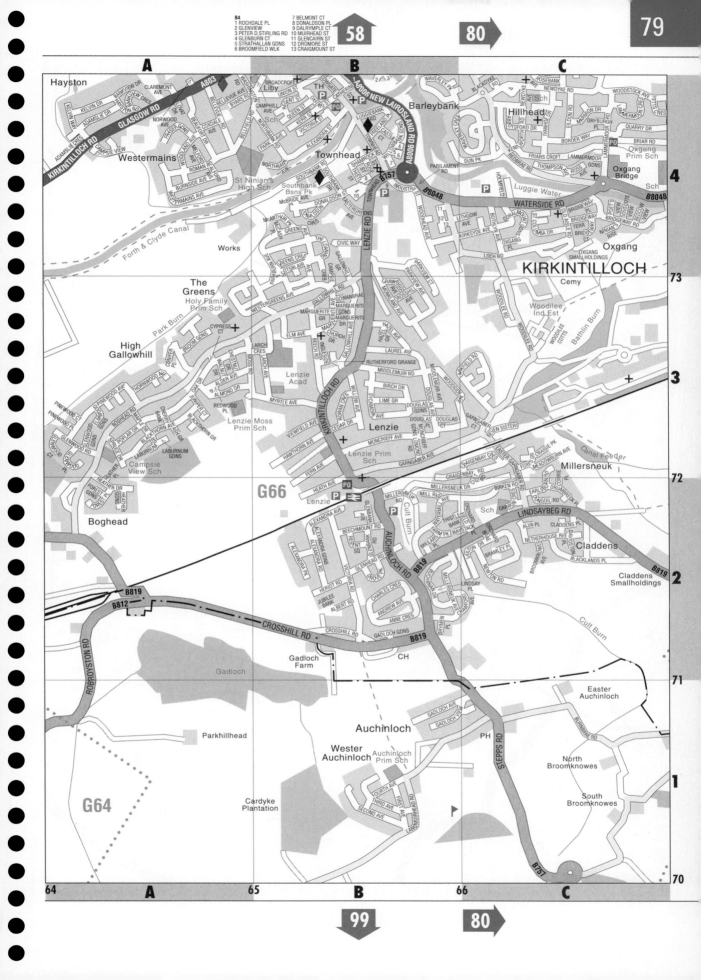

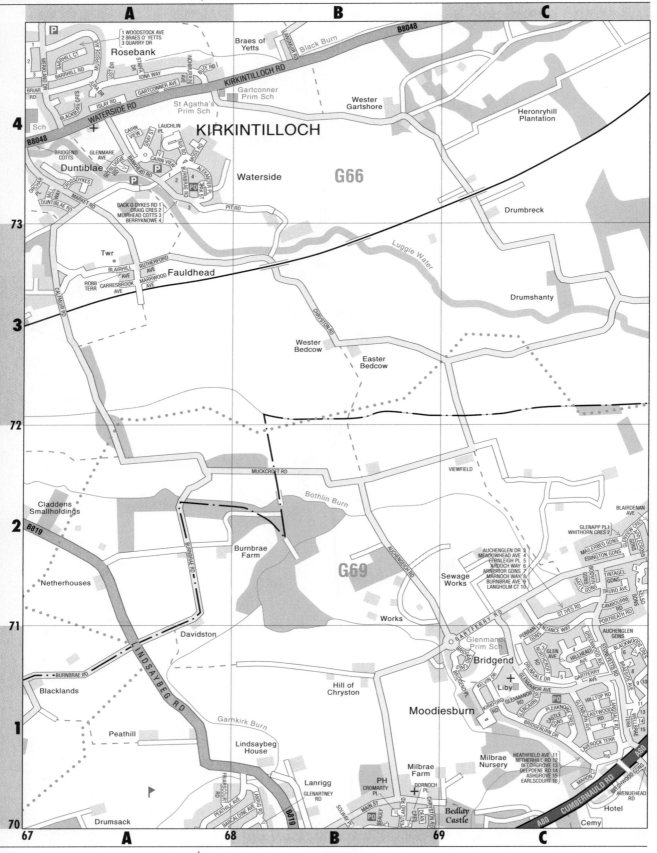

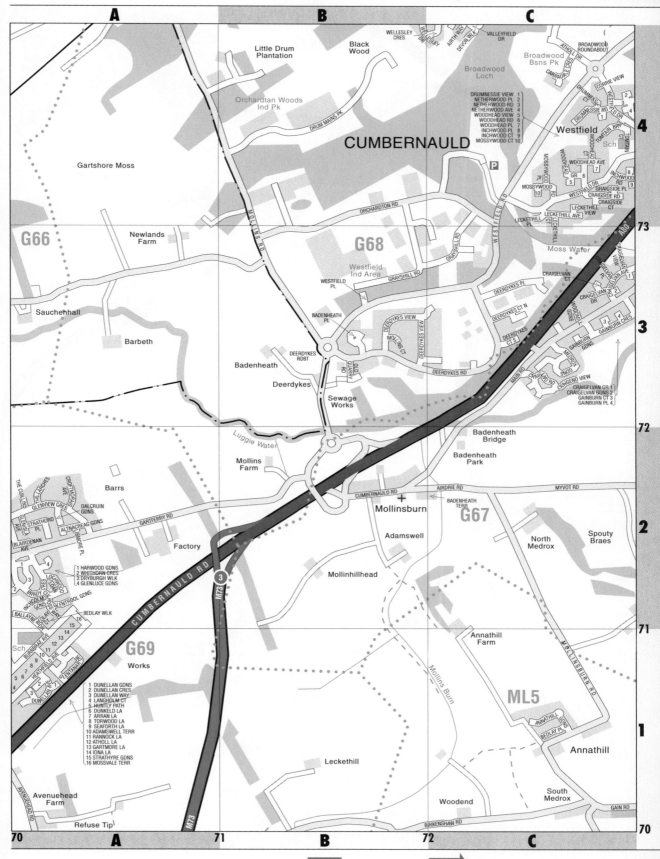

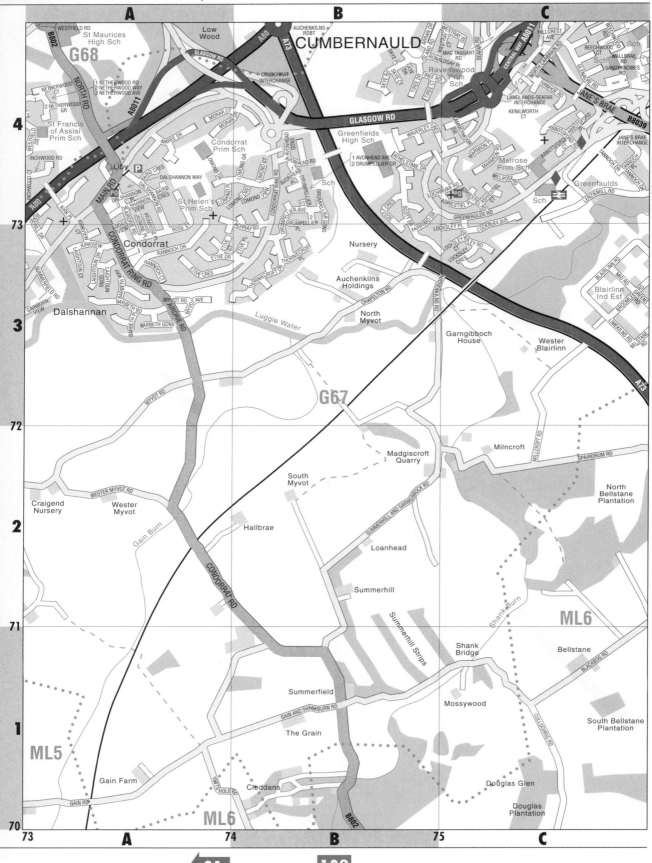

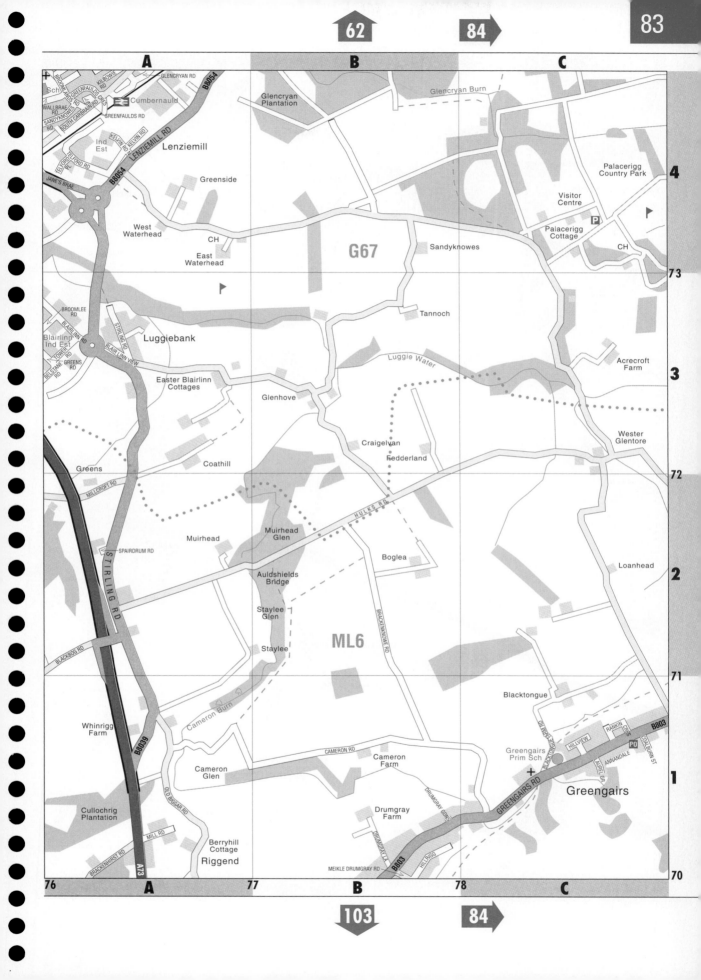

83
63

A B C

4

Palacerigg Country Park

Fannyside Lochs

Fannyside Mill

Jawhills

River Avon

Thieves Hill

Garbethill Burn

Fannyside Lodge

73

G67

Herd's Hill

West Fannyside

FK1

Scar Hill

Toddle Knowe

Bog Bridge

3

Luggie Water

Avon Water

Black Hill

Blackhill

72

Torbrex

Bogside

Netherton of Glentore

Easter Glentore

B803

2

Shielhill Burn

Langdales

DERVAIG GDNS

LUCKENHILL DR

AVON AVE

SCAMADALE RD

Easter Glentore

GREENGAIRS RD

ML6

HM Remand Inst

Upperton Farm

Meadowfield

71

THE CRESCENT

B803

PH

1

Avalon

Greendykeside

BRIDGE ST

70

79 A 80 B 81 C

83
104

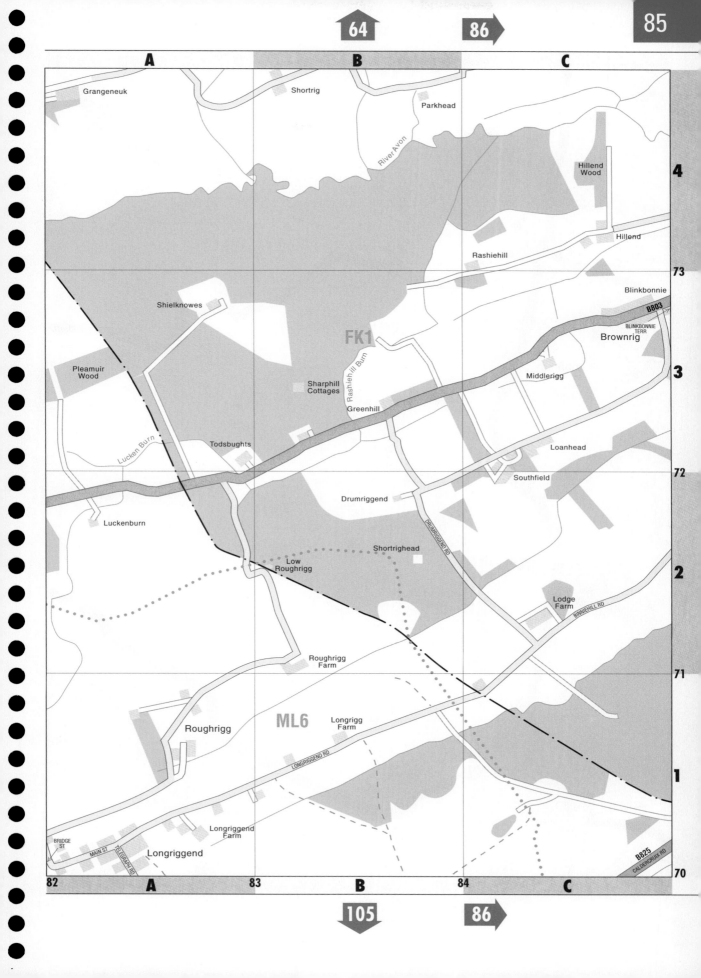

Grangeneuk

Shortrig

Parkhead

River Avon

Hillend
Wood

4

Rashiehill

Hillend

73

Blinkbonnie

Shielknowes

B803

BLINKBONNIE
TERR

Brownrig

FK1

Middlerigg

Pleamuir
Wood

Sharphill
Cottages

Greenhill

Rashiehill Burn

3

Lucken Burn

Todsbughts

Loanhead

Southfield

72

Drumriggend

Luckenburn

DRUMRIGGEND RD

Shortrighead

Low
Roughrigg

Lodge
Farm

BINNIEHILL RD

2

Roughrigg
Farm

71

Roughrigg

ML6

Longrigg
Farm

LONGRIGGEND RD

1

BRIDGE
ST

MAIN ST

TELEGRAPH RD

Longriggend

Longriggend
Farm

B825

CALDERCRUIX RD

70

85
65

River Avon

Wester Jaw

Redbrae

Wester Loanrigg

B803

BALMULZIER RD

Balmulzier

Loanrigg

4

MANSE PL

THORNDENE TERR

MOSSCASTLE RD

PH

Slamannan Prim Sch

Liby

HIGH ST

NEW ST

KIRK PATH

PO

AVONBRIDGE RD

Hillhead

73

Blinkbonnie

BANK ST

BENNIE TERR

GOWANLEA DR

B8022

Peatrigend

Crossburn

B803

BLINKBONNIE TERR

BALQUHATSTONE

SOUTHFIELD DR

DRUMCLAIR AVE

CASTLE HILL

RASHIEHILL

AITKEN DR

BALCASTLE

BIRNIE

WELL RD

OH HOO CRES

Balquhatstone House

Wester Crosshill

B8022

Crosshill

Culloch Burn

THE RUMLIE

3

Balcastle House

Slamannan

STATION RD

Wester Arnloss

North Arnloss

LINTVIEW

Binniehill Farm

Balquhatstone Mains

FK1

South Arnloss

Binniehill

STATION ROW

BINNIEHILL RD

72

Salterhill Farm

2

B825

Easter Drumclair

CAMERON TERR

THOMPSON PL

Low Limerigg

Loch House

SLAMANNAN RD

71

PO

Limerigg

Little Black Loch

High Limerigg

B8022

Barnsmuir

1

Limerigg Prim Sch

LOCHSIDE RD

Blackloch

B825

CALDERCRUIX RD

Holehousemuir

Stoneridge

Black Loch

70

A B C

Lower Boxton

BOXTON RD

Boagstown

B8028

Hareburn

North Bankhead

Windy-yett

Avonview

Avonbridge

4

Balmitchell

Manse

Whinny Knowes

B8028

South Bankhead

River Avon

73

Neucks Cottages

Neucks

FK1

Bogo

THE NEUCKS

Summerhouse

AVON FK

SLAMANNAN RD

B825

3

Avonbridge Prim Sch

Babbithill

B8022

Crossroads

Craigend

Edinburgh STREET ATLAS

Bulliondale

72

Dykehead

Holehouse

Lin Mill Burn

Redhall

Wester Holehouse

North East Holehouse

Elrigside Wood

2

South Holehouse

Linhouse Farm

Easter Greenhill

East Plantation

Wester Greenhill

Drumtassie Burn

71

Barns

Westfield

North Rhodens Plantation

1

88

A

89

B

90

C

70

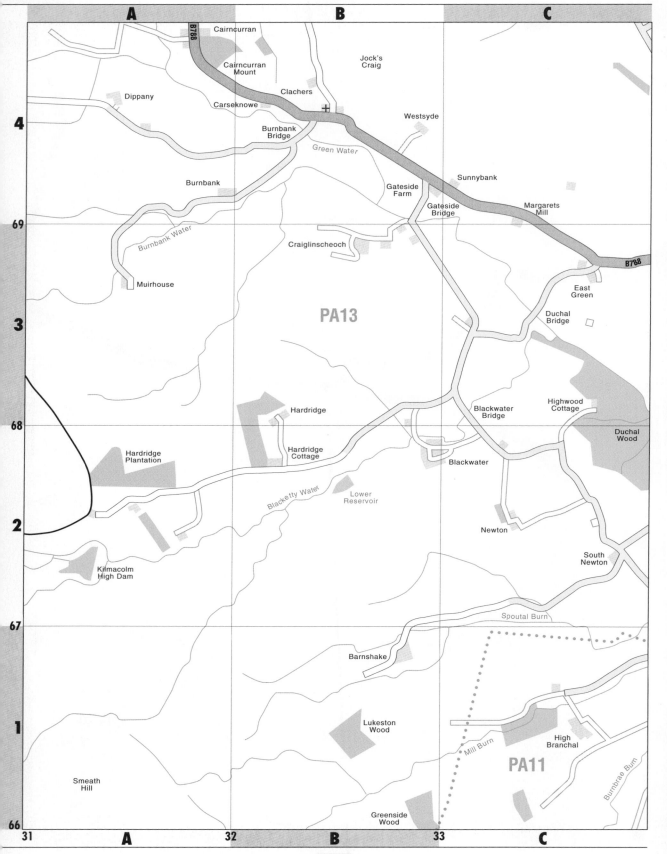

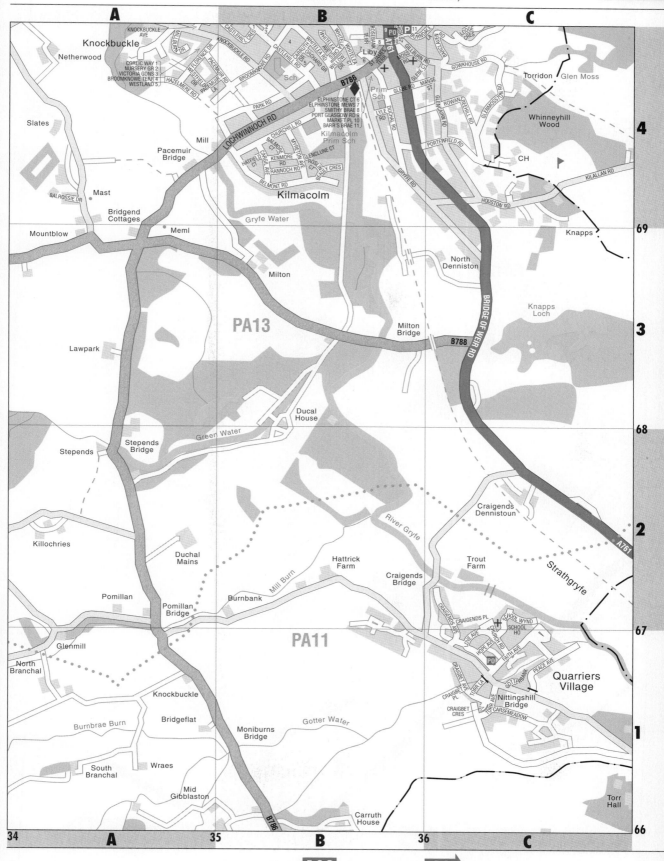

← 89
70

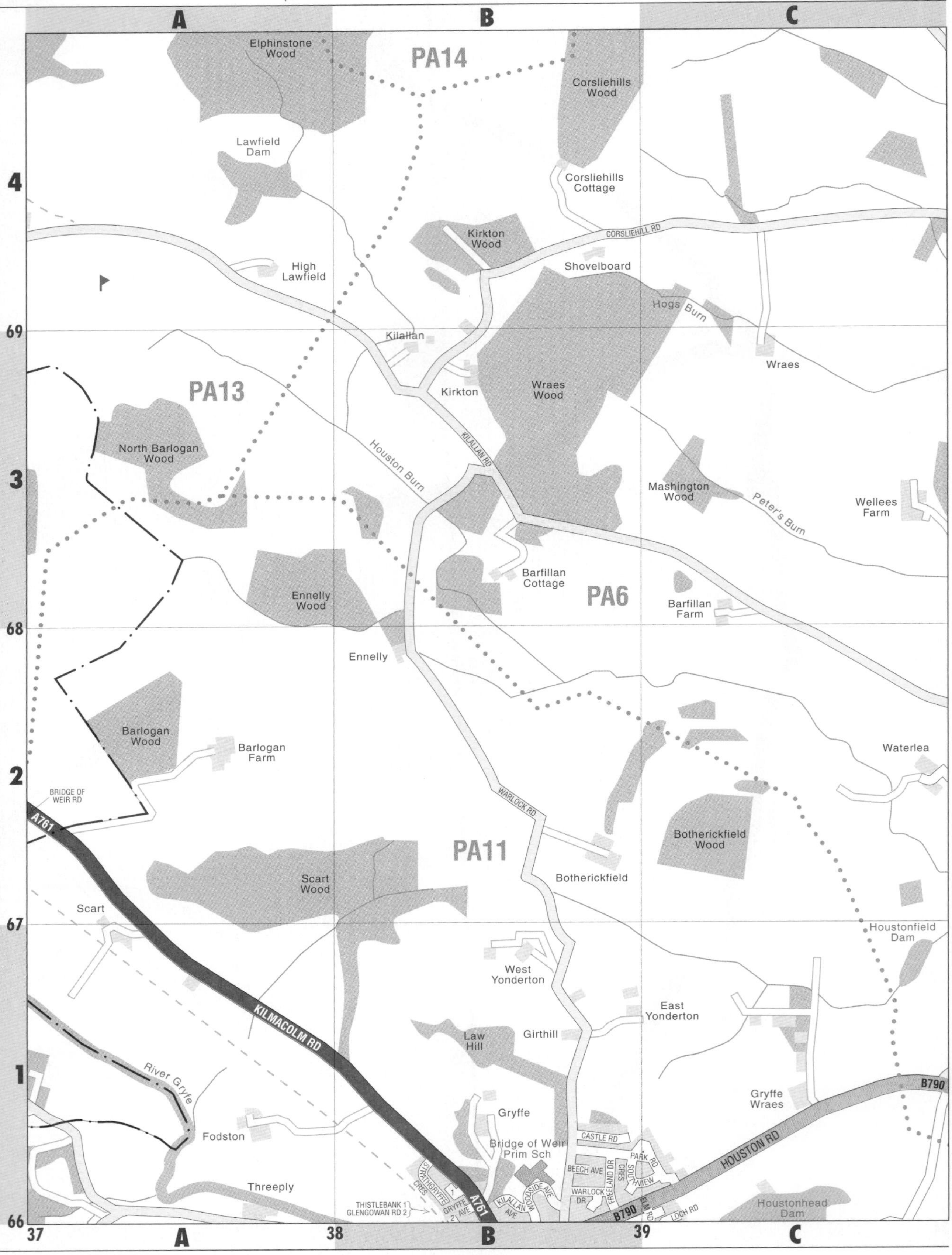

A B C

PA14

Elphinstone Wood

Corsliehills Wood

Lawfield Dam

Corsliehills Cottage

Corsliehill Rd

4

Kirkton Wood

Shovelboard

Hogs Burn

High Lawfield

69

Kilallan

Wraes

PA13

Kirkton

Wraes Wood

North Barlogan Wood

Houston Burn

KILALLAN RD

3

Mashington Wood

Peter's Burn

Wellees Farm

Ennelly Wood

Barfillan Cottage

PA6

Barfillan Farm

68

Ennelly

Barlogan Wood

Barlogan Farm

Waterlea

2

BRIDGE OF WEIR RD

A761

WARLOCK RD

PA11

Botherickfield Wood

Scart Wood

Botherickfield

Houstonfield Dam

67

Scart

West Yonderton

East Yonderton

KILMACOLM RD

Law Hill

Girthill

B790

1

River Gryfe

Gryffe Wraes

HOUSTON RD

Fodston

Gryffe

CASTLE RD

Threeply

Bridge of Weir Prim Sch

BEECH AVE

WARLOCK DR

Houstonhead Dam

THISTLEBANK 1
GLENGOWAN RD 2

A761

KILALLAN AVE

PARK RD

B790

LOCH RD

66
37 A 38 B 39 C

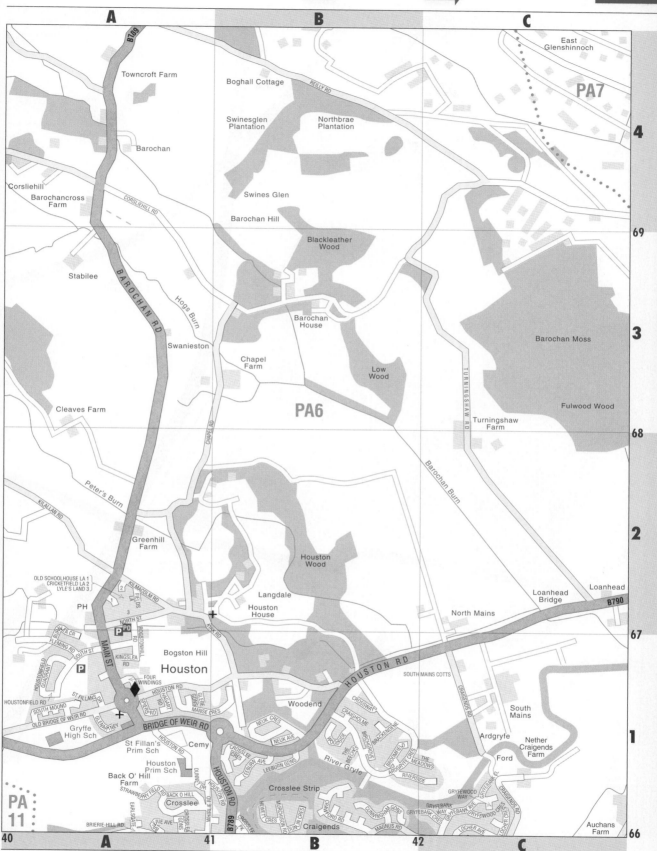

A   B   C

PA8

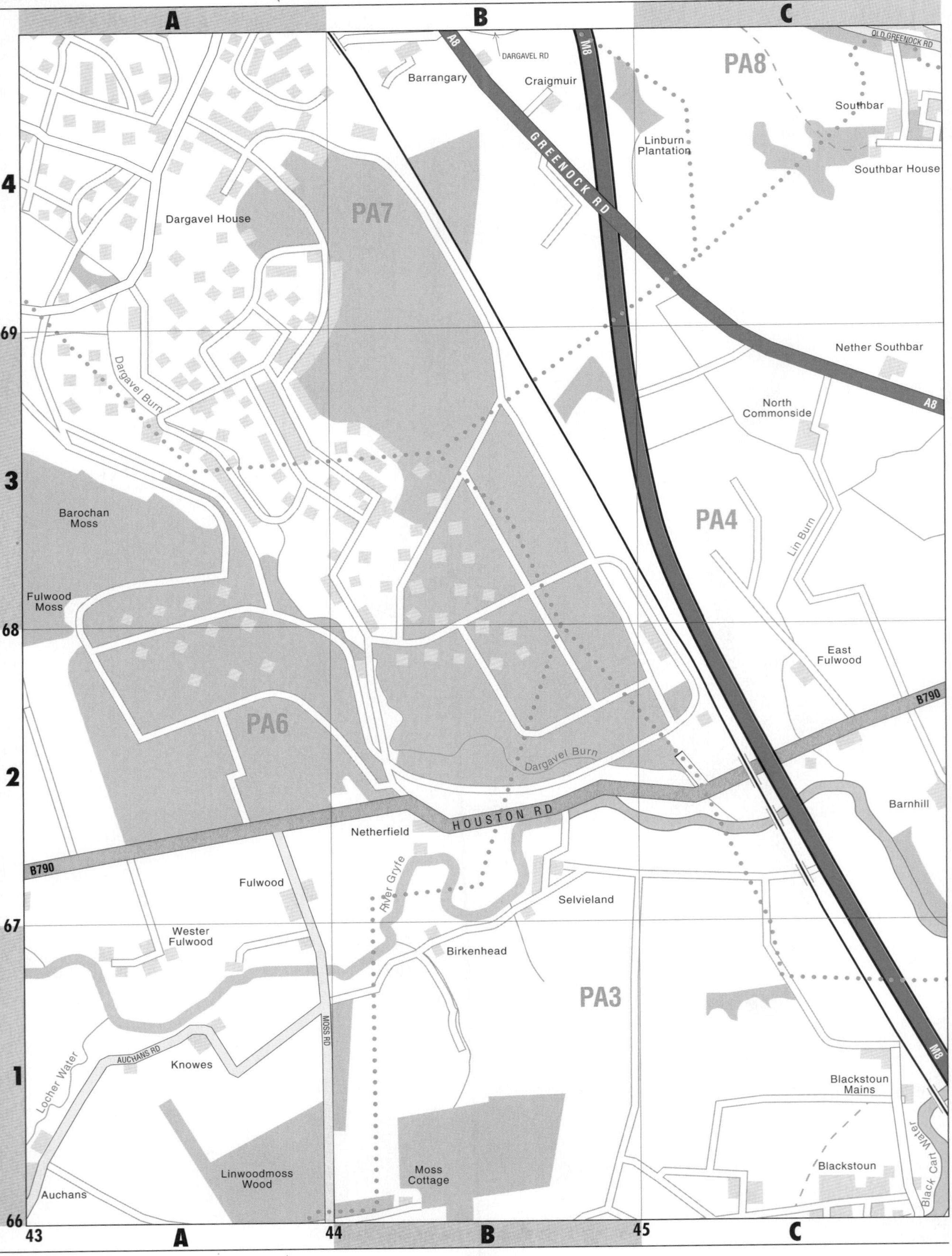

OLD GREENOCK RD

Southbar

Linburn
Plantation

Southbar House

4

Dargavel House

PA7

A8

DARGAVEL RD

Barrangary

Craigmuir

GREENOCK RD

M8

69

Nether Southbar

A8

Dargavel Burn

North
Commonside

Lin Burn

3

Barochan
Moss

PA4

Fulwood
Moss

68

East
Fulwood

B790

PA6

Dargavel Burn

2

Barnhill

HOUSTON RD

Netherfield

B790

Fulwood

River Gryfe

Selvieland

67

Wester
Fulwood

Birkenhead

PA3

MOSS RD

AUCHANS RD

1

Locher Water

Knowes

Blackstoun
Mains

M8

Auchans

Linwoodmoss
Wood

Moss
Cottage

Blackstoun

Black Cart Water

66

43   A   44   B   45   C

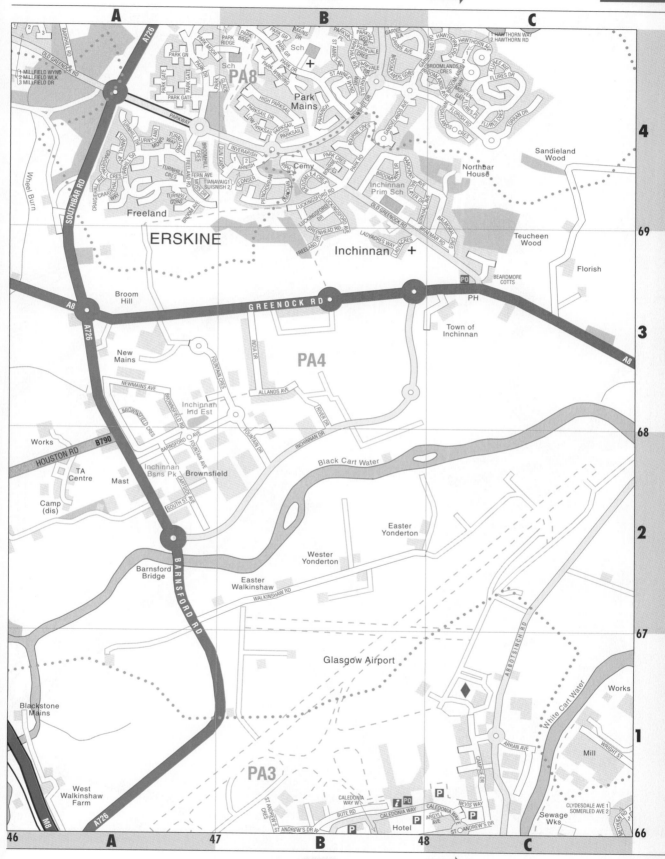

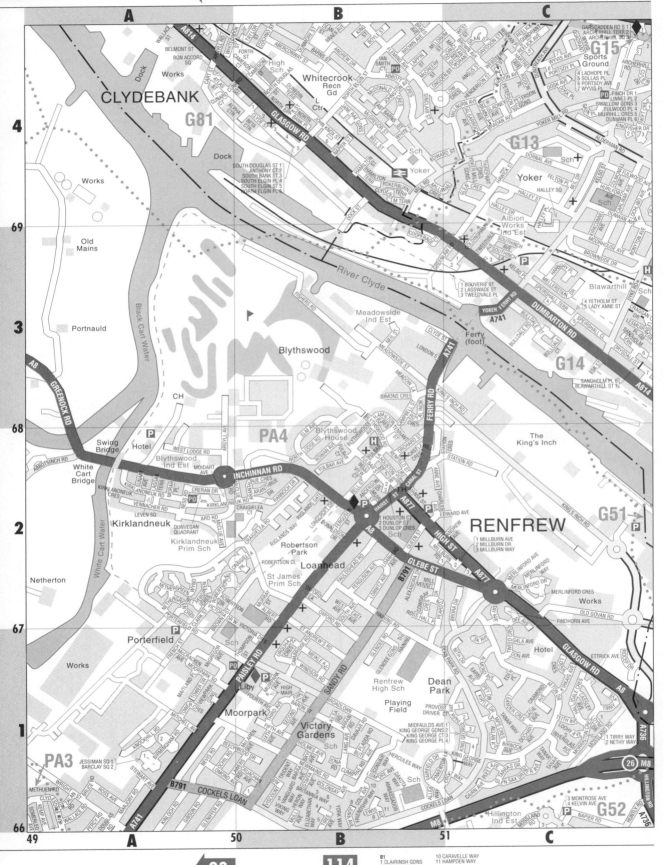

B1
1 CLAIRINSH GDNS
2 HERALD WAY
3 ARGOSY WAY
4 LANCASTER WAY
5 WELLINGTON WAY
6 ANSON WAY
7 HALIFAX WAY
8 STIRLING WAY
9 LYSANDER WAY
10 CARAVELLE WAY
11 HAMPDEN WAY

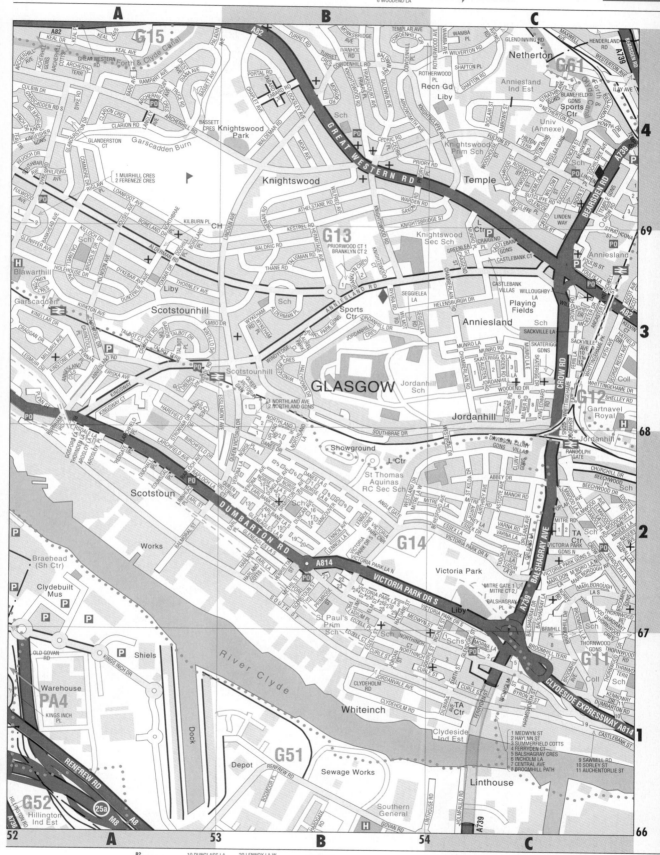

75

96

95

C3
1 CHAMBERLAIN LA
2 AUSTEN LA
3 BORDEN LA
4 SELBORNE PLACE LA
5 SELBORNE PL
6 WOODEND LA

7 MILNER LA
8 KING EDWARD LA
9 SOUTHBRAE LA
10 FERN COTTS
11 ALBANY COTTS
12 ALGAS COTTS

C4
1 TEMPLE LOCKS CT
2 TEMPLE LOCKS PL
3 WALDO ST
4 STRATHCONA DR

B2
1 DANES AVE
2 UPLAND LA
3 DANES LA N
4 VERONA GDNS
5 DUNGLASS LA N
6 ORMISTON LA N
7 DUNCAN LA N
8 VANCOUVER LA
9 LENNOX LA W

10 DUNGLASS LA
11 EARLBANK LA N
12 ORMISTON LA
13 DUNGLASS LA S
14 ORMISTON LA S
15 DUNCAN LA S
16 NORSE LA S
17 VANCOUVER LA
18 EARLBANK LA N
19 DUNCAN LA

20 LENNOX LA W
21 PRIMROSE CT
22 BOWLING GREEN LA
23 BOWLING GREEN RD
24 LIME LA
25 ELM LA W
26 ELM LA E
27 VICTORIA PARK ST
28 WESTLAND DRIVE LA
29 HALDANE LA

A2
1 DEVONSHIRE GDNS
2 DEVONSHIRE GDNS LA
3 WESTBOURNE TERR LA S
4 KINGSBOROUGH GDNS
5 TURNBERRY AVE
6 HILLSIDE GARDENS LA

7 MONKSCROFT AVE
8 KIRKMICHAEL GDNS
9 KIRKMICHAEL GATE
10 THORNWOOD DR
11 BLAIRATHOLL GDNS
12 TIBBERMORE RD
13 QUEENSBOROUGH GDNS

14 PRINCES GARDENS LA
B3
1 THORNBRIDGE AVE
2 BELLSHAUGH PL
3 GARRIOCH CRES
4 GARRIOCH QUADRANT
5 WYNDFORD PL

B3
6 DUNBEITH PL
7 LATHERTON DR
8 INVERSHIN DR
9 CARRBRIDGE DR
10 TOWIE PL
11 KELVINDALE PL

12 GLENFINNAN PL
13 STRATHY PL
14 STRATHCARRON PL
15 KIRKHILL PL
16 KIRKHILL PL
17 GARRIOCH GATE

95 | 76

Map area (Glasgow districts G61, G13, G12, G11, G51, G3, G4, G20, G22, G23)

A81 / A739 / A82 / A814 / A804

Univ of Glasgow (Veterinary Medicine)
Dawsholm Park
Playing Fields
River Kelvin
Kelvin Walkway
Dalsholm Ind Est
Maryhill
Forth & Clyde Canal
MARYHILL RD
Western Necropolis
Crem
Cemy
Gilshochill
Cadder
Kelvindale
G20
Ruchill Prim Sch
Ruchill Park
Chapel Street Ind Est
North Kelvin
Gartnavel Royal
Gartnavel General
Glasgow Homeopathic
Hyndland
Kelvinside
Cleveden Sec Sch
GREAT WESTERN RD
Glasgow Bot Gdns
Botanic Gardens
Hillhead
Kelvinbridge
Partickhill
Partick
Burgh Hall
Kelvinhall
Western
Univ
Kelvingrove
Kelvingrove Museum & Art Gall
Kelvinhaugh
The Queen Mother's
CLYDESIDE EXPRESSWAY
River Clyde
Univ Campus
G4
Kelvingrove Park
Kelvin Walkway
240

B2
1 KERSLAND LA
2 SANDRINGHAM LA
3 VINICOMBE LA
4 BURGH LA
5 CRESSWELL LA
6 GREAT GEORGE LA
7 DOWANSIDE LA
8 RUTHVEN LA
9 SALTOUN LA

10 GROSVENOR CRES
11 OBSERVATORY LA
12 GROSVENOR CRES LA
13 GROSVENOR TERR
14 MARCHMONT TERR
15 BOWMONT GDNS
16 VICTORIA CRES PL
17 BEAUMONT GATE
18 FOREMOUNT TERR LA
19 CROWN CIR

20 PRINCE'S PL
21 KENSINGTON GATE
22 KENSINGTON GATE LA
23 LORRAINE RD
24 LORRAINE GDNS
25 LORRAINE GDNS LA
26 WESTBOURNE GDNS LA
27 WESTBOURNE GDNS N
28 WESTBOURNE GDNS S
29 WESTBOURNE TERR LA N

30 LANCASTER TERR LA
31 LANCASTER TERR
32 GREAT WESTERN TERR LA
33 GREAT WESTERN TERR
34 REDLANDS TERR
35 LOWTHER TERR
36 BELHAVEN TERR W
37 BELHAVEN TERR W LA
38 ROSSLYN TERR
39 BELHAVEN TERR LA

40 BELHAVEN TERR
41 KIRKLEE TERR RD
42 KIRKLEE QUADRANT
43 GREAT WESTERN TERR
44 REDLANDS TERR LA
B2
1 SOUTHPARK LA
2 OAKFIELD LA
3 ETON LA

4 BOTHWELL LA
5 CALEDONIAN CRES
6 WEST PRINCE'S ST
7 WESTBANK CT
8 WILLOWBANK CRES
9 HOLYROOD QUADRANT
10 NAPIERSHALL PL
11 PARK TERR LA
12 LA BELLE PL
13 LA BELLE ALLEE

14 N CLAREMONT ST
15 KELVINGROVE LA
16 PARKGROVE TERR LA
17 CRAIGMADDIE TERR LA
C2
1 YARROW GDNS LA
2 JEDBURGH GDNS
3 LOTHIAN GDNS
4 CLOUSTON CT
5 OBAN LA

6 QUEEN MARGARET CT
7 KELVINSIDE GDNS LA
8 KELVINSIDE TERR W
9 KELVINSIDE TERR S
10 DOUNE QUADRANT
11 ALFRED LA
12 COLEBROOKE ST

C4
1 FORRESTER CT
2 MUIRPARK TERR
3 HUNTERSHILL RD
4 FULMAR CT
5 RAVENS CT
6 HILLCROFT TERR
7 MILTON DR
8 COLSTON PL
9 EVERARD PL
10 BISHOPSGATE PL
11 NEWBOLD AVE
12 SOUTHVIEW CT
13 STRATHKELVIN AVE

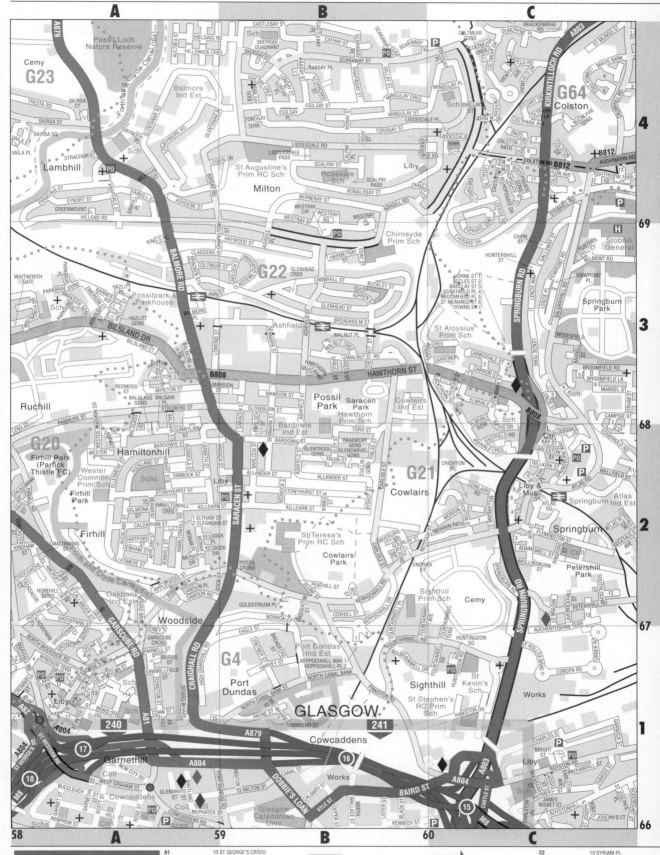

For full street detail of the highlighted area see pages 240 and 241.

A1
1 SEAMORE ST
2 BURNBANK PL
3 BURNBANK TERR
4 WINDSOR ST
5 CROMWELL LA
6 MELROSE ST
7 QUEEN'S CRES
8 ST GEORGE'S PL
9 CLARENDON PL
10 ST GEORGE'S CROSS
11 GLADSTONE ST
12 GLENFARG ST
13 ST PETER'S PATH
14 MANRESA PL
15 DUNDASHILL

C2
1 GOURLAY ST
2 VALLEYFIELD ST
3 PALERMO ST
4 SPRINGBURN WAY
5 VULCAN ST
6 COWLAIRS RD
7 ANGUS ST
8 KEMP ST
9 SPRINGVALE TERR
10 SYRIAM PL
11 CROFTBANK ST
12 SOUTHLOCH GDNS
13 AUCHINLOCH ST

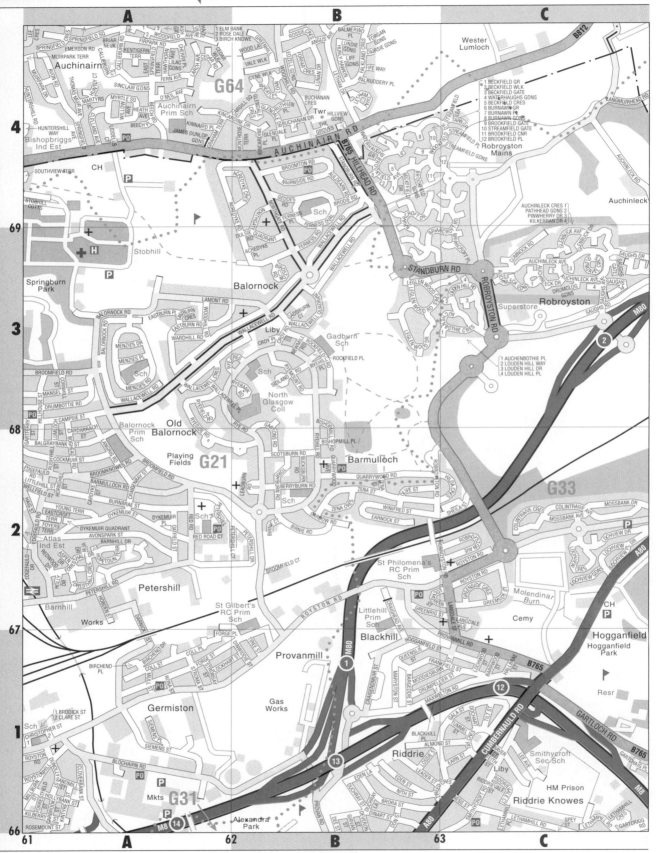

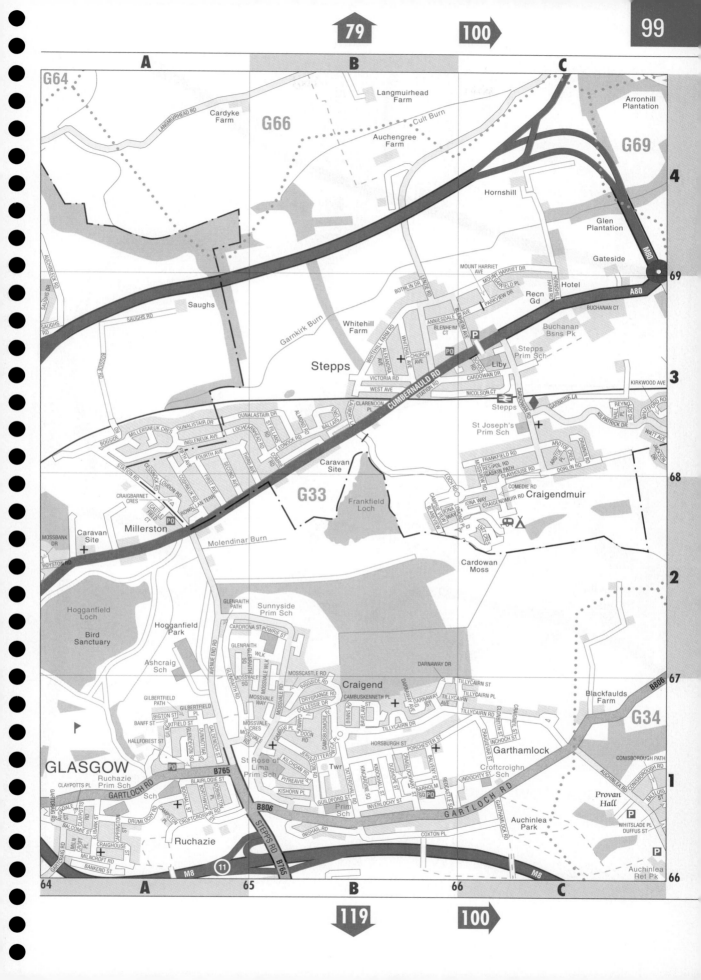

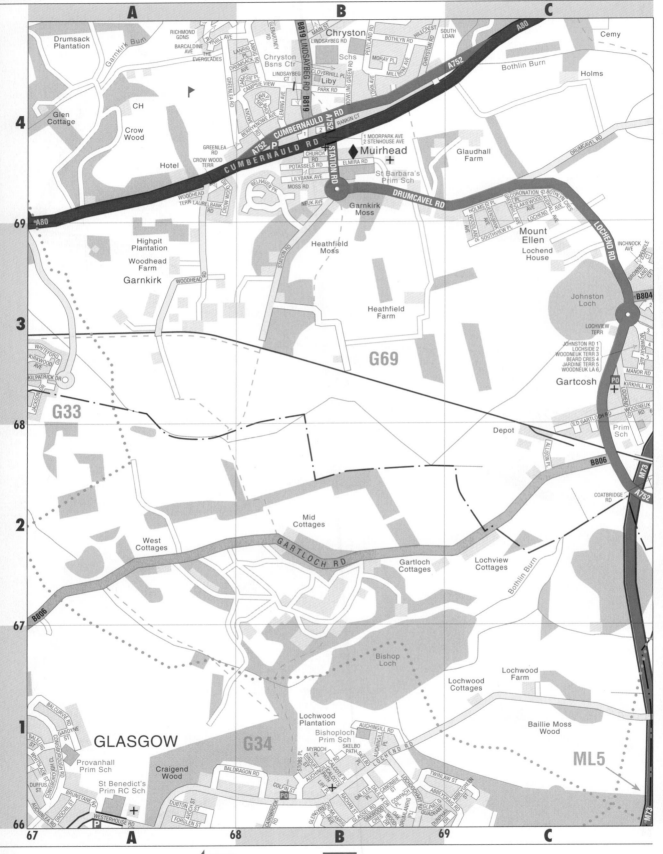

99
80

A B C

Drumsack Plantation
Garnkirk Burn
RICHMOND GDNS
BARCALDINE AVE
THE EVERGLADES
CRHILL AVE
Chryston
MAIN ST
LINDSAYBEG RD
PENTLAND RD
BOTHLYN RD
HILLCREST
SOUTH LOAN
A80
Cemy
Bothlin Burn
Holms

CH
LANRIG PL
LAURIG RD
GLENARTNEY RD
GLENALMOND RD
Chryston Bsns Ctr
Schs
MORAY PL
MILLBRAE AVE
CHRISTON RD
A752

4
Glen Cottage
Crow Wood
DRUMSACK AVE
CAMPSIE PL
CAMPSIE VIEW
GREENLEA RD
LINDSAYBEG CT
B819 LINDSAYBEG RD
Liby
CLOVERHILL PL
BOWLING GREEN RD
PARK RD
LORN AVE
A80
A752
Bothlin Burn
DRUMCAVEL RD

Hotel
GREENLEA RD
CROW WOOD TERR
FLEMING AVE
BERRYKNOWE AVE
A752 CUMBERNAULD RD
CUMBERNAULD RD
P
CHURCH RD
STATION RD
A752
RANKIN CT
1 2
1 MOORPARK AVE
2 STENHOUSE AVE
Muirhead
ELMIRA RD
St Barbara's Prim Sch
Glaudhall Farm

69
A80
WOODHEAD TERR LAURELBANK RD
BELHAVEN PK
POTASSELS RD
LILYBANK AVE
MOSS RD
NEUK AVE
Garnkirk Moss
DRUMCAVEL RD
HOLMS PL
QUEENSLAND RD
SOUTHVIEW PL
SLAKIEWOOD AVE
GREENHILL PL
CORONATION
BOTHLYN CRES
AUCHINAIRN AVE
AVE
LOCHEND
Mount Ellen
Lochend House
LOCHEND RD
INCHNOCK AVE
BROWNS LANE CT
PENDALE
B804

3
Highpit Plantation
Woodhead Farm
Garnkirk
WOODHEAD
STATION RD
Heathfield Moss
Heathfield Farm
G69
WOODLANDS
Johnston Loch
LOCHVIEW TERR
JOHNSTON RD 1
LOCHSIDE 2
WOODNEUK TERR 3
BEARD CRES 4
JARDINE TERR 5
WOODNEUK LA 6
MOWBRA AVE
MANOR RD
B804

WHITEFORD
KIRKWOOD AVE
KILPATRICK DR
Gartcosh
PO
KIRKHILL RD
WOODNEUK RD
LOCHEND RD

68
G33
JACKSON ST
Depot
OLD GARTLOCH RD
ALLISON PL
B806
Prim Sch
MT73
COATBRIDGE RD
A752

2
West Cottages
Mid Cottages
GARTLOCH RD
Gartloch Cottages
Lochview Cottages
Bothlin Burn

67
B806
Bishop Loch
Lochwood Cottages
Lochwood Farm
Baillie Moss Wood

1
GLASGOW
BALCURVIE RD
GARDYNE
BALLIG ST
WHITSLADE ST
CONISBROUGH RD
Lochwood Plantation
Bishoploch Prim Sch
AUCHINGILL RD
SKELBO PATH
SKELBO PL
AUCHINGILL PL
AUCHINGILL RD
LOCHEND RD
TWINLAW ST
ML5
Provanhall Prim Sch
Craigend Wood
G34
BALDRAGON RD
STOBS PL
MYROCH PL
DAIL LEA
COYTES
DRUMKINNON
AUCHINGILL RD
DIAL PL
CAMONNIE
CAMBUSNETHAN
CORRACHAN
ABBEYDALE RD
ABBEYGREEN ST
St Benedict's Prim RC Sch
DUFFUS ST
BRUNSTANE ST
COLFIN ST
PO
CARIBRIDGON RD
GLENGYRE ST
DRUM LARIG
GNEL
AVE
RACHAN ST
GLASSEL RD
OAKWOOD
OAK
CRES
CORPACH
DRUMLANRIG
QUADRANT
DUNDAFF
DR

66
67
AUCHINLEA RD
DRICHIL ST
P
WESTERHOUSE RD
DUBTON ST
AVOCH ST
FORGLEN ST
BALDRAGON RD
68
B
69
MT73

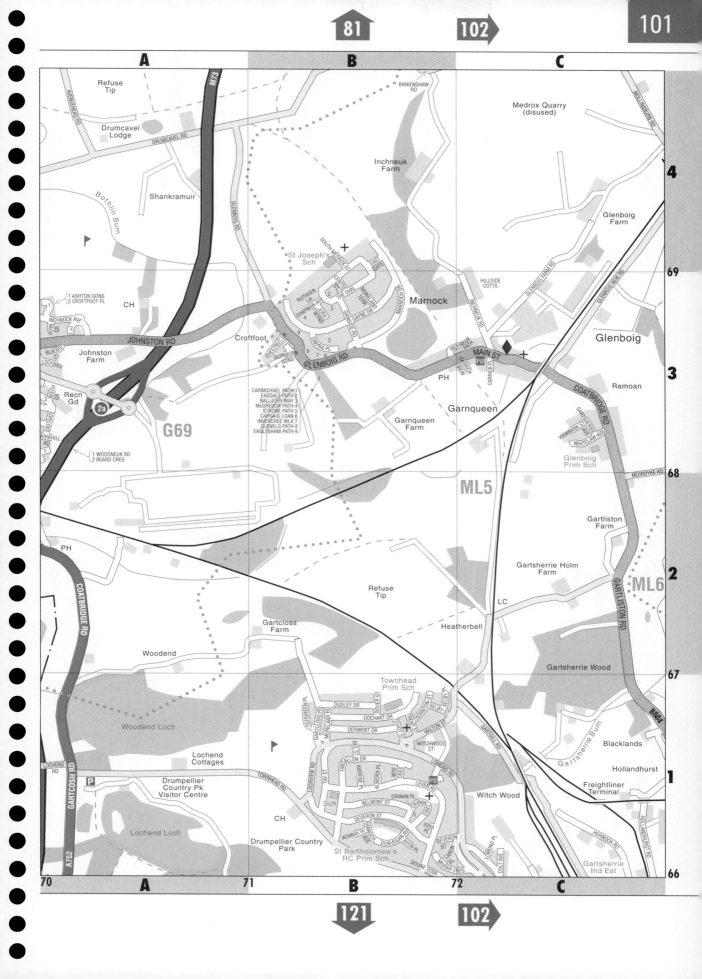

A

B

C

Refuse Tip

BIRKENSHAW RD

Medrox Quarry (disused)

MT73

DRUMCAVEL RD

Drumcavel Lodge

AIRDRIEHEAD RD

GLENBOIG RD

Inchneuk Farm

Glenboig Farm

MOLLINSBURN RD

4

Bothlin Burn

Shankramuir

SOUTH MEDROX ST

St Joseph's Sch

HILLSIDE COTTS

GLENBOIG FARM RD

GLENBOIG NEW RD

69

CH

1 ASHTON GDNS 2 CROFTFOOT PL

INCHNOCK AVE

FERN GR

RUTHVEN LA

CHAPMAN AVE

CENTRE

THE OVAL

EAST GATE

MONKLAND TERR

MARNOCK DR

GAYNE DR

Marnock

INCHNEUK RD

Glenboig

JOHNSTON RD

Croftfoot

CHESTNUT GR

GLENBURN GDNS

DAYRIA PL

GRINSIDE RD

INCHNEUK PATH

GARRICK VIEW

MAIN ST

PO

COATBRIDGE RD

Ramoan

Johnston Farm

BLADES CT

LOCHSIDE

EASTGATE

BEECH CT

GLENBOIG RD

CARMICHAEL PATH 1
EASDALE PATH 2
BALLATER WAY 3
McGREGOR PATH 4
STRONE PATH 5
CARSAIG LOAN 6
INVERCREE WLK 7
GLENELG PATH 8
EAGLESHAM PATH 9

PH

CARRICK PL

PH

Garnqueen

GARTSHERRIE AVE

VIEWBANK AVE

WHITELAW AVE

Glenboig Prim Sch

3

Recn Gd

2a

KIRKHILL RD

G69

Garnqueen Farm

MUIRDYKE RD

68

1 WOODNEUK RD 2 BEARD CRES

ML5

Gartliston Farm

PH

ML6

GARTLISTON RD

2

Gartsherrie Holm Farm

Refuse Tip

LC

Heatherbell

Gartcloss Farm

COATBRIDGE RD

Woodend

Gartsherrie Wood

67

B804

Woodend Loch

Townhead Prim Sch

HIGHGREEN PL

GARTCLOSS RD

DUDLEY DR

DOVER ST

MERKLAND RD

DOCHART DR

DERWENT DR

TEVIOT ST

FRITH ST

SELBY ST

WILTON ST

WITCHWOOD CT

GARBILL RD

Gartsherrie Burn

Blacklands

Lochend Cottages

LOCHEND RD

P

Drumpellier Country Pk Visitor Centre

GARTCOSH RD

TOWNHEAD RD

LOCHVIEW RD

TAY ST

DEE ST

TARF ALLON DR

KATRINE PL

ALMOND PL

WYE CRES

LOMOND RD

LEVEN RD

PO

Hollandhurst

Freightliner Terminal

Witch Wood

HOLLANDHURST RD

1

CH

Sch

CRINAN PL

BELMONT ST

CRUBAN ST

IONA PL

DEVERON ST

LOMOND PL

COLT AVE

HORNOCK RD

A752

Lochend Loch

Drumpellier Country Park

DEVERON ST

ACHRAY PL

RANNOCH AVE

DUNVEGAN AVE

AVON PL

DOUNE TERR

MOHAR CRES

St Bartholomew's RC Prim Sch

Gartsherrie Ind Est

66

A

B

C

70

71

72

101 82

A B C

G67

Gaindydykehead

East Lodge Wood

Foot o' Loan Wood

East Gartmillan

Shank Burn

4 LC

Greenfoot

West Gartmillan

Ardaryth

Glenmill Wood

Drumbowie Farm

Callochrig

CALLOCHRIG RD

BRACKENHIRST RD

GLENBOIG NEW RD

MOLLINSBURN RD

69 ML5

Haggmuir Farm

MOLLINSBURN RD

CONDORRAT RD

Refuse Tip

3 Gas Storage Depot

Brackenhirst

MUIRDYKE RD

YETTS HOLE RD

Ryden Mains

New Monkland

DUNNET AVE 1
STRATHYRE GDNS 2
HAWKWOOD RD 3

GRANTOWN GDNS

ARRAN DR

BADENOCH RD

AVE

BARONY

TREE

CLYDE

CRATHIE DR

B803

68 Gartverrie Burn

ML6

Cemy

New Monkland Prim Sch

WINDSOR DR

IRVINE CRES

DUNVEGAN

RAEBOG RD

Rochsoles

BURNLIP RD

Palace

RYDEN MAINS RD

CLEDDANS VIEW

QUARRYSIDE ST

MACARTHUR AVE

ARTHUR PL

KIRKSTYLE PL

B802

B803

PH

LOCHBUIE LA

MELDRUM MAINS

LOCHVIEW ST

PO

GLENVIEW ST

GLENWELL ST

Blackwalk Plantation

2 Gartverrie Farm

Copse Wood

Cromlet

Braidenhill Farm

B802

Glenmavis

Dryflat

COATBRIDGE RD

CH

STRATMUNGO CRES 1
STAINEYBRAES PL 2
DYKEHEAD CRES 3
CRAIGMOCHAN AVE 4

BLUEBELL WAY

SPRINGHOLM DR

67 Virtuewell Glen

GLENMAVIS RD

Golfhill Prim Sch

LOCHEARN CRES

CARLOCH CRES

LOCH LOCH

TUNNEL RD

DYKEHEAD RD

CROWHILL

RAEBOG CRES

KIRKSTYLE CRES

ROCHSOLES DR

QUADRANT

Kippsbyre

BALLOCHNEY LA 5
LEVEN QUADRANT 6
LAIDON RD 7
KATRINE CRES 8

Burnfoot

LUBNAIG PL

MORAR CRES

LOMOND

LAGGAN QUADRANT

BALLOCHNEY RD

RANNOCH RD

BALLOCHNEY ST

TAYSIDE

ARRAN DR

COMMONHEAD AVE

COMMONHEAD LA 9
SOUTH COMMONHEAD AVE 10
QUARRY RD 11

Acad

1 ML5

Kipps

North Burn

METHVEN TERR

NORTHBURN RD

WAVERLEY ST

B803

Greenhill Ind Est

Greenhill

Greenhill Bsns Ctr

1 CHASSELS ST
2 BRUCE ST
3 GREENSIDE ST
4 BURNBANK ST

Works

B804 GARTLISTON RD

COLTSWOOD RD B804

BURNSIDE RD

CAMERON ST

WHINHALL RD

WHINHALL AVE

LAIND RD

WILSON ST

Sch

BEECHBANK

B802

HUNTER

66

73 A 74 B 75 C

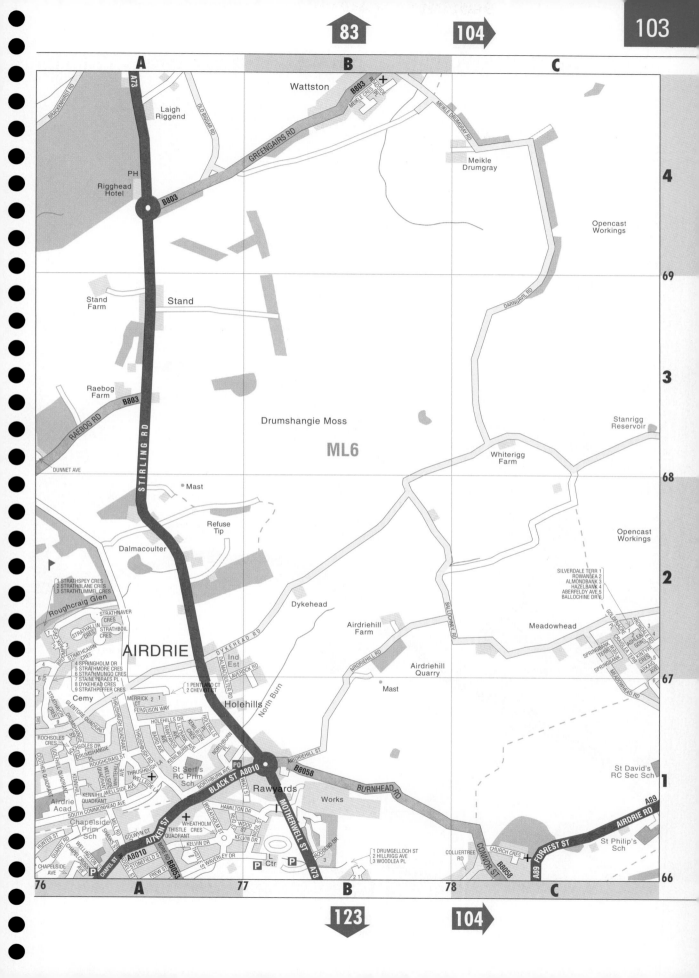

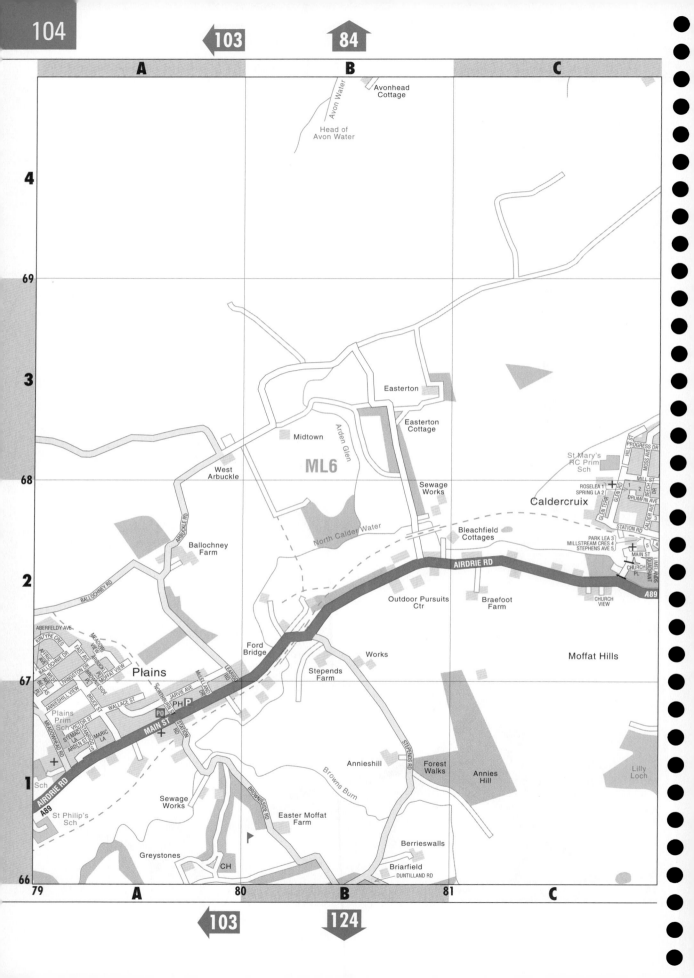

103

84

A B C

4

69

3

Avonhead
Cottage

Avon Water

Head of
Avon Water

Easterton

Easterton
Cottage

Midtown

Arden Glen

ML6

West
Arbuckle

68

ARBUCKLE RD

Ballochney
Farm

Sewage
Works

North Calder Water

St Mary's
RC Prim
Sch

ST PROGRESS DR

MOSS ST

MILL ST

GLEN TERR

GLEN RD

BEECH DR

DRUMFIN AVE

CALDER AVE

ROSELEA 1
SPRING LA 2

Caldercruix

STATION RD

Bleachfield
Cottages

PARK LEA 3
MILLSTREAM CRES 4
STEPHENS AVE 5

MAIN ST

CHURCHART
PL

LIMELANDS
QUADRANT

2

BALLOCHNEY RD

AIRDRIE RD

Outdoor Pursuits
Ctr

Braefoot
Farm

CHURCH
VIEW

A89

Moffat Hills

ABERFELDY AVE

KINTYRE CRES

NEFRIL AVE

MEADOW AVE

EAST AVE

ARBUCKLE

MOFFAT VIEW

Ford
Bridge

Works

LEA RIDGE RD

Lilly
Loch

BALLOCHNIE DR

ANNIESHILL VIEW

LIVINGSTON ST

BROWNSIDE

BRUCE ST

MCLELLAND
DR

JARVIE AVE

NORTHBURN AVE

Plains

Stepends
Farm

Plains
Prim
Sch

ST VICTOR ST

ST MAC
LA

CAMBUS
LA

ARDEN LA

MARIC LA

WALLACE ST

MEADOWHEAD RD

PO

PH P

STATION RD

MAIN ST

Annieshill

STEPENDS RD

Forest
Walks

Annies
Hill

1

AIRDRIE RD

A89

Sch

St Philip's
Sch

Sewage
Works

BROWNSIDE RD

Easter Moffat
Farm

Browns Burn

Berrieswalls

Briarfield

DUNTILLAND RD

Greystones

CH

66

79 A 80 B 81 C

103

124

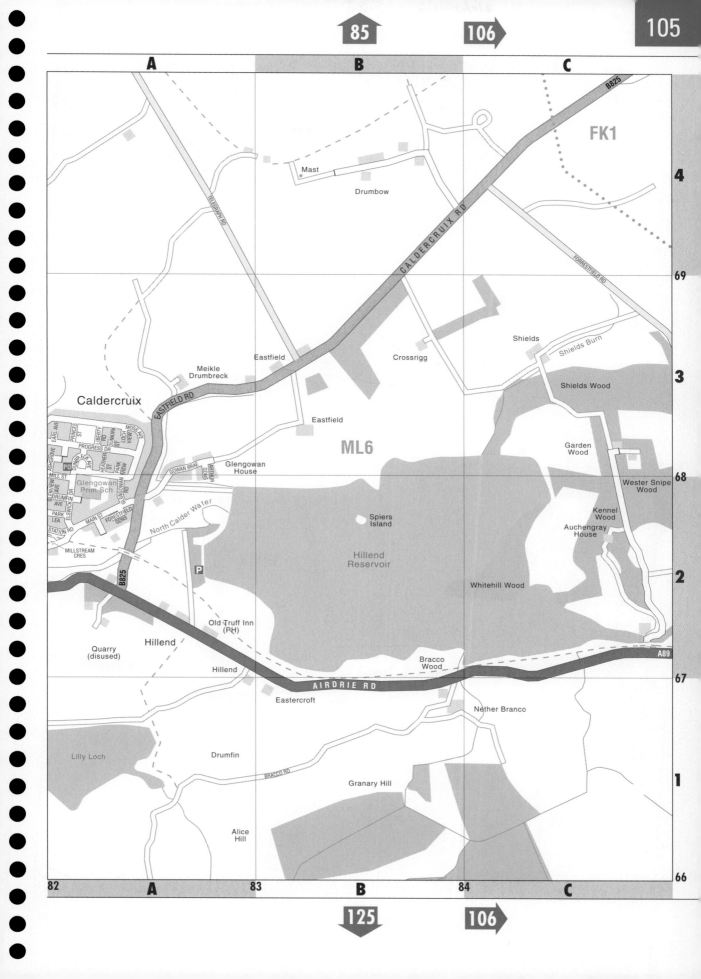

105
86

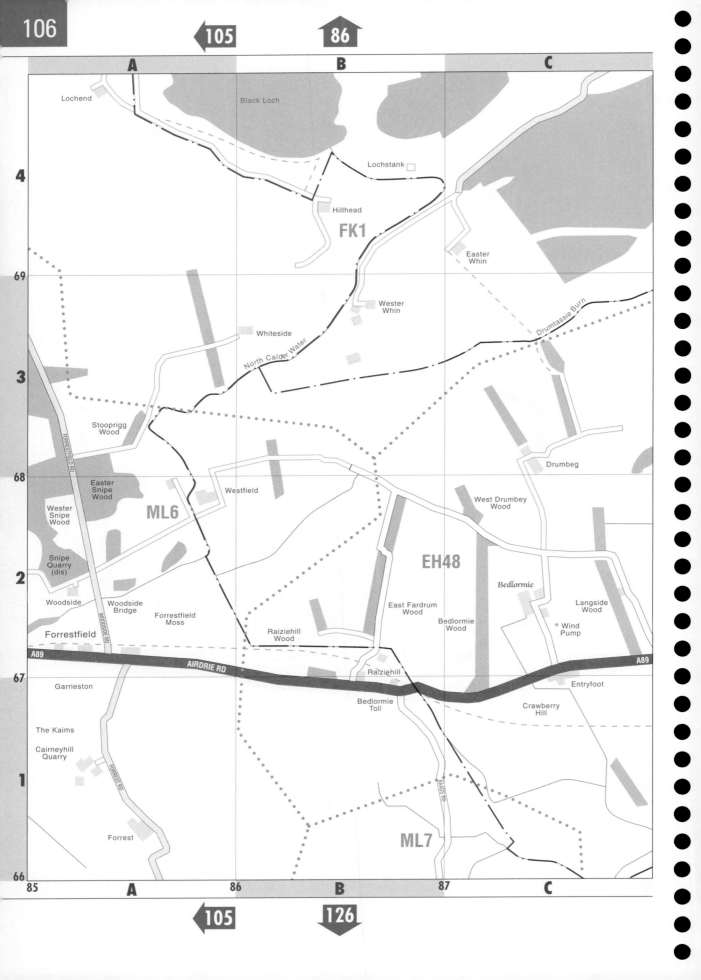

A   B   C

4

Lochend

Black Loch

Lochstank

Hillhead

FK1

Easter
Whin

69

Wester
Whin

Drumtassie Burn

Whiteside

North Calder Water

3

Stooprigg
Wood

Drumbeg

68

Easter
Snipe
Wood

Westfield

West Drumbey
Wood

Wester
Snipe
Wood

ML6

EH48

Bedlormie

2

Snipe
Quarry
(dis)

East Fardrum
Wood

Langside
Wood

Woodside

Woodside
Bridge

Forrestfield
Moss

Raiziehill
Wood

Bedlormie
Wood

Wind
Pump

Forrestfield

FORRESTFIELD RD

WOODSIDE RD

A89   AIRDRIE RD   A89

67

Garrieston

Raiziehill

Entryfoot

Bedlormie
Toll

Crawberry
Hill

The Kaims

Cairneyhill
Quarry

FORREST RD

BLAIRS RD

1

Forrest

ML7

66

85   A   86   B   87   C

105
126

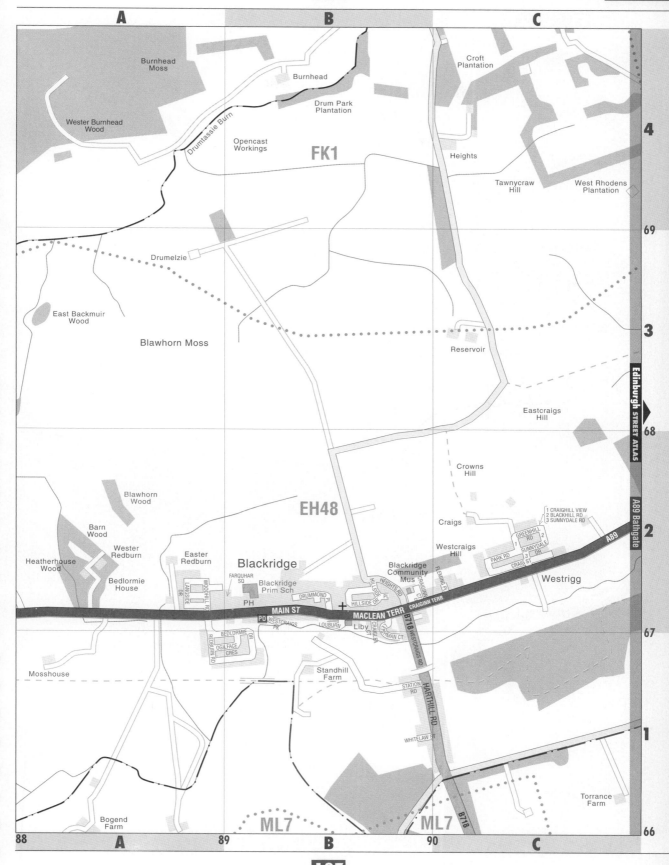

A B C

Burnhead
Moss

Burnhead

Croft
Plantation

Drum Park
Plantation

4

Wester Burnhead
Wood

Drumtassie Burn

Opencast
Workings

FK1

Heights

Tawnycraw
Hill

West Rhodens
Plantation

69

Drumelzie

3

East Backmuir
Wood

Blawhorn Moss

Reservoir

Edinburgh STREET ATLAS

Eastcraigs
Hill

A89 Bathgate

68

Crowns
Hill

Blawhorn
Wood

EH48

Craigs

1 CRAIGHILL VIEW
2 BLACKHILL RD
3 SUNNYDALE RD

Barn
Wood

Westcraigs
Hill

GREENHILL
RD

SUNNYDALE
DR

2

Heatherhouse
Wood

Wester
Redburn

Easter
Redburn

Blackridge

PARK RD

CRAIG ST

A89

Bedlormie
House

FARQUHAR
SQ

Blackridge
Prim Sch

Blackridge
Community
Mus

Westrigg

WOODHILL RD

LANGSIDE
DR

PH

DRUMMOND
PL

HILLSIDE RD

HEIGHTS RD

FLEMING PL

CRAIGINN TERR

MAIN ST

HILLSIDE DR

HILLSIDE
PL

CRAIGIN TERR

PO

WESTCRAIGS
PK

LOUBURN

MACLEAN TERR

B718

WESTCRAIGS RD

67

BEDLORMIE DR

REDBURN RD

OGILFACE
CRES

Liby

CRAIGLEA

CRESHMAN CT

Mosshouse

Standhill
Farm

STATION
RD

HARTHILL RD

WHITELAW ST

1

B718

Torrance
Farm

Bogend
Farm

ML7

ML7

B718

66

88 A 89 B 90 C

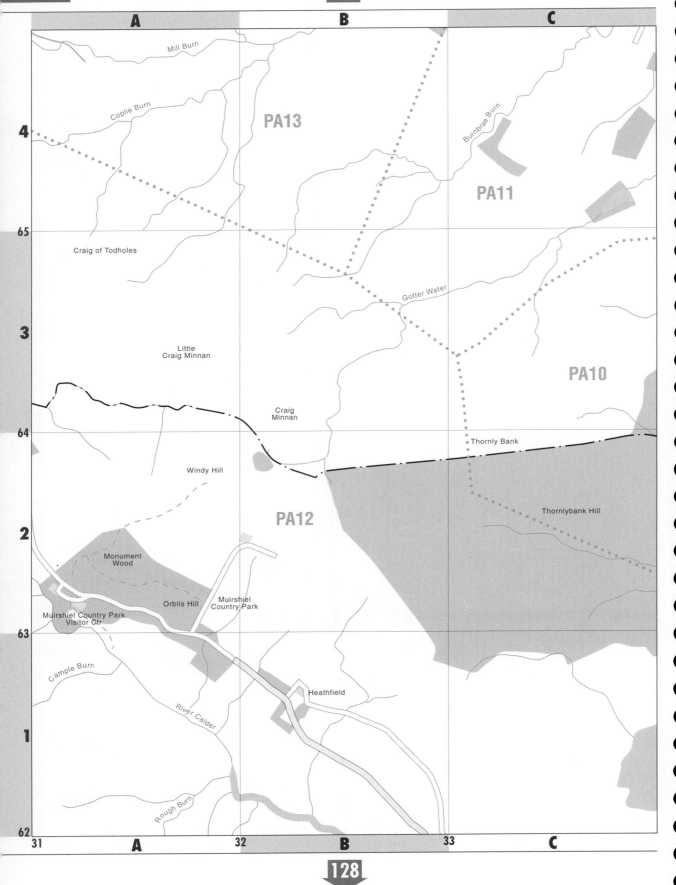

A   B   C

Mill Burn

Coplie Burn

PA13

Burnbrae Burn

PA11

4

65

Craig of Todholes

Gotter Water

3

Little
Craig Minnan

PA10

Craig
Minnan

64

Thornly Bank

Windy Hill

Thornlybank Hill

PA12

2

Monument
Wood

Orblis Hill   Muirshiel
Country Park

Muirshiel Country Park
Visitor Ctr

63

Cample Burn

River Calder

Heathfield

1

Rough Burn

62
31   A   32   B   33   C

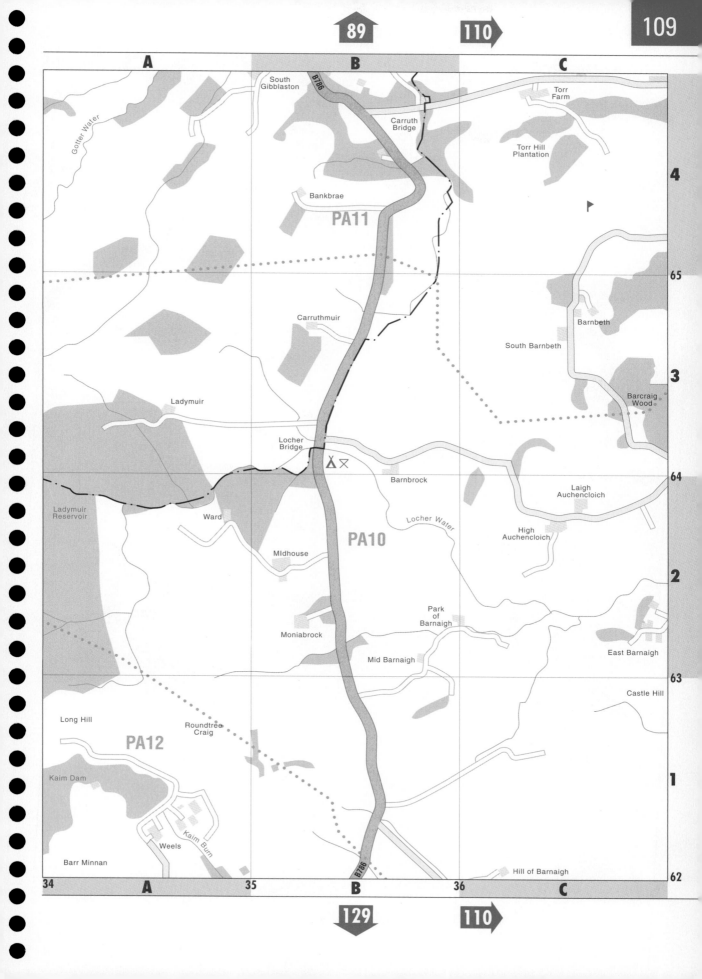

109
90

A B C

4

65

3

64

2

63

1

62

37 A 38 B 39 C

WOODSIDE AVE
HOUSTON RD
B790
WARLOCK RD
ELM RD
MIMOSA RD
LOCH RD
MILL OF GRYFFE RD
GRYFFE GR
GLEN GOWAN RD
KILMACOLM RD
A761
TORR RD
LOMOND CRES
THRIPLEE RD
KENBANK RD
HORSEWOOD RD
FETLAR RD
CARRUTH RD
BARCRAIG RD
GLEN BRAE
KENBANK CRES
Maxwell PL
Liby
PO
Main St
MILL BRAE
BACK RD
Church Manse La
St Mungos Rd
Linwhytes Cres Rd
Church
St Machars Rd
Hillview Rd
Lintwhite Ct
Broom Pl
Moss Rd
Peat La
Gore
Bridge of Weir
Houstonhead Dam
Goldenlee Farm
Houstonhead
River Gryfe
Coalbog

Threeplands
Golf Course Rd
CH
Clevans Rd
Lawmarnock Cres
Anna Ave
Lawmarnock Rd
Clevans
Donaldfield Rd
Lawmarnock Ho
Troon Dr
Kelso Ave
Prieston Rd
Ranfurly Ct
Collace Ave
Hazelwood La
Hazelwood Ave
Castle Terr
Montrose Terr
Bonar Cres
Ranfurly Pl
Watt Rd
Watt La
Bonar La
Ranfurly Rd
Bankend Rd
North View Rd
Kilbarchan Rd
Crosslee Rd
Bridge of Weir Rd
A761

Pow Burn
Southbrae Ave
Rosemount La
Dalmahoy Cres
Bellfield Cres
Glendentan Rd
Bassie Dr
St Andrews Dr
Sunningdale Dr
Turnberry Dr
Ranfurly Castle (rems of)
CH
PA11
Kilgraston Rd
Hazelwood Rd
Earl Pl
Shillingworth Pl
The Grove
Eldin Pl
Ranfurly
Manswrae
Works
Mill Dam

Lochend

Barcraig Wood
Carslaverock Hill
Mill Dam
Pannell Farm
Penwold House

Laigh Auchensale
Locher Water
Whinnerston
Shillingworth

High Auchensale

Auchensale Bridge
Harelaw
The Braes
Locher Rd

Lawmarnock Wood
Monkland
Forehouse
Shuttle St

Law

Lawmarnock
PA10
Forehouse Rd
Wardhouse Farm

Dampton Farm
Glentyan House
Bank Brae

Marshall Moor
Burntshields Rd
Gladstone
Auchenames

Burntshields

Meikle Burntshields
High Overton
Auchenames Cottage

Bower
Low Overton
Huthead
Kibbleston Rd

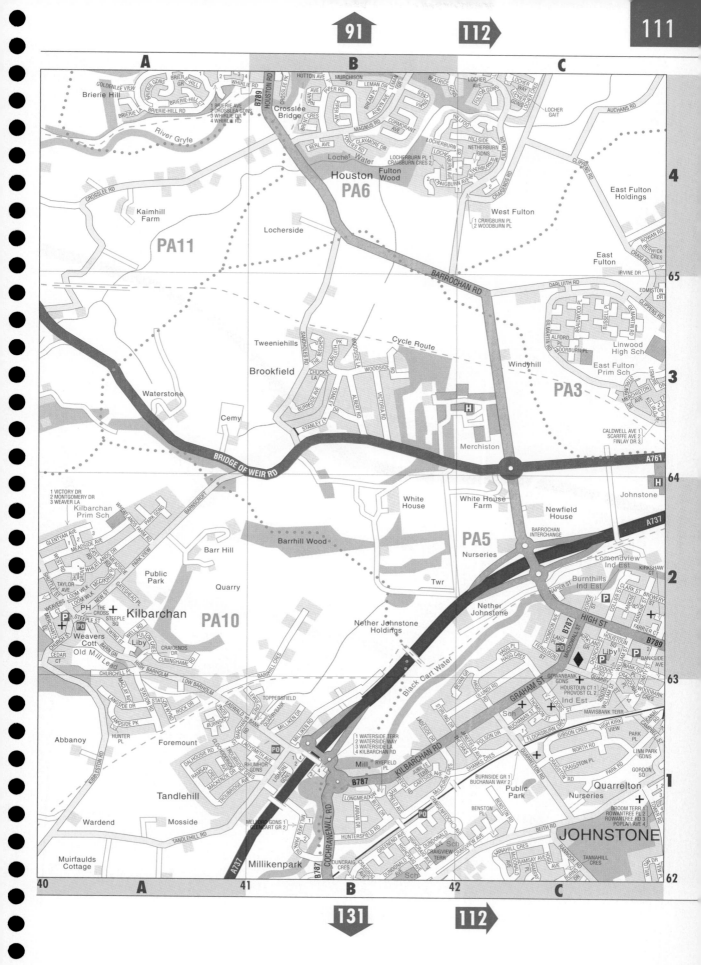

A   B   C

PA6

East Fulton Holdings

Linwood Moss

Candrens

4

Middleton

MIDDLETON RD

ROWAN RD

Sports Ctr

A737

65

Clippens Sch

PA3

Sewage Works

Clippens
1 LOANHEAD LA
2 LOANHEAD AVE

Linwood

St Brendan's High Sch

Black Cart Water

CANDREN RD

Mossedge Ind Est

PA1

The Phoenix Bsns Pk

3

Mill

GRIFFEN AVE

Phoenix Leisure Pk

The Phoenix Ret Pk

PEGASUS AVE

Liby

Linclive Terr

1 BURNBRAE AVE
2 ARDLAMONT SQ

A761

SATURN AVE

GRIFFEN RD

PA1

Superstore

A761 BRIDGE OF WEIR RD

A761

LINWOOD RD

Linclive Interchange

64

A737

LYON RD

WEST AVE

BURNBRAE DR

St James Bsns Ctr

Works

Barskiven Hill

FISHER DR

WHITES BRIDGE CL

Sewage Works

Linwood Ind Est

BURNBRAE RD

BARONSCOURT RD

LINWOOD RD

A761

JOHNSTONE

Old Patrick Water

Cycle Track

1 BREWERY ST
2 CO-OPERATIVE TERR

BARONSCOURT GDNS

B789

FERGUSLIE

Super store

2

PA5

Cemy

CANAL GDNS

BURNBRAE DR

B789

NEWTON TERR

Cycle Track

MAIN RD

Elderslie Golf Course

NEWTON DR

CASTLE GDNS

HIGH ST

B789 THORN BRAE

Sch

THORNHILL

Liby

STODDARD SQ

Roundhill Plantation

FILBAR RD

GREEN ST

PEACOCK

63

Johnstone Thorn Ct

Elderslie

GLEN GDNS

Wallace Prim Sch

KINGS CRES

GREENHILL CRES

BYRES RD

FULBAR GDNS 1
KATRINE DR 2
LOCHALSH DR 3

H

CHERRYWOOD

PARK AVE

QUEEN'S DR

EAZELWOOD

PA2

WATERMILL GR

GIFFORD WYND

DEE AVE

ALMOND AVE

Newton Wood

HELMSDALE DR

SPRINGVALE DR

TWEED DR

Cemy

HILLVIEW RD

BARDRAIN AVE

GLENPATRICK RD

FORTH AVE

DON AVE

SPEY AVE

BEAULY DR

BREDILAND RD

1

ABBEY RD

Elderslie

NEWLANDS GDNS

TUMMELL WAY 4
ESK WAY 5
RYE WAY 6
LEVEN WAY 7
MANNERING WAY 8
JARVIE WAY 9
DINMONT WAY10
DINMONT AVE 11
DURWARD WAY 12
KENILWORTH WAY 13
KENILWORTH WAY 14
IVANHOE WAY 15
AMOCHRIE WAY 16

AMOCHRIE WAY

LOCKSLEY AVE

IVANHOE DR

MONTROSE AVE

DURWARD CRES

Liby

Sch

Johnstone Castle

Auchenlodmont Prim Sch

1 ROWANTREE RD
2 TOWER PL
3 TOWER RD

GLENPATRICK BLDGS

Works

62

43   A   44   B   45   C

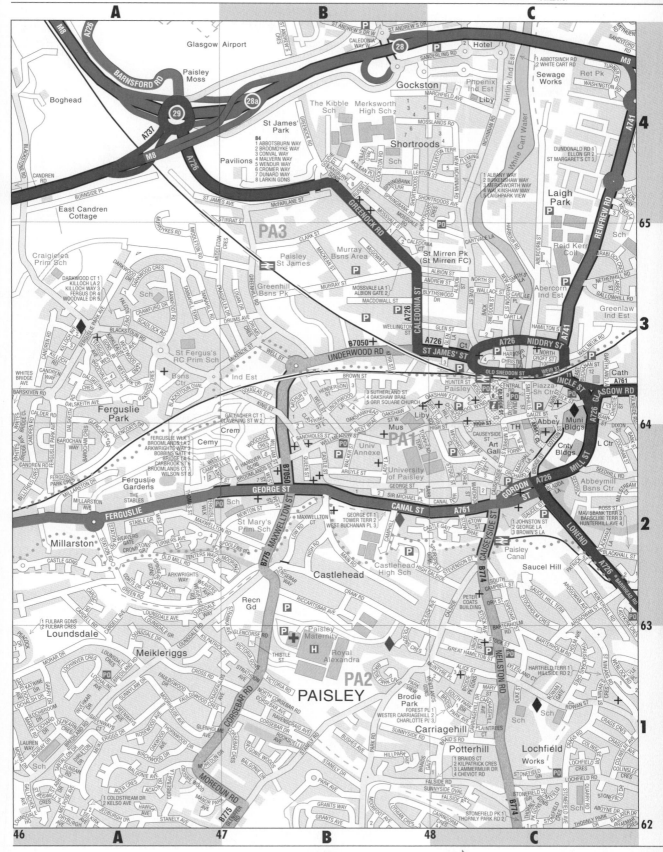

C3
1 BLACKLAW LA
2 MONCRIEFF ST
3 STONEY BRAE
4 BACK SNEDDON ST
5 MAXWELL ST
6 MEETINGHOUSE LA

7 COUNTY SQ
8 COUNTY PL
9 CENTRAL WAY
10 BRICK LA
11 WALLNEUK
12 EAST BUCHANAN MEWS
13 MILLAR ST

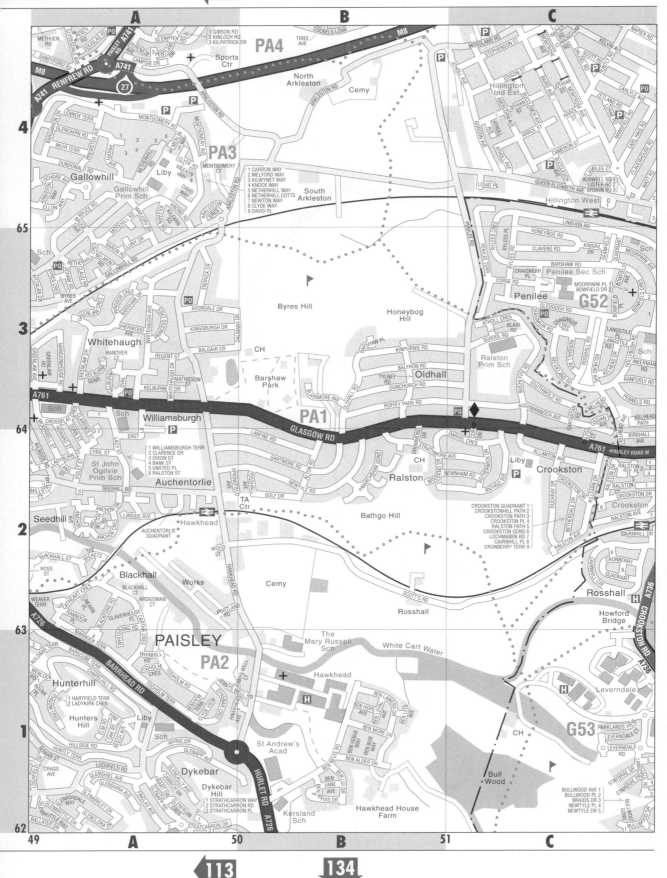

95

116

C4
1 LINTHOUSE BLDGS
2 HOLMFAULD RD
3 HOLMFAULDHEAD PL
4 CLACHAN DR
5 CARMOUTH GDNS
6 FAIRFIELD PL

7 FAIRFIELD GDNS
8 ELDERPARK GR
9 CROSSLOAN TERR

115

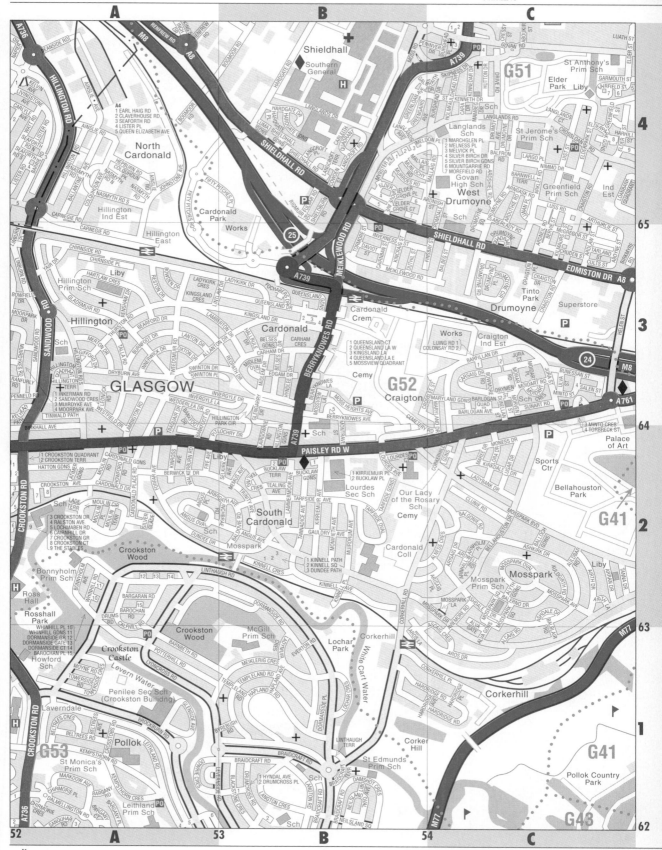

A1
1 BULLWOOD DR
2 BULLWOOD CT
3 BALLOCHMYLE DR
4 DEVOL CRES
5 LEITHLAND AVE
6 LEVERNSIDE CRES

135

116

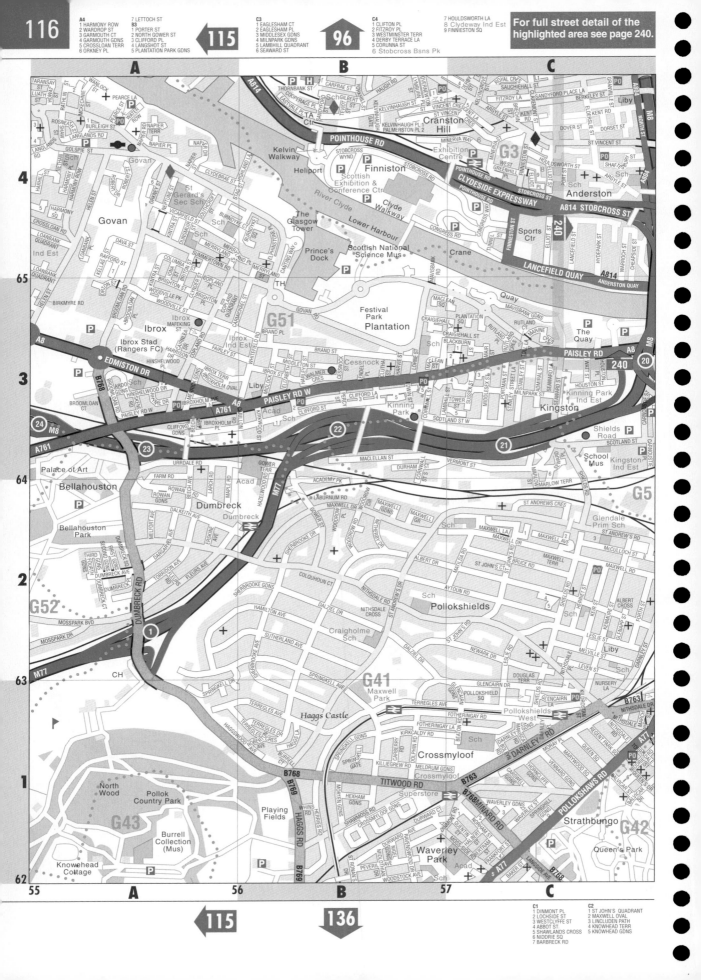

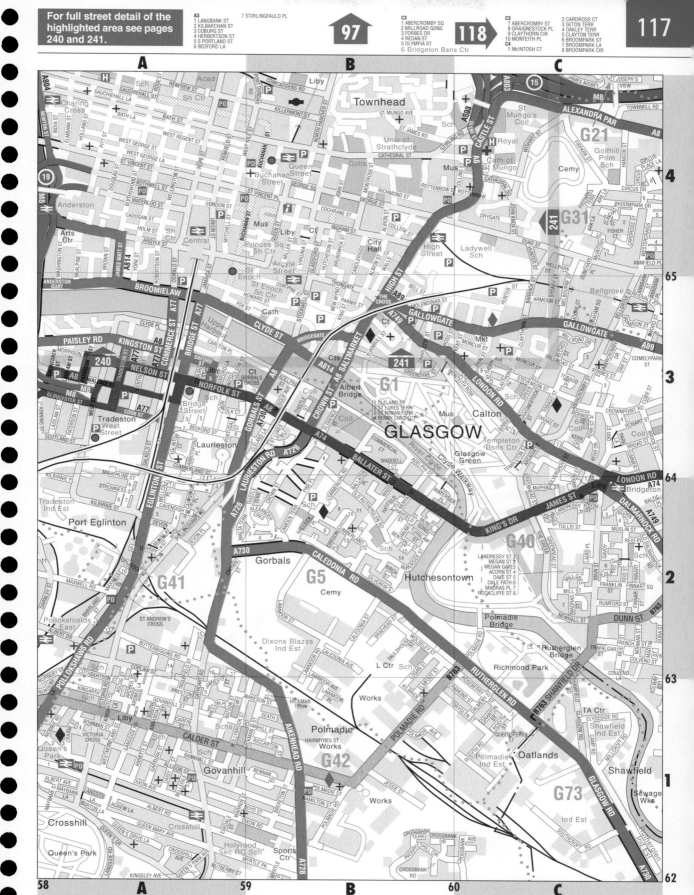

For full street detail of the highlighted area see pages 240 and 241.

A3
1 LANGBANK ST
2 KILBARCHAN ST
3 COBURG ST
4 ROBERTSON ST
5 S PORTLAND ST
6 BEDFORD LA
7 STIRLINGFAULD PL

97

C3
1 ABERCROMBY SQ
2 MILLROAD GDNS
3 FORBES DR
4 REDAN ST
5 OLYMPIA ST
6 Bridgeton Bsns Ctr

118

C3
7 ABERCROMBY ST
8 GRAIGNESTOCK PL
9 CLAYTHORN CIR
10 MONTEITH PL
C4
1 McINTOSH CT

C2
2 CARDROSS CT
3 SETON TERR
4 OAKLEY TERR
5 CLAYTON TERR
6 BROOMPARK ST
7 BROOMPARK LA
8 BROOMPARK CIR

A1
1 TORRISDALE ST
2 PRINCE EDWARD ST
3 ALLISON PL
4 CHAPMAN ST
5 JAMIESON CT
6 HOLLYBROOK PL
A2
1 SURREY LA
2 SALISBURY ST

3 SURREY ST
4 ABBOTSFORD PL
5 CAVENDISH CT
6 FALFIELD ST
7 FRANCIS ST
8 RITCHIE ST
9 LAUDER ST
10 CARDWELL ST
11 ST ANDREW'S RD
12 MUIRHOUSE ST

13 BUTTERFIELD PL
14 ANNANDALE ST
15 LARKFIELD ST
16 ROBSON GR
17 MORGAN MEWS
B2
1 SANDIEFIELD RD
2 SOUTHSIDE CRES
3 HANDEL PL
4 KIDSTON TERR

5 KIDSTON PL
6 NABURN GATE
7 GILMOUR PL
8 HUTCHINSON TOWN CT
9 CUMBERLAND ARC
10 SANDYFAULDS SQ
11 QUEEN ELIZABETH SQ
12 SANDYFAULDS ST
13 CUMBERLAND PL
14 SNOWDON PL

15 SNOWDON ST

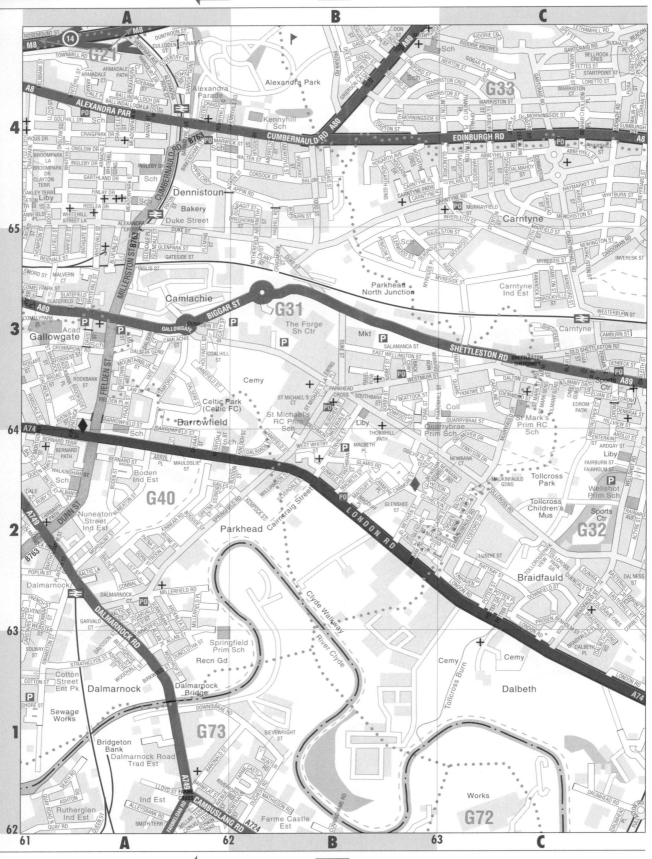

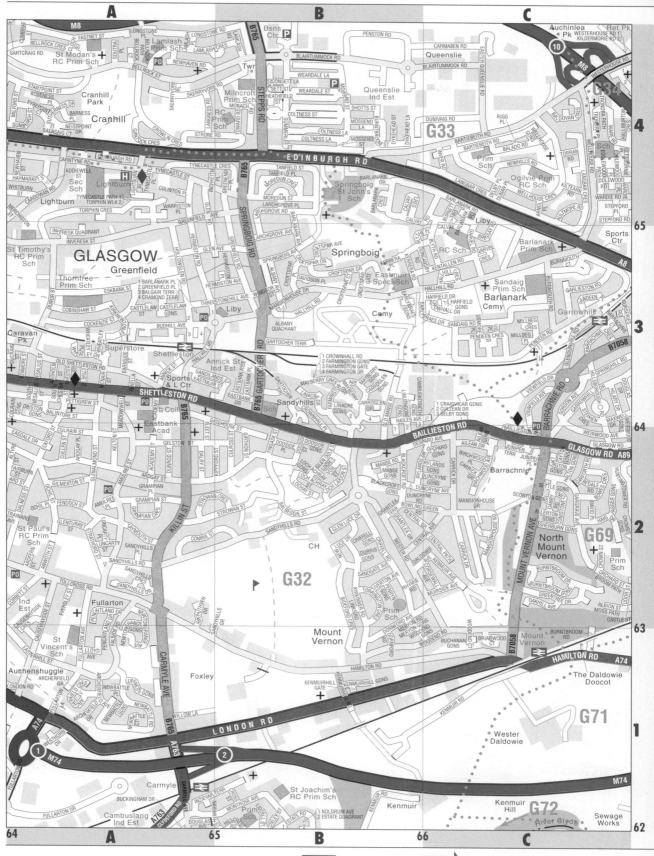

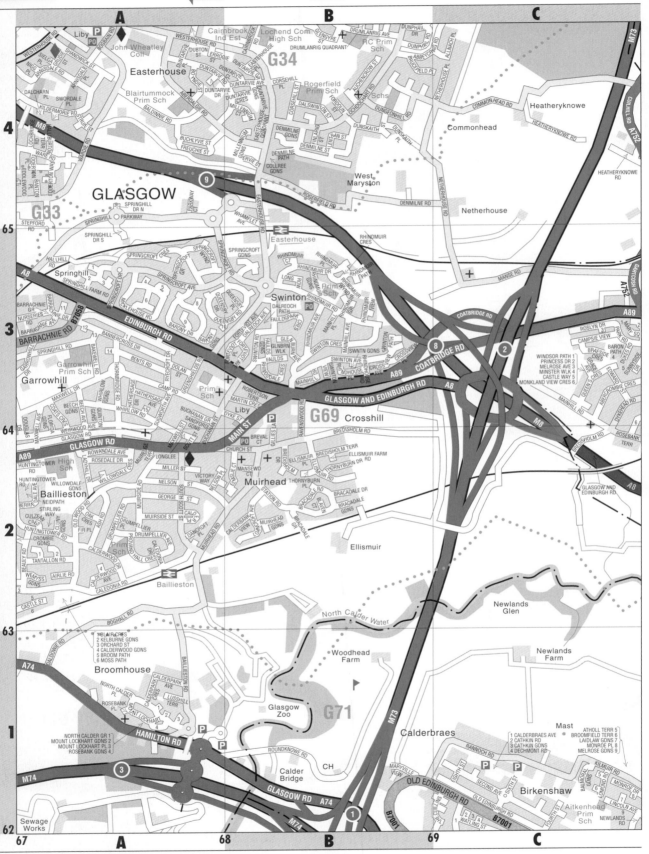

A3
1 SPRINGHILL FARM PL
2 SPRINGHILL FARM WAY
3 SPRINGHILL FARM GR
4 MICKLEHOUSE PL
5 MICKLEHOUSE OVAL
6 MICKLEHOUSE WYND
7 THORNBRIDGE AVE
8 BARONY CT
9 BARONY WYND
10 QUEENSBY AVE
11 BARRACHNIE PL
12 BANNERCROSS GDNS
13 BANNERCROSS AVE
14 THORNBRIDGE GDNS
15 HATHERSAGE GDNS

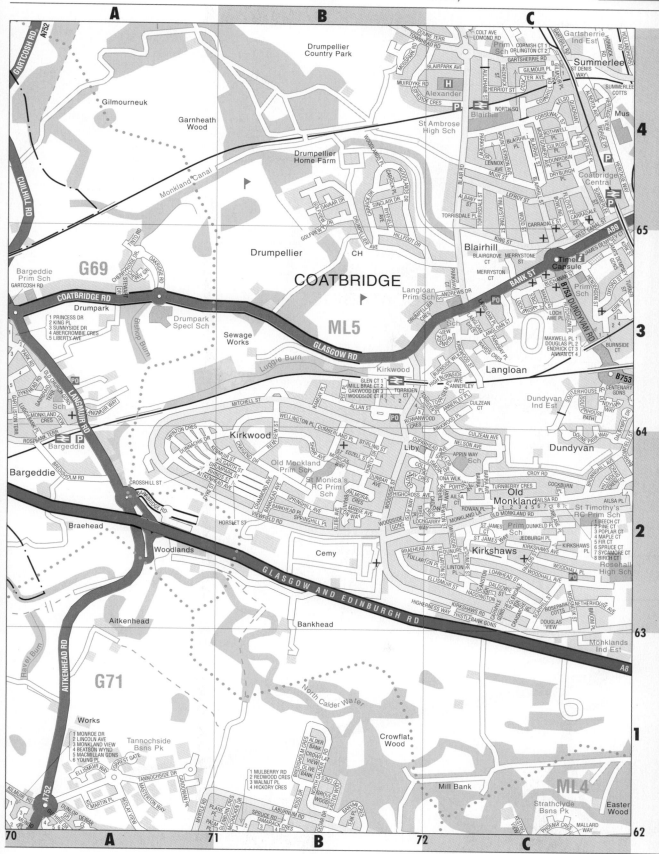

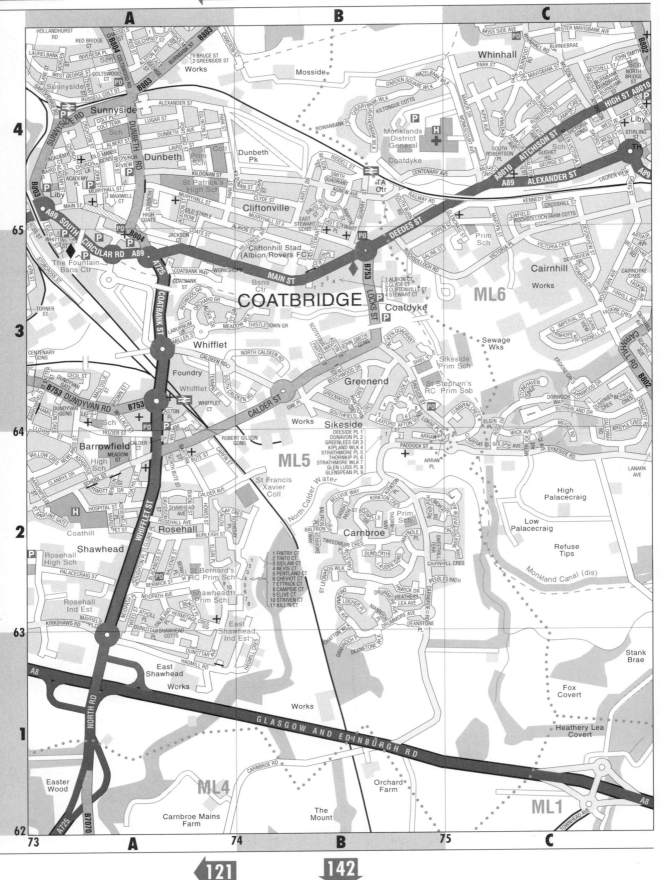

A4
1 ANDERSON LA
2 AULD'S BRAE
3 PARKHEAD LA
4 OLD CROSS
5 ANDERSON ST
6 MANSE PL

7 BAILLIES LA
8 SOUTH NIMMO ST
9 ALBERT CRES
10 ST ANDREW'S GDNS

B4
1 KINGSTON AVE
2 COLSTON PL
3 COLSTON ROW
4 COLSTON TERR
5 MEADOWSIDE GDNS
6 MEADOWSIDE PL

103

124

C4
1 CAMERON CT
2 OGILVIE CT
3 ERSKINE CT
4 INNES CT
5 BRUCE CT
6 FINLAYSON QUADRANT

7 WESTER MOFFAT CRES
8 MOORPARK AVE
9 CRAIGNURE CRES

123

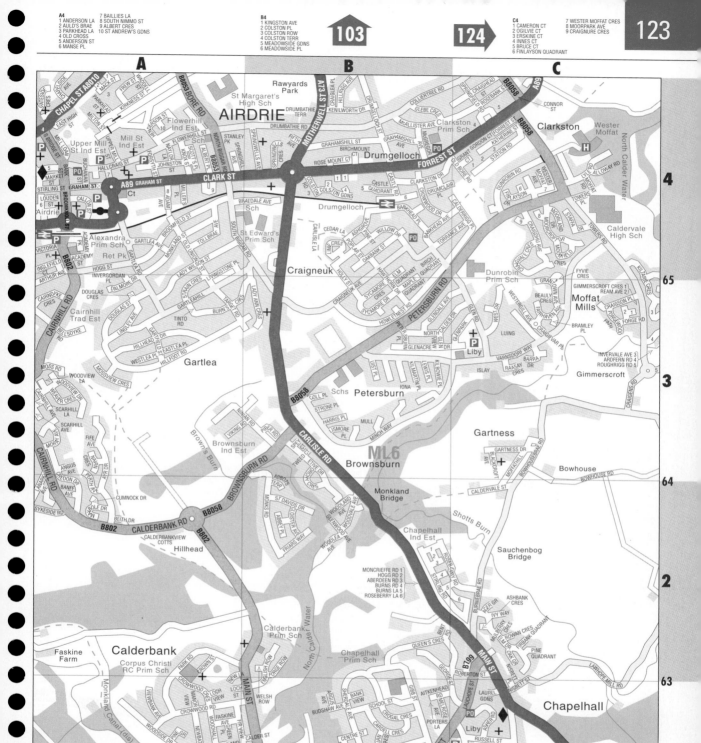

A B C

4

BROWNIESIDE RD

STEPENDS RD

Lochhill

DUNTILLAND RD

Browns Burn

Wester Bracco

Springbank Quarry (disused)

Lady Bell's Moss

65

KILMAHA CRES
BURNWOOD DR
INVERVALE AVE
ACHNASHEEN RD
ARDFERN RD
BALLOCH RD
DYSART WAY

Burn Wood

ROUGHRIGG RD

3

ML6

Works

Roughrigg Reservoir

BOWHOUSE RD

Clattering Burn

DUNSISTON RD

Easter Dunsyston

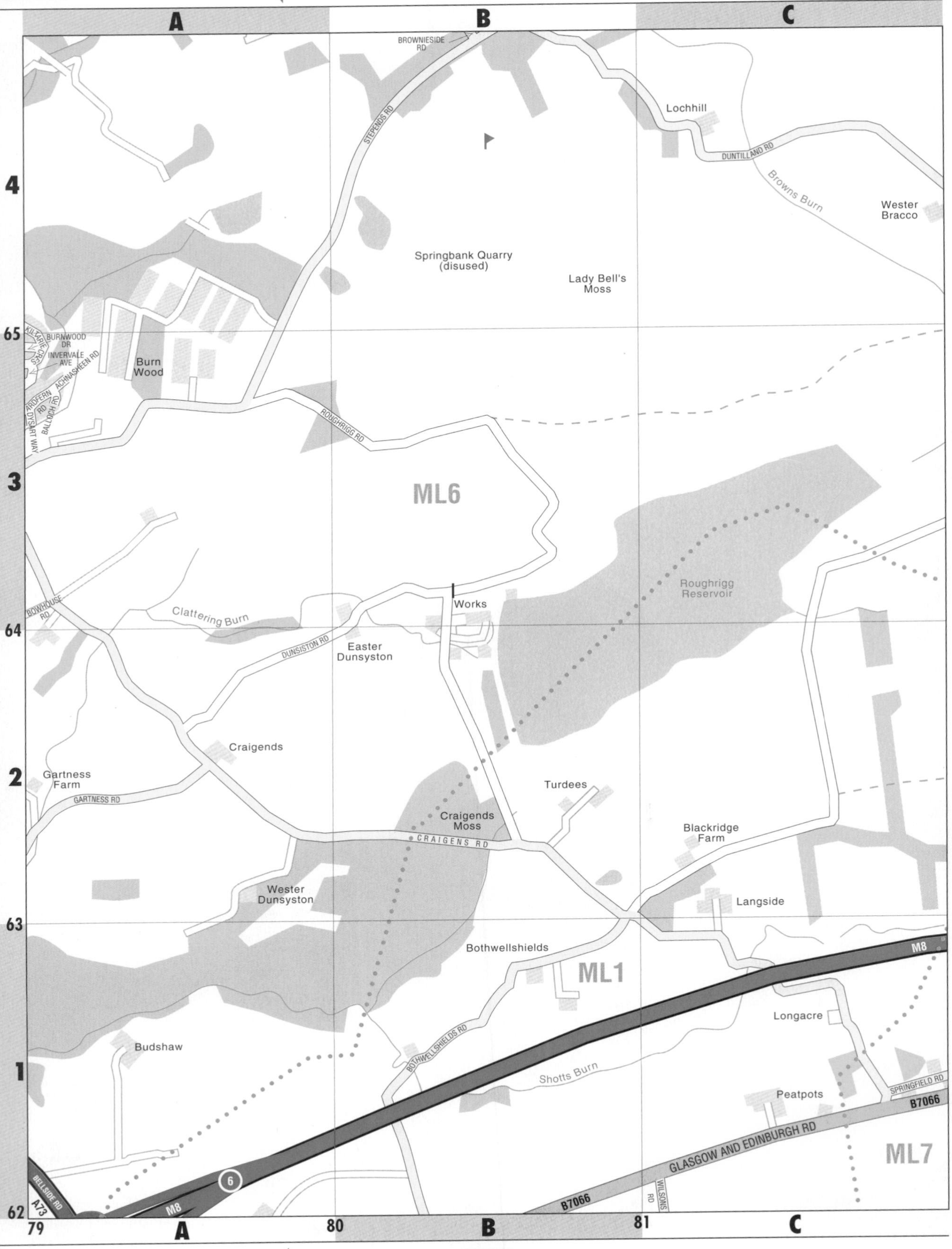

64

Craigends

2

Gartness Farm

GARTNESS RD

Craigends Moss

CRAIGENS RD

Turdees

Blackridge Farm

Langside

63

Wester Dunsyston

Bothwellshields

ML1

BOTHWELLSHIELDS RD

Longacre

1

Budshaw

Shotts Burn

Peatpots

SPRINGFIELD RD

B7066

M8

GLASGOW AND EDINBURGH RD

ML7

62

A73

BELLSIDE RD

M8

6

B7066

WILSONS RD

79 A 80 B 81 C

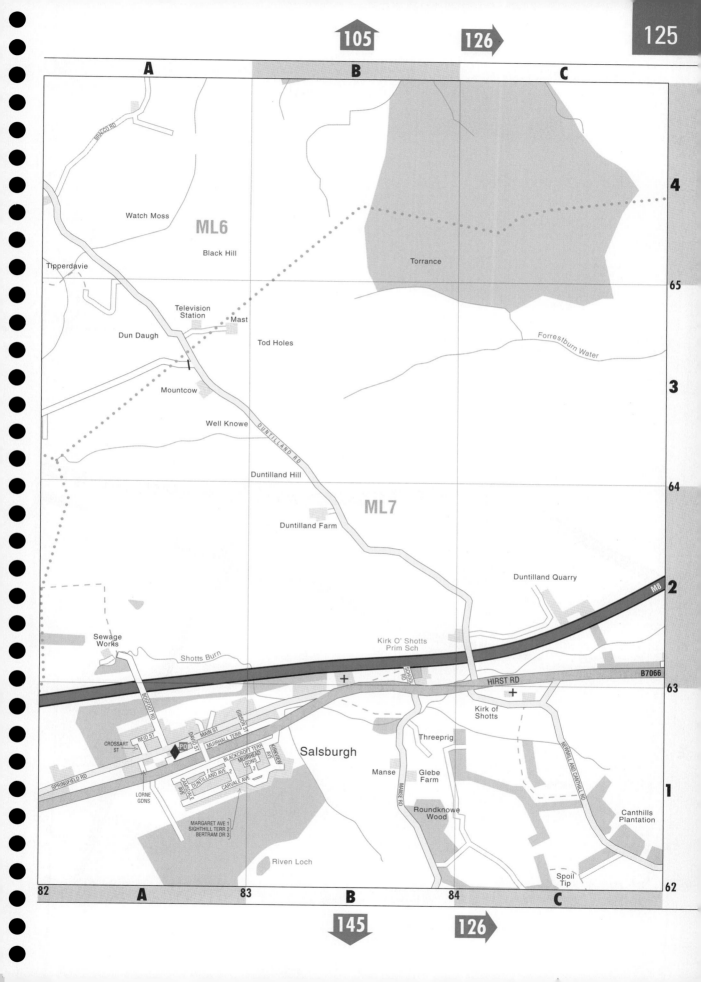

125
106

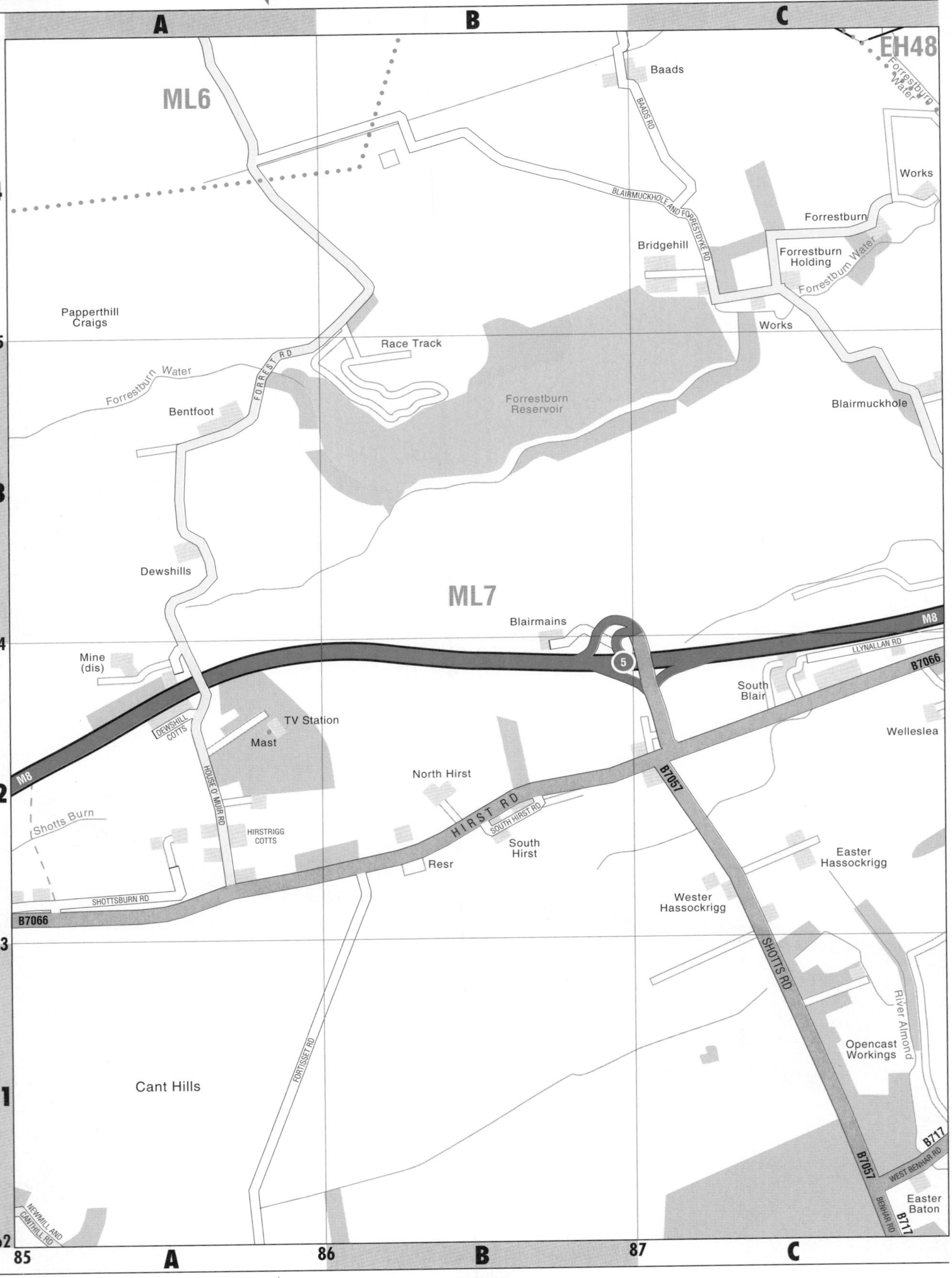

A **B** **C**

EH48

ML6

Baads

BAADS RD

Forrestburn Water

BLAIRMUCKHOLE AND FORRESTDYKE RD

Works

Bridgehill

Forrestburn

Forrestburn Holding

Forrestburn Water

4

Papperthill Craigs

Works

65

Forrestburn Water

FORREST RD

Race Track

Forrestburn Reservoir

Blairmuckhole

Bentfoot

3

Dewshills

ML7

Blairmains

M8

LLYNALLAN RD

64

Mine (dis)

5

B7066

South Blair

DEWSHILL COTTS

TV Station

Welleslea

HOUSE O MUIR RD

Mast

North Hirst

B7057

2

M8

HIRST RD

SOUTH HIRST RD

Shotts Burn

HIRSTRIGG COTTS

South Hirst

Easter Hassockrigg

Resr

Wester Hassockrigg

SHOTTS RD

63

B7066

SHOTTSBURN RD

River Almond

FORTISSET RD

Opencast Workings

1

Cant Hills

B7717

B7057

WEST BENHAR RD

Easter Baton

B7717

BENHAR RD

NEWMILL AND CANTHILL RD

62

85 **A** 86 **B** 87 **C**

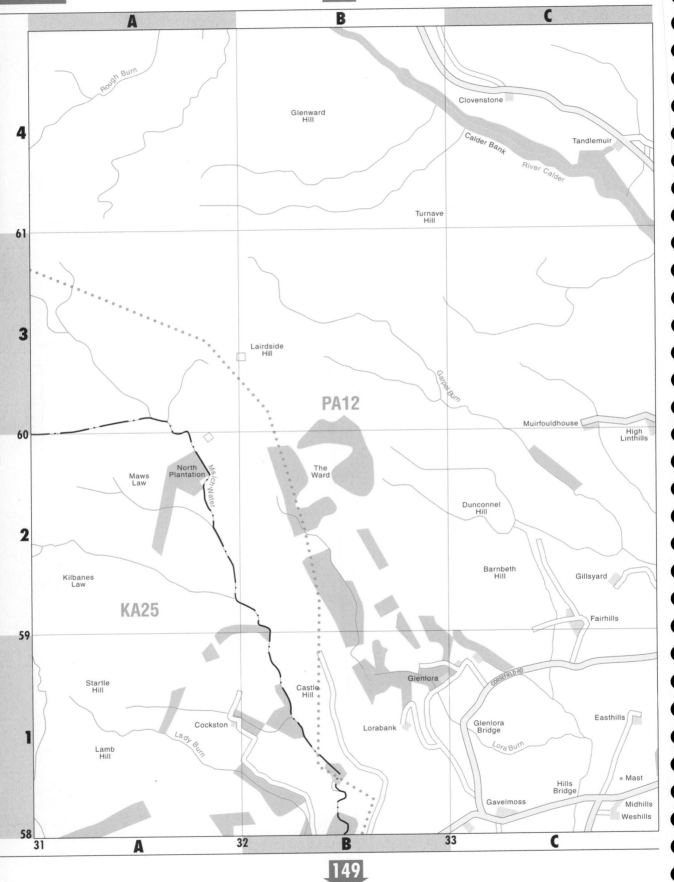

A   B   C

4

Rough Burn

Glenward
Hill

Clovenstone

Calder Bank

Tandlemuir

River Calder

Turnave
Hill

61

3

Lairdside
Hill

Garpel Burn

PA12

Muirfouldhouse

High
Linthills

60

North
Plantation

Maws
Law

Maich Water

The
Ward

Dunconnel
Hill

2

Kilbanes
Law

KA25

Barnbeth
Hill

Gillsyard

Fairhills

59

Startle
Hill

Glenlora

CORSEFIELD RD

Easthills

Castle
Hill

1

Cockston

Lady Burn

Lorabank

Glenlora
Bridge

Lora Burn

Lamb
Hill

Mast

Hills
Bridge

Gavelmoss

Midhills

Weshills

58

31   A   32   B   33   C

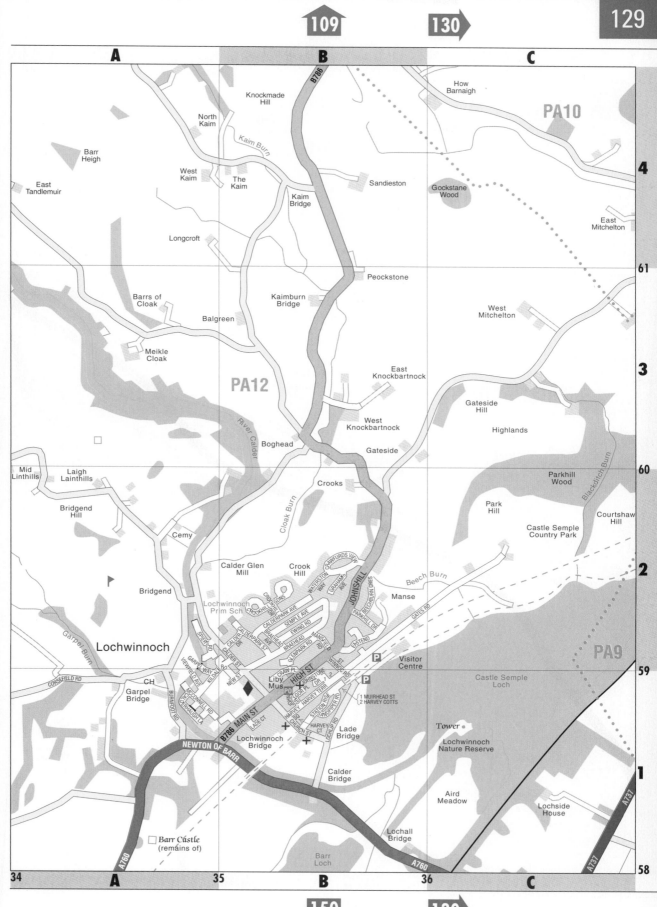

A   B   C

4

61

PA10

How
Barnaigh

Knockmade
Hill

North
Kaim

Kaim Burn

Barr
Heigh

West
Kaim

The
Kaim

Kaim
Bridge

Sandieston

Gockstane
Wood

East
Mitchelton

East
Tandlemuir

Longcroft

Peockstone

West
Mitchelton

3

Barrs of
Cloak

Kaimburn
Bridge

Balgreen

Meikle
Cloak

PA12

East
Knockbartnock

Gateside
Hill

Highlands

West
Knockbartnock

Boghead

Gateside

60

River Calder

Mid
Linthills

Laigh
Lainthills

Crooks

Parkhill
Wood

Park
Hill

Blackditch Burn

Bridgend
Hill

Cloak Burn

Castle Semple
Country Park

Courtshaw
Hill

Cemy

2

Calder Glen
Mill

Crook
Hill

Beech Burn

Bridgend

CRAWFURDS VIEW

WATERSTON WAY

GRAHAMS AVE

JOHNSHILL

Manse

Lochwinnoch
Prim Sch

CROOKHILL DR

CALDERPARK AVE

SEMPLE AVE

EWING RD

BRAEHEAD

MANSFIELD

PARKHILL DR

BEECHBURN CRES

Garpel Burn

SPIERS RD

CALDER DR

BRAEHEAD

GLENPARK AVE

MANSE RD

WINNOCH RD

EASTEND

GATES RD

PA9

Lochwinnoch

Castle Semple
Loch

59

GARPEL WAY

VIEWFIELD AVE

KILDAL

NEW ST

CALDER ST

CRAW PL

HIGH ST

JOHNSTONE DR

P

P

Visitor
Centre

CH

CORSEFIELD RD

BURNFOOT RD

MCCONNELL RD

LOCHBAR AVE

Liby
Mus

PO

GASGOR PL

HARVEY TERR

HARVEY CT

STATION RSE

MOSSPIER RD

1 MUIRHEAD ST
2 HARVEY COTTS

Garpel
Bridge

LADE CT

HARVEY CT

CHURCH RD

LOCH LIP RD

Tower

B786 MAIN ST

Lochwinnoch
Bridge

Lochwinnoch
Nature Reserve

NEWTON OF BARR

Lade
Bridge

Calder
Bridge

Aird
Meadow

1

Lochside
House

Barr Castle
(remains of)

Lochall
Bridge

A760

Barr
Loch

A760

A737

A737

58

34   A   35   B   36   C

← 129
↑ 110

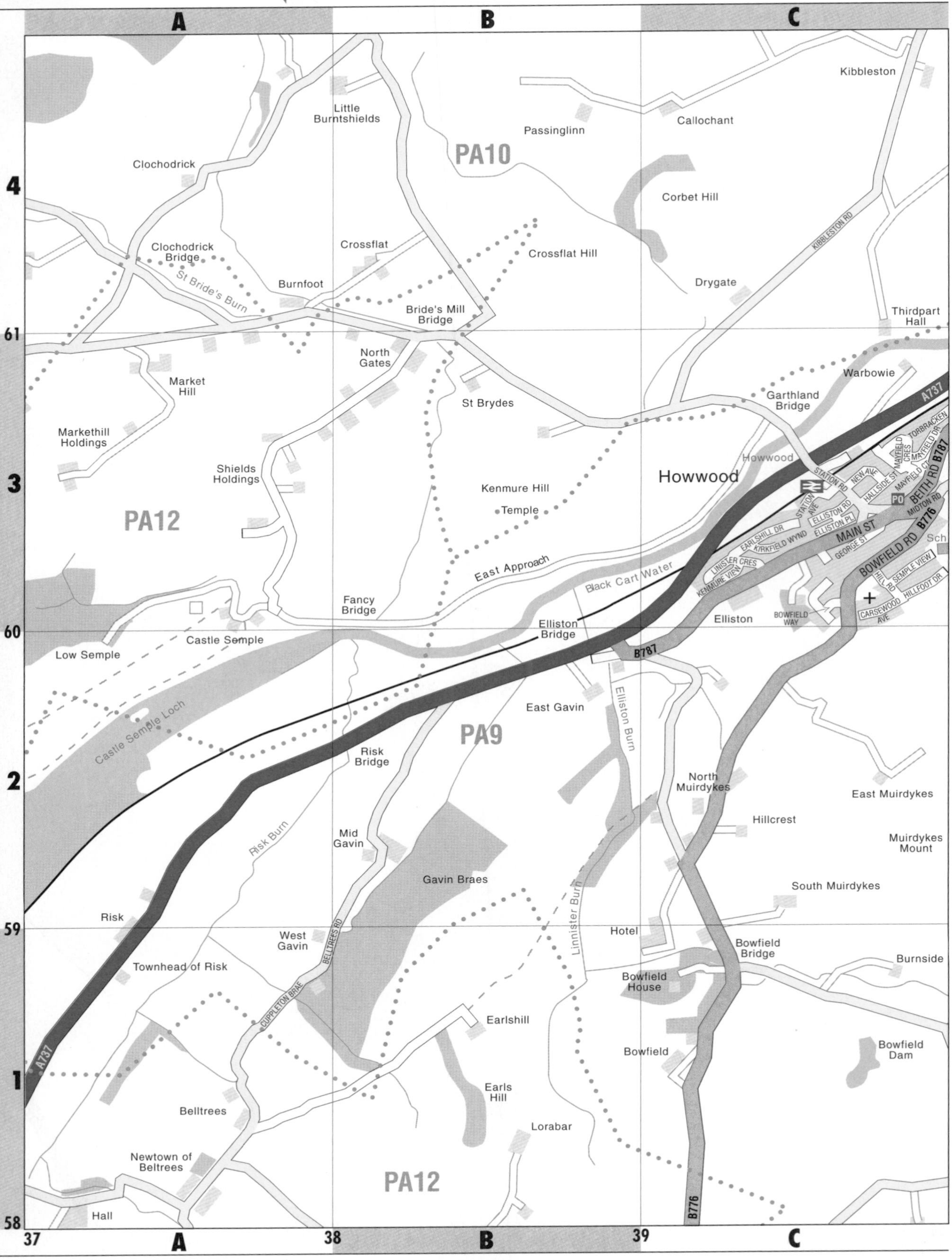

A   **B**   **C**

Kibbleston

Little Burntshields

Passinglinn

Callochant

PA10

Clochodrick

Corbet Hill

4

Clochodrick Bridge

Crossflat

Crossflat Hill

Kibbleston Rd

St Bride's Burn

Burnfoot

Drygate

Thirdpart Hall

Bride's Mill Bridge

61

North Gates

Warbowie

Market Hill

St Brydes

Garthland Bridge

Howwood

Markethill Holdings

Shields Holdings

Kenmure Hill

Station Rd

New Av

Mayfield St

Torbracken

PA12

Temple

Howwood

Mayfield Cres

Midton Rd

Beith Rd

B787

3

Earlshill Dr

Elliston Rd

Elliston Pl

Kirkfield Wynd

B776

Main St

East Approach

Black Cart Water

Linister Cres

George St

Bowfield Rd

Semple View

Sch

Kenmure View

Fancy Bridge

Elliston Bridge

Elliston

Bowfield Way

Carsewood Ave

Hillfoot Dr

60

Castle Semple

Low Semple

B787

East Gavin

Elliston Burn

Castle Semple Loch

Risk Bridge

PA9

North Muirdykes

East Muirdykes

2

Risk Burn

Hillcrest

Muirdykes Mount

Mid Gavin

Gavin Braes

South Muirdykes

Risk

West Gavin

Beltrees Rd

Linnister Burn

Hotel

Bowfield Bridge

Burnside

59

Townhead of Risk

A737

Cuppleton Brae

Earlshill

Bowfield House

Bowfield

Bowfield Dam

1

Earls Hill

Belltrees

Lorabar

B776

Newtown of Beltrees

PA12

58

Hall

37   38   39

A   **B**   **C**

← 129
↓ 151

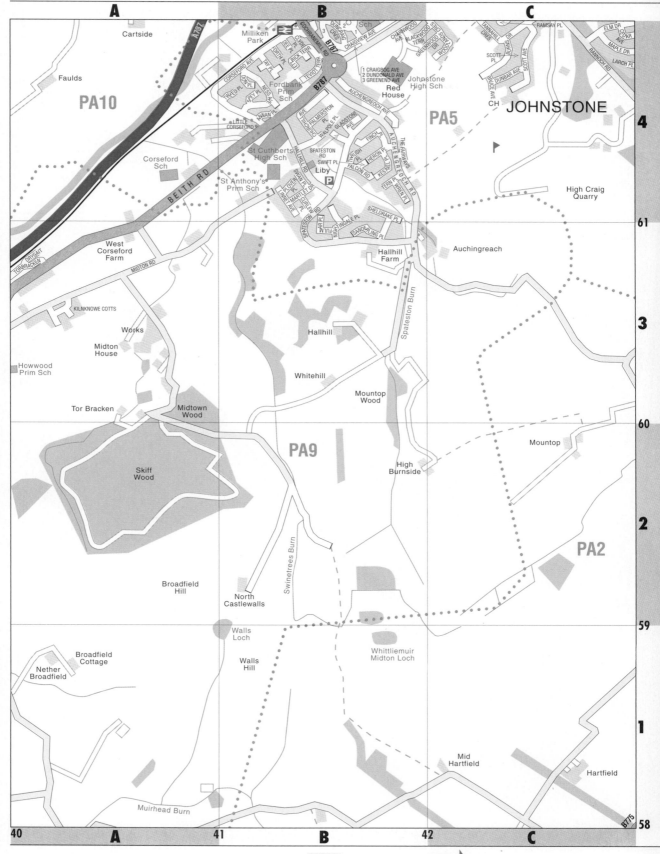

111
132
152
132

Cartside

Faulds

PA10

Milliken Park

Corseford Sch

Fordbank Prim Sch

LITTLE CORSEFORD

St Cuthberts High Sch

St Anthony's Prim Sch

CORSEFORD AVE

Sch

CRAIGVIEW AVE

1 CRAIGBOG AVE
2 DUNDONALD AVE
3 GREENEND AVE

Johnstone High Sch

Red House

CH

JOHNSTONE

PA5

RAMSAY PL

ELM DR

MAPLE DR

SCOTT PL

SCOTT AVE

High Craig Quarry

SPATESTON RD

Liby

AUCHENGREOCH AVE

THE FAIRWAYS

SHELDRAKE PL

Hallhill Farm

Auchingreach

Spateston Burn

West Corseford Farm

MIDTON RD

BEITH RD

DRYGAIT

TORBRACKEN

KILNKNOWE COTTS

Works

Midton House

Howwood Prim Sch

Tor Bracken

Midtown Wood

Skiff Wood

Hallhill

Whitehill

Mountop Wood

Mountop

PA9

High Burnside

Broadfield Hill

North Castlewalls

Swinetrees Burn

Walls Loch

Walls Hill

Whittliemuir Midton Loch

PA2

Broadfield Cottage

Nether Broadfield

Mid Hartfield

Hartfield

Muirhead Burn

A   **B**   **C**

4

PA5

ELM DR · PO · SYCAMORE · BALMORAL RD
CEDAR AVE · MAPLE DR
LABURNUM · ACACIA PL · HOLLY PL
LARCH · CHESTNUT · JUNIPER PL

Craigston Wood

Craigbog

Windyhill

Glenpatrick

Leitchland Farm

Mackiesmill

Low Bardrain

GLENPATRICK RD

LEITCHLAND RD

MACKIE'S MILL RD

Sch

Foxbar

MANNERING WAY

SPEY AVE · TEVIOT AVE · KENILWORTH AVE
ETTRICK OVAL · ROTHERWOOD · IVANHOE RD · AINCRIEF RD
WOODSTOCK WAY
WOODSTOCK AVE
MONTROSE WAY
WAVERLEY RD
MOGARTH AVE

CORNISH DR · GLENDOWER WAY · ROTHWICK WAY
GILFILLAN WAY
ASHTON WAY · SPENCER DR · FINDHOH AVE
BREGHIN · KEPSTON CT · IDLESDALE · BARRENWOOD
ALLOT CT
HAZELWOOD

1 ROTHERWOOD WAY
2 OLIPHANT CT
3 MONTROSE CT
4 HERIOT WAY
5 OLIPHANT OVAL
6 HEBROT CT
7 MARMION CT
8 MONTROSE WAY

MARMION WAY

HERIOT WAY

ROXBURGH RD
MAGDALEN WAY
GLENALLAN WAY
ABBOTSFORD CRES
ROWANLEA
ROSEDALE AVE

FOXBAR DR
FOXBAR RD
FOXBAR CRES

DURROCKSTOCK RD
ROADEN AVE
WAVERLEY WAY
TALFORD
HOLLOWS AVE
HOLLOWS CRES
DURROCKSTOCK CRES 9
DURROCKSTOCK WAY 10

SERGEANT LAW RD

B775

61

Wester Craigenfeoch

Highcraig Wood

High Craigenfeoch

3

Old Patrick Water

Bardrain Wood

Mast

PA2

Craigmuir

Robertson Park

P

60

High Bardrain Wood

GLENIFFER RD

Mast

Sergeant Law

Masts

Sergeantlaw

P

SERGEANT LAW RD

2

Bent Farm

Bent Bridge

Brownside

Lapwing Lodge

Thornliemuir

59

Caplaw Dam

Caplaw

CAPLAW RD

G78

Mossneuk Farm

1

Caplaw Bridge

SHILFORD RD

Greenfieldmuir

58

B775

43   **A**   44   **B**   45   **C**

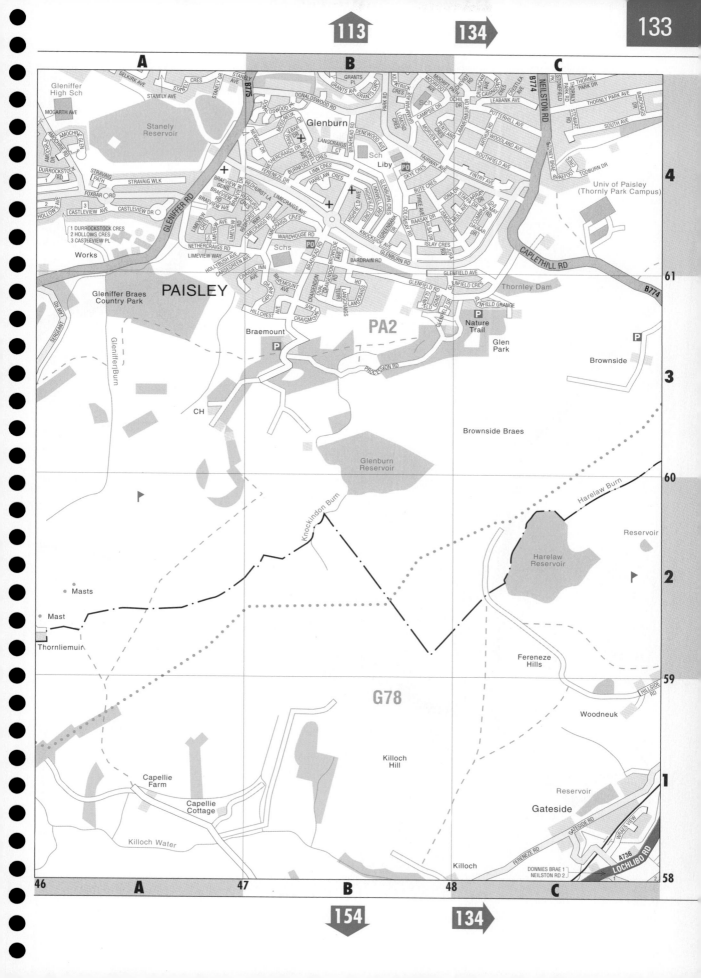

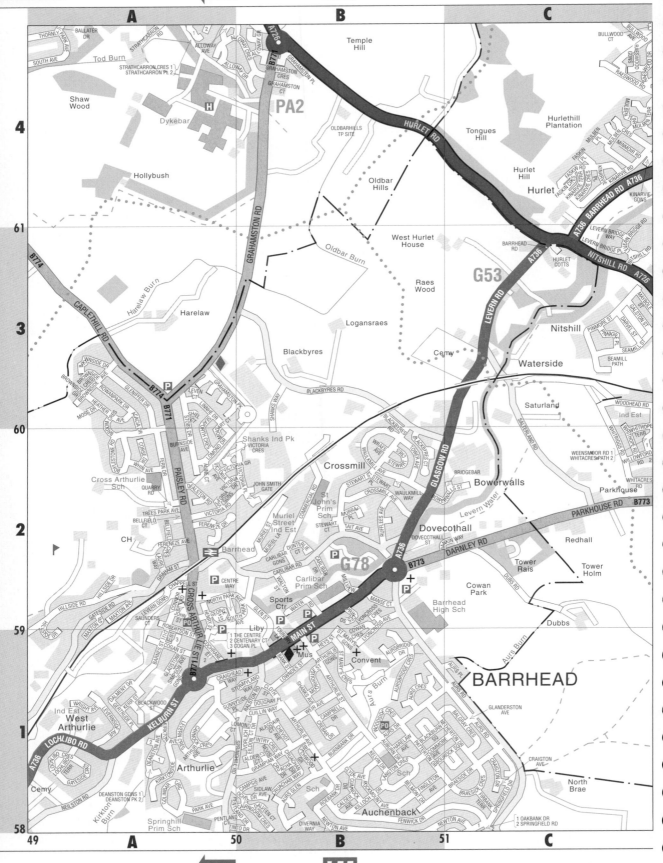

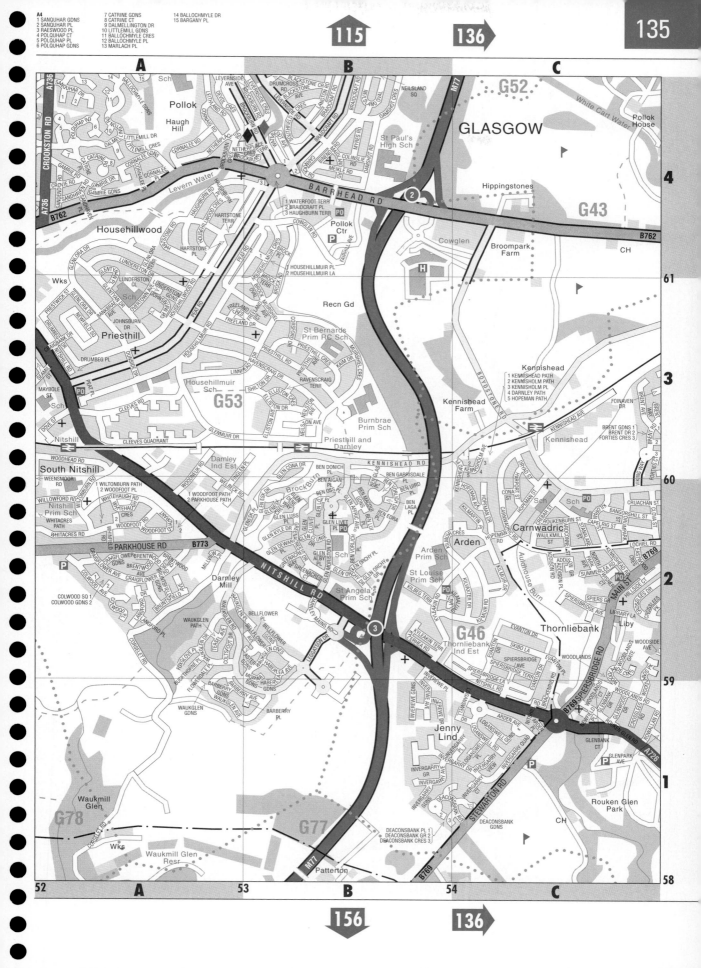

115
136
156
136

A4
1 SANQUHAR GDNS
2 SANQUHAR PL
3 RAESWOOD PL
4 POLQUHAP CT
5 POLQUHAP PL
6 POLQUHAP GDNS

7 CATRINE GDNS
8 CATRINE CT
9 DALMELLINGTON DR
10 LITTLEMILL GDNS
11 BALLOCHMYLE CRES
12 BALLOCHMYLE PL
13 MARLACH PL

14 BALLOCHMYLE DR
15 BARGANY PL

GLASGOW

Pollok
Haugh
Hill

Pollok
House

G52

White Cart Water

G43

CROOKSTON RD

A736

B762

Levern Water

BARRHEAD RD

1 WATERFOOT TERR
2 BRAIDCRAFT PL
3 HAUGHBURN TERR

Pollok
Ctr

St Paul's
High Sch

Hippingstones

Househollwood

Hartstone
Terr

Hartstone
Pl

1 HOUSEHILLMUIR PL
2 HOUSEHILLMUIR LA

Cowglen

Broompark
Farm

CH

61

Wks

Priesthill

St Bernards
Prim RC Sch

Recn Gd

Kennishead

1 KENNISHEAD PATH
2 KENNISHOLM PATH
3 KENNISHOLM PL
4 DARNLEY PATH
5 HOPEMAN PATH

3

MAYBOLE
ST
Sch

Househollmuir
Sch

G53

Priesthill
Terr

Ravenscraig
Terr

Kennishead
Farm

FOINAVEN

Nitshill

Priesthill and
Darnley

Burnbrae
Prim Sch

KENNISHEAD RD

Kennishead

60

South Nitshill

Darnley
Ind Est

1 WOODFOOT PATH
2 PARKHOUSE PATH

Brockburn

BEN DONICH
PL

BEN GABRISDALE

1 WILTONBURN PATH
2 WOODFOOT PL

Carnwadric

WEENSMOOR
RD

Nitshill
Prim Sch

WHITACRES
PATH

WHITACRES RD

Arden
Prim Sch

Arden

PARKHOUSE RD

B773

NITSHILL RD

Auldhouse Burn

B769

Darnley
Mill

St Angela's
Prim Sch

Thornliebank
Ind Est

St Louise
Prim Sch

G46

Thornliebank

Liby

59

Waukglen
Path

Bellflower
Pl

Spiersbridge
Ave

WOODSIDE
AVE

Barberry
Pl

Jenny
Lind

STEWARTON RD

GLENBANK
CT

GLENPARK
AVE

A726

1

Waukmill
Glen

G78

Rouken Glen
Park

CH

G77

Wks

Waukmill Glen
Resr

DEACONSBANK PL 1
DEACONSBANK GR 2
DEACONSBANK CRES 3

DEACONSBANK
GDNS

Patterton

M77

B769

58

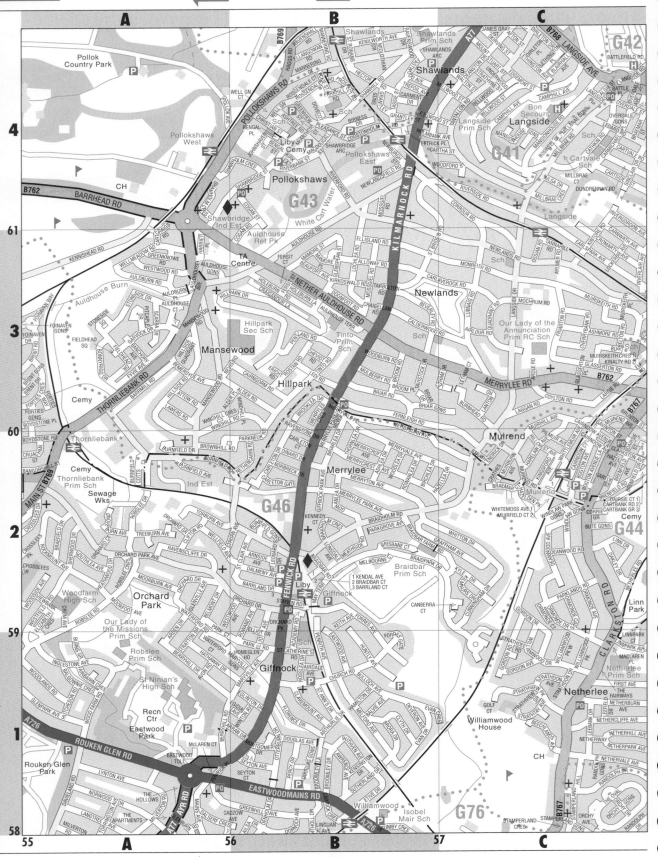

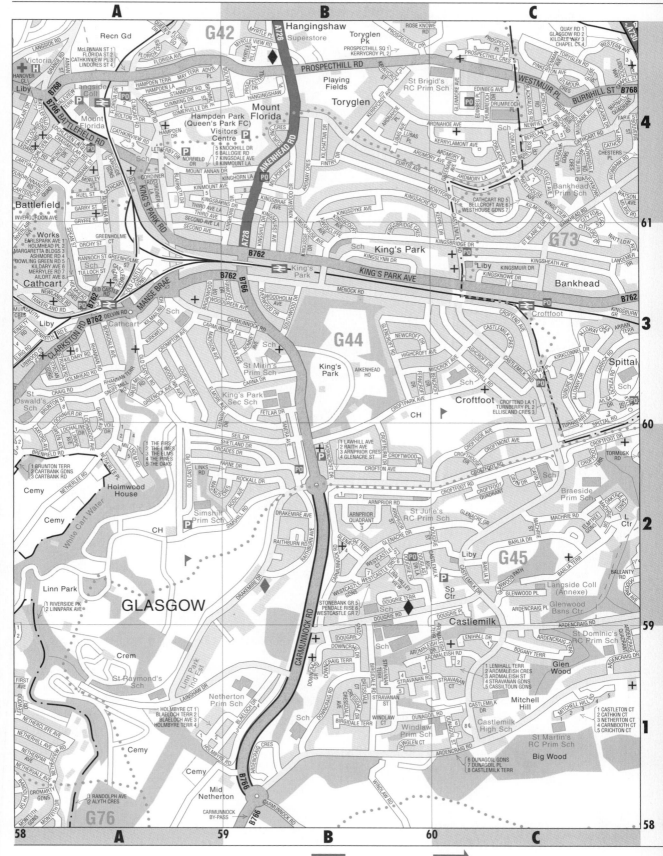

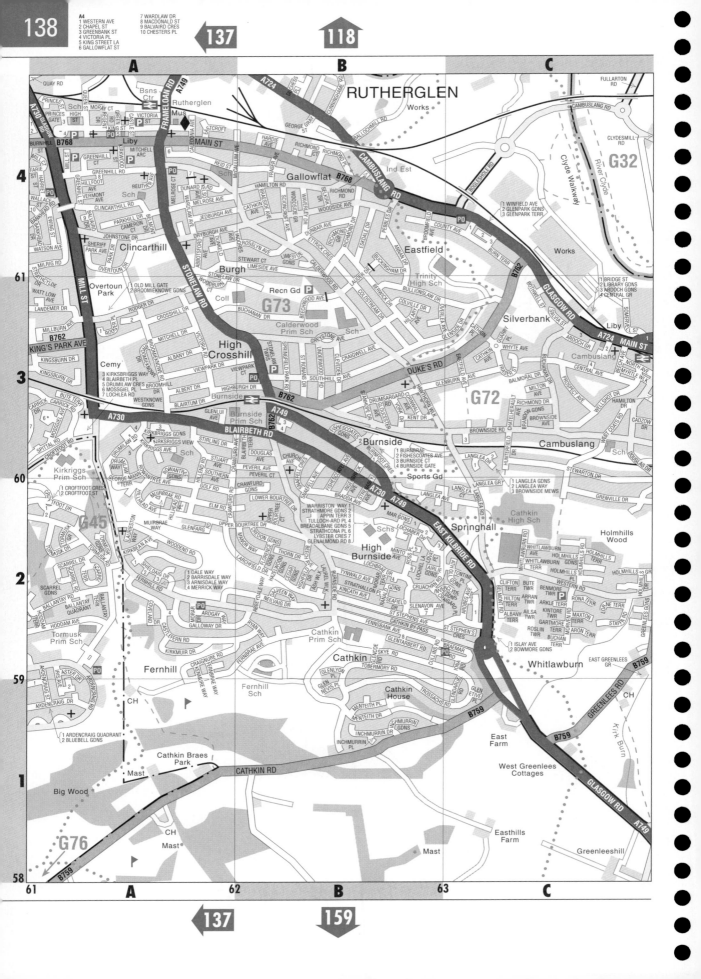

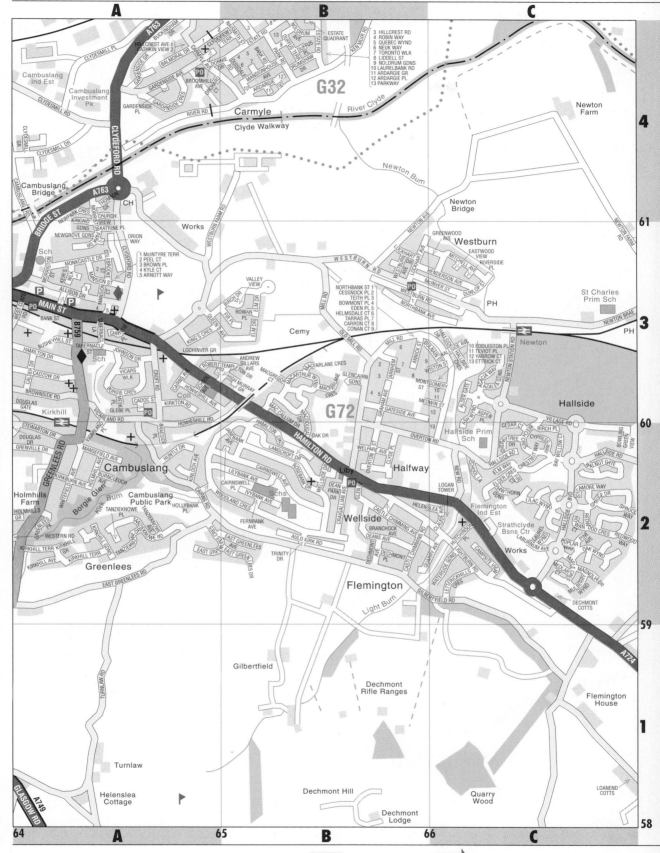

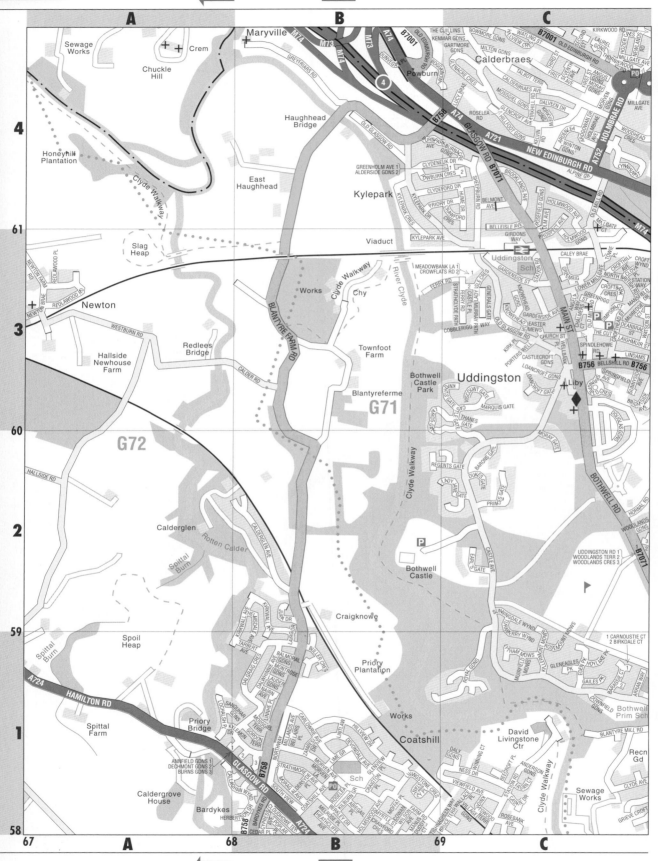

121
142

A4
1 YOUNG PL
2 WALKER PATH
3 CRIGHTON GN
4 MUIRHEAD GATE
5 PRENTICE LA
6 HADDOW GR
7 CAMPSIE VIEW
8 OCHIL VIEW
9 KILPATRICK WAY
10 RUSSELL GDNS
11 BAILLE WYND

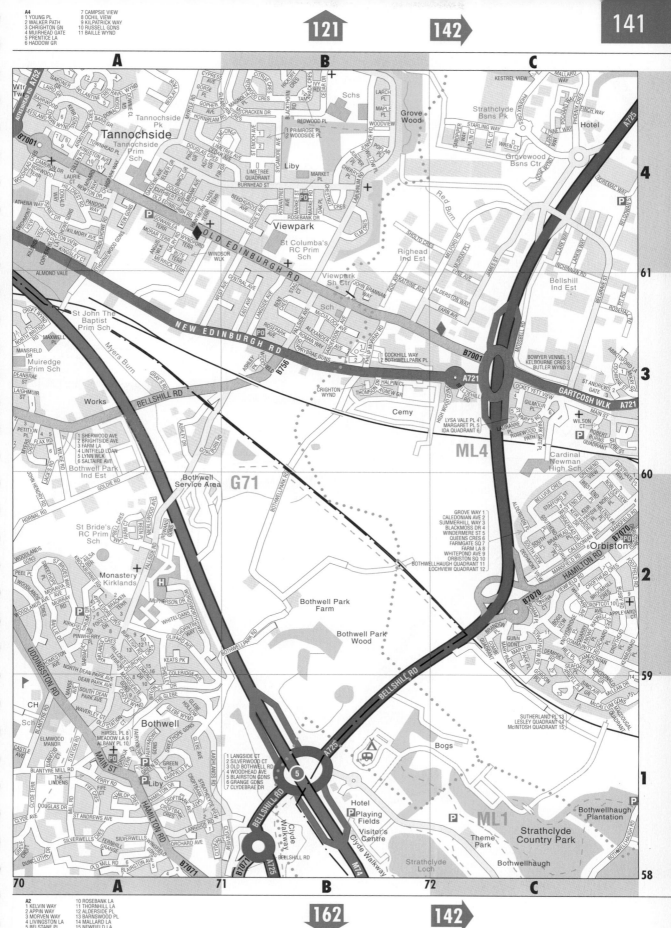

A2
1 KELVIN WAY
2 APPIN WAY
3 MORVEN WAY
4 LIVINGSTON LA
5 BELSTANE PL
6 KATRINE WAY
7 RANNOCH WAY
8 CARRICK WAY
9 TANTALLON RD
10 ROSEBANK LA
11 THORNHILL LA
12 ALDERSIDE PL
13 BARNSWOOD PL
14 MALLARD LA
15 NEWFIELD LA
16 HOZIER PL

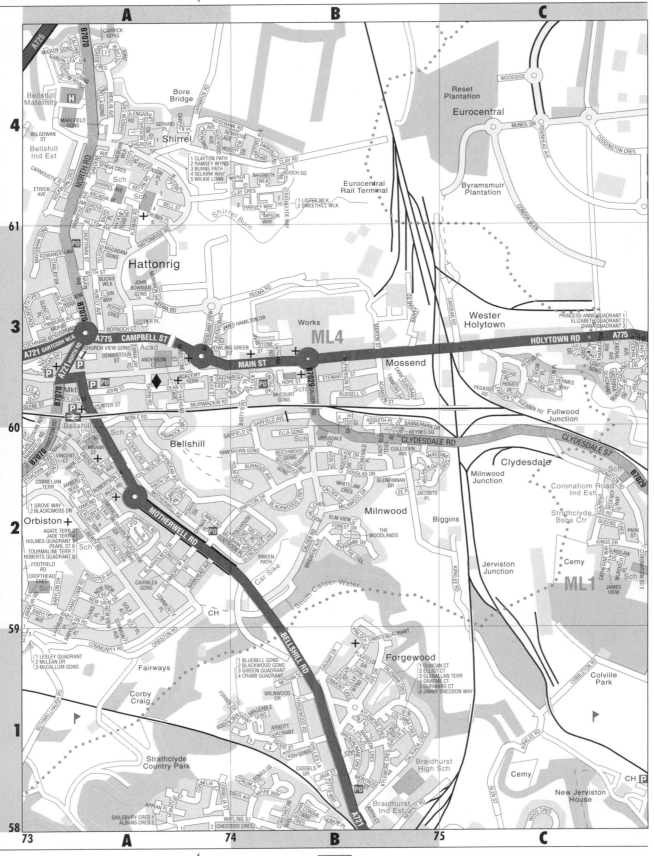

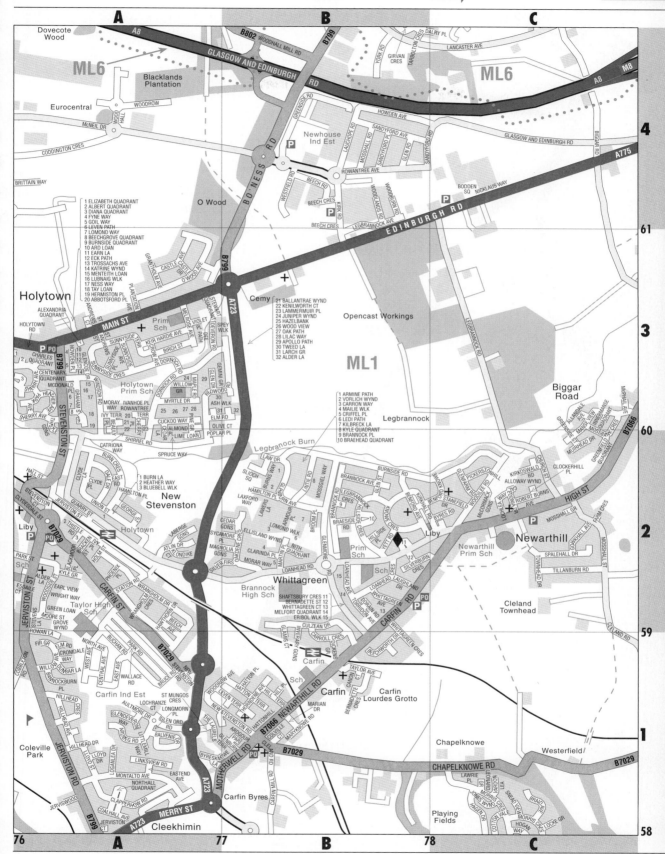

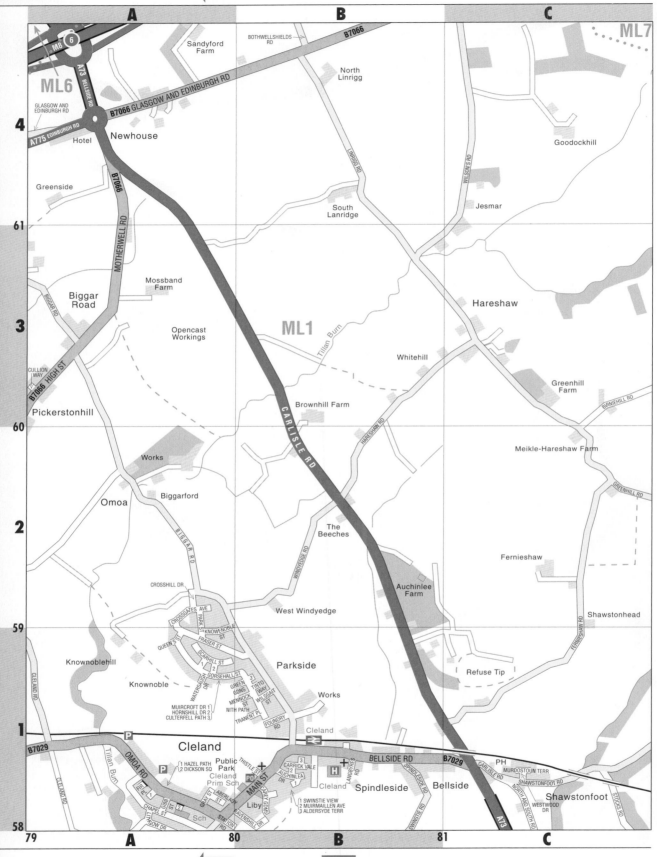

143
124

A
B
C

ML7

M8 6

A73

ML6 BELLSIDE RD

GLASGOW AND EDINBURGH RD

GLASGOW AND
EDINBURGH RD

B7066 GLASGOW AND EDINBURGH RD

BOTHWELLSHIELDS RD

B7066

North
Linrigg

Sandyford
Farm

Goodockhill

4

A775 EDINBURGH RD

Hotel

Newhouse

WILSON'S RD

B7066

Jesmar

Greenside

MOTHERWELL RD

LINRIGG RD

South
Lanridge

61

BIGGAR RD

Biggar
Road

Mossband
Farm

Hareshaw

ML1

Tillan Burn

Whitehill

3

CULLION
WAY

B7066 HIGH ST

Opencast
Workings

CARLISLE RD

Greenhill
Farm

BURNIEHILL RD

Pickerstonhill

Brownhill Farm

HARESHAW RD

60

Works

Meikle-Hareshaw Farm

GREENHILL RD

Omoa

Biggarford

BIGGAR RD

The
Beeches

Fernieshaw

GREENHILL RD

2

WINDYEDGE RD

CROSSHILL DR

CROSSGATES AVE

PARK ST

West Windyedge

Auchinlee
Farm

FERNIESHAW RD

Shawstonhead

KNOWNOBLE ST

Parkside

59

QUEEN ST

FRASER ST

Knownoblehill

SCARHILL ST

GORSEHALL ST

Refuse Tip

Knownoble

WATERSLEUGH DR

GREEN
GDNS

MENNOCK ST

NITH PATH

TINTO WAY

WILSGATE ST

Works

MUIRCROFT DR 1
HORNSHILL DR 2
CULTERFELL PATH 3

TRANENT PL

FOUNDRY RD

1

B7029

Cleland

Cleland

OMOA RD

Tillan Burn

CLELAND RD

P

P

PO

1 HAZEL PATH
2 DICKSON SQ

Public
Park

Cleland
Prim Sch

THISTLE ST

MAIN ST

CARRICK VALE

AUCHINLEA DR

BELLSIDE RD

B7029

LANGBYRES RD

SPINDLESIDE RD

CARLISLE RD

PH

MURDOSTOUN TERR

SHAWSTONFOOT RD

H

Cleland

Spindleside

Bellside

NORTH AND SOUTH RD

STOCKS RD

Shawstonfoot

GRAY ST

LABERLADE ST

ABERLADY GDNS

Liby

Sch

CHAPEL ST

GLASGOW DR

STATION RD

RAVENSHILL DR

SWINSTIE RD

SWINSTIE RD

1 SWINSTIE VIEW
2 MUIRMAILLEN AVE
3 ALDERSYDE TERR

A73

WESTWOOD DR

58

79
80
81

A
B
C

143
165

A
B
C

Spoil Tip
Well Hill

Westfield
Fortissat View

MANSE RD

Roughdike
Mains

4

Jersay

Tillan Burn

61

Law's Castle

MUIREDGE AND JERSY RD

ML7

Pell Hill

3

BIRNIEHILL RD

Pellhill Wood

Mine (dis)

Muirhouse

Heatherhead Plantation

Hareshaw Moss

60

ML1

2

GREENHILL RD

Mast

Home Farm

Hartwood

ASHGROVE

HOME FARM RD

Hartwood

MUIREDGE AND JERSY RD

Penty

H

CANTHILL GDNS

NEWMILL GDNS

GDNS

59

HARTWOOD GDNS

Hill of Murdostoun

Penty Wood

HARTWOOD RD

BOWHOUSEBOG RD

SHAWSTONFOOT RD

FOULBURN RD

Newmill Cottage

1

MILL RD

Big Wood

Newmill Wood

MURDOSTOUN RD

Muiredge Wood

ML2

ALLANTON RD

58

82
A
83
B
84
C

A   B   C

4

Shepherd's Hill

MUIREDGE AND JERSY RD

Hillhead Plantation

FORTISSAT RD

Easter Fortissat

Fortissat

B717

BENHAR RD

HM Prison

Hillhouseridge

61

NEWMILL AND CANTHILL RD

BURNS PL
BYRON RD

Works

CALDERHEAD RD

MOSSBAND LA

BUTE CRES
GRAYSTONELEE RD
RIMMON
LOMOND RD
CRES
GARRY WAY
LEVEN PL
FRUGHT PL
BAL LOCH RD
ST JAMES RD
FYNE LA
KATRINE RD
LAGGAN PATH
LAGGAN RD
PENMACHAR ST
MODONNAH PL
MODONNAH
PL

3

Pell Hill

Pell Wood

SHOTSKIRK RD

DEAS RD

Bridge End

MINARD RD

ST CATHERINES CRES

BURNSIDE CRES
DEN LA
SPRINGBANK AVE
KILFINAN RD
BATON RD
ALEXANDER RD
HIRST GDNS

THOMSON TERR

HILLHOUSERIDGE RD

EARN TERR

TAY PL
TAY CRES
RADINOL
AVE
RADING
PL
DYRIG ST
INVERNIP DR

INNELLAN CRES

Shotts

SUNNYBANK

Works

B717

ABBOTSFORD CRES

1 AFFRIC LOAN
2 MONTEITH WLK
3 BROOM WYND

ML7
Dykehead

Mossband Wood

QUARRY RD
NITHSDALE
MORNAY WAY
NITHSDALE ST
BERTRAM ST
QUARRY PL
PARK RD
HUNTER PL
HUNTER ST
BON ACCORD CRES
WINDSOR PL
HILL PL
JAMIESON
WINDSOR ST

Prim Sch

FORREST ST

BERTRAM
RD

Calderhead High Sch

Works

60

H

Hartwoodhill

QUARRY PL
ST JOHN SMITH ST
KING ST
CLIVE ST
CALEDONIA RD
GREENWOOD ST

REGAL GR

KIRK PL
SCHOOL ST
GILBURN PL

Liby

BENHAR RD

Janefield

HARTWOOD RD

PARKSIDE RD
CLYDE PL
CURRIESIDE PL
UNITY PK
ALBERT ST
ROBERT ST
CURRIESIDE AVE
ERSKINE WAY
STATION RD

Sch

HIGH ST

STATION RD

CHURCHYARD CT 1
NEW CENTURY DR 2

FOUNDRY RD

GLEN RD
PARK CT

Calderhead

2

Sewage Works

South Calder Water

Burnbrae

BURNBRAE RD

Rosehall

ROSEHALL RD

East Tarbrax

59

CANTHILL GDNS

Hartwood

Parkfoot

HARTWOOD GDNS

West Tarbrax

B717

Mast

A71

1

BOWHOUSEBOG OR LIQUO

BOWHOUSEBOG RD

OLD MILL RD

Coal Burn

ALLANTON RD

East Redmire

A71

Redmyre Bridge

58

85   A   86   B   87   C

A

B

C

Fauldhouse

4

B717

BENHAR RD

CH

61

Edinburgh STREET ATLAS

South Calder Water

Starryshaw Farm

Stanebent

3

Spoil Heap

Cairneyhead

Stane

STABLE RY

Torbothie

ML7

60

GRAY ST

HIGH ST

CEDAR WK

CHARLES ST

ROMAN CRES

TORBOTHIE RD

HAZEL GR

CLYDE DR

CALDER DR

KELVIN DR

HAWTHORN DR

Stane Prim Sch

SOUTHFIELD AVE

SOUTHFIELD RD

SOUTHFIELD CRES

Torbothie

2

EH47

MANSE RD

CHARLOTTE ST

CEMETERY RD

NEVIS PL

2 GARTEN DR

3

Cemy

1 ETIVE WLK
2 UIG WAY
3 GAIR WYND
4 BOWMORE WLK
5 TORRIN LOAN
6 SPRINGHILL VIEW
7 DORNIE WYND
8 MORAR WAY
9 COIRE LOAN
10 SUNA PATH
11 SALEN LOAN

PO

MAIN ST

SANDYHILL AVE

REDMANS RD

LOCHABER CRES

TULLOCH RD

SWIRE GDNS

APPIN TERR

MELFORD AVE

WYVIS PL

LONICH PL

LAGGAN AVE

SANDYVALE PL

Stane

BRIDGE PL

NAZAR CT

KNOLL CROFT

LANSDOWNE CRES

HUNTLY TERR

BLINNY CT 1
TARBRAX PATH 2

B7010

BLACKHILL ST

SPRINGHILL RD

Springhill

B7010

59

BELMONT DR

BROWN ST

BERRYHILL PL

BEECHMOUNT CT

ELMWOOD RD

B715 HEADLESSCROSS RD

STANE RD

LARCHFIELD PATH

MULDRON TERR

NORTHFIELD AVE

Works

Springhill

SPRINGHILL AND LEADLOCH RD

A71 Livingston, Edinburgh

Works

Knowton Farm

Lingore Linn

A71

1

88

A

89

B

90

C

58

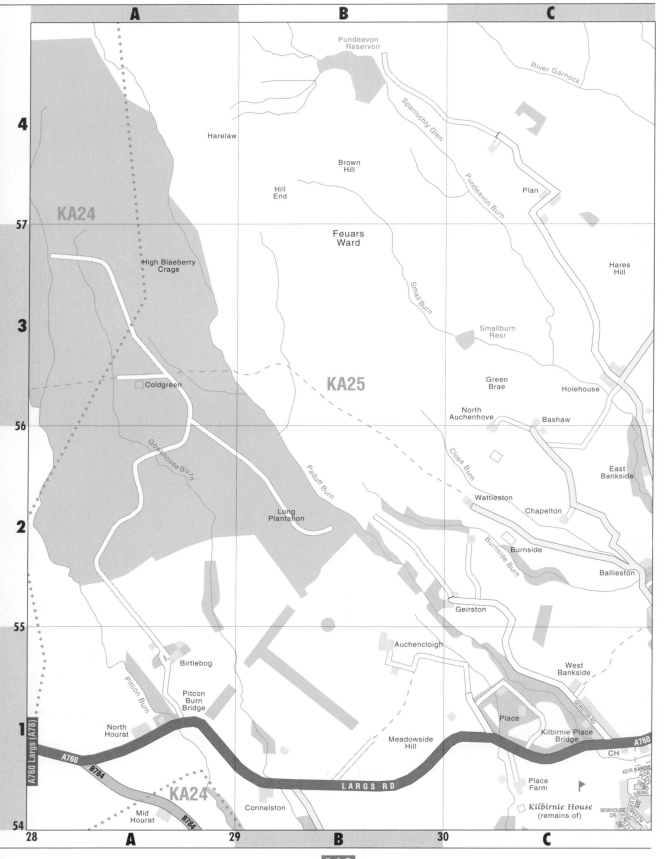

A   B   C

4

KA24

57

High Blaeberry
Crags

Harelaw

Pundeavon
Reservoir

River Garnock

Sparrochly Glen

Brown
Hill

Hill
End

Plan

Pundeavon Burn

3

Feuars
Ward

Small Burn

Smallburn
Resr

Hares
Hill

Coldgreen

KA25

Green
Brae

Holehouse

North
Auchenhove

Bashaw

East
Bankside

56

Gowkhouse Burn

Paduff Burn

Close Burn

Wattieston

Chapelton

2

Long
Plantation

Burnside Burn

Burnside

Ballieston

Geirston

55

Auchencloigh

West
Bankside

Birtlebog

Pitcon Burn

Pitcon
Burn
Bridge

GEIRSTON RD

A760

1

A760 Largs (A78)

North
Hourat

A760

B784

Largs Rd

Meadowside
Hill

Place

Kilbirnie Place
Bridge

CH

KEIR HARDIE RD

KA24

Connelston

Place
Farm

Kilbirnie House
(remains of)

NEWHOUSE
DR

B784

Mid
Hourat

54

28   A   29   B   30   C

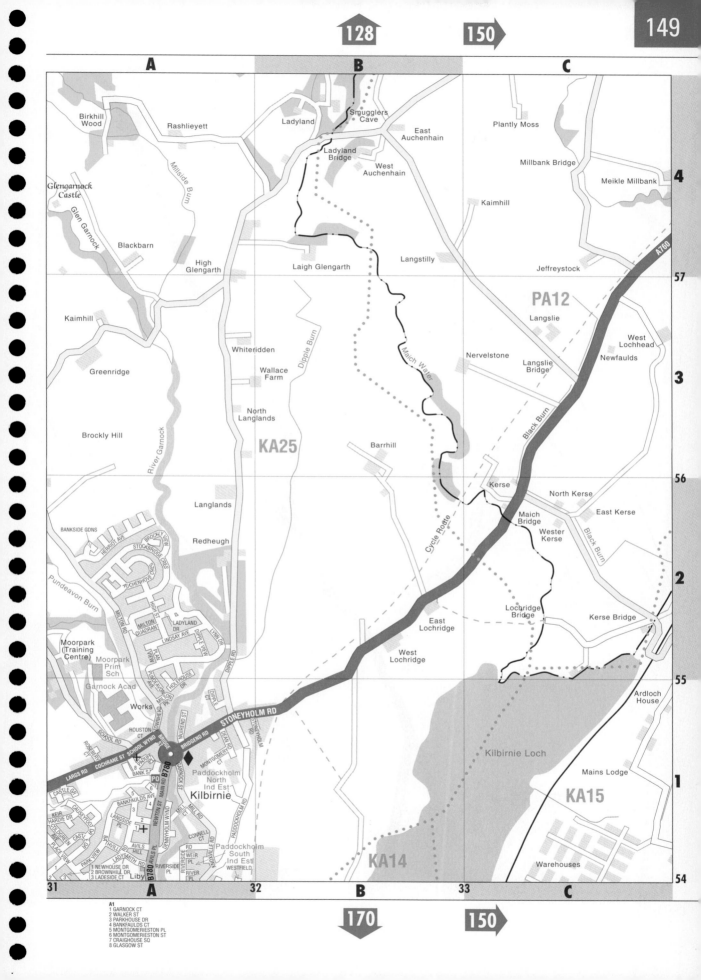

A   B   C

Birkhill Wood
Rashlieyett
Ladyland
Smugglers Cave
East Auchenhain
Plantly Moss
Millbank Bridge
Meikle Millbank
4
Glengarnock Castle
Glen Garnock
Millside Burn
Ladyland Bridge
West Auchenhain
Kaimhill
Blackbarn
High Glengarth
Laigh Glengarth
Langstilly
Jeffreystock
A760
57
Kaimhill
Dipple Burn
Maich Water
Langslie
PA12
West Lochhead
Greenridge
Whiteridden
Wallace Farm
Nervelstone
Langslie Bridge
Newfaulds
3
North Langlands
Black Burn
River Garnock
Brockly Hill
KA25
Barrhill
Kerse
North Kerse
East Kerse
56
Langlands
Cycle Route
Maich Bridge
Wester Kerse
Black Burn
Redheugh
Bankside Gdns
Brockly View
Stocabridge Cres
Auchenhove Cres
Pundeavon Burn
Milton Rd
Herriot Ave
Milton Quadrant
Ladyland Dr
Lindsay Ave
Plan View
Lynn Cr
Dipple Rd
Dipple View
Lochridge Bridge
Kerse Bridge
2
Moorpark (Training Centre)
Moorpark Prim Sch
Dipple Pl
Holehouse Dr
Dipple Ct
East Lochridge
West Lochridge
55
Garnock Acad
Works
Stoneyholm Rd
Stoneyholm Rd
Ardloch House
School Rd
Houston Ct
Cochrane St
School Wynd
Bridge
Bridgend Rd
Tram Rd
Montgomery Ct
Mill Rd
Paddockholm Rd
Kilbirnie Loch
Mains Lodge
1
Rosebery Ct
Largs Rd
Bank St
Avils Pl
B780
P.O.
Main Rd
Garnock St
Muirend St
Montgomerieston St
Paddockholm North Ind Est
KA15
Castle Gt
Keir Hardie Dr
Causeyfoot Dr
Cargill Ogren
Bankfaulds Ave
Newton St
Dennyholm Wynd
Connell Ct
Kilbirnie
Langside Pl
Bathville Pl
Park View
Ladysmith Rd
Avils Hill
Knoxville Rd
Paddockholm South Ind Est
Westfield
Warehouses
Place Rd
Riverside Pl
Weir Pl
River Pl
Liby
B780
A   B   C
KA14
31   32   33

54

A1
1 GARNOCK CT
2 WALKER ST
3 PARKHOUSE DR
4 BANKFAULDS CT
5 MONTGOMERIESTON PL
6 MONTGOMERIESTON ST
7 CRAIGHOUSE SQ
8 GLASGOW ST

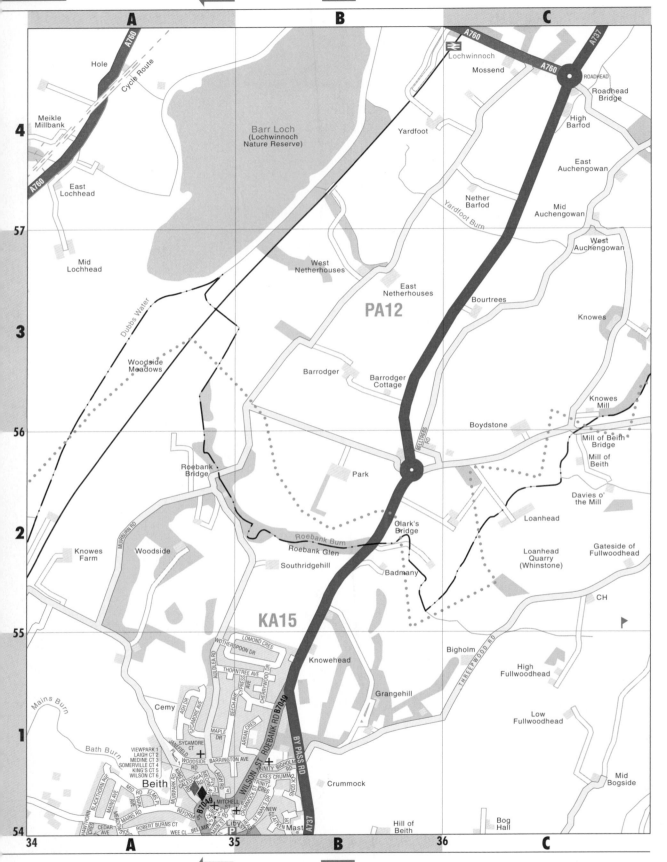

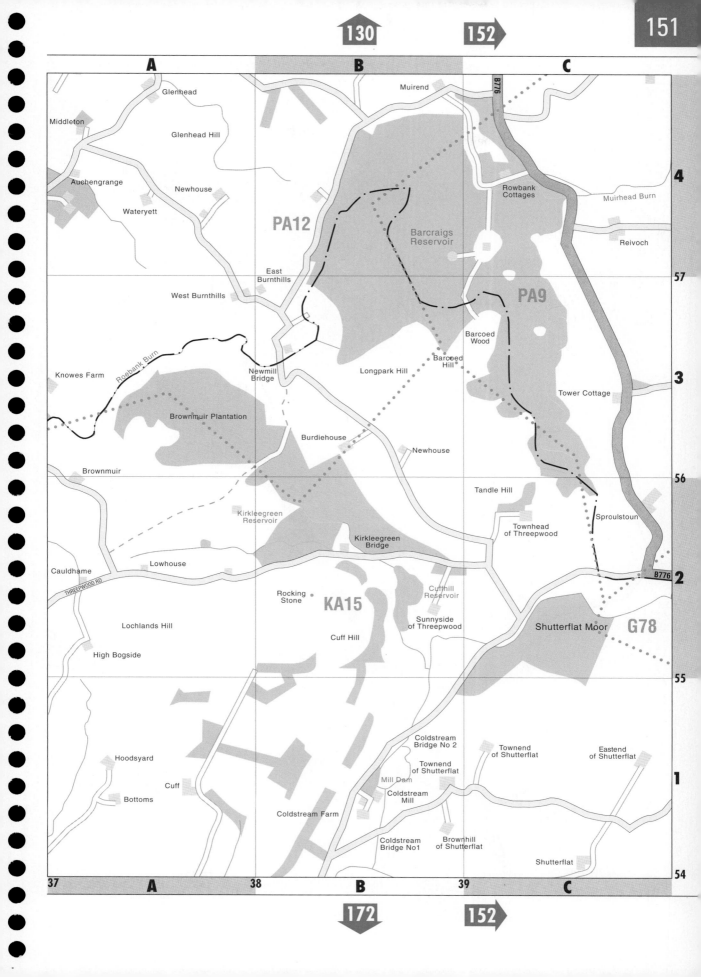

A
B
C

4
57
3
56
2
55
1
54

Glenhead
Middleton
Glenhead Hill
Muirend
B776

Auchengrange
Newhouse
Rowbank
Cottages
Muirhead Burn

Wateryett
PA12
Barcraigs
Reservoir
Reivoch

East
Burnthills
West Burnthills
PA9

Knowes Farm
Roebank Burn
Newmill
Bridge
Longpark Hill
Barcoed
Wood
Barcoed
Hill
Tower Cottage

Brownmuir Plantation
Burdiehouse
Newhouse

Brownmuir
Tandle Hill
Sproulstoun

Kirkleegreen
Reservoir
Townhead
of Threepwood
B776

Cauldhame
Lowhouse
THREEPWOOD RD
Kirkleegreen
Bridge
Cuffhill
Reservoir

Rocking
Stone
KA15
Sunnyside
of Threepwood
Shutterflat Moor
G78

Lochlands Hill
Cuff Hill

High Bogside

Hoodsyard
Coldstream
Bridge No 2
Townend
of Shutterflat
Eastend
of Shutterflat

Cuff
Townend
of Shutterflat

Bottoms
Mill Dam
Coldstream
Mill

Coldstream Farm
Coldstream
Bridge No1
Brownhill
of Shutterflat

Shutterflat

37
38
39
A
B
C

A
B
C

Rashiefield Bridge

PA2

Springside

Old Patrick Water

Plymuir Bridge

4

PA9

57

Windy Hill

Top of Auchenbathie

Tophouse

Windyhill

Hartfield Moss

Muirhouse Farm

3

56

Riglaw

GLENIFFER RD

G78

Caldwell Law

Greenside

Caldwell-law Wood

2

B776

Rigfoot Farm

Braco

Dunsmore Bridge

Old Barn Farm

Bowfield

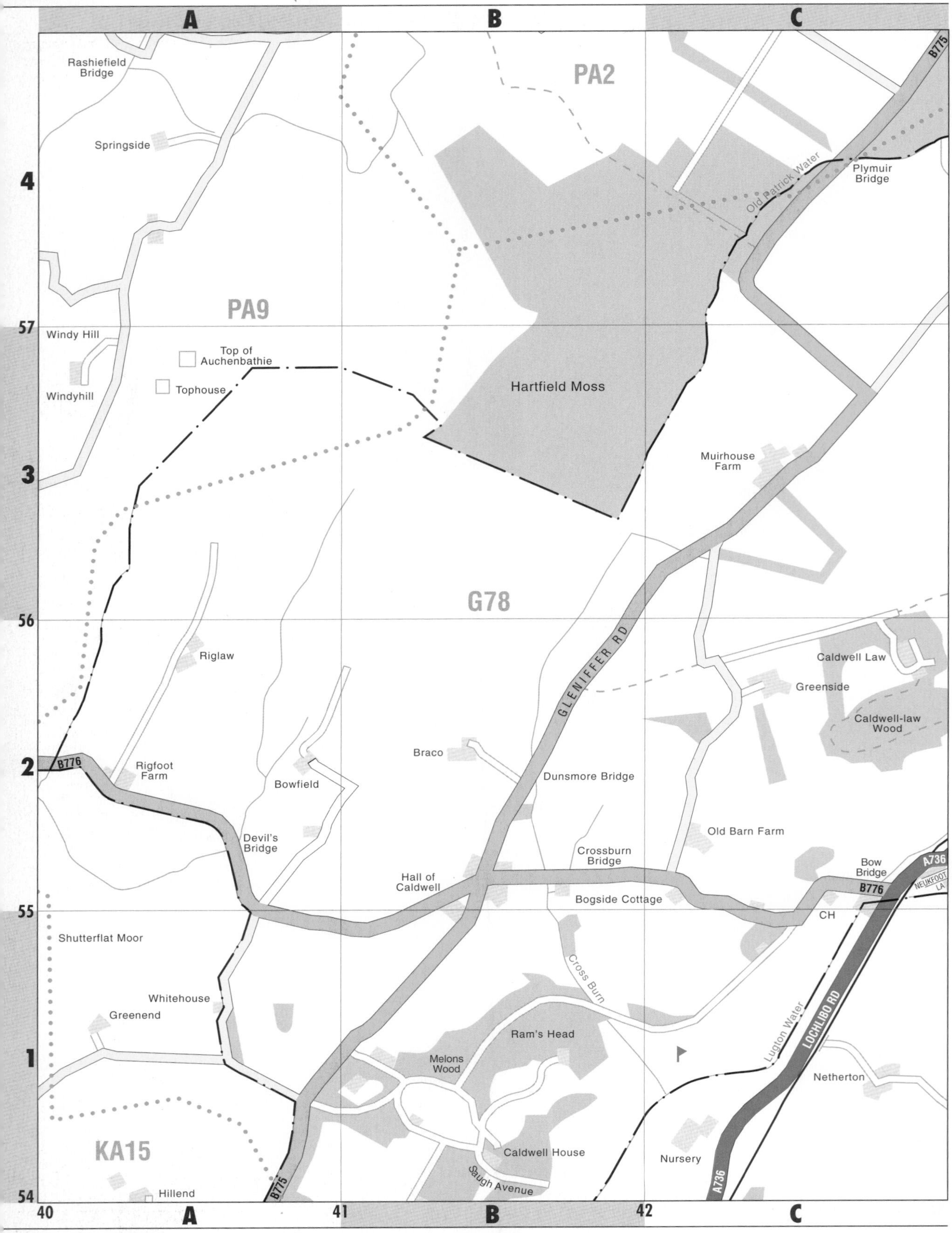

Devil's Bridge

Crossburn Bridge

Bow Bridge

A736

NEUKFOOT LA

Hall of Caldwell

Bogside Cottage

B776

55

Shutterflat Moor

Cross Burn

CH

LOCHLIBO RD

Lugton Water

Whitehouse

Greenend

Ram's Head

1

Melons Wood

Netherton

KA15

Nursery

Caldwell House

A736

Hillend

Saugh Avenue

54

40
41
42

A
B
C

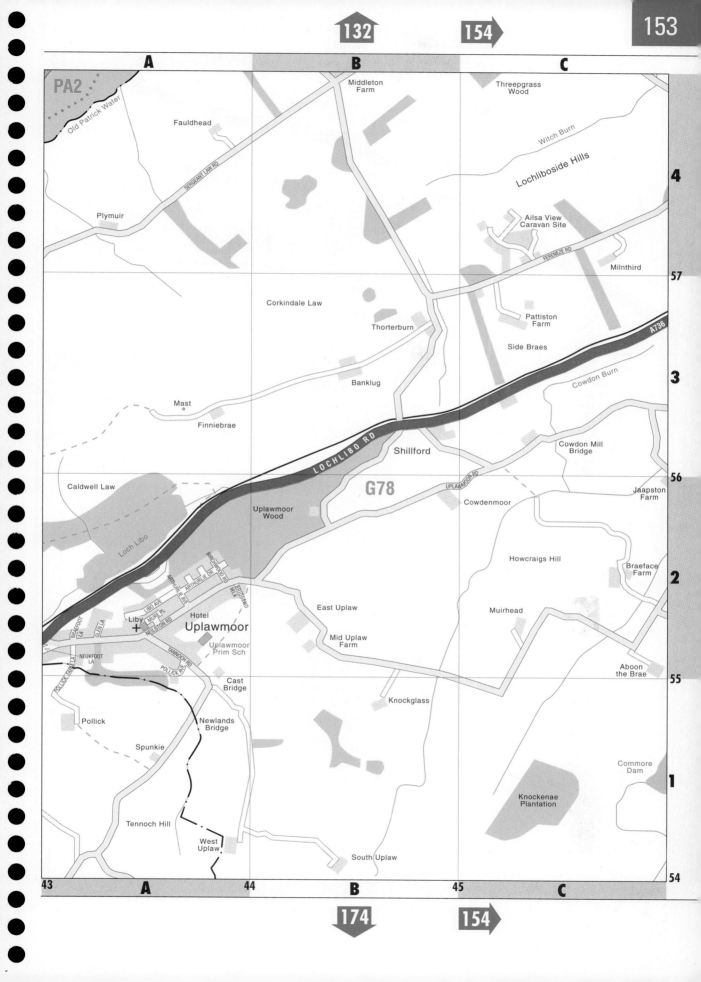

A   B   C

PA2

Old Patrick Water

Fauldhead

Middleton Farm

Threepgrass Wood

Witch Burn

Plymuir

Lochliboside Hills

4

Ailsa View Caravan Site

FERENEZE RD

Milnthird

SERGEANT LAW RD

57

Corkindale Law

Pattiston Farm

Thorterburn

Side Braes

A736

Banklug

Cowdon Burn

3

Mast

Finniebrae

LOCHLIBO RD

Shillford

Cowdon Mill Bridge

Caldwell Law

56

UPLAWMOOR RD

Jaapston Farm

G78

Uplawmoor Wood

Cowdenmoor

Loch Libo

Howcraigs Hill

Braeface Farm

2

BIRCHWOOD RD

ARTHURLIE DR

ARTHURLIE AVE

East Uplaw

Muirhead

LIBO AVE

Liby

MURE PL

Hotel

BRIDGRAND WLK

NEILSTON RD

Uplawmoor

Mid Uplaw Farm

Aboon the Brae

55

BRAEFOOT LA

GLEN LA

TANNOCH RD

Uplawmoor Prim Sch

NEUKFOOT LA

POLLICK AVE

Cast Bridge

Knockglass

POLLICK PARK LA

Commore Dam

1

Pollick

Newlands Bridge

Spunkie

Knockenae Plantation

Tennoch Hill

West Uplaw

South Uplaw

54

43   A   44   B   45   C

A   B   C

Killoch

Auchentiber

Works

A736

DENNIES BRAE

Nether Kirkton

Foreside

FERENEZE RD

STATION BRAE

LOCHLIBO RD

NEILSTON RD

GLENIFFER VIEW

LOW BROADLE RD

ROBERTSON CRES

BARR AVE

MANSE RD

KIRK

GLEBE

KIRK HILL

INGLEBY PL

HARTFIELD CRES

McDONALD PL

NEILSTON RD

SYKES TERR

SPRINGFIELD RD

4

Mast

Cowdon Burn

Mill (dis)

BROADLIE RD

HOLEHOUSE BRAE

St Thomas Sch

Chapel

KIRKSTYLE

KIRKTONFIELD RD

Liby L Ctr

MADRAS PL

GLEN AVE

DUNCARNOCK CRES

KIRKTON FIELD

KIRKTONFIELD DR

Kirktonfield Bridge

CROFTHEAD COTTS

HILLSIDE RD

RILLSIDE CRES

BRAEHEAD AVE

BRAEHEAD

LEA AVE

BANKS ST

CROSS

MAIN ST

STATION RD

PD DUMDOUALD RD

DUNCARNOCK CRES

Factory

57

A736

Holehouse

MOLENDINAR TERR

ALEXANDER TERR

MILLVIEW TERR

MAKEFIELD

HOLEHOUSE TERR

BRIG O' LEA TERR

WELL RD

MAIN ST

Neilston

LUCKIESFAULD

MACLELLAN RD

Neilston

Neilston Prim Sch

Neilston House

GLENBURN WAY

GLENLIVET RD

GLEN MARK RD

GLEN MUIR RD

GLEN LYON RD

GLEN CREPAN CRES

GROVE

LYNE

GLEN TARBERT

HARELAW AVE

COMMORE PL

KINGSTON AVE

DOUBLE EDGES RD

LOANFOOT AVE

CRAIG RD

VIGNOL

Kirkton Dam

KIRKTON RD

Kirkton Bridge

Dyke Greenhill

UPLAWMOOR RD

Smiddyhill

Brimstone Bridge

GLEN DOLL RD

GLEN FINLET RD

GLEN ISLA

GLEN SHEE AVE

GLEN ROY DR

GLEN FANNICS

GLEN FALLOCH CRES

KINGSTON RD

G78

Kirkton Burn

Loanfoot

Dyke Hill

3

Crumyards

Levern Water

Kilburn

Water Works

P

56

Jaapston Farm

Neilstonside Bridge

Neilstonside Hill

Water Works

Craig of Neilston

Craig of Neilston

Muirhead

2

Neilstonside

Neilston Pad

Barr Hill

Snypes Dam

Snypes

Low Walton

North Walton

Waterside

Craighall Dam

55

Commore

Drumler Craigs

1

Commore Dam

Harelaw

P

West Walton

G77

Straun Hill

High Walton

Commore Bridge

Levern Water

Walton Burn

Walton Glen

54

46   A   47   B   48   C

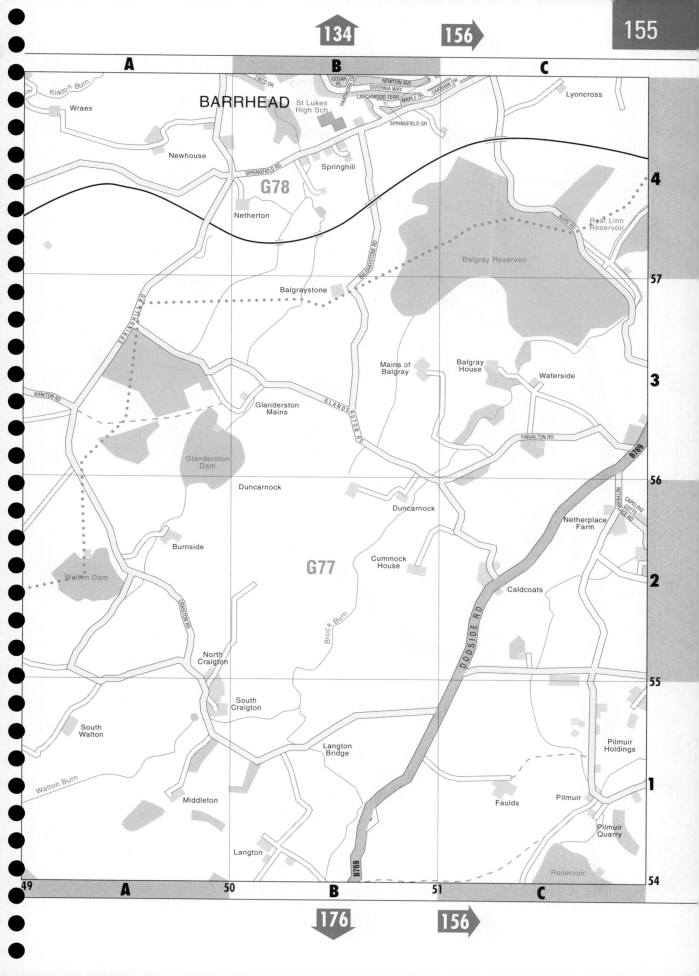

A
B
C

Kirkton Burn
Wraes

BARRHEAD
St Lukes High Sch

TINTO DR
CEDAR PL
NEWTON AVE
DIVERNIA WAY
HAWTHORN DR
LARCHWOOD TERR
MAPLE DR
OAKBANK DR
SPRINGFIELD GR
Lyoncross

Newhouse

SPRINGFIELD RD
Springhill

G78

Netherton

BALGRAYSTONE RD

AURS RD

Ryat Linn Reservoir

4

Balgray Reservoir

57

Balgraystone

SPRINGHILL RD

Mains of Balgray
Balgray House
Waterside

KIRKTON RD
GLANDERSTON RD

Glanderston Mains

FINGALTON RD

B769

3

Glanderston Dam

Duncarnock

56

Duncarnock

NETHERPLACE RD
CAPELRIG COTTS
Netherplace Farm

Burnside

G77

Cummock House

Walton Dam

Caldcoats

2

North Craigton

DODSIDE RD

South Craigton

55

South Walton

Langton Bridge

Pilmuir Holdings

Walton Burn

Middleton

Faulds
Pilmuir

1

Brock Burn

Pilmuir Quarry

Langton

B769

Reservoir

54

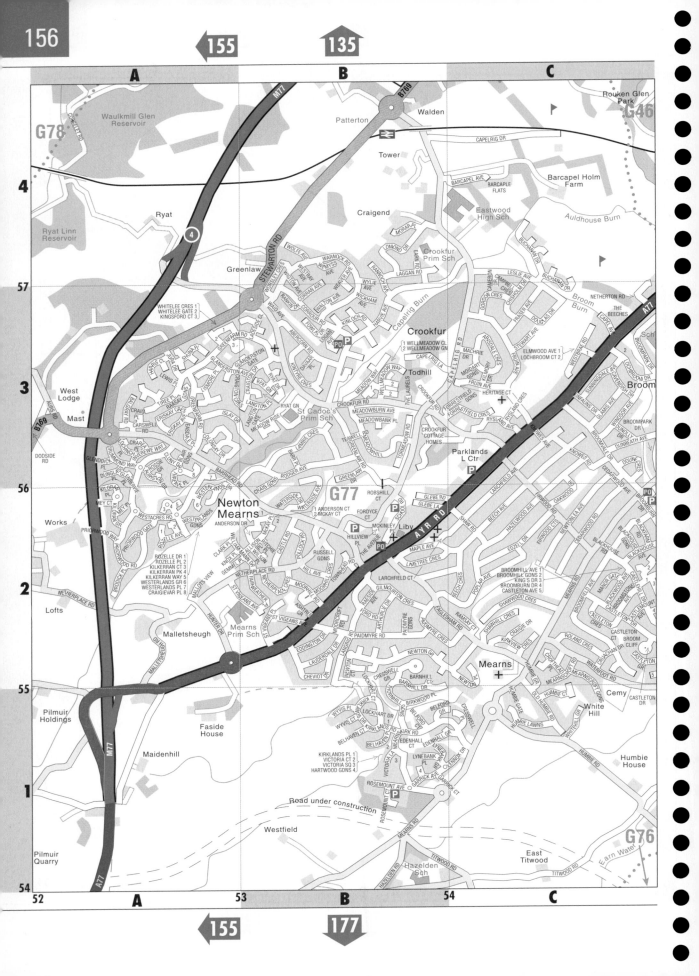

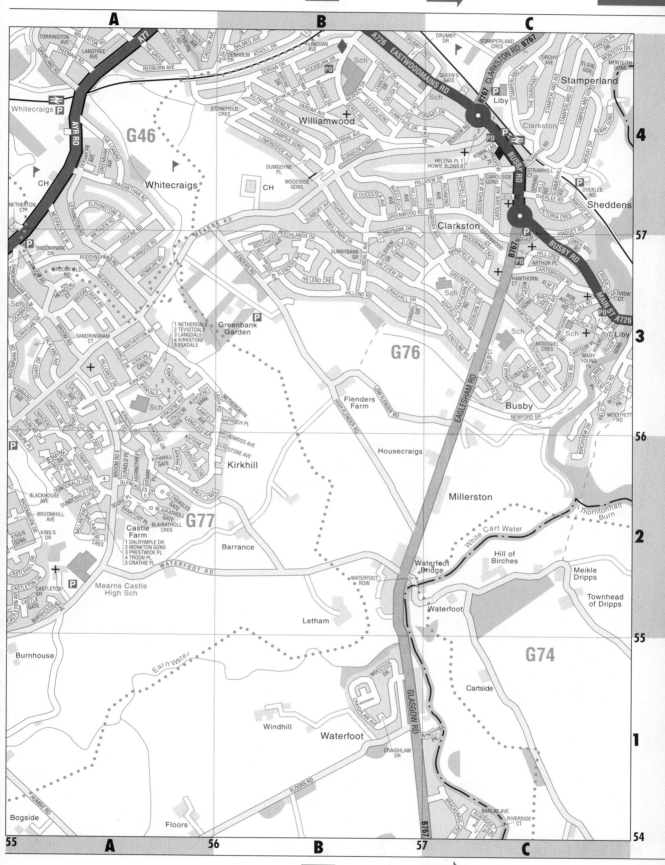

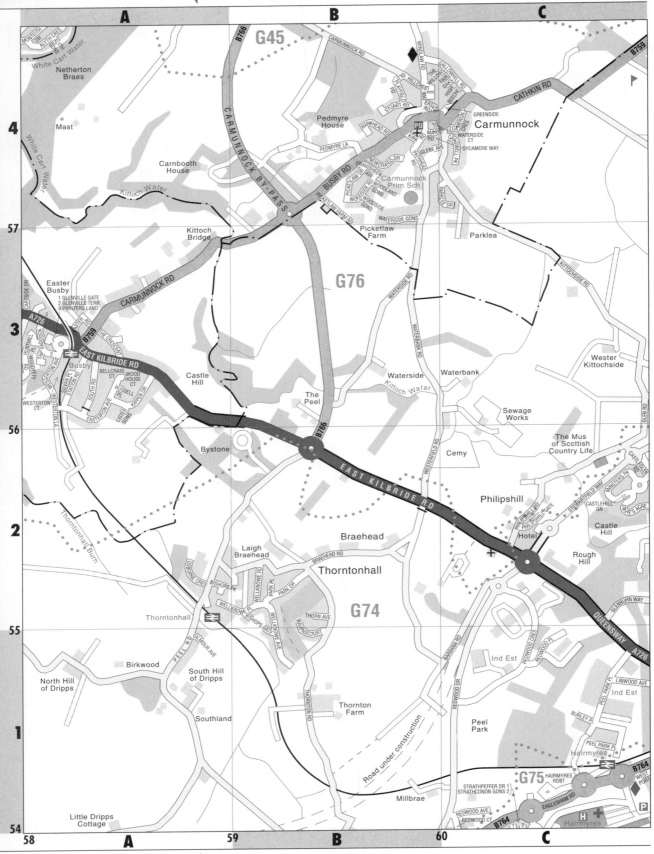

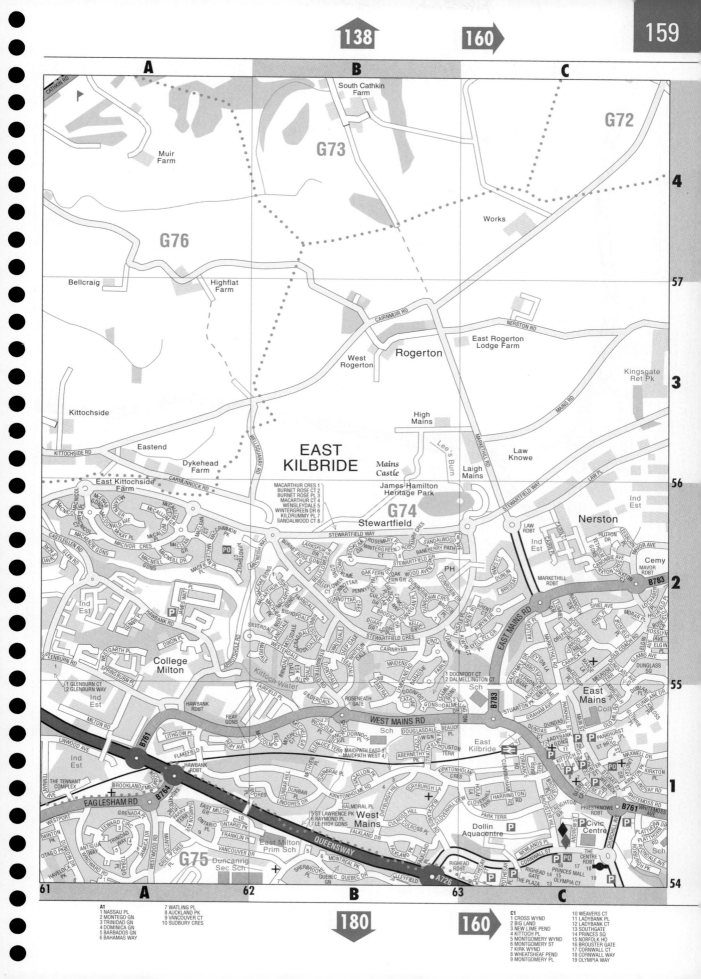

A1
1 NASSAU PL
2 MONTEGO GN
3 TRINIDAD GN
4 DOMINICA GN
5 BARBADOS GN
6 BAHAMAS WAY
7 WATLING PL
8 AUCKLAND PK
9 VANCOUVER CT
10 SUDBURY CRES

C1
1 CROSS WYND
2 BIG LAND
3 NEW LIME PEND
4 KITTOCH PL
5 MONTGOMERY WYND
6 MONTGOMERY ST
7 KIRK WYND
8 WHEATSHEAF PEND
9 MONTGOMERY PL
10 WEAVERS CT
11 LADYBANK PL
12 LADYBANK CT
13 SOUTHGATE
14 PRINCES SQ
15 NORFOLK HO
16 BROUSTER GATE
17 CORNWALL CT
18 CORNWALL WAY
19 OLYMPIA WAY

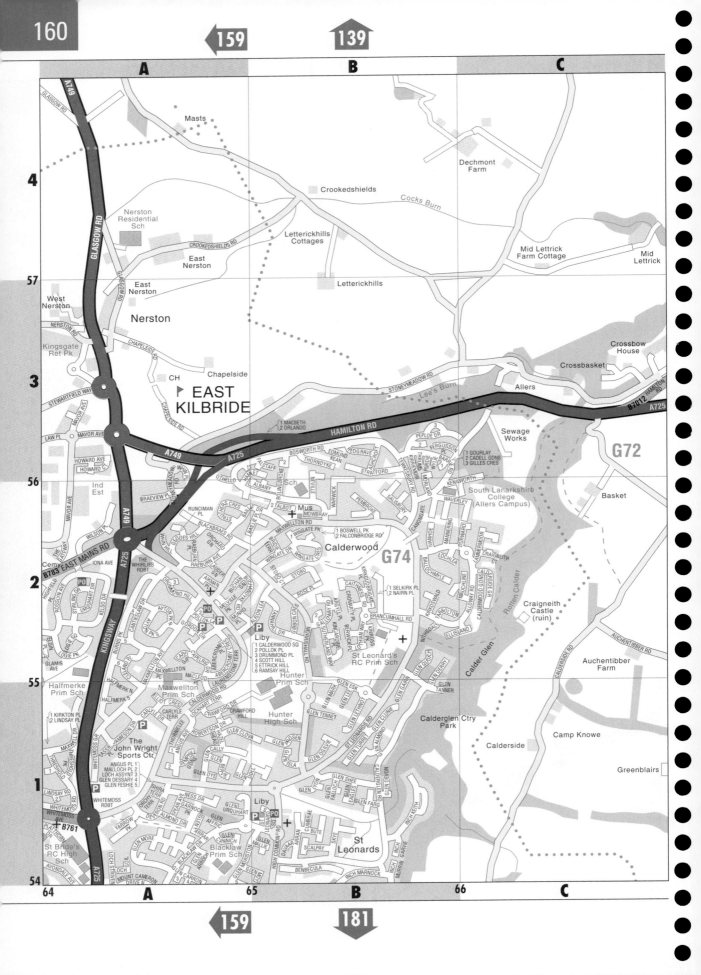

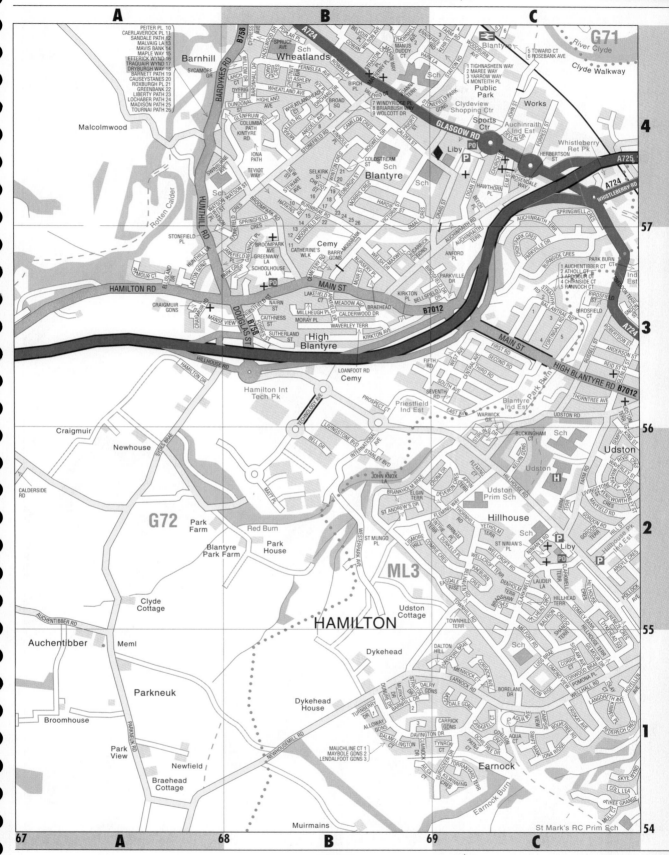

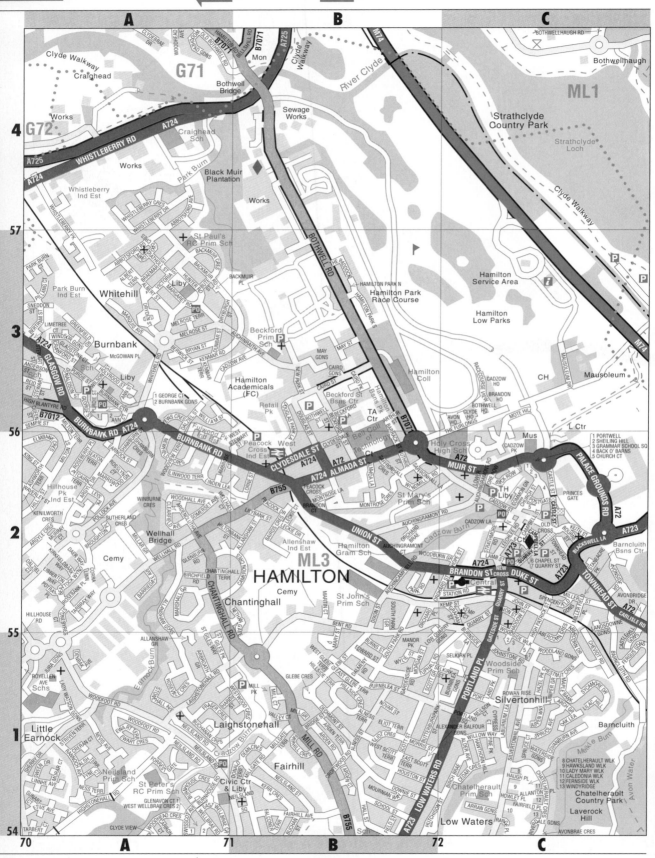

C1
1 BROWN ST
2 CENTENARY GDNS
3 WEAVERS CT
4 WOODSIDE CT
5 WOODSIDE AVE
6 CARLTON CT
7 WILTON CT

142

164 →

C3
1 BRANDON ARC
2 OAKFIELD DR
3 WATSONVILLE PK
4 WINDMILL CT
5 MACDONALD ST
6 McCLURG CT
7 ELVAN TWR
8 KERR GRIEVE CT
9 CALDER TWR
10 AVON TWR
11 CLYDE TWR
12 ELLIS WAY
13 BLAIR PATH

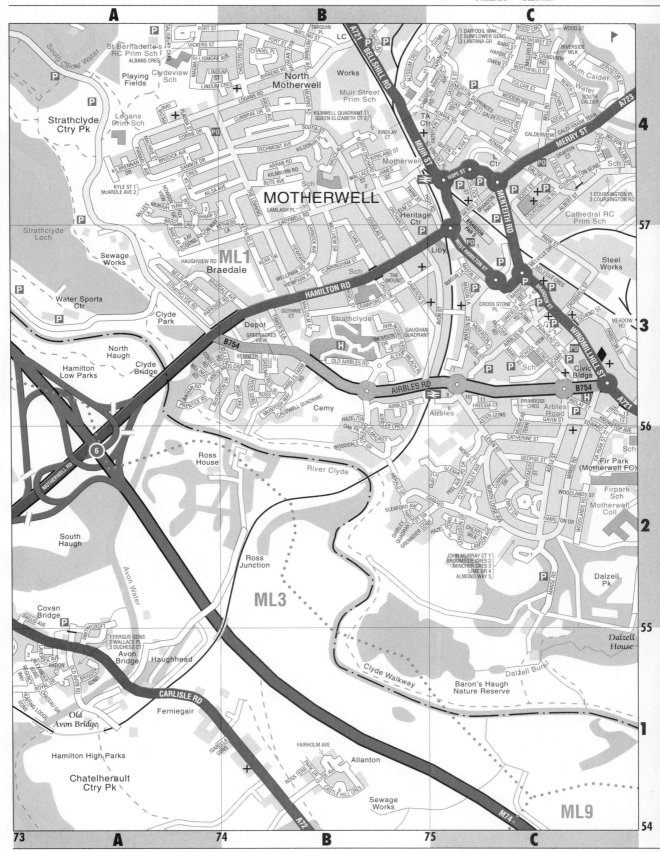

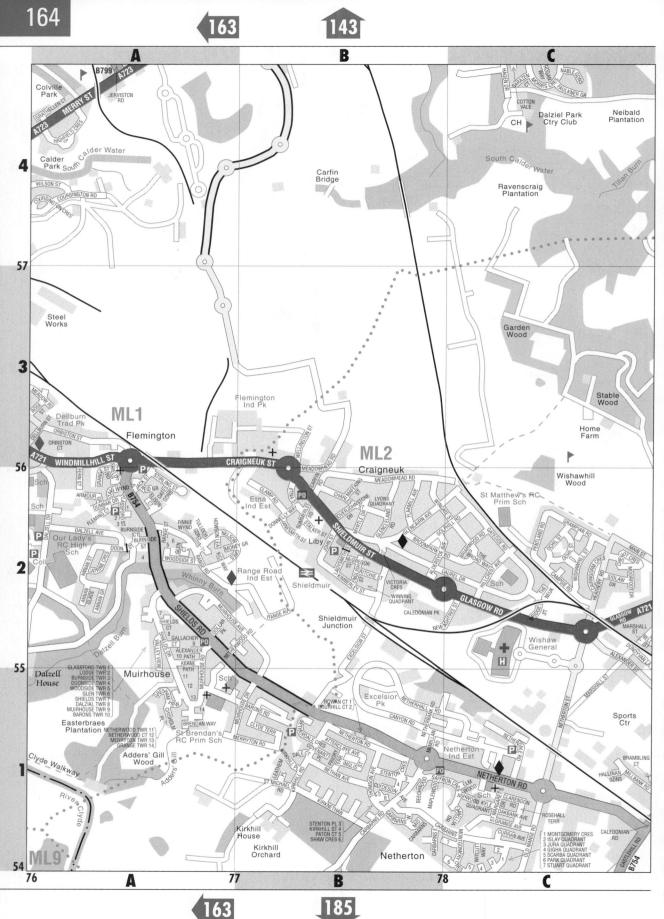

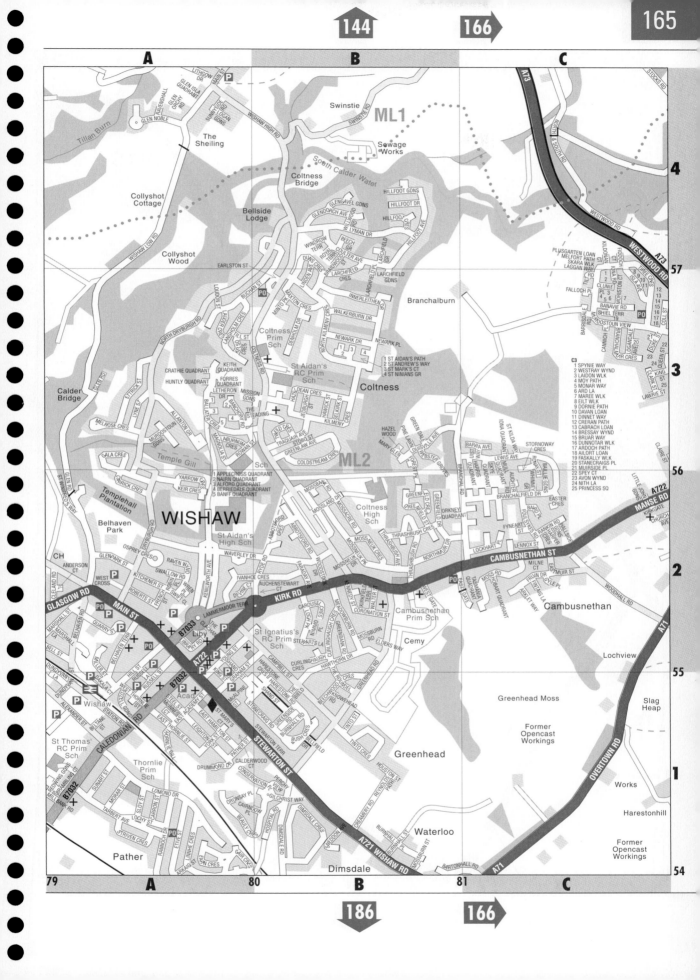

165
145

A   B   C

ML1

Mill

Easterhouse

ALLANTON RD

MILL RD

SUMMERHILL PL

WOOD VIEW CALDER RD

AUCHTERBURN RD

COLTNESS AVE

MILL RD

ALLANDALE ST

Brucefield

Crosshill

WILSON RD

A71

4

Mill

Murdostoun Castle

ML7

STOCKS RD

South Calder Water

Kennel Knowe Wood

Murdostoun Bridge

MURDOSTOUN RD

ALLANTON RD

+

UNDERWOOD DR

DEVINE CT

MURRAY CRES

MCGARRISON

MCMAHON DR

2

57

Bonkle

1 AITKEN CL
2 ROBERT WYND
3 DARRAGH GN

CHURCH RD

BROWNHILL VIEW

CAIRNEY PL

East Crindledyke

BOLEYN CT

BONDS DR

WOODSIDE CRES

MEADOWFIELD PL

Sharnothshield Small Holdings

Calkers Wood

CALDER AVE

N.MICHAEL AVE

EASTWOOD DR

NORTHWOOD DR

ABERNETHYN RD

FIRTREE RD

FIRTREE PL

ALCATH RD

Crindledyke

Gallow Hill

LE VIEW

MURDOSTOUN VIEW

CLYDE WLK

KING ST

PRINCE ST

TAY LA

WEST PL

BAILLIESMUIR PL

CHRINDLEDYKE CRES

MURRHOUSE AVE

BONKLE RD

BONKLE GDNS

YOUNG ST

GOODARD

BROWN WLK

HAWTHORN AVE

LYNWOOD

HAWTHORNBANK

BRAEDALE AVE

BRAEDALE PL

BRAEDALE CRES

ALCHTER

Sharnothshield

3

WESTWOOD RD

STEWART CRES

PARK DR

Cathburn Holdings

CATHBURN RD

MILL RD

St Brigid's RC Prim Sch

NEWTON DR

PO

+

Newmains

ML2

56

CLAIRE ST

A722 MANSE RD

HOPE ST

PARKVIEW ST

A71

A73

Liby

CHURCH AVE

SCHOOL RD

Sch

1 MANSE MEWS
2 BROWN ST

Works

Morningside Farm

Watstonfoot

VICTORIA ST

Morningside Prim Sch

SCHOOL RD

Torbush

Woodside Farm

2

OVERTOWN RD

A71

WOODHALL RD

MAIN ST

Works

MORNINGSIDE RD

Watstonmids

Opencast Workings

+

Morningside

55

Slag Heap

Chapel

CHAPEL RD

Holmhill

1

Harestonhill

Watstonheads

Herdshill

A73

Bogside Farm

ML8

54

82   A   83   B   84   C

165
187

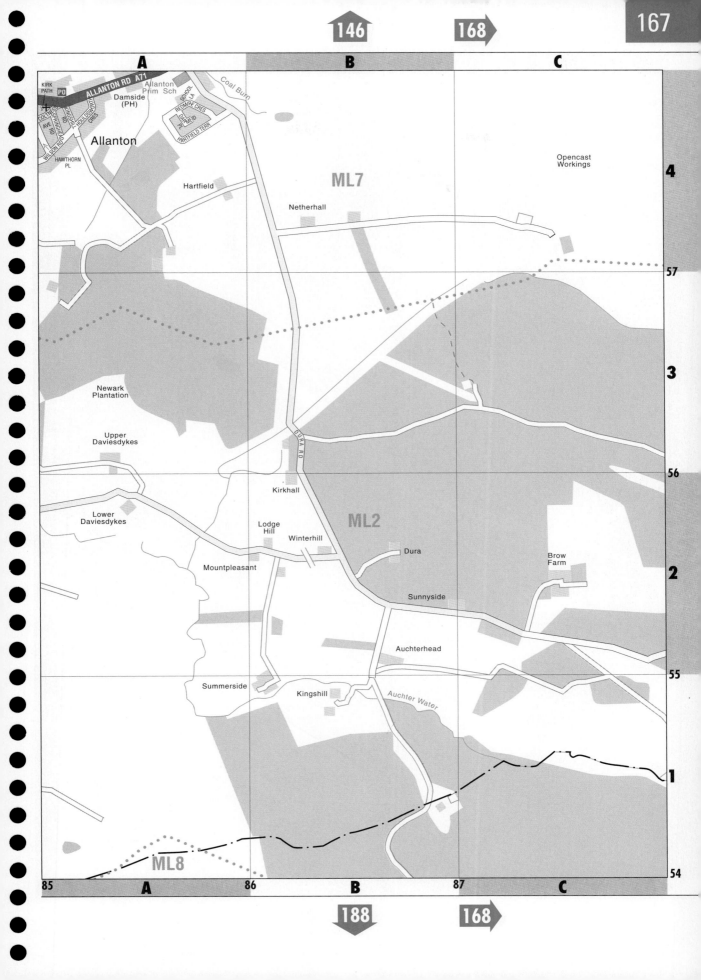

A   B   C

ALLANTON RD A71
KIRK PATH
PO
Allanton Prim Sch
Damside (PH)
SCHOOL LA
REDMIRE CRES
Allanton
COLTNESS AVE RD
SPRINGHEAD
HOLLOSKIRTH CRES
WILSON RD
HAWTHORN PL
HARTFIELD TERR
DYKEHEAD PL
Coal Burn

Hartfield

4

ML7

Netherhall

Opencast Workings

57

Newark Plantation

3

Upper Daviesdykes

DURA RD

56

Kirkhall

Lower Daviesdykes

ML2

Lodge Hill

Winterhill

Dura

Brow Farm

Mountpleasant

2

Sunnyside

Auchterhead

55

Summerside

Kingshill

Auchter Water

1

ML8

54

85   A   86   B   87   C

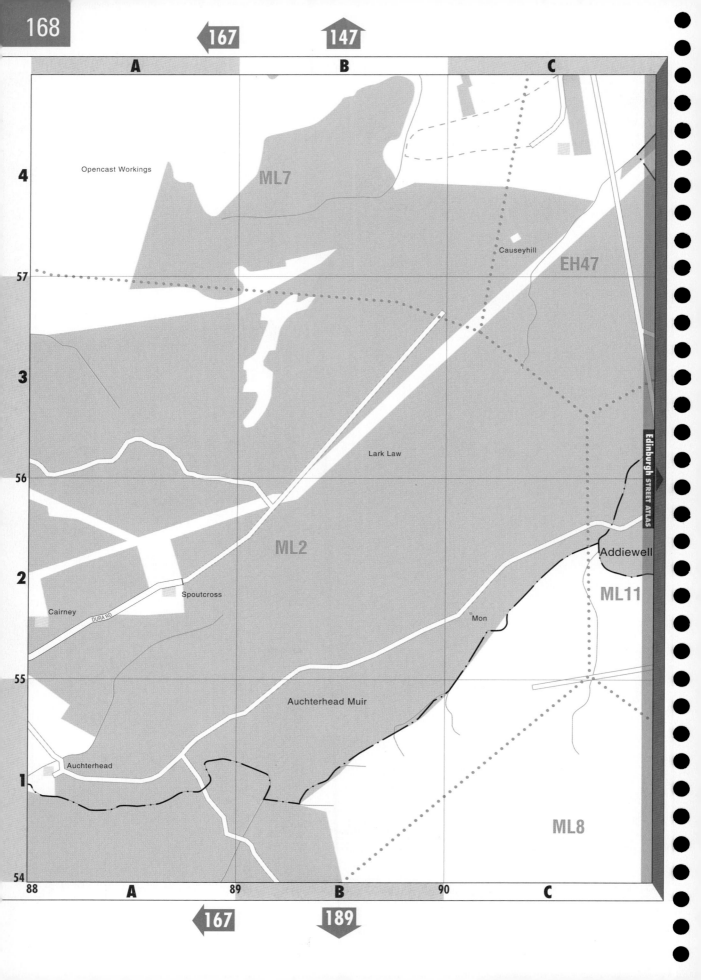

A B C

4

Opencast Workings

ML7

Causeyhill

EH47

57

3

Lark Law

Edinburgh STREET ATLAS

56

ML2

Addiewell

2

ML11

Spoutcross

Cairney

DURA RD

Mon

55

Auchterhead Muir

1

Auchterhead

ML8

54

88 89 90

A B C

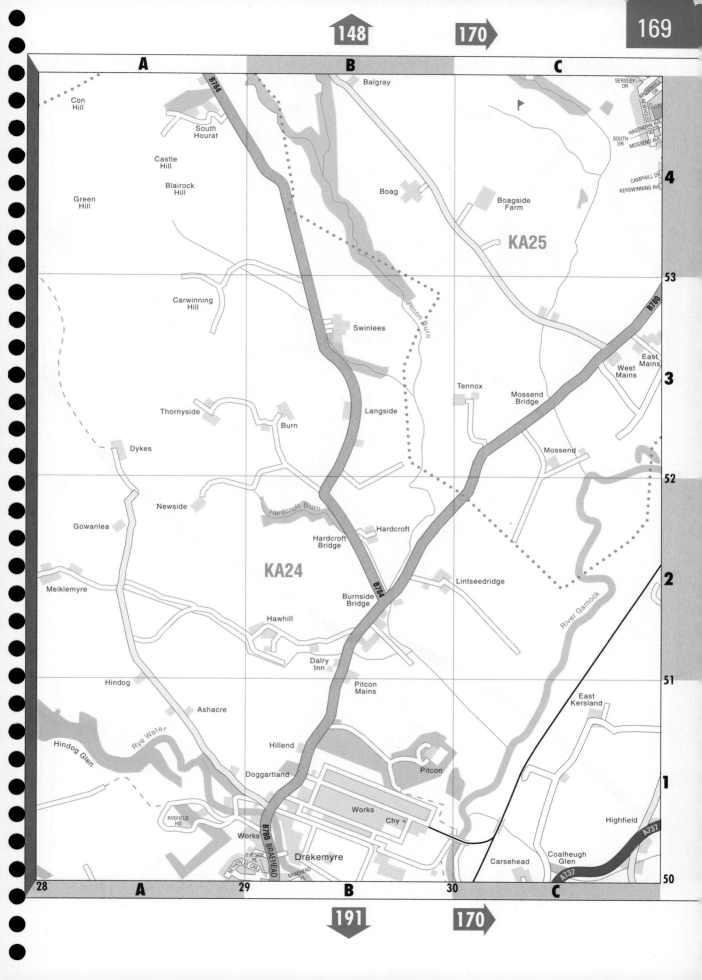

A B C

Con Hill

South Hourat

Castle Hill

Blairock Hill

Green Hill

Balgray

Boag

Boagside Farm

SERSLEY DR
BROWNHILL DR
NEWHOUSE
Sch
HAGTHORN AVE

SOUTH DR
MOSSEND AVE

CAMPHILL DR
KERSWINNING AVE

4

KA25

Carwinning Hill

Swinlees

Pitcon Burn

B780

53

East Mains
West Mains

3

Thornyside

Burn

Langside

Tennox

Mossend Bridge

Mossend

Dykes

Newside

Hardcroft Burn

Hardcroft

52

Gowanlea

KA24

Hardcroft Bridge

Meiklemyre

Hawhill

Burnside Bridge

B784

Lintseedridge

River Garnock

2

Dalry Inn

Hindog

Ashacre

Pitcon Mains

51

East Kersland

Rye Water

Hillend

Pitcon

Hindog Glen

Doggartland

Works
Chy

Carsehead

Highfield

1

RYEFIELD HO

Works

RYESIDE PL
NETKELEE CRES

B780 BRAEHEAD

Drakemyre

BRAEHEAD PL

Coalheugh Glen

A737

A737

50

A
B
C

169
149

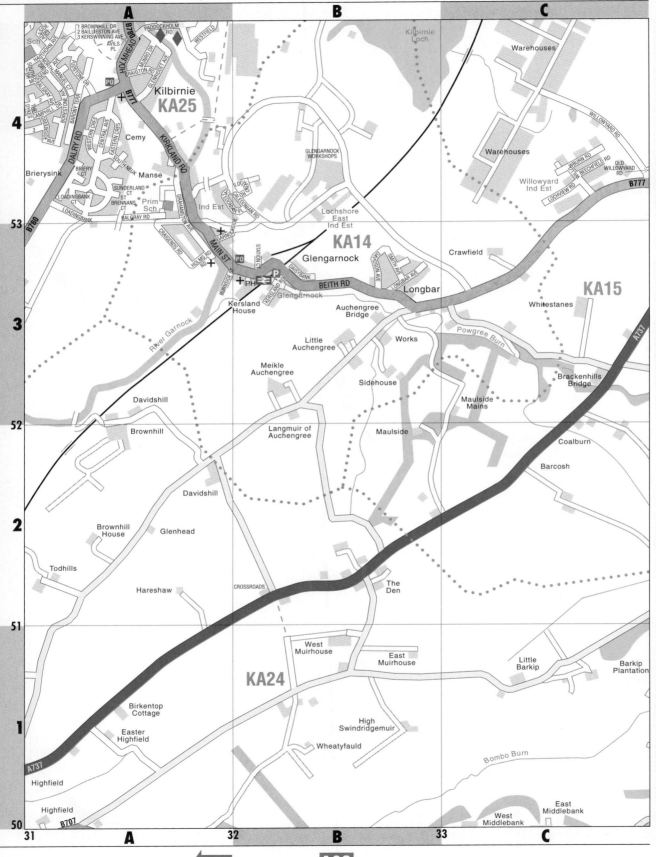

169
192

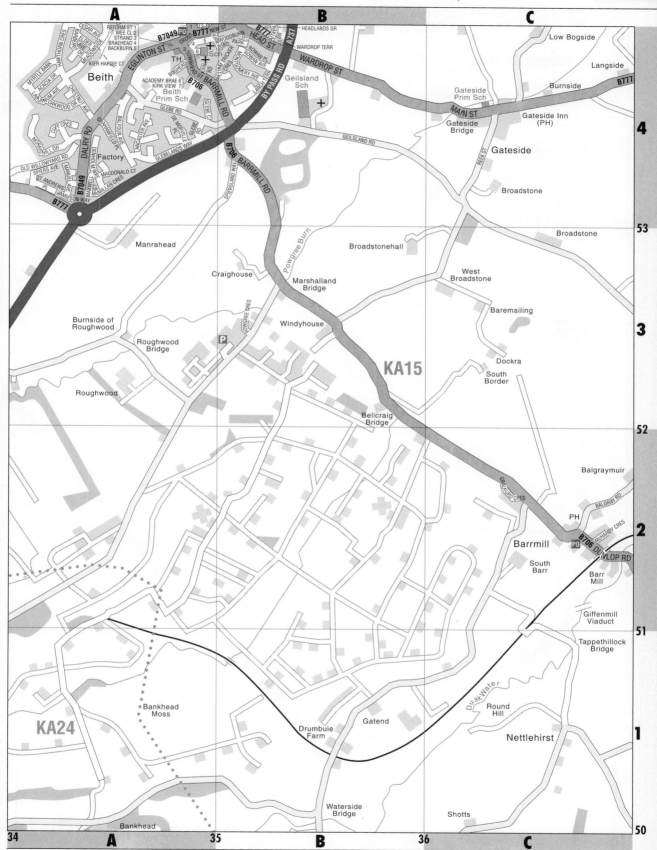

A   B   C

Beith

REFORM ST 1
WEE CL 2
STRAND 3
BRAEHEAD 4
BACKBURN 5

CEDAR AVE
WEE CL
BARBER BRAE DR
ELDER AVE
MEADOWSIDE

B7049
EGLINTON ST

PO
B777

New St

HEAD ST

A737
HEADLANDS GR

WARDROP TERR

Low Bogside

Langside

Burnside

B777

MYRTLE BANK
HAWTHORN CRES
ACACIA DR

KIER HARDIE CT

TH
ACADEMY BRAE 6
KIRK VIEW 7
Beith
Prim Sch

Sch
WOODBURN
REID PARK
ROWAN PL
ROWAN AVE
MONTGOMERY AVE
LARGS TER

Geilsland
Sch

Gateside
Prim Sch

MAIN ST

Gateside
Bridge

Gateside Inn
(PH)

Gateside

Broadstone

Broadstone

AILSA DR
LAUN AVE
OAKWOOD DR

CHESTNUT AVE

GLEBE RD

DE MORVILLE
PL

WARDROP ST

GEILSLAND RD

REEK ST

4

CAVE CRES

DALRY RD

BALFOUR AVE

LANCASTER AVE

GLEBE CT

GLEBELANDS WAY

B706

B706

BARRMILL RD

Factory

MORRIS RD
SPIERS AVE
ST ANDREWS
PL

MAXWELL
MANSE AVE
JAMIESON WAY

MACDONALD CT
MCMILLAN CRES

B7049

B777

OLD WILLOWYARD RD

Manrahead

Craighouse

BY PASS RD

SPIERSLAND WAY

POWGREE CRES

Powgree Burn

Marshalland
Bridge

Broadstonehall

West
Broadstone

Baremailing

53

3

Burnside of
Roughwood

Roughwood
Bridge

P

Windyhouse

KA15

Dockra

South
Border

Roughwood

Bellcraig
Bridge

52

Balgraymuir

CRAIGURD CRES

BALGRAY RD

PH

MCHARDY CRES

2

Barrmill

South
Barr

B706 DUNLOP RD

PO

Barr
Mill

Giffenmill
Viaduct

Tappethillock
Bridge

51

KA24

Bankhead
Moss

Drumbuie
Farm

Gatend

DUSK WATER

Round
Hill

Nettlehirst

1

Waterside
Bridge

Shotts

Bankhead

50

34   A   35   B   36   C

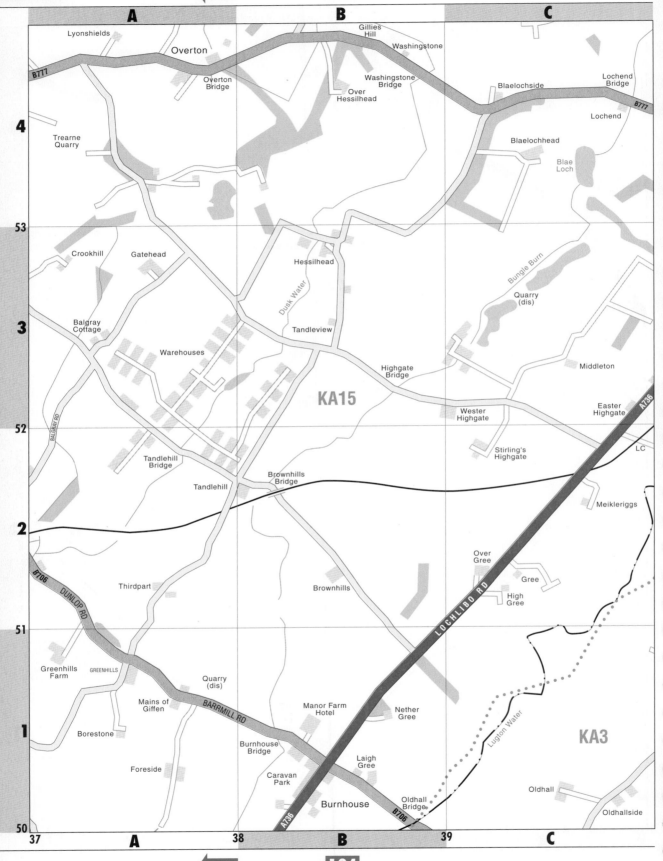

A
B
C

Lyonshields
Overton
Gillies Hill
Washingstone
Washingstone Bridge
Lochend Bridge
B777
Overton Bridge
Over Hessilhead
Blaelochside
Lochend
4
Trearne Quarry
Blaelochhead
Blae Loch
B777
53
Crookhill
Gatehead
Hessilhead
Bungle Burn
Quarry (dis)
Dusk Water
3
Balgray Cottage
Tandleview
Middleton
Warehouses
Highgate Bridge
KA15
Wester Highgate
Easter Highgate
A736
52
Tandlehill Bridge
Stirling's Highgate
LC
Tandlehill
Brownhills Bridge
Meiklerriggs
BALGRAY RD
2
Over Gree
Thirdpart
Brownhills
Gree
LOCHLIBO RD
B706
High Gree
51
DUNLOP RD
Greenhills Farm
GREENHILLS
Quarry (dis)
Nether Gree
Lugton Water
KA3
Mains of Giffen
BARRMILL RD
Manor Farm Hotel
1
Borestone
Burnhouse Bridge
Laigh Gree
Oldhall
Foreside
Caravan Park
A736
Oldhall Bridge
B706
Oldhallside
Burnhouse
50
37
A
38
B
39
C

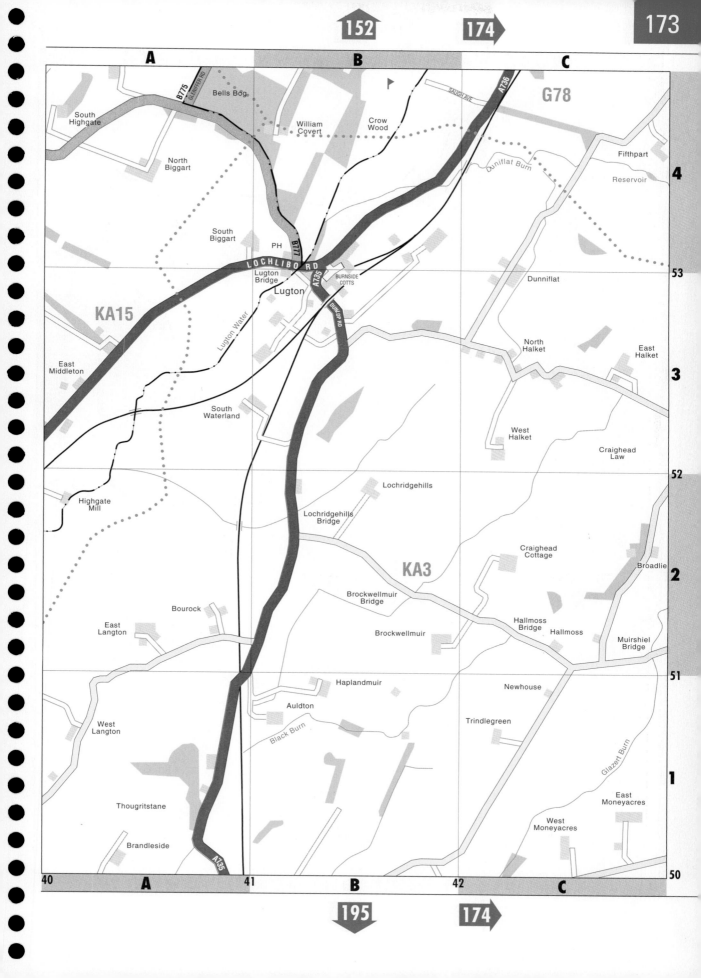

A B C

GLENIFFER RD
B775

Bells Bog

SAUGH AVE
A736
G78

South Highgate

William Covert

Crow Wood

Fifthpart

Duniflat Burn

Reservoir

North Biggart

4

South Biggart

PH

LOCHLIBO RD

B771

53

Lugton Bridge

Lugton

A735

BURNSIDE COTTS

Dunniflat

KA15

Lugton Water

DUNLOP RD

North Halket

East Halket

East Middleton

South Waterland

West Halket

3

Craighead Law

Highgate Mill

52

Lochridgehills

Lochridgehills Bridge

Craighead Cottage

Broadlie

KA3

2

Bourock

Brockwellmuir Bridge

Hallmoss Bridge

Hallmoss

Muirshiel Bridge

East Langton

Brockwellmuir

Haplandmuir

Newhouse

51

West Langton

Auldton

Trindlegreen

Black Burn

Glazert Burn

1

Thougritstane

East Moneyacres

West Moneyacres

Brandleside

A135

40 A 41 B 42 C 50

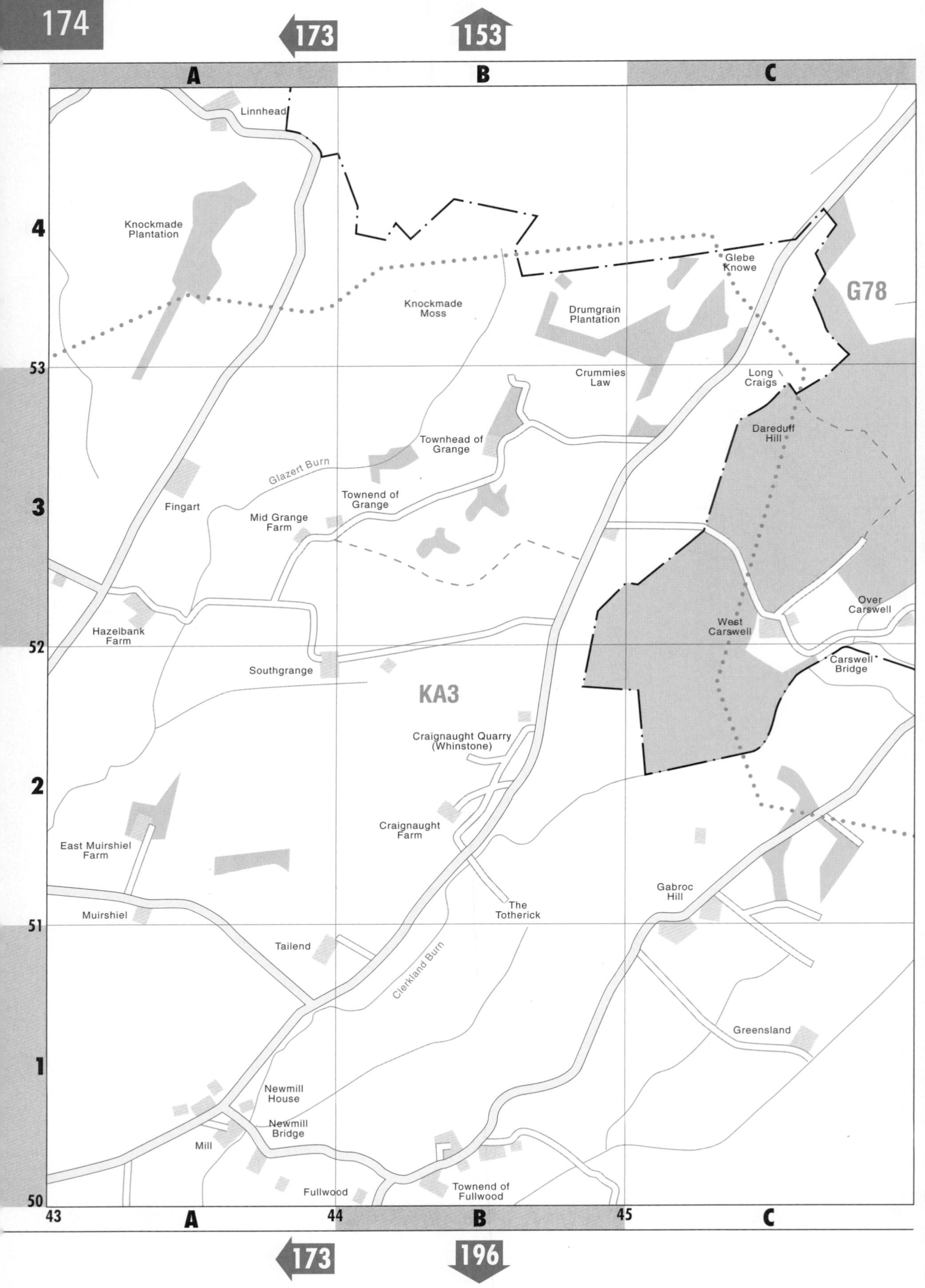

173
153

A B C

Linnhead

4

Knockmade
Plantation

Knockmade
Moss

Drumgrain
Plantation

Glebe
Knowe

G78

53

Crummies
Law

Long
Craigs

Townhead of
Grange

Dareduff
Hill

Glazert Burn

3

Fingart

Townend of
Grange

Mid Grange
Farm

Over
Carswell

West
Carswell

52

Hazelbank
Farm

Southgrange

Carswell
Bridge

KA3

Craignaught Quarry
(Whinstone)

2

East Muirshiel
Farm

Craignaught
Farm

Gabroc
Hill

Muirshiel

The
Totherick

51

Tailend

Clerkland Burn

Greensland

1

Newmill
House

Newmill
Bridge

Mill

50

Fullwood

Townend of
Fullwood

43 A 44 B 45 C

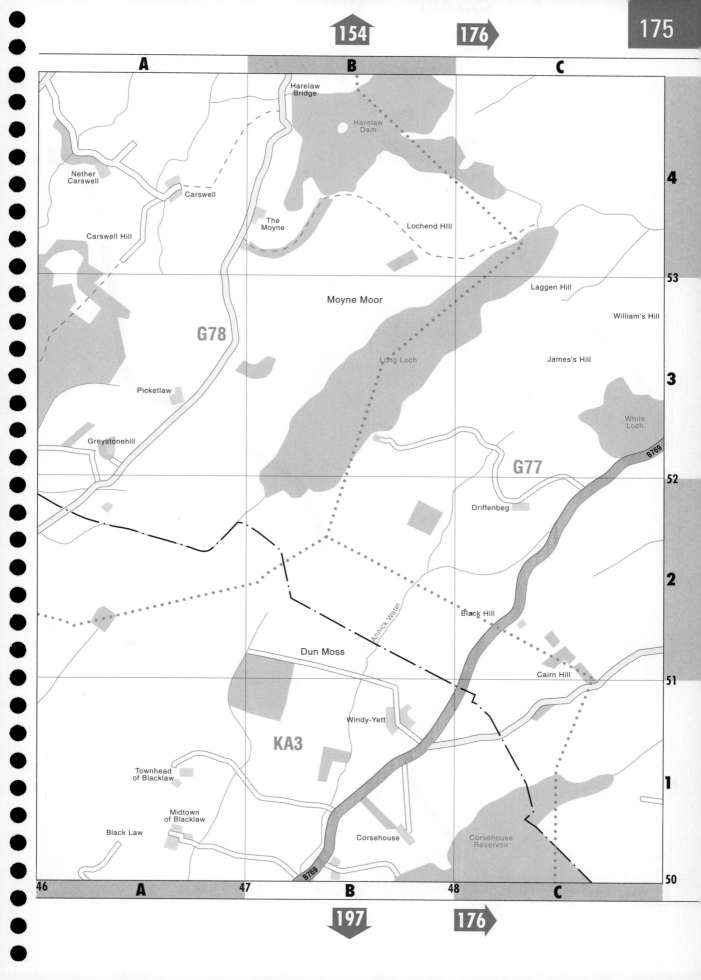

A

B

C

Harelaw
Bridge

Harelaw
Dam

4

Nether
Carswell

Carswell

The
Moyne

Lochend Hill

Carswell Hill

53

Moyne Moor

Laggen Hill

G78

William's Hill

James's Hill

3

Picketlaw

Long Loch

White
Loch

B769

Greystonehill

G77

52

Driffenbeg

2

Annick Water

Black Hill

Dun Moss

Cairn Hill

51

Windy-Yett

KA3

1

Townhead
of Blacklaw

Midtown
of Blacklaw

Black Law

Corsehouse

Corsehouse
Reservoir

B769

50

46

A

47

B

48

C

175
155

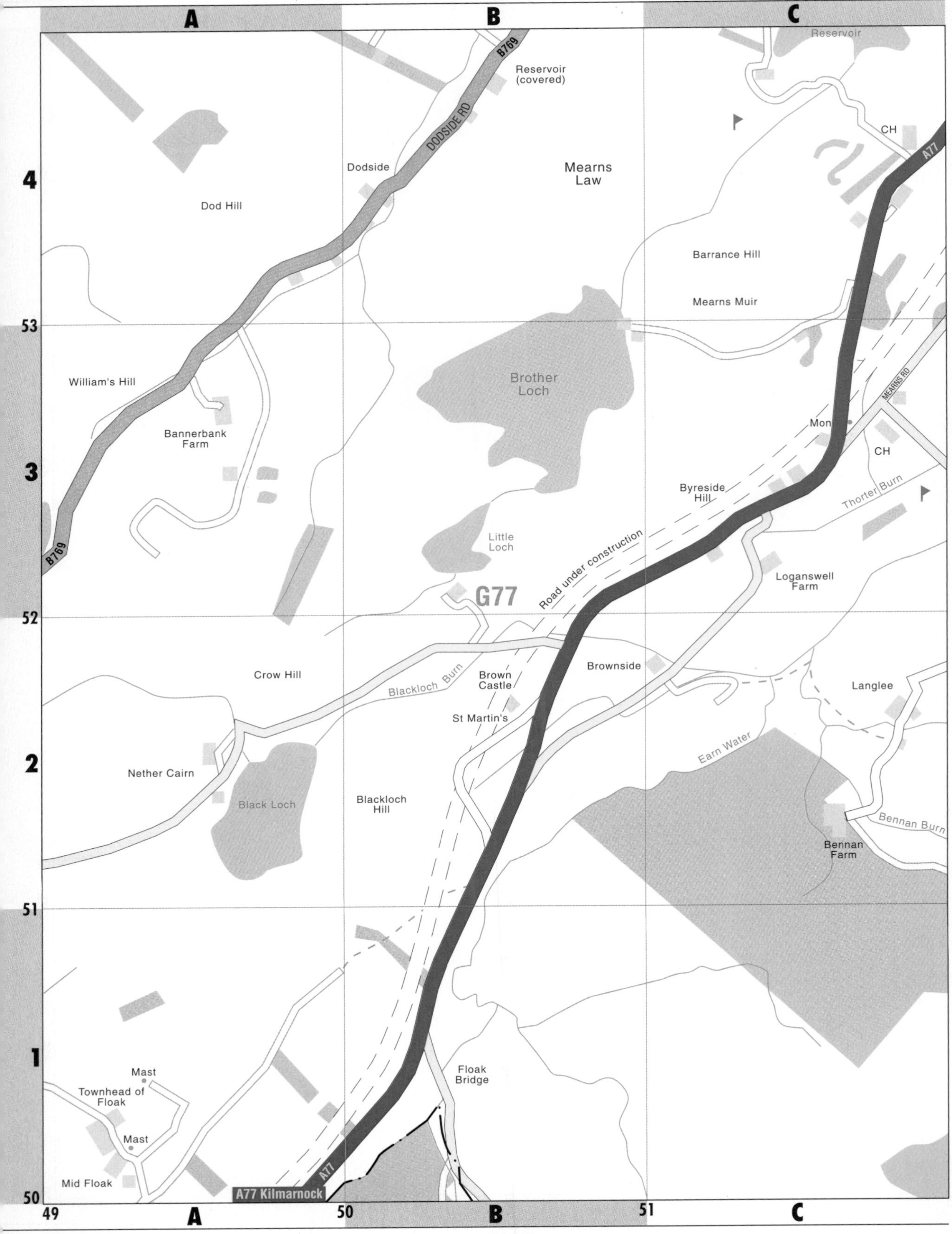

A   B   C

B769

Reservoir

Reservoir
(covered)

DODSIDE RD

Dodside

Mearns
Law

CH

A77

4

Dod Hill

Barrance Hill

Mearns Muir

53

William's Hill

Brother
Loch

MEARNS RD

Mon

CH

Byreside
Hill

Thorter Burn

3

Bannerbank
Farm

B769

Little
Loch

Road under construction

Loganswell
Farm

52

G77

Crow Hill

Blackloch Burn

Brown
Castle

Brownside

Langlee

2

St Martin's

Earn Water

Nether Cairn

Black Loch

Blackloch
Hill

Bennan Burn

Bennan
Farm

51

1

Mast

Townhead of
Floak

Floak
Bridge

Mast

A77

50

Mid Floak

49   A   50   B   51   C

175

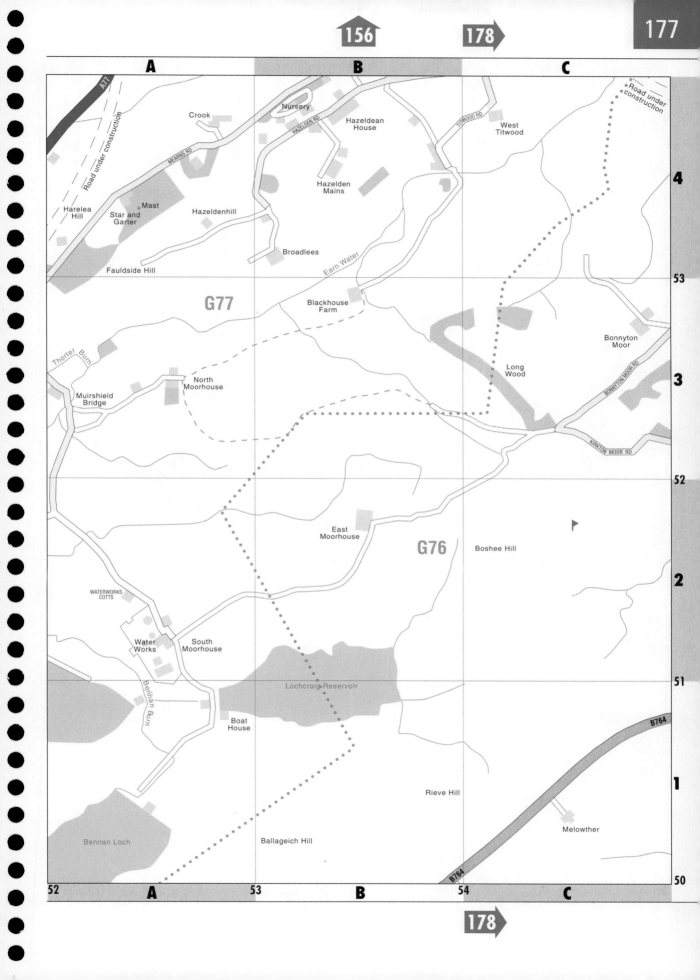

A   B   C

Road under construction

A77

Crook

Nursery

Hazeldean House

Hazelden Mains

TINWOOD RD

West Titwood

HAZELDEN RD

MEARNS RD

Harelea Hill

Mast

Star and Garter

Hazeldenhill

Broadlees

4

Fauldside Hill

Earn Water

53

G77

Blackhouse Farm

Bonnyton Moor

Thorter Burn

North Moorhouse

Long Wood

3

Muirshield Bridge

BONNYTON MOOR RD

KIRKTON MOOR RD

52

East Moorhouse

G76

Boshee Hill

WATERWORKS COTTS

2

Water Works

South Moorhouse

51

Bennan Burn

Lochcraig Reservoir

Boat House

B764

1

Rieve Hill

Melowther

Bennan Loch

Ballageich Hill

B764

50

52   A   53   B   54   C

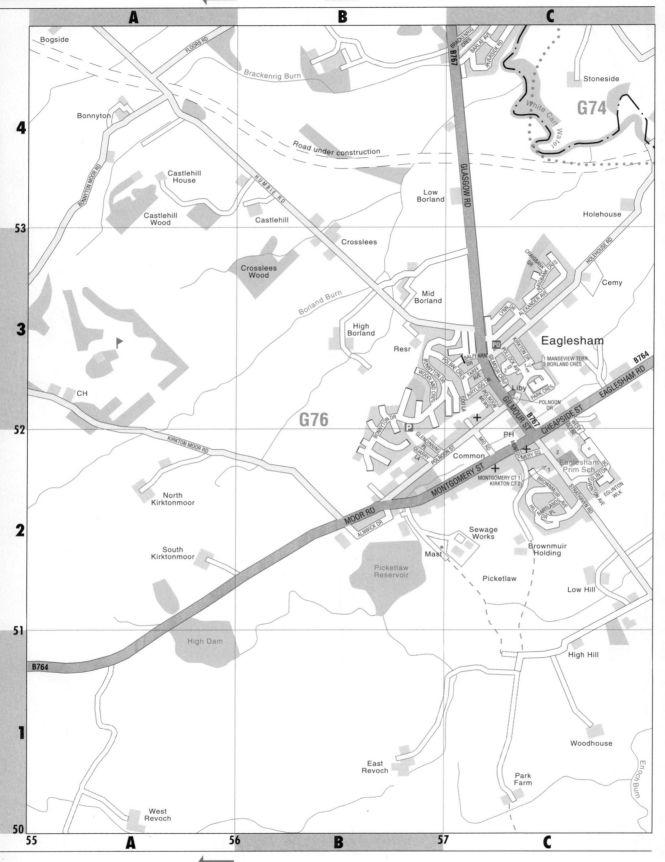

A B C

4

Bogside

Brackenrig Burn

B767

BRACKENRIG CRES
BARLAE AVE
RIVERSIDE RD

Stoneside

G74

White Cart Water

Bonnyton

Road under construction

Low
Borland

GLASGOW RD

Holehouse

53

Castlehill
House

HUMBIE RD

Castlehill
Wood

Castlehill

Crosslees

Crosslees
Wood

Borland Burn

Mid
Borland

Holehouse

HOLEHOUSE RD

Cemy

CRANBANK GR
CRANBANK CRES

3

BONNYTON MOOR RD

High
Borland

Resr

LYNN DR
ALEXANDER AVE
KIRKTON DR
PO
POLLOCK PVT

Eaglesham

1 MANSEVIEW TERR
2 BORLAND CRES

B764

EAGLESHAM RD

CH

G76

BALFEARN DR
POLBAE CRES
TARFF
AIRYLIGG DR
COOLA
GILMOUR CRAIG
POLNOON MEWS

Liby

PARK CRES

POLNOON
DR

B767

GILMOUR ST

CHEAPSIDE ST

52

KIRKTON MOOR RD

BONNYTON DR
WOODLAND CRES
GLENONNING
PL
P
POLNOON ST
QUARRY
LA

Common

MID RD

PH

MONTGOMERY SQ

2
1

Eaglesham
Prim Sch

WEST
GR
EGLINTON
RD
WIKTON AVE
EGLINTON
WLK
STRATHAVEN RD

North
Kirktonmoor

MOOR RD

MONTGOMERY ST

MONTGOMERY CT 1
KIRKTON CT 2

ALNWICK DR

2
1
BROWNMUIR AVE
BARTLANDS AVE
HILL
DR
PL

2

South
Kirktonmoor

Sewage
Works

Mast

Picketlaw
Reservoir

Picketlaw

Brownmuir
Holding

Low Hill

51

High Dam

High Hill

B764

1

Woodhouse

East
Revoch

Park
Farm

Enoch Burn

50

West
Revoch

55 A 56 B 57 C

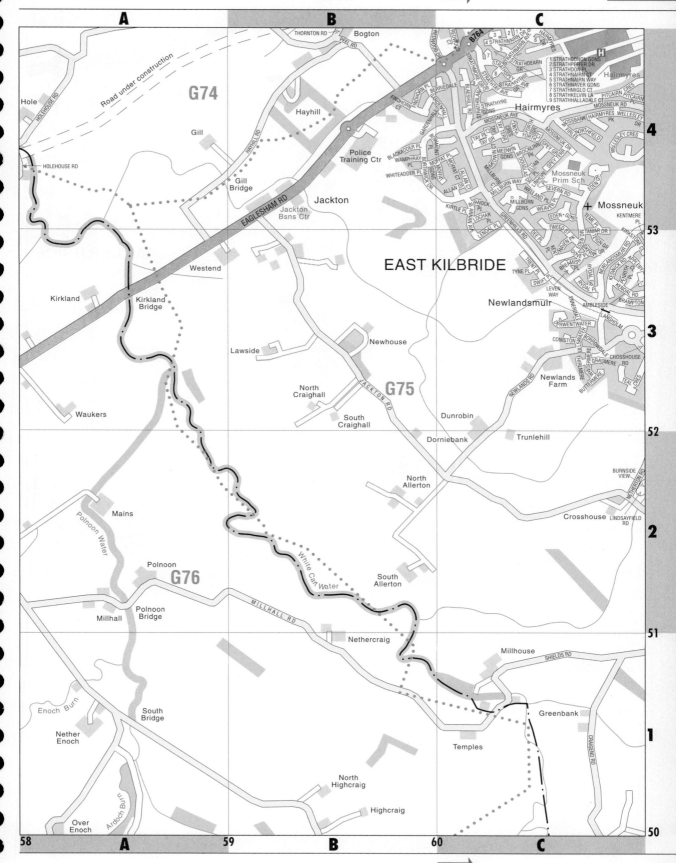

A   B   C

Hole

Road under construction

G74

HOLEHOUSE RD

THORNTON RD   Bogton
PEEL RD
Gill   Hayhill

B764
HACKSTON PL   REDHOLM CT
FINDHORN PL   STRATHCONON GR
STRATHDEE DR   STRATHYRE AVE
1 STRATHCONON GDNS
2 STRATHPEFFER DR
3 STRATHDOON PL
4 STRATHNAIRN CT
5 STRATHNAIRN WAY
6 STRATHNAVER GDNS
7 STRATHMIGLO CT
8 STRATHKELVIN LA
9 STRATHHALLADALE CT
H
Hairmyres

Gill Bridge

Jackton
Jackton Bsns Ctr

HAYHILL RD
EAGLESHAM RD

Police
Training Ctr

Westend

Kirkland

Kirkland Bridge

Waukers

Lawside

Newhouse

North Craighall

South Craighall

G75

JACKTON RD

EAST KILBRIDE

Newlandsmuir

Mossneuk
Prim Sch
Mossneuk

Hairmyres PK   WELLESLEY

Newlands Farm

Dunrobin

Dorniebank

Trunlehill

Crosshouse
RD

North Allerton

Mains

Polnoon Water

Polnoon

G76

Millhall

Polnoon Bridge

White Cart Water

MILLHALL RD

South Allerton

Nethercraig

Millhouse
SHIELDS RD

Crosshouse   LINDSAYFIELD RD

BURNSIDE VIEW

WETHERTON RD

Enoch Burn

South Bridge

Nether Enoch

Ardoch Burn

Over Enoch

North Highcraig

Highcraig

Temples

Greenbank

CRAIGEND RD

4
53
3
52
2
51
1
50

58   A   59   B   60   C

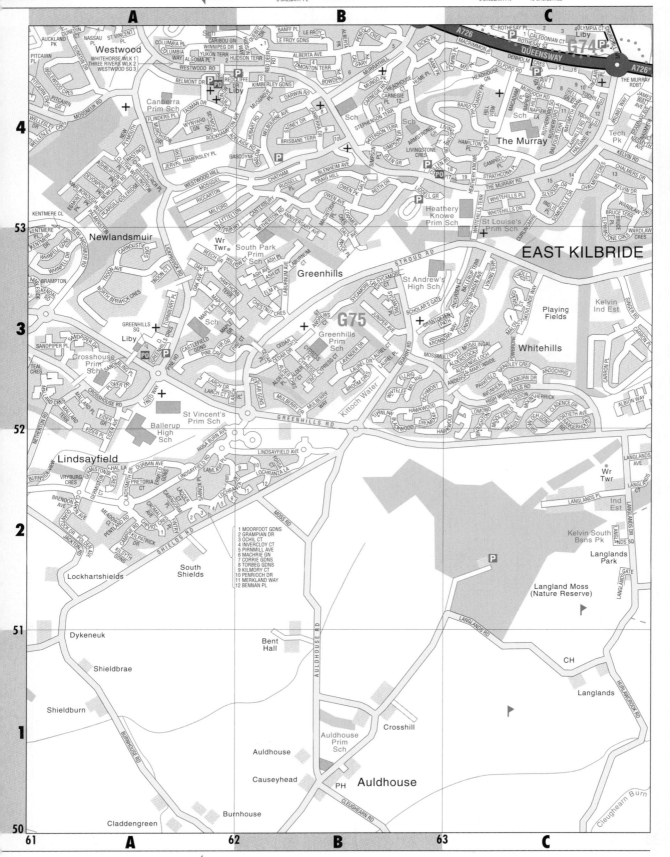

179
159

B4
1 ALBERTA CRES
2 BARKLY TERR
3 BUNBURY TERR
4 LETHBRIDGE PL
5 ALBERTA PL
6 CALGARY PL
7 MELBOURNE GN
8 SYDNEY PL
9 COOLGARDIE PL
10 COOLGARDIE GN
11 STEPHENSON PL
12 STEPHENSON SQ

C4
1 THE PLAZA
2 SOUTHGATE MALL
3 THE OLYMPIA
4 OLYMPIA ARC
5 DENHOLM GN
6 SINCLAIR PK
7 MUIRHOUSE LA
8 HENRY BELL GN
9 FREELAND LA
10 TELFORD TERR
11 SYMINGTON SQ
12 TODHILLS
13 SHEILDHILL

14 SOMERVILLE LA
15 SOMERVILLE TERR
16 HEATHER GR
17 THE MURRAY SQ
18 CULLEN LA
19 STRATHCONA LA

1 MOORFOOT GDNS
2 GRAMPIAN DR
3 OCHIL CT
4 INVERCLOY CT
5 PIRNMILL AVE
6 MACHRIE GN
7 CORRIE GDNS
8 TORBEG GDNS
9 KILMORY CT
10 PENRIOCH DR
11 MERKLAND WAY
12 BENNAN PL

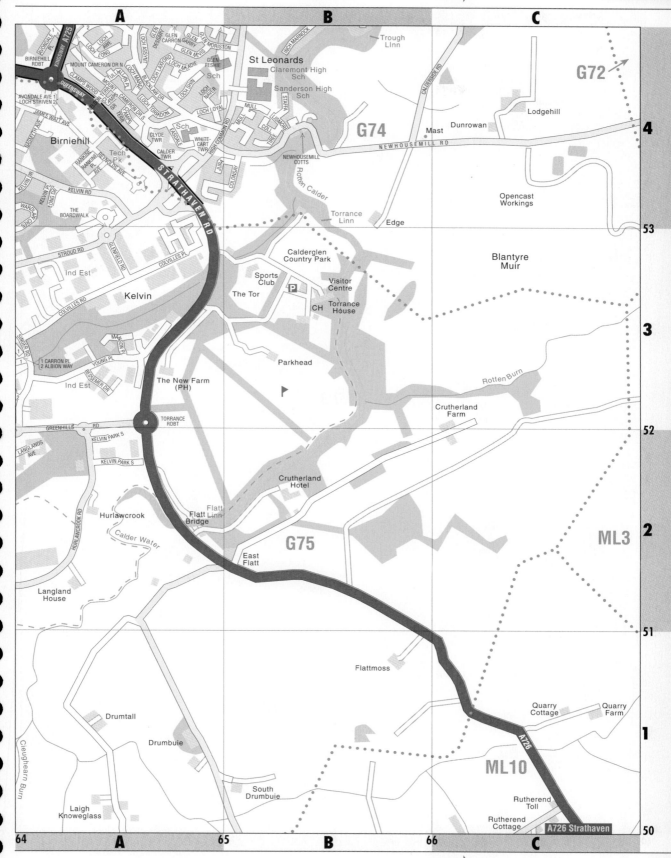

A   B   C

↑ 160

AVONDALE AV
BIRNIEHILL RDBT
KINGSWAY A725
AVONDALE AVE 1
LOCH STRIVEN 2
QUEENSWAY
CLAIMS WOOD
Birniehill
JAMES WATT AVE
INSHKEITH AVE
Tech Pk
BANKINE
RANKINE
REYNOLDS AVE
KELVIN DR
LONG DR
KELVIN RD
WARD CRES
THE BOARDWALK
STROUD RD
GLENFIELD RD
COLVILLES PL
Ind Est
Kelvin
COLVILLES RD
RANGER RD
MANSON PL
YOUNG PL
BESSEMER DR
1 CARRON PL
2 ALBION WAY
Ind Est
The New Farm (PH)
GREENHILLS RD
TORRANCE RDBT
KELVIN PARK S
LANGLANDS AVE
KELVIN PARK S
HURLAWCROOK RD
Hurlawcrook
Calder Water
Langland House
Cieughearn Burn
Drumtall
Drumbuie
Laigh Knoweglass
South Drumbuie

MOUNT CAMERON DR N
GLEN ESK
GLEN CARRON
GLEN MORISTON
GLEN GARRY
GLEN MEVIS
GLEN DESSARY
GLEN FESHIE
Sch
LOCH ASS'NT
LOCH LONG
LOCH AVE
LOCH LAXFORD
LOCH MAREE
LOCH MCADIE
LOCH SHIN
LOCH MAREE
LOCH LOYAL
MOUNT CAMERON DR S
MOUNT CAMERON DR S
CAMPS
CAMERON DR S
CALTON PL
MULL
HIGH COMMON RD
JURA
COLONSAY
Sch
CLYDE TWR
CALDER TWR
WHITE-CART TWR
ST LEONARDS
Claremont High Sch
Sanderson High Sch
MULL
STAFFA
COLL
TIREE
ISMORE
LINCH MARNOCK
Trough Linn
Rotten Calder
NEWHOUSEMILL COTTS
Torrance Linn
Edge
Calderglen Country Park
Sports Club
The Tor
P
Visitor Centre
CH
Torrance House
Parkhead
Crutherland Farm
Rotten Burn
Crutherland Hotel
Flatt
Flatt Linn Bridge
East Flatt
Flattmoss
Quarry Cottage
Quarry Farm
A726
Rutherend Toll
Rutherend Cottage
A726 Strathaven

STRATHAVEN RD

G74
Mast
Dunrowan
Lodgehill
NEWHOUSEMILL RD
CALDERSIDE RD
Opencast Workings
Blantyre Muir
G72
ML3
G75
ML10

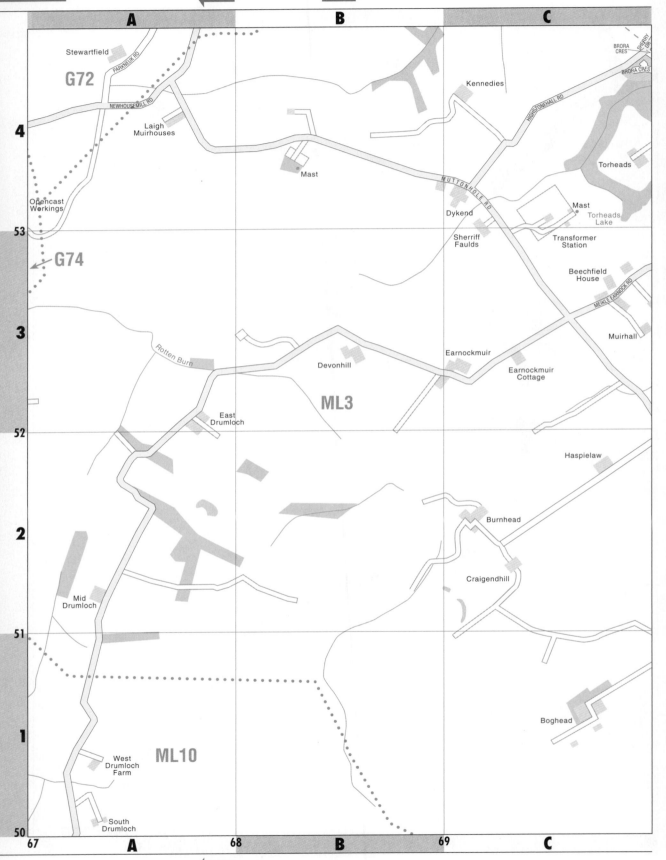

181

161

A

B

C

Stewartfield

PARKNEUK RD

G72

NEWHOUSEMILL RD

Laigh
Muirhouses

4

Mast

Kennedies

HIGHSTONEHALL RD

BRORA
CRES

SHERRY DR

BRORA CRES

Torheads

Opencast
Workings

MUTTONHOLE RD

Dykend

Mast

Torheads
Lake

53

G74

Sherriff
Faulds

Transformer
Station

Beechfield
House

MEIKLE EARNOCK RD

Rotten Burn

3

Devonhill

Earnockmuir

Earnockmuir
Cottage

Muirhall

ML3

East
Drumloch

52

Haspielaw

Burnhead

2

Craigendhill

Mid
Drumloch

51

Boghead

1

West
Drumloch
Farm

ML10

South
Drumloch

50

67

A

68

B

69

C

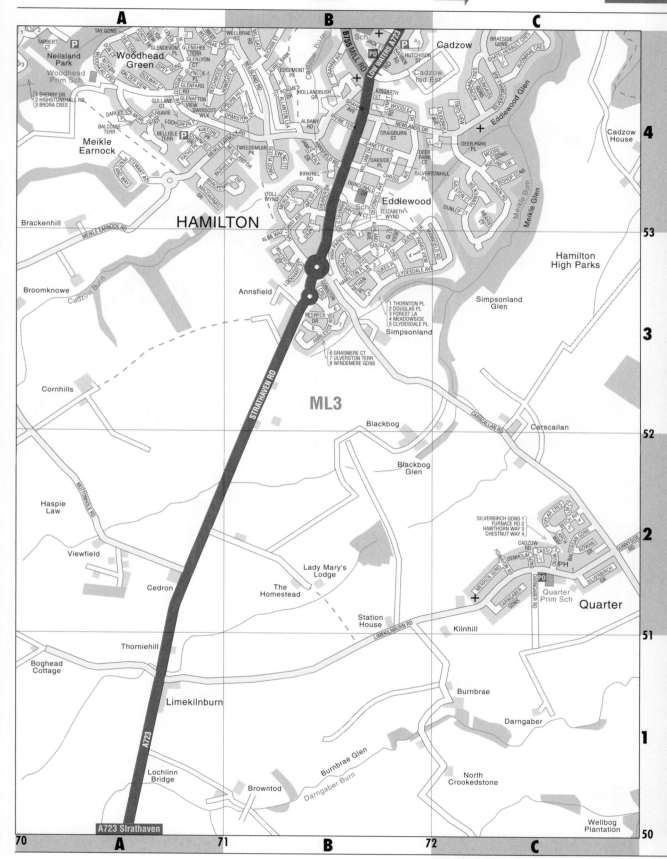

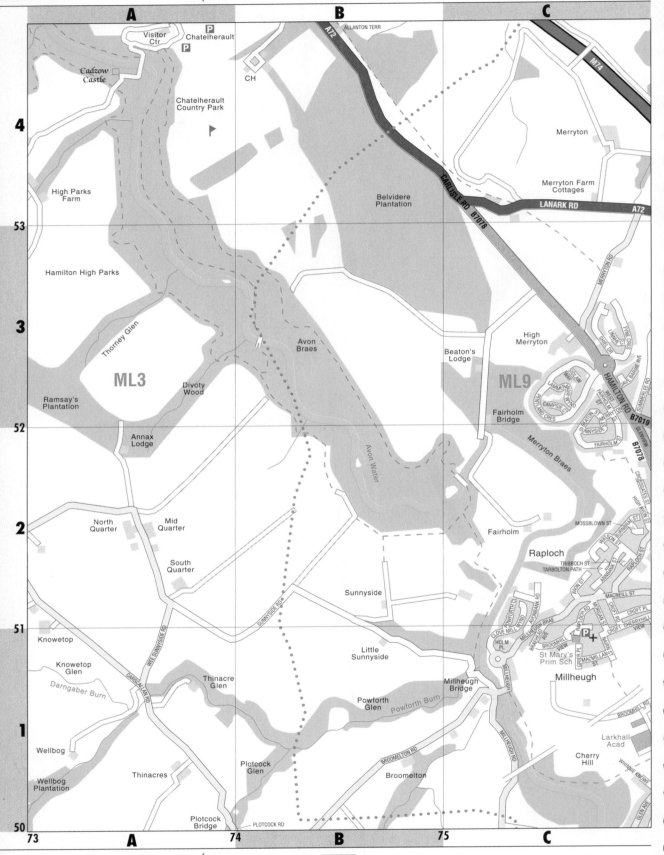

183
163

A **B** **C**

ALLANTON TERR

Visitor Ctr

P Chatelherault

P

Cadzow Castle

CH

Chatelherault Country Park

MERRYTON RD

Merryton

M74

A72

CARLISLE RD B7078

Belvidere Plantation

High Parks Farm

LANARK RD   A72

Merryton Farm Cottages

53

Hamilton High Parks

3

Thorney Glen

Avon Braes

High Merryton

Beaton's Lodge

HAMILTON RD

ML3

Divoty Wood

ML9

Ramsay's Plantation

Fairholm Bridge

B7019

52

Annax Lodge

Avon Water

Merryton Braes

B7078

MOSSBLOWN ST

2

North Quarter

Mid Quarter

Fairholm

Raploch

TRIBBOCH ST

TARBOLTON PATH

South Quarter

Sunnyside

SUNNYSIDE RD

MACNEILL ST

CROFT PL

51

Knowetop

Little Sunnyside

St Mary's Prim Sch

Millheugh

Knowetop Glen

WEE SUNNYSIDE RD

Thinacre Glen

CARSCALLAN RD

Powforth Glen

Millheugh Bridge

Darngaber Burn

Powforth Burn

MILLHEUGH RD

Larkhall Acad

1

Wellbog

Cherry Hill

Wellbog Plantation

Thinacres

Plotcock Glen

BROOMELTON RD

Broomelton

GLEN AVE

50

Plotcock Bridge

PLOTCOCK RD

73   **A**   74   **B**   75   **C**

183
198

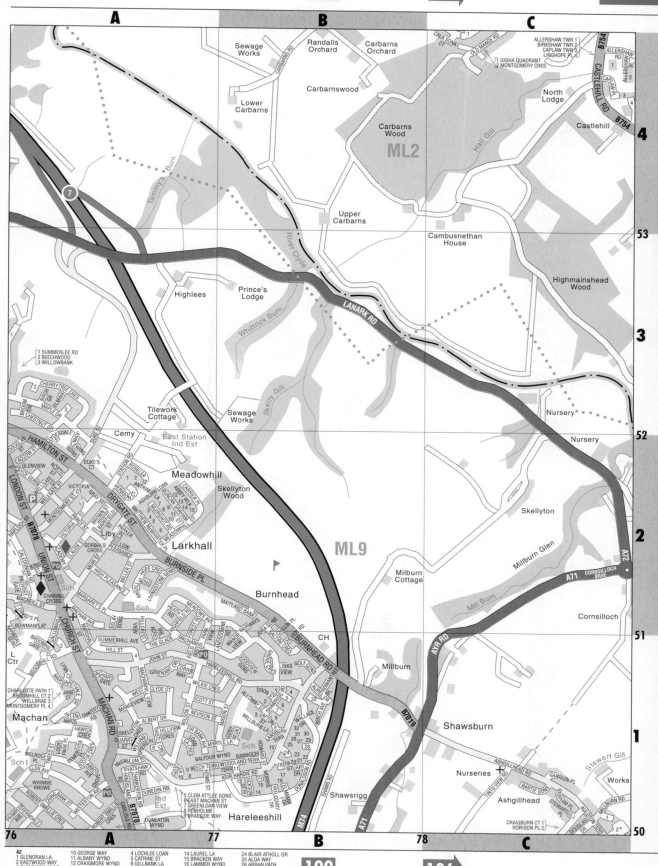

A2
1 GLENORAN LA
2 EASTWOOD WAY
3 GLENBURN WYND
4 PORTLAND WYND
5 SIGHTHILL LOAN
6 PARKNOOK WAY
7 LOMOND WLK
8 HOZIER LOAN
9 CRAIGIE LA

10 GEORGE WAY
11 ALBANY WYND
12 CRAIGMORE WYND
13 BURNS LOAN
14 BANK WAY
15 BRAESIDE LA
B1
1 LOANING
2 LOVAT PATH
3 BALMORAL PATH

4 LOCHLEE LOAN
5 CATRINE ST
6 GILLBANK LA
7 CARRICK ST
8 WINDSOR PATH
9 WOODBURN TERR
10 MOSSGIEL LA
11 BERTRAM ST
12 HAZELDENE LA
13 ROSEMOUNT LA

14 LAUREL LA
15 BRACKEN WAY
16 LAMMER WYND
17 CAMERONIAN WAY
18 GLEN FRUIN DR
19 ST ANDREWS PATH
20 LAWRIE WAY
21 KATRIONA PATH
22 CAMERON PATH
23 TRINITY WAY

24 BLAIR ATHOLL DR
25 ALOA WAY
26 ARRAN PATH
27 DALSERF PATH
28 BANNOCKBURN DR
29 LOCHNAGAR WAY
30 FLEMING WAY
31 BRUCE'S LOAN
32 MAXWELL PATH
33 HAWTHORN GDNS

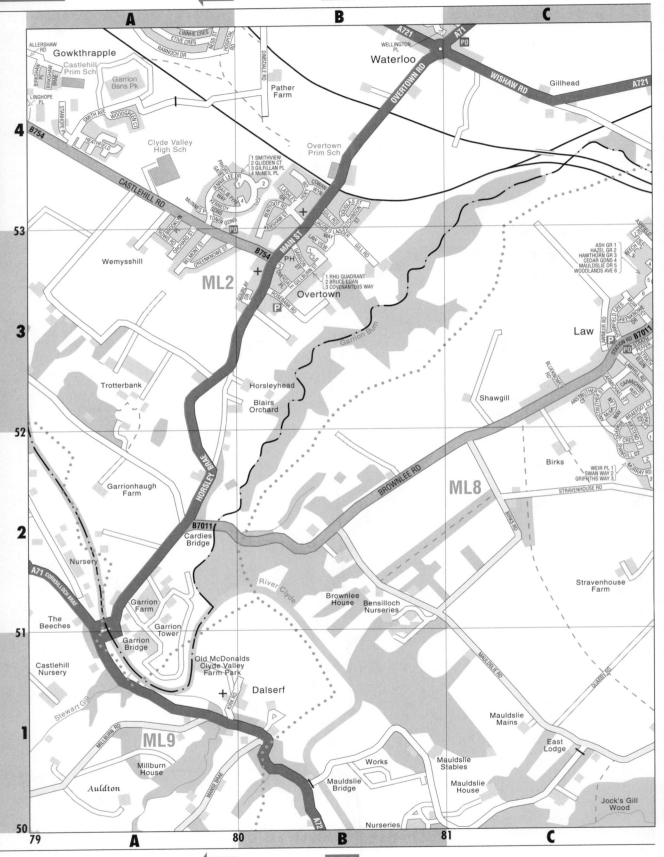

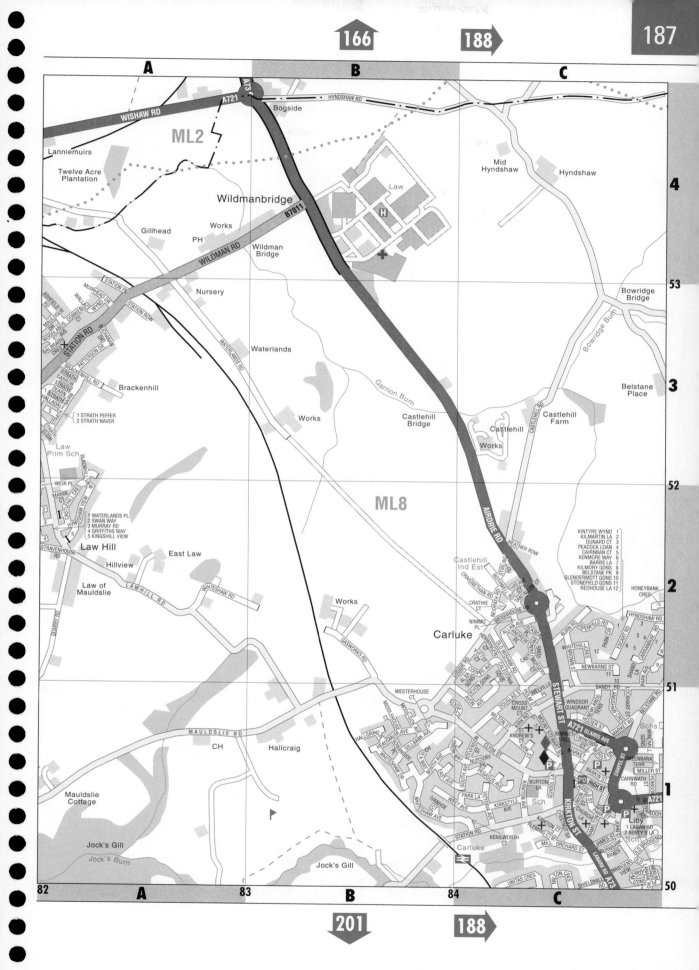

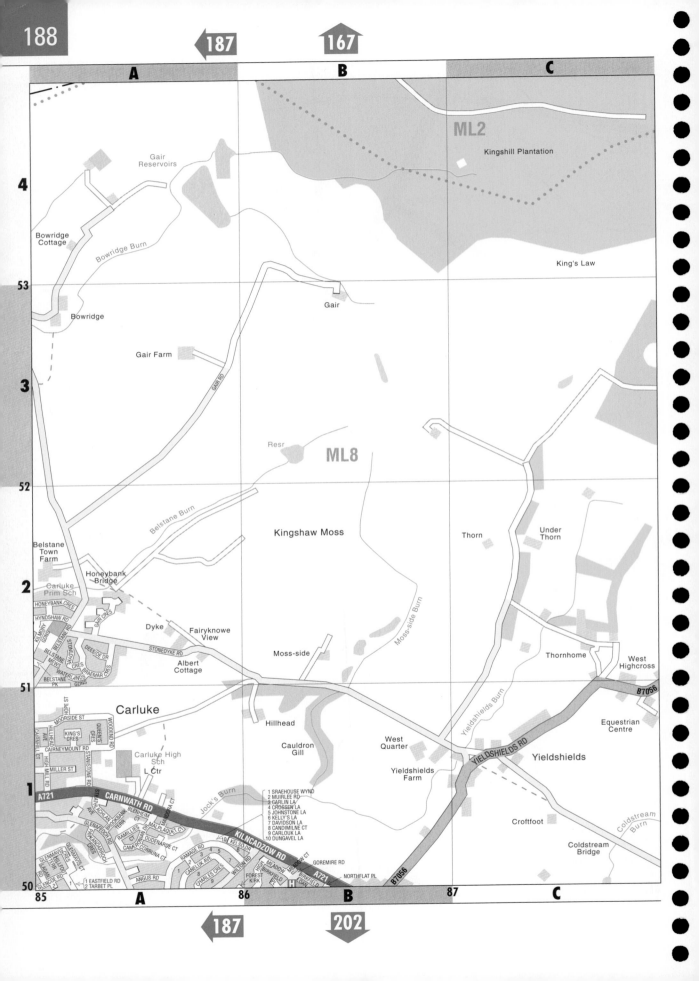

ML2

Kingshill Plantation

Gair Reservoirs

King's Law

Bowridge Cottage

Bowridge Burn

4

53

Bowridge

Gair

Gair Farm

GAIR RD

3

Resr

ML8

Belstane Burn

52

Kingshaw Moss

Thorn

Under Thorn

Belstane Town Farm

Honeybank Bridge

2

Carluke Prim Sch

HONEYBANK CRES

HYNDSHAW RD

KILMORY GDNS

GAIR CRES

STONEDYKE RD

Dyke

Fairyknowe View

STONEDYKE RD

Moss-side Burn

Moss-side

Thornhome

West Highcross

BELSTANE RD

DEESIDE DR

CRES BRAEMAR CRES

Albert Cottage

BELSTANE MEWS

WATERLANDS

BELSTANE PK

GDNS

51

Yieldshields Burn

B7056

Carluke

HOPE ST

MOORSIDE ST

QUEEN'S CRES

WOODEND RD

Hillhead

Cauldron Gill

West Quarter

YIELDSHIELDS RD

Equestrian Centre

Yieldshields

KING'S CRES

HILLHEAD AVE

CAIRNHILL CT

CAIRNEYMOUNT RD

HIGH MILL RD

MILLER ST

STANISTONE RD

Carluke High Sch

L Ctr

Yieldshields Farm

1

A721

CARNWATH RD

Jock's Burn

1 SRAEHOUSE WYND
2 MUIRLEE RD
3 CARLIN LA
4 CROSSEN LA
5 JOHNSTONE LA
6 KELLY'S LA
7 DAVIDSON LA
8 CANDIMILNE CT
9 CARLOUK LA
10 DUNGAVEL LA

Croftfoot

Coldstream Burn

STRATHCLYDE AVE

BROOKBANK

BLENHEIM

GLENAEROW RD

MALPLAQUET CT

MANDORA CT

KILNCADZOW RD

KELSO DR

Coldstream Bridge

RAMILLIES CT

OUDENARDE CT

CORRUNA CT

BAMAGE RD

WILTON RD

MEADOW ST

BIRKFIELD DR

GOREMIRE RD

A721

NORTHFLAT PL

B7056

GLENMAVIS

PHILLIPS

LASWADE

GLENMAVIS DR

GLENCOE RD

CAMERON DR

CANDLUK AVE

CHARLES CRES

HIGH BIRKFIELD PL

MEADOW CT

ANGUS RD

Forest Kirk

H

1 EASTFIELD RD
2 TARBET PL

50

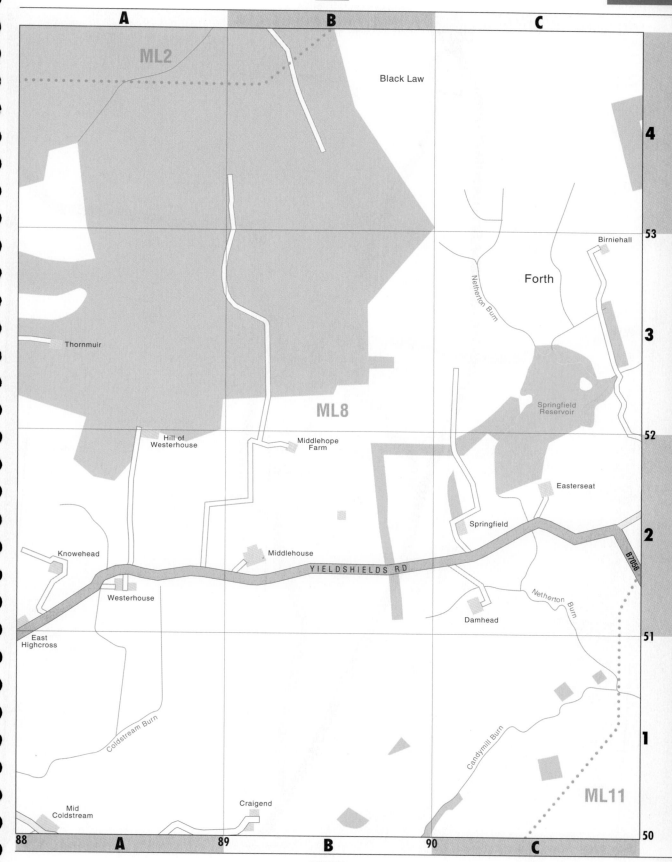

ML2

Black Law

ML8

Thornmuir

Hill of
Westerhouse

Middlehope
Farm

Forth

Birniehall

Netherton Burn

Springfield
Reservoir

Easterseat

Springfield

Knowehead

Middlehouse

YIELDSHIELDS RD

Westerhouse

Damhead

Netherton Burn

East
Highcross

Coldstream Burn

Candymill Burn

Mid
Coldstream

Craigend

ML11

B7056

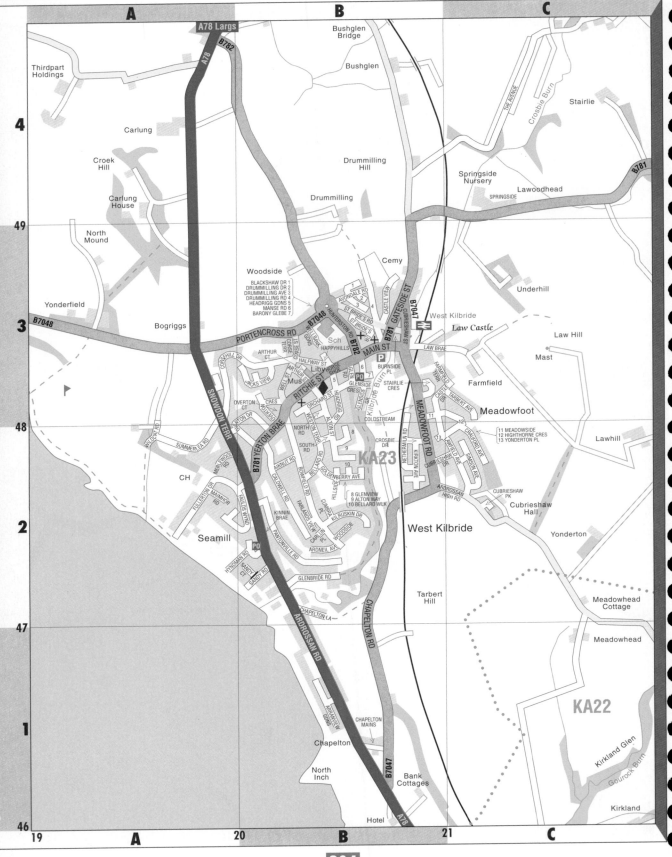

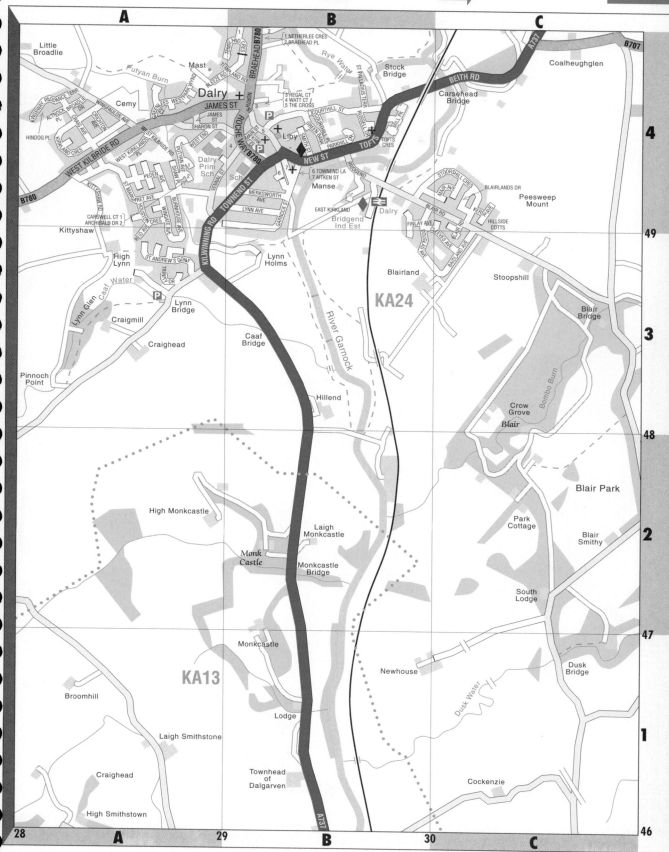

191
170

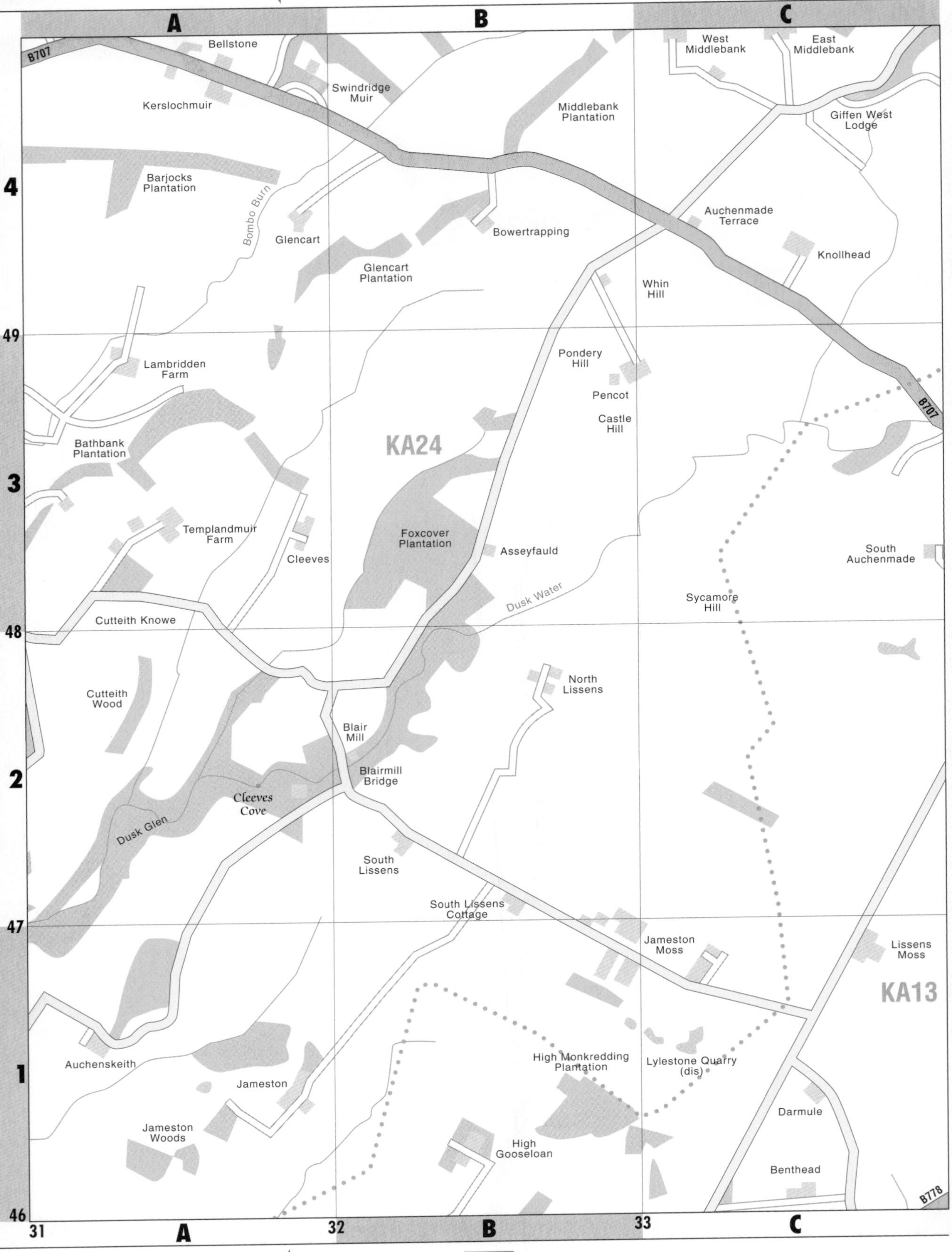

A **B** **C**

B707

Bellstone

Kerslochmuir

Swindridge Muir

Middlebank Plantation

West Middlebank

East Middlebank

Giffen West Lodge

Barjocks Plantation

Bombo Burn

Glencart

Bowertrapping

Auchenmade Terrace

Knollhead

Glencart Plantation

Whin Hill

4

49

Lambridden Farm

KA24

Pondery Hill

Pencot

Castle Hill

B707

Bathbank Plantation

South Auchenmade

3

Templandmuir Farm

Cleeves

Foxcover Plantation

Asseyfauld

Dusk Water

Sycamore Hill

Cutteith Knowe

48

Cutteith Wood

North Lissens

Blair Mill

Blairmill Bridge

2

Dusk Glen

Cleeves Cove

South Lissens

South Lissens Cottage

47

Jameston Moss

Lissens Moss

KA13

Auchenskeith

Jameston

High Monkredding Plantation

Lylestone Quarry (dis)

Darmule

1

Jameston Woods

High Gooseloan

Benthead

B778

46

31 **A** 32 **B** 33 **C**

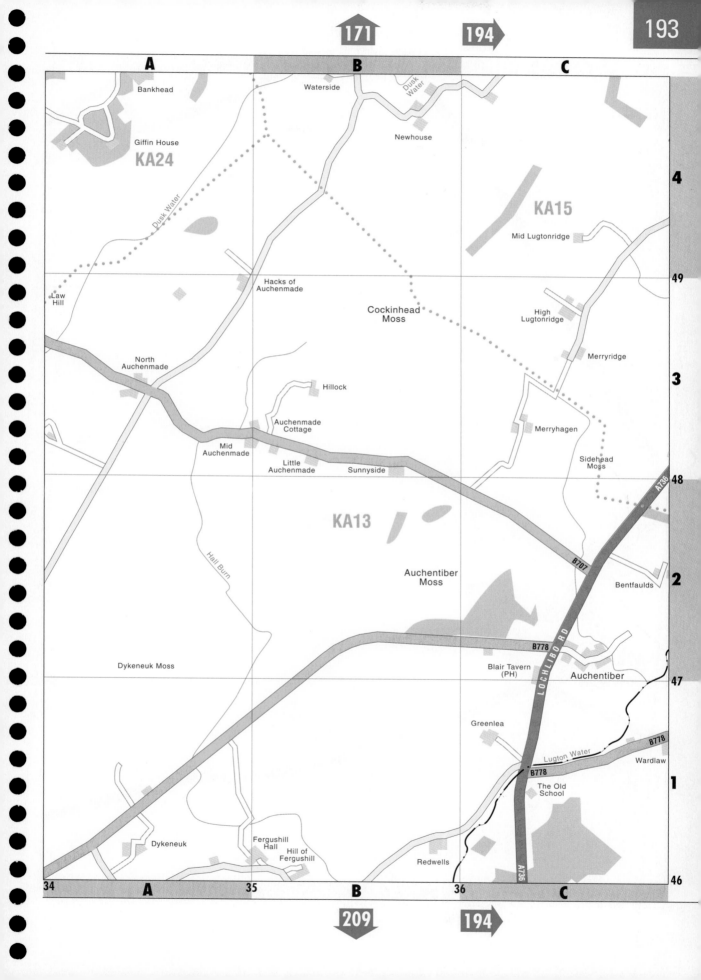

A B C

Bankhead

Waterside

Dusk Water

Newhouse

Giffin House

KA24

4

KA15

Mid Lugtonridge

Dusk Water

49

Hacks of Auchenmade

Law Hill

Cockinhead Moss

High Lugtonridge

Merryridge

North Auchenmade

3

Hillock

Auchenmade Cottage

Merryhagen

Mid Auchenmade

Little Auchenmade

Sunnyside

Sidehead Moss

A736

48

KA13

Hall Burn

Auchentiber Moss

B707

Bentfaulds

2

B778

LOCHLIBO RD

Dykeneuk Moss

Blair Tavern (PH)

Auchentiber

47

Greenlea

B778

Lugton Water

Wardlaw

B778

The Old School

1

Dykeneuk

Fergushill Hall

Hill of Fergushill

Redwells

A736

46

34 A 35 B 36 C

A B C

4

South
Nettlehurst

Nettlehurst

Lugtonridge

Lugtonridge

Deepstone

Sidehead

3

48

KA13

47

B778

Wardlaw

1

Law

46

37

A736

LOCHLIBO RD

KA15

East
Lugtonridge

Lugton Water

49

Loanhead

Braehead

Leahead

Thorn

KA3

Glazert Burn

Waterside
House

Ravenslie

Cauldhame
Farm

Brae

South
Brae

Bowhouse
Farm

Bloakholmes

Townend
of Kirkwood

East
Bloakhillhead

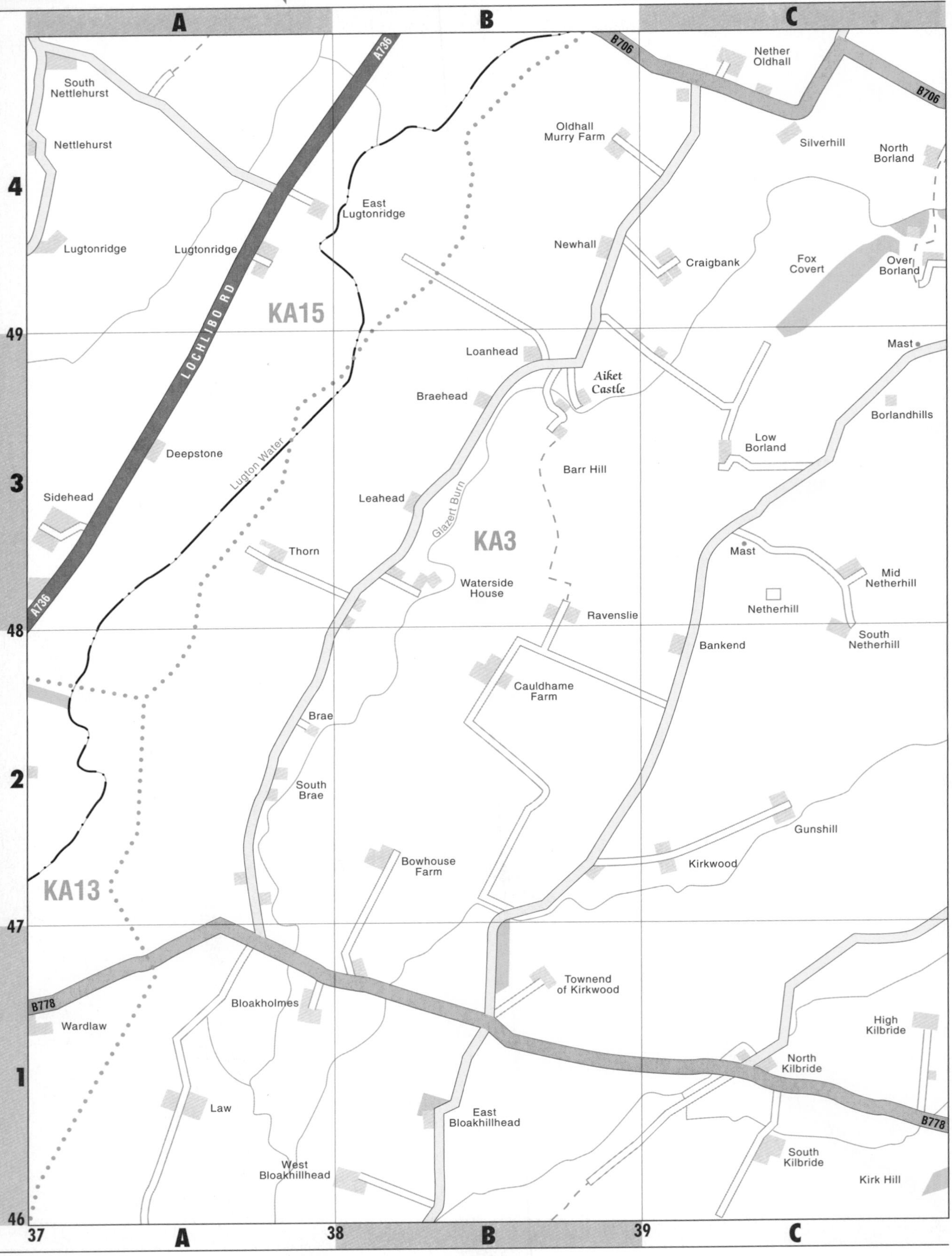

West
Bloakhillhead

B706

Nether
Oldhall

Oldhall
Murry Farm

Newhall

Craigbank

Aiket
Castle

Barr Hill

Silverhill

North
Borland

Fox
Covert

Over
Borland

Mast

Low
Borland

Borlandhills

Mast

Netherhill

Bankend

Mid
Netherhill

South
Netherhill

Gunshill

Kirkwood

High
Kilbride

North
Kilbride

South
Kilbride

Kirk Hill

B778

2

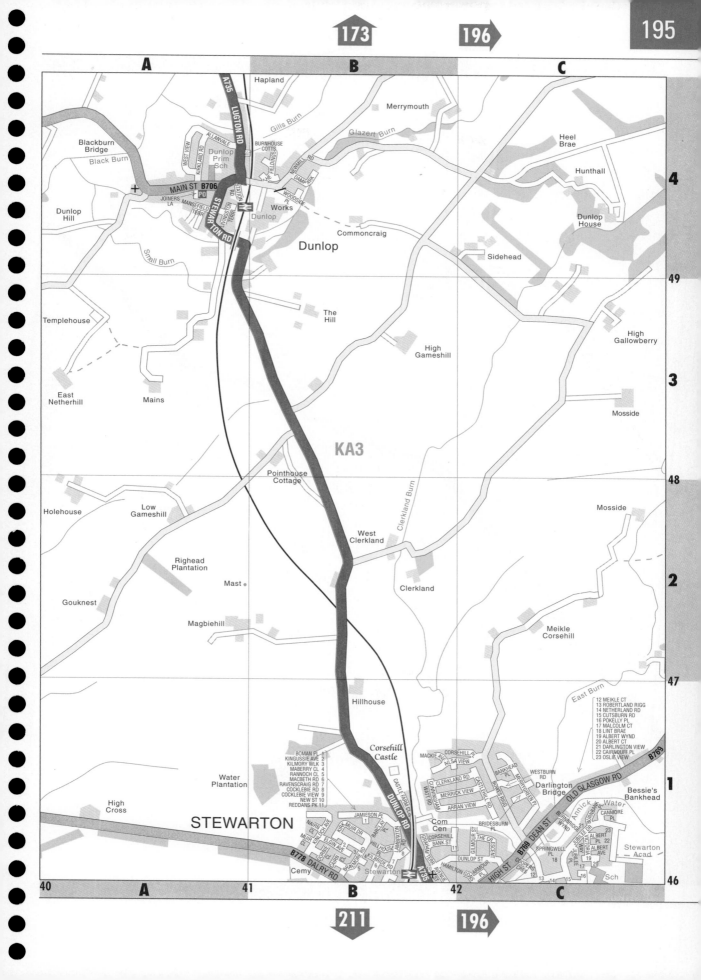

A   B   C

Hapland

Merrymouth

Gills Burn

Glazert Burn

Heel Brae

Blackburn Bridge

Black Burn

LUGTON RD

A735

ALLANVALE

WEST VIEW

KIRKLAND RD

Dunlop Prim Sch

BURNHOUSE COTTS

NEWMILL RD

DAMPRK

Hunthall

Dunlop Hill

MAIN ST B706

PO

STATION RD

THE FIELDINGS

STEWARTON RD

WOODSIDE PL

Works

Dunlop

4

JOINERS LA

MANSEFIELD TERR

RENSMITH RD

Dunlop House

Dunlop Hill

Small Burn

Dunlop

Commoncraig

Sidehead

Dunlop House

49

Templehouse

The Hill

High Gameshill

High Gallowberry

East Netherhill

Mains

KA3

Mosside

3

Holehouse

Low Gameshill

Pointhouse Cottage

Clerkland Burn

Mosside

48

Righead Plantation

West Clerkland

Gouknest

Mast

Clerkland

Meikle Corsehill

2

Magbiehill

Hillhouse

47

High Cross

Water Plantation

Corsehill Castle

CASTLE FARM CL

DUNLOP RD

East Burn

12 MEIKLE CT
13 ROBERTLAND RIGG
14 NETHERLAND RD
15 CUTSBURN RD
16 POKELLY PL
17 MALCOLM CT
18 LINT BRAE
19 ALBERT WYND
20 ALBERT CT
21 DARLINGTON VIEW
22 CAIRNDUFF PL
23 OSLIE VIEW

B769

MACKIE AVE

CORSEHILL PL

NILSA VIEW

BANKHEAD PL

Westburn RD

Darlington Bridge

OLD GLASGOW RD

Bessie's Bankhead

Annick Water

1

BOMAN PL 1
KINGUSSIE AVE 2
KILMORY WLK 3
MABERRY CL 4
RANNOCH CL 5
MACBETH RD 6
RAVENSCRAIG RD 7
COCKLEBIE RD 8
COCKLEBIE VIEW 9
NEW ST 10
REDDANS PK 11

CLERKLAND RD

CUNNINGHAM WATT RD

MERRICK VIEW

ARRAN VIEW

CASTLEHILL RD

BONES RIGG

TERRA GREEN PL

DEAN ST

B769

CANMORE PL

JAMIESON PL

Com Cen

Corsehill Bank St

BRIDESBURN PL

HIGH ST

JUBILEE PL

ALBERT PL 23
VICTORIA AVE
ALBERT 22
PL
ALBERT 20
AVE 19

STEWARTON

NAIRN AVE

KIRK MUIR DR

ELGIN AVE

BARCLAY

HILLHOUSE

LAMBIE ST

NITHSDALE RD

THE CRESCENT

DUNLOP ST

HAMILTON GO

GILMOUR

SPRINGWELL PL

CROFTS CRES

Stewarton Acad

MUIR CL

BONNIE AVE

CAIRN CL

KILBRIDE RD

KILBRIDE RD

ARMOUR

Sch

B778 DALRY RD

Cemy

Stewarton

A735

40   41   42   46

A   B   C

195 174

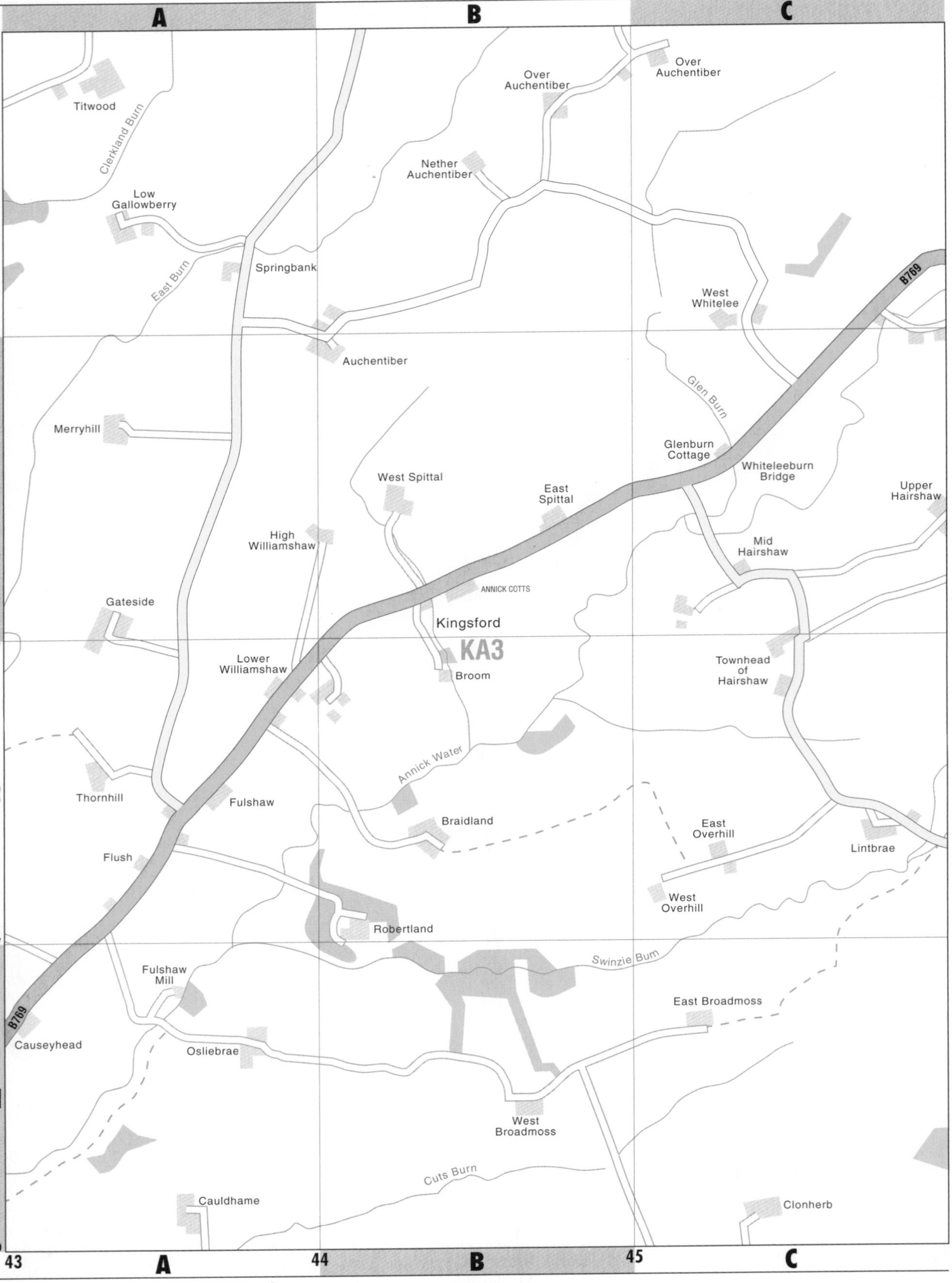

A B C

Titwood

Clerkland Burn

Low
Gallowberry

East Burn

Springbank

4

Over Auchentiber

Over
Auchentiber

Nether
Auchentiber

B769

West
Whitelee

49

Auchentiber

Glen Burn

Merryhill

West Spittal

East
Spittal

Glenburn
Cottage

Whiteleeburn
Bridge

Upper
Hairshaw

3

High
Williamshaw

Mid
Hairshaw

ANNICK COTTS

Gateside

Kingsford

KA3

Townhead
of Hairshaw

48

Lower
Williamshaw

Broom

Annick Water

Thornhill

Fulshaw

Braidland

East
Overhill

Lintbrae

2

Flush

West
Overhill

Robertland

Swinzie Burn

47

Fulshaw
Mill

East Broadmoss

B769

Causeyhead

Osliebrae

West
Broadmoss

1

Cuts Burn

Cauldhame

Clonherb

46

43 A 44 B 45 C

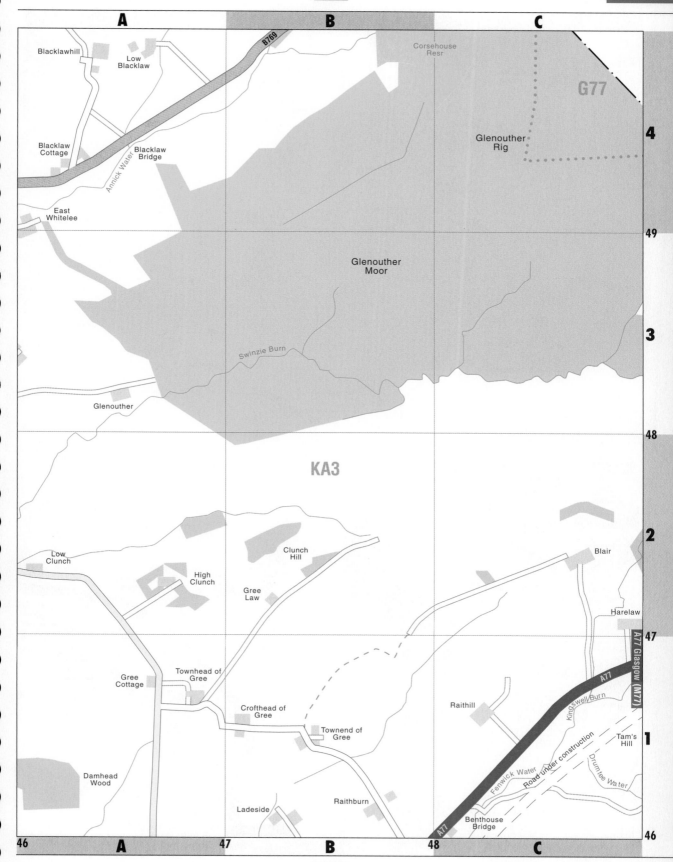

G77

Corsehouse Resr

Glenouther Rig

Glenouther Moor

KA3

Blacklawhill

Low Blacklaw

B769

Blacklaw Cottage

Blacklaw Bridge

Annick Water

East Whitelee

Swinzie Burn

Glenouther

Low Clunch

High Clunch

Clunch Hill

Gree Law

Blair

Harelaw

A77 Glasgow (M77)

A77

Gree Cottage

Townhead of Gree

Crofthead of Gree

Townend of Gree

Raithill

Kingswell Burn

Road under construction

Tam's Hill

Drumtee Water

Damhead Wood

Ladeside

Raithburn

Fenwick Water

A77

Benthouse Bridge

4

49

3

48

2

47

1

46

A 46   47   B   48   C

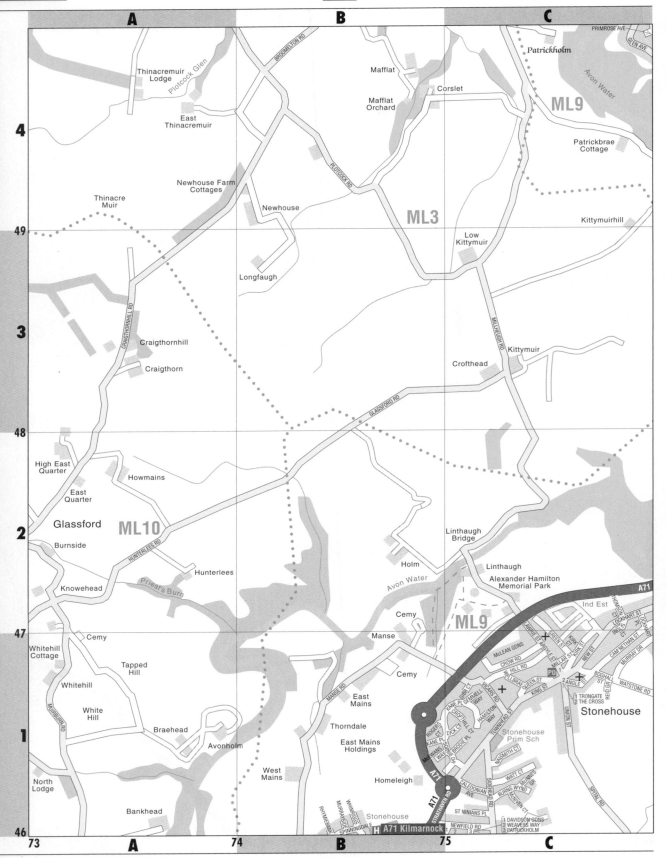

A

B

C

Primrose Ave

Glen Ave

Patrickholm

Thinacremuir Lodge

Plotcock Glen

Mafflat

Corslet

ML9

Avon Water

East Thinacremuir

Mafflat Orchard

Patrickbrae Cottage

Broomelton Rd

Plotcock Rd

Newhouse Farm Cottages

Newhouse

ML3

Kittymuirhill

Thinacre Muir

49

Longfaugh

Low Kittymuir

Craigthornhill Rd

Millheugh Rd

Kittymuir

3

Craigthornhill

Crofthead

Craigthorn

Glassford Rd

48

High East Quarter

Howmains

East Quarter

Glassford

ML10

Linthaugh Bridge

Hunterlees Rd

Burnside

Holm

Linthaugh

2

Avon Water

Alexander Hamilton Memorial Park

Knowehead

Hunterlees

Priest's Burn

Cemy

ML9

A71

Manse

Ind Est

Cemy

Whitehill Cottage

47

Manse Rd

Cemy

Stonehouse

Tapped Hill

McLean Gdns

Crow Rd

Hill Rd

W J L Brae

Queen St

King St

Trongate

The Cross

Whitehill

East Mains

Kane Gibb Ct

Gemmell Way

Crofthill Ct

Dick Ct

Vicars Rd

Hamilton St

Townhead St

Angle

1 Tronage

2 The Cross

White Hill

Thorndale

Rogers

Kane Pl

McEwans Way

Brodie Pl

Caledonian Ave

Stonehouse Prim Sch

Nasmith Ct

Watstone Rd

Boghall Rd

Murray Dr

Cam Nethan St

Ingles

New St

Kirk St

Lockhart Pl

Lockhart St

Thorniston

Red Gr

Union St

Braehead

Avonholm

1

East Mains Holdings

Watt Ct

Burns Wynd

McAtyres Gr

Septal Rd

Mair Burn Rd

West Mains

Homeleigh

Sidehead Rd

McInnes Ct

North Lodge

A71

Strathaven Rd

St Ninians Pl

1 Davidson Gdns

2 Weavers Way

3 Patruckholm

Bankhead

Rhymerbank

Murrayside

Winnings

Spinningdale

Stonehouse

Newfield Rd

H A71 Kilmarnock

1 Davidson Gdns

2

3

A71

46

73

A

74

B

75

C

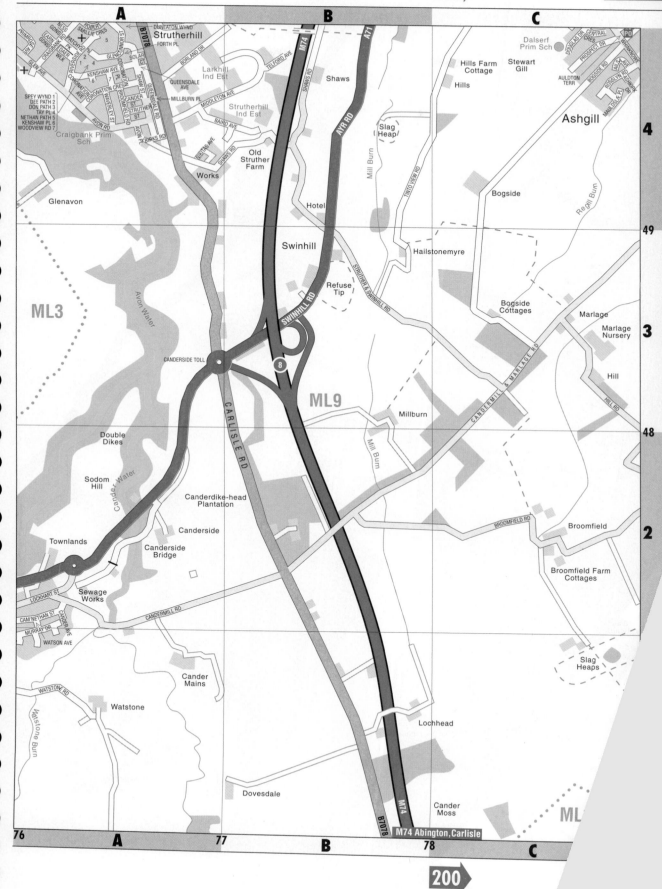

A B C

DUNEATON WYND
Strutherhill
FORTH PL
B7078

SPEY WYND 1
DEE PATH 2
DON PATH 3
TAY PL 4
NETHAN PATH 5
KENSHAW PL 6
WOODVIEW RD 7

Larkhill Ind Est
Queensdale Ave
MILLBURN PL
Strutherhill Ind Est
BAIRD AVE
Craigbank Prim Sch

Shaws

Hills Farm Cottage
Hills
Stewart Gill
Dalserf Prim Sch
AULDTON TERR

Ashgill

Glenavon
Works
Old Struther Farm
Hotel
Slag Heap
Mill Burn
Bogside
Regill Burn

4

Swinhill
Hailstonemyre
49

ML3
SWINHILL RD
Refuse Tip
STRUTHER & SWINHILL RD
Bogside Cottages
Marlage
Marlage Nursery

3

CANDERSIDE TOLL
8
ML9
Millburn
CANDERMILL & MARLAGE RD
Hill
HILL RD

Double Dikes
CARLISLE RD
48

Sodom Hill
Cander Water
Canderdike-head Plantation
Broomfield RD
Broomfield

2

Townlands
Canderside
Canderside Bridge
LOCHART ST
Sewage Works
CANDERMILL RD
Broomfield Farm Cottages

CAM'NETHAN ST
CANDER AVE
MURRAY DR
WATSON AVE
Cander Mains
Slag Heaps

WATSTONE RD
Watstone
Watstone Burn
Lochhead

Dovesdale
M74
B7078
Cander Moss
ML

199
186
199

A
B
C

4

Over Dalserf
MANSE BRAE
NURSERY DR
Meadowbank Farm
Over Dalserf Cottages
Woodside House
NETHERBURN RD
CANDERMILL AND MARLAGE RD

Nursery
A72
Nurseries
Hotel
Rosebank
Nursery
Dalpatrick
LANARK RD

Jock's Burn
Gillbank
Milton-Lockhart Farm
River Clyde
Sandilandgate

49

Refuse Tip

West High Overton

Overton Farm

3

North Netherburn

Works

ML9

ML8

Sandyholm

Glenharvie

Braeholm

48

Hill Cottages

PH

Overton Rd
HOLY COMB
FIVE WAYS RD
PO

Lockhart's Knowe

HILL RD

South Netherburn Farm
BROOMFIELD RD
Bellhaven
CROSSING LA
ELLIOT PL
STATION RD

Netherburn
ANNABELLA RD
Broomfield St
High Overton St
CRAIGNETHAN CRES

A72

2

Threepwood Moss
STATION CT
Netherburn Prim Sch

1

Dalserf Burn
DRAFFAN RD

Draffanmuir

ML11

Nethan Craigs
Craignethan Burn
River Nethan

P
Craignethan Castle
CORRA MILL RD

1
46

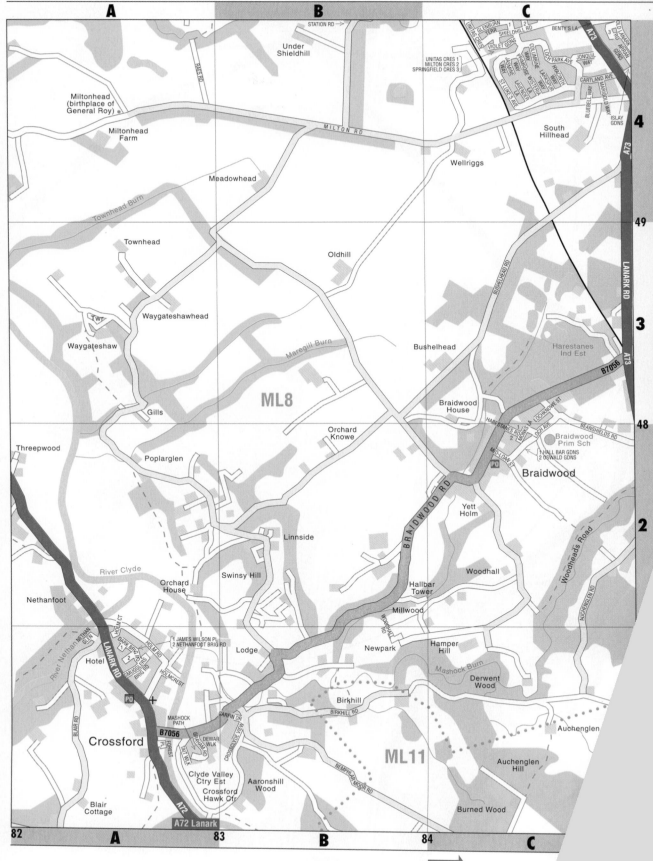

201
188

A

B

C

Crawforddyke Prim Sch

GLENCOE RD
ELMBANK ST
LANKSFIELD DR
EASTFIELD RD
OLD LANARK RD
CALDWELL RD
GLENORCHAD RD
RAMAGE RD
CAM UK
KIRK
FOREST
KYRK
HIGH MEADOW
NORTHFLAT PL
ROY WAY

A721

B7056

YIELDSHIELDS RD

Burnhead

WILTON RD
KIMBERLY RD
MAVIN LOAN
LEEMUIR VIEW

Cemy
Roadmeetings

HILLHOUSE GATE
HAYWARD AVE
HAYWARD CT

HAYWARD
HAYWARD

Burnhead
Bridge

Coldstream
Reservoir

West
Coldstream

ELDERSLEA RD
CARRADALE
SKIPNESS AVE
BARMORE AVE

SAMSON CRES
BUCHANAN DR
CUMMING AVE
SAMSON LA

7 CAMERON RD
8 BRAEHEAD LOAN
9 CHARLES CRES

FORRESTLEA RD
CARNOCH GDNS
GOREMIRE RD

Carluke

4

MAYFIELD GDNS

A73

1 SAUCHIESMOOR RD
2 THORNLEA ST
3 BEECHFIELD DR
4 ISLAY GDNS
5 JURA GDNS
6 GIGHA GDNS

Headsmuir

KILNCADZOW RD

Gowanside

Langshaw

BOGHALL RD

Gateside

A721

49

Fiddler Burn

Nursery

Leemuir

3

PH

B7056

Lee
Meadow

ML8

Nellfield
House

48

A73

OLD LANARK RD

Crossgates

Cartland Muir
Plantation

Crossgates
Plantation

MEADOW RD

2

AUCHENGLEN RD

Nursery

Lee Burn

Craigen Hill

March
Bridge

47

West Wood

Leewood
House

LANARK RD

Mast

MOOR RD

ML11

1

The Lee

New Greentowers
Farm

OLD LANARK RD

Castlehill

46

Brocklinn
Glen

Brocklinn Burn

A73

Brocklinn
Bridge

Cartland

CARTLAND RD
GREENTOWERS RD

86

B

87

C

201
214

East Coldstream

Callagreen

Craighead

Gowanside

Candymill Burn

Hill Rigg
• Mast

KILNCADZOW RD

• Mast

Greenbank Farm

Back Burn

Westtown

Midtown
Kilncadzow

CARNWATH RD

Hill of Kilncadzow

CRAIGENHILL RD

ML8

ML11

Hole

Muirhead

Drums

A721

A721 Carstairs

Colielaw Cottage

Collielaw

Tinto View

Birkenhead

Fullwood

MOOR RD

WHITELEES RD

Wellh

Fullwood Burn

Cleghorn

4

49

3

48

2

A

B

C

4

45

3

44

2

1

Glenhead

Kirkland

South
Inch

KA23

P

P

P

Gourock Burn

KA22

Glenfoot
House Hotel

Boydston
Braes

Scart
Rock

Boydston
Shore

A78

North
Islet

East
Islet

Broad
Rock

Horse
Isle
(Nature Reserve)

Camp
Wood

1

46

20

B

21

C

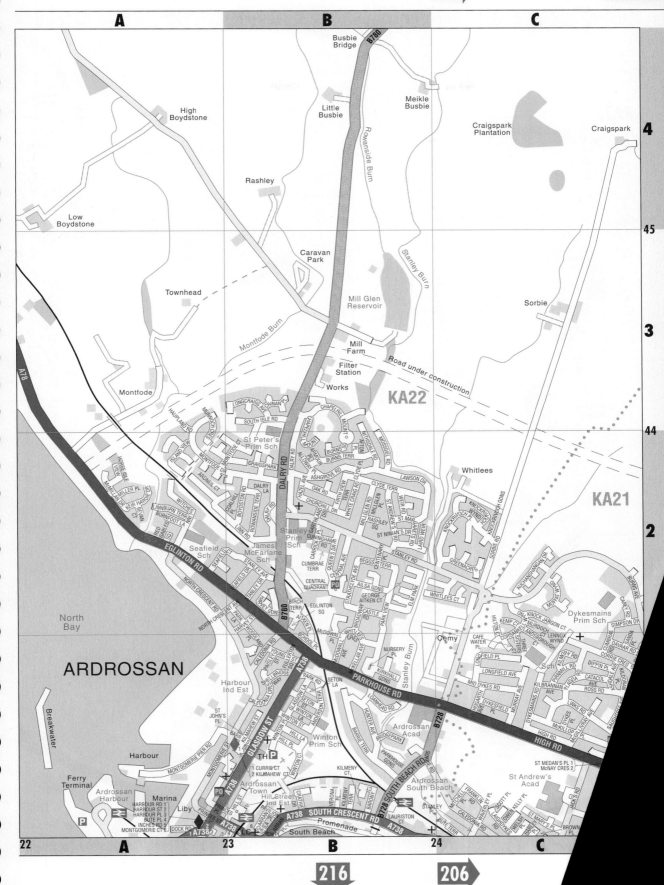

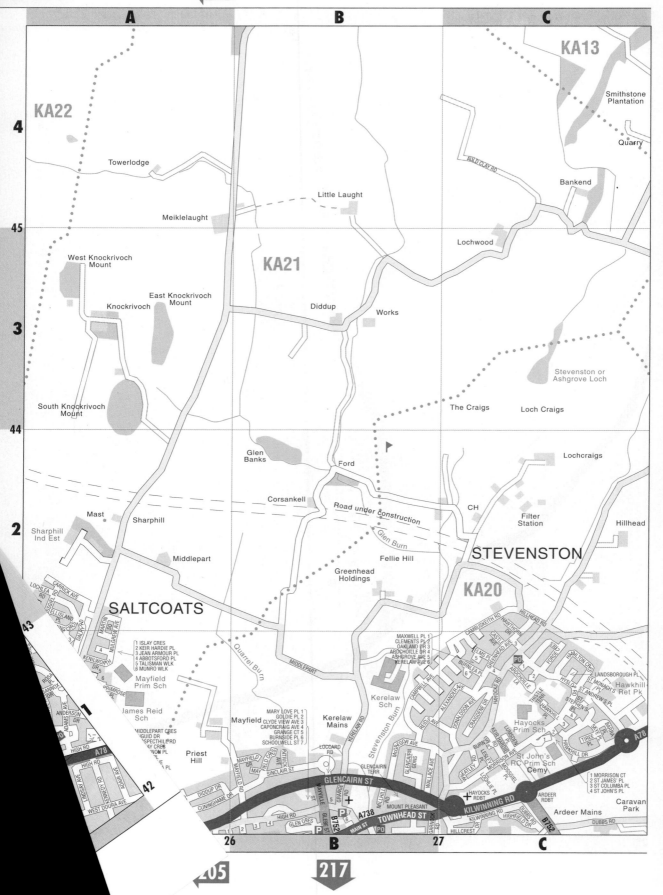

205

A

B

C

KA13

Smithstone
Plantation

4

KA22

Quarry

Towerlodge

AULD CLAY RD

Bankend

Little Laught

Meiklelaught

Lochwood

45

West Knockrivoch
Mount

KA21

East Knockrivoch
Mount

Knockrivoch

Diddup

Works

3

Stevenston or
Ashgrove Loch

South Knockrivoch
Mount

The Craigs

Loch Craigs

44

Lochcraigs

Glen
Banks

Ford

Corsankell

Road under construction

CH

Filter
Station

Hillhead

Mast

Sharphill

Glen Burn

2

Sharphill
Ind Est

Middlepart

Fellie Hill

STEVENSTON

Greenhead
Holdings

KA20

CARRICK AVE

SALTCOATS

LOCHLEA
RD

DALRY RD

ELLISLAND DR

KINGS

MARTIN SQ

MILLGREW AVE

MAXWELL PL 1
CLEMENTS PL 2
OAKALND DR 3
ARDCHOILLE DR 4
ASHGROVE AVE 5
KERELAW AVE 6

CAMBUSKEITH RD

HAWTHORN

HILLHEAD RD

43

1 ISLAY CRES
2 KEIR HARDIE PL
3 JEAN ARMOUR PL
4 ABBOTSFORD PL
5 TALISMAN WLK
6 MUNRO WLK

KENILWORTH
DR

Quarrel Burn

MIDDLEPART

BURNLEA PL

ELMS PL

GREENHEAD RD

CASTLE

AVE

LANDSBOROUGH PL

Hawkhill
Ret Pk

Mayfield
Prim Sch

PRIMROSE
PL

James Reid
Sch

Kerelaw
Sch

CAMPBELL AVE

ALEXANDER AVE

ARDCHOILLE
LA

HYSLOP

ST MONACH'S

Hayocks
Prim Sch

ST ANDREW'S PL

MIDDLEPART CRES
GUID DR
SPECTHILL RD
AY CRES
NON PL
PL

MARY LOVE PL 1
GOLDIE PL 2
CLYDE VIEW AVE 3
CAPONCRAIG AVE 4
GRANGE CT 5
BURNSIDE PL 6
SCHOOLWELL ST 7

Mayfield

Kerelaw
Mains

KERELAW RD

REID AVE

DONALDSON AVE

CRAIGDENE DR

MCGREGOR AVE

KEATLEY

BURN

STEPHEN ST

TIREE

BERN

ANDERSON
DR

RIGG

LANNOX

ADAMS DR

HIGH RD

1

Priest
Hill

MAYFIELD
CRES

GAY

KELLY AVE

PATRICK ST

SINCLAIR ST

LOCCARD
RD

GLENCAIRN
TERR

Stevenston Burn

WALLACE AVE

GLENCAIRN GDNS

LESLIE

LOCHWE PL

St John's
RC Prim Sch
Cemy

1 MORRISON CT
2 ST JAMES' PL
3 ST COLUMBA PL
4 ST JOHN'S PL

Caravan
Park

HIGH RD

LINDSAY RD

KENNEDY RD

ADAIR AVE

WEST DOURA AVE

GLENCAIRN ST

DIDDUP DR

CUNINGHAME RD

MAYFIELD RD

GRANGE

GLEN CRES

HIGH RD

GLEBE ST

MAIN ST

MOUNT PLEASANT

MILLHILL

P

TOWNHEAD ST

A738

HAYOCKS
RDBT

KILWINNING RD

KILWINNING RD

HIGHFIELD DR

ARDEER
RDBT

Ardeer Mains

A78

DUBBS RD

42

Priest
Hill

P

B752

PO

HILLCREST

GARNOCK
RD

B752

A78

26

B

27

C

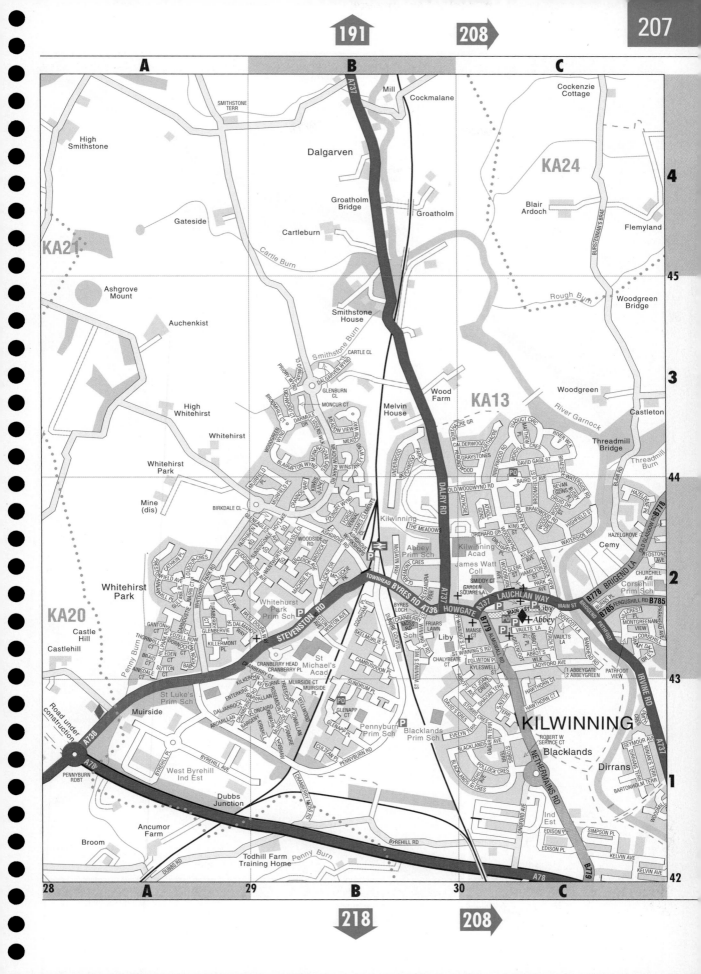

207
192

A   **B**   **C**

Barneyhill
Plantation

KA24

Rough Burn

4

Laigh
Gooseloan

Lylestone
Farm

Monkredding
House

LYLESTONE
TERR

Clonbeith
Castle
(remains of)

Lylestone
Cottage

Sevenacres
Wood

B778

Outer
Ardoch

Monkreddan
Kennels

45

Threadmill Burn

Hullerhill

Ardoch

Crofthead

Sevenacres
Mains

Bannoch Burn

Sevenacres
Mill

3

Bannoch

KA13

High Moncur

Burrowland

44

B778

Redston

Bannoch
Bridge

Nursery

Corsehillmuir
Plantation

Mid Moncur

Windyhall

HAZELGROVE AVE
REDSTONE AVE
CHURCHILL AVE
McGAVIN AVE
KEIR HARDIE
BANNOCH GDNS
BANNOCH PL
BANNOCH PL
BANNOCH RD
Sch
FIVE ROADS

Broomhill

North
Fergushill

Lugton Water

2

B785 FERGUSHILL RD

MONTGOMERIE TERR
QUEEN'S PL
LOVE ST
QUEEN ST
MONCUR RD
HUNTER PL
CORSEHILL
WEIRSTON RD

South
Fergushill

PARKHEAD AVE

Eglinton
Kennels

43

+

Benslie
Fauld

BANNOCH RD

Eglinton
Country Park

Benslie Wood

Chapelholms
Wood

North
Millburn

The
Millburn
(PH)

Weirston

1

Ladyha' Park

KA12

Eglinton
Castle
(remains of)

B785

AT37
WOODMILL
IRVINE RD

Kilwinning
Gates

KA11

Auchenwinsey

1 KELVIN AVE
2 WATERCUT RD

Millburn
Lodge

42

AT37

Factory

31   **A**   **32**   **B**   **33**   **C**

207
219

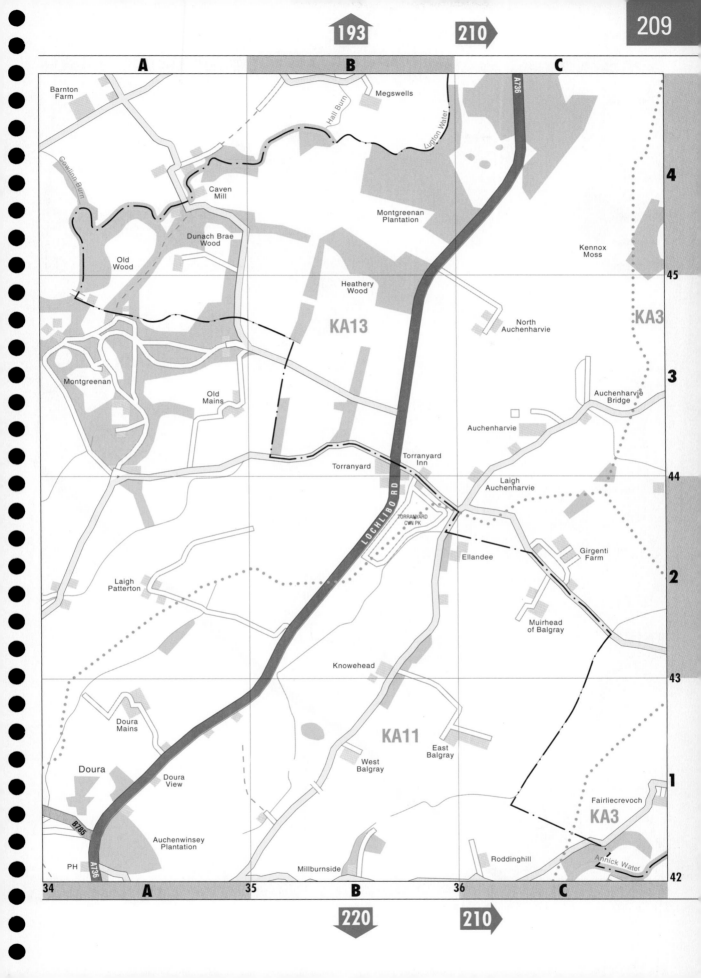

A
B
C

Barnton
Farm

Megswells

Hall Burn

A736

Cowlian Burn

Caven
Mill

Montgreenan
Plantation

4

Dunach Brae
Wood

Kennox
Moss

Old
Wood

45

Heathery
Wood

KA13

North
Auchenharvie

KA3

Montgreenan

Old
Mains

Auchenharvie
Bridge

3

Auchenharvie

Torranyard
Inn

Torranyard

Laigh
Auchenharvie

44

LOCHLIBO RD

TORRANYARD
CVN PK

Ellandee

Girgenti
Farm

Laigh
Patterton

Muirhead
of Balgray

2

Knowehead

43

Doura
Mains

KA11

Doura

West
Balgray

East
Balgray

1

Doura
View

Fairliecrevoch

KA3

B785

Auchenwinsey
Plantation

Roddinghill

Annick Water

A736

PH

Millburnside

42

34
A
35
B
36
C

← 209
194 ↑

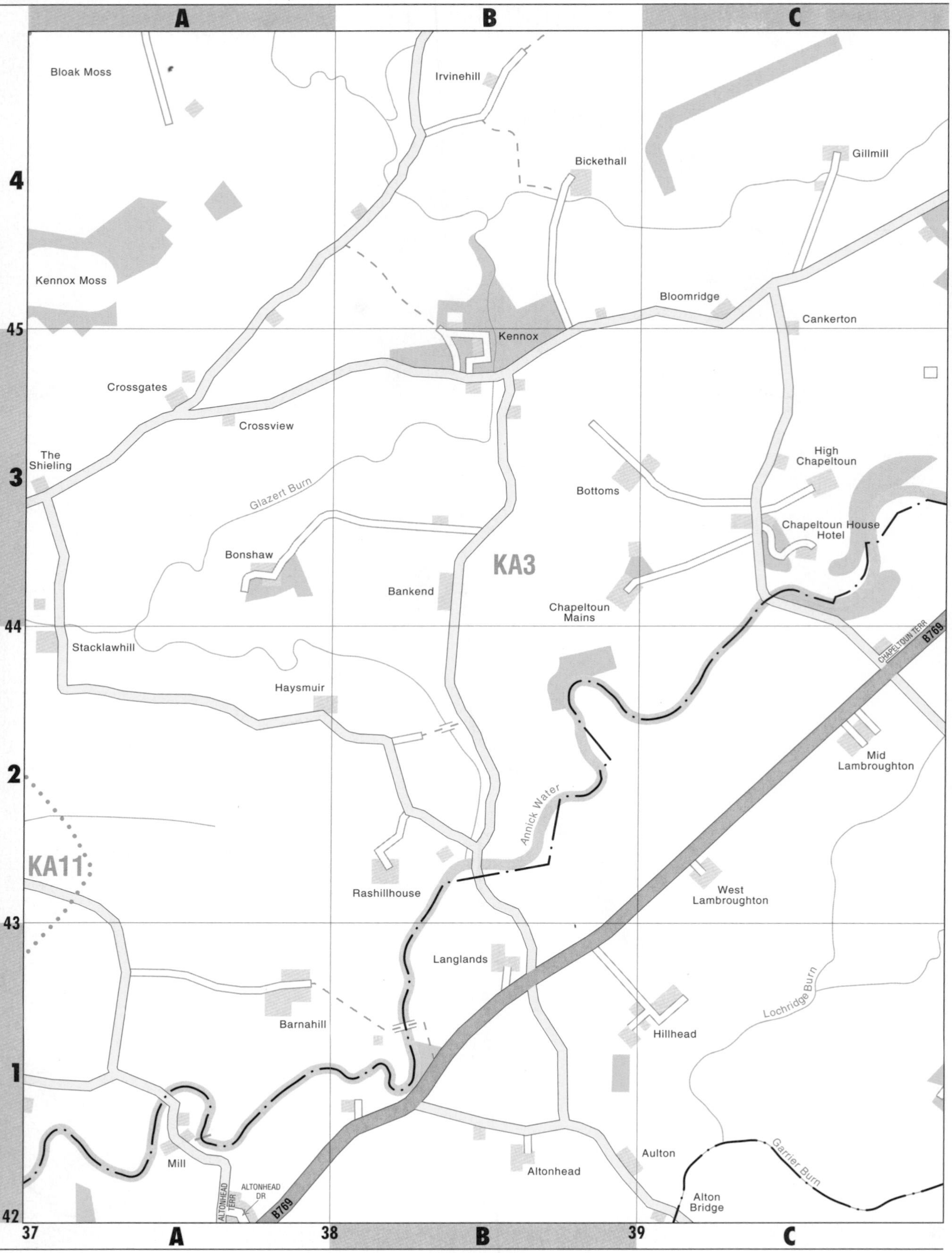

A   **B**   **C**

Bloak Moss

Irvinehill

Bickethall

Gillmill

4

Kennox Moss

Bloomridge

Cankerton

45

Crossgates

Crossview

High
Chapeltoun

The
Shieling

Glazert Burn

Bottoms

Chapeltoun House
Hotel

3

Bonshaw

KA3

Bankend

Chapeltoun
Mains

CHAPELTOUN TERR

B769

44

Stacklawhill

Mid
Lambroughton

Haysmuir

2

Annick Water

KA11

West
Lambroughton

Rashillhouse

43

Langlands

Lochridge Burn

Barnahill

Hillhead

1

Aulton

Garrier Burn

Mill

ALTONHEAD TERR

ALTONHEAD
DR

B769

Altonhead

Alton
Bridge

42

37   **A**   **38**   **B**   **39**   **C**

← 209
221 ↓

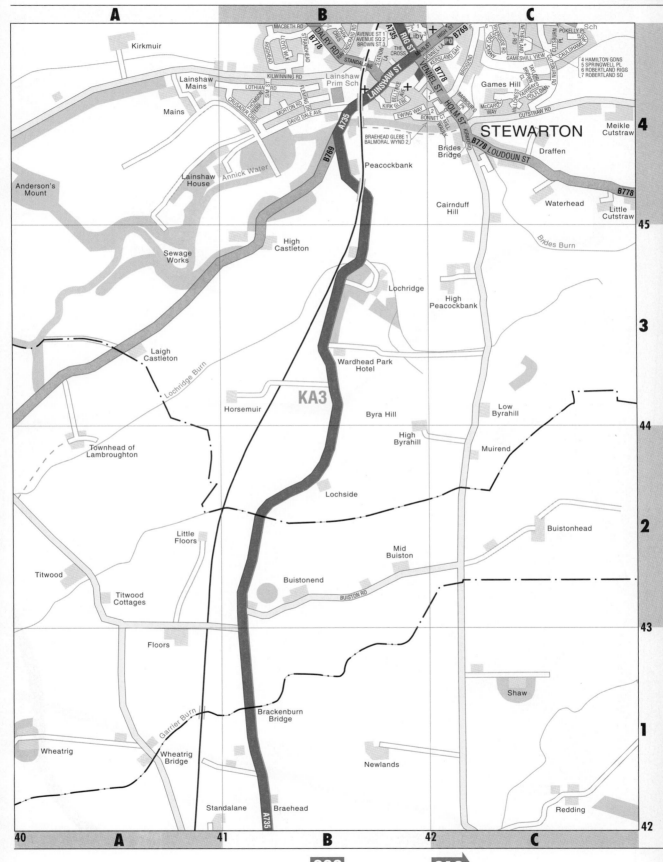

Kirkmuir

MACBETH RD
DALRY RD
B778
Lainshaw Mains
KILWINNING RD
Lainshaw Prim Sch
Mains
MORTON ST
CRUSADER CRES
LOTHIAN
DAVID DALE AVE
FLEMING DR
LLOYD WK
RIGGHEAD
STRANDHEAD
PARK
RENNIE STG RD
AVENUE ST 1
AVENUE SQ 2
BROWN ST 3
STANDALANE
STATION
A735
THE CROSS
MAIN ST
HIGH ST
VENNEL LA
KERSLAND GATT
LAINSHAW ST
BELLTREE
KIRK GLEBE
EWING WAY
BONNET
VENNEL ST
HOLM ST
BRIDGEND
B778
PO
HIGH ST
B769

Sch
POKELLY PL
NETHERLAND
ANNICK CRESCENT RD
RIVERSIDE RD
GAMESHILL VIEW
CUTSBURN RD
CAULDHAME
NUMBER 1 ST
4 HAMILTON GDNS
5 SPRINGWELL PL
6 ROBERTLAND RIGG
7 ROBERTLAND SQ

Games Hill

STEWARTON

Meikle Cutstraw

4

Anderson's Mount

Lainshaw House

Annick Water

A735
B769

Peacockbank

Brides Bridge

BARBIEUR
McCAROL WAY
FAIRWAYS BRAEHEAD
COLEDOAM
CUTSTRAW RD

B778 LOUDOUN ST

Draffen

Waterhead

B778

Little Cutstraw

Sewage Works

High Castleton

Cairnduff Hill

Brides Burn

45

Laigh Castleton

Lochridge Burn

Lochridge

High Peacockbank

3

Horsemuir

KA3

Wardhead Park Hotel

Byra Hill

Low Byrahill

44

Townhead of Lambroughton

High Byrahill

Muirend

Lochside

Little Floors

Mid Buiston

Buistonhead

2

Titwood

Buistonend

BUISTON RD

Titwood Cottages

43

Floors

Shaw

Garrier Burn

Brackenburn Bridge

1

Wheatrig

Wheatrig Bridge

Newlands

Redding

Standalane   A735   Braehead

42

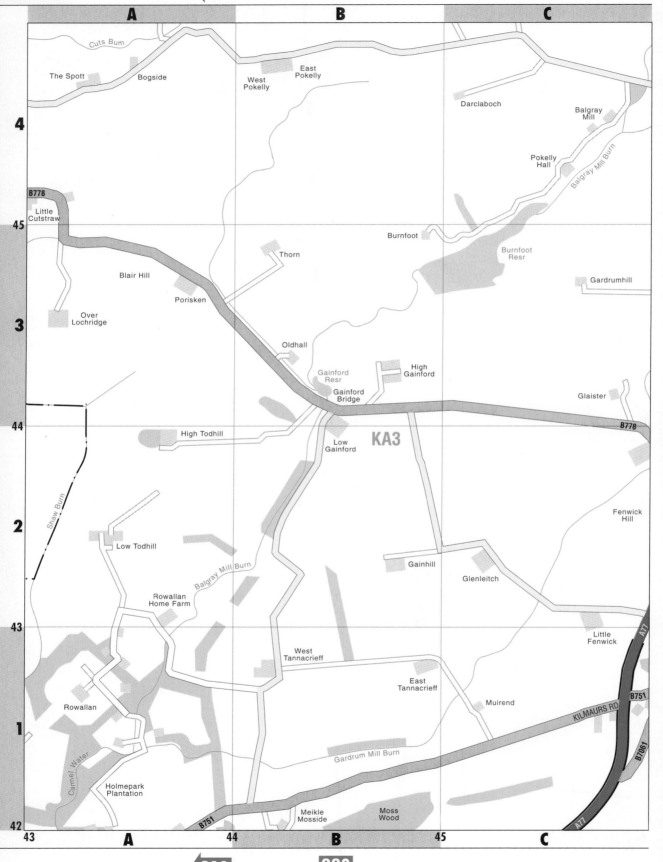

A   B   C

Cuts Burn

The Spott   Bogside   West Pokelly   East Pokelly   Darclaboch   Balgray Mill

4

Pokelly Hall   Balgray Mill Burn

B778

Little Cutstraw   Burnfoot   Burnfoot Resr

45

Thorn   Gardrumhill

Blair Hill

Porisken

Over Lochridge   3

Oldhall

Gainford Resr   High Gainford   Glaister

Gainford Bridge

44   High Todhill   Low Gainford   KA3   B778

Shaw Burn

Fenwick Hill

2   Low Todhill   Gainhill   Glenleitch

Balgray Mill Burn

Rowallan Home Farm

43   Little Fenwick

West Tannacrieff

East Tannacrieff   Muirend   A77

B751

Rowallan   KILMAURS RD   B7061

1

Camel Water   Gardrum Mill Burn

Holmepark Plantation

42   Meikle Mosside   Moss Wood   A77

43   A   44   B   45   C

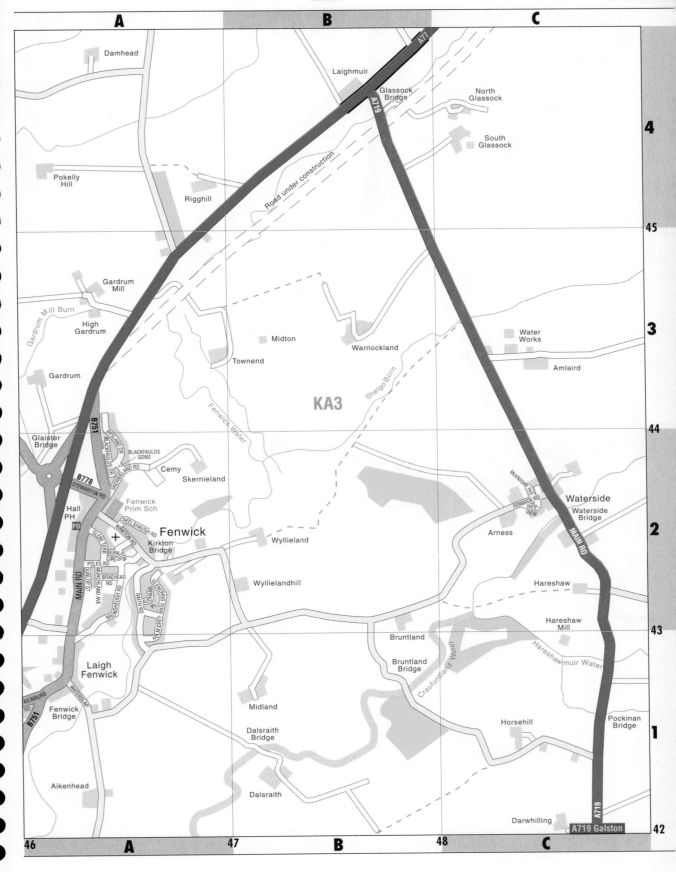

A   B   C

Damhead

Laighmuir

A77

Glassock
Bridge

North
Glassock

A719

South
Glassock

4

Pokelly
Hill

Rigghill

Road under construction

45

Gardrum
Mill Burn

Gardrum
Mill

High
Gardrum

Midton

Townend

Warnockland

Water
Works

3

Shelgo Burn

Amlaird

Gardrum

Fenwick Water

KA3

B751

Glaister
Bridge

BYELAND DR
BLACKFAULDS DR
SKERNIELAND RD

BLACKFAULDS
GDNS

Cemy

Skernieland

44

B778

STEWARTON RD

Fenwick
Prim Sch

McKNIGHT AVE
FENWICK RD
WEST
VIEW

Waterside

Waterside
Bridge

Hall
PH
PO

CREELSHAUGH RD

KIRKTON RD

Fenwick

Kirkton
Bridge

Wyllieland

Arness

2

GLEBE TERR

KIRKTON
PL

MAIN RD

POLES RD
MURCHLAND AVE
DUNLOP ST

BRAEHEAD
RD

MARSHLEIGH RD

GLENCRANG TERR

RAITH RD

HELM CRES

Wyllielandhill

Hareshaw

MAIN RD

Laigh
Fenwick

WATERSLAP

Bruntland

Bruntland
Bridge

Craufurdland Water

Hareshaw
Mill

Hareshaw muir Water

43

KILMAURS RD

B751

Fenwick
Bridge

Midland

Horsehill

Pockinan
Bridge

1

Dalsraith
Bridge

Aikenhead

Dalsraith

A719

Darwhilling

A719 Galston

42

46   A   47   B   48   C

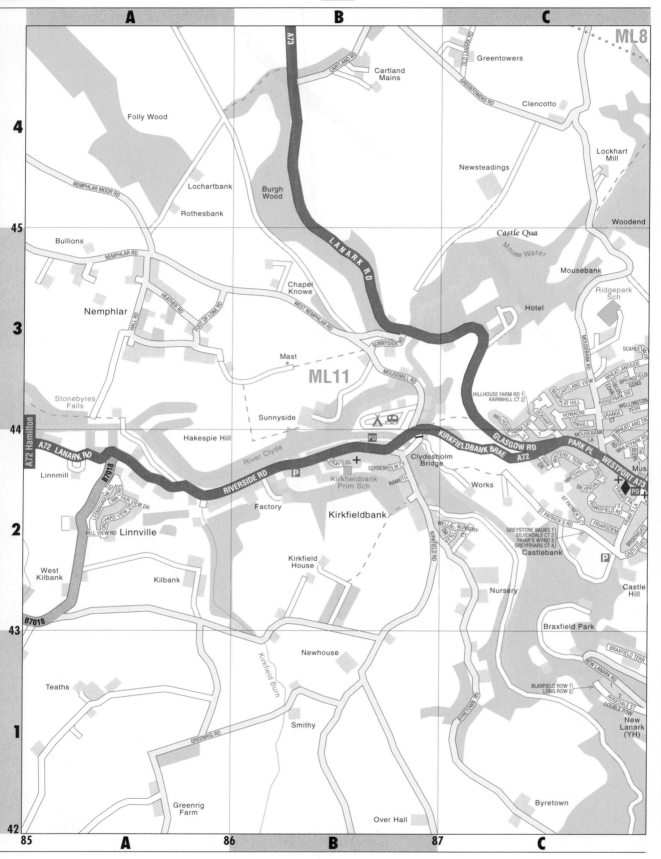

202

ML8

ML11

A **B** **C**

4

45

3

44

2

43

1

42

85   **A**   86   **B**   87   **C**

Greentowers
Old Lanark Rd
Greentowers Rd
Clencotto
Cartland
Mains
Cartland Rd
Newsteadings
Lockhart
Mill
Woodend
Folly Wood
Burgh
Wood
Castle Qua
Mouse Water
Nemphlar Moor Rd
Lochartbank
Mousebank
Rothesbank
Ridgepark
Sch
Bullions
Nemphlar Rd
Chapel
Knowe
West Nemphlar Rd
Hotel
Mousebank Rd
Heather Rd
Foot of Loan Rd
Wall Rd
Nemphlar
Sunnyside Rd
Scarletmuir
Wheatlandside
Springfield
Gdns
Cartland View
Westfields
Loan
Ridgepark Dr
Wellington
Terr
Grange
Ct
Wheatland Dr
Mast
Mousemill Rd
Hillhouse Farm Rd 1
Kairnhill Ct 2
Howacre
Kirkhill
Flat Hill
Mansewood
Wheatpark Pl
The
Glebe
Stonebyres
Falls
Sunnyside
Hillhouse Farm Ditt
Lockhart Rd
Glasgow Rd
Park Pl
Westport A73
Mus
A72 Hamilton
Hakespie Hill
Kirkfieldbank Brae
A72
Whitehill Terr
Park Dr
A72 Lanark Rd
River Clyde
Clydesholm
Bridge
Whitehill Cres
Friars Pk
PO
B7018
Linnmill
Riverside Rd
Gray's Cl
Clydesholm Ct
Ramoth
Works
Silverdale Ct
Friarsfield Rd
St Patrick's Rd
St Patrick's Rd
Friarsdene
Kirkfieldbank
Prim Sch
Factory
Kirkfieldbank
Castlegate
Linn Cres
Linn Fair View Dr
Orchard View Dr
Greystone Bauks 1
Silverdale Ct 2
Friar's Wynd 3
Greyfriars Ct 4
Broomgate
Hill View Rd
Linnville
Kirkfield
House
Wellbill
Nursery
Ct
Castlebank
West
Kilbank
Kilbank
Kirkfield Rd
Nursery
Castle
Hill
B7018
Braxfield Park
Braxfield Terr
Teaths
Newhouse
Kirkfield Burn
New Lanark Rd
Blaxfield Row 1
Long Row 2
Rosedale St
Double Row
Byretown Rd
Greenrig Rd
Smithy
New
Lanark
(YH)
Greenrig
Farm
Over Hall
Byretown

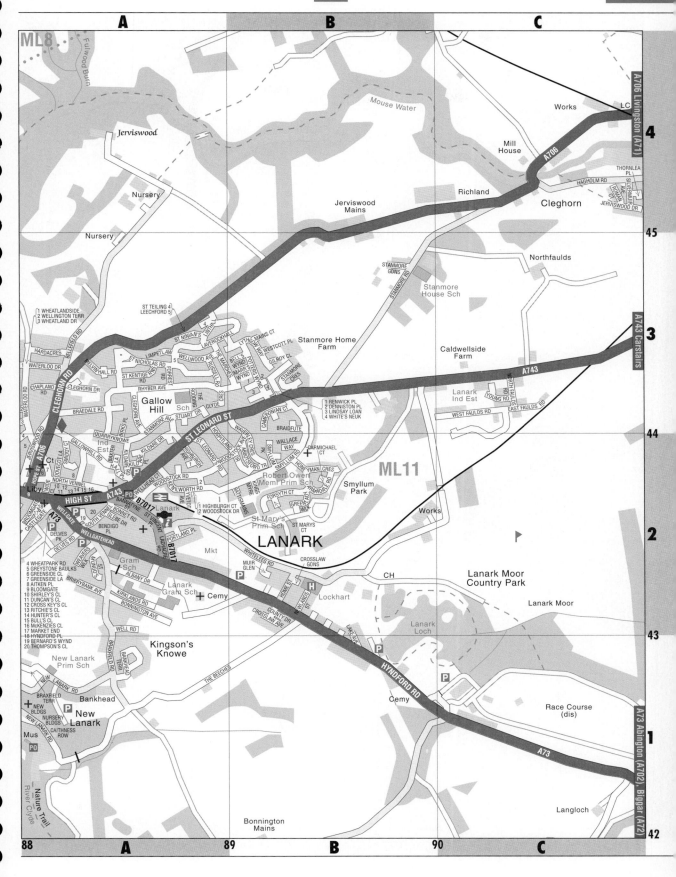

ML8

Fullwood Burn

Jerviswood

Mouse Water

Works

LC

A706 Livingston (A71)

Mill House

4

Nursery

Jerviswood Mains

Richland

THORNLEA PL
HAGHOLM RD
SILVERMUIR AVE
IRONMAN CT
JERVISWOOD DR

Cleghorn

Nursery

A706

45

STANMORE GDNS
STANMORE RD

Northfaulds

1 WHEATLANDSIDE
2 WELLINGTON TERR
3 WHEATLAND DR

ST TEILING 4
LEECHFORD 5

Stanmore House Sch

Caldwellside Farm

A743 Carstairs

3

HARDACRES
BELLEFIELD RD
WATERLOO DR
CLEGHORN RD
CHAPLAND RD
WATERLOO RD
KELVIN HALL RD
ST NICHOLAS RD
ST KENTIGERN RD
RHYBER AVE
LIMPETLAW
FORRES
WELLWOOD AVE
RUSSELL RD
THE HARDIES
LINTHU
LYTH MAINS CT
WESTCOTT PL
POTTERS WYND
GILROY CL
STANMORE CRES

Stanmore Home Farm

A743

Lanark Ind Est

NORTH FAULDS RD
YOUNG RD

BRAEDALE RD
CLEGHORN AVE
BIRKS PL
STUART DR
THE CLYDE

Gallow Hill

Sch

1 RENWICK PL
2 DENNISTON PL
3 LINDSAY LOAN
4 WHITE'S NEUK

WEST FAULDS RD

EAST FAULDS RD

44

QUARRYKNOWE
Ind Est
GALLOWHILL RD
SMIDDY CT
KILDARE DR
HALL RD
KILDARE RD
STANMORE AVE
HOSPITLAND
WOODSTOCK RD
LEONARD
HIGHBURGH
WAVERLEY CRES
ABBOTSFORD RD
SMYLLUM
CAMERONIAN CT

WALLACE WAY

CARMICHAEL CT

ML11

Caldwellside

ST LEONARD ST

BRAIDFUTE

HONEYMAN CRES

Smyllum Park

Works

A706
Ct
DOVECOTE LA
WIDE
HOPE ST
NORTH VENNEL
11 12 13 14 15 16

Liby

BANNATYNE
BONNET RD
WELLGATE CT
KENILWORTH RD
KINGS
BRITISHMAINS
FORSYTH CT
GREEN WK

Robert Owen Meml Prim Sch

HIGH ST
A743 PO
B7017
Lanark

1 HIGHBURGH CT
2 WOODSTOCK DR

St Mary's Prim Sch
ST MARYS CT

BROOMGATE
CASTLEGATE
WELLGATE
SOUTH VENNEL
BENDIGO
PORTLAND PL
A73
DELVES PK
DELVES RD
WELLGATEHEAD
BLEBE DR
B7017
GLEBE DR
VINCENT ST
LADYACRE RD
BERNARD'S WYND
THOMPSON'S CL

i

LANARK

H

CROSSLAW GDNS

Lanark Moor Country Park

2

4 WHEATPARK RD
5 GREYSTONE BAULKS
6 GREENSIDE CL
7 GREENSIDE LA
8 AITKEN PL
9 BLOOMGATE
10 SHIRLEY'S CL
11 DUNCAN'S CL
12 CROSS KEY'S CL
13 RITCHIE'S CL
14 HUNTER'S CL
15 BULL'S CL
16 McKENZIES CL
17 MARKET END
18 HYNDFORD PL
19 BERNARD'S WYND
20 THOMPSON'S CL

BRIERYBANK AVE
ST MUNGOS
WEAVERS WK
ALBANY DR
Gram Sch
KIRKLANDS RD
BONNINGTON AVE

Lanark Gram Sch
Cemy

Mkt

MUIR GLEN
WHITELEES RD
HOME ST
NEWLANDS ST
COUNTY DR
LANE AVE
CROSSLAW AVE

Lockhart

CH

Lanark Moor

Lanark Loch

43

BRAXFIELD RD
BANKHEAD TERR

Kingson's Knowe

THE BEECHES

New Lanark Prim Sch

HYNDFORD RD

P

Cemy

P

Race Course (dis)

1

NEW LANARK RD
BRAXFIELD TERR
NEW BLDGS
NURSERY BLDGS
CAITHNESS ROW

Bankhead

New Lanark

A73

Mus

PO

Nature Trail

River Clyde

Langloch

Bonnington Mains

42

88   A   89   B   90   C

205

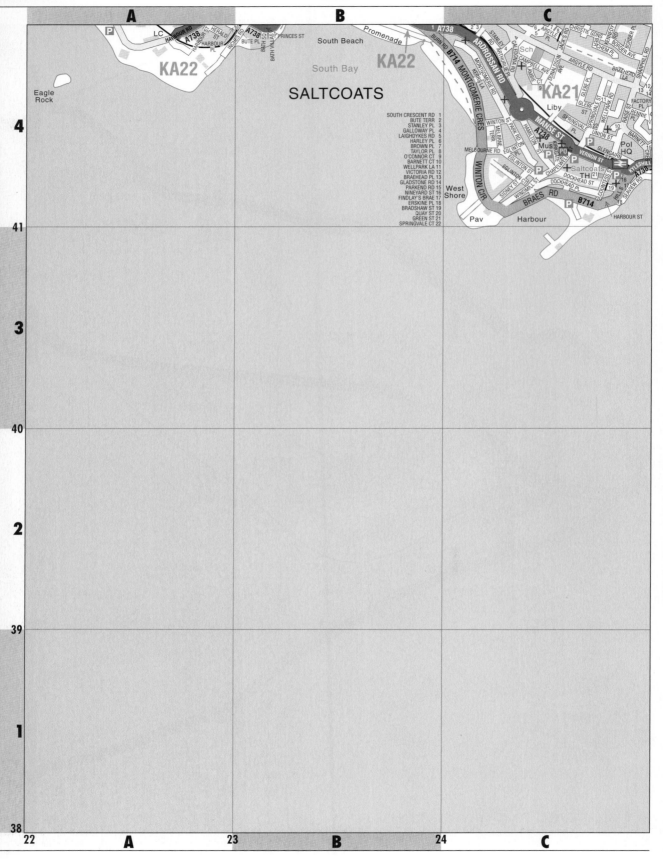

SALTCOATS

SOUTH CRESCENT RD 1
BUTE TERR 2
STANLEY PL 3
GALLOWAY PL 4
LAIGHDYKES RD 5
HARLEY PL 6
BROWN PL 7
TAYLOR PL 8
O'CONNOR CT 9
BARNETT CT 10
WELLPARK LA 11
VICTORIA RD 12
BRAEHEAD PL 13
GLADSTONE RD 14
PARKEND RD 15
NINEYARD ST 16
FINDLAY'S BRAE 17
ERSKINE PL 18
BRADSHAW ST 19
QUAY ST 20
GREEN ST 21
SPRINGVALE CT 22

DUBBS RD

Penny Burn

BYREHILL RD

A78

B779

Nethermains
Bridge

WATERCUT RD

Garnock Floods
Nature Reserve

KA13

Refuse
Tip

B779

4

41

KA20

GARNOCK RD

WEST RD

MISK RD

POWER PLANT RD

POWER PLANT RD

NORTH RING RD

CENTRAL AVE

SOUVENIRS RD

River Garnock

CH

3

P

P

Works

BURMA RD

ACIDS RD

SOUTH RING RD

WORKSHOP RD

WORKSHOP RD

Stevenston
Site

KA12

Bogside

40

PROPULSION RD

NEW HILL RD

Bogside
Race Course
(disused)

Crooky's
Point

River Irvine

2

WHARF RD

Bogside
Flats

39

1

The Big Idea
(Inventor Ctr)

Irvine
Harbour

River Irvine

HARBOUR ST

Arts
Ctr

P

BEACH DR

Magnum
L Ctr

38

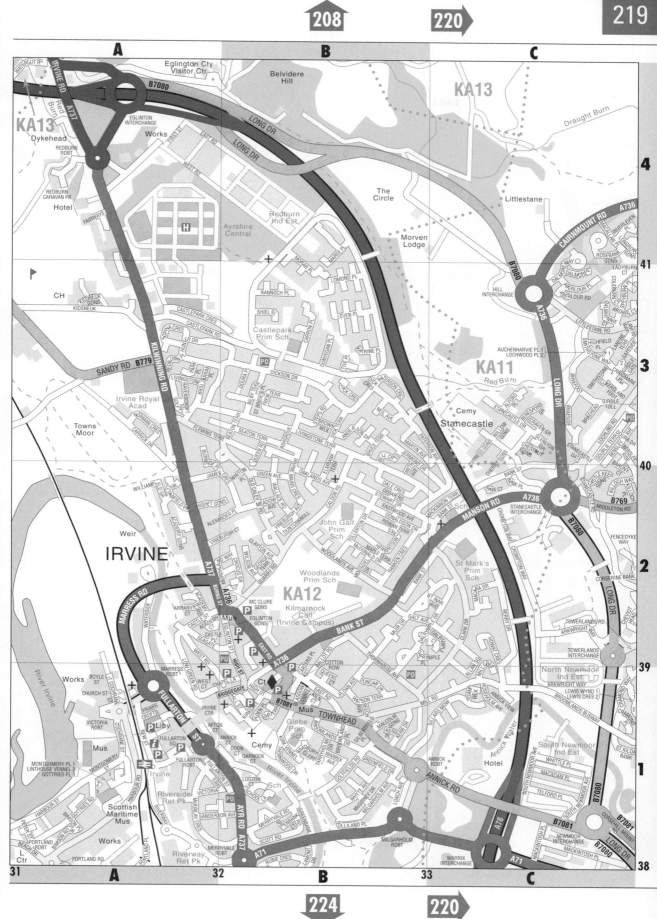

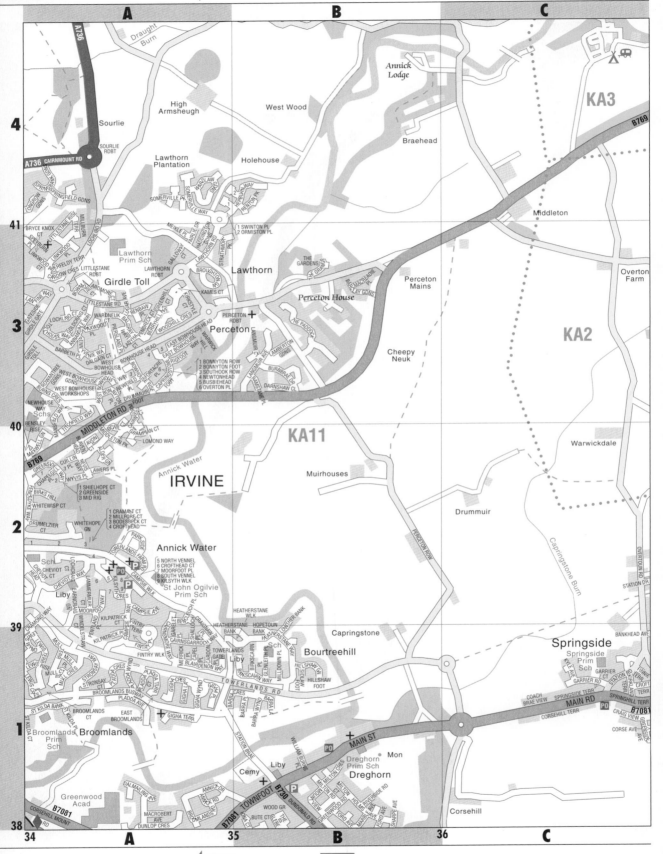

219 209

Map labels

A736 Draught Burn Sourlie High Armsheugh West Wood Annick Lodge KA3 B769 Braehead Cairnmount Rd A736 Lawthorn Plantation Holehouse Middleton Overton Farm 41 Bryce Knox Ct Lawthorn Prim Sch 1 Swinton Pl 2 Ormiston Pl The Gardens Perceton Mains Girdle Toll Lawthorn Perceton House Cheepy Neuk KA2 3 Perceton Rdbt Perceton 1 Bonnyton Row 2 Bonnyton Foot 3 Southook Row 4 Newtonhead 5 Busbiehead 6 Overton Pl West Bowhouse Workshops 40 Middleton Rd KA11 Warwickdale B769 Muirhouses Drummuir IRVINE Annick Water 2 1 Shielhope Ct 2 Greenside 3 Mid Rig 1 Cramat Ct 2 Millfore Ct 3 Bodesbeck Ct 4 Crofthead Capringstone Burn Station Dr Annick Water 5 North Vennel 6 Crofthead Ct 7 Moorfoot Pl 8 South Vennel 9 Kilsyth Wlk St John Ogilvie Prim Sch Liby Heatherstane Wlk 39 Capringstone Springside Bankhead Ave Kilpatrick Bourtreehill Springside Prim Sch Towerlands Rd Main Rd B7081 Broomlands Broomlands Prim Sch Gigha Terr Main St Mon Corsehill Terr Corse Ave 1 Liby Dreghorn Prim Sch Dreghorn Greenwood Acad B7081 Townfoot B7081 B730 Dundonald Rd Corsehill 38 Corsehill Mount 34 35 36

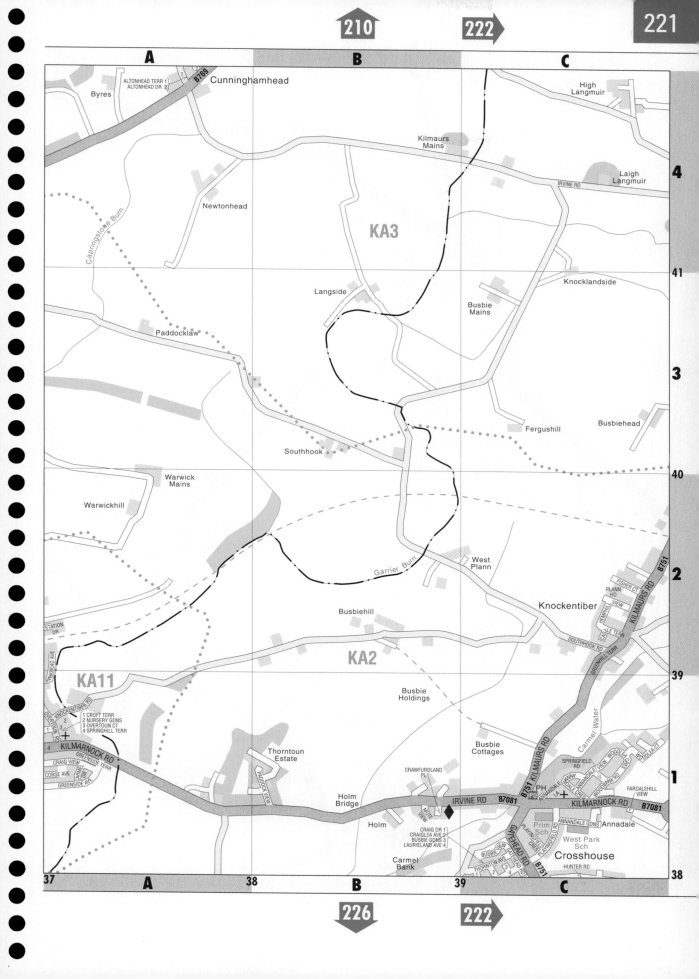

ALTONHEAD TERR 1
ALTONHEAD DR 2
B769
Cunninghamhead
Byres

High Langmuir

Kilmaurs Mains

Newtonhead

Laigh Langmuir

IRVINE RD

4

Capringstone Burn

KA3

Knocklandside

41

Langside

Busbie Mains

Paddocklaw

Fergushill

Busbiehead

3

Southhook

Warwick Mains

40

Warwickhill

Garrier Burn

West Plann

B751

2

PLANN HO

FISHER CT

HEMPHILL VIEW

CASTLE TERR

KILMAURS RD

Busbiehill

Knockentiber

SOUTHHOOK RD

STATION DR

GREENWALL TERR

KNOCKENTIBER RD

KA2

39

BOYDHEAD AVE

OVERTOUN RD

KA11

1 CROFT TERR
2 NURSERY GDNS
3 OVERTOUN CT
4 SPRINGHILL TERR

Busbie Holdings

Carmel Water

KILMAURS RD

GREENSIDE TERR

KILMARNOCK RD

Thorntoun Estate

Busbie Cottages

Springfield RD

CRAWFURDLAND PL

1

CRAIG VIEW
CORSE AVE
GREENSIDE AVE

PADDOCK VIEW

WOODLEA CRES

Fardalehill VIEW

PH

PO

Prim Sch

Annandale

KILMARNOCK RD

B7081

ANNANDALE GDNS

Holm Bridge

Holm

MUTE VIEW

IRVINE RD

B7081

CRAIG DR 1
CRAIGLEA AVE 2
BUSBIE GDNS 3
LAURIELAND AVE 4

West Park Sch

Carmel Bank

GATEHEAD RD

PLAYINGFIELD RD

BUSBIE GREEN

THORNTON AVE

Crosshouse

B751

HUNTER RD

38

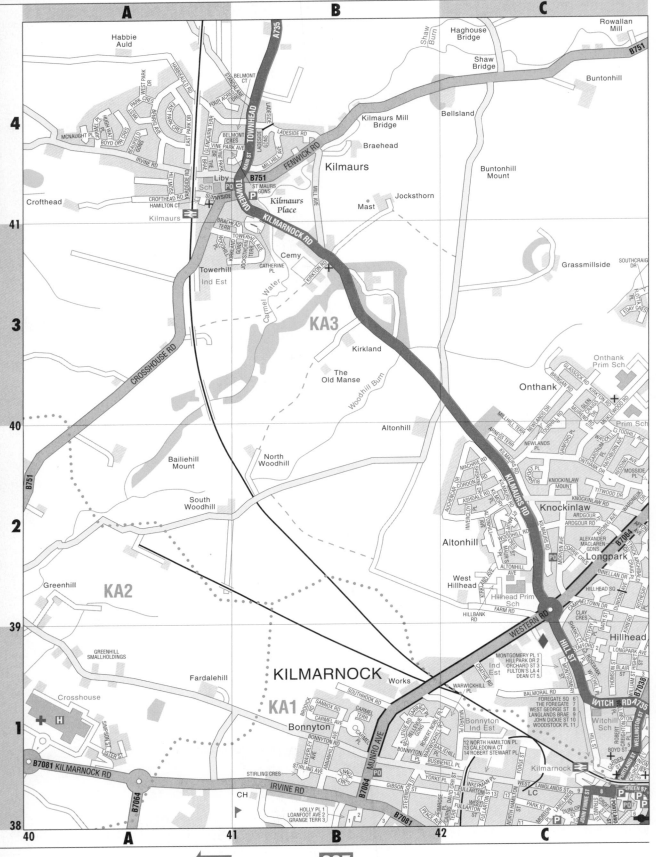

A   B   C

Habbie Auld

Rowallan Mill

B751

Shaw Burn

Haghouse Bridge

Shaw Bridge

Buntonhill

4

McNAUGHT PL

BELMONT CT

FOUR ACRE DR

STANDALANE DR

LADESIDE GDNS

Kilmaurs Mill Bridge

Bellsland

Braehead

Kilmaurs

Buntonhill Mount

41

Crofthead

Kilmaurs Place

Jocksthorn

Mast

Grassmillside

SOUTHCRAIG DR

KA3

Towerhill Ind Est

Cemy

CATHERINE PL

KIRKTON RD

Kirkland

The Old Manse

Onthank Prim Sch

3

CROSSHOUSE RD

Carmel Water

Woodhill Burn

Onthank

Prim Sch

40

Baillehill Mount

North Woodhill

Altonhill

B751

South Woodhill

Knocknilaw Mount

Knocknilaw

2

KA2

Greenhill

Altonhill

KILMAURS RD

West Hillhead

Longpark

B7064

Hillhead Prim Sch

HILLBANK RD

FARM RD

Hillhead

39

Greenhill Smallholdings

WESTERN RD

HILL ST

Fardalehill

KILMARNOCK

Works

Ind Est

WARWICKHILL PL

BALMORAL RD

Crosshouse

H

KA1

Bonnyton

CARMEL TERR

SOUTHHOOK RD

Bonnyton Ind Est

Kilmarnock

1

B7081 KILMARNOCK RD

B7064

MUNRO AVE

IRVINE RD

CH

STIRLING CRES

B7081

38

40   A   41   B   42   C

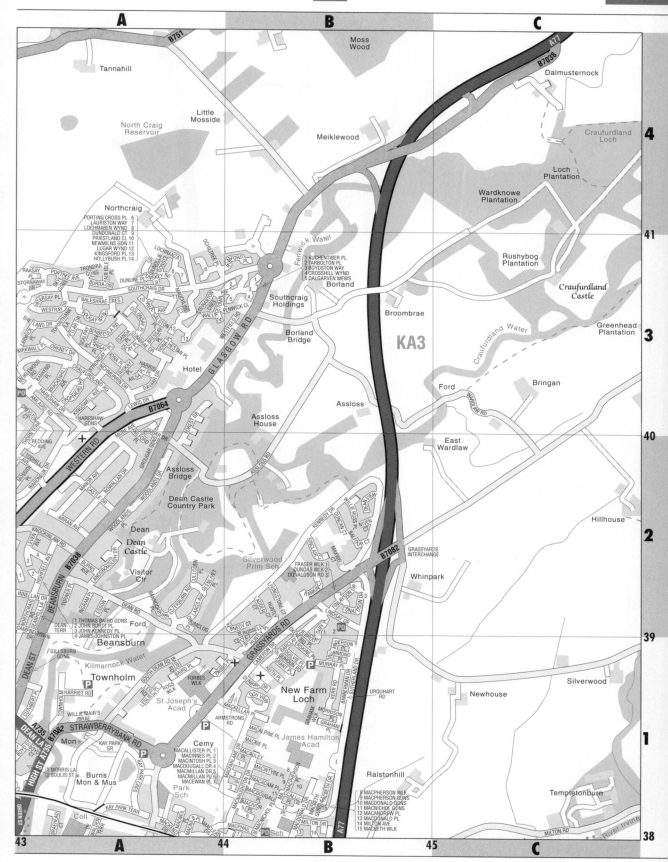

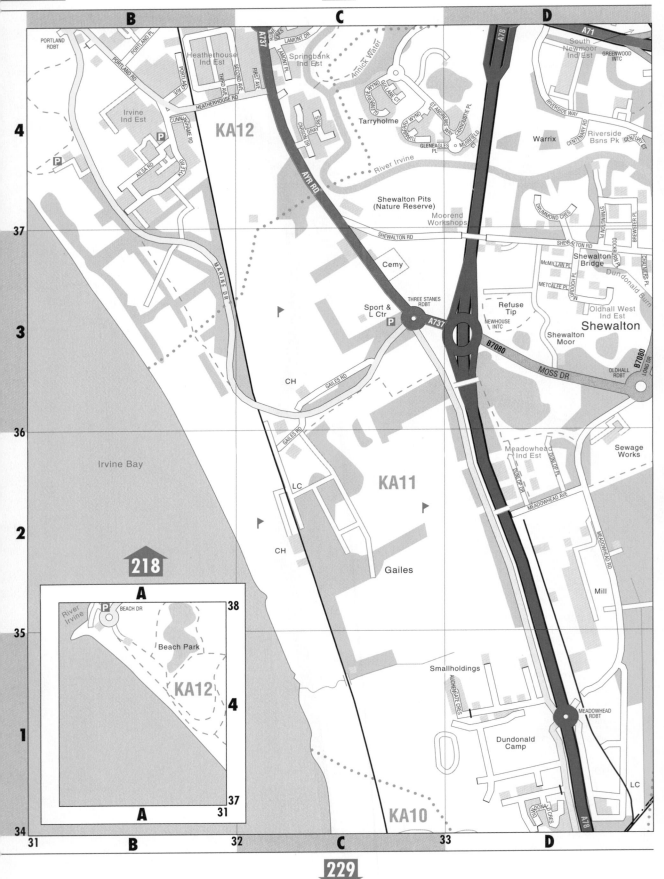

218

Irvine Bay

KA12

Irvine Ind Est

PORTLAND RDBT

PORTLAND RD

PORTLAND AVE

SECOND AVE

THIRD AVE

FIRST AVE

HEATHERHOUSE RD

Heatherhouse Ind Est

AILSA RD

KYLE DR

CUNNINGHAME RD

MARINE DR

AYR RD

Springbank Ind Est

LAMONT DR

LAMONT PL

CARSON DR

GRAY

Tarryholme

Annick Water

River Irvine

TURNBERRY WYND

GILLANE CT

ST ANDREWS WAY

CARNOUSTIE PL

MUIRFIELD

GLENEAGLES PL

A78

A71

South Newmoor Ind Est

GREENWOOD INTC

RIVERSIDE WAY

CENTENARY RD

Riverside Bsns Pk

Warrix

CENTURY RD

CENTURY CT

DRUMMOND CRES

Shewalton Pits
(Nature Reserve)

Moorend
Workshops

SHEWALTON RD

SHEWALTON RD

Shewalton
Bridge

McMILLAN PL

METCALFE PL

MURDOCH PL

BREWSTER PL

CHALMERS PL

Dundonald Burn

Cemy

Sport &
L Ctr

THREE STANES
RDBT

A737

A737

Refuse
Tip

NEWHOUSE
INTC

B7080

Oldhall West
Ind Est

Shewalton

Shewalton
Moor

OLDHALL
RDBT

B7080

MOSS DR

CH

GAILES RD

LONG DR

KA12

KA11

LC

GAILES RD

CH

Gailes

Meadowhead
Ind Est

DUNLOP PL

DUNLOP DR

MEADOWHEAD AVE

MEADOWHEAD RD

Sewage
Works

Mill

River Irvine

BEACH DR

Beach Park

KA12

Smallholdings

AUCHENGATE CRES

Dundonald
Camp

MEADOWHEAD
RDBT

LC

A78

KA10

SIDONA CRES

SIDONA CT CRES

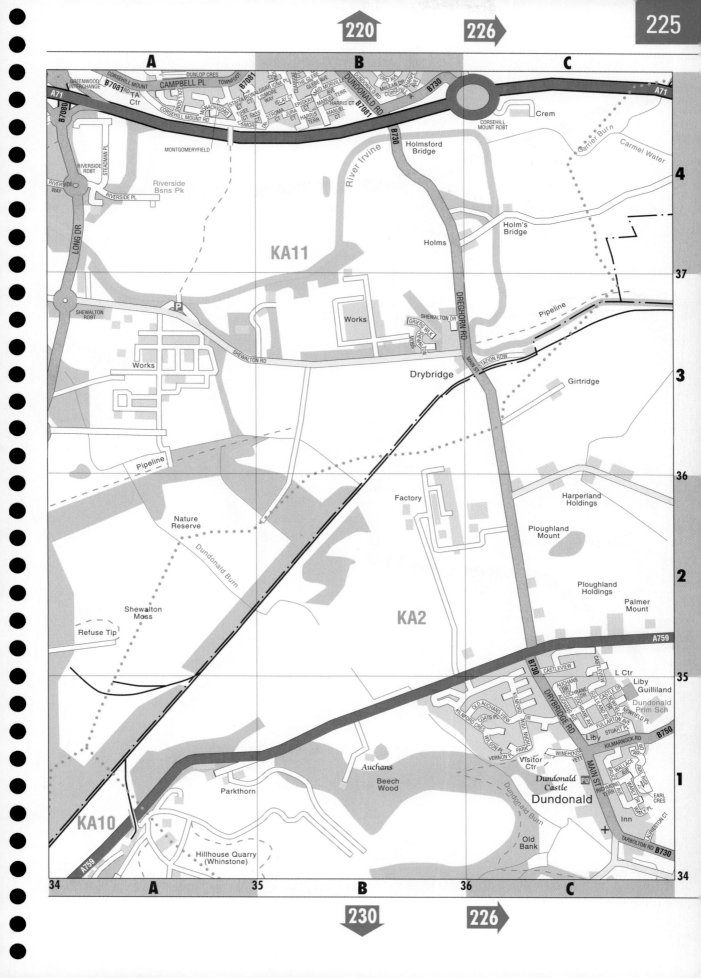

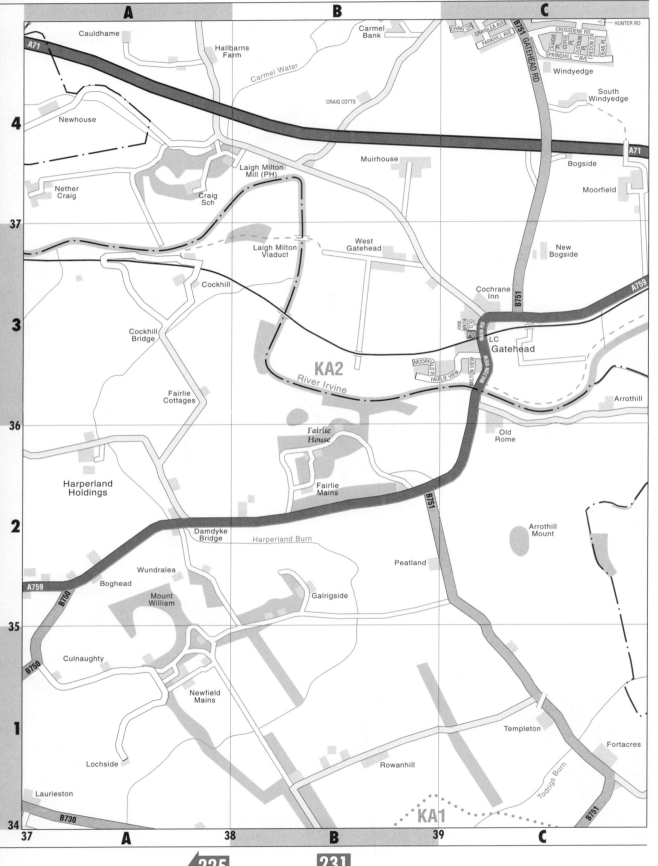

225
221

A71 Cauldhame
Hallbarns Farm
Carmel Bank
Carmel Water
CRAIG DR
CRAIGLEA AVE
PARKHILL AVE
B751
GATEHEAD RD
CROSSDENE RD.
HUNTER RD
CRAIGIE PL
CORSE PL
LOUDOUN PL
CREDON DR
DEAN PL
SPRINGHILL AVE
Windyedge

CRAIG COTTS
South Windyedge

Newhouse
4
Muirhouse
A71
Bogside
Moorfield

Laigh Milton Mill (PH)
Nether Craig
Craig Sch
West Gatehead
New Bogside

37
Laigh Milton Viaduct
Cochrane Inn
B751
A759

Cockhill
OLD ROME WAY
MAIN RD
PO
3
Cockhill Bridge
KA2
River Irvine
LC Gatehead
MOORFIELD
FAIRLIE VIEW
MILTON VIEW
Arrothill

Fairlie Cottages
36
Fairlie House
Old Rome

Harperland Holdings
Fairlie Mains
B751
Arrothill Mount

2
Damdyke Bridge
Harperland Burn
Peatland

Wundralea
A759
Boghead
B750
Galrigside
Mount William

35
Culnaughty

Newfield Mains
1
B750
Templeton
Fortacres

Lochside
Rowanhill
Todrigs Burn
B751

Laurieston
B730
KA1
34
37
A
38
B
39
C

225
231

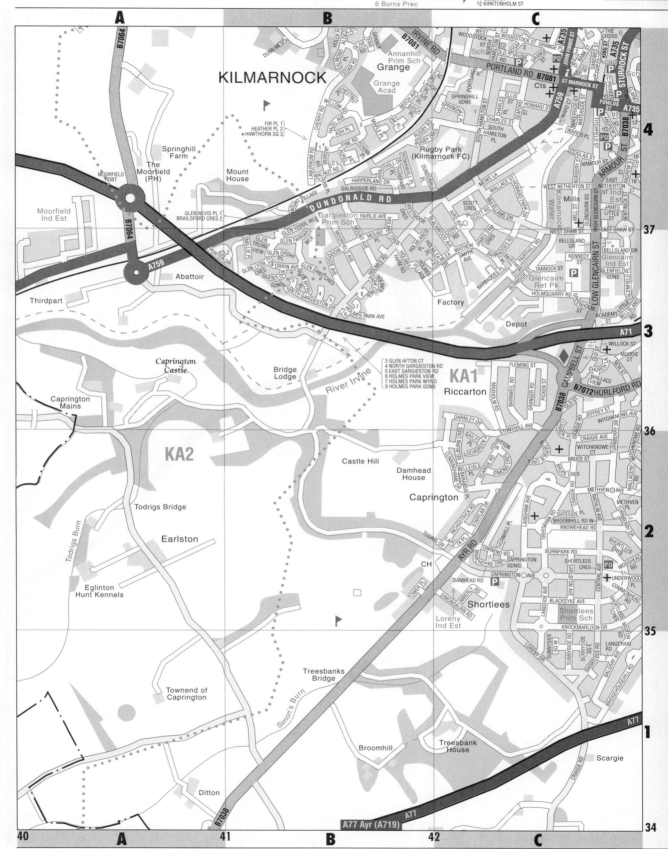

222

228

C4
1 SOUTH HAMILTON CT
2 EAST WOODSTOCK CT
3 BANK PL
4 COLLEGE WYND
5 LOW CHURCH LA
6 Burns Prec

C4
7 SANDBED LA
8 WATER LA
9 BRIDGE LA
10 ST MARNOCK PL
11 QUEEN ST
12 KIRKTONHOLM ST

13 GALLION WLK
14 KIRKTONHOLM PL
15 ST ANDREW'S WLK
16 RICHARDLAND RD
17 BREWERY RD

KILMARNOCK

Grange

Annanhill
Prim Sch

Grange
Acad

Springhill
Farm

Mount
House

FIR PL 1
HEATHER PL 2
HAWTHORN SQ 3

The Moorfield
(PH)

Moorfield
RDBT

Moorfield
Ind Est

GLEN NEVIS PL 1
BRAILSFORD CRES 2

Thirdpart

Abattoir

Rugby Park
(Kilmarnock FC)

Gargieston
Prim Sch

Fairlie Ave

PORTLAND RD

St Marnock St

Cts

Mills

St Ind
Est

West Netherton St

East
Netherton

West Shaw St

East Shaw St

Bellsland
Gr

Bellsland
Ind Est

Glencairn
Ind Est

Glenfield
Gdns

Glencairn
Ret Pk

Factory

Depot

A71

DUNDONALD RD

3 GLEN AFTON CT
4 NORTH GARGIESTON RD
5 EAST GARGIESTON RD
6 HOLMES PARK VIEW
7 HOLMES PARK WYND
8 HOLMES PARK GDNS

Caprington
Castle

Bridge
Lodge

River Irvine

Caprington
Mains

KA2

KA1

Riccarton

FLEMING ST

Castle Hill

Damhead
House

Caprington

Todrigs Bridge

Earlston

Eglinton
Hunt Kennels

Shortlees
Prim Sch

CH

AYR RD

Caprington
Gdns

Shortlees

Loreny
Ind Est

Townend of
Caprington

Treesbanks
Bridge

Broomhill

Treesbank
House

Scargie

Ditton

A77 Ayr (A719)

A77

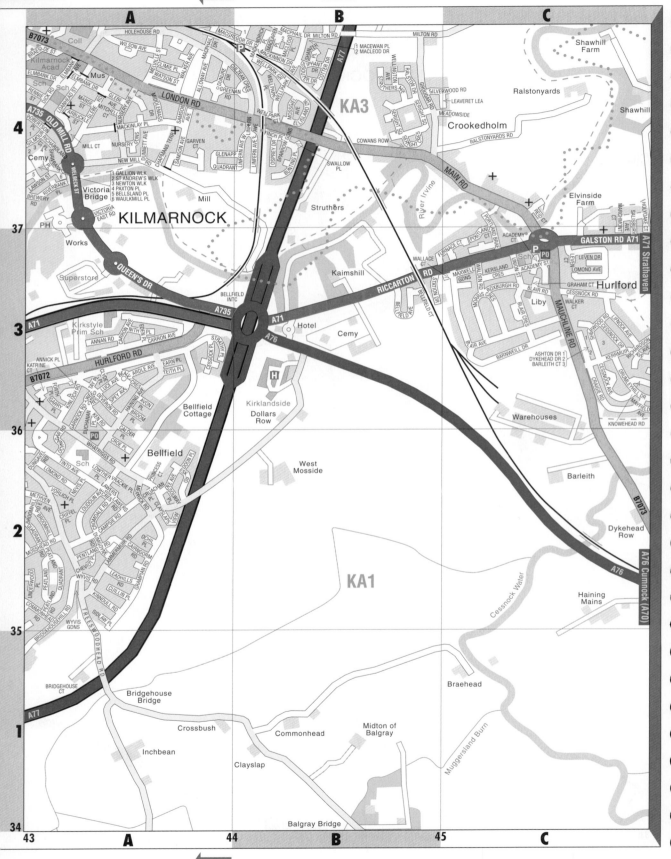

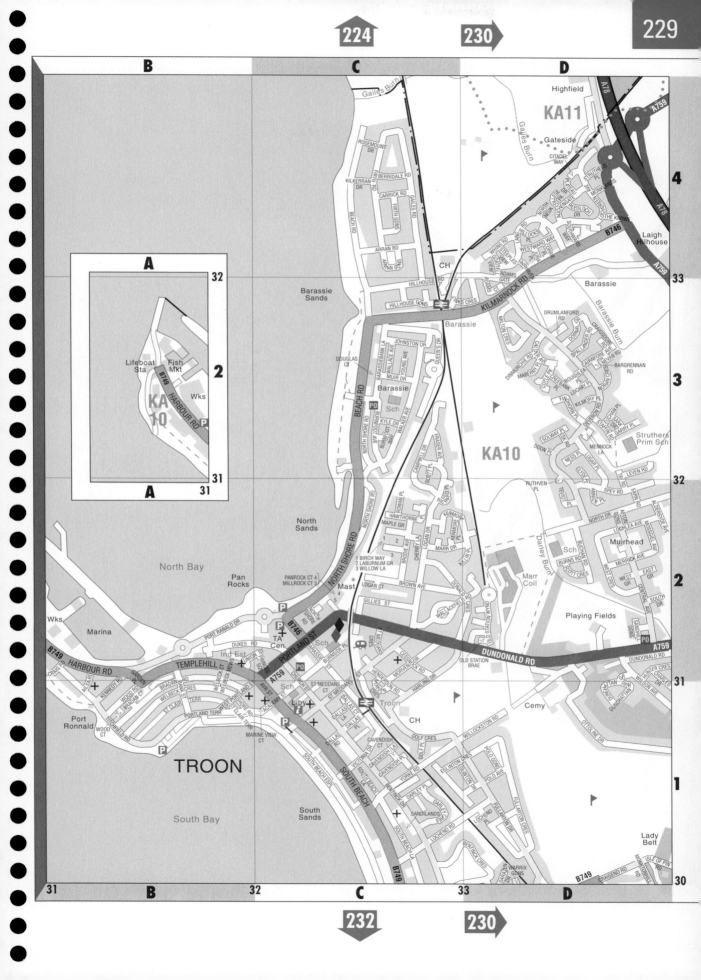

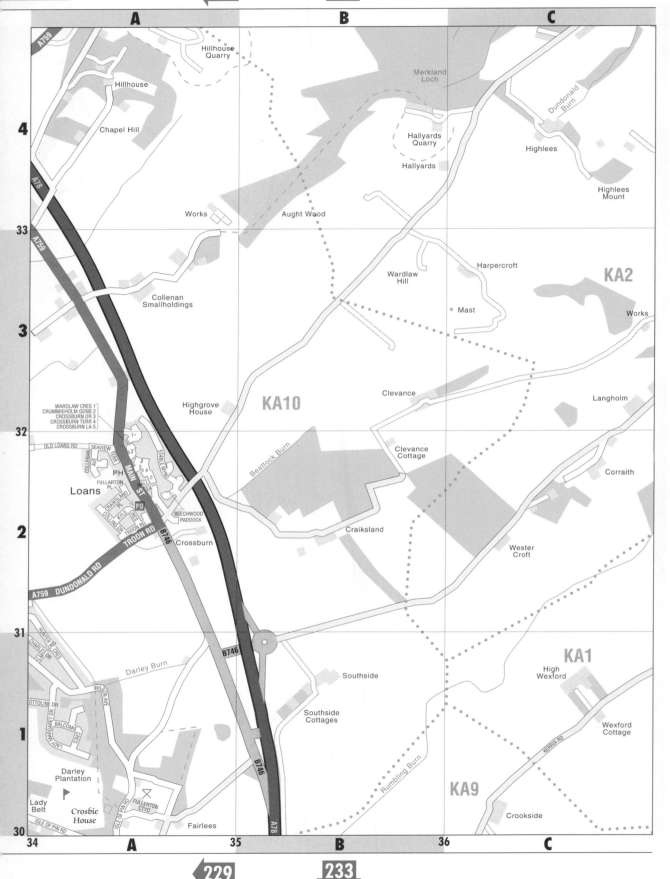

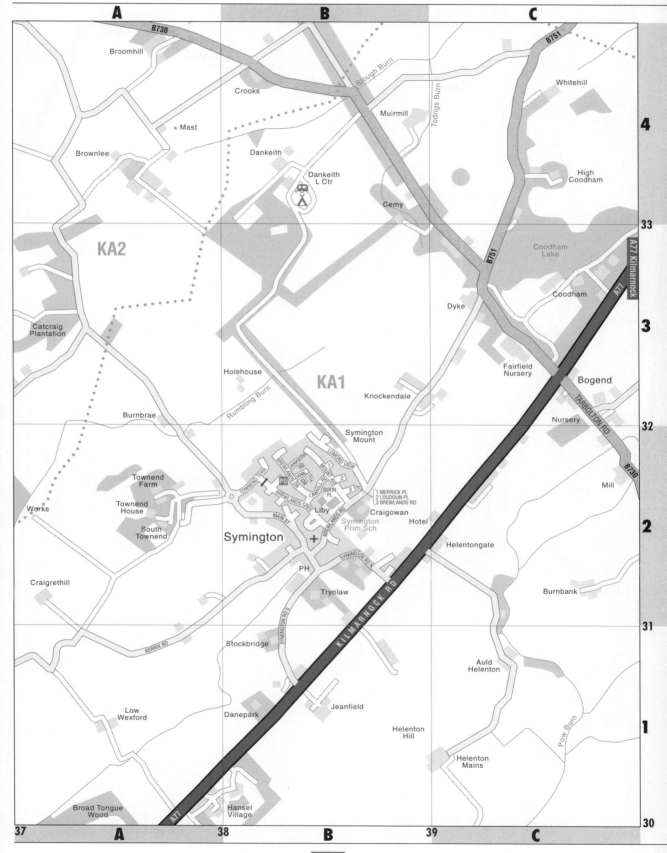

229

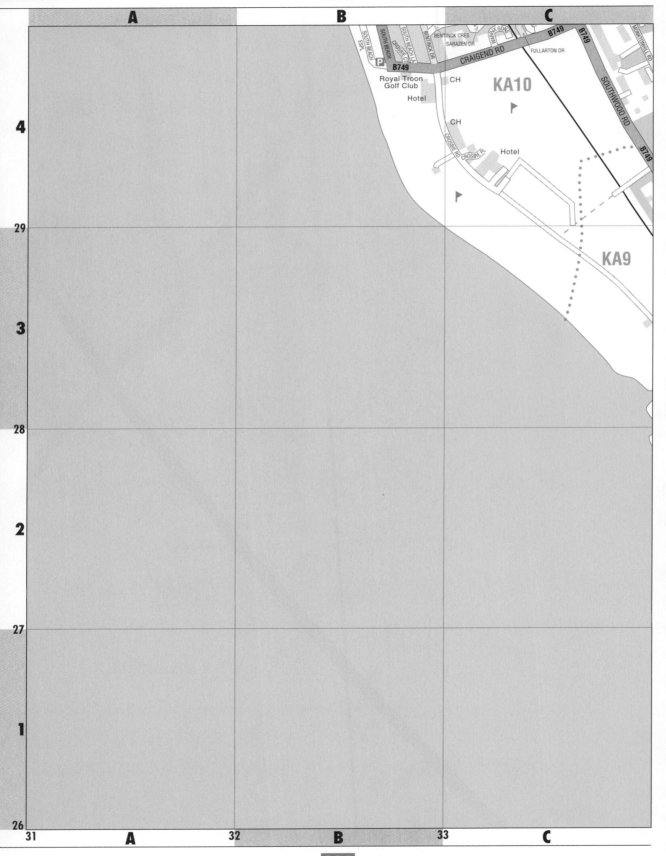

235

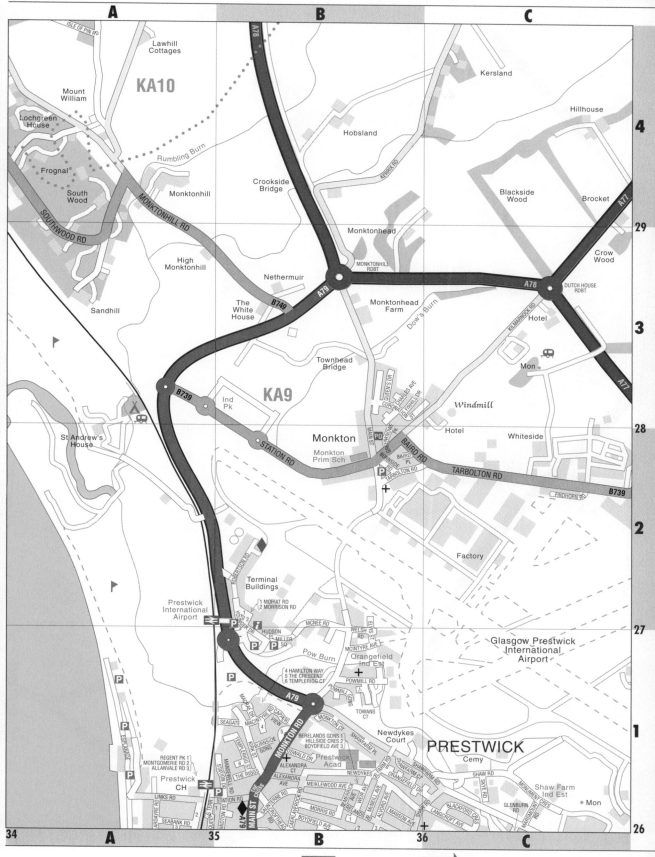

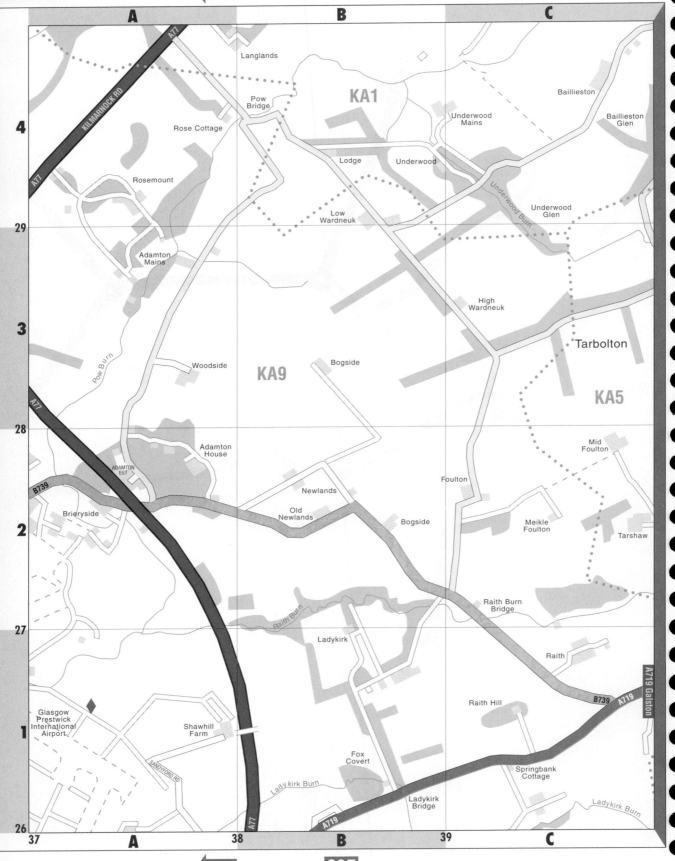

A

B

C

Langlands

KA1

Baillieston

Pow
Bridge

Underwood
Mains

Baillieston
Glen

4

Rose Cottage

Underwood

Rosemount

Lodge

Underwood
Glen

Underwood Burn

29

Low
Wardneuk

Adamton
Mains

High
Wardneuk

3

Tarbolton

Woodside

Bogside

KA9

KA5

Pow Burn

28

Mid
Foulton

Adamton
House

Foulton

A77

Newlands

B739

Brieryside

Old
Newlands

Bogside

Meikle
Foulton

Tarshaw

2

Raith Burn
Bridge

27

Raith Burn

Ladykirk

Raith

A719 Galston

Raith Hill

Glasgow
Prestwick
International
Airport

Shawhill
Farm

B739

A719

1

Fox
Covert

Springbank
Cottage

SANDYFORD RD

Ladykirk Burn

Ladykirk Burn

Ladykirk
Bridge

A77

A719

26

37

A

38

B

39

C

KILMARNOCK RD

A77

A B C

4

25

3

24

2

23

1

22

North
Breakwater

KA8

Dock

Ayr Harbour

South
Pier

SALTPANS RD

LIMEKILN RD

SHORE RD

ELMBANK
ST

WEIR RD

GLEBE RD

GLEBE CRES

WAGGON RD

GRIFFIN
DOCK RD

YORK STREET
LA

TAYLOR
ST

GREEN ST LA

GREEN ST

GREEN ST LA

BACK PEEBLES ST

PEEBLES ST

WEIR RD

WELFER ST

Bens
Pk

OSWALD LA

SPUR RD

YORK ST LA

YORK ST

CHURCHILL
TWR

YORK PL

NORTH HARBOUR ST

CROWN ST

Ind
Est

MAIN ST

CRES

DAMSIDE

PO

A79

A79

KING ST

P

A713

18 17
SOUTH
BEACH RD

16 15

River Ayr

SOUTH HARBOUR ST

Liby

JOHN ST

P

Citadel
L Ctr

ESPLANADE

SEABANK
RD

ARRAN TERR

MONTGOMERIE TERR

EGLINTON PL

Ayr
Acad

B748

NEW BRIDGE ST

HIGH ST

TH
10

Ct

Auld
Brig

A719

AYR
KA7

CROMWELL RD

ALLISON

EGLINTON TERR

CITADEL

13 12 11

4

F

C

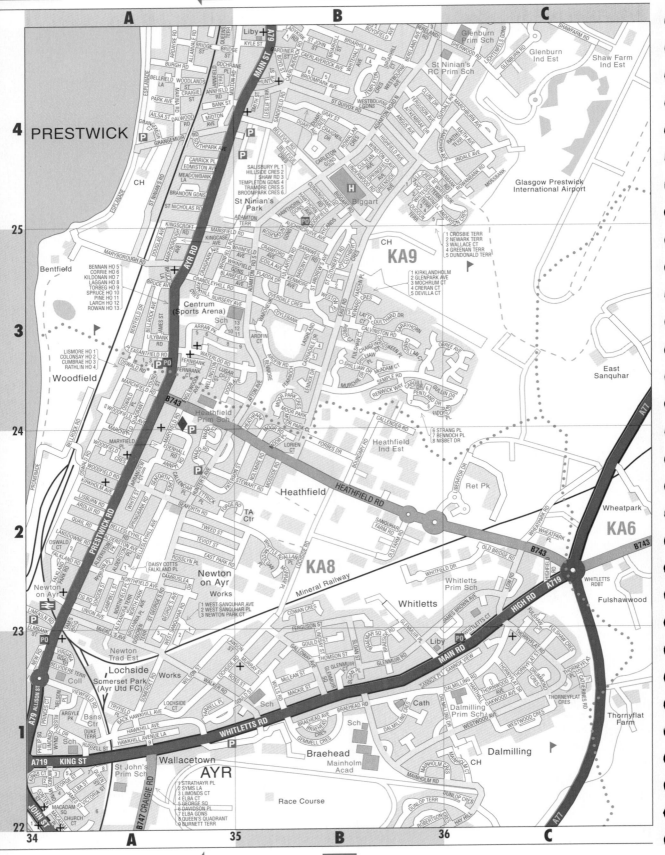

235
233

A
B
C

4 PRESTWICK

Liby
KYLE ST
A79
QUEENS DR

CH

Bentfield

25

Woodfield

3

LISMORE HO 1
COLONSAY HO 2
CUMBRAE HO 3
RATHLIN HO 4

BENNAN HO 5
CORRIE HO 6
KILDONAN HO 7
LAGGAN HO 8
TORBEG HO 9
SPRUCE HO 10
PINE HO 11
LARCH HO 12
ROWAN HO 13

SALISBURY PL 1
HILLSIDE CRES 2
SHAW RD 3
TEMPLETON GDNS 4
TRAMORE CRES 5
BROOMPARK CRES 6.

St Ninian's
Park

Centrum
(Sports Arena)

AYR RD

B743

Heathfield
Prim Sch

St Ninian's
RC Prim Sch

H
Biggart

Glenburn
Prim Sch

Glenburn
Ind Est

Shaw Farm
Ind Est

CH

KA9

1 CROSBIE TERR
2 NEWARK TERR
3 WALLACE CT
4 GREENAN TERR
5 DUNDONALD TERR

1 KIRKLANDHOLM
2 GLENPARK AVE
3 MOCHRUM CT
4 CRERAN CT
5 DEVILLA CT

East
Sanquhar

6 STRANG PL
7 BENNOCH PL
8 NISBET DR

24

Heathfield

HEATHFIELD RD

Heathfield
Ind Est

Ret Pk

Wheatpark

KA6

B743

A77

2

Newton
on Ayr

KA8

Newton
on Ayr
Works

1 WEST SANQUHAR AVE
2 WEST SANQUHAR PL
3 NEWTON PARK CT

Mineral Railway

Whitletts

Whitletts
Prim Sch

Liby

MAIN RD

Whitletts
RDBT

Fulshawwood

HIGH RD

A719

23

PRESTWICK RD

Newton
Trad Est

Lochside

Somerset Park
(Ayr Utd FC)

Works

Braehead

Dalmilling
Prim Sch

Cath

Thornyflat
Farm

Dalmilling

CH

1

WHITLETTS RD

A79
KING ST
A719

Wallacetown

St John's
Prim Sch

AYR

1 STRATHAYR PL
2 SYMS LA
3 LIMONDS CT
4 ELBA CT
5 GEORGE SQ
6 DAVIDSON PL
7 ELBA GDNS
8 QUEEN'S QUADRANT
9 BURNETT TERR

Mainholm
Acad

Race Course

22

235
239

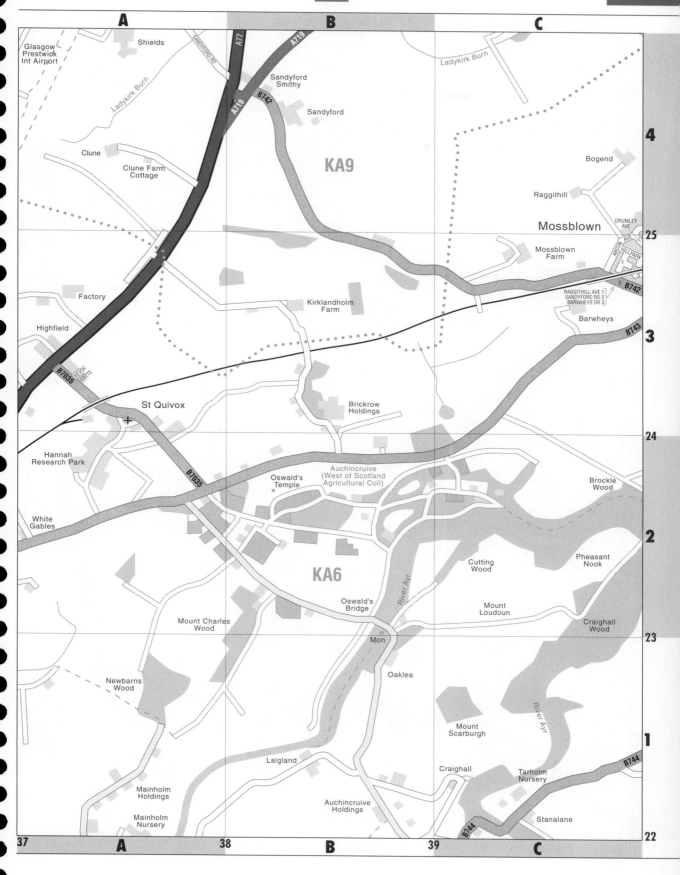

A **B** **C**

Glasgow Prestwick Int Airport

Shields

Sandyford Smithy

Ladykirk Burn

A77

A719

B742

Sandyford

Ladykirk Burn

Bogend

4

Clune

Clune Farm Cottage

KA9

Raggithill

Mossblown

DRUMLEY AVE

25

Mossblown Farm

Factory

Kirklandholm Farm

ARGON AVE

HILLPARK

B742

Highfield

RAGGITHILL AVE 1
SANDYFORD RD 2
BARWHEYS DR 3

Barwheys

B7035

KEVOC COTTS

B743

3

St Quivox

Brickrow Holdings

24

Hannah Research Park

B7035

Oswald's Temple

Auchincruive (West of Scotland Agricultural Coll)

Brockle Wood

White Gables

Cutting Wood

Pheasant Nook

2

KA6

Oswald's Bridge

Mount Loudoun

Craighall Wood

Mount Charles Wood

Mon

23

Oaklea

Newbarns Wood

River Ayr

Mount Scarburgh

1

Laigland

River Ayr

B744

Mainholm Holdings

Craighall

Tarholm Nursery

Stanalane

Mainholm Nursery

Auchincruive Holdings

B144

22

37 **A** **38** **B** **39** **C**

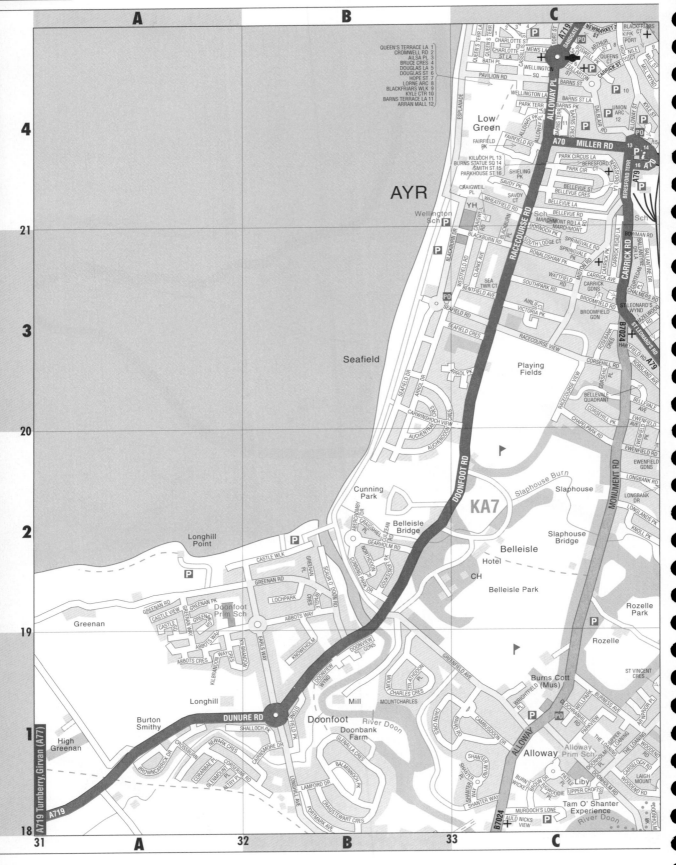

Queen's Terrace La 1
Cromwell Rd 2
Ailsa Pl. 3
Bruce Cres 4
Douglas La 5
Douglas St 6
Hope St 7
Lorne Arc 8
Blackfriars Wlk 9
Kyle Ctr 10
Barns Terrace La 11
Arran Mall 12

Low Green

AYR

Wellington Sch

Seafield

KA7

Cunning Park

Belleisle Bridge

Belleisle

Belleisle Park

Rozelle Park

Rozelle

Greenan

Longhill Point

Longhill

Burton Smithy

High Greenan

Doonfoot Prim Sch

DUNURE RD

Doonfoot

Doonbank Farm

River Doon

Burns Cott (Mus)

Alloway Prim Sch

Alloway

Liby

Tam O' Shanter Experience

Slaphouse

Slaphouse Bridge

Playing Fields

A719 Turnberry, Girvan (A77)

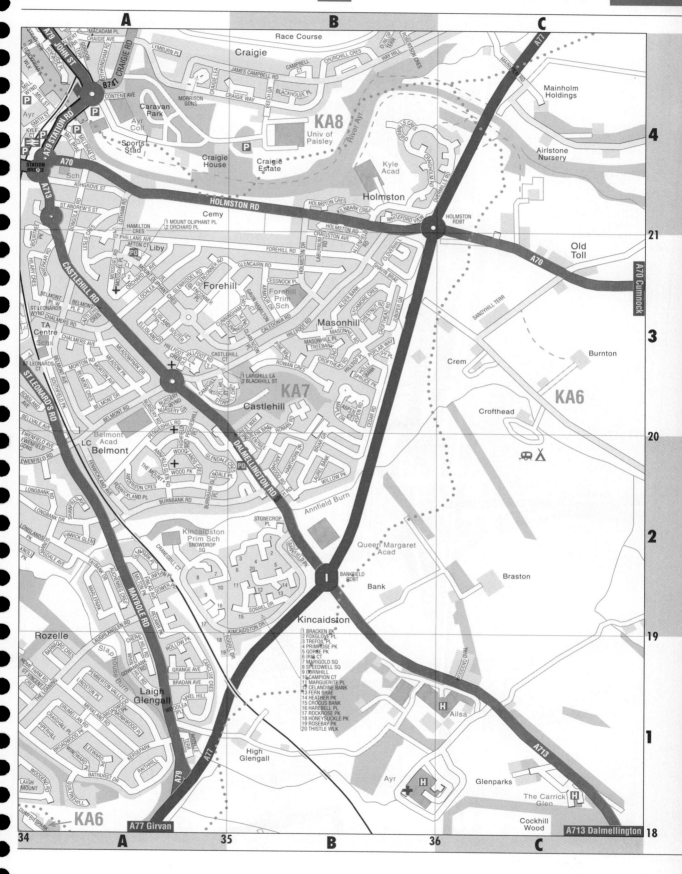

Scale: 7 inches to 1 mile
0 110 yards 220 yards
0 125 m 250 m

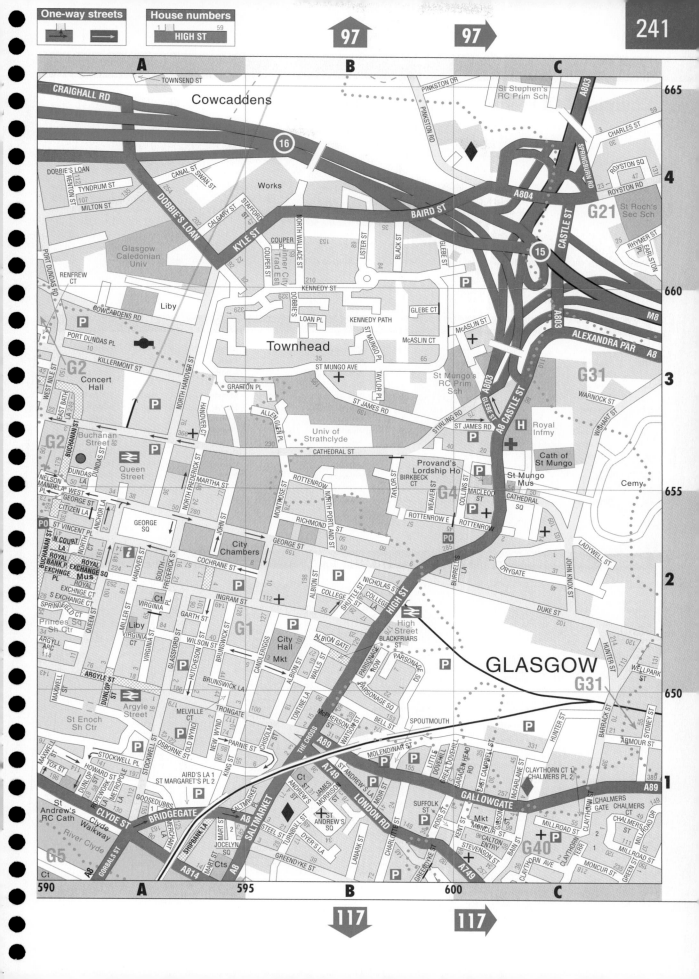

Index

Church Rd **6** Beckenham BR2..........**53** C6

Place name
May be abbreviated on the map

Location number
Present when a number indicates the place's position in a crowded area of mapping

Locality, town or village
Shown when more than one place has the same name

Postcode district
District for the indexed place

Page and grid square
Page number and grid reference for the standard mapping

Public and commercial buildings are highlighted in magenta   **Places of interest** are highlighted in blue with a star★

Abbreviations used in the index

Acad	Academy	Comm	Common	Gd	Ground	L	Leisure	Prom	Promenade
App	Approach	Cott	Cottage	Gdn	Garden	La	Lane	Rd	Road
Arc	Arcade	Cres	Crescent	Gn	Green	Liby	Library	Recn	Recreation
Ave	Avenue	Cswy	Causeway	Gr	Grove	Mdw	Meadow	Ret	Retail
Bglw	Bungalow	Ct	Court	H	Hall	Meml	Memorial	Sh	Shopping
Bldg	Building	Ctr	Centre	Ho	House	Mkt	Market	Sq	Square
Bsns, Bus	Business	Ctry	Country	Hospl	Hospital	Mus	Museum	St	Street
Bvd	Boulevard	Cty	County	HQ	Headquarters	Orch	Orchard	Sta	Station
Cath	Cathedral	Dr	Drive	Hts	Heights	Pal	Palace	Terr	Terrace
Cir	Circus	Dro	Drove	Ind	Industrial	Par	Parade	TH	Town Hall
Cl	Close	Ed	Education	Inst	Institute	Pas	Passage	Univ	University
Cnr	Corner	Emb	Embankment	Int	International	Pk	Park	Wk, Wlk	Walk
Coll	College	Est	Estate	Intc	Interchange	Pl	Place	Wr	Water
Com	Community	Ex	Exhibition	Junc	Junction	Prec	Precinct	Yd	Yard

Index of localities, towns and villages

Argyle Cres *continued*
Hamilton ML3 .161 C2
Argyle Dr ML3 .162 A2
Argyle Gdns G66 .57 C4
Argyle Pk KA8 .236 A1
Argyle Pl Kilsyth G65 .60 C4
Saltcoats KA21 .216 C4
Argyle Rd Gourock PA19 .44 C3
Saltcoats KA21 .216 C4
Argyle St Glasgow G2 .240 C2
Glasgow, Anderston G3 .240 A2
Greenock PA15 .45 C3
Paisley PA1 .113 B2
Stonehouse ML9 .198 C1
Argyle St E G84 .16 B1
Argyle St W G84 .16 B1
Argyle Street Sta G1 .241 A1
Argyll Arc G1 .241 A2
Argyll Ave Dumbarton G82 .50 B2
Falkirk FK2 .42 B3
Renfrew PA3 .93 C1
Renfrew, Kirklandneuk PA4 .94 A2
Stirling FK8 .2 B1
Argyll Ct ML7 .127 C3
Argyll Est G83 .27 B4
Argyll Gdns ML9 .185 A2
Argyll Pl Alloa FK10 .10 B4
Bellshill ML4 .141 C1
Dumbarton G82 .50 B2
East Kilbride G74 .160 B2
Argyll Rd Bearsden G61 .75 C4
Clydebank G81 .74 B1
Rosneath G84 .15 A2
Argyll St Alexandria G83 .27 B4
Alloa FK10 .10 B4
Arisaig Dr Bearsden G61 .76 A2
Glasgow G52 .115 C2
Arisaig Pl G52 .115 C2
Arisdale Cres G77 .156 C3
Ark La G31 .117 C4
Arkaig Ave ML6 .103 C2
Arkaig Pl G77 .157 A2
Arkaig St ML2 .165 A1
Arkle Terr G72 .138 C2
Arkleston Cres PA3 .114 A4
Arkleston Prim Sch PA4 .94 B1
Arkleston Rd PA3,PA4 .114 A4
Arklet Rd G51 .115 C4
Arklet Way ML2 .165 C2
Arkwright Way KA11 .219 C2
Arkwrights Way PA1 .113 A2
Arlington St G3 .240 A4
Armadale Ct G31 .118 A4
Armadale Path G31 .118 A4
Armadale Pl
Glasgow G31 .118 A4
Greenock PA15 .45 C2
Armadale Rd
Lanark ML11 .215 B2
Rhu G84 .15 C2
Armadale St G31 .118 A4
Armine Path ML1 .143 B2
Armour Ave Airdrie ML6 .122 C4
Cowie FK7 .12 B4
Armour Ct Blantyre G72 .161 A3
Kirkintilloch G66 .59 A1
Armour Dr Ayr KA7 .239 B3
Kirkintilloch G66 .59 A1
Armour Gdns G66 .59 A1
Armour Gr ML1 .164 A2
Armour Mews FK5 .23 B2
Armour Pl
Ardrossan KA22 .205 B2
Johnstone PA5 .112 A2
Johnstone, Linwood PA5 .112 B3
Kirkintilloch G66 .59 A1
Motherwell ML1 .143 B2
Stewarton KA3 .195 C1
Armour Sq PA5 .112 A2
Armour St
Glasgow G4, G31 .241 C1
Johnstone PA5 .112 A2
Kilmarnock KA1 .227 C4
Armstrong Cres G71 .141 A4
Armstrong Gr G75 .180 B4
Armstrong Rd
Helensburgh G84 .25 B4
Kilmarnock KA3 .223 B1
Arnbrae Rd G65 .36 A1
Arness Terr KA3 .222 C2
Arngask Rd G51 .115 C4
Arnhall Pl G52 .115 C2
Arnhem St G72 .139 B3
Arnholm Pl G52 .115 C2
Arnisdale Pl G34 .120 A4
Arnisdale Rd G34 .120 A4
Arnisdale Way G73 .138 A2
Arnish PA4 .93 B4
Arniston St G32 .118 C4
Arniston Way PA3 .114 A4
Arnol Pl G33 .119 C4
Arnold Ave G64 .78 A1
Arnold St G20 .97 A3
Arnot St FK1 .42 B2
Arnothill FK1 .42 A2
Arnothill Bank 6 FK1 .42 A2
Arnothill Ct FK1 .41 C3
Arnothill Gdns FK1 .42 A2
Arnothill La FK1 .41 C2
Arnothill Mews FK1 .42 A2
Arnott Dr ML5 .122 A2
Arnott Quadrant ML1 .142 B1
Arnott Way G72 .139 A3
Arnprior Cres G44 .137 B2
Arnprior Gdns G69 .80 C1
Arnprior Pl KA7 .238 C1
Arnprior Quadrant G45 .137 B2
Arnprior Rd G45 .137 B2
Arnprior St G45 .137 B2
Arns Gr FK10 .9 C4
Arnside Ave G46 .136 B2
Arnswell FK10 .5 B1
Arnum Gdns ML8 .187 C1
Arnum Pl ML8 .187 C1
Arnwood Dr G12 .96 A3
Aron Terr G72 .138 C2
Arondale Rd ML6 .103 C2
Aros Dr G52 .115 C1
Aros La G52 .115 B1
Aros Rd G84 .15 B3
Arran G74 .160 B1
Arran Ave
Coatbridge ML5 .122 B2
Dumbarton G82 .49 B3
Kilmarnock KA3 .223 A2
Port Glasgow PA14 .69 A4
Renfrew PA3 .93 C1
Arran Cres KA15 .150 B1
Arran Ct Alloa FK10 .10 A3
Stevenston KA20 .217 B4
Arran Dr Airdrie ML6 .102 C1
Cumbernauld G67 .82 B4
Glasgow G52 .115 C2
Glasgow, Giffnock G46 .136 B1
Glenmavis ML6 .102 C3
Johnstone PA5 .111 B1
Kirkintilloch G66 .58 C1
Paisley PA2 .133 C4
Arran Gdns Carluke ML8 .201 C4
Hamilton ML3 .162 C1
Troon KA10 .229 C4
Arran La Ardrossan KA22 .205 B1
Moodiesburn G69 .81 A1
Arran Mall KA7 .238 C4
Arran Path 26 ML9 .185 B1
Arran Pk KA9 .236 A3
Arran Pl Ardrossan KA22 .205 B1
Clydebank G81 .74 B1
Coatbridge ML6 .122 B2
Irvine KA12 .219 A3
Linwood PA3 .112 A3
Saltcoats KA21 .206 A1
Arran Rd Gourock PA19 .44 B3
Motherwell ML1 .163 B4
Renfrew PA4 .94 B1
Troon KA10 .229 C4
Arran Terr Ayr KA7 .235 C1
Falkirk FK1 .41 B2
Rutherglen G73 .137 C3
Arran Twr G72 .138 C2
Arran View 14 Kilsyth G65 .60 B4
Stewarton KA3 .195 C1
Arran Way G72 .140 C1
Arranview Ct Ayr KA8 .236 A2
Irvine KA12 .219 A2
Arranview Gdns KA23 .190 B1
Arranview St ML6 .123 C1
Arrochar Ct G23 .96 C4
Arrochar Dr G23 .76 B1
Arrochar Path 6 G23 .76 B1
Arrochar St G23 .76 B1
Arrol Cres FK10 .10 B4
Arrol Dr KA7 .238 B3
Arrol Pk KA7 .238 C3
Arrol Pl G40 .118 A2
Arrol St G52 .114 C4
Arrothill Dr KA1 .227 B4
Arrotshole Ct G74 .159 A2
Arrotshole Rd G74 .159 A2
Arrowsmith Ave G13 .95 B4
Artarman Rd G84 .15 C2
Arthur Ave Airdrie ML6 .123 A3
Barrhead G78 .134 A1
Arthur Ct KA23 .190 B3
Arthur Gdns ML6 .105 A3
Arthur Pl G76 .157 C3
Arthur Rd PA2 .133 C4
Arthur St Alexandria G83 .27 C2
Ayr KA7 .238 C4
Clarkston G76 .157 C3
Glasgow G3 .96 B1
Greenock PA15 .46 A2
Hamilton ML3 .162 B3
Paisley PA1 .113 B3
Saltcoats KA21 .217 A4
Stevenston KA20 .217 B4
West Kilbride KA23 .190 B3
Arthur's Dr FK5 .23 C1
Arthurlie Ave
Barrhead G78 .134 B1
Uplawmoor G78 .153 A2
Arthurlie Dr
Glasgow G46 .136 B1
Newton Mearns G77 .156 B2
Uplawmoor G78 .153 A2
Arthurlie Gdns G78 .134 B1
Arthurlie Pl KA21 .216 C4
Arthurlie St
Barrhead G78 .134 B1
Glasgow G51 .115 C4
Arthurston Rd G83 .28 A4
Artizan Br G82 .49 C2
Arundel Dr
Bishopbriggs G64 .78 A2
Glasgow G42 .137 A4
Ascaig Cres G52 .115 C1
Ascog Rd G61 .75 C1
Ascog St G42 .117 A1
Ascot G12 .96 A3
Ascot Ave G12 .95 C3
Ash Ave G75 .180 B3
Ash Ct G75 .180 B3
Ash Dr KA15 .150 A1
Ash Gr Alloa FK10 .10 B3
Bishopbriggs G64 .98 A4
Kirkintilloch G66 .79 A3
Ash Gr *continued*
Law ML8 .186 C3
Stenhousemuir FK5 .23 C1
Uddingston G71 .141 A4
Ash Pl Banknock FK4 .38 C1
East Kilbride G75 .180 B3
Johnstone PA5 .112 A1
Kilmarnock KA1 .227 B4
Ash Rd Clydebank G81 .74 A3
Cumbernauld G67 .62 C3
Dumbarton G82 .49 C2
Glasgow G69 .120 A2
Ash Terr FK8 .6 C3
Ash Wlk Motherwell ML1 .143 A3
Rutherglen G73 .138 B2
Ash Wynd G72 .139 C3
Ashbank Cres ML6 .123 C2
Ashbrae Gdns FK7 .7 A1
Ashburn Gate PA19 .44 B4
Ashburn Gdns
Gourock PA19 .44 B4
Milngavie G62 .54 C1
Ashburn Loan ML9 .185 A2
Ashburn Rd G62 .54 C1
Ashburton La G12 .96 A3
Ashburton Pk G75 .180 A4
Ashburton Rd G12 .96 A3
Ashby Cres G13 .75 C1
Ashcraig Sch G33 .99 A2
Ashcroft G74 .160 B3
Ashcroft Ave G66 .57 C4
Ashcroft Dr G44 .137 C3
Ashcroft Wlk G66 .57 C4
Ashdale Ave KA21 .205 C1
Ashdale Dr G52 .115 C2
Ashdale Rd KA3 .222 C2
Ashdene St G22 .97 A4
Asher Rd ML6 .123 C1
Ashfield G64 .78 A2
Ashfield Cotts G83 .20 A2
Ashfield Rd
Clarkston G76 .157 C3
Law ML8 .187 A3
Milngavie G62 .55 A1
Ashfield St G22 .97 B2
Ashfield Sta G22 .97 B3
Ashgill Pl G22 .97 B3
Ashgill Rd G22 .97 B4
Ashgillhead Rd ML9 .185 C1
Ashgrove Airdrie ML6 .123 B4
Caldercruix ML6 .105 A3
Coatbridge ML5 .122 A2
Hartwood ML7 .145 C2
Irvine KA12 .219 B3
Moodiesburn G69 .80 C1
Ashgrove Ave
Gourock PA19 .44 B4
Stevenston KA20 .206 C1
Ashgrove La PA14 .47 B1
Ashgrove Rd
Ardrossan KA22 .205 B2
Bellshill ML4 .142 A4
Kilwinning KA13 .207 B2
Ashgrove St Ayr KA7 .239 A4
Glasgow G73 .118 A1
Ashgrove Workshops
KA13 .207 B2
Ashiestiel Ct G67 .82 C4
Ashiestiel Pl G67 .82 C4
Ashiestiel Rd G67 .82 C4
Ashkirk Dr Ashgill ML9 .199 C4
Glasgow G52 .115 C2
Ashland Ave ML3 .183 B3
Ashlea Dr G46 .136 B2
Ashlea Gdns ML6 .103 C2
Ashley Dr G71 .141 A3
Ashley La G3 .240 A4
Ashley Pk G71 .141 B3
Ashley Pl G72 .161 B4
Ashley Rise G83 .27 C1
Ashley St Bonnybridge FK4 39 C3
Glasgow G3 .240 A4
Ashley Terr FK10 .10 A4
Ashmore Rd G43 .136 C3
Ashton Dr
Helensburgh G84 .25 B4
Hurlford KA1 .228 C3
Ashton Gdns G69 .101 A3
Ashton Gn G74 .159 C1
Ashton La N G12 .96 B1
Ashton Pl PA19 .44 B4
Ashton Rd Glasgow G12 .96 B1
Gourock PA19 .44 B4
Rutherglen G73 .118 A1
Ashton St ML1 .142 B1
Ashton Terr PA19 .44 B4
Ashton View G82 .49 A2
Ashton Way PA2 .132 C4
Ashtree Ct G60 .73 A3
Ashtree Gr G77 .156 B2
Ashtree Rd G43 .136 B4
Ashvale Cres G21 .97 C2
Ashwood ML2 .164 C1
Ashwood Gdns G13 .95 C3
Ashworth Terr ML3 .162 A2
Aspen Ct KA7 .239 B3
Aspen Dr G21 .98 A2
Aspen Pl
Cambuslang G72 .139 C3
Johnstone PA5 .112 A1
Aspen Rd KA7 .239 B3
Aspen Way ML3 .162 C1
Asquith Pl ML4 .142 B3
Assloss Rd KA3 .223 B2
Aster Dr G45 .138 A2
Aster Gdns Glasgow G53 .135 B2
Motherwell ML1 .163 C3
Athelstane Dr G67 .82 B4
Athelstane Rd G13 .95 B4
Athena Way G71 .141 A4
Athole Gdns G12 .96 B2
Athole La Glasgow G12 .96 B2
Gourock PA16 .44 B2
Athole St G84 .16 C1
Athole Terr PA16 .44 B2
Atholl Ave Paisley G52 .114 C4
Torrance G64 .57 A1
Atholl Cres PA1 .114 C3
Atholl Ct G66 .59 A1
Atholl Dr Cumbernauld G68 81 C4
Rutherglen G46 .157 B4
Atholl Gdns Bearsden G61 75 C4
Bishopbriggs G64 .77 C2
Kilwinning KA13 .207 C2
Rutherglen G73 .138 C2
Atholl La G69 .81 A1
Atholl Pl Coatbridge ML5 .122 A2
Linwood PA3 .112 A3
Stirling FK8 .1 C1
Atholl Prep Sch G62 .55 A2
Atholl St ML3 .162 A3
Atholl Terr G71 .120 C1
Atlas Ind Est G21 .97 C2
Atlas Pl G21 .97 C2
Atlas Rd G21 .97 C2
Atlas Sq G21 .97 C2
Atlas St G81 .94 A4
Atlin Dr ML1 .143 A2
Atrium Way FK4 .40 A2
Attercliffe Ave ML2 .164 B1
Attlee Ave G81 .74 C1
Attlee Pl G81 .74 C1
Attow Rd G43 .136 A3
Auburn Dr G78 .134 B1
Auchans Ave KA2 .225 C1
Auchans Dr KA2 .225 C1
Auchans Pl KA3 .213 A2
Auchans Rd PA6 .92 A1
Auchanshangan Dr
KA21 .205 C2
Auchenback Prim Sch
G78 .134 B1
Auchenbeg Cres KA7 .239 A2
Auchenbothie Cres G33 .98 C3
Auchenbothie Pl G33 .98 C3
Auchenbothie Rd PA14 .68 C3
Auchencar Dr KA3 .222 C2
Auchencrow St G34 .120 B4
Auchencruive G62 .76 B4
Auchendarroch St PA15 .46 B2
Auchendavie Rd G66 .59 A1
Auchendoon Cres KA7 .238 B2
Auchendores Ave PA14 .69 A4
Auchenfoil La PA14 .68 B4
Auchenfoil Rd
Port Glasgow PA14 .67 C3
Port Glasgow, Devol PA14 .68 B4
Auchengate KA10 .229 D4
Auchengate Cres KA11 .224 D1
Auchengeich Rd G69 .80 B2
Auchengilloch G75 .180 C3
Auchenglen Dr G69 .80 C1
Auchenglen Gdns G69 .80 C1
Auchenglen Rd ML8 .201 C2
Auchengreoch Ave PA5 .131 B4
Auchengreoch Rd PA5 .131 B4
Auchenharvie Acad
KA21 .217 A4
Auchenharvie Pl
Irvine KA11 .219 C3
Stevenston KA20 .206 A1
Auchenharvie Rd KA21 .217 A4
Auchenhove Cres KA25 .149 A2
Auchenhowie Rd G62 .76 B4
Auchenkilns Holdings
G68 .61 B1
Auchenkilns Rd G67 .82 B3
Auchenkilns Rdbt G67 .82 B4
Auchenleck La PA14 .68 C4
Auchenleck Rd PA14 .68 C4
Auchenlodment Prim Sch
PA5 .112 A1
Auchenlodment Rd PA5 .112 A1
Auchenreoch G66 .59 A3
Auchenreoch Ave G82 .50 A3
Auchenstewart Ct ML2 .165 B2
Auchentibber Rd G72 .161 A2
Auchentiber Pl KA3 .223 B3
Auchentorlie Quadrant
PA1 .114 A2
Auchentorlie St G11 .95 C1
Auchentoshan Ave G81 .73 C3
Auchentoshan Sch G81 .73 C3
Auchentoshan Terr G21 .97 C1
Auchentrae Cres KA7 .238 B3
Auchentyre Pl FK2 .24 B2
Auchinairn Prim Sch
G64 .98 A4
Auchinairn Rd G64 .98 B4
Auchinbaird FK10 .5 B1
Auchinbee Farm Rd G68 61 A2
Auchinbee Way G68 .61 A2
Auchincampbell Rd
ML3 .162 B2
Auchincarroch Rd
Bonhill G83 .28 A4
Gartocharn G83 .20 C2
Auchincloch Dr FK4 .38 C1
Auchincruive (West of
Scotland Agricultural Coll)
KA6 .237 B2
Auchincruive Ave KA9 .236 B3
Auchineden Ct G61 .75 B4
Auchingill Pl G34 .100 B1
Auchingill Rd G34 .100 B1
Auchingramont Ct ML3 .162 B2
Auchingramont Rd ML3 162 B2
Auchingramount Ct
ML3 .162 C2
Auchinlea Dr ML1 .144 B1
Auchinlea Rd G34 .99 C1
Auchinlea Ret Pk G34 .99 C1
Auchinleck Ave G33 .98 C3
Auchinleck Cres G33 .98 C3
Auchinleck Dr G33 .98 C3
Auchinleck Gdns G33 .98 C3
Auchinleck Rd
Clydebank G81 .74 A4
Glasgow G33 .98 C4
Auchinleck Terr G81 .74 A4
Auchinloch Prim Sch
G66 .79 B1
Auchinloch Rd G66 .79 B2
Auchinloch St 13 G21 .97 C2
Auchinraith Ave ML3 .162 B3
Auchinraith Prim Sch
G72 .161 B4
Auchinraith Rd G72 .161 C3
Auchinraith Terr G72 .161 C3
Auchinvole Cres G65 .60 A4
Auchmannoch Ave PA1 .114 C3
Auchmead Rd PA16 .44 C2
Auchmountain Rd
Greenock PA15 .46 C1
Greenock, Bridgend PA15 .46 B2
Port Glasgow PA15 .67 C4
Auchnacraig Rd G81 .74 B4
Auchneagh Ave PA16 .45 A2
Auchneagh Cres PA16 .45 A2
Auchneagh Farm La
PA16 .45 A3
Auchneagh Farm Rd
PA16 .45 A3
Auchneagh Rd PA16 .45 A2
Auchter Ave ML2 .166 B3
Auchter Rd ML2 .165 C2
Auchterburn Rd ML7 .166 C4
Auckland Pk 8 G75 .159 A1
Auckland Pl G81 .73 B2
Auckland St G22 .97 A2
Auld Brig Rd FK10 .10 A3
Auld Clay Rd KA21 .206 C4
Auld Kirk Mus* G66 .58 B1
Auld Kirk Rd G72 .139 B2
Auld NIck's View KA7 .238 C1
Auld Rd The G67 .62 A2
Auld St G81 .73 C2
Auld's Brae 2 ML6 .123 A4
Auldbar Rd G52 .115 C2
Auldbar Terr PA2 .114 A1
Auldburn Rd G43 .136 A3
Auldearn Rd G21 .98 B4
Auldgirth Rd G52 .115 C2
Auldhame St ML5 .121 C4
Auldhouse Ave G43 .136 A3
Auldhouse Ct G43 .136 A3
Auldhouse Gdns G43 .136 A3
Auldhouse Prim Sch
G75 .180 B1
Auldhouse Rd
East Kilbride G75 .180 B1
Glasgow G43 .136 B3
Auldhouse Ret Pk G43 .136 B3
Auldhouse Terr G43 .136 B3
Auldlea Rd KA15 .150 A1
Auldmurroch Dr G62 .54 B1
Auldton Terr ML9 .185 C1
Aultbea St G22 .97 A4
Aultmore Dr ML1 .143 A1
Aultmore Rd G33 .119 C4
Aurs Cres G78 .134 B1
Aurs Dr G78 .134 B1
Aurs Glen G78 .134 B1
Aurs Pl G78 .134 C1
Aurs Rd G78 .134 C1
Aursbridge Cres G78 .134 B1
Aursbridge Dr G78 .134 B1
Austen La 2 G13 .95 C3
Austen Rd G13 .95 C3
Austine Dr ML3 .183 C4
Aven Dr FK2 .42 C2
Avenel Rd G13 .75 C1
Avenue End Rd G33 .99 A2
Avenue Pk FK9 .1 C4
Avenue Sq KA3 .211 B4
Avenue St Glasgow G40 .118 A3
Rutherglen G73 .118 A1
Stewarton KA3 .195 B1
Avenue The Bridge of A FK9 2 A4
Falkirk FK2 .24 B1
Newton Mearns G77 .156 B2
West Kilbride KA23 .190 C4
Avenuehead Rd G69 .101 A4
Avenuepark St G20 .96 C3
Aviemore Gdns G61 .76 A3
Aviemore Rd G52 .115 C2
Avils Hill KA25 .149 A1
Avils Pl KA25 .149 A1
Avoch St G34 .100 A1
Avon Ave Bearsden G61 .76 A2
Carluke ML8 .187 C1
Longriggend ML6 .84 B2
Avon Ct Falkirk FK1 .42 B1
Irvine KA11 .220 A2
Avon Dr Bellshill ML4 .142 B2
Linwood PA3 .112 A3
Avon Ho ML3 .162 C3
Avon Pk FK1 .87 C3
Avon Pl Coatbridge ML5 .101 B1
Kilmarnock KA1 .228 A3
Larkhall ML9 .199 A4

Avon Rd Bishopbriggs G64 .98 A4
Glasgow G46 .136 A1
Larkhall ML9 .199 A4
Avon St Denny FK6 .21 B2
Hamilton ML3 .162 C2
Larkhall ML9 .184 C2
Motherwell ML1 .163 C3
Avon Twr [10] ML1 .163 C3
Avon Wynd [23] ML2 .165 C3
Avonbank Cres ML3 .183 C4
Avonbank Gdns FK6 .21 B2
Avonbank Rd
Larkhall ML9 .184 C2
Rutherglen G73 .137 C4
Avonbrae Cres ML3 .183 C4
Avonbridge Dr ML3 .162 C2
Avonbridge Prim Sch
FK1 .87 C3
Avonbridge Rd FK1 .86 A4
Avondale Ave G74 .159 C1
Avondale Dr PA1 .114 A3
Avondale Pl G74 .181 A4
Avondale Rd KA23 .190 B3
Avondale St G33 .99 A1
Avonhead G75 .180 C3
Avonhead Ave G67 .82 B4
Avonhead Gdns G67 .82 B4
Avonhead Pl G67 .82 B4
Avonhead Rd G67 .82 B4
Avonmouth Pl PA19 .44 C3
Avonside Dr FK6 .21 B3
Avonside Gr ML3 .162 C2
Avonspark St G21 .98 A2
Aylmer Rd G43 .136 C3
Ayr Acad KA7 .235 C1
Ayr Coll KA8 .239 A4
Ayr Coll (Newton Annexe)
KA8 .236 A1
Ayr Dr ML6 .123 A3
Ayr Gram Prim Sch KA7 238 C4
Ayr Hospl KA6 .239 B1
Ayr La PA16 .44 C2
Ayr Rd Ashgill ML9 .185 C1
Irvine KA11,KA12 .224 C4
Kilmarnock KA1 .227 C2
Newton Mearns G77 .156 B2
Prestwick KA9 .236 A3
Rutherglen G46 .157 A4
Ayr St Glasgow G21 .97 C2
Troon KA10 .229 C1
Ayr Sta KA7 .239 A4
Ayr Terr PA16 .44 C2
Ayrshire Central Hospl
KA12 .219 A4
Ayton Pk N G74 .160 A2
Ayton Pk S G74 .160 A2
Aytoun Dr PA8 .72 C2
Aytoun Rd G41 .116 C2
Azalea Gdns G72 .139 C3

B

Baads Rd EH48,ML7 .106 B1
Baberton Way KA13 .207 A2
Babylon Ave ML4 .142 A2
Babylon Dr ML4 .142 A2
Babylon Pl ML4 .142 A2
Babylon Rd ML4 .142 A2
Back Cswy G31 .118 B3
Back Hawkhill Ave KA8 .236 A1
Back Main St KA8 .235 C1
Back O Dykes Rd G66 .80 A4
Back O Hill PA6 .91 A3
Back O' Hill Ind Est FK8 .2 A1
Back o' Hill Rd
Fluchter G64 .56 C1
Stirling FK8 .2 A1
Back O'Barns ML3 .162 C2
Back Peebles St KA8 .235 C1
Back Rd Alva FK12 .4 C4
Bridge of W PA11 .110 B4
Back Row ML3 .162 C2
Back Sneddon St PA3 .113 C3
Back St G82 .27 B1
Back Wlk FK8 .7 A4
Backbrae St G65 .60 B4
Backburn KA15 .171 A4
Backmuir Cres ML3 .162 A3
Backmuir Pl ML3 .162 A3
Backmuir Rd Glasgow G15 75 A2
Hamilton ML3 .162 A3
Backwood Ct FK10 .10 C3
Badenheath Pl G68 .81 B3
Badenheath Terr G67 .81 C2
Badenoch Rd G66 .59 B1
Bagnell St G21 .97 C3
Bahamas Way [6] G75 .159 A1
Baidland Ave KA24 .191 C3
Bailie Dr G61 .75 B4
Bailie Fyfe Way ML2 .186 A4
Bailiehill Pl KA1 .222 B1
Baille Wynd [11] G71 .141 A4
Baillie Dr Bothwell G71 .141 A2
East Kilbride G74 .160 B2
Baillie Gdns ML2 .165 C2
Baillie Pl G74 .160 B2
Baillie Waugh Rd FK7 .7 B2
Baillies La [7] ML6 .123 A4
Bailliesmuir Pl ML2 .166 A3
Baillieston Ave KA25 .170 A4
Baillieston Rd
Glasgow G32 .119 C2
Glasgow, Broomhouse
G71 .120 A1
Baillieston Sta G69 .120 A2
Bain Cres G84 .16 C2
Bain St G40 .241 C1
Bain Way G83 .27 C3
Bainfield Rd G82 .48 A4
Baingle Brae FK10 .4 A2
Baingle Cres FK10 .4 A2
Bainsford Prim Sch FK2 .42 A4
Bainsford St G32 .118 C3
Baird Ave Airdrie ML6 .103 A1
Helensburgh G84 .16 A1
Kilwinning KA13 .207 C2
Larkhall ML9 .199 B4
Paisley G52 .114 C4
Baird Brae G4 .97 A2
Baird Cres Alexandria G83 .27 B4
Cumbernauld G67 .82 A4
Baird Ct G81 .74 A1
Baird Dr Bearsden G61 .75 B3
Erskine PA8 .72 C2
Baird Hill G75 .180 C4
Baird Meml Prim Sch
G67 .82 B4
Baird Pl Bellshill ML4 .142 A4
Kilmarnock KA3 .223 A1
Monkton KA9 .233 B2
Wishaw ML2 .165 C2
Baird Rd Ayr KA7 .238 C1
Kilmarnock KA3 .223 A1
Monkton KA9 .233 B2
Baird St Coatbridge ML5 .122 A4
Falkirk FK1 .41 B3
Glasgow G4 .241 B4
Baird Terr ML7 .127 B3
Bairds Cres ML3 .162 B2
Bairdsland View ML4 .142 A3
Bairns Ford Ave FK2 .42 A4
Bairns Ford Ct FK2 .42 A4
Bairns Ford Dr FK2 .42 A4
Baker St Glasgow G41 .116 C1
Greenock PA15 .46 A2
Stirling FK8 .7 A4
Bakewell Rd G69 .120 A3
Balaclava St G2, G3 .240 B2
Balado Rd G33 .119 C4
Balbakie Rd ML7 .127 C3
Balbeg St G51 .115 C3
Balbeggie St G32 .119 B2
Balblair Rd G52 .115 C1
Balcarres Ave G12 .96 B3
Balcary Pl ML6 .123 C1
Balcastle Gdns G65 .36 A1
Balcastle Rd Kilsyth G65 .36 A1
Slamannan FK1 .86 A3
Balcomie Cres KA10 .230 A1
Balcomie St G33 .99 A1
Balcomie Terr ML3 .183 A4
Balcurvie Rd G34 .100 A1
Baldernock Prim Sch
G64 .56 A1
Baldernock Rd G62 .55 B1
Baldinnie Rd G34 .120 A4
Baldoran Dr G66 .58 A3
Baldorran Cres G68 .61 A2
Baldovan Cres G33 .119 C4
Baldovie Rd G52 .115 B2
Baldragon Rd G34 .100 B1
Baldric Rd G13 .95 B3
Baldwin Ave G13 .95 B4
Balerno Dr G52 .115 C2
Baleshrae Cres KA3 .223 A3
Balfearn Dr G76 .178 C3
Balfleurs St G62 .55 A1
Balfluig St G34 .99 C1
Balfour Ave KA15 .171 A4
Balfour Cres Plean FK7 .12 B2
Stenhousemuir FK5 .23 B1
Balfour Ct KA3 .223 B2
Balfour St Alloa FK10 .10 B4
Bannockburn FK7 .7 B1
Bonnybridge FK4 .39 C3
Glasgow G20 .96 B3
Port Glasgow PA14 .47 A1
Stirling FK8 .1 C1
Balfour Terr G75 .180 C4
Balfour Wynd ML9 .185 A1
Balfron Cres ML3 .161 C2
Balfron Dr ML5 .122 B2
Balfron Pl ML5 .122 B2
Balfron Rd Glasgow G51 .115 C4
Greenock PA15 .46 B1
Paisley PA1 .114 B3
Balgair Dr PA1 .114 A3
Balgair Pl G22 .97 A2
Balgair St G22 .97 A2
Balgair Terr G32 .119 A3
Balglass Gdns G22 .97 A2
Balglass St G22 .97 A3
Balgonie Ave PA2 .113 A1
Balgonie Dr PA2 .113 B1
Balgonie Rd G52 .115 C2
Balgonie Woods PA2 .113 B1
Balgownie Cres G46 .136 A1
Balgray Ave
Kilbirnie KA25 .170 A4
Kilmarnock KA1 .227 C1
Balgray Cres G78 .134 C1
Balgray Rd Barrmill KA15 172 A3
Glengarnock KA14,KA25 .170 A4
Newton Mearns G77 .156 A3
Balgray Way KA11 .220 A3
Balgraybank St G21 .98 A2
Balgrayhill Rd G21 .97 C3
Balgraystone Rd G77,
G78 .155 B4
Balintore St G32 .119 A3
Baliol La G3 .240 A4
Baliol St G3 .240 A4
Baljaffray Prim Sch G61 .75 B4
Baljaffray Rd G61 .75 A4
Ballachalairy Yett G63 .30 B2
Ballagan Pl G62 .54 B1
Ballaig Ave G61 .75 B3
Ballaig Cres G33 .99 B3
Ballantay Quadrant G45 138 A2
Ballantay Rd G45 .138 A2
Ballantay Terr G45 .138 A2
Ballantine Ave G52 .115 A4
Ballantine Dr KA7 .238 C3
Ballantrae G74 .159 B1
Ballantrae Cres G77 .157 A2
Ballantrae Dr G77 .157 A2
Ballantrae Rd G72 .161 C3
Ballantyne Dr La KA7 .238 C3
Ballater Cres ML2 .165 A3
Ballater Dr Bearsden G61 .76 A1
Inchinnan PA4 .93 B4
Paisley PA2 .114 A1
Stirling FK9 .2 B2
Ballater Pl G5 .117 B2
Ballater St G5 .117 B2
Ballater Way ML5 .101 B3
Ballayne Dr G69 .81 A2
Ballengeich Pass FK8 .2 A1
Ballengeich Rd FK8 .1 C1
Ballentrae Wynd ML1 .143 A3
Ballerup High Sch G75 .180 A2
Ballerup Terr G75 .180 C3
Ballewan Cres G63 .31 A2
Ballindalloch Dr G31 .118 A4
Ballindalloch La G31 .118 A4
Ballinkier Ave FK4 .38 C2
Balloch Castle★ G83 .19 B1
Balloch Castle Ctry Pk★
G83 .19 B1
Balloch Gdns G52 .115 C2
Balloch Holdings G68 .61 A1
Balloch Rd Airdrie ML6 .124 A3
Balloch G83 .27 B4
Cumbernauld G68 .61 B1
Greenock PA15 .46 A1
Shotts ML7 .146 C3
Balloch Rdbt G68 .61 A1
Balloch Sta G83 .27 C4
Balloch View G67 .61 C1
Ballochmill Rd G73 .138 B4
Ballochmyle G74 .160 B2
Ballochmyle Cres [11]
G53 .135 A4
Ballochmyle Dr [14] G53 .135 A4
Ballochmyle Gdns G53 .135 A4
Ballochmyle Pl [12] G53 .135 A4
Ballochney La ML6 .102 C1
Ballochney Rd ML6 .103 C2
Ballochney St ML6 .102 C1
Ballochnie Dr ML6 .104 A2
Ballochyle Pl PA19 .43 C3
Ballogie Rd G44 .137 A4
Ballot Rd KA12 .219 B2
Balmalloch Prim Sch
G65 .36 B1
Balmalloch Rd G65 .36 B1
Balmartin Rd G23 .76 B1
Balmedie PA8 .73 A1
Balmeg Ave G46 .157 B4
Balmerino Pl G64 .98 B4
Balminnoch Pk KA7 .238 B1
Balmoral Ave ML6 .102 C3
Balmoral Cres
Coatbridge ML5 .121 B2
Inchinnan PA4 .93 C3
Balmoral Dr Bearsden G61 76 A1
Bishopton PA7 .72 B1
Cambuslang G72 .138 C3
Falkirk FK1 .41 C2
Glasgow G32 .139 A4
Balmoral Gdns
Blantyre G72 .140 B1
Uddingston G71 .120 C1
Balmoral Path [3] ML9 .185 B1
Balmoral Pl
East Kilbride G74 .159 B1
Gourock PA19 .43 C3
Stenhousemuir FK5 .23 C2
Stirling FK8 .7 A4
Balmoral Rd
Elderslie PA5 .112 A1
Kilmarnock KA3 .222 C1
Balmoral St Falkirk FK1 .41 C2
Glasgow G14 .95 A2
Balmoral Wynd KA3 .211 C4
Balmore Ct PA13 .89 B4
Balmore Dr ML3 .183 A4
Balmore Ind Est G22 .97 A4
Balmore Pl G22 .97 A3
Balmore Rd Glasgow G22 .97 A3
Greenock PA15 .46 B1
Bardowie G62,G64 .77 B4
Balmore Sq G22 .97 A3
Balmuildy Prim Sch G64 .77 C2
Balmuildy Rd G64 .77 B3
Balmulzier Rd FK1 .86 A4
Balornock Prim Sch G21 98 A2
Balornock Rd G21 .98 A3
Balquhatstone Cres FK1 .86 A3
Balquhidderock FK7 .7 B2
Balrossie Dr PA13 .89 A4
Balruddery Pl G64 .98 B4
Balshagray Ave G11,G14 .95 C2
Balshagray Cres G14 .95 C1
Balshagray Dr G11 .95 C2
Balshagray La G11 .95 C2
Balshagray Pl G11 .95 C2
Baltersan Gdns ML3 .183 C2
Baltic Ct G40 .118 A2
Baltic La G40 .118 A2
Baltic Pl G40 .117 C2
Baltic St G40 .118 A2
Balure Cres FK7 .8 B2
Balure St G31 .118 B4
Balvaird Cres [9] G73 .138 A4
Balvaird Dr G73 .138 A4
Balvenie Dr ML1 .143 A1
Balvenie St ML5 .122 A2
Balveny St G33 .99 B1
Balvicar Dr G42 .116 C1
Balvicar St G42 .116 C1
Balvie Ave Glasgow G15 .75 A1
Glasgow, Giffnock G46 .136 B1
Balvie Cres G62 .54 C1
Balvie Rd G62 .54 C1
Banavie Rd Glasgow G11 .96 A2
Wishaw ML2 .165 C3
Banchory Ave
Glasgow G43 .136 A3
Glenmavis ML6 .102 C3
Inchinnan PA4 .93 B4
Banchory Cres G61 .76 A1
Banchory Pl FK10 .4 B2
Banchory Prim Sch FK10 .4 B2
Banchory Rd ML2 .165 A3
Bandeath Ind Est
Fallin FK7 .8 C2
Throsk FK7 .9 A3
Bandeath Rd FK7 .8 B2
Baneberry Path G74 .159 B2
Banff Ave ML6 .123 A2
Banff Pl East Kilbride G75 180 B4
Greenock PA16 .44 B3
Banff Quadrant ML2 .165 A3
Banff Rd PA16 .44 B3
Banff St G33 .99 A1
Bangorshill St G46 .135 C2
Bank Ave G62 .55 A2
Bank Ct KA12 .219 C2
Bank Pk G75 .180 B4
Bank Pl Irvine KA12 .219 C2
[3] Kilmarnock KA1 .227 C4
Shotts ML7 .146 C2
Bank Rd Glasgow G32 .139 B4
Harthill ML7 .127 C3
Bank St Airdrie ML6 .123 A4
Alexandria G83 .27 C3
Alloa FK10 .10 A3
Barrhead G78 .134 B1
Cambuslang G72 .139 A3
Coatbridge ML5 .121 C3
Falkirk FK1 .42 A3
Glasgow G12 .96 C1
Greenock PA15 .45 C2
Irvine KA12 .219 B2
Kilbirnie KA25 .149 A1
Kilmarnock KA1 .227 C4
Neilston G78 .154 B4
Paisley PA1 .113 C3
Prestwick KA9 .236 A4
Slamannan FK1 .86 A3
Stirling FK8 .7 A4
Troon KA10 .229 B1
Bank View ML6 .123 B1
Bank Way [14] ML9 .185 A2
Bankbrae Ave G53 .135 A3
Bankend Pl KA3 .223 A3
Bankend Rd
Bridge of W PA11 .110 C4
Dumbarton G82 .49 C2
Bankend St G33 .99 A1
Bankfaulds Ave KA25 .149 A1
Bankfaulds Ct [4] KA25 .149 A1
Bankfield Dr ML3 .183 B4
Bankfield Pk KA7 .239 B2
Bankfield Rdbt KA7 .239 B2
Bankfoot Dr G52 .115 A3
Bankfoot Pl G77 .157 A2
Bankfoot Rd
Glasgow G52 .115 A2
Paisley PA3 .113 A3
Bankglen Rd G15 .75 A2
Bankhall St G42 .117 A1
Bankhead Ave
Airdrie ML6 .123 B4
Bellshill ML4 .142 A2
Coatbridge ML5 .121 B2
Glasgow G13 .95 A3
Springside KA11 .221 A1
Bankhead Cres FK4 .39 B3
Bankhead Dr G73 .138 A4
Bankhead Pl Airdrie ML6 123 B4
Coatbridge ML5 .121 B2
Stewarton KA3 .195 C1
Bankhead Prim Sch
Glasgow G13 .95 A3
Glasgow, Bankhead G73 .137 C4
Bankhead Rd
Carmunnock G76 .158 B4
Fishcross FK10 .5 B2
Kilwinning KA13 .207 C2
Kirkintilloch G66 .80 A4
Rutherglen G73 .137 C4
Bankhead Terr ML11 .215 A1
Bankholm Pl G76 .157 C3
Bankier Prim Sch FK4 .38 C2
Bankier Rd FK4 .38 C2
Bankier Terr FK4 .38 C2
Banknock St G32 .118 C3
Banks Rd G66 .58 C1
Banks View FK2 .14 C2
Bankside FK2 .42 B4
Bankside Ave PA5 .111 C2
Bankside Ct FK6 .21 C1
Bankside Gdns KA25 .149 A2
Bankside Ind Est FK2 .42 B4
Banktop Pl PA5 .111 C2
Bankview Cres G66 .79 A4
Bankview Dr G66 .79 A4
Bannachra Cres G83 .27 B3
Bannachra Dr G84 .16 A1
Bannatyne Ave G31 .118 A4
Bannatyne St ML11 .215 A2
Banner Dr G13 .75 B1
Banner Rd G13 .75 B1
Bannercross Ave [13]
G69 .120 A3
Bannercross Dr G69 .120 A3
Bannercross Gdns [12]
G69 .120 A3
Bannerman Dr
Bellshill ML4 .142 B3
Kilmarnock KA3 .223 B1
Bannerman High Sch
G69 .120 A2
Bannerman Pl G81 .74 A1
Bannoch Gdns KA13 .208 A2
Bannoch Pl KA13 .208 A2
Bannoch Rd KA13 .208 A2
Bannock Rd FK7 .8 B2
Bannockburn Cross FK7 .7 C1
Bannockburn Dr [28]
ML9 .185 B1
Bannockburn Heritage Ctr★
FK7 .7 A1
Bannockburn High Sch
FK7 .7 B1
Bannockburn Hospl FK7 .11 C4
Bannockburn Pl
Kilmarnock KA3 .223 A2
Motherwell ML1 .143 A1
Bannockburn Prim Sch
FK7 .7 C1
Bannockburn Rd
Cowie FK7 .12 B4
Stirling FK7 .7 B2
Bannockburn St PA16 .45 B2
Bannockburn Station Rd
FK7 .8 A2
Bantaskin Prim Sch FK1 .41 C2
Bantaskin St G20 .96 B4
Bantaskine Dr FK1 .41 C2
Bantaskine Gdns FK1 .41 C2
Bantaskine Rd FK1 .41 C2
Bantaskine St FK1 .41 C2
Banton Pl
Bonnybridge FK4 .40 A2
Glasgow G33 .120 A4
Banton Prim Sch G65 .37 C2
Banton Rd G65 .37 B1
Banyan Cres G71 .121 B1
Bar Hill Pl G65 .60 A4
Bar Hill Roman Fort★
G65 .60 A2
Barassie G74 .159 B2
Barassie Cres G68 .61 C3
Barassie Ct G72 .140 C1
Barassie Dr PA11 .110 B3
Barassie Pl KA1 .227 C2
Barassie Prim Sch
KA10 .229 C3
Barassie St KA10 .229 C2
Barassie Sta KA10 .229 C3
Barassiebank La KA10 .229 C3
Barbadoes Pl KA1 .227 C3
Barbadoes Rd KA1 .227 C3
Barbados Gn [5] G75 .159 A1
Barbae Pl G71 .141 A2
Barbana Rd G74 .158 C1
Barbegs Cres G65 .60 C2
Barberry Ave G53 .135 A1
Barberry Dr KA15 .171 A4
Barberry Gdns G53 .135 A1
Barberry Pl G53 .135 B1
Barbeth Gdns G67 .82 A3
Barbeth Pl
Cumbernauld G67 .82 A3
Irvine KA11 .220 A3
Barbeth Rd G67 .82 A3
Barbeth Way G67 .82 A3
Barbour Ave FK7 .7 B2
Barbour's Pk KA3 .211 C4
Barbreck Rd [7] G42 .116 C1
Barcaldine Ave G69 .80 A1
Barcapel Ave G77 .156 C4
Barcaple Flats G77 .156 C4
Barclaven Rd PA13 .89 C4
Barclay Ave PA5 .112 A1
Barclay Ct G60 .73 A3
Barclay Dr
Helensburgh G84 .16 B2
Kilmarnock KA3 .223 B1
Barclay Gdns KA11 .220 B3
Barclay Pl KA3 .195 B1
Barclay Rd ML1 .163 A3
Barclay Sq PA4 .94 A1
Barclay St Glasgow G21 .97 C3
Old Kilpatrick G60 .73 A3
Barcloy Pl ML6 .123 C1
Barcraigs Dr PA2 .133 C4
Bard Ave G13 .95 A4
Bardowie Ind Est G22 .97 B2
Bardowie St G22 .97 A2
Bardrain Ave PA5 .112 B1
Bardrain Rd PA2 .133 B4
Bardrainney Ave PA14 .68 C4
Bardrill Dr G64 .77 C1
Bardykes Rd G72 .161 A4
Barefield St ML9 .185 A2
Barfillan Dr G52 .115 C3
Bargany Ct G53 .115 A1
Bargany Pl G53 .115 A1
Bargany Rd G53 .115 A1
Bargaran Rd G53 .115 A2
Bargarran Prim Sch PA8 .72 C1
Bargarran Rd PA8 .72 C2

Bargarron Dr PA3 ...114 A4
Barge Ct G84 ...15 B3
Bargeddie Prim Sch
G69 ...121 A3
Bargeddie St G33 ...98 B1
Bargeddie Sta G69 ...121 A2
Bargeny KA13 ...207 A1
Bargrennan Rd KA10 ...229 D3
Barhill La G65 ...59 C2
Barhill Rd PA8 ...73 A1
Barhill Terr G65 ...60 A2
Barholm Sq G33 ...99 B1
Barke Rd G67 ...62 A2
Barkin Ct FK1 ...42 A1
Barkly Terr [2] G75 ...180 B4
Barlae Ave G76 ...178 C4
Barlanark Ave G32 ...119 B3
Barlanark Cres G33 ...119 B4
Barlanark Dr G33 ...119 B4
Barlanark Pl
Glasgow G33 ...119 C4
Glasgow, Greenfield G32 ...119 A3
Barlanark Prim Sch
G33 ...119 C3
Barlanark Rd G33 ...119 C4
Barlandfauld St G65 ...60 C4
Barleith Ct KA1 ...228 C3
Barleyhill FK4 ...40 A3
Barlia Dr G45 ...137 C2
Barlia St G45 ...137 C2
Barlia Terr G45 ...137 C2
Barloan Cres G82 ...50 A3
Barloan Pl G82 ...50 A3
Barloch Ave G62 ...55 A1
Barloch Rd G62 ...55 A1
Barloch St G22 ...97 B2
Barlogan Ave G52 ...115 C3
Barlogan Quadrant G52 115 C3
Barmore Ave ML8 ...202 A4
Barmouth Ave PA19 ...44 C3
Barmulloch Prim Sch
G21 ...98 B2
Barmulloch Rd G21 ...98 A2
Barn Gn PA10 ...111 A2
Barn Rd FK8 ...7 A4
Barnard Gdns G64 ...78 A2
Barnardo's Lecropt Project
FK9 ...1 C4
Barnbeth Rd G53 ...115 A1
Barncluith Bsns Ctr
ML3 ...162 C2
Barncluith Rd ML3 ...162 C1
Barnego Rd FK6 ...21 B2
Barnes Rd G20 ...97 A3
Barnes St G78 ...134 A1
Barness Pl G33 ...119 A4
Barnett Cres KA21 ...216 C4
Barnett Ct KA21 ...216 C4
Barnett Path G72 ...161 B4
Barnflat St G73 ...118 A1
Barnford Cres KA7 ...239 A1
Barnhill Ct G77 ...156 B2
Barnhill Dr Hamilton ML3 161 B1
Newton Mearns G77 ...156 B2
Tullibody FK10 ...4 B1
Barnhill Rd G82 ...50 B2
Barnhill St PA15 ...46 B2
Barnhill Sta G21 ...98 A2
Barnkirk Ave G15 ...75 A2
Barns Cres KA7 ...238 C4
Barns Pk KA7 ...238 C4
Barns St Ayr KA7 ...238 C4
Clydebank G81 ...94 B4
Barns Street La KA7 ...238 C4
Barns Terr KA7 ...238 C4
Barns Terrace La KA7 ...238 C4
Barnscroft PA10 ...111 A2
Barnsdale Rd FK7 ...7 A2
Barnsford Ave PA4 ...93 A2
Barnsford Rd PA3,PA4 ...93 A2
Barnswood Pl [13] G71 ...141 A2
Barnton La FK1 ...42 A2
Barnton St Glasgow G32 ...118 C4
Stirling FK8 ...7 A4
Barnweil Rd
Kilmarnock KA1 ...227 C3
Prestwick KA9 ...236 B3
Barnweill Dr KA1 ...228 C3
Barnwell Rd FK9 ...2 B2
Barnwell Terr G51 ...115 C4
Barochan Cres PA3 ...113 A2
Barochan Pl G53 ...115 A2
Barochan Rd
Bellshill ML4 ...142 B3
Bishopton PA6 ...71 A1
Glasgow G53 ...115 A2
Houston PA6 ...91 A3
Barochan Way PA3 ...113 A2
Baron Ct ML3 ...163 A1
Baron Path G69 ...120 C3
Baron Rd PA3 ...114 A3
Baron St PA4 ...94 B1
Baron's Haugh Nature
Reserve* ML1 ...163 C1
Baronald Dr G12 ...96 A3
Baronald Gate G12 ...96 A3
Baronald St G73 ...118 A1
Barone Dr G76 ...157 B4
Baronhall Dr G72 ...161 B4
Baronhill G67 ...62 A3
Barons Gate G71 ...140 C2
Barons Rd ML1 ...164 B1
Barons Twr ML1 ...164 A2
Baronscourt Dr PA1 ...112 C2
Baronscourt Gdns PA1 ...112 C2
Baronscourt Rd PA1 ...112 C2
Barony Ct
Ardrossan KA22 ...205 B1
Barony Ct *continued*
[8] Glasgow G69 ...120 A3
Irvine KA11 ...219 C3
Barony Dr G69 ...120 A3
Barony Gdns G69 ...120 A3
Barony Glebe KA23 ...190 B3
Barony Pl G68 ...60 C1
Barony Rd KA9 ...236 B3
Barony Terr KA25 ...170 A4
Barony Wynd [9] G69 ...120 A3
Barr Ave G78 ...154 C4
Barr Cres G81 ...74 A3
Barr Farm Rd G65 ...60 C4
Barr Gr G71 ...141 A4
Barr Pl
Newton Mearns G77 ...156 B3
Paisley PA1 ...113 B2
Barr St Ardrossan KA22 ...205 B1
Glasgow G20 ...97 A2
Motherwell ML1 ...163 C4
Barr Terr G74 ...159 C1
Barr's Brae
Kilmacolm PA13 ...69 B1
Port Glasgow PA14 ...68 B4
Barra Ave
Coatbridge ML5 ...121 C2
Renfrew PA4 ...94 B1
Wishaw ML2 ...165 C3
Barra Cres Irvine KA11 ...220 B1
Old Kilpatrick G60 ...73 B3
Barra Dr ML6 ...123 C3
Barra Gdns G60 ...73 B3
Barra La KA11 ...220 B1
Barra Pl Coatbridge ML5 ...121 C2
Irvine KA11 ...220 B1
Stenhousemuir FK5 ...24 A2
Stevenston KA20 ...206 C1
Barra Rd G60 ...73 B3
Barra St G20 ...96 B4
Barra Wynd KA11 ...220 B1
Barrachnie Ave G69 ...120 A3
Barrachnie Cres G69 ...119 C3
Barrachnie Ct G69 ...119 C3
Barrachnie Dr G69 ...120 A3
Barrachnie Gr G69 ...120 A3
Barrachnie Pl [11] G69 ...120 A3
Barrachnie Rd G69 ...119 C3
Barrack St Glasgow G4 ...241 C1
Hamilton ML3 ...162 B2
Barraston Rd G64 ...57 A1
Barrbridge Rd G69 ...121 A2
Barrcraig Rd PA11 ...110 B4
Barrhead High Sch G78 134 B2
Barrhead Rd
Glasgow G53 ...135 B4
Newton Mearns G77 ...156 A3
Paisley PA2 ...114 A1
Barrhead Sta G78 ...134 A2
Barrhill Cres PA10 ...111 B2
Barrhill Ct G66 ...80 A4
Barrhill Rd Erskine PA8 ...93 A4
Gourock PA19 ...44 B4
Kirkintilloch G66 ...80 A4
Barrie Quadrant G81 ...74 A2
Barrie Rd
East Kilbride G74 ...160 B3
Glasgow G52 ...115 A4
Stenhousemuir FK5 ...23 C2
Barrie St ML1 ...163 C3
Barrie Terr KA22 ...205 B1
Barriedale Ave ML3 ...162 A2
Barrington Ave KA15 ...150 A1
Barrington Dr G4 ...96 C1
Barrisdale Rd
Glasgow G20 ...96 B4
Wishaw ML2 ...165 C3
Barrisdale Way G73 ...138 A2
Barrland Ct G46 ...136 B2
Barrland Dr G46 ...136 B2
Barrland St G41 ...117 A2
Barrmill Rd Beith KA15 ...171 B4
Burnhouse KA15 ...172 A1
Glasgow G43 ...136 A3
Barrochan Intc PA5 ...111 C2
Barrochan Rd PA3,PA5,
PA6 ...111 C3
Barrowfield Prim Sch
G40 ...118 A3
Barrowfield St
Coatbridge ML5 ...121 C2
Glasgow G40 ...118 A3
Barrpath G65 ...60 C4
Barrs Brae La PA14 ...47 B1
Barrs Cres G82 ...48 A4
Barrs Ct G82 ...26 A1
Barrs La ML8 ...187 C2
Barrs Terr G82 ...48 A4
Barrwood Pl G71 ...141 A4
Barrwood St G33 ...98 C1
Barry Gdns G72 ...161 B3
Barsail Prim Sch PA8 ...93 B4
Barscube Ave PA14 ...68 C4
Barscube Terr PA2 ...114 A1
Barshaw Dr PA1 ...114 A3
Barshaw Pl PA1 ...114 B3
Barshaw Rd G52 ...114 C3
Barskiven Rd PA1,PA3 ...112 C2
Barterholm Rd PA2 ...113 C1
Bartholomew St G40 ...118 A2
Bartie Gdns ML9 ...185 C1
Bartiebeith Rd G33 ...119 C4
Bartlands Pl G76 ...178 C2
Barton Ave G83 ...28 A4
Bartonhall Rd ML2 ...165 B1
Bartonholm Terr KA13 ...207 C1
Barty's Rd ML4 ...142 B3
Barwheys Dr KA6 ...237 C3
Barwood Hill G82 ...50 A3
Bassett Ave G13 ...95 A4
Bassett Cres G13 ...95 A4
Bastion Wynd FK8 ...7 A4
Bath La G2 ...240 B3
Bath Pl KA7 ...238 C4
Bath Sq KA22 ...216 B4
Bath St Glasgow G2 ...240 C3
Gourock PA19 ...44 C4
Kilmarnock KA3 ...222 C1
Bath Villas KA22 ...216 B4
Bathgate St G31 ...118 A3
Bathgo Ave PA1 ...114 C2
Bathurst Dr KA7 ...239 A1
Bathville Rd KA25 ...149 A1
Baton Rd ML7 ...146 B3
Batson St G42 ...117 A1
Batterflats Gdns FK7 ...6 C3
Batterflats Ho FK7 ...6 C3
Battery Park Ave PA16 ...45 A4
Battery Park Dr PA16 ...45 A4
Battismains ML11 ...215 B2
Battle Pl G42 ...136 C4
Battlefield Ave G42 ...137 A4
Battlefield Gdns G42 ...137 A4
Battlefield Prim Sch
G42 ...136 C4
Battlefield Rd G42 ...137 A4
Bavelaw St G33 ...99 B1
Bawhirley Rd PA15 ...46 B2
Baxter Cres FK6 ...21 B1
Baxter La Alexandria G83 ...27 C4
Lanark ML11 ...215 A2
Baxter St Fallin FK7 ...8 B2
Greenock PA15 ...46 B2
Baxter's Wynd FK1 ...42 A2
Bay St PA14 ...47 B1
Bay View Rd PA19 ...44 C4
Bay Willow Ct G72 ...139 C2
Bayfield Ave G15 ...75 A2
Bayfield Terr G15 ...75 A2
Bayne St FK8 ...2 A1
Beach Dr KA12 ...218 C1
Beach Pk* KA12 ...224 A4
Beach Rd KA10 ...229 C3
Beacon Pl G33 ...118 C4
Beaconcroft FK9 ...2 B4
Beaconhurst Sch FK9 ...2 B3
Beaconsfield Rd G12 ...96 A3
Beagle Cres KA7 ...238 B2
Bean Row FK1 ...42 A2
Beansburn KA3 ...223 A2
Beanshields Rd ML8 ...201 C2
Beard Cres G69 ...100 C3
Beardmore Cotts PA4 ...93 C3
Beardmore Pl G81 ...73 C2
Beardmore St G81 ...73 C2
Beardmore Way G81 ...73 B1
Bearford Dr G52 ...115 A3
Bearhope St PA15 ...45 C3
Bearsden Acad G61 ...75 C3
Bearsden Bath Ho* G61 75 C3
Bearsden Prim Sch G61 ...75 C2
Bearsden Rd G13 ...95 C4
Bearsden Sta G61 ...75 C2
Bearside Rd FK7 ...7 A2
Beaton Ave FK7 ...7 B1
Beaton Rd Balloch G83 ...27 C4
Glasgow G41 ...116 C1
Beaton St ML9 ...184 C3
Beaton Terr KA12 ...219 B3
Beatrice Dr ML1 ...142 C3
Beatrice Gdns PA6 ...111 B4
Beatson Wynd G71 ...121 A1
Beattock St G31 ...118 B3
Beattock Wynd ML3 ...162 A2
Beatty Ave FK8 ...2 A1
Beatty Pl G84 ...17 A1
Beatty St G81 ...73 C2
Beauclerc St FK12 ...5 A4
Beaufield Gdns KA3 ...222 A4
Beaufort Ave G43 ...136 B3
Beaufort Dr Falkirk FK2 ...24 A2
Kirkintilloch G66 ...79 A4
Beaufort Gdns G64 ...77 C1
Beauly Cres Airdrie ML6 ...123 C3
Kilmacolm PA13 ...89 B4
Kilmarnock KA1 ...228 A3
Newton Mearns G77 ...157 A2
Wishaw ML2 ...165 A1
Beauly Ct FK1 ...42 B1
Beauly Dr PA2 ...112 C1
Beauly Pl Chryston G69 ...80 B1
Coatbridge ML5 ...122 A2
East Kilbride G74 ...159 B1
[14] Glasgow G20 ...96 B3
Motherwell ML1 ...143 A3
Beauly Rd G69 ...120 A2
Beaumont Dr FK2 ...24 A1
Beaumont Gate [17] G12 ...96 B2
Beckfield Cres G33 ...98 B4
Beckfield Dr G33 ...98 B4
Beckfield Gate G33 ...98 B4
Beckfield Gr G33 ...98 B4
Beckfield Wlk G33 ...98 B4
Beckford La ML3 ...162 B3
Beckford Prim Sch ML3 162 B3
Beckford St ML3 ...162 B3
Beckford St Bsns Ctr
ML3 ...162 B3
Beda Pl FK7 ...8 B3
Bedale Rd G69 ...119 C2
Bedcow View G66 ...79 C4
Bedford Ave G81 ...74 B1
Bedford Ct FK10 ...10 A3
Bedford La [6] G5 ...117 A3
Bedford Pl FK10 ...10 A3
Bedford St Glasgow G5 ...117 A3
Greenock PA16 ...45 B4
Bedlay Ct G69 ...81 A2
Bedlay Pl ML5 ...81 C1
Bedlay View G71 ...141 A4
Bedlay Wlk G69 ...81 A2
Bedlormie Dr EH48 ...107 B1
Beech Ave Bearsden G61 ...76 A4
Beith KA15 ...150 A1
Bridge of W PA11 ...90 B1
Elderslie PA5 ...112 B1
Glasgow G69 ...120 A3
Glasgow, Dumbreck G41 ...116 A2
Irvine KA12 ...219 B1
Kilmarnock KA1 ...227 B4
Larkhall ML9 ...185 B1
Motherwell ML1 ...143 A2
Newton Mearns G77 ...156 C2
Paisley PA2 ...114 A1
Plean FK7 ...12 B2
Quarter ML3 ...183 C2
Rutherglen, Cambuslang
G72 ...138 C3
Rutherglen, High Burnside
G73 ...138 B2
Beech Cres
Cambuslang G72 ...139 C2
Denny FK6 ...21 B2
Larbert FK5 ...41 B4
Motherwell ML1 ...143 B4
Newton Mearns G77 ...156 C2
Beech Ct ML5 ...121 C2
Beech Dr
Caldercruix ML6 ...104 C2
Clydebank G81 ...74 A3
Beech Gdns G69 ...120 A3
Beech Gr Ayr KA8 ...239 B4
East Kilbride G75 ...180 A3
Gartcosh G69 ...101 A3
Law ML8 ...186 C3
Rhu G84 ...15 B3
Wishaw ML2 ...165 B4
Beech La FK9 ...2 A2
Beech Pl Bishopbriggs G64 98 A4
Blantyre G72 ...161 C4
Gourock PA19 ...44 B3
Beech Rd
Bishopbriggs G64 ...98 A4
Johnstone PA5 ...111 B1
Kirkintilloch G66 ...79 B3
Motherwell ML1 ...143 B4
Beech Terr ML9 ...185 A1
Beechbank Ave ML6 ...102 C1
Beechburn Cres PA12 ...129 B2
Beeches Ave G81 ...73 C3
Beeches Rd G81 ...73 C3
Beeches Terr G81 ...74 A3
Beeches The
Brookfield PA5 ...111 B3
Houston PA6 ...91 B1
Lanark ML11 ...215 A1
Newton Mearns G77 ...156 C3
Beechfield Dr ML8 ...202 A4
Beechfield Rd KA15 ...170 C4
Beechgrove G69 ...80 C1
Beechgrove Ave G71 ...141 B4
Beechgrove Pl G84 ...25 B4
Beechgrove Quadrant
ML1 ...143 A3
Beechgrove St G40 ...118 A1
Beechlands Ave G44 ...136 C1
Beechlands Dr G76 ...157 B3
Beechmount Ct ML7 ...147 A1
Beechmount Rd G66 ...79 B2
Beechtree Terr G66 ...58 B3
Beechwood Alloa FK10 ...5 B1
Kilwinning KA13 ...207 B3
Larkhall ML9 ...185 A3
Wishaw ML2 ...164 B1
Beechwood Ave
Clarkston G76 ...157 B3
Hamilton ML3 ...183 A4
Langbank PA14 ...70 B4
Rutherglen G73 ...138 B3
Beechwood Cres ML2 ...165 B1
Beechwood Ct
Bearsden G61 ...75 C2
Cumbernauld G67 ...61 C1
Cumbernauld G67 ...82 C4
Beechwood Dr
Bonhill G83 ...28 A1
Coatbridge ML5 ...122 B3
Glasgow G11 ...95 C2
Renfrew PA4 ...94 B1
Beechwood Gdns
Bellshill ML4 ...142 B2
Moodiesburn G69 ...80 C1
Stirling FK8 ...7 A3
Beechwood Gr G78 ...134 B1
Beechwood La G61 ...75 C2
Beechwood Paddock
KA10 ...230 A2
Beechwood Pl
Bellshill ML4 ...142 B2
Glasgow G11 ...95 C2
Beechwood Rd G67 ...82 C4
Beechworth Dr ML1 ...143 B1
Beecroft Pl G72 ...140 C1
Begg Ave FK1 ...41 C2
Beggs Terr KA22 ...205 B2
Beil Dr G13 ...94 C4
Beith Dr ML6 ...123 A2
Beith Prim Sch KA15 ...171 A4
Beith Rd Dalry KA24 ...191 C4
Glengarnock KA14 ...170 B3
Greenock PA16 ...45 C1
Johnstone PA5 ...111 C1
Beith St G11 ...96 A1
Belford Ct G77 ...156 B1
Belford Gr G77 ...156 B1
Belgowan St ML4 ...141 C4
Belgrave La G12 ...96 C2
Belgrave St ML4 ...141 C3
Belhaven Ct G77 ...156 B1
Belhaven Pk G69 ...100 B4
Belhaven Pl G77 ...156 B1
Belhaven Rd
Hamilton ML3 ...161 C2
Wishaw ML2 ...165 A2
Belhaven St PA14 ...47 A1
Belhaven Terr
[40] Glasgow G12 ...96 B2
Wishaw ML2 ...165 A2
Belhaven Terr W [36] G12 ...96 B2
Belhaven Terrace La [39]
G12 ...96 B2
Belhaven Terrace West La [37]
G12 ...96 B2
Bell Coll of Technology
ML3 ...162 B2
Bell Cres KA12 ...219 B3
Bell Dr ML3 ...161 B2
Bell Gn E G75 ...180 C4
Bell Gn W G75 ...180 C4
Bell St Airdrie ML6 ...122 C4
Bellshill ML4 ...142 A4
Clydebank G81 ...94 B4
Glasgow G1 ...241 B1
Greenock PA15 ...46 C1
Renfrew PA4 ...94 B2
Wishaw ML2 ...165 A2
Bell Trees Rd PA9 ...130 B1
Bell View Ct PA4 ...94 B2
Bell's Wynd Falkirk FK1 ...42 A2
Lanark ML11 ...215 B3
Bellahouston Acad G41 116 B3
Bellahouston Acad Annexe
G51 ...116 B3
Bellahouston Dr G52 ...115 C2
Bellahouston Prim Sch
G51 ...116 B3
Bellairs Pl G72 ...140 B1
Bellard Rd KA23 ...190 B2
Bellard Wlk KA23 ...190 B2
Bellas Pl ML6 ...104 A1
Bellcraig Ct G76 ...158 A3
Belleaire Dr PA16 ...45 B4
Bellefield Rd ML11 ...215 A3
Belleisle Ave G71 ...140 C4
Belleisle Cl KA13 ...207 B2
Belleisle Cres PA11 ...110 B3
Belleisle Dr G68 ...61 C2
Belleisle Gdns G68 ...61 C2
Belleisle Gr G68 ...61 C2
Belleisle Pk* KA7 ...238 C2
Belleisle Pl Gourock PA19 ...44 A3
Kilmarnock KA1 ...227 C2
Belleisle St G42 ...117 A1
Bellesleyhill Ave KA8 ...236 A2
Bellesleyhill Rd KA8 ...236 A2
Bellevale Quadrant KA7 238 C3
Bellevue Ave G66 ...79 A4
Bellevue Cres Ayr KA7 ...238 C4
Prestwick KA9 ...236 B4
Bellevue Gdns KA1 ...222 B1
Bellevue La KA7 ...238 C4
Bellevue Rd Alloa FK10 ...9 C3
Ayr KA7 ...238 C4
Kilmarnock KA1 ...222 B1
Kirkintilloch G66 ...79 A4
Prestwick KA9 ...236 B4
Bellevue St Ayr KA7 ...238 C4
Falkirk FK1 ...42 B2
Bellfield Ave KA1 ...228 B3
Bellfield Cres G78 ...134 A2
Bellfield Ct
Barrhead G78 ...134 A2
Hurlford KA1 ...228 B3
Bellfield Dr ML2 ...165 B1
Bellfield Intc KA1 ...228 B3
Bellfield La KA9 ...236 A4
Bellfield Prim Sch KA1 ...228 A2
Bellfield Rd
Bannockburn FK7 ...7 C1
Kirkintilloch G66 ...79 A4
Stirling FK8 ...7 A3
Bellfield St G31 ...118 A3
Bellflower Ave G53 ...135 B2
Bellflower Ct G74 ...159 B2
Bellflower Gdns G53 ...135 B2
Bellflower Gr G74 ...159 B2
Bellflower Pl G53 ...135 B2
Bellgrove St G31 ...117 C3
Bellgrove Sta G31 ...117 C3
Bellisle Terr ML3 ...183 A4
Bellrock Ave KA9 ...236 A3
Bellrock Cres G33 ...119 A4
Bellrock Ct G33 ...119 A4
Bellrock Path G33 ...119 A4
Bellrock Rd KA8 ...236 A2
Bellrock St G33 ...119 A4
Bellscroft Ave G73 ...137 C4
Bellsdyke Hospl FK5 ...23 B3
Bellsdyke Rd Airdrie ML6 123 A3
Falkirk FK2 ...24 B3
Stenhousemuir FK5 ...23 B2
Bellsdyke Rdbt FK5 ...23 A2
Bellsfield Dr G72 ...161 C3
Bellshaugh Gdns G12 ...96 B3
Bellshaugh La G12 ...96 B3
Bellshaugh Pl [2] G12 ...96 B3
Bellshaugh Rd G12 ...96 B2
Bellshill Acad ML4 ...142 A3
Bellshill Ind Est ML4 ...141 C3

Branchton Sta PA16 44 C2
Brancumhall Rd G74 160 B2
Brand Pl G51 116 B3
Brand St G51 116 B3
Brandon Arc 1 ML1 163 C3
Brandon Ct ML3 162 B2
Brandon Dr G61 75 C4
Brandon Gdns
  Cambuslang G72 138 C3
  Prestwick KA9 236 A4
Brandon Ho ML3 162 C3
Brandon Par E ML1 163 C4
Brandon Par S ML1 163 C3
Brandon Pl ML4 141 C2
Brandon St Glasgow G31 117 C3
  Hamilton ML3 162 C2
  Motherwell ML1 163 C3
Brandon Way ML5 121 B2
Brandyhill FK10 5 C2
Brankholm Brae ML3 161 B2
Branklyn Cres G13 95 B3
Branklyn Ct G13 95 B3
Brannock Ave ML1 143 B2
Brannock High Sch
  ML1 143 B2
Brannock Pl ML1 143 B2
Brannock Rd ML1 143 B2
Branshill Pk FK10 10 A4
Branshill Rd FK10 10 A4
Brassey St G20 96 C3
Braxfield Rd ML11 215 A1
Braxfield Terr ML11 214 C1
Breadalbane Cres ML1 142 B1
Breadalbane Gdns G73 138 B2
Breadalbane St G3 240 A3
Breadie Dr G62 75 C4
Bream Pl PA6 111 B4
Breamish Pl G75 179 C3
Brechin Rd G64 78 B1
Brechin St G3 116 C4
Breck Ave PA2 132 B4
Brediland Prim Sch
  PA2 113 A1
Brediland Rd
  Linwood PA3 112 A3
  Paisley PA2 112 C1
Bredin Way ML1 163 A4
Bredisholm Cres G71 121 B1
Bredisholm Dr G69 120 B2
Bredisholm Rd
  Bargeddie G69 121 A2
  Coatbridge G69 120 C2
  Glasgow G69 120 B2
Bredisholm Terr G69 120 B2
Brendan Way ML1 164 A1
Brendon Ave G75 180 A2
Brenfield Ave G44 136 C2
Brenfield Dr G44 136 C2
Brenfield Rd G44 137 A2
Brent Ave G46 135 C3
Brent Cres PA6 111 B4
Brent Ct G74 159 C2
Brent Dr G46 135 C3
Brent Gdns G46 135 C3
Brent Rd
  East Kilbride G74 159 C2
  Glasgow G46 135 C3
Brent Way G46 135 C3
Brentham Ave FK8 7 A3
Brentham Cres FK8 7 A3
Brentwood Ave G53 135 A2
Brentwood Dr G53 135 A2
Brentwood Sq G53 135 A2
Brereton St G42 117 B1
Breslin Terr ML7 127 B3
Bressay G74 159 C2
Bressay Pl KA3 223 A3
Bressay Rd G33 119 C3
Bressay Wynd 14 ML2 165 C3
Breton Ct FK1 42 B2
Breval Cres G81 74 A4
Breval Ct G69 120 B2
Brewery Rd 17 KA1 227 C4
Brewery St PA5 111 C2
Brewlands Cres KA1 231 B2
Brewlands Dr KA1 231 B2
Brewlands Rd KA1 231 B2
Brewster Ave PA3 114 A4
Brewster Pl Denny FK6 21 B1
  Irvine KA11 224 D3
Briar Bank G66 58 A3
Briar Dr G81 74 A2
Briar Gdns G43 136 B3
Briar Gr Ayr KA7 239 B2
  Glasgow G43 136 B3
Briar Neuk G64 98 A4
Briar Pl PA19 44 B3
Briar Rd Glasgow G43 136 B3
  Kirkintilloch G66 79 C4
Briarbush Way G72 161 B4
Briarcroft Dr G33 98 B4
Briarcroft Pl G33 98 C3
Briarcroft Rd G33 98 C3
Briarhill Ct KA9 236 B4
Briarhill Rd KA9 236 B4
Briarhill St KA9 236 B4
Briarlea Dr G46 136 B2
Briars Rd FK10 4 C1
Briarwell La G62 55 A1
Briarwell Rd G62 55 A1
Briarwood Ct G32 119 C1
Briarwood Rd ML2 164 C2
Brick La 10 PA3 113 C3
Bridesburn Pl KA3 195 C1
Bridge Cres FK6 21 B1
Bridge End ML7 146 B3
Bridge La
  9 Kilmarnock KA1 227 C4
  Paisley PA2 113 A2
Bridge of Allan Prim Sch
  FK9 2 A3
Bridge of Allan Sta FK9 1 C4
Bridge of Weir Prim Sch
  PA11 90 B1
Bridge of Weir Rd
  Bridge of W PA11 110 C4
  Brookfield PA3,PA5,PA11 111 B3
  Houston PA6 91 A1
  Kilmacolm PA13 89 C3
  Linwood PA3 112 A3
Bridge Pl Denny FK6 21 B1
  Milngavie G62 55 A1
  Shotts ML7 147 A2
Bridge Rd PA14 68 C4
Bridge St Alexandria G83 27 C2
  Bonnybridge FK4 40 A3
  Cambuslang G72 139 A3
  Clydebank G81 73 C2
  Dumbarton G82 49 C2
  Glasgow G5 240 C1
  Hamilton ML3 162 B1
  Kilbirnie KA25 149 A1
  Linwood PA3 112 B3
  Longriggend ML6 84 C1
  Paisley PA1 113 C2
  Prestwick KA9 236 A4
  Wishaw ML2 164 C2
Bridge Street Underground
  Sta G5 117 A3
Bridge Terr 10 FK10 10 A3
Bridgebar St G78 134 C2
Bridgeburn Dr G69 80 C1
Bridgeford Ave ML4 142 B4
Bridgegait G62 76 B4
Bridgegate Glasgow G1 241 A1
  Irvine KA12 219 B1
Bridgehaugh Rd FK9 2 A1
Bridgehouse Ct KA1 228 A1
Bridgehousehill Rd KA1 227 C1
Bridgend Bishopton PA7 72 A2
  Dalry KA24 191 B4
  Kilwinning KA13 207 C2
  Stewarton KA3 211 C4
Bridgend Ave PA14 68 C4
Bridgend Cotts G66 80 A4
Bridgend Cres G69 80 C1
Bridgend Ct G68 38 C1
Bridgend Ind Est KA24 191 B4
Bridgend La KA13 207 C2
Bridgend Pl G69 80 C1
Bridgend Rd
  Greenock PA15 46 B1
  Kilbirnie KA25 149 A1
Bridgend View ML8 187 C1
Bridgend Wlk G78 153 A2
Bridgepark KA22 205 B1
Bridgeton Bsns Ctr 6
  G40 117 C3
Bridgeton Sta G40 117 C2
Bridgewater Ind Pk PA8 73 B1
Bridgewater Sh Ctr PA8 73 B1
Bridgeway Ct G66 79 C4
Bridgeway Pl G66 79 C4
Bridgeway Rd G66 79 C4
Bridgeway Terr G66 79 C4
Bridie Terr G74 160 B2
Brierie Ave PA6 91 A1
Brierie Gdns PA6 111 A4
Brierie La PA6 111 A4
Brierie-Hill Ct PA6 111 A4
Brierie-Hill Gr PA6 111 A4
Brierie-Hill Rd PA6 111 A4
Briery Ct KA25 170 A4
Brierybank Ave ML11 215 A2
Brig O'Lea Terr G78 154 B3
Brig-O-Doon Gr FK7 12 C4
Brigbrae Ave ML4 142 B2
Brigham Pl G23 96 C4
Bright St G21 97 C1
Brighton Pl G51 116 A3
Brighton St G51 116 A3
Brightside Ave
  Port Glasgow PA14 69 A4
  Uddingston G71 140 C3
Brigside Gdns ML3 163 A1
Bringan Rd KA3 222 C3
Brisbane Ct G46 136 B2
Brisbane Rd PA7 72 A2
Brisbane St Clydebank G81 73 B2
  Glasgow G42 137 A4
  Greenock PA16 45 B3
Brisbane Terr G75 180 B4
Britannia Pl KA8 236 A1
Britannia Way PA4 94 B1
Briton St G51 116 A4
Broad Sq G72 161 B4
Broad St Alloa FK10 10 A3
  Denny FK6 21 C1
  Glasgow G40 118 A3
  Stirling FK8 7 A4
Broad Way The ML2 164 C2
Broadcroft
  Kirkintilloch G66 79 B4
  4 Kirkintilloch, Eastside
  G66 58 B1
Broadcroft Rd 5 G66 58 B1
Broadfield Ave PA14 69 A4
Broadford St G4 97 B1
Broadford Terr PA16 44 C2
Broadholm Prim Sch
  G15 75 A2
Broadholm St G22 97 B3
Broadleys Ave G64 77 C1
Broadleys Rd FK7 7 B4
Broadleys Rdbt FK7 7 B3
Broadlie Ct G78 154 B4
Broadlie Dr Dalry KA24 191 A4
  Glasgow G13 95 A3
Broadlie Rd G78 154 B4
Broadloan PA4 94 B1
Broadmeadow Ind Est
  G82 49 C3
Broadmoss Ave G77 157 B2
Broadside Pl FK6 21 B1
Broadstone Ave PA14 47 A1
Broadway KA22 205 B2
Broadwood Bsns Pk G68 81 C4
Broadwood Dr G44 137 A3
Broadwood Pk KA7 239 A1
Broadwood Rdbt G68 81 C4
Broadwood Stad (Clyde &
  Airdrieonians FC's) G68 60 C1
Brock Oval G53 135 B3
Brock Pl Glasgow G53 135 B4
  Stirling FK7 7 A1
Brock Rd G53 135 B3
Brock Terr G53 135 B3
Brockburn Cres G53 135 A4
Brockburn Rd G53 135 B4
Brockburn Terr G53 135 B4
Brocklinn Pk G75 179 C4
Brockly View KA25 149 A2
Brockville Pk (Falkirk FC)
  FK1,FK2 42 A3
Brockville St G32 118 C3
Brodick Ave
  Kilwinning KA13 207 B2
  Motherwell ML1 163 A4
Brodick Cl KA13 207 B2
Brodick Dr
  East Kilbride G74 159 B2
  Gourock PA19 43 C3
  Helensburgh G84 16 C2
Brodick Pl Falkirk FK1 41 B2
  Newton Mearns G77 156 A2
Brodick Rd KA1 222 B1
Brodick St G21 98 A1
Brodie Ave KA10 229 C2
Brodie Park Ave PA2 113 C1
Brodie Park Cres PA2 113 B1
Brodie Park Gdns PA2 113 C1
Brodie Pl
  East Kilbride G74 159 B2
  Kilmarnock KA3 223 B1
  Stonehouse ML9 198 C1
Brodie Rd G21 98 B4
Brodie St FK2 42 A4
Brogan Cres ML1 163 A4
Broich The FK12 4 C4
Bron Way G67 62 A1
Bronte Pl FK5 24 A2
Brook St Alva FK10,FK12 5 A3
  Clydebank G81 73 C2
  Glasgow G40 117 C3
  Menstrie FK11 3 C3
Brookbank Terr ML8 188 A1
Brooke Ave G83 28 A4
Brookfield Ave G33 98 B4
Brookfield Cnr G33 98 B4
Brookfield Dr G33 98 B4
Brookfield Gate G33 98 B4
Brookfield Gdns G33 98 B4
Brookfield Pl Alva FK12 5 A3
  Glasgow G33 98 C4
Brookfield Rd PA14 68 C4
Brooklands
  Alexandria G83 27 B3
  East Kilbride G74 159 A1
Brooklands Ave G71 140 C4
Brooklea Dr G46 136 B3
Brooklime Dr G74 159 B2
Brooklime Gdns G74 159 B2
Brooklyn Pl ML2 186 A4
Brookside St G40 118 A3
Broom Ave PA8 93 A4
Broom Cliff G77 156 C2
Broom Cres
  Barrhead G78 134 A3
  East Kilbride G75 180 B3
Broom Ct FK7 7 B2
Broom Dr Clydebank G81 74 A2
  Larkhall ML9 185 A3
Broom Gdns G66 79 A3
Broom Path G69 119 C2
Broom Pk E FK11 4 A3
Broom Pk W FK11 4 A3
Broom Pl
  Bridge of W PA11 110 C4
  Coatbridge ML5 121 C2
  Glasgow G43 136 B3
  Kilmarnock KA1 228 A3
  Motherwell ML1 143 B2
Broom Rd
  Cumbernauld G67 62 B3
  Glasgow G43 136 B3
  Newton Mearns G77 157 A3
  Rosneath G84 15 A2
  Stirling FK7 7 B2
Broom Rd E G77 157 A2
Broom Terr PA5 112 A1
Broom Wynd ML7 146 C3
Broomage Ave FK5 23 A2
Broomage Cres FK5 23 A2
Broomage Dr FK5 23 A2
Broomage Pk FK5 23 B1
Broomberry Dr PA19 44 C4
Broomburn Dr G77 157 A2
Broomcroft Rd G77 157 A3
Broomdyke Way 2 PA3 113 B4
Broomelton Rd ML3,ML9 184 B1
Broomfauld Gdns G82 50 A2
Broomfield PA6 91 B1
Broomfield Ave
  Cambuslang G72 138 B4
  Newton Mearns G77 156 C2
Broomfield Ct G21 98 B2
Broomfield Gdn KA7 238 C3
Broomfield Gdns G84 15 B4
Broomfield La G21 97 C3
Broomfield Pl G21 97 C3
Broomfield Rd Ayr KA7 238 C3
  Glasgow G21 98 A2
  Netherburn ML9 199 C2
  Netherburn, Strutherhill
  ML9 199 A4
  Rutherglen G46 157 A3
Broomfield St
  Airdrie ML6 123 A4
  Kilwinning KA13 207 C2
  Netherburn ML9 200 B2
Broomfield Terr G71 120 C1
Broomfield Wlk 6 G66 79 B4
Broomgate ML11 215 A2
Broomhill Ave
  Glasgow G32 139 A4
  Glasgow, Whiteinch G11 95 C1
  Larbert FK5 23 A1
  Newton Mearns G77 156 C2
Broomhill Cres
  Bellshill ML4 141 C2
  Bonhill G83 28 A1
  Erskine PA8 93 A4
Broomhill Ct
  Kilwinning KA13 207 B3
  Larkhall ML9 185 A1
Broomhill Dr
  Dumbarton G82 50 A3
  Glasgow G11 95 C2
  Rutherglen G73 138 A3
Broomhill Farm Mews
  G66 58 C1
Broomhill Gate ML9 185 A1
Broomhill Gdns
  Glasgow G11 95 C2
  Newton Mearns G77 156 C2
Broomhill La G11 95 C1
Broomhill Path G11 95 C1
Broomhill Pl Denny FK6 21 B2
  Glasgow G11 95 C1
  Stirling FK7 6 C3
Broomhill Prim Sch G11 95 C2
Broomhill Prim Sch Annexe
  G11 95 C2
Broomhill Quadrant
  KA1 228 A2
Broomhill Rd
  Bonnybridge FK4 40 A2
  Larkhall ML9 185 A1
Broomhill Rd E KA1 228 A2
Broomhill Rd W KA1 227 C2
Broomhill St
  Greenock PA15 45 C2
  Harthill ML7 127 B3
Broomhill Terr G11 95 C1
Broomhill View ML9 184 C1
Broomhill Way PA15 45 C2
Broomieknowe FK10 4 B2
Broomieknowe Dr G73 138 A3
Broomieknowe Rd G73 138 A3
Broomielaw G1, G2 240 C1
Broomknoll St ML6 123 A4
Broomknowe G68 61 B2
Broomknowe Rd PA13 89 B4
Broomknowe Terr PA13 89 B4
Broomknowes Ave G66 79 C2
Broomknowes Prim Sch
  G21 98 A2
Broomknowes Rd G21 98 A2
Broomland Ct PA1 113 B2
Broomlands Ave PA8 93 C4
Broomlands Busway
  KA11 220 A1
Broomlands Cres PA8 93 C4
Broomlands Ct KA11 220 A1
Broomlands Dr KA12 219 B1
Broomlands Gdns PA8 93 B4
Broomlands La PA1 113 A2
Broomlands Pl KA12 219 B1
Broomlands Prim Sch
  KA11 220 A1
Broomlands Rd
  Cumbernauld G67 83 A4
  Irvine KA11 220 A1
Broomlands St PA1 113 B2
Broomlands Way PA8 93 C4
Broomlea Cres PA4 93 B4
Broomlea Sch G11 95 C1
Broomlee Rd G67 82 C3
Broomley Cres G83 27 B4
Broomley Dr G46 136 B1
Broomley La G46 136 B1
Broomloan Ct G51 116 A3
Broomloan Pl G51 116 A3
Broomloan Rd G51 116 A3
Broompark Ave
  Blantyre G72 161 B3
  Prestwick KA9 236 B4
Broompark Cir 8 G31 117 C4
Broompark Cres
  Airdrie ML6 103 A2
  Prestwick KA9 236 B4
Broompark Dr
  Glasgow G31 117 C4
  Inchinnan PA4 93 B4
  Newton Mearns G77 157 A3
Broompark Gdns FK6 21 C1
Broompark La 7 G31 117 C4
Broompark Rd
  Blantyre G72 161 B4
Broompark Rd *continued*
  Wishaw ML2 164 B2
Broompark St 6 G31 117 C4
Broomridge Rd FK7 7 A2
Broomside Cres ML1 163 C2
Broomside Pl FK5 23 B1
Broomside Rd FK4 40 A2
Broomside St ML1 163 C2
Broomstone Ave G77 156 C2
Broomton Rd G21 98 B4
Broomvale Dr G77 156 C3
Broomward Dr PA5 112 A2
Brora Cres ML3 182 C4
Brora Dr Bearsden G61 76 A2
  Glasgow G46 136 B1
  Renfrew PA4 94 C2
Brora Gdns G64 78 A1
Brora Rd G64 78 A1
Brora St G33 98 B1
Brosdale Ct FK1 42 A1
Brougham St PA16 45 C4
Broughton G75 180 C3
Broughton Dr G23 96 C4
Broughton Gdns G23 76 C1
Broughton Gn KA11 220 A3
Broughton Pl
  Coatbridge ML5 122 A2
  Hamilton ML3 162 A2
Broughton Rd G23 76 C1
Broun Dr KA7 238 C1
Brouster Gate 16 G74 159 C1
Brouster Hill G74 159 C1
Brouster Pl G74 159 C1
Brown Ave Alloa FK10 4 C1
  Clydebank G81 94 C4
  Dumbarton G82 50 B2
  Stirling FK9 2 A1
  Troon KA10 229 C2
Brown Pl
  Cambuslang G72 139 A3
  Saltcoats KA21 205 C1
Brown Rd G67 61 C1
Brown St Balloch G83 28 A4
  Carluke ML8 187 C2
  Coatbridge ML5 122 A3
  Falkirk FK1 41 B3
  Glasgow G2 240 B2
  Greenock PA15 46 B2
  1 Hamilton ML3 162 C1
  Larkhall ML9 185 A2
  Motherwell ML1 163 C4
  Paisley PA1 113 B3
  Port Glasgow PA14 47 A1
  Renfrew PA4 94 A2
  Shotts ML7 147 A2
  Stewarton KA3 211 B4
  Wishaw ML2 166 A2
Brown Wlk Irvine KA12 219 B3
  Wishaw ML2 166 A3
Brown's La PA1 113 C2
Browncarrick Dr KA7 238 A1
Brownhill Dr KA25 169 C4
Brownhill Rd G43 136 A2
Brownhill View ML2 166 B3
Brownieside Pl ML6 104 A2
Brownieside Rd ML6 104 B1
Brownlee Rd ML8 186 B2
Brownlie St G42 137 A4
Brownmuir Ave G76 178 C2
Brownsburn Ind Est
  ML6 123 A3
Brownsburn Rd ML6 123 B3
Brownsdale Rd G73 137 C4
Brownsfield Cres PA4 93 A3
Brownsfield Rd PA4 93 A3
Brownshill Ave ML5 121 C2
Brownside Ave
  Barrhead G78 134 A3
  Cambuslang G72 138 C3
Brownside Cres G78 134 A3
Brownside Dr
  Barrhead G78 134 A3
  Glasgow G13 94 C3
Brownside Gr G78 134 A3
Brownside Mews G72 138 C3
Brownside Rd G72 138 C3
Brownsland Ct G69 100 C3
Browside Ave PA2 133 B4
Bruar Way 15 ML2 165 C3
Bruart Ave FK5 23 C2
Bruce Ave
  Dundonald KA2 225 C1
  Johnstone PA5 131 C4
  Motherwell ML1 163 B4
  Paisley PA3 114 A4
  Prestwick KA9 236 A3
Bruce Cres 13 Ayr KA7 235 C1
  Falkirk FK2 24 A2
  Kilmarnock KA1 227 C2
  Plean FK7 12 B2
Bruce Ct 5 ML6 123 C4
Bruce Dr Fallin FK7 8 B3
  Stenhousemuir FK5 23 C2
Bruce Gate FK2 14 B1
Bruce La KA9 236 A3
Bruce Loan ML2 186 B3
Bruce Pl G75 180 C4
Bruce Rd Bishopton PA7 72 A2
  Glasgow G41 116 C2
  Motherwell ML1 143 A1
  Paisley PA3 114 A4
  Renfrew PA4 94 A1
Bruce St Alloa FK10 10 B4
  Bannockburn FK7 7 C1
  Bellshill ML4 142 A3
  Clydebank G81 74 A1
  Coatbridge ML5 122 A4
  Dumbarton G82 50 A1

Carfin Lourdes Grotto★
ML1 143 B1
Carfin Mill Rd ML1 143 B1
Carfin Rd
Motherwell ML1 143 B2
Wishaw ML2 164 B2
Carfin St Coatbridge ML5 122 A2
Glasgow G42 117 A1
Motherwell ML1 143 A2
Carfin Sta ML1 143 B1
Carfrae St G3 116 B4
Cargil Ave PA13 89 B4
Cargill Dr KA9 236 B3
Cargill Sq G64 98 B4
Carham Cres G52 115 B3
Carham Dr G52 115 B3
Caribou Gn G75 180 A4
Carillon Rd G51 116 B3
Carisbrooke Cres G64 78 A2
Carlaverock Rd G43 136 C3
Carleith Ave G81 73 C3
Carleith Prim Sch G81 73 C3
Carleith Quadrant G51 115 B4
Carleith Terr G81 73 C3
Carleston St G21 97 C2
Carleton Ct G46 136 B2
Carleton Dr G46 136 B2
Carleton Gate G46 136 B2
Carleton Gdns KA9 236 B4
Carlibar Ave G13 94 C4
Carlibar Dr G78 134 B2
Carlibar Gdns G78 134 B2
Carlibar Prim Sch G78 134 B2
Carlibar Rd G78 134 B2
Carlie Ave FK9 2 A3
Carlile Pl PA3 113 C3
Carlin La ML8 188 A1
Carlin's Pl G66 57 B4
Carlisle La ML6 123 B4
Carlisle Rd Airdrie ML6 123 B3
Cleland ML1 144 B3
Hamilton ML3 163 A1
Larkhall ML3,ML9 184 C4
Stonehouse ML9 199 B2
Carlisle St G21, G22 97 B2
Carlouk La ML8 188 A1
Carlowrie Ave G72 140 B1
Carlton Ct Glasgow G5 240 C1
6 Hamilton ML3 162 C1
Carlton Pl G5 240 C1
Carluke High Sch ML8 188 A1
Carluke Prim Sch ML8 188 A2
Carluke Sta ML8 187 C1
Carlung Pl KA23 190 B2
Carlyle Ave G52 114 C4
Carlyle Dr G74 160 A1
Carlyle Terr
East Kilbride G74 160 A1
Rutherglen G73 118 A1
Carmaben Rd G33 119 C4
Carman Rd Cardross G82 48 B4
Renton G82 27 B1
Carman View G82 50 A3
Carmel Ave KA1 222 B1
Carmel Dr KA11 221 A1
Carmel Pl
Kilmarnock KA1 222 B1
Kilmaurs KA3 222 A4
Carmel Terr KA1 222 B1
Carment Dr Glasgow G41 136 B4
Stevenston KA20 217 C4
Carmichael Ct
Bridge of A FK9 2 A4
Lanark ML11 215 B2
Carmichael Path ML5 101 B3
Carmichael Pl G42 136 C4
Carmichael St
Glasgow G51 116 B3
Greenock PA16 45 B3
Law ML8 186 C3
Carmichael Way ML8 186 C3
Carmona Dr G83 28 A4
Carmuirs Ave FK1 41 B3
Carmuirs Dr FK1 41 B3
Carmuirs Prim Sch FK1 41 B3
Carmuirs St FK1 41 B3
Carmunnock By-Pass
G76 158 B4
Carmunnock La G44 137 B3
Carmunnock Prim Sch
G76 158 B4
Carmunnock Rd
Clarkston G76 158 A3
Glasgow G44 137 B3
Carmyle Ave G32 139 A4
Carmyle Gdns ML5 121 C2
Carmyle Pl KA20 217 B4
Carmyle Prim Sch G32 119 B1
Carmyle Sta G32 119 A1
Carna Dr G44 137 B3
Carnarvon St G3 240 A4
Carnaughton Pl FK12 4 C3
Carnbooth Ct G45 137 C1
Carnbroe Prim Sch ML5 122 B2
Carnbroe Rd ML5 122 B2
Carneddans Rd G62 54 B2
Carnegie Dr FK1 41 B3
Carnegie Hill G75 180 B4
Carnegie Pl G75 180 B4
Carnegie Rd G52 115 A3
Carnell Cres KA9 236 B4
Carnell Terr KA9 236 B4
Carnoch St 11 G23 76 B1
Carnock Cres G78 134 A1
Carnock Gdns G62 54 C1
Carnock Rd G53 135 B4
Carnock St Cowie FK7 12 C4
Greenock PA15 46 A2
Carnoustie Ave PA19 44 A3
Carnoustie Cres
Bishopbriggs G64 78 B1
East Kilbride G75 180 A3
Carnoustie Ct
Bothwell G72 140 C1
Kilwinning KA13 207 A2
Carnoustie Pl
Bellshill ML4 142 A4
Glasgow G5 116 C3
Irvine KA11 224 D4
Carnoustie St G5 116 C3
Carnoustie Way G68 61 C3
Carntyne Ind Est G32 118 C3
Carntyne Path G32 118 B4
Carntyne Pl G32 118 B4
Carntyne Prim Sch G33 118 B4
Carntyne Rd G32 118 C4
Carntyne Sta G32 118 C3
Carntynehall Rd G32 118 C3
Carnwadric Prim Sch
G46 135 C2
Carnwadric Rd G46 135 C2
Carnwath Ave G43 136 C3
Carnwath Rd
Carluke ML8 188 A1
Kilncadzow ML8 203 B3
Caroline Cres FK12 4 C3
Caroline St G31 118 C3
Carolside Ave G76 157 C4
Carolside Dr G15 75 A2
Carolside Gdns G76 157 C4
Carolside Prim Sch
G76 157 C3
Carousel Cres ML2 165 B2
Carpenters Wynd FK10 9 C3
Carr Quadrant ML4 142 B3
Carradale Ave FK1 41 B2
Carradale Cres G68 81 C4
Carradale Dr KA9 236 B3
Carradale Gdns
Bishopbriggs G64 78 B1
Carluke ML8 202 A4
Carradale Pl PA3 112 A3
Carradale St ML5 121 C4
Carranbuie Rd ML8 187 C2
Carrbridge Dr 9 G20 96 B3
Carresbrook Ave G66 80 A3
Carriagehill Ave PA2 113 C1
Carriagehill Dr PA2 113 C1
Carrick Ave Ayr KA7 238 C3
Saltcoats KA21 206 A2
Carrick Cres
Glasgow G46 136 B1
Wishaw ML2 165 A2
Carrick Ct Kirkintilloch G66 59 A1
Stirling FK7 7 B3
Carrick Dr
Coatbridge ML5 121 B4
Glasgow G32 119 C2
Irvine KA12 219 A3
Rutherglen G73 138 A3
Carrick Gdns Ayr KA7 238 C3
Bellshill ML4 142 A4
Blantyre G72 161 B3
Carluke ML8 202 A4
Hamilton ML3 161 C1
Carrick Glen Hospl The
KA6 239 C1
Carrick Gr G32 119 C2
Carrick La PA16 44 C2
Carrick Pk KA7 238 C3
Carrick Pl
Ardrossan KA22 205 B2
Bellshill ML4 142 A4
Coatbridge ML5 121 B4
Falkirk FK2 24 A2
Falkirk, Tamfourhill FK1 41 B2
Glenboig ML5 101 C3
Larkhall ML9 185 A2
Prestwick KA9 236 A4
Carrick Rd Ayr KA7 238 C3
Bishopbriggs G64 78 B1
Bishopton PA7 72 B1
Cumbernauld G67 62 A2
East Kilbride G74 159 C2
Rutherglen G73 137 C3
Troon KA10 229 C4
Carrick Road La KA7 238 C3
Carrick St Ayr KA7 238 C4
Glasgow G2 240 B2
7 Larkhall ML9 185 B1
Carrick Terr
Dumbarton G82 49 A2
Greenock PA16 44 C2
Carrick Vale ML1 144 B1
Carrick View ML5 101 C3
Carrick Way 8 G71 141 A2
Carrickarden Rd G61 75 C2
Carrickstone Rd G68 61 C2
Carrickstone Rdbt G68 61 C3
Carrickstone View G68 61 C3
Carrington St G4 96 C1
Carrochan Cres G83 27 C4
Carrochan Rd G83 27 C4
Carroglen Gdns G32 119 B3
Carroglen Gr G32 119 B3
Carroll Cres ML1 143 B1
Carron Ave KA1 228 A3
Carron Cres Bearsden G61 75 B2
Bishopbriggs G64 78 A1
Glasgow G22 97 B3
Kirkintilloch G66 79 C2
Carron Ct
Cambuslang G72 139 B3
Hamilton ML3 162 A1
Carron Dr PA7 72 B1
Carron Pl Coatbridge ML5 101 B1
Carron Pl *continued*
East Kilbride G75 180 C3
Glasgow G22 97 C3
Irvine KA12 219 B3
Stirling FK7 7 A1
Carron Prim Sch FK2 24 A1
Carron Rd FK2 42 A4
Carron St Glasgow G22 97 C3
Wishaw ML2 165 A1
Carron Way
Motherwell ML1 143 B2
Paisley PA3 114 A4
Carronbank Ave FK2 24 A1
Carronbank Cres FK6 21 C2
Carronbank Ct FK2 24 A1
Carrongrange Ave FK5 23 C1
Carrongrange Gdns FK5 23 C1
Carrongrange Gr FK5 23 C1
Carrongrange Rd FK5 23 C1
Carrongrange Sch FK5 23 C1
Carrongrove Ave FK2 24 A1
Carrongrove Bsns Pk
FK2 24 A1
Carrongrove Rd FK2 24 A1
Carronhall Ave FK2 24 B2
Carronlea Dr FK2 24 A1
Carronshore Prim Sch
FK2 24 B2
Carronshore Rd FK2 24 A1
Carronside Pl FK6 21 C2
Carronside St FK2 42 A4
Carronvale Ave FK5 23 B1
Carronvale Rd FK5 23 B1
Carronview FK5 23 B1
Carrour Gdns G64 77 C1
Carruth Dr PA13 89 B4
Carruth Rd PA11 110 B4
Carsaig Ct FK9 2 A3
Carsaig Dr G52 115 C3
Carsaig Loan ML5 101 B3
Carscallan Rd ML3 183 C3
Carse Terr FK10 9 C4
Carse View FK2 14 C2
Carsebridge Ct FK10 10 B4
Carsebridge Rd FK10 10 B4
Carsegreen Ave PA2 133 A4
Carseloch Rd KA7 238 C1
Carsemeadow PA11 89 C1
Carseview Bannockburn FK7 7 C1
Tullibody FK10 4 A1
Carseview Dr G61 76 A3
Carsewood Ave PA9 130 C3
Carson Dr KA12 224 C4
Carson Rd G83 27 C4
Carstairs St G40 118 A1
Carswell Ct KA24 191 A4
Carswell Gdns G41 116 C1
Carswell Rd G77 156 A3
Cart La PA3 113 C3
Cart St G81 94 A4
Cartbank Gdns G44 137 A2
Cartbank Gr G44 136 C2
Cartbank Rd G44 136 C2
Cartcraigs Rd G43 136 A3
Carters Pl KA12 219 B1
Cartha Cres PA2 114 A2
Cartha St G41 136 C4
Cartland Ave ML8 201 C4
Cartland Rd ML11 214 B4
Cartland View ML11 214 C3
Cartle Cl KA13 207 B3
Cartsbridge Rd G76 157 C3
Cartsburn St PA15 46 A2
Cartsdyke Ave PA15 46 B2
Cartsdyke Sta PA15 46 B2
Cartside Ave
Inchinnan PA4 93 A2
Johnstone PA5 111 B1
Cartside Dr G76 158 A3
Cartside Pl G76 157 C3
Cartside Quadrant G42 137 A4
Cartside Rd G76 157 C3
Cartside St G42 136 C4
Cartvale La PA3 113 C3
Cartvale Rd G42 137 A4
Cartvale Sch G42 136 C4
Cartview Ct G76 157 C3
Carvale Ave ML7 125 A1
Carwinshoch View KA7 238 B3
Carwood Ct PA15 46 B2
Carwood St PA15 46 B2
Cask Cres FK8 7 B4
Caskie Dr G72 140 C1
Cassels Gr ML1 142 B1
Cassels St Carluke ML8 187 C1
Motherwell ML1 163 C4
Cassillis St KA7 238 C4
Cassiltoun Gdns G45 137 B1
Cassley Ave PA4 94 C1
Castburn Rd G67 62 C3
Castings Ave FK2 42 A4
Castings Ct Falkirk FK2 42 A4
Falkirk, Middlefield FK2 42 C3
Castings Dr FK2 42 A3
Castings Rd FK2 42 C3
Castle Ave Airth FK2 14 C2
Balloch G83 19 C1
Bothwell G71 140 C2
Elderslie PA5 112 A1
Falkirk FK2 24 B2
Helensburgh G84 16 A1
Motherwell ML1 143 A3
Stevenston KA20 206 C1
Castle Bsns Pk The FK9 1 C1
Castle Chimmins Ave
G72 139 B2
Castle Chimmins Rd
G72 139 B2
Castle Cres Bishopton PA7 72 A1
Denny FK6 21 B1
Falkirk FK2 42 B4
Torwood FK5 22 C4
Castle Ct Cumbernauld G68 62 C4
Falkirk FK2 42 B4
Kirkintilloch G66 79 B4
Menstrie FK11 3 C3
Stirling FK8 7 A4
Castle Dr Airth FK2 14 C2
Dundonald KA2 225 C1
Falkirk FK2 42 B4
Kilbirnie KA25 149 A1
Kilmarnock KA3 223 A2
Motherwell ML1 143 A3
Stenhousemuir FK5 23 C1
West Kilbride KA23 190 B3
Castle Farm Cl KA3 195 B1
Castle Gait PA1 113 C2
Castle Gate
Newton Mearns G77 157 A2
Uddingston G71 140 C3
Castle Gdns Chryston G69 80 C1
Gourock PA19 44 C4
Paisley PA2 113 A2
Castle Gr Kilbirnie KA25 149 A1
Kilsyth G65 36 B1
Castle Keep Gdns KA11 219 C2
Castle Levan Manor
PA19 43 C3
Castle Mains Rd G62 54 B1
Castle Pl Falkirk FK2 42 B4
Irvine KA12 219 A2
Uddingston G71 140 C3
Castle Quadrant ML6 123 B4
Castle Rd Airdrie ML6 123 B4
Ardrossan KA22 205 B2
Bridge of W PA11 90 B1
Dumbarton G82 50 A1
Elderslie PA5 112 B2
Falkirk FK2 42 B4
Greenock PA15 46 B1
Menstrie FK11 3 C3
Newton Mearns G77 156 B2
Port Glasgow PA14 47 B1
Stirling FK9 2 B2
Castle Semple Country Pk★
PA12 129 C2
Castle Semple Loch Visitor
Ctr★ PA12 129 B2
Castle Sq Ayr KA7 238 A2
Clydebank G81 73 C2
Castle St Alloa FK10 10 A3
Chapelhall ML6 123 B1
Clydebank G81 73 C2
Dumbarton G82 49 C2
Glasgow G4 241 C3
Glasgow, Baillieston G69 120 A2
Glasgow, Kelvinhaugh G11 96 B1
Hamilton ML3 162 C2
Irvine KA12 219 A2
Paisley PA1 113 B2
Rutherglen G73 138 A4
Castle Terr
Bridge of W PA11 110 C4
Denny FK6 21 B1
Knockentiber KA2 221 C2
Castle Vale FK9 2 A2
Castle View Airth FK2 14 B1
Ayr KA7 238 A2
Fallin FK7 8 B2
West Kilbride KA23 190 B3
Wishaw ML2 166 A3
Castle Way
Coatbridge G69 120 C3
Cumbernauld G67 62 B2
Castle Wlk KA7 238 B2
Castle Wynd
Bothwell G71 141 A1
Quarter ML3 183 C2
Stirling FK8 7 A4
Castlebank Cres G11 96 A1
Castlebank Ct G13 95 C3
Castlebank Gdns G13 95 C3
Castlebank St G11 96 A1
Castlebank Villas G13 95 C3
Castlebay Dr G22 77 B1
Castlebay Pl G22 97 B4
Castlebay St G22 97 B4
Castlebrae G82 49 B3
Castlebrae Gdns G44 137 A3
Castlecary Rd G68 62 B4
Castlecroft Gdns G71 140 C3
Castlefern Rd G73 138 A2
Castlefield Ct G33 99 A2
Castlefield Gdns G75 180 A3
Castlefield Prim Sch
G75 180 A3
Castlegait FK8 7 A4
Castlegate ML11 215 A2
Castleglen Rd G74 159 A2
Castlegreen Cres G82 50 A1
Castlegreen Gdns G82 50 A1
Castlegreen La G82 50 A1
Castlegreen St G82 50 A1
Castlehead High Sch
PA1 113 B2
Castlehill Ave
Port Glasgow PA14 69 A4
Slamannan FK1 86 A3
Castlehill Cres Ayr KA7 239 A3
Banknock FK4 38 C1
Chapelhall ML6 123 C1
Hamilton ML3 162 C2
Hamilton, Allanton ML3 163 B1
Kilmacolm PA13 89 B4
Law ML8 187 A2
Renfrew PA4 94 B2
Castlehill Ct KA7 239 A3
Castlehill Dr G77 156 C2
Castlehill Gdns ML3 162 C1
Castlehill Gn G74 158 C2
Castlehill Ind Est ML8 187 C2
Castlehill Prim Sch
Bearsden G61 75 B3
Wishaw ML2 186 A4
Castlehill Quadrant G82 49 B3
Castlehill Rd Ayr KA7 239 A3
Bearsden G61 75 B3
Carluke ML8 187 C3
Dumbarton G82 49 B3
Kilmacolm PA13 89 B4
Overtown ML2 186 A4
Stewarton KA3 195 C1
Castlehill View G65 36 B1
Castleknowe Gdns ML8 187 C2
Castlelaurie St FK2 42 B4
Castlelaw Gdns G32 119 A3
Castlelaw St G32 119 A3
Castlemilk Arc G45 137 B2
Castlemilk Cres G44 137 C3
Castlemilk Dr G45 137 C2
Castlemilk High Sch
G45 137 C1
Castlemilk Rd G44 137 C3
Castlemilk Terr G45 137 C1
Castlemount Ave G77 156 C2
Castlepark Cres KA12 219 A3
Castlepark Prim Sch
KA12 219 B3
Castlepark Rd KA12 219 A3
Castlerankine Rd FK6 21 B1
Castleton Ave
Bishopbriggs G64 97 C4
Newton Mearns G77 157 A2
Castleton Cres G77 156 C2
Castleton Ct
Glasgow G45 137 C1
Newton Mearns G77 156 C2
Castleton Dr G77 156 C2
Castleton Gr G77 156 C2
Castleton Prim Sch G45 137 B2
Castleview
Clachan of C G66 32 C2
Cumbernauld G68 62 C4
Dundonald KA2 225 C2
Castleview Ave PA2 133 A4
Castleview Dr
Bridge of A FK9 2 A4
Paisley PA2 133 A4
Castleview Pl PA2 133 A4
Castleview Terr FK4 39 A2
Catacol Ave KA21 205 C1
Cath of St Mungo★ G4 241 C3
Cathay St G22 97 B4
Cathburn Rd ML2 166 B3
Cathcart Bldgs PA15 46 A2
Cathcart Cres PA2 114 A2
Cathcart Pl G73 137 C4
Cathcart Rd
Glasgow G42 117 A1
Rutherglen G73 137 C4
Cathcart Sq PA15 45 C3
Cathcart St 10 Ayr KA7 235 C1
Greenock PA15 46 A3
Cathcart Sta G44 137 A3
Cathedral RC Prim Sch
ML1 163 C4
Cathedral Sq G4 241 C2
Cathedral St G1, G4 241 B3
Catherine Pl KA3 222 B3
Catherine St
Bannockburn FK7 7 B1
Kirkintilloch G66 79 B4
Motherwell ML1 163 C2
Catherine Way ML1 142 C2
Catherine's Wlk G72 161 B3
Cathkin Ave
Rutherglen G72 138 C3
Rutherglen, Gallowflat
G73 138 B4
Cathkin By-Pass G73 138 B2
Cathkin Cres G68 61 C2
Cathkin Ct G45 137 C1
Cathkin Dr G76 157 B4
Cathkin Gdns G71 120 C1
Cathkin High Sch G72 138 C2
Cathkin Pl
Cambuslang G72 138 C3
Kilwinning KA13 207 A2
Cathkin Prim Sch G73 138 B2
Cathkin Rd Glasgow G42 136 C4
Rutherglen G73 138 B1
Uddingston G71 120 C1
Cathkin View G32 139 A4
Cathkinview Pl G42 137 A4
Cathkinview Rd G42 137 A4
Catrine G74 159 B1
Catrine Cres ML1 164 A2
Catrine Ct 8 G53 135 A4
Catrine Gdns 7 G53 135 A4
Catrine St 5 ML9 185 B1
Catriona Pl G82 50 B1
Catriona Way ML1 143 A2
Catter Gdns G62 54 C2
Cauldhame Cres FK7 6 B3
Cauldhame Rigg KA3 211 C4
Cauldstream Pl G62 54 C1
Causeway The FK9 2 B3
Causewayhead Rd FK9 2 B2
Causewayside Cres G32 119 A2
Causewayside St G32 119 A1
Causeyfoot Dr KA25 149 A1

Craigton Dr
Barrhead G78 .134 C1
Glasgow G51 .115 C3
Newton Mearns G77 .156 B3
Craigton Gdns G62 .54 C1
Craigton Ind Est G52 .115 C3
Craigton Pl Blantyre G72 140 B1
Glasgow G51 .115 C3
Craigton Prim Sch G52 .115 C3
Craigton Rd
Glasgow G51 .115 C4
Kilbirnie KA25 .170 A4
Milngavie G62 .54 C2
Neilston G77 .155 A2
Craigton St G81 .74 B4
Craigvale Cres ML6 .123 C4
Craigvicar Gdns G32 .119 B2
Craigview FK10 .5 B1
Craigview Ave PA5 .111 C1
Craigview Rd ML1 .163 C4
Craigview Terr PA5 .111 B1
Craigward FK10 .10 A3
Craigweil Pl KA7 .238 C4
Craigweil Rd KA7 .238 C4
Craigwell Ave G73 .138 B3
Craiksland Pl KA10 .230 A2
Crail St G31 .118 B3
Cramalt Ct KA11 .220 A2
Crammond Ave ML5 .121 B2
Cramond Ave PA4 .94 C1
Cramond Ct FK1 .42 A1
Cramond Pl KA11 .219 C1
Cramond St G5 .117 C1
Cramond Terr G32 .119 A3
Cramond Way KA11 .219 C1
Cranberry Moss Rd
Kilwinning KA13 .207 B2
Kilwinning KA13,KA20 .207 B1
Cranberry Rd KA13 .207 A1
Cranborne Rd G12 .96 A3
Cranbrooke Dr G20 .96 B4
Crandleyhill Rd KA9 .236 A3
Cranesbill Ct KA7 .239 A2
Crannog Ct G82 .50 C1
Crannog Rd G82 .50 C1
Crannog Way KA13 .207 B2
Cranston St G3 .240 A2
Cranworth La G12 .96 B2
Cranworth St G12 .96 B2
Crarae Ave G61 .75 C1
Crathes Ave FK5 .24 A2
Crathes Ct G44 .136 C2
Crathie Ct ML8 .187 C2
Crathie Dr
Ardrossan KA22 .205 B1
Denny FK6 .21 B2
Glasgow G11 .96 A1
Glenmavis ML6 .102 C2
Crathie Pl G77 .157 A2
Crathie Quadrant ML2 .165 A3
Crathie Rd KA3 .222 C1
Crauford Ave KA23 .190 C2
Craufurd Cres KA15 .171 C2
Craufurdland Rd KA3 .223 A3
Craven Gr KA11 .219 C3
Craw Pl PA12 .129 B1
Craw Rd PA2 .113 B2
Crawberry Rd PA15 .46 A1
Crawford Ave
Kirkintilloch G66 .79 C2
Prestwick KA9 .236 B3
Crawford Cres
Blantyre G72 .140 B1
Uddingston G71 .140 C4
Crawford Dr
East Kilbride G74 .160 A1
Glasgow G15 .75 A1
Helensburgh G84 .16 C2
Crawford Hill G74 .160 A1
Crawford Rd Houston PA6 .91 B1
Milngavie G62 .54 C2
Crawford Sq FK2 .14 B2
Crawford St Glasgow G11 .96 A1
Hamilton ML3 .162 A3
Motherwell ML1 .163 B3
Port Glasgow PA14 .47 B1
Crawforddyke Prim Sch
ML8 .202 A4
Crawfurd Ave G73 .138 A3
Crawfurd Dr PA3 .113 A3
Crawfurd Gdns G73 .138 B2
Crawfurd Rd G73 .138 A2
Crawfurd St PA15 .45 C3
Crawfurdland Pl KA2 .221 B1
Crawfurds View PA12 .129 B2
Crawhin Gdns PA15 .45 B2
Crawriggs Ave G66 .79 B3
Creamery Rd ML2 .165 B1
Crebar Dr G78 .134 B1
Crebar St G46 .135 C2
Credon Dr Airdrie ML6 .123 A2
Crosshouse KA2 .226 C4
Credon Gdns G73 .138 B2
Cree Ave G64 .78 B1
Cree Gdns G32 .118 C3
Cree Pl G75 .159 A1
Creebank Pl KA10 .229 D3
Creelshaugh Rd KA3 .213 A2
Creighton Gr G74 .159 C1
Creigton Ct KA3 .223 A3
Creinch Dr G83 .19 C1
Creran Ct Hamilton ML3 .162 A1
Prestwick KA9 .236 B3
Creran Dr Denny FK6 .39 B3
Renfrew PA4 .94 A2
Creran Path 12 ML2 .165 C3
Crescent Rd G13 .95 A3
Crescent St PA15 .46 A2
Crescent The
Clarkston G76 .158 A3
Clydebank G81 .73 C2
Longriggend ML6 .84 B1
Prestwick KA9 .233 B1
Stewarton KA3 .195 C1
Cressdale Ave G45 .137 B1
Cressdale Ct G45 .137 B1
Cressdale Dr G45 .137 B1
Cresswell Gr G77 .156 B2
Cresswell La G12 .96 B2
Cresswell Pl G77 .156 C1
Cresswell St 5 G12 .96 B2
Cressy St G51 .115 C4
Crest Ave G13 .95 A4
Crestlea Ave PA2 .133 C4
Creteil Ct FK1 .42 B2
Creveul Ct G83 .27 C3
Crichton Ave KA24 .191 A4
Crichton Ct G45 .137 C1
Crichton Pl G21 .97 C2
Crichton St
Coatbridge ML5 .122 A4
Glasgow G21 .97 C2
Cricketfield La PA6 .91 A2
Crieff Ave ML6 .123 B1
Criffel Pl Kilmarnock KA1 228 A2
Motherwell ML1 .143 B2
Criffell Gdns G32 .119 B2
Criffell Rd G32 .119 B2
Crighton Wynd ML4 .141 B3
Crimea St G2 .240 B2
Crimond Pl Kilsyth G65 .36 A1
Shieldhill FK1 .66 C4
Crinan Cres ML5 .101 B1
Crinan Gdns G64 .78 B1
Crinan Pl
Ardrossan KA22 .205 B3
Bellshill ML4 .142 A2
Coatbridge ML5 .101 B1
Crinan Rd G64 .78 B1
Crinan St G31 .118 A4
Crindledyke Cres ML2 .166 A3
Cringate Gdns FK7 .7 C1
Cripps Ave G81 .74 B1
Crisswell Cl PA16 .44 B1
Crisswell Cres PA16 .44 B1
Crocus Bank KA7 .239 B2
Crocus Gr KA12 .219 B2
Croe Pl KA1 .228 A2
Croft ML9 .184 C1
Croft Pl ML9 .184 C2
Croft Rd Balmore G64 .77 C4
Cambuslang G72 .139 A3
East Kilbride G75 .180 C4
Larkhall ML9 .184 C2
Croft St Alexandria G83 .27 C2
Kilmarnock KA1 .222 C1
Croft Terr KA11 .220 C1
Croft Way PA4 .94 C1
Croft Wynd G71 .141 A3
Croft's Rd FK10 .4 A2
Croftbank Ave G71 .141 A1
Croftbank Cres
Bothwell G71 .141 A1
Uddingston G71 .140 C3
Croftbank Gate G71 .141 A1
Croftbank St 11 G21 .97 C2
Croftburn Dr G44 .137 B2
Croftcot Ave ML4 .141 C2
Croftcroighn Rd G33 .99 A1
Croftcroighn Sch G33 .99 C1
Croftend Ave G44 .137 C3
Croftend La G44 .137 C3
Croftfoot Cres G45 .138 A2
Croftfoot Dr G45 .137 C2
Croftfoot Pl Denny FK6 .21 B2
Gartcosh G69 .101 A3
Croftfoot Quadrant G45 137 C2
Croftfoot Rd G44 .137 C2
Croftfoot Sch G44 .137 C3
Croftfoot St G45 .138 A2
Croftfoot Sta G44 .137 C3
Croftfoot Terr G45 .137 C2
Crofthead KA11 .220 A2
Crofthead Ave KA3 .223 A3
Crofthead Cotts G78 .154 B4
Crofthead Cres ML4 .141 C2
Crofthead Ct Irvine KA11 220 A2
Stirling FK8 .2 A1
Crofthead Dr G66 .33 B1
Crofthead Pl
Bellshill ML4 .141 C2
Newton Mearns G77 .156 C2
Crofthead Rd Ayr KA7 .239 B3
Kilmaurs KA3 .222 A4
Prestwick KA9 .233 B1
Stirling FK8 .2 A1
Crofthead St G71 .140 C3
Crofthill Ave G71 .140 C3
Crofthill Ct ML9 .198 C1
Crofthill Rd G44 .137 C3
Crofthouse Dr G44 .137 C2
Croftmont Ave G44 .137 C2
Croftmoraig Ave G69 .81 A2
Crofton Ave G44 .137 B2
Croftpark Ave G44 .137 B3
Croftpark Cres G72 .161 C3
Croftpark Rd G81 .74 A4
Croftpark St ML4 .142 A3
Croftshaw Rd FK12 .5 A4
Croftside Ave G44 .137 C2
Croftspar Ave G32 .119 B3
Croftspar Ct G32 .119 B3
Croftspar Dr G32 .119 B3
Croftspar Gate G32 .119 B3
Croftspar Gr G32 .119 B3
Croftspar Pl G32 .119 B3
Croftwood G64 .78 A2
Croftwood Ave G44 .137 B2
Croftwood Rd ML3 .162 B1
Crogal Cres ML6 .123 B1
Cromalt Ave G75 .180 A2
Cromalt Cres G61 .75 B4
Cromarty Ave
Bishopbriggs G64 .78 B1
Glasgow G43 .136 C3
Cromarty Cres G61 .75 C4
Cromarty Gdns G76 .137 A1
Cromarty Pl Chryston G69 .80 B1
East Kilbride G74 .160 B2
Cromarty Rd ML6 .122 C3
Crombie Gdns G69 .120 A2
Cromdale Rd
Kilmarnock KA1 .228 A2
Port Glasgow PA14 .69 A3
Cromdale St G51 .115 C4
Cromdale Way ML1 .143 A1
Cromer Way 6 PA3 .113 B4
Crompton Ave G44 .137 A3
Crompton Way KA12 .219 C2
Cromptons Gr PA1 .113 A2
Cromwell Dr FK1 .42 B2
Cromwell La 5 G20 .97 A1
Cromwell Rd Ayr KA7 .235 C1
Falkirk FK1 .42 B2
Cromwell Rd W FK1 .42 B2
Cromwell St G20 .97 A1
Crona Dr ML3 .161 C2
Cronberry Quadrant
G52 .114 C2
Cronberry Terr G52 .114 C2
Cronin Pl ML4 .142 A4
Cronulla Pl G65 .60 C4
Crookedshields Rd G72,
G74 .160 A4
Crookfur Cottage Homes
G77 .156 B3
Crookfur Prim Sch G77 .156 B4
Crookfur Rd G77 .156 B3
Crookhill Dr PA12 .129 B2
Crookhill Gdns PA12 .129 B2
Crookston Ave G52 .115 A2
Crookston Castle★ G53 115 A1
Crookston Ct G52 .115 A2
Crookston Dr PA1,G52 .114 C2
Crookston Gdns G52 .114 C2
Crookston Gr G52 .115 A2
Crookston Path G52 .114 C2
Crookston Pl G52 .114 C2
Crookston Quadrant
G52 .115 A2
Crookston Rd G53 .135 A4
Crookston Sta G52 .114 C2
Crookston Terr G52 .115 A2
Crookstonhill Path G52 114 C2
Crophill FK10 .5 B1
Crosbie Ct KA10 .232 B4
Crosbie Dr Paisley PA2 .132 C4
West Kilbride KA23 .190 B2
Crosbie La G20 .96 B4
Crosbie Pl KA10 .232 C4
Crosbie Rd KA10 .232 C4
Crosbie St G20 .96 B4
Crosbie Terr KA9 .236 B4
Crosbie Wood PA2 .113 A1
Crosbies Ct FK8 .7 A4
Cross KA15 .171 A4
Cross Arthurlie Sch
G78 .134 A2
Cross Arthurlie St G78 .134 A2
Cross Brae FK1 .66 B3
Cross Ct G64 .77 C1
Cross Gates ML4 .142 A2
Cross House Stables & Riding
Sch★ G66 .32 B2
Cross Key's Cl ML11 .215 A2
Cross Rd PA2 .113 A1
Cross Shore St PA15 .46 A3
Cross St Falkirk FK2 .24 A1
Glasgow G32 .119 B1
Cross Stone Pl ML1 .163 C3
Cross The Dalry KA24 .191 B4
Glasgow G1 .241 B1
Kilmarnock KA1 .227 C4
Prestwick KA9 .233 B1
Stewarton KA3 .211 B4
Stonehouse ML9 .198 C1
Cross Wynd 1 G74 .159 C1
Crossart St ML7 .125 A1
Crossbank Ave G42 .117 C1
Crossbank Dr G42 .117 B1
Crossbank Rd G42 .117 B1
Crossbank Terr G42 .117 B1
Crossburn KA7 .238 A1
Crossburn Ave G62 .54 C1
Crossburn Dr KA10 .230 A2
Crossburn La KA10 .230 A2
Crossburn Terr KA10 .230 A2
Crossclyde View ML8 .201 B1
Crossdene Rd KA2 .226 C4
Crossdykes G66 .80 A4
Crossen La ML8 .188 A1
Crossflat Cres PA1 .114 A3
Crossford Dr 8 G23 .76 C1
Crossford Hawk Ctr★
ML8 .201 A1
Crossgate G66 .58 B1
Crossgates PA7 .72 A2
Crossgates Ave ML1 .144 A2
Crossgates St ML9 .184 C2
Crosshill Ave
Glasgow G42 .117 A1
Kirkintilloch G66 .79 B3
Crosshill Dr Cleland ML1 144 A2
Rutherglen G73 .138 A3
Crosshill Pl PA14 .68 C4
Crosshill Rd
Bishopbriggs G64,G66 .78 C3
Kirkintilloch G66 .79 B2
Port Glasgow PA14 .68 C3
Port Glasgow, Boglestone
PA14 .68 C4
Crosshill St Airdrie ML6 .122 C4
Coatbridge ML5 .121 A2
Lennoxtown G66 .33 B1
Motherwell ML1 .163 C3
Crosshill Sta G42 .117 A1
Crosshill Wynd KA3 .223 B3
Crosshouse Hospl KA2 .222 A1
Crosshouse Prim Sch
Crosshouse KA2 .221 C1
East Kilbride G75 .180 A3
Crosshouse Rd
Clachan of C G66 .33 A2
East Kilbride G75 .180 A3
Kilmaurs KA3 .222 A3
Crossing La ML9 .200 A2
Crosslaw Ave ML11 .215 B2
Crosslaw Gdns ML11 .215 B2
Crosslea Gdns PA6 .91 A1
Crosslee Cres PA6 .91 B1
Crosslee Pk PA6 .111 B4
Crosslee Rd PA11 .111 A4
Crosslee St G52 .115 B3
Crosslees Dr G46 .135 C2
Crosslees Pk G46 .135 C2
Crosslees Rd G46 .135 C1
Crosslet Ave G82 .50 B2
Crosslet Ct G82 .50 A2
Crosslet Pl G82 .50 A2
Crosslet Rd G82 .50 A2
Crossloan Rd G51 .115 C4
Crossloan Terr 5 G51 .116 A4
Crossmill Ave G78 .134 B2
Crossmount Ct ML8 .187 C1
Crossmyloof Gdns G41 .116 B1
Crossmyloof Sta G41 .116 C1
Crosspoint Dr 7 G23 .76 C1
Crossroads KA24 .170 B2
Crosstobs Rd G53 .115 A1
Crossveggate Bsns Pk
G62 .55 A1
Crossview Ave G69 .120 B3
Crossview Pl G69 .120 B3
Crossways PA6 .91 B1
Crosveggate G62 .55 A1
Crovie Rd G53 .135 A4
Crow Ave ML1 .143 A3
Crow Rd Glasgow G11 .96 A1
Lennoxtown G66 .33 A3
Stonehouse ML9 .198 C1
Crow Wood Rd G69 .100 A4
Crow Wood Terr G69 .100 A4
Crowflat View G71 .121 B1
Crowflats Rd G71 .140 C3
Crowhall Dr G33 .119 C3
Crowhill Cres ML6 .102 C1
Crowhill Rd G64 .97 C4
Crowhill St G22 .97 B3
Crowlin Cres G33 .119 A4
Crown Ave G81 .74 A2
Crown Cir 19 G12 .96 B2
Crown Gdns Alloa FK10 .9 C4
Glasgow G12 .96 B2
Crown Rd N G12 .96 B2
Crown Rd S G12 .96 B2
Crown St Ayr KA8 .235 C1
Calderbank ML6 .123 A2
Coatbridge ML5 .122 B4
Glasgow G69 .119 C2
Glasgow, Gorbals G1,G5 .117 B3
Greenock PA15 .45 C3
Crown Terr G12 .96 B2
Crownest Loan FK5 .23 C1
Crownhall Pl G32 .119 B3
Crownhall Rd G32 .119 B3
Crownpoint Rd G40 .117 C3
Crowwood Cres ML6 .123 A1
Crowwood Dr ML6 .123 B4
Crowwood Rd ML6 .123 A1
Croy G74 .159 B2
Croy Ave G77 .157 A3
Croy Hill Roman Fort★
G68 .61 A3
Croy Pl G21 .98 B3
Croy Rd Coatbridge ML5 .121 C2
Glasgow G21 .98 B3
Croy Sta G68 .60 C2
Cruachan Ave
Paisley PA2 .133 C4
Renfrew PA4 .94 B1
Stirling FK9 .2 A2
Cruachan Ct FK1 .42 B1
Cruachan Dr
Barrhead G78 .134 B1
Newton Mearns G77 .156 C2
Cruachan Pl KA1 .228 A2
Cruachan Rd
Bearsden G61 .75 A4
Rutherglen G73 .138 B2
Cruachan St G46 .135 C2
Cruachan Way G78 .134 B1
Cruckburn Wynd FK7 .6 C2
Cruden St G51 .115 C3
Cruickshank Dr FK1 .66 B3
Cruikshank's Ct FK6 .21 C1
Crum Ave G46 .136 A2
Crum Cres FK7 .7 B1
Crummieholm Gdns
KA10 .230 A2
Crummock Gdns KA15 .150 B1
Crummock St KA15 .150 B1
Crusader Ave G13 .75 B1
Crusader Cres KA3 .211 B4
Cubie St G40 .117 C3
Cubrieshaw Dr KA23 .190 B2
Cubrieshaw Pk KA23 .190 C2
Cubrieshaw St KA23 .190 B3
Cuckoo Way ML1 .143 A3
Cuff Cres KA15 .171 A4
Cuilhill Rd G69 .121 A4
Cuillin Ct FK1 .42 B1
Cuillin Pl Chapelhall ML6 .123 C1
Irvine KA11 .220 A2
Kilmarnock KA1 .228 A2
Cuillin Way G78 .134 B1
Cuillins Ave PA14 .68 C3
Cuillins The
Moodiesburn G69 .81 A2
Uddingston G71 .120 C1
Cuilmuir Terr G65 .60 C2
Cuilmuir View G65 .60 C3
Cuilt Pl G63 .31 A2
Cuilts Rd G63 .30 A2
Culbin Dr G13 .95 A4
Cullen PA8 .73 A2
Cullen La 18 G75 .180 C4
Cullen Pl G71 .141 A4
Cullen Rd
East Kilbride G75 .180 B4
Motherwell ML1 .163 B3
Cullen St Alexandria G83 .27 B4
Glasgow G32 .119 A2
Cullin Gdns G22 .97 B2
Cullins Rd G73 .138 B2
Cullion Way ML1 .144 A3
Culloch Rd Bearsden G61 .75 B4
Slamannan FK1 .86 A3
Cullochrig Rd G67 .82 C1
Culloden Ave ML4 .142 B2
Culloden Pl KA3 .223 A2
Culloden St G31 .118 A4
Culmore Pl FK1 .42 C1
Culrain Gdns G32 .119 A3
Culrain St G32 .119 A2
Culross Hill G74 .159 B1
Culross Pl
Coatbridge ML5 .121 C4
East Kilbride G74 .159 B1
Culross St G32 .119 B2
Culross Way G69 .81 A2
Cult Rd G66 .79 C2
Cultenhove Cres FK7 .7 A2
Cultenhove Pl FK7 .7 A2
Cultenhove Rd FK7 .7 A2
Culterfell Path ML1 .144 B1
Cults St G51 .115 C3
Culvain Ave G61 .75 A4
Culvain Pl FK1 .42 B1
Culzean ML6 .102 C3
Culzean Ave
Coatbridge ML5 .121 C2
Prestwick KA9 .236 B4
Culzean Cres
Glasgow G69 .120 A2
Kilmarnock KA3 .228 B4
Newton Mearns G77 .157 A2
Culzean Ct ML5 .121 C3
Culzean Dr
East Kilbride G74 .159 B2
Glasgow G32 .119 B2
Gourock PA19 .43 C3
Motherwell ML1 .143 B2
Culzean Pl
East Kilbride G74 .159 B2
Kilwinning KA13 .207 B1
Stenhousemuir FK5 .23 C2
Culzean Rd KA7 .238 B2
Cumberland Arc 9 G5 .117 B2
Cumberland Ave G84 .16 A2
Cumberland Pl
Coatbridge ML5 .121 B2
13 Glasgow G5 .117 B2
Cumberland Rd
Greenock PA16 .44 C2
Rhu G84 .15 B3
Cumberland St
Glasgow G5 .117 B2
Glasgow, Laurieston G5 .117 A3
Cumberland Terr G84 .15 B3
Cumberland Wlk PA16 .44 C2
Cumbernauld Airport
G68 .62 A4
Cumbernauld Coll G67 .61 C1
Cumbernauld High Sch
G67 .62 B1
Cumbernauld Prim Sch
G67 .62 A2
Cumbernauld Rd
Chryston G69 .100 B4
Cumbernauld G67 .81 B2
Glasgow G31,G33 .118 B4
Haggs FK4 .39 A2
Moodiesburn G68,G69 .81 A2
Stepps G33 .99 B3
Cumbernauld Sta G67 .83 A4
Cumbrae G74 .160 B1
Cumbrae Ave PA14 .69 A4
Cumbrae Cres ML5 .122 C3
Cumbrae Cres N G82 .49 B3
Cumbrae Cres S G82 .49 B3
Cumbrae Ct
Clydebank G81 .74 A1
Irvine KA11 .225 B4
Cumbrae Dr Falkirk FK1 .41 B2
Kilmarnock KA3 .223 A3
Motherwell ML1 .163 B4
Cumbrae Ho KA9 .236 A3

Cumbrae Pl
Coatbridge ML5 122 C2
Gourock PA19 44 B3
West Kilbride KA23 190 B2
Cumbrae Rd Paisley PA2 133 C4
Renfrew PA4 94 B1
Saltcoats KA21 205 C1
Cumbrae St G33 119 A4
Cumlodden Dr G20 96 B4
Cumming Ave ML8 202 B4
Cumming Dr G42 137 A4
Cumnock Dr Airdrie ML6 123 A2
Barrhead G78 134 B1
Hamilton ML3 161 B1
Cumnock Rd G33 98 C3
Cumroch Rd G66 33 B1
Cunard Ct G81 94 A4
Cunard St G81 94 A4
Cuninghame Dr KA20 206 A1
Cuninghame Rd
Ardrossan KA22 205 B2
Kilbarchan PA10 111 A2
Saltcoats KA21 217 A4
Cunning Park Dr KA7 238 B2
Cunningair Dr ML1 163 C2
Cunningham Cres KA7 239 B3
Cunningham Dr
Clydebank G81 73 C3
Glasgow G46 136 C2
Harthill ML7 127 B3
Cunningham Gdns
Falkirk FK2 42 C3
Houston PA6 91 B1
Cunningham Pl KA7 239 B3
Cunningham Rd
Paisley G52 114 C4
Stenhousemuir FK5 24 A2
Stirling FK7 7 B4
Cunningham St ML1 163 B3
Cunningham Watt Rd
KA3 195 B1
Cunninghame Dr KA1 227 C2
Cunninghame Rd
East Kilbride G74 159 C1
Irvine KA12 224 B4
Prestwick KA9 236 B4
Rutherglen G73 138 B4
Cupar Dr PA16 44 C2
Cuparhead Ave ML5 121 C2
Cuppleton Brae PA9 130 A1
Curfew Rd G13 75 B1
Curle St G14 95 B1
Curlew Cres PA16 45 A2
Curlew La PA16 45 A2
Curlew Pl PA5 131 B4
Curling Cres G44 137 B4
Curlinghaugh Cres ML2 165 B2
Curlingmire G75 180 C4
Curran Ave ML2 164 C1
Currie Ct KA22 205 B1
Currie St G20 96 C3
Currieside Ave ML7 146 C2
Currieside Pl ML7 146 B2
Curtecan Pl KA7 238 C3
Curtis Ave G44 137 B4
Curzon St G20 96 C3
Cushenquarter Dr FK7 12 B2
Custom House Mus★
PA15 46 A3
Custom House Quay Ret Pk
PA15 46 A3
Customhouse Pl PA15 46 A3
Custonhall Pl FK6 21 B1
Cut The G71 140 C3
Cuthbert Pl KA3 223 A1
Cuthbert St G71 141 A4
Cuthbertson Prim Sch
G42 117 A2
Cuthbertson St G42 117 A1
Cuthelton Dr G31 118 C2
Cuthelton St G31 118 B2
Cuthelton Terr G31 118 B2
Cutsburn Pl KA3 211 C4
Cutsburn Rd KA3 211 C4
Cutstraw Rd KA3 211 C4
Cutty Sark Pl G82 50 B1
Cuttyfield Pl FK2 24 B2
Cypress Ave Beith KA15 150 B1
Blantyre G72 140 B1
Uddingston G71 141 A4
Cypress Cres G75 180 B3
Cypress Ct
East Kilbride G75 180 B3
Hamilton ML3 162 C1
Kirkintilloch G66 79 A3
Cypress Gdns KA11 219 C3
Cypress Pl G75 180 B3
Cypress St G22 97 B3
Cypress Way G72 139 C2
Cyprus Ave PA5 112 A1
Cyril St PA1 114 A2

D

Daer Ave PA4 94 C1
Daer Way ML3 162 A2
Daer Wlk ML9 199 A4
Daffodil Way ML1 163 C4
Dairsie Ct G44 136 C2
Dairsie Gdns G64 98 B4
Dairsie House Sch G43 136 C3
Dairsie St G44 136 C2
Daisy Cotts KA8 236 A2
Daisy St G42 117 A1
Daisybank KA14 170 B3
Dakala Ct ML2 165 A1
Dakota Way PA4 94 B1
Dalbeattie Braes ML6 123 C1
Dalbeth Pl G32 118 C1
Dalbeth Rd G32 118 C1
Dalblair Rd KA7 238 C4
Dalcharn Pl G34 120 A4
Dalcross St G11 96 B1
Dalcruin Gdns G69 81 A2
Dalderse Ave FK2 42 A3
Daldowie Ave G32 119 B2
Daldowie Doocot The★
G69 119 C1
Daldowie Rd G71 120 A1
Daldowie St ML5 121 C2
Dale Ave G75 180 B3
Dale Cres KA12 219 B2
Dale Ct ML2 164 B1
Dale Dr ML1 143 A2
Dale Path G40 117 C2
Dale St G40 118 A2
Dale Way G73 138 A2
Daleview Ave G12 96 A3
Daleview Dr G76 157 B3
Daleview Gr G76 157 B3
Dalfoil Ct PA1 114 C2
Dalgain Ct KA11 220 A3
Dalgarroch Ave G81 94 C4
Dalgarven Mews KA3 223 B3
Dalgarven Mill★ KA13 207 B4
Dalgarven Wynd KA13 207 B3
Dalgleish Ave G81 73 C3
Dalgleish Ct FK8 7 A4
Dalgraig Cres G72 140 B1
Dalhousie Gdns G64 78 A1
Dalhousie La G3 240 B4
Dalhousie Rd PA10 111 A1
Dalhousie St G3 240 C4
Dalilea Dr G34 100 B1
Dalilea Pl G34 100 B1
Dalintober St G5 240 B1
Daljarrock KA13 207 A1
Dalkeith Ave
Bishopbriggs G64 78 A2
Glasgow G41 116 A2
Dalkeith Rd G64 78 A2
Dallas Ct KA10 229 C1
Dallas La KA10 229 C1
Dallas Pl KA10 229 C1
Dallas Rd KA10 229 C1
Dalmacoulter Rd ML6 103 A2
Dalmahoy Cres PA11 110 B3
Dalmahoy St G32 118 C4
Dalmahoy Way KA13 207 A2
Dalmailing Ave KA11 220 A1
Dalmally St Glasgow G20 96 C2
Greenock PA15 46 C1
Dalmarnock Ct G40 118 A2
Dalmarnock Prim Sch
G40 118 A2
Dalmarnock Rd G40 118 A2
Dalmarnock Road Trad Est
G73 118 A1
Dalmarnock Sta G40 118 A2
Dalmary Dr PA1 114 A3
Dalmellington Ct
East Kilbride G74 159 B1
Hamilton ML3 161 B1
Dalmellington Dr
East Kilbride G74 159 B1
9 Glasgow G53 135 A4
Dalmellington Rd
Ayr KA7 239 B2
Glasgow G53 115 A1
Dalmeny Ave G46 136 B2
Dalmeny Dr G78 134 A1
Dalmeny Rd ML3 162 B1
Dalmeny St G5 117 C1
Dalmilling Cres KA8 236 B1
Dalmilling Dr KA8 236 C1
Dalmilling Rd KA8 236 C1
Dalmoak Rd PA15 46 B1
Dalmonach Rd G83 27 C2
Dalmore Cres G84 16 A2
Dalmore Dr Airdrie ML6 123 A3
Alva FK12 4 C3
Dalmore Pl KA11 219 C3
Dalmore Way KA11 219 C3
Dalmorglen Pk FK7 6 C3
Dalmuir Sta G81 73 C2
Dalnair Pl G62 54 B1
Dalnair St G3 96 B1
Dalness St G32 119 A2
Dalnottar Ave G60 73 A3
Dalnottar Dr G60 73 A3
Dalnottar Gdns G60 73 A3
Dalnottar Hill Rd G60 73 A3
Dalnottar Terr G60 73 A3
Dalreoch Ave G69 120 B3
Dalreoch Ct G82 49 B2
Dalreoch Path G69 120 B3
Dalreoch Prim Sch G82 49 B3
Dalreoch Sta G82 49 C2
Dalriada Cres ML1 142 B1
Dalriada Dr G64 78 B4
Dalriada Rd PA16 44 B2
Dalriada St G40 118 B2
Dalry Gdns ML3 161 B1
Dalry La KA22 205 B2
Dalry Pl ML6 143 C4
Dalry Prim Sch KA24 191 A4
Dalry Rd Ardrossan KA22 205 B2
Beith KA15 171 A4
Kilbirnie KA25 170 A4
Kilwinning KA13 207 B2
Saltcoats KA21 206 A1
Stewarton KA3 195 B1
Dalry Rd *continued*
Uddingston G71 141 A4
Dalry St G32 119 A2
Dalry Sta KA24 191 B4
Dalrymple Ct
Irvine KA12 219 C2
9 Kirkintilloch G66 79 B4
Dalrymple Dr
Coatbridge ML5 121 C2
East Kilbride G74 159 C1
Newton Mearns G77 157 A2
Dalrymple Pl KA12 219 B2
Dalrymple St PA15 46 A3
Dalserf Cres G46 136 A1
Dalserf Ct G31 118 A3
Dalserf Gdns G31 118 A3
Dalserf Path 27 ML9 185 B1
Dalserf Prim Sch ML9 199 C4
Dalserf St G31 118 A3
Dalsetter Ave G15 75 A1
Dalsetter Pl G15 75 A1
Dalshannon Pl G67 82 A4
Dalshannon Rd G67 82 A4
Dalshannon View G67 82 A4
Dalshannon Way G67 82 A4
Dalsholm Ave G20 96 A4
Dalsholm Ind Est G20 96 A4
Dalskeith Ave PA3 113 A3
Dalskeith Cres PA3 113 A3
Dalskeith Rd PA3 113 A3
Dalswinton St G34 120 B4
Dalton Ave G81 74 C1
Dalton Hill ML3 161 C1
Dalton St G31 118 C3
Dalvait Ct G83 27 C4
Dalvait Gdns G83 27 C4
Dalvait Rd G83 27 C4
Dalveen Ct G78 134 B1
Dalveen Dr G71 140 C4
Dalveen Quadrant ML5 122 B3
Dalveen St G32 118 C3
Dalveen Way G73 138 B2
Dalwhinnie Ave G72 140 B1
Dalwhinnie Ct KA11 219 C3
Dalwood Rd KA9 236 A4
Daly Gdns G72 140 C1
Dalzell Ave ML1 164 A2
Dalzell Dr ML1 164 A2
Dalzell Pk★ ML1 163 C2
Dalzial Twr ML1 164 A2
Dalziel Ct ML3 162 A2
Dalziel Dr G41 116 B2
Dalziel High Sch ML1 163 B3
Dalziel Rd G52 114 C4
Dalziel St Hamilton ML3 162 A3
Motherwell ML1 163 C4
Damhead Rd KA1 227 C2
Dampark KA3 195 B4
Damshot Cres G53 115 B1
Damshot Rd G53 135 B4
Damside KA8 235 C1
Danby Rd G69 119 C2
Danes Ave 1 G14 95 B2
Danes Cres G14 95 A3
Danes Dr G14 95 B2
Danes La N 3 G14 95 B2
Danes La S G14 95 B2
Daniel McLaughlin Pl
G66 58 C1
Dankeith Dr KA1 231 B2
Dankeith Rd KA1 231 B2
Darg Rd KA20 217 B4
Dargarvel Ave G41 116 A2
Dargavel Ave PA7 72 A2
Dargavel Rd PA7,PA8 72 B1
Dark Brig Rd ML8 201 A1
Darkwood Cres PA3 113 A3
Darkwood Ct PA3 113 A3
Darkwood Dr PA3 113 A3
Darleith Rd
Alexandria G83 27 C3
Cardross G82 26 A1
Darleith St G32 118 C3
Darley Cres KA10 229 C1
Darley Pl Hamilton ML3 183 A4
Troon KA10 229 C1
Darley Rd G68 61 C3
Darlington View KA3 195 C1
Darluith Pk PA5 111 B3
Darluith Rd PA3 111 C3
Darmeid Pl ML7 167 A4
Darmule Dr KA13 207 B3
Darnaway Ave G33 99 B1
Darnaway Dr G33 99 B1
Darnaway St G33 99 B1
Darndaff Rd PA15 46 A1
Darngaber Gdns ML3 183 C2
Darngaber Rd ML3 183 C2
Darngavil Rd ML6 103 C3
Darnick St G21 98 A1
Darnley Cres G64 77 C2
Darnley Dr KA1 227 C3
Darnley Gdns G41 116 C1
Darnley Ind Est G53 135 A3
Darnley Mains Rd G53 135 B2
Darnley Path G46 135 C3
Darnley Pl G41 116 C1
Darnley Prim Sch No 1
G53 135 B2
Darnley Rd
Barrhead G78 134 C2
Glasgow G41 116 C1
Darnley St Glasgow G41 116 C2
Stirling FK8 7 A4
Darnshaw Cl KA11 220 B3
Darrach Dr FK6 21 A1
Darragh Gn ML2 166 A3
Darroch Ave PA19 44 C4
Darroch Dr Erskine PA8 72 C2
Gourock PA19 44 C4
Darroch Way G67 62 A2
Dartford St G22 97 A2
Dartmouth Ave PA19 44 C3
Darvel Ave KA3 223 A3
Darvel Cres PA1 114 C2
Darvel Dr G77 157 A3
Darvel St G53 134 C3
Darwin Pl G81 73 B2
Darwin Rd G75 180 B4
Dava St G51 116 A4
Davaar G74 160 B1
Davaar Dr
Coatbridge ML5 121 B4
Kilmarnock KA3 223 A3
Motherwell ML1 142 B1
Paisley PA2 133 C4
Davaar Pl Falkirk FK1 41 B2
Newton Mearns G77 156 B3
Davaar Rd Greenock PA16 44 B2
Renfrew PA4 94 B1
Saltcoats KA21 205 C1
Davaar St G40 118 A2
Davan Loan 10 ML2 165 C3
Dave Barrie Ave ML9 184 C3
Daventry Dr G12 96 A3
Davey St PA16 45 B3
David Dale Ave KA3 211 B4
David Gage St KA13 207 C3
David Livingstone Ctr★
G72 140 C1
David Livingstone Meml Prim
Sch G72 140 B1
David Orr St KA1 222 C1
David Pl Glasgow G69 119 C2
Paisley PA3 114 A4
David St Coatbridge ML5 122 B4
Glasgow G40 118 A3
Salsburgh ML7 125 A1
David Way PA3 114 A4
David's Cres KA13 207 B1
David's Loan FK2 24 B1
Davidson Ave KA14 170 B3
Davidson Cres G65 59 C2
Davidson Dr PA19 44 C4
Davidson Gdns G14 95 C2
Davidson La ML8 188 A1
Davidson Pl Ayr KA8 236 A1
Glasgow G32 119 A3
Davidson Quadrant G81 73 C4
Davidson Rd G83 27 C4
Davidson St Airdrie ML6 122 C4
Bannockburn FK7 7 B1
Clydebank G81 94 C4
Coatbridge ML5 122 A2
Glasgow G40 118 A2
Davidston Pl G66 79 C2
Davie's Acre G74 158 C2
Davieland Rd G46 136 A1
Davies Dr G83 27 C3
Davies Quadrant ML1 142 B1
Davies Row FK6 21 C1
Davington Dr ML3 161 B1
Daviot St G51 115 B3
Dawsholm Rd G20 96 A4
Dawson Ave Alloa FK10 9 C4
East Kilbride G75 159 A1
Dawson Pl G4 97 A2
Dawson Rd G4 97 A2
Dawson St FK2 42 A4
De Morville Pl KA15 171 A4
De Walden Terr KA3 223 A1
Deacons Rd G65 60 C4
Deaconsbank Ave G46 135 C1
Deaconsbank Cres G46 135 B1
Deaconsbank Gdns G46 135 C1
Deaconsbank Gr G46 135 B1
Deaconsbank Pl G46 135 B1
Dealston Rd G78 134 A2
Dean Castle★ KA3 223 A2
Dean Castle Ctry Pk★
KA3 223 A2
Dean Cres Chryston G69 80 B1
Hamilton ML3 162 B1
Stirling FK8 2 B1
Dean Ct KA3 222 C1
Dean La KA3 223 A1
Dean Park Ave G71 141 A1
Dean Park Dr G72 139 B2
Dean Park Rd PA4 94 C1
Dean Pl KA2 226 C4
Dean Rd Kilbirnie KA25 149 A1
Kilmarnock KA3 223 A2
Dean St Bellshill ML4 142 A3
Clydebank G81 74 B1
Kilmarnock KA3 223 A1
Stewarton KA3 195 C1
Dean Terr KA3 223 A2
Dean View KA3 223 B2
Deanbank Sch ML5 101 B1
Deanbrae St G71 140 C3
Deanfield Quadrant
G52 114 C3
Deanhill La KA3 223 A2
Deans Ave G72 139 B2
Deanside Rd G52 115 A4
Deanston Ave G78 134 A1
Deanston Dr G41 136 C4
Deanston Gdns G78 134 A1
Deanston Gr ML5 121 C2
Deanston Pk G78 134 A1
Deanstone Pl ML5 122 B2
Deanstone Wlk ML5 122 B1
Deanwood Ave G44 136 C2
Deanwood Rd G44 136 C2
Deas Rd ML7 146 B3
Dechmont G75 180 B3
Dechmont Ave
Cambuslang G72 139 B2
Motherwell ML1 163 B4
Dechmont Cotts G72 139 C2
Dechmont Gdns G72 140 B1
Dechmont Pl G72 139 B2
Dechmont Rd G71 120 C1
Dechmont St
Glasgow G31 118 B2
Hamilton ML3 162 B1
Dechmont View
Bellshill ML4 141 C2
Uddingston G71 141 A4
Dee Ave Kilmarnock KA1 228 A2
Paisley PA2 112 C1
Renfrew PA4 94 C2
Dee Dr PA2 112 C1
Dee Path Larkhall ML9 199 A4
Motherwell ML1 143 A3
Dee Pl East Kilbride G75 179 C3
Johnstone PA5 131 B4
Dee St Coatbridge ML5 101 B1
Glasgow G33 118 B4
Greenock PA16 45 A3
Shotts ML7 146 B3
Dee Terr ML3 183 A4
Deedes St ML6 122 B3
Deep Dale G74 159 B2
Deepdene Rd
Bearsden G61 75 B1
Chryston G69 80 C1
Deer Park Ave KA20 217 C4
Deer Park Ct ML3 183 B4
Deer Park Pl ML3 183 C4
Deer Path ML7 127 C3
Deer Pk FK10 5 C1
Deerdykes Ct N G68 81 C3
Deerdykes Ct S G68 81 C3
Deerdykes Pl G68 81 C3
Deerdykes Rd G68,G69 81 C3
Deerdykes Rdbt G68 81 B3
Deerdykes View G68 81 B3
Deerpark Prim Sch FK10 5 C1
Deeside Dr ML8 188 A2
Deeside Pl ML5 122 B2
Delfie Dr PA16 45 A2
Delhi Ave G81 73 B2
Dell The Bellshill ML4 142 B2
Newton Mearns G77 157 A3
Dellburn St ML1 164 A3
Dellburn Trad Pk ML1 164 A3
Dellingburn St PA15 46 A2
Delny Pl G33 119 C4
Delph Rd FK10 4 B1
Delphwood Cres FK10 4 B1
Delves Pk ML11 215 A2
Delves Rd ML11 215 A2
Delvin Rd G44 137 A3
Dempsey Rd ML4 141 C2
Dempster St PA15 45 C2
Den La ML7 146 B3
Denbak Ave ML3 162 A1
Denbeck St G32 118 C3
Denbrae St G32 118 C3
Denewood Ave PA2 133 B4
Denham St G22 97 A2
Denholm Cres G75 180 C4
Denholm Dr
Glasgow G46 136 B1
Wishaw ML2 165 B3
Denholm Gdns
Greenock PA16 45 B3
Quarter ML3 183 C2
Denholm Gn 5 G75 180 C4
Denholm St PA16 45 B3
Denholm Terr
Greenock PA16 45 B3
Hamilton ML3 161 C2
Denholm Way KA15 171 A4
Denmark St G22 97 B2
Denmilne Gdns G34 120 B4
Denmilne Path G34 120 B4
Denmilne Rd G34 120 B4
Denmilne St G34 120 B4
Denniston Pl ML11 215 B3
Dennistoun Cres G84 25 B4
Dennistoun Rd PA14 70 B4
Dennistoun St ML4 142 A3
Denny High Sch FK6 39 C4
Denny Prim Sch FK6 21 B1
Denny Rd Denny FK4,FK6 39 C3
Larbert FK5 23 A1
Denny Tank Mus★ G82 50 A2
Dennyholm Wynd KA25 149 A1
Dennystoun Forge G82 49 C2
Denovan Rd FK6 21 C2
Dentdale G74 159 B2
Deramore Ave G46 157 A4
Derby St G3 116 C4
Derby Terrace La 4 G3 116 C4
Deroran Pl FK8 6 C3
Derrywood Rd G66 58 B3
Dervaig Gdns ML6 84 B2
Derwent Ave FK1 41 C2
Derwent Dr ML5 101 B1
Derwent St G22 97 A2
Derwentwater G75 179 C3
Despard Ave G32 119 C2
Despard Gdns G32 119 C2
Deveron Ave G46 136 B1
Deveron Cres ML3 161 C2
Deveron Rd Bearsden G61 75 B1
East Kilbride G74 160 A1
Kilmarnock KA1 228 A3
Motherwell ML1 143 A3
Troon KA10 229 D3
Deveron St
Coatbridge ML5 101 B1

Deveron St *continued*
Glasgow G33 98 B1
Devilla Ct KA9 236 B3
Devine Ct ML2 165 A2
Devine Gr ML2 166 A4
Devlin Gr G72 161 C4
Devol Ave PA14 47 A1
Devol Cres G53 135 A4
Devol Rd PA14 68 B3
Devon Ct FK10 4 A1
Devon Dr Bishopton PA7 72 B2
Tullibody FK10 4 C2
Devon Gdns
Bishopbriggs G64 77 C2
Carluke ML8 187 C1
Devon Pl Cambus FK10 4 A1
Glasgow G41 117 A2
Devon Rd Alloa FK10 10 B3
Greenock PA16 44 B2
Devon St G5 117 A2
Devon Village FK10 5 C2
Devon Way ML1 163 A3
Devon Wlk G68 81 C4
Devonbank FK10 5 C2
Devondale Ave G72 140 B1
Devonhill Ave ML3 183 B4
Devonport Pk G75 180 A4
Devonshire Gardens La 2
G12 96 A2
Devonshire Gdns 1 G12 96 A2
Devonshire Terr G12 96 A2
Devonshire Terrace La
G12 96 A2
Devonview Pl ML6 122 C3
Devonview St ML6 122 C3
Devonway FK10 10 C3
Dewar Cl G71 121 A1
Dewar Wlk ML8 201 A1
Dewshill Cotts ML7 126 A2
Dhuhill Dr E G84 16 C2
Diamond St ML4 142 A2
Diana Ave G13 95 A4
Diana Quadrant ML1 143 A3
Diana Vernon Ct G84 25 A4
Dick Cres KA12 219 B3
Dick Ct ML9 198 C1
Dick Inst Mus★ KA1 228 A4
Dick Quad G82 48 A4
Dick Rd KA1 228 A4
Dick St G20 96 C2
Dick Terr KA12 219 B3
Dickburn Cres FK4 39 C3
Dickens Ave G81 74 A2
Dickens Gr ML1 143 B1
Dickies Wells FK12 5 B4
Dicks Pk G75 180 B4
Dickson Dr KA12 219 B3
Dickson Sq ML1 144 A1
Dickson St ML9 185 B1
Diddup Dr KA20 206 A1
Differ Ave G65 59 C1
Dillichip Cl G83 27 C1
Dillichip Gdns G83 27 C2
Dillichip Loan G83 27 C2
Dillichip Terr G83 27 C2
Dilwara Ave G14 95 C1
Dimity St PA5 111 C2
Dimsdale Cres ML2 165 B1
Dimsdale Rd ML2 165 B1
Dinard Dr G46 136 B2
Dinart St G33 98 B1
Dinduff St G34 100 B1
Dingwall Dr PA16 44 C2
Dinmont Ave PA2 112 C1
Dinmont Cres ML1 142 B1
Dinmont Pl 1 G41 116 C1
Dinmont Rd G41 116 B1
Dinmont Way PA2 112 C1
Dinmurchie Rd KA10 229 D3
Dinnet Way 11 ML2 165 C3
Dinwiddie St G21 98 B1
Dinyra Pl ML5 101 B3
Dippin Pl KA21 205 C1
Dipple Ct KA25 149 A1
Dipple Pl G15 75 A1
Dipple Rd KA25 149 A2
Dipple View KA25 149 A2
Dirleton Dr Glasgow G41 136 C4
Paisley PA2 113 A1
Dirleton Gate G61 75 B1
Dirleton Gdns FK10 9 C4
Dirleton La FK10 9 C3
Dirleton Pl G41 136 C4
Dirrans Terr KA13 207 C1
Ditton Dr KA1 227 C2
Divernia Way G78 155 B4
Diverswell FK10 5 B1
Divert Rd PA19 44 B3
Divert Wlk PA19 44 B3
Dixon Ave Dumbarton G82 49 C2
Glasgow G42 117 A1
Dixon Dr G82 49 B1
Dixon Pl G74 159 A2
Dixon Rd Glasgow G42 117 B2
Helensburgh G84 16 C2
Dixon St Coatbridge ML5 122 A2
Glasgow G1 240 C1
Hamilton ML3 162 B2
Paisley PA1 113 C2
Dixons Blazes Ind Est
G42,G5 117 B2
Dobbie Ave FK5 23 B1
Dobbie's Loan G4 241 A4
Dobbie's Loan Pl G4 241 B3
Dobbies Ct ML8 187 A3
Dochart Ave PA4 94 C1
Dochart Dr ML5 101 B1
Dochart Pl FK1 42 B1
Dochart St G33 98 C1
Dock Breast PA15 46 A3
Dock Rd KA22 205 A1
Dock St Clydebank G81 94 B4
Falkirk FK2 24 B1
Dockhead Pl KA21 216 C4
Dockhead St KA21 216 C4
Dodhill Pl G13 95 A3
Dodside Gdns G32 119 B2
Dodside Pl G32 119 B2
Dodside Rd G77 155 C2
Dodside St G32 119 B2
Dolan St G69 120 A3
Dollan Aquacentre G74 159 C1
Dollar Ave FK2 42 A4
Dollar Gdns FK2 42 A4
Dollar Ind Est FK1,FK2 42 A3
Dollar Pk ML1 164 A2
Dollar Terr G20 96 B4
Dolphin Rd G41 116 B1
Dominica Gn 4 G75 159 A1
Don Ave PA4 94 C1
Don Ct ML3 183 A4
Don Dr PA2 112 C1
Don Path ML9 199 A4
Don Pl PA5 131 B4
Don St Glasgow G33 98 C1
Greenock PA16 45 B3
Donald Cres KA10 229 C2
Donald Terr ML3 162 B1
Donald Way G71 141 A4
Donald's Ct PA15 46 A3
Donaldfield Rd PA11 110 A4
Donaldson Ave Alloa FK10 4 C1
Kilsyth G65 60 C4
Saltcoats KA21 216 C4
Stevenston KA20 206 C1
Donaldson Cres G66 79 B4
Donaldson Dr
Irvine KA12 219 B2
Kilmarnock KA3 223 B2
Renfrew PA4 94 B2
Donaldson Gn G71 141 A4
Donaldson Pl
Cambusbarron FK7 6 B3
8 Kirkintilloch G66 79 B4
Donaldson Rd
Kilmarnock KA3 223 B2
Larkhall ML9 185 B1
Donaldson St
Hamilton ML3 162 A3
Kirkintilloch G66 79 B4
Donaldswood Pk PA2 133 B4
Donaldswood Rd PA2 133 B4
Doncaster St G20 97 A2
Dongola Rd KA7 239 A4
Donnelly Way ML2 164 B2
Donnies Brae G78 154 C4
Donnini Ct 18 KA7 235 C1
Doo'cot Brae FK10 10 A4
Doon Ave KA9 236 A3
Doon Cres G61 75 B2
Doon Ct KA12 219 B1
Doon Pl Kilmarnock KA1 228 A2
Kirkintilloch G66 58 C1
Saltcoats KA21 206 A2
Symington KA1 231 B2
Troon KA10 229 D3
Doon Rd G66 59 A1
Doon Side G67 62 A1
Doon St Clydebank G81 74 B2
Larkhall ML9 185 B1
Motherwell ML1 164 A2
Doon Way G66 59 A1
Doonfoot Ct G74 159 B1
Doonfoot Gdns G74 159 B1
Doonfoot Prim Sch KA7 238 A2
Doonfoot Rd Ayr KA7 238 C2
Glasgow G43 136 B3
Doonholm Pl KA7 238 C1
Doonholm Rd KA7 238 C1
Doonside Twr ML1 164 A2
Doonview Gdns KA7 238 B1
Doonview Wynd KA7 238 B1
Dora St G40 117 C2
Dorain Rd ML1 143 B2
Dorchester Ave G12 96 A3
Dorchester Ct G12 96 A3
Dorchester Pl G12 96 A3
Dorian Dr G76 157 B4
Dorlin Rd G33 99 C3
Dormanside Ct G53 115 A2
Dormanside Gate G53 115 A2
Dormanside Gr G53 115 A2
Dormanside Pl G53 115 B1
Dormanside Rd G53 115 B2
Dornal Ave G13 94 C4
Dornal Dr KA10 229 D3
Dornford Ave G32 119 B2
Dornford Rd G32 119 B2
Dornie Cl KA3 195 B1
Dornie Dr G32 139 A4
Dornie Path 9 ML2 165 C3
Dornie Wynd ML7 147 A2
Dornoch Ave G46 136 B1
Dornoch Ct Bellshill ML4 142 A3
Kilwinning KA13 207 A2
Dornoch Pk KA7 238 C3
Dornoch Pl
Bishopbriggs G64 78 B1
Chryston G69 80 B1
East Kilbride G74 159 B1
Dornoch Rd Bearsden G61 75 B1
Motherwell ML1 143 A3
Dornoch St G40 117 C3
Dornoch Way
Airdrie ML6 122 C3
Cumbernauld G68 62 A3
Dorrator Ct FK1 41 C3
Dorrator Rd FK1 41 C3
Dorset Rd PA16 44 C2
Dorset Sq G3 240 A3
Dorset St G3 240 A3
Dosk Ave G13 94 C4
Dosk Pl G13 94 C4
Double Edges Rd G78 154 B3
Double Row ML11 214 C1
Dougalston Ave G62 55 A1
Dougalston Cres G62 55 A1
Dougalston Gdns N G62 55 A1
Dougalston Gdns S G62 55 A1
Dougalston Rd G23 76 C1
Douglas Acad G62 54 B2
Douglas Ave Dalry KA24 191 B3
Elderslie PA5 112 A1
Glasgow G46 136 B1
Glasgow, Carmyle G32 119 A1
Kirkintilloch G66 79 B3
Langbank PA14 70 B4
Prestwick KA9 236 A3
Rutherglen G73 138 B3
Douglas Cres
Airdrie ML6 123 A3
Bishopton PA8 72 C2
Hamilton ML3 183 B3
Uddingston G71 141 A4
Douglas Ct
Kirkintilloch G66 79 B3
Troon KA10 229 C3
Douglas Dr Ashgill ML9 199 C4
Bellshill ML4 142 B2
Bothwell G71 141 A1
Cambuslang G72 138 C3
Clydebank G15 74 C1
East Kilbride G75 179 C4
Glasgow G69 119 C3
Helensburgh G84 16 B2
Newton Mearns G77 156 C3
Stirling FK7 7 B2
Douglas Dr E G84 16 C2
Douglas Drive La G45 137 B2
Douglas Gate G72 139 A3
Douglas Gdns
Bearsden G61 75 C2
Glasgow G46 136 B1
Kirkintilloch G66 79 B3
Uddingston G71 140 C3
Douglas La Ayr KA7 238 C4
Glasgow G2 240 B3
Douglas Muir Dr G62 54 B2
Douglas Muir Gdns G62 54 B2
Douglas Muir Pl G62 54 B2
Douglas Muir Rd
Clydebank G81 74 B4
Milngavie G62 54 B1
Douglas Park Cres G61 76 A3
Douglas Park La ML3 162 B2
Douglas Pl Bearsden G61 75 C3
Coatbridge ML5 121 C3
Hamilton ML3 183 B3
Kirkintilloch G66 79 B3
Stenhousemuir FK5 23 C2
Douglas Rd
Dumbarton G82 50 A2
Renfrew PA4 114 A4
Douglas St Airdrie ML6 123 A3
Ayr KA7 238 C4
Bannockburn FK7 7 C1
Blantyre G72 161 B3
Carluke ML8 187 C1
Glasgow G2 240 B3
Hamilton ML3 162 B2
Kilmarnock KA1 227 C4
Larkhall ML9 185 A2
Milngavie G62 55 A1
Motherwell ML1 163 B3
Paisley PA1 113 B3
Stirling FK8 2 A1
Uddingston G71 141 A4
Wishaw ML2 186 B4
Douglas Terr
Glasgow G41 116 C1
Stirling FK7 6 C3
Douglas View ML5 121 C2
Douglasdale G74 159 B1
Douglaston Woodland Wlk★
G62 55 B1
Dougliehill Pl PA14 68 B4
Dougliehill Rd PA14 68 A4
Dougliehill Terr PA14 68 B4
Dougray Pl G78 134 B1
Dougrie Dr G45 137 B2
Dougrie Gdns G45 137 B1
Dougrie Pl G45 137 C2
Dougrie Rd G45 137 B2
Dougrie St G45 137 C2
Dougrie Terr G45 137 B2
Doune Cres
Bishopbriggs G64 78 A2
Chapelhall ML6 123 B1
Newton Mearns G77 156 C3
Stenhousemuir FK5 24 A2
Doune Gardens La G20 96 C2
Doune Gdns Glasgow G20 96 C2
Gourock PA19 44 A3
Doune Park Way ML5 121 C2
Doune Quadrant 10 G20 96 C2
Doune Terr ML5 101 B1
Doura Dr KA11 219 C3
Doura Pl KA12 219 B3
Dove Pl G75 179 C3
Dove St G53 135 A3
Dove Wynd ML4 141 C4
Dovecot G43 136 B4
Dovecot La
Kilwinning KA13 207 C2
Dovecot La *continued*
Lanark ML11 215 A2
Dovecot Pl FK10 4 A2
Dovecot Rd FK10 4 A2
Dovecote View G66 79 C4
Dovecothall St G78 134 B2
Dovecotwood G65 36 B1
Dovehill FK10 10 A4
Doveholm G82 50 A3
Doveholm Ave G82 50 A3
Dover St Coatbridge ML5 101 B1
Glasgow G3 240 A3
Dowan Pl FK7 6 C3
Dowan Rd G62 55 C1
Dowanfield Rd G67 61 C1
Dowanhill Prim Sch G11 96 B1
Dowanhill St G11 96 B1
Dowanside La 7 G12 96 B2
Dowanside Rd G12 96 B2
Dower Pl FK2 14 B2
Downcraig Dr G45 137 B1
Downcraig Gr G45 137 B1
Downcraig Rd G45 137 B1
Downcraig Terr G45 137 B1
Downfield Dr ML3 183 A4
Downfield Gdns G72 140 C1
Downfield St G32 118 C2
Downhill St G12 96 B2
Downie St ML3 162 B1
Downiebrae Rd G73 118 A1
Downs Cres FK10 9 C3
Downs St G21 97 C3
Dowrie Cres G53 115 A1
Dr Campbell Ave FK7 12 B4
Draffan Rd ML9 200 A1
Draffen Ct ML1 163 C4
Draffen St ML1 163 C4
Drake St G40 117 C3
Drakemire Ave G45 137 B2
Drakemire Dr G45 137 B2
Dreghorn Prim Sch
KA11 220 B1
Dreghorn Rd KA11 225 B3
Dreghorn St G31 118 B4
Dresling Rd PA15 45 C2
Drimnin Rd G33 99 C3
Drip Rd FK8,FK9 1 C1
Drive David Gray G66 59 A1
Drive Rd G51 115 C4
Drochil St G34 100 A1
Dromore St 12 G66 79 B4
Drossie Rd FK1 42 A2
Drove Hill G68 61 A2
Drove Loan FK4,FK6 39 C3
Drove Loan Cres FK6 39 C4
Druid Dr KA13 207 C2
Drum Mains Pk G68 81 B4
Drumadoon Dr G84 16 C1
Drumaling Terr G66 57 C4
Drumbathie Rd ML6 123 B4
Drumbathie Terr ML6 123 B4
Drumbeg Dr G53 135 A3
Drumbeg Pl G53 135 A3
Drumbeg Terr G62 54 B1
Drumbottie Rd G21 98 A3
Drumbreck Pl G66 79 C2
Drumbrock Rd G62 54 B1
Drumby Cres G76 157 B4
Drumby Dr G76 157 B4
Drumcarn Dr G62 54 C1
Drumcavel Rd G69 100 C4
Drumchapel Gdns G15 75 A1
Drumchapel High Sch
G15 75 A2
Drumchapel Hospl G15 75 A1
Drumchapel Pl G15 75 A1
Drumchapel Rd G15 75 A1
Drumchapel Sh Ctr G15 74 C2
Drumchapel Sta G15 75 A1
Drumclair Ave FK1 86 A3
Drumclair Pl ML6 123 B4
Drumclog Ave G62 55 A2
Drumclog Gdns G33 98 C3
Drumclog Pl KA3 223 A2
Drumcross Pl G53 115 B1
Drumcross Rd
Bowling G60 72 B2
Glasgow G53 115 B1
Drumduff G75 180 B3
Drumellan Rd KA7 239 A1
Drumelzier Ct KA11 220 A2
Drumfin Ave ML6 104 C2
Drumfork Ct G84 25 A4
Drumfork Rd G84 25 B4
Drumfrochar Pl PA15 45 C2
Drumfrochar Rd PA15 45 C2
Drumfrochat Sta PA15 45 B2
Drumgarve Ct G84 16 B1
Drumgelloch St ML6 123 B4
Drumgelloch Sta ML6 123 B4
Drumglass View G65 60 C2
Drumgray Gdns ML6 83 B1
Drumgray La ML6 83 B1
Drumgrew Rdbt G68 60 A1
Drumhead Pl G32 118 C1
Drumhead Rd G32 118 C1
Drumhill G66 59 A1
Drumilaw Cres G73 138 A3
Drumilaw Rd G73 138 A3
Drumilaw Way G73 138 A3
Drumillan Hill PA16 44 B1
Drumkinnon Rd G83 27 B4
Drumlaken Ave 1 G23 76 B1
Drumlaken Ct 2 G23 76 B1
Drumlaken Path 7 G23 76 B1
Drumlaken Pl 5 G23 76 B1
Drumlaken St G23 76 B1
Drumlanford Rd KA10 229 D3
Drumlanrig Pl
Glasgow G34 100 B1
Stenhousemuir FK5 23 C2
Drumlanrig Quadrant
G34 120 B4
Drumley Ave KA6 237 C3
Drumleyhill Dr KA1 228 C3
Drumlin Dr G62 76 A4
Drumloch Gdns G75 180 C3
Drumlochy Rd G33 99 A1
Drummilling Ave KA23 190 B3
Drummilling Dr KA23 190 B3
Drummilling Rd KA23 190 B3
Drummond Ave G73 137 C4
Drummond Cres
Ayr KA8 236 C1
Irvine KA11 224 D4
Drummond Dr
Paisley PA1 114 B2
Wishaw ML2 165 A1
Drummond Hill G74 160 A2
Drummond Ho G67 62 A2
Drummond La FK8 7 A3
Drummond Pl
Blackridge EH48 107 B2
Bonnybridge FK4 40 A4
East Kilbride G74 160 A2
Falkirk FK1 41 C1
Kilmarnock KA3 223 B1
Stirling FK8 7 A3
Drummond Place La FK8 7 A3
Drummond St PA16 45 B2
Drummond Way G77 156 A3
Drummore Ave ML5 122 B2
Drummore Rd G15 75 A2
Drummore Sch G15 75 B2
Drummuir Foot KA11 220 A3
Drumnessie Ct G68 81 C4
Drumnessie Rd G68 81 C4
Drumnessie View G68 81 C4
Drumore Ave ML6 123 B1
Drumover Dr G31 118 C2
Drumoyne Ave G51 115 C4
Drumoyne Cir G51 115 C3
Drumoyne Dr G51 115 C4
Drumoyne Pl G51 115 C3
Drumoyne Prim Sch
G51 115 C4
Drumoyne Quadrant
G51 115 C3
Drumoyne Rd G51 115 C4
Drumoyne Sq G51 115 C4
Drumpark Specl Sch
G69 121 A3
Drumpark St
Coatbridge ML5 121 B2
Glasgow G46 135 C2
Stirling FK7 7 A2
Drumpellier Ave
Coatbridge ML5 121 B3
Cumbernauld G67 82 B4
Glasgow G69 120 A2
Drumpellier Country Pk★
ML5 101 B1
Drumpellier Country Pk
Visitor Ctr★ ML5 101 A1
Drumpellier Cres ML5 121 B3
Drumpellier Ct G67 82 B4
Drumpellier Ctry Pk★
ML5 121 B4
Drumpellier Gdns G67 82 B4
Drumpellier Gr G67 82 B4
Drumpellier Pl
Cumbernauld G67 82 B4
Glasgow G69 120 A2
Drumpellier Rd G69 120 A2
Drumpellier St G33 98 B1
Drumreoch Dr G42 137 C4
Drumreoch Pl G42 137 C4
Drumriggend Rd FK1 85 B2
Drumry Prim Sch G15 74 C2
Drumry Rd G81 74 B2
Drumry Rd E G15 74 C1
Drumry Sta G81 74 B1
Drums Ave PA3 113 B3
Drums Cres PA3 113 B3
Drums Rd G53 115 A2
Drums Terr PA16 45 A4
Drumsack Ave G69 100 B4
Drumsargard Rd G73 138 B3
Drumshangie Pl ML6 103 A1
Drumshangie St ML6 103 A1
Drumshantie Rd PA19 44 C3
Drumshantie Terr PA19 44 C4
Drumshaw Dr G32 139 B4
Drumslea PA16 45 B4
Drumtrocher St G65 60 B4
Drumvale Dr G69 80 C1
Drury St G2 240 C2
Dryad St G46 135 C3
Drybridge Rd KA2 225 C1
Dryburgh Ave Denny FK6 21 B1
Paisley PA2 113 A1
Rutherglen G73 138 A4
Dryburgh Gdns G20 96 C2
Dryburgh Hill G74 159 B1
Dryburgh La G74 159 B1
Dryburgh Pl
Coatbridge ML5 121 C4
Kirkintilloch G66 79 C4
Dryburgh Rd
Bearsden G61 75 B3
Wishaw ML2 165 A2
Dryburgh St ML3 162 A3
Dryburgh Way G72 161 B4

Dryburgh Wlk G69 81 A2
Dryburn Ave G52 115 A3
Dryden St ML3 162 A3
Drygait PA9 131 A3
Drygate G4 241 C2
Drygate St ML9 185 A2
Drygrange Rd G33 99 B1
Drymen Pl G66 79 B2
Drymen Rd Balloch G83 19 C1
Bearsden G61 75 C2
Drymen St G52 115 C3
Drymen Wynd G61 75 C2
Drynoch Pl G22 97 A4
Drysdale St Alloa FK10 10 A3
Glasgow G14 94 C3
Duart Ave KA9 236 B4
Duart Cres KA9 236 B4
Duart Dr
East Kilbride G74 159 B2
Elderslie PA5 112 B1
Newton Mearns G77 157 A3
Duart St G20 96 B4
Dubbs Rd
Kilwinning KA13 207 A1
Port Glasgow PA14 68 C4
Stevenston KA20 206 C1
Dubs Rd G78 134 C2
Dubton St G34 100 A1
Duchal Rd PA13 89 B4
Duchal St PA14 68 B4
Duchall Pl G14 95 A2
Duchess Ct ML3 163 A1
Duchess Dr G84 16 A2
Duchess Pal G73 138 B4
Duchess Pk G84 16 A2
Duchess Rd G73 118 B1
Duchray Dr PA1 114 C2
Duchray La G33 98 B1
Duchray St G33 98 B1
Ducraig St G32 119 A3
Duddingston Ave KA13 207 A2
Dudhope St G33 99 B1
Dudley Dr
Coatbridge ML5 101 B1
Glasgow G12 96 A2
Dudley La G12 96 A2
Duff Cres FK8 1 C1
Duff Pl Kilmarnock KA3 223 B2
Saltcoats KA21 206 A1
Duff St PA15 46 A3
Duffus Pl G32 139 B4
Duffus St G34 100 A1
Duffus Terr G32 139 B4
Duguid Dr KA21 206 A1
Duich Gdns G23 76 C1
Duisdale Rd G32 139 B4
Duke St Alva FK12 5 A4
Bannockburn FK7 7 B1
Denny FK6 21 B1
Glasgow G31 118 A3
Hamilton ML3 162 C2
Larkhall ML9 185 A2
Motherwell ML1 163 C4
Paisley PA2 113 C1
Wishaw ML2 165 C3
Duke Street Sta G31 118 A4
Duke Terr KA8 236 A1
Duke's Ct ML9 185 A2
Duke's Rd G72,G73 138 B3
Dukes Gate G71 140 C2
Dukes Pl ML3 183 B3
Dukes Rd Coatbridge G69 120 C3
Troon KA10 229 B2
Dulatur Rd G68 61 B3
Dullatur Rdbt G68 61 C3
Dulnain St G72 139 C3
Dulsie Rd G21 98 B3
Dumbain Cres G83 28 A4
Dumbain Rd G83 20 A1
Dumbarton Acad G82 50 A2
Dumbarton Castle★ G82 49 B2
Dumbarton Central Sta
G82 49 C2
Dumbarton Cottage Hospl
G82 49 C3
Dumbarton East Sta G82 50 A2
Dumbarton Joint Hospl
G82 49 B2
Dumbarton Rd
Bowling G60 72 B4
Cambusbarron FK8 6 C4
Clydebank G60,G81 73 B2
Glasgow G14 94 C3
Glasgow, Partick G11 96 A1
Milton G82 50 C1
Stirling FK8 7 A4
Dumbreck Ave G41 116 A2
Dumbreck Ct G41 116 A2
Dumbreck Marsh Nature
Reserve★ G65 60 A4
Dumbreck Pl G41 116 A2
Dumbreck Rd G41 116 A2
Dumbreck Sq G41 116 A2
Dumbreck Sta G41 116 B2
Dumbreck Terr G65 59 C4
Dumbrock Cres G63 31 B2
Dumbrock Dr G63 31 A2
Dumbrock Rd G63 31 B2
Dumbuck Cres G82 50 B1
Dumbuck Gdns G82 50 A1
Dumbuck Rd G82 50 A2
Dumbuie Ave G82 50 A2
Dumfries Cres ML6 122 C3
Dumfriespark KA6 239 A1
Dumgoyne Ave G62 54 C1
Dumgoyne Dr G61 75 B4
Dumgoyne Gdns G62 54 C1
Dumgoyne Pl G76 157 B4
Dumgoyne Rd KA1 228 A2
Dumyat Ave FK10 4 A1
Dumyat Dr FK1 41 C2
Dumyat Rd Alva FK12 4 C3
Menstrie FK11 3 C3
Stirling FK9 2 B2
Dumyat Rise FK5 23 B3
Dumyat St FK10 4 C1
Dun Cann PA4 93 B4
Dun Pk G66 79 C4
Dunagoil Gdns G45 137 C1
Dunagoil Pl G45 137 C1
Dunagoil Rd G45 137 B1
Dunagoil St G45 137 C1
Dunalastair Dr G33 99 B3
Dunalistair Dr G33 99 A3
Dunan Pl G33 119 C4
Dunard Ct ML8 187 C2
Dunard Prim Sch G20 96 C2
Dunard Rd G73 138 A4
Dunard St G20 96 C2
Dunard Way 7 PA3 113 B4
Dunaskin St G11 96 B1
Dunavon Pl ML5 122 B2
Dunbar Ave
Coatbridge ML5 121 B2
Johnstone PA5 131 C4
Rutherglen G73 138 B4
Stenhousemuir FK5 23 C2
Dunbar Dr
Kilmarnock KA3 223 B1
Motherwell ML1 164 A2
Dunbar Gate FK6 21 C2
Dunbar Hill G74 159 B1
Dunbar La ML1 143 A1
Dunbar Pl G74 159 B1
Dunbar Rd PA2 113 A1
Dunbar St ML3 162 A3
Dunbeath Ave G77 156 C3
Dunbeith Pl 6 G20 96 B3
Dunbeth Ave ML5 122 A4
Dunbeth Ct ML5 122 A4
Dunbeth Rd ML5 122 A4
Dunblane Dr G74 159 C1
Dunblane Pl
Coatbridge ML5 121 C2
East Kilbride G74 159 C1
Dunblane St G4 240 C4
Dunbrach Rd G68 61 B1
Dunbreck Ave ML6 105 A3
Dunbritton Rd G82 50 B2
Duncairn Ave FK4 39 C3
Duncan Ave Falkirk FK2 24 A2
Glasgow G14 95 B2
Duncan Ct
Kilmarnock KA3 223 B2
Motherwell ML1 142 B1
Duncan Dr KA12 219 B1
Duncan Graham St ML9 185 A2
Duncan La 19 G14 95 B2
Duncan La N 7 G14 95 B2
Duncan La S 15 G14 95 B2
Duncan McIntosh Rd
G68 62 B4
Duncan Rd
Helensburgh G84 16 C2
Port Glasgow PA14 47 A1
Duncan St
Bonnybridge FK4 39 C3
Clydebank G81 74 A2
Greenock PA15 45 C3
Duncan's Cl ML11 215 A2
Duncanrig Sec Sch G75 159 B1
Duncansby Rd G33 119 B3
Duncanson Ave FK10 10 A4
Duncarnock Ave G78 154 C4
Duncarnock Cres G78 154 C4
Duncarron Ind Est FK6 21 C1
Duncarron Pl FK6 21 C1
Dunchattan Gr KA10 229 D1
Dunchattan Pl G31 117 C4
Dunchattan St G31 117 C4
Dunchattan Way KA10 229 D1
Dunchurch Rd PA1 114 B3
Dunclutha Dr G71 141 A1
Dunclutha St G40 118 A1
Duncolm Pl G62 54 B1
Duncombe Ave G81 74 A4
Duncombe St G20 96 B4
Duncombe View G81 74 B2
Duncraig Cres PA5 131 B4
Duncrub Dr G64 77 C1
Duncruin St G20 96 B4
Duncruin Terr G20 96 B4
Duncryne Ave G32 119 C2
Duncryne Gdns G32 119 C2
Duncryne Pl G64 97 C4
Duncryne Rd
Alexandria G83 27 C3
Gartocharn G83 20 C4
Glasgow G32 119 B2
Dundaff Ct FK6 21 B1
Dundaff Hill G68 61 B1
Dundarroch St FK5 23 A1
Dundas Ave G64 78 A4
Dundas Cotts FK4 39 A1
Dundas Ct G74 159 C1
Dundas La G1 241 A3
Dundas Pl G74 159 C1
Dundas Rd FK9 2 A2
Dundas St G1 241 A3
Dundas Wlk KA3 223 B2
Dundashill 15 G4 97 A1
Dundasvale Ct G4 240 C4
Dundee Ct FK2 42 A4
Dundee Dr G52 115 A2
Dundee Path G52 115 B2
Dundee Pl FK2 42 A4
Dundonald Ave PA5 111 B1
Dundonald Castle★
KA2 225 C1
Dundonald Cres
Newton Mearns G77 157 A2
Troon KA11 224 D1
Dundonald Ct KA3 223 A3
Dundonald Dr ML3 183 B4
Dundonald Pl
Kilmarnock KA1 227 B4
Neilston G78 154 B4
Dundonald Prim Sch
KA2 225 C1
Dundonald Rd
Glasgow G12 96 B2
Irvine KA11 220 B1
Kilmarnock KA1,KA2 227 B4
Paisley PA3 114 A4
Troon KA10 229 D2
Dundonald St G72 161 B4
Dundrennan Rd G42 136 C4
Dundyvan Gate ML5 122 A3
Dundyvan Gdns ML5 122 A3
Dundyvan Ind Est ML5 121 C3
Dundyvan La ML2 165 A1
Dundyvan Rd ML5 121 C3
Dundyvan St ML2 165 A1
Dundyvan Way ML5 121 C3
Dunean St G4 96 C1
Dunearn Pl PA2 114 A2
Duneaton Wynd ML9 185 A1
Dunedin Ct G75 180 A4
Dunedin Dr G75 180 A4
Dunedin Rd ML9 185 A1
Dunedin Terr G81 94 B4
Dunellan Ave G69 81 A1
Dunellan Cres G69 81 A1
Dunellan Dr G81 74 A4
Dunellan Gdns G69 81 A1
Dunellan Rd G62 54 B1
Dunellan St G52 115 C3
Dunellan Way G69 81 A1
Dungavel Gdns ML3 183 C4
Dungavel La ML8 188 A1
Dungavel Rd KA1 228 A2
Dungeonhill Rd G34 120 B4
Dunglass Ave
East Kilbride G74 159 C2
Glasgow G14 95 B2
Dunglass La 10 G14 95 B2
Dunglass La N 5 G14 95 B2
Dunglass La S 13 G14 95 B2
Dunglass Pl Milngavie G62 54 C2
Newton Mearns G77 156 A3
Dunglass Rd PA7 72 B1
Dunglass Sq G74 159 C2
Dunglass View G63 31 B2
Dungoil Ave G68 61 A2
Dungoil Rd G66 79 C2
Dungourney Dr PA16 45 B4
Dungoyne St G20 96 B4
Dunholme Pk G81 73 B2
Dunipace Prim Sch FK6 21 B2
Dunira St G32 118 C2
Dunivaig Rd G33 119 C4
Dunkeld Ave G73 138 A4
Dunkeld Dr G61 76 A2
Dunkeld Gdns G64 78 A1
Dunkeld La G69 81 A1
Dunkeld Pl
Coatbridge ML5 121 C2
Falkirk FK2 24 B1
Hamilton ML3 161 C2
Newton Mearns G77 157 A2
Dunkeld St G31 118 B2
Dunkenny Rd G15 74 C2
Dunkenny Sq G15 74 C2
Dunkirk St ML6 105 A3
Dunlin East Kilbride G74 159 C2
Glasgow G12 96 A3
Dunlin Cres PA6 91 B1
Dunlin Ct ML4 141 C4
Dunlop Cres Ayr KA8 236 C1
Bothwell G71 141 A1
Irvine KA11 220 A1
Renfrew PA4 94 B2
Dunlop Ct ML3 183 C4
Dunlop Dr KA11 224 D2
Dunlop Gr G71 121 A1
Dunlop Halt KA3 195 A4
Dunlop Pl Irvine KA11 224 D2
Milngavie G62 54 C2
Dunlop Prim Sch KA3 195 A4
Dunlop Rd Barrmill KA15 172 A2
Lugton KA3 173 B3
Stewarton KA3 195 B1
Dunlop St
Cambuslang G72 139 C3
Fenwick KA3 213 A2
Glasgow G1 241 A1
Greenock PA16 45 B2
Kilmarnock KA1 222 C1
Linwood PA3 112 B3
Renfrew PA4 94 B2
Stewarton KA3 195 C1
Dunlop Terr KA8 236 B1
Dunmar Cres FK10 4 C1
Dunmar Dr FK10 4 C1
Dunmore Dr G62 76 B4
Dunmore St G81 94 B4
Dunn Mews KA1 227 B4
Dunn St Clydebank G81 73 C3
Clydebank, Dalmuir G81 73 C2
Glasgow G40 118 A2
Greenock PA15 45 C2
Dunn St *continued*
Paisley PA1 114 A2
Dunn Terr ML7 127 C3
Dunnachie Dr ML5 121 A2
Dunnet Ave ML6 102 C3
Dunnet Dr PA6 91 A1
Dunnett Ave KA1 228 A4
Dunnichen Gdns G64 78 B1
Dunnikier Wlk G68 60 C1
Dunning Pl FK2 24 B1
Dunnotar Wlk 16 ML2 165 C3
Dunnottar Cres G74 159 B2
Dunnottar Dr FK5 23 C2
Dunnottar St
Bishopbriggs G64 78 B1
Glasgow G33 99 A1
Dunns Wood Rd G67 62 B3
Dunollie Gdns KA3 223 A3
Dunolly Dr G77 156 C3
Dunolly St G21 98 A1
Dunoon Ave KA3 222 C2
Dunottar Ave ML5 122 A1
Dunottar Pl ML5 122 A2
Dunphail Dr G34 100 B1
Dunphail Rd G34 120 B4
Dunragit St G31 118 B4
Dunrobin Ave
Elderslie PA5 112 B1
Stenhousemuir FK5 23 C3
Dunrobin Cres G74 159 B2
Dunrobin Ct
Clydebank G81 74 A1
East Kilbride G74 159 B2
Dunrobin Dr
East Kilbride G74 159 B2
Gourock PA19 43 C3
Dunrobin Pl ML5 121 C4
Dunrobin Prim Sch
ML6 123 C4
Dunrobin Rd ML6 123 C4
Dunrobin St G31 118 A3
Dunrod Hill G74 159 C2
Dunrod St G32 119 A2
Duns Cres ML2 165 B4
Duns Path ML5 122 B2
Dunscore Brae ML3 161 C1
Dunside Dr G53 135 A3
Dunsiston Rd ML6 124 A2
Dunskaith Pl G34 120 B4
Dunskaith St G34 120 B4
Dunskey Rd KA3 223 A3
Dunsmore Rd PA7 72 A2
Dunsmuir St G51 116 A4
Dunster Gdns G64 78 A2
Dunster Rd FK9 2 B2
Dunswin Ave G81 73 C2
Dunsyre Pl G23 76 C1
Dunsyre St G33 118 C4
Duntarvie Ave G34 120 B4
Duntarvie Cl G34 120 B4
Duntarvie Cres G34 120 B4
Duntarvie Dr G34 120 A4
Duntarvie Gdns G34 120 B4
Duntarvie Gr G34 120 B4
Duntarvie Pl G34 120 A4
Duntarvie Rd G34 120 A4
Dunterlie Ave G13 95 A3
Dunterlie Ct G78 134 B2
Duntiblae Rd G66 80 A4
Duntiglennan Rd G81 74 A3
Duntilland Ave ML7 125 A1
Duntilland Rd
Airdrie ML6 124 C4
Salsburgh ML6,ML7 125 B3
Duntocher Rd
Bearsden G61 75 A3
Clydebank G81 74 C4
Clydebank, Radnor Pk G81 74 A2
Duntonknoll KA12 219 B2
Duntreath Ave G15, G13 74 C1
Duntreath Dr G15 74 C1
Duntreath Gdns G15 74 C1
Duntreath Gr G15 74 C1
Duntreath Terr G65 60 B4
Duntroon Pl ML4 142 A2
Duntroon St G31 118 A4
Dunure Cres FK4 40 A3
Dunure Cts KA13 207 B2
Dunure Dr Hamilton ML3 161 B1
Kilmarnock KA3 228 A4
Newton Mearns G77 157 A3
Rutherglen G73 137 C3
Dunure Pl
Coatbridge ML5 121 C2
Kilmarnock KA3 223 A3
Newton Mearns G77 157 A2
Dunure Rd KA7 238 B1
Dunure St
Bonnybridge FK4 40 A3
Coatbridge ML5 121 C2
Glasgow G20 96 B4
Dunvegan ML6 102 C2
Dunvegan Ave
Coatbridge ML5 101 B1
Elderslie PA5 112 B1
Gourock PA19 43 C3
Stenhousemuir FK5 23 C2
Dunvegan Ct FK10 10 A3
Dunvegan Dr
Bishopbriggs G64 78 A2
Falkirk FK2 24 B1
Newton Mearns G77 157 A3
Stirling FK9 2 A2
Dunvegan Pl
Bonnybridge FK4 39 C3
East Kilbride G74 159 B2
Irvine KA12 219 B3
Uddingston G71 140 B4
Dunvegan Quadrant PA4 94 A2
Dunwan Ave G13 94 C4
Dunwan Pl G13 94 C4
Dura Rd ML2,ML7 167 B3
Durban Ave Clydebank G81 73 B2
East Kilbride G75 180 A2
Durham Rd PA16 44 C3
Durham St G41 116 B3
Durisdeer Dr ML3 161 C1
Durness Ave G61 76 A2
Duror St G32 119 A3
Durris Gdns G32 119 B2
Durrockstock Cres PA2 132 C4
Durrockstock Rd PA2 132 C4
Durrockstock Way PA2 132 C4
Durward G74 160 C2
Durward Ave G41 116 B1
Durward Cres PA2 112 C1
Durward Ct Glasgow G41 116 B1
Motherwell ML1 142 B1
Durward Way PA2 112 C1
Dutch House Rdbt KA9 233 C3
Duthie Rd PA19 45 A4
Duthil St G51 115 B3
Dyce Ave ML6 122 C2
Dyce La G11 96 A1
Dyer's La G1 241 B1
Dyers' Wynd PA1 113 C3
Dyfrig St Blantyre G72 161 B4
Shotts ML7 146 C3
Dyke Rd G13 95 A4
Dyke St Coatbridge ML5 121 A2
Glasgow G69 120 B3
Dykebar Ave G13 95 A3
Dykebar Cres PA2 114 A1
Dykebar Hospl PA2 134 A4
Dykehead Cres ML6 102 C1
Dykehead Dr KA1 228 C3
Dykehead La G33 119 B4
Dykehead Prim Sch
ML7 146 C3
Dykehead Rd
Airdrie ML6 103 A2
Bargeddie G69 121 A3
Dullatur G68 61 B3
Queenzieburn G65 59 C4
Dykehead Sq ML3 161 C2
Dykehead St G33 119 B4
Dykemuir Pl G21 98 A2
Dykemuir Quadrant G21 98 A2
Dykemuir St G21 98 A2
Dykeneuk Rd PA14 68 B4
Dykes Pl KA21 205 C1
Dykes The KA25 170 A4
Dykesfield Pl KA21 205 C1
Dykesmains Prim Sch
KA21 205 C2
Dykesmains Rd KA21 205 C1
Dysart Ct G68 60 C1
Dysart Way ML6 124 A3

E

Eagle Cres G61 75 A3
Eagle St G4 97 B1
Eaglesham Ct 1 G51 116 C3
Eaglesham Path ML5 101 B3
Eaglesham Pl 2 G51 116 C3
Eaglesham Prim Sch
G76 178 C2
Eaglesham Rd
Clarkston G76 157 C3
East Kilbride GL75,GL76 179 B4
Newton Mearns G77 156 B2
Earl Ave ML6 105 A3
Earl Cres KA2 225 C1
Earl Dr KA2 225 C1
Earl Haig Rd G52 114 C4
Earl La G14 95 B2
Earl Of Mar Ct FK10 10 A3
Earl Pl Bridge of W PA11 110 B3
Glasgow G14 95 B2
Earl Rise KA2 225 C1
Earl St G14 95 A2
Earl View ML1 143 A2
Earl's Gate G71 140 C2
Earl's Hill G68 61 A2
Earlbank Ave G14 95 B2
Earlbank La N
11 Glasgow G14 95 B2
18 Glasgow G14 95 B2
Earlbank La S G14 95 B2
Earls Ct FK10 10 A3
Earls Way KA7 238 B1
Earlsburn Ave FK7 7 A2
Earlsburn Rd G66 79 C2
Earlscourt G69 80 C1
Earlsgate PA6 91 A1
Earlshill Dr
Bannockburn FK7 7 C1
Howwood PA9 130 C3
Earlspark Ave G43 136 C3
Earlston Ave Glasgow G21 97 C1
Kilmarnock KA1 227 C2
Earlston Cres ML5 122 B2
Earlston Pl G21 241 C4
Earlston St ML2 165 B3
Earlybraes Dr G33 119 C3
Earlybraes Gdns G33 119 B3
Earn Ave Bearsden G61 76 A2
Bellshill ML4 141 C3
Renfrew PA4 94 C1
Earn Cres ML2 165 A1
Earn Ct FK10 10 B3
Earn Gdns ML9 199 A4
Earn La ML1 143 A3
Earn Pl Denny FK6 39 B3

Earn Pl *continued*
Kilmarnock KA1 228 A3
Earn Rd
Newton Mearns G77 156 B4
Troon KA10 229 D2
Earn St G33 98 C1
Earn Terr ML7 146 C3
Earncraig Gn KA11 220 A2
Earnhill La PA16 44 B3
Earnhill Pl PA16 44 B3
Earnhill Rd PA16 44 B3
Earnock Ave ML1 163 B3
Earnock High Sch ML3 162 A1
Earnock Rd ML3 161 C1
Earnock St Glasgow G33 98 B2
Hamilton ML3 162 A2
Earnside St G32 119 A3
Easdale G74 181 A4
Easdale Dr G32 119 A2
Easdale Path
Coatbridge ML5 122 B2
Glenboig ML5 101 B3
Easdale Pl G77 156 A3
Easdale Rise ML3 161 C2
East Academy St ML2 165 A1
East Ave Carluke ML8 187 B1
Hamilton G72 161 C3
Motherwell ML1 143 A1
Plains ML6 104 A2
Renfrew PA4 94 B2
Uddingston G71 141 B3
East Barmoss Ave PA14 68 C4
East Barns St G81 94 B4
East Bath La G2 241 A3
East Blackhall St PA15 46 A2
East Boreland Pl FK6 21 C1
East Bowhouse Head
KA11 220 A3
East Bowhouse Way
KA11 220 A3
East Breast PA15 46 A3
East Bridge St FK1 42 B2
East Broomlands KA11 220 A1
East Buchanan Mews 12
PA1 113 C3
East Buchanan St PA1 113 C3
East Burnside St 2 G65 60 B4
East Campbell St G1 241 C1
East Castle St FK10 10 A3
East Crawford St PA15 46 B2
East Dean St ML4 142 A3
East Dr FK5 23 B1
East Faulds Rd ML11 215 C3
East Fulton Prim Sch
PA3 111 C3
East Gargieston Ave
KA1 227 B3
East Gate Glenboig ML5 101 B4
Wishaw ML2 165 B2
East George St ML5 122 A4
East Glebe Terr ML3 162 B1
East Gr KA10 229 D2
East Greenlees Ave G72 139 B2
East Greenlees Cres
G72 139 B2
East Greenlees Dr G72 139 B2
East Greenlees Gr G72 138 C2
East Greenlees Rd G72 139 A2
East Hallhill Rd G33 120 B3
East Hamilton St
Greenock PA15 46 B2
Wishaw ML2 165 A1
East High St Airdrie ML6 123 A4
Kirkintilloch G66 58 B1
East India Breast PA15 46 A3
East Kilbride Rd
Rutherglen G73 138 C2
Thorntonhall G74,G76 158 B2
East Kilbride Sta G74 159 C1
East Kirkland KA24 191 B4
East La PA1 114 A2
East Lennox Dr G84 16 C2
East Link Rd FK9 2 B3
East Machan St ML9 185 A1
East Main St ML7 127 C3
East Mains FK11 4 A3
East Mains Rd G74 159 C2
East Milton Gr G75 159 A1
East Milton Prim Sch
G75 159 B1
East Montrose St G84 16 C1
East Murrayfield FK7 7 C1
East Netherton St KA1 227 C4
East Park Cres KA3 222 A4
East Park Dr KA3 222 A4
East Park Rd KA8 236 A2
East Plean Prim Sch FK7 12 B2
East Princes St G84 16 B1
East Rd Irvine KA12 219 A4
Irvine KA12 219 B2
Kilbarchan PA10 111 A2
Motherwell ML1 143 A2
Port Glasgow PA14 68 C4
Prestwick KA9 236 B3
East Rossdhu Dr G84 16 C2
East Scott Terr ML3 162 B1
East Shaw St
Greenock PA15 45 C3
Kilmarnock KA1 227 C3
East Shawhead Ind Est
ML5 122 A2
East Springfield Terr
G64 98 A4
East St PA14,PA15 46 C1
East Station Ind Est
ML9 185 A2
East Stewart Gdns ML5 122 B4
East Stewart Pl ML5 122 B4
East Stewart St
Coatbridge ML5 122 B3
Greenock PA15 46 A2
East Stirling St FK12,FK13 5 A4
East Thomson St G81 74 A2
East Thornlie St ML2 165 A1
East Vennel FK10 10 A3
East Wellbrae Cres ML3 162 A1
East Wellington St G31 118 B3
East William St PA15 46 B2
East Woodside Ave PA14 69 A4
East Woodstock Ct 2
KA1 227 C4
Eastbank Acad G32 119 A2
Eastbank Dr G32 119 B3
Eastbank Pl G32 119 B3
Eastbank Prim Sch G32 119 B3
Eastbank Rise G32 119 B3
Eastburn Cres G21 98 A3
Eastburn Dr FK1 42 B2
Eastburn Pl G21 98 A3
Eastburn Rd G21 98 A3
Eastcote Ave G14 95 C2
Eastcroft G73 138 A4
Eastcroft St FK5 23 A1
Eastcroft Terr G21 98 A2
Eastend PA12 129 B2
Eastend Ave ML1 143 A1
Easter Carmuirs Prim Sch
FK1 41 A3
Easter Cornton Rd FK9 2 A2
Easter Craigs G31 118 A4
Easter Cres ML2 165 C2
Easter Garngaber Rd
G66 79 C3
Easter Livilands FK7 7 B2
Easter Mews G71 140 C3
Easter Queenslie Rd
G33 119 C4
Easter Rd Clarkston G76 158 A3
Shotts ML7 146 B3
Easter Wood Cres G71 121 B1
Eastergreens Ave G66 79 B4
Easterhill Pl G32 118 C2
Easterhill Rd G84 16 C2
Easterhill St G32 119 A1
Easterhouse Pl G34 120 B4
Easterhouse Quadrant
G34 120 B4
Easterhouse Rd G34 120 B4
Easterhouse Sta G69 120 B3
Eastermains G66 59 A1
Eastern Cres KA25 170 A4
Easterton Ave G76 158 A3
Easterton Cres FK7 12 C4
Easterton Dr FK7 12 C4
Easterton Gr FK7 12 C4
Easterton Stables★ G66 32 B2
Eastfield Ave G72 138 C3
Eastfield Cres G82 50 A1
Eastfield Pl G82 50 A1
Eastfield Prim Sch G68 61 A1
Eastfield Rd
Caldercruix ML6 105 A3
Carluke ML8 202 A4
Cumbernauld G68 61 B2
Glasgow G21 97 C2
Eastfield Terr ML4 142 B2
Eastgate G69 101 A3
Easthall Prim Sch G34 119 C4
Eastlea Pl ML6 123 A3
Eastmuir Specl Sch
G33 119 B3
Eastmuir St Glasgow G32 119 A3
Wishaw ML2 165 C2
Easton Ct FK8 2 A1
Easton Dr FK1 66 B4
Easton Pl ML5 122 A3
Eastside G66 58 B1
Eastside Ind Est G66 58 B1
Eastvale Pl G3 116 B4
Eastwood Ave
Glasgow G41 136 B4
Glasgow, Giffnock G46 136 B1
Irvine KA12 219 B2
Eastwood Cres G46 135 C2
Eastwood Dr ML2 166 A3
Eastwood High Sch
G77 156 C4
Eastwood La G84 25 A4
Eastwood Rd G69 80 C1
Eastwood Toll G46 136 A1
Eastwood View G72 139 C3
Eastwood Way 2 ML9 185 A2
Eastwoodmains Rd
Clarkston G76 157 B4
Glasgow G46 136 B1
Easwald Bank PA10 111 B1
Ebenezer Pl FK1 66 C3
Ebroch Dr G65 60 C4
Ebroch Pk G65 60 C4
Eccles Ct FK7 7 A2
Eccles St G22 97 C3
Eck Path ML1 143 A3
Eckford St G32 119 A2
Eday Cres KA3 222 C3
Eday St G22 97 B3
Edderton Pl G34 120 A4
Edderton Way G34 120 A4
Eddington Dr G77 156 B2
Eddleston Pl G72 139 C3
Eddlewood Ct G33 120 A4
Eddlewood Path G33 119 C4
Eddlewood Pl G33 119 C4
Eddlewood Rd G33 119 C4
Eden Ct KA13 207 A2
Eden Dr G75 179 C3
Eden Gdns G75 179 C4
Eden Gr G75 179 C4
Eden La G33 98 B1
Eden Pk G72 140 C1
Eden Pl Cambuslang G72 139 B3
Kilmarnock KA1 228 A3
Renfrew PA4 94 C1
Eden Rd FK10 9 C4
Eden St G33 98 B1
Edenhall Ct G77 156 B1
Edenhall Gr G77 156 B1
Edenhall Rd KA8 236 A2
Edenkill Pl G63 31 B2
Edenside G68 62 A4
Edenwood St G31 118 C3
Edgam Dr G52 115 B3
Edgefauld Ave G21 97 C2
Edgefauld Dr G21 97 C2
Edgefauld Pl G21 97 C3
Edgefauld Rd G21 98 A2
Edgehill La G11 96 A2
Edgehill Rd Bearsden G61 75 C3
Glasgow G11 96 A2
Edgemont Pk ML3 183 B4
Edgemont St G41 136 C4
Edinbarnet Prim Sch
G81 74 B4
Edinbeg Ave G42 137 C4
Edinbeg Pl G42 137 C4
Edinburgh Dr PA19 43 C3
Edinburgh Rd
Glasgow G33 119 B4
Harthill ML7 127 B3
Motherwell ML1 143 B4
Edington Gdns G69 80 C2
Edington St G4 97 A1
Edison Pl KA13 207 C1
Edison St G52 114 C4
Edmiston Ave KA9 236 A4
Edmiston Dr
Glasgow G51 116 A3
Linwood PA3 112 A3
Edmonstone Dr G65 60 B4
Edmonton Terr G75 180 B4
Edmund Kean G74 160 B3
Edrom Ct G32 118 C3
Edrom Path G32 118 C3
Edrom St G32 118 C3
Edward Ave Renfrew PA4 94 C2
Stenhousemuir FK5 23 C2
Stirling FK8 2 B1
Edward Dr G84 16 B2
Edward Pl FK2 24 C2
Edward Rd FK8 2 A1
Edward St Clydebank G81 94 B4
Coatbridge G69 120 C3
Hamilton ML3 162 B1
Kilsyth G65 36 B1
Motherwell ML1 163 C2
Edwin St G51 116 B3
Edzell Ct G14 95 B1
Edzell Dr Elderslie PA5 112 B1
Newton Mearns G77 156 C2
Edzell Gdns
Bishopbriggs G64 98 B4
Wishaw ML2 165 A1
Edzell Pl G14 95 B2
Edzell Row KA13 207 A2
Edzell St Coatbridge ML5 121 B2
Glasgow G14 95 B1
Egidia Ave G46 136 B1
Egilsay Cres G22 97 B4
Egilsay Pl G22 97 B4
Egilsay St G22 97 B4
Egilsay Terr G22 97 B4
Eglinton Cty Visitor Ctr★
KA12 219 A4
Eglinton Cres KA10 229 C1
Eglinton Ct Glasgow G5 117 A3
Saltcoats KA21 216 C4
Eglinton Ctry Pk KA13 208 A1
Eglinton Dr
Eaglesham G76 178 C2
Glasgow G46 136 B1
Troon KA10 229 D1
Eglinton Gdns KA12 219 B2
Eglinton Intc KA12 219 A4
Eglinton Pl Ayr KA7 235 C1
Kilwinning KA13 207 C2
Saltcoats KA21 216 C4
Eglinton Rd KA22 205 A2
Eglinton Sq KA22 205 B2
Eglinton St Beith KA15 171 A4
Coatbridge ML5 122 A4
Glasgow G5 117 A2
Irvine KA12 219 B2
Saltcoats KA21 216 C4
Eglinton Terr KA7 235 C1
Eglinton Wlk G76 178 C2
Egmont Pk G75 180 A4
Eider G12 96 A4
Eider Ave G75 180 A3
Eider Gr G75 180 A3
Eider Pl G75 180 A2
Eighth St G71 120 C1
Eildon Cres ML6 123 C1
Eildon Dr G78 134 B1
Eildon Rd G66 79 C4
Eileen Gdns G64 78 A1
Eilt Wlk 8 ML2 165 C3
Elba Ct KA8 236 A1
Elba Gdns KA8 236 A1
Elba St KA8 236 A1
Elcho St G40 117 C3
Elder Ave KA15 171 A4
Elder Cres G72 139 C2
Elder Gr G71 141 A4
Elder Grove Ave G51 115 B4
Elder Grove Ct G51 115 B4
Elder Grove Pl G51 115 B4
Elder Park Prim Sch
G51 115 C4
Elder St G51 115 C4
Elderbank G61 75 C2
Elderpark Gdns G51 115 C4
Elderpark Gr 8 G51 115 C4
Elderpark St G51 115 C4
Elders Way ML2 165 B2
Elderslea Rd ML8 202 A4
Elderslie Cres KA1 227 C2
Elderslie Hospl PA5 112 B1
Elderslie St G3 240 A3
Eldin Pl Bridge of W PA11 110 C3
Elderslie PA5 112 A1
Eldon Ct G11 96 A1
Eldon Gdns G64 77 C1
Eldon Pl PA16 45 B4
Eldon St Glasgow G3 96 C1
Greenock PA16 45 B4
Elgin Ave
East Kilbride G74 159 C2
Stewarton KA3 195 B1
Elgin Dr FK7 7 B2
Elgin Gdns G76 157 C4
Elgin Pl Airdrie ML6 122 C3
Coatbridge ML5 122 A2
East Kilbride G74 159 C2
Falkirk FK1 42 B2
Kilsyth G65 36 B1
Elgin Rd G61 75 C4
Elgin Terr ML3 161 C2
Elgin Way ML4 142 A3
Elibank St G33 99 A1
Elie St G11 96 B1
Elim Dr FK1 66 B3
Eliot Cres ML3 162 B1
Eliot Terr ML3 162 B1
Elison Ct ML1 164 A2
Elive Ct ML5 122 A2
Elizabeth Ave
Milton of C G66 58 A3
Stenhousemuir FK5 23 B1
Elizabeth Cres Falkirk FK1 41 A3
Glasgow G46 136 A2
Elizabeth Quadrant
ML1 142 C3
Elizabeth St
Glasgow G51 116 B3
Stirling FK8 7 A3
Elizabeth Wynd ML3 183 B4
Elizabethan Way PA4 94 B1
Ella Gdns ML4 142 B2
Ellangowan Rd
Glasgow G41 136 B4
Milngavie G62 55 A1
Ellergreen Rd G61 75 C2
Ellerslie St PA5 112 A2
Ellesmere St G22 97 A2
Elliot Ave Glasgow G46 136 B2
Paisley PA2 132 C4
Elliot Cres G74 160 A1
Elliot Dr G46 136 B2
Elliot Pl Glasgow G3 116 C4
Netherburn ML9 200 A2
Elliot St G3 116 C4
Elliot Terr FK2 42 A4
Ellis St Coatbridge ML5 122 A3
Kilmarnock KA1 227 C4
Ellis Way 12 ML1 163 C3
Ellisland
East Kilbride G74 160 C2
Kirkintilloch G66 59 A1
Ellisland Ave G81 74 B2
Ellisland Cres G73 137 C3
Ellisland Dr Blantyre G72 161 A3
Kilmarnock KA3 228 B4
Kirkintilloch G66 59 A1
Ellisland Pl Ayr KA7 239 A3
Saltcoats KA21 206 A2
Ellisland Rd
Clarkston G76 157 C3
Cumbernauld G67 62 A1
Glasgow G43 136 B3
Ellisland Sq KA7 239 A3
Ellisland Wynd ML1 143 B2
Ellismuir Farm Rd G69 120 B2
Ellismuir Pl G69 120 B2
Ellismuir Rd G69 120 B2
Ellismuir St ML5 121 C2
Ellismuir Way G71 121 A1
Elliston Ave G53 135 B3
Elliston Cres G53 135 B3
Elliston Dr G53 135 B3
Elliston Pl PA9 130 C3
Elliston Rd PA9 130 C3
Ellon Dr PA3 112 A3
Ellon Gr PA3 113 C4
Ellon Way PA3 114 A4
Ellrig G75 180 B3
Elm Ave Kirkintilloch G66 79 B3
Renfrew PA4 94 B2
Elm Bank
Bishopbriggs G64 78 A1
Kirkintilloch G66 58 B1
Elm Cres G71 141 B4
Elm Ct ML3 183 C2
Elm Dr Cambuslang G72 139 B3
Chapelhall ML6 123 C2
Cumbernauld G67 62 C2
Johnstone PA5 112 A1
Elm Gdns Bearsden G61 75 C3
Troon KA10 230 A1
Elm Gr Alloa FK10 10 B3
Langbank PA14 70 B4
Stenhousemuir FK5 23 B1
Elm La E 26 G14 95 B2
Elm La W 25 G14 95 B2
Elm Pk KA22 205 B2
Elm Pl G75 180 B3
Elm Quadrant ML6 123 B4
Elm Rd Bridge of W PA11 110 C4
Clydebank G81 74 A3
Dumbarton G82 49 C2
Motherwell ML1 143 A1
Motherwell ML1 143 A3
Paisley PA2 114 A1
Rutherglen G73 138 A2
Elm St Blantyre G72 161 C4
Clarkston G76 157 C3
Coatbridge ML5 122 B3
Glasgow G14 95 B2
Lennoxtown G66 57 C4
Motherwell ML1 163 B4
Stirling FK8 1 C1
Elm Terr PA19 44 C3
Elm View Ct ML4 142 B2
Elm Way G72 139 C2
Elm Wlk G61 75 C3
Elmbank FK11 4 A3
Elmbank Ave
Kilmarnock KA1 228 A4
Uddingston G71 141 A4
Elmbank Cres
Bonnybridge FK4 39 B3
Glasgow G2 240 B3
Hamilton ML3 162 A2
Elmbank Dr
Alexandria G83 27 C3
Kilmarnock KA1 228 A4
Larkhall ML9 185 B1
Elmbank Rd
Langbank PA14 70 B4
Stirling FK7 7 A2
Elmbank St Ayr KA8 236 A2
Bellshill ML4 142 A2
Carluke ML8 202 A4
Glasgow G2 240 B3
Elmbank Street La G2 240 B3
Elmbank Terr KA12 219 B2
Elmfoot St G5 117 B1
Elmhurst ML1 163 B2
Elmira Rd G69 100 B4
Elmore Ave G44 137 A3
Elms Pl Beith KA15 150 A1
Stevenston KA20 206 C1
Elms The G44 137 A2
Elmslie Ct G69 120 B2
Elmtree Gdns G45 137 C2
Elmvale Prim Sch G22 97 C3
Elmvale Row G21 97 C3
Elmvale St G21 97 C3
Elmway ML9 185 A3
Elmwood ML2 164 C1
Elmwood Ave
Glasgow G11 95 C2
Newton Mearns G77 156 C3
Elmwood Ct G71 141 A1
Elmwood Gdns G66 79 A3
Elmwood La G14 95 C2
Elmwood Manor G71 141 A1
Elmwood Rd ML7 147 A1
Elphin St G23 76 B1
Elphinstone Cres
Airth FK2 14 C2
East Kilbride G75 180 C3
Elphinstone Ct PA13 89 B4
Elphinstone Mews PA13 89 B4
Elphinstone Pl G51 116 B4
Elphinstone Rd G46 157 A4
Elrig Rd G44 137 A3
Elsinore Path G75 180 C3
Elspeth Gdns G64 78 B1
Elswick Dr ML6 105 A2
Eltham St G22 97 A2
Elvan Pl G75 179 C4
Elvan St Glasgow G32 118 C3
Motherwell ML1 163 B3
Elvan Twr 7 ML1 163 C3
Elvis St KA9 233 B1
Embo Dr G13 95 A3
Emerald Terr ML4 142 A2
Emerson Rd G64 78 A1
Emerson Rd W G64 78 A1
Emerson St G20 97 A3
Emily Dr ML1 163 C2
Emma Jay Rd ML4 142 A3
Empire Way ML1 142 B1
Empress Ct PA15 46 A2
Empress Dr G84 16 A2
Empress Rd G84 15 B3
Endfield Ave G12 96 A3
Endrick Bank G64 78 A2
Endrick Ct ML5 121 C3
Endrick Dr Balloch G83 19 C1
Bearsden G61 75 C2
Denny FK6 39 C3
Paisley PA1 114 A3
Endrick Gdns G62 54 C1
Endrick Pl FK7 7 A2
Endrick Rd PA15 46 A1
Endrick St G21 97 B2
Endrick Way G83 27 C3
Engelen Dr FK10 10 A3
Engels St G83 27 C4
Englewood Ave KA8 236 A3
English Row ML6 123 B2
English St ML2 164 B2
Ennerdale G75 179 C3
Ennisfree Rd G72 161 B4
Ensay St G22 97 B4
Enterkin St G32 118 C2
Enterkine KA13 207 A1

Fin – Gal 263

Fintry Rd PA15 46 A1
Fintry Terr KA11 220 A2
Fintry Wlk KA11 220 A1
Fir Bank KA7 239 B3
Fir Bank Ave ML9 185 A1
Fir Ct Cambuslang G72 139 C2
Coatbridge ML5 121 C2
Fir Dr G75 180 A3
Fir Gr Motherwell ML1 143 A1
Uddingston G71 141 B4
Fir La FK5 23 B1
Fir Park St ML1 163 C2
Fir Pk (Motherwell FC) ML1 163 C2
Fir Pl Cambuslang G72 139 B3
Cleland ML1 144 A1
Glasgow G69 120 A2
Johnstone PA5 112 A1
Kilmarnock KA1 227 B4
Fir St PA15 46 C1
Fir Terr PA19 44 B3
Fir View ML6 123 A1
Firbank Ave G64 78 A4
Firbank Quadrant ML6 123 C2
Firbank Terr G78 134 C1
Firdon Cres G15 75 A1
Firhill Ave ML6 122 C3
Firhill Dr KA9 233 B3
Firhill Pk (Partick Thistle FC) G20 97 A2
Firhill Rd G20 97 A2
Firhill St G20 97 A2
Firlee G75 179 C4
Firpark Rd G64 98 A4
Firpark Sch ML1 163 C2
Firpark St G31 117 C4
Firpark Terr
Cambusbarron FK7 6 B3
Glasgow G31 117 C4
Firs Cres FK7 7 B1
Firs Entry FK7 7 B1
Firs Pk (East Stirlingshire FC) FK2 42 B3
Firs Rd FK10 4 B1
Firs St FK2 42 B3
Firs The Bannockburn FK7 7 B1
Glasgow G44 137 A2
First Ave Alexandria G83 27 C3
Bearsden G61 76 A2
Dumbarton G82 50 B1
Glasgow G44 136 C1
Irvine KA12 224 C4
Kirkintilloch G66 79 B1
Millerston G33 99 A2
Renfrew PA4 94 B1
Stevenston KA20 217 C4
Uddingston G71 140 C4
First Gdns G41 116 A2
First Rd G72 161 C3
First St Irvine KA12 219 A4
Uddingston G71 140 C4
First Terr G81 74 A2
Firth Cres PA19 44 B3
Firth Gdns KA10 229 C4
Firth Rd KA10 229 C4
Firth View Terr KA22 205 B2
Firthview Terr G82 49 B2
Firtree Pl ML2 166 A3
Firtree Rd ML2 166 A3
Firwood Cts G77 156 C2
Firwood Dr G44 137 B3
Firwood Rd G77 156 C2
Fischer Gdns PA1 112 C3
Fishcross Prim Sch FK10 5 B2
Fisher Ave Kilsyth G65 60 B4
Paisley PA1 112 C2
Fisher Cres G81 74 A3
Fisher Ct Glasgow G31 117 C4
Knockentiber KA2 221 C2
Fisher Dr PA1 112 C2
Fisher Pl G84 17 A1
Fisher St ML9 185 A1
Fisher Way PA1 112 C2
Fishers Rd PA4 94 B3
Fisherwood Rd G83 27 C4
Fishescoates Ave G73 138 B3
Fishescoates Gdns G73 138 B3
Fitzalan Dr PA3 114 A3
Fitzalan Rd PA4 94 A1
Fitzroy La G3 116 C4
Fitzroy Pl 2 G3 116 C4
Five Roads KA13 208 A2
Five Ways Rd ML9 200 B2
Flakefield G74 159 A1
Flanders St G81 74 B4
Flanigan Gr ML4 142 A3
Flatterton La PA16 44 B1
Flatterton Rd PA16 44 B1
Flax Mill Rd ML7 127 C3
Flax Rd G71 141 A3
Flaxfield Gr ML1 142 B1
Flaxmill Ave ML2 164 B2
Fleck Ave KA21 206 A1
Fleet Ave PA4 94 C1
Fleet St G32 119 A2
Fleming Ave
Chryston G69 100 B4
Clydebank G81 94 B4
Fleming Cres KA21 206 A2
Fleming Ct Carluke ML8 187 C1
Clydebank G81 74 A1
Hamilton ML3 161 C2
Motherwell ML1 164 A2
Fleming Dr
Stenhousemuir FK5 24 A2
Stewarton KA3 211 B4
Fleming Gdns FK1 41 C3
Fleming Pl
Blackridge EH48 107 C2
East Kilbride G75 180 C4
Fleming Rd Bellshill ML4 142 A4
Bishopton PA7 72 A2
Cumbernauld G67 61 C1
Houston PA6 91 A1
Fleming St Glasgow G31 118 A3
Kilmarnock KA1 227 C3
Paisley PA3 113 C4
Fleming Terr KA12 219 A3
Fleming Way
Hamilton ML3 161 C2
30 Larkhall ML9 185 B1
Flemington Ind Est G72 139 C2
Flemington Ind Pk ML1 164 B3
Flemington St G21 97 C2
Flenders Ave G76 157 B3
Flenders Rd G76 157 B3
Fletcher Ave PA19 44 C4
Fleurs Ave G41 116 A2
Fleurs Rd G41 116 A2
Flinders Pl G75 180 A4
Flint Cres FK7 12 B4
Flint Mill La PA15 46 A1
Flloyd St ML5 121 C4
Floors Rd G76 157 B1
Floors St PA5 111 C1
Floors Street Ind Est PA5 111 C1
Floorsburn Cres PA5 111 C1
Flora Gdns G64 78 B1
Florence Dr
Glasgow G46 136 B1
Kilmacolm PA13 89 A4
Florence Gdns G73 138 B2
Florence St Glasgow G5 117 B3
Greenock PA16 45 A2
Florida Ave G42 137 A4
Florida Cres G42 137 A4
Florida Dr G42 137 A4
Florida Gdns G69 120 A3
Florida Sq G42 137 A4
Florida St G42 137 A4
Florish Rd PA8 93 C4
Flotta Pl KA3 222 C3
Flowerdale Pl G53 135 A2
Flowerhill Ind Est ML6 123 A4
Flowerhill St ML6 123 A4
Flures Ave PA8 93 C4
Flures Cres PA8 93 C4
Flures Dr PA8 93 C4
Flures Pl PA8 93 C4
Fochabers Dr G52 115 B3
Fogo Pl G20 96 B3
Foinaven Dr G46 136 A3
Foinaven Gdns G46 136 A3
Foinaven Way G46 136 A3
Foinavon Rd ML3 183 C2
Foot Of Lone Rd ML11 214 A3
Footfield Rd ML4 141 C2
Forbes Cres FK5 23 B1
Forbes Ct FK2 42 C3
Forbes Dr Ayr KA8 236 B2
3 Glasgow G40 117 C3
Motherwell ML1 142 B1
Forbes Pl
Kilmarnock KA3 223 A1
Paisley PA1 113 C2
Forbes Rd FK1 42 B2
Forbes St Alloa FK10 9 C3
Glasgow G40 117 C3
Forbes Wlk KA3 223 A1
Ford Ave KA11 225 B4
Ford Rd Bonnybridge FK4 40 A3
Glasgow G12 96 B2
Newton Mearns G77 156 B2
Fordbank Prim Sch PA5 131 B4
Forde Cres KA20 206 C1
Fordneuk St G40 118 A3
Fordoun St G34 120 B4
Fordyce Ct G77 156 B2
Fordyce Gdns FK1 41 C2
Fordyce St G11 96 B1
Fore Row ML3 162 C2
Fore St Glasgow G14 95 B2
Port Glasgow PA14 47 B1
Forebraes FK10 10 A4
Foregate Sq KA1 222 C1
Foregate The KA1 222 C1
Forehill Prim Sch KA7 239 B3
Forehill Rd KA7 239 B3
Forehouse Rd PA10 110 B2
Foremount Terrace La 18 G12 96 B2
Forest Ave ML3 183 B3
Forest Dr Bellshill ML4 142 B2
Bothwell G71 141 A2
Forest Gdns G66 79 A2
Forest Gr KA3 223 A3
Forest Kirk ML8 202 A4
Forest La ML3 183 B3
Forest Pk ML2 165 B3
Forest Pl Crossford ML8 201 A1
Kirkintilloch G66 79 A2
Paisley PA2 113 C1
Forest Rd
Cumbernauld G67 62 C3
Larkhall ML9 185 A2
Forest View G67 62 B2
Forest Walks★ G66 57 A3
Forest Way KA7 239 B3
Forester Gr FK10 4 C1
Forestfield Gdns ML6 105 A2
Foresthall Cres G21 98 A2
Foresthall Dr G21 98 A2
Forfar Ave G52 115 A2
Forfar Cres G64 98 B4
Forfar Rd PA16 44 C2
Forgan Gdns G64 98 B4
Forge Dr ML5 121 C4
Forge Pl G21 98 A1
Forge Rd Airdrie ML6 123 C3
Ayr KA8 236 A2
Forge Row ML6 123 B2
Forge Sh Ctr The G31 118 B3
Forge St Glasgow G21 98 A1
Kilmarnock KA1 222 C1
Forge Vennal KA13 207 B2
Forgewood Path ML6 123 C3
Forgewood Rd ML1 142 B1
Forglen Cres FK9 2 A3
Forglen Rd FK9 2 A3
Forglen St G34 100 A1
Formakin Estate Walks★ PA7 71 B1
Formby Dr G23 76 B1
Forres Ave G46 136 B2
Forres Cres ML4 142 A3
Forres Gate G46 136 B1
Forres Quadrant ML2 165 A3
Forres St Blantyre G72 161 B3
1 Glasgow G23 76 C1
Forrest Dr G61 75 A4
Forrest Gate
Hamilton ML3 162 A1
Uddingston G71 121 A1
Forrest Pl ML7 127 C3
Forrest Rd
Forrestfield ML6 106 A1
Lanark ML11 215 A3
Salsburgh ML7 126 A3
Stirling FK8 2 A1
Forrest St Airdrie ML6 123 B4
Blantyre G72 161 C4
Glasgow G40 118 A3
Shotts ML7 146 C3
Forrester Ct 1 G64 97 C4
Forrester Pl FK2 14 B2
Forrestfield Cres G77 156 C3
Forrestfield Gdns G77 156 C3
Forrestfield Rd ML6 106 A3
Forrestfield St G21 98 A1
Forrestlea Rd ML8 202 A4
Forsa Ct G75 180 B2
Forsyth Ct ML11 215 B2
Forsyth Gr PA16 45 B3
Forsyth St Airdrie ML6 123 A4
Greenock PA16 45 B3
Fort Matilda Pl PA16 45 A4
Fort Matilda Sta PA16 45 A4
Fort Matilda Terr PA16 45 A4
Fort St Ayr KA7 235 C1
Motherwell ML1 163 B4
Fortacre Pl KA11 220 A3
Forteviot Ave G69 120 B3
Forteviot Pl G69 120 B3
Forth Ave Larbert FK5 23 A2
Paisley PA2 112 C1
Forth Cres Alloa FK10 10 B3
East Kilbride G75 179 C4
Stirling FK8 7 A4
Forth Ct East Kilbride G75 179 C4
Stirling FK8 2 A1
Forth Gr G75 179 C4
Forth Pk FK9 2 A3
Forth Pl Johnstone PA5 131 B4
Kilmarnock KA1 228 A3
Larkhall ML9 199 A4
Stirling FK8 7 A4
Forth Rd Bearsden G61 75 B1
Torrance G64 78 A4
Forth St Cambus FK10 9 A4
Clydebank G81 94 B4
Fallin FK7 8 B2
Glasgow G41 116 C2
Greenock PA16 45 A3
Stirling FK8 2 A1
Forth Terr ML3 183 A4
Forth Valley Coll of Nursing & Midwifery FK1 42 A2
Forth View FK8 2 A1
Forthbank (Stirling Albion FC) FK7 7 C4
Forthbank Ind Est FK10 10 A2
Forthvale FK11 4 A3
Forthvale Ct FK9 2 A1
Forthview FK7 7 C1
Forthview Ct FK1 41 C1
Forties Cres G46 136 A3
Forties Gdns G46 136 A3
Forties Rd PA6 111 B4
Forties Way G46 136 A3
Fortieth Ave G75 180 C3
Fortingale Ave G12 96 B3
Fortingale Pl G12 96 B3
Fortingall Rd G72 161 C3
Fortissat Ave ML7 146 B3
Fortisset Rd ML7 126 A1
Fortrose St G11 96 A1
Fortuna Ct FK1 42 B2
Forum Pl ML1 142 B1
Forum Sh Ctr The PA15 45 C3
Fossil Gr G66 59 A1
Foswell Dr G15 74 C3
Foswell Pl G15 74 C3
Fotheringay La G41 116 B1
Fotheringay Rd G41 116 C1
Fothringham Rd KA8 239 A4
Foulburn Rd ML7,ML2, ML1 145 B1
Foulis La G13 95 C3
Foulis St G13 95 C3
Foulsykes Rd ML2 165 C2
Foundry La G78 134 B1
Foundry Loan FK5 23 A1
Foundry Rd
Bonnybridge FK4 40 A3
Cleland ML1 144 B1
Shotts ML7 146 C2
Foundry St FK2 42 A4
Foundry Wynd KA13 207 B2
Fountain Ave PA4 93 A2
Fountain Bsns Ctr The ML5 122 A3
Fountain Cres PA4 93 B3
Fountain Dr PA4 93 B2
Fountain Rd FK9 2 A4
Fountainwell Ave G21 97 B2
Fountainwell Dr G21 97 B1
Fountainwell Pl G21 97 B2
Fountainwell Rd G21 97 B1
Fountainwell Sq G21 97 C1
Fountainwell Terr G21 97 C1
Four Acres Dr KA3 222 A4
Four Windings PA6 91 A1
Fourth Ave
Dumbarton G82 50 B1
Kirkintilloch G66 79 B1
Millerston G33 99 A3
Renfrew PA4 94 B1
Fourth Gdns G41 116 A2
Fourth St G71 120 C1
Fowlds St KA1 227 C4
Fowlis Dr G77 156 B3
Fox Gr ML1 163 A4
Fox St Glasgow G1 240 C1
Greenock PA16 45 B4
Foxbar Cres PA2 132 C4
Foxbar Dr Glasgow G13 95 A3
Paisley PA2 132 C4
Foxbar Rd PA2 132 C4
Foxes Gr G66 79 C3
Foxglove Pl Ayr KA7 239 B2
Glasgow G53 135 A2
Foxhills Pl G23 76 C1
Foxley St G32 119 B1
Foyers Terr G21 98 A2
Franchi Dr FK5 23 C3
Francis St 7 G5 117 A2
Frankfield Rd G33 99 C3
Frankfield St G33 98 C1
Frankfort St G41 116 C1
Franklin Pl G75 159 A1
Franklin Rd KA21 205 C1
Franklin St G40 117 C2
Fraser Ave Bishopton PA7 72 A2
Dumbarton G82 50 B2
Johnstone PA5 112 A1
Newton Mearns G77 156 C3
Rutherglen G73 138 B4
Troon KA10 229 C3
Fraser Cres ML3 162 A1
Fraser Gdns G66 79 A4
Fraser Pl FK9 2 A2
Fraser St
Cambuslang G72 138 C3
Cleland ML1 144 A1
Fraser Wlk KA3 223 B2
Frazer Ave G84 16 A2
Frazer St G40 118 A3
Frederick St ML5 121 C4
Freeland Cres G53 135 A3
Freeland Ct G53 135 B3
Freeland Dr
Bridge of W PA11 90 B1
Glasgow G53 135 A3
Inchinnan PA4 93 B3
Freeland La 9 G75 180 C4
Freeland Pl G66 79 B4
Freeland Rd PA8 93 A4
Freelands Cres G60 73 B3
Freelands Ct G81 73 B2
Freelands Rd G60 73 B2
Freesia Ct ML1 163 C3
French St Clydebank G81 73 C2
Glasgow G40 117 C2
Renfrew PA4 94 A1
Wishaw ML2 165 A2
Freuchie St G34 120 A4
Frew Terr KA12 219 B3
Friar Ave G64 78 A2
Friar's La ML11 214 C2
Friar's Wynd ML11 214 C2
Friars Croft Irvine KA12 219 A1
Kirkintilloch G66 79 C4
Friars Lawn KA13 207 B2
Friars Pk ML11 214 C2
Friars Pl G13 95 B4
Friars St FK8 7 A4
Friars Way ML6 123 B2
Friarscourt Ave G13 95 B4
Friarscourt Rd G69 80 A1
Friarsdene ML11 214 C2
Friarsfield Rd ML11 214 C2
Friarton Rd G43 136 C3
Friendship Gdns FK2 24 B2
Friendship Way PA4 94 B1
Frobisher Ave FK1 41 C2
Frobisher Pl G84 17 A1
Frood St ML1 142 B1
Fruin Ave G77 156 C3
Fruin Dr ML2 165 C2
Fruin Rd G15 74 C1
Fruin Rise ML3 161 C1
Fruin St G22 97 B2
Fudstone Dr KA25 170 A4
Fulbar Ave PA4 94 B2
Fulbar Cres PA2 112 C1
Fulbar Ct PA4 94 B2
Fulbar Gdns PA2 112 C1
Fulbar La PA4 94 B2
Fulbar Rd Glasgow G51 115 B4
Paisley PA2 112 C2
Fulbar St PA4 94 B2
Fullarton Ave
Dundonald KA2 225 C1
Glasgow G32 119 A1
Fullarton Cres KA10 229 D1
Fullarton Ct KA1 222 C1
Fullarton Dr
Glasgow G32 119 A1
Troon KA10 229 D1
Fullarton La G32 119 A1
Fullarton Pl
Coatbridge ML5 121 C2
Stevenston KA20 217 B4
Troon KA10 230 A2
Fullarton Rd
Cumbernauld G68 61 C3
Glasgow G32 119 A1
Prestwick KA9 236 B3
Fullarton Rdbt KA12 219 A1
Fullarton Sq KA12 219 A1
Fullarton St Ayr KA7 238 C4
Coatbridge ML5 121 C2
Irvine KA12 219 A1
Kilmarnock KA1 222 C1
Fullers Gate G81 74 B4
Fullerton Ctyd KA10 230 A1
Fullerton Dr KA23 190 A2
Fullerton La PA15 46 C2
Fullerton Sq KA22 205 B1
Fullerton St PA3 113 B4
Fullerton Terr PA3 113 C4
Fulmar Ct 4 G64 97 C4
Fulmar Pk G74 159 B2
Fulmar Pl PA5 131 B3
Fulshaw Cres KA8 236 C1
Fulshaw Ct KA9 236 B3
Fulshaw Pl KA8 236 C2
Fulton Cres PA10 111 A2
Fulton Dr PA6 111 C4
Fulton Gdns PA6 111 C4
Fulton Rd G62 55 A1
Fulton St G13 95 C4
Fulton's La KA3 222 C1
Fulwood Ave Glasgow G13 94 C4
Linwood PA3 112 A3
Fulwood Pk Ind Est ML3 162 A2
Fulwood Pl G13 94 C4
Furlongs The ML3 162 C3
Furnace Ct KA1 228 C3
Furnace Rd ML3 183 C2
Fyfe Park Terr PA14 47 C1
Fyfe Shore Rd PA14 47 C1
Fyffe Park Rd PA14 47 C1
Fyne Ave ML4 141 C3
Fyne Cres ML9 184 C3
Fyne Ct ML3 162 A1
Fyne La ML7 146 C3
Fyne Way ML1 143 A3
Fyneart St ML2 165 C2
Fynloch Pl G81 73 C4
Fyvie Ave G43 136 A3
Fyvie Cres ML6 123 C3

G

Gaberston Ave FK10 10 B4
Gabriel St PA15 46 A1
Gadburn Sch G21 98 B3
Gadie Ave PA4 94 C1
Gadie St G33 118 B4
Gadloch Ave G66 79 B1
Gadloch Gdns G66 79 B2
Gadloch St G22 97 B3
Gadloch View G66 79 B1
Gadsburn Ct G21 98 B3
Gadshill St G21 97 C1
Gael St PA16 45 B2
Gagarin Terr KA13 207 C1
Gailes Pk G72 140 C1
Gailes Pl KA1 227 C2
Gailes Rd
Cumbernauld G68 61 C3
Irvine KA11 224 C3
Troon KA10 229 C4
Gailes St G40 118 A2
Gain & Shankburn Rd G67 82 B1
Gain Rd G67, ML5 82 A1
Gainburn Cres G67 81 C3
Gainburn Ct G67 81 C3
Gainburn Gdns G67 81 C3
Gainburn Pl G67 81 C3
Gainburn View G67 82 A3
Gainford Pl KA3 222 C2
Gainside Rd ML5 101 B3
Gair Cres Carluke ML8 188 A2
Wishaw ML2 165 A1
Gair Rd ML8 188 A3
Gair Wynd ML7 147 A2
Gairbraid Ave G20 96 B3
Gairbraid Ct G20 96 B3
Gairbraid Pl G20 96 B3
Gairbraid Terr G69 121 A3
Gairdoch Dr FK2 24 B2
Gairdoch St FK2 42 A4
Gairloch Gdns G66 59 A1
Gaitskell Ave G83 27 B4
Gala Ave PA4 94 C1
Gala Cres ML2 165 A3
Gala St G33 98 C1
Galbraith Cres ML8 187 A3
Galbraith Dr
Glasgow G51 115 C4

Galbraith Dr *continued*
Milngavie G62 .75 C4
Galdenoch St G33 .99 A1
Gallacher Ave PA2 .113 A1
Gallacher Cres G83 .19 C1
Gallacher Ct
Motherwell ML1 .164 A2
Paisley PA1 .113 B3
Gallacher Way G82 .27 B1
Gallahill Ave PA14 .69 A4
Gallamuir Dr FK7 .12 B2
Gallamuir Rd FK7 .12 B3
Gallan Ave 3 G23 .76 C1
Gallion Wlk 13 KA1 .227 C4
Galloway Ave Ayr KA8 .236 B1
Hamilton ML3 .183 B4
Galloway Ct
Falkirk FK1,FK2 .42 A3
Irvine KA11 .220 A3
Galloway Dr G73 .138 A2
Galloway Pl KA21 .216 C4
Galloway Rd Airdrie ML6 122 C2
East Kilbride G74 .160 B2
Galloway St Falkirk FK1 .42 A3
Glasgow G21 .97 C3
Gallowflat St 6 G73 .138 A4
Gallowgate G1,G4,G40 .117 C3
Gallowhill ML9 .185 A1
Gallowhill Ave G66 .79 B3
Gallowhill Gr G66 .79 B4
Gallowhill Prim Sch
PA3 .114 A4
Gallowhill Rd
Carmunnock G76 .158 C4
Kirkintilloch G66 .79 B3
Lanark ML11 .215 A2
Paisley PA3 .114 A3
Galrigside Rd KA1 .227 B4
Galston Ave G77 .157 A3
Galston Ct ML3 .183 C4
Galston Pl KA3 .223 A3
Galston Rd KA1 .228 C3
Galston St G53 .134 C3
Galt Ave KA12 .219 B2
Galt Pl G75 .180 B4
Galt St PA15 .46 B2
Gambeson Cres FK7 .7 B2
Gameshill View KA3 .211 C4
Gamrie Dr G53 .135 A4
Gamrie Gdns G53 .135 A4
Gamrie Rd G53 .135 A4
Gannochy Dr G64 .78 B1
Gantock Cres G33 .119 A4
Ganton Ct KA13 .207 A2
Garden Ct 5 KA8 .235 C1
Garden Pl KA10 .229 B2
Garden Square La KA13 207 C2
Garden Square Wlk
ML6 .122 B4
Garden St Ayr KA8 .235 C1
Falkirk FK1 .42 B3
Kilmarnock KA3 .222 C1
Garden Terr FK1 .42 B3
Garden Veteran's Cotts
PA8 .72 C3
Gardenhall G75 .179 C4
Gardenhall Ct G75 .179 C4
Gardens The KA11 .220 B3
Gardenside ML4 .142 A2
Gardenside Ave
Glasgow G32 .139 A4
Uddingston G71 .140 C3
Gardenside Cres G32 .139 A4
Gardenside Pl G32 .139 A4
Gardenside Rd ML3 .162 B1
Gardenside St G71 .140 C3
Gardiner St KA9 .236 B4
Gardner Gr G71 .141 A4
Gardner St G11 .96 A1
Gardrum Gdns FK1 .66 B4
Gardrum Pl KA3 .222 C2
Gardyne St G34 .100 A1
Gare Rd G84 .15 A2
Garelet Pl KA11 .220 A1
Gareloch Ave PA2 .113 A1
Gareloch Cl PA15 .46 A1
Gareloch Cres ML6 .102 C1
Gareloch La PA14 .68 B4
Gareloch Rd
Greenock PA15 .46 A2
Port Glasgow PA14 .68 C4
Rhu G84 .15 C2
Garfield Ave ML4 .142 B3
Garfield Dr ML4 .142 B2
Garfield Pl G33 .99 C3
Garfield St G31 .118 A3
Garforth Rd G69 .119 C2
Gargieston Prim Sch
KA2 .227 B3
Gargrave Ave G69 .119 C2
Garion Dr G13 .95 A3
Garlieston Rd G33 .119 C3
Garmouth Ct 3 G51 .116 A4
Garmouth Gdns 4 G51 .116 A4
Garmouth St G51 .115 C4
Garnet St G3 .240 B4
Garnetbank Prim Sch
G3 .240 B4
Garnethill Convent Sec RC
Sch G3 .240 B4
Garnethill St G3 .240 B4
Garngaber Ave G66 .79 B3
Garngaber Ct G66 .79 C3
Garngrew Rd FK4 .38 C2
Garnhall Ditch★ G68 .38 C1
Garnhall Farm Rd G68 .62 C4
Garnie Ave PA8 .93 B4
Garnie La PA8 .93 B4
Garnie Oval PA8 .73 B1
Garnie Pl PA8 .73 B1
Garnieland Rd PA8 .73 B1
Garnkirk La G33 .99 C3
Garnock Acad KA25 .149 A1
Garnock Ct Irvine KA12 .219 B1
1 Kilbirnie KA25 .149 A1
Garnock Pk G74 .160 A1
Garnock Rd
Kilmarnock KA1 .228 A3
Stevenston KA20 .217 B4
Stevenston, Stevenston Site
KA20 .218 B3
Garnock St Dalry KA24 .191 B4
Glasgow G21 .97 C1
Kilbirnie KA25 .149 A1
Garnock View KA13 .207 C2
Garnockside KA14 .170 A3
Garpel Way PA12 .129 A1
Garrallan KA13 .207 B1
Garraway Pl G84 .16 C1
Garraway Rd G84 .16 C1
Garrel Gr G65 .36 B1
Garrell Ave G65 .36 B1
Garrell Pl G65 .60 B4
Garrell Rd G65 .60 B4
Garrell Way
Cumbernauld G67 .61 C1
Kilsyth G65 .60 B4
Garrick Ave G77 .156 B1
Garrick Ct G77 .156 B1
Garrier Ct KA11 .220 C1
Garrier Pl KA1 .222 B1
Garrier Rd KA11 .220 C1
Garrioch Cres 3 G20 .96 B3
Garrioch Dr G20 .96 B3
Garrioch Gate 17 G20 .96 B3
Garrioch Quadrant 4
G20 .96 B3
Garrioch Rd G20 .96 B3
Garriochmill Rd G20 .96 C2
Garrion Bsns Pk ML2 .186 A4
Garrion Pl ML9 .185 C1
Garrion St ML2 .186 B3
Garrison Pl FK1 .42 A3
Garrowhill Dr G69 .119 C3
Garrowhill Halt G33 .119 C3
Garrowhill Prim Sch
G69 .120 A3
Garry Ave G61 .76 A1
Garry Dr PA2 .113 A1
Garry Pl Falkirk FK1 .42 A2
Kilmarnock KA1 .228 A3
Troon KA10 .229 D3
Garry St G44 .137 A4
Garry Way ML7 .146 C3
Garryhorn KA9 .236 B3
Garscadden Prim Sch
G13 .94 C4
Garscadden Rd G15 .75 A1
Garscadden Rd S
Glasgow G13 .95 A4
Glasgow G15 .94 C4
Garscadden Sta G14 .95 A3
Garscadden View G81 .74 B2
Garscube Cross G4 .97 A1
Garscube Mill G61 .76 A1
Garscube Rd G4, G20 .97 A1
Garshake Ave G82 .50 B3
Garshake Rd G82 .50 B3
Garshake Terr G82 .50 B3
Gartartan Rd PA1 .114 C3
Gartcarron Hill G68 .61 B2
Gartchaig Pl G33 .98 C1
Gartcloss Rd ML5 .101 B1
Gartclush Gdns FK7 .11 C4
Gartconnell Dr G61 .75 C3
Gartconnell Gdns G61 .75 C3
Gartconnell Rd G61 .75 C3
Gartconner Ave G66 .80 A4
Gartconner Prim Sch
G66 .80 A4
Gartcosh Prim Sch G69 100 C2
Gartcosh Rd ML5 .101 A1
Gartcosh Wlk ML4 .141 C3
Gartcows Ave FK1 .42 A2
Gartcows Cres FK1 .42 A2
Gartcows Dr FK1 .42 A2
Gartcows Gdns FK1 .41 C2
Gartcows Pl FK1 .42 A2
Gartcows Rd FK1 .42 A2
Gartcraig Rd G33 .118 C4
Garten Dr ML7 .147 A2
Gartferry Ave G69 .80 C1
Gartferry Rd G69 .80 C1
Gartferry St G21 .98 A2
Gartfield St ML6 .123 A3
Gartgill Rd ML5 .101 C1
Garth St G1 .241 A2
Garthamlock Prim Sch
G33 .99 B1
Garthamlock Rd G33 .99 C1
Garthill Gdns FK1 .42 A2
Garthill La FK1 .42 A2
Garthland Dr
Ardrossan KA22 .205 B2
Glasgow G31 .118 A4
Garthland La PA1 .113 C3
Gartlea Ave ML6 .123 A4
Gartlea Rd ML6 .123 A4
Gartleahill ML6 .123 A3
Gartliston Rd ML5 .101 C2
Gartliston Terr G69 .121 A3
Gartloch Rd G69 .100 B2
Gartly St G44 .136 C2
Gartmore Gdns G71 .140 C4
Gartmore La G69 .81 A1
Gartmore Rd PA1 .114 B2
Gartmore Terr G72 .138 C2
Gartmorn Rd FK10 .5 B1
Gartnavel General Hospl
G12 .96 A2
Gartnavel Royal Hospl
G12 .96 A2
Gartness Dr ML6 .123 C3
Gartness Rd ML6 .124 A2
Gartocher Dr G32 .119 B3
Gartocher Rd G32 .119 B3
Gartocher Terr G32 .119 B3
Gartons Rd G21 .98 B2
Gartsherrie Ave ML5 .101 C3
Gartsherrie Ind Est ML5 101 C1
Gartsherrie Prim Sch
ML5 .121 C4
Gartsherrie Rd ML5 .121 C4
Gartshore Cres G65 .59 C1
Gartshore Gdns G68 .60 C1
Garturk St
Coatbridge ML5 .122 A2
Glasgow G42 .117 A1
Garvald Ct G40 .118 A2
Garvald La FK6 .21 B1
Garvald Rd FK6 .39 B4
Garvald St Glasgow G40 .118 A2
Greenock PA15 .46 B2
Garvally Cres FK10 .10 A4
Garve Ave G44 .137 A3
Garvel Cres G33 .119 C3
Garvel Deaf Ctr PA16 .44 C3
Garvel Dr PA15 .45 B2
Garvel Pl G62 .54 B1
Garvel Rd Glasgow G33 .119 C3
Milngavie G62 .54 C1
Garven Ct KA1 .228 A4
Garven Rd KA20 .217 C3
Garvie Ave PA19 .44 C3
Garvin Lea ML4 .142 A4
Garvock Dr Glasgow G43 136 A3
Greenock PA15 .45 C2
Garwhitter Dr G62 .55 A1
Gas St PA5 .112 A2
Gascoyne G75 .180 B4
Gask Pl G13 .94 C4
Gaskin Path G33 .99 C3
Gasworks Rd ML8 .187 B2
Gatehead Rd KA2 .221 C1
Gatehouse St G32 .119 B2
Gates Rd PA12 .129 B2
Gateshead Pl PA10 .111 A2
Gateside KA11 .219 C3
Gateside Ave
Bonnybridge FK4 .40 B3
Cambuslang G72 .139 B3
Greenock PA16 .45 A2
Kilsyth G65 .60 A4
Gateside Cres
Airdrie ML6 .123 A4
Barrhead G78 .134 A1
Gateside Gdns PA16 .45 A2
Gateside Gr PA16 .45 A2
Gateside Pk G65 .60 A4
Gateside Pl KA1 .227 C2
Gateside Prim Sch
KA15 .171 C4
Gateside Rd
Barrhead G78 .134 A1
Stirling FK7 .7 A2
Wishaw ML2 .164 C2
Gateside Sch for the Deaf
PA2 .133 B4
Gateside St Glasgow G31 118 A3
Hamilton ML3 .162 C2
West Kilbride KA23 .190 B3
Gateway Ctr (Nat Pk Visitor
Ctr)★ G83 .19 B1
Gateway The G74 .160 A2
Gaughan Quadrant ML1 163 B3
Gauldry Ave G52 .115 B2
Gauze St PA1 .113 C3
Gavell Rd G65 .59 B3
Gavin Hamilton Ct KA7 .239 B3
Gavin St ML1 .163 C3
Gavin's Mill Rd G62 .55 A1
Gavinburn Gdns G60 .73 A4
Gavinburn Pl G60 .73 A4
Gavinburn Prim Sch G60 72 C4
Gavinburn St G60 .73 A4
Gavins Rd Alloa FK10 .4 C1
Clydebank G81 .74 A3
Gavinton St G44 .136 C3
Gayne Dr ML5 .101 B3
Gean Ct G67 .62 C2
Gean Rd FK10 .9 C4
Gearholm Rd KA7 .238 B2
Geary St 13 G23 .76 B1
Geddes Hill G74 .160 A2
Geddes Rd G21 .98 B4
Geelong Gdns G66 .33 B1
Geils Ave G82 .50 B1
Geils Quadrant G82 .50 B2
Geilsland Rd KA15 .171 B4
Geilsland Sch KA15 .171 B4
Geilston House & Gdns★
G82 .25 D1
Geilston Pk G82 .48 A4
Geirston Rd KA25 .148 C1
Gelston St G32 .119 A2
Gemini Gr ML1 .143 A3
Gemmel Pl G77 .156 B2
Gemmell Cres KA8 .236 B1
Gemmell Way ML9 .198 C1
General Roy Way ML8 .202 B4
Generals Gate G71 .140 C3
Gentle Row G81 .73 C3
George Aitken Ct KA22 .205 B2
George Ave G81 .74 B2
George Cres G81 .74 B2
George Ct Hamilton ML3 .162 A3
Paisley PA1 .113 B2
George Gray St G73 .138 B4
George La PA1 .113 C2
George Laing Ct FK5 .23 C1
George Mann Terr G73 .138 A2
George Pl PA1 .113 C2
George Rd PA19 .44 C3
George Reith Ave G12 .95 C3
George Sq Ayr KA8 .236 A1
Glasgow G2 .241 A2
Greenock PA15 .45 C3
George St Airdrie ML6 .122 C4
Alexandria G83 .27 C2
Alva FK12 .5 A3
6 Ayr KA8 .235 C1
Ayr KA8 .236 A1
Barrhead G78 .134 A2
Chapelhall ML6 .123 B2
Falkirk FK2 .42 A3
Glasgow G1 .241 B2
Glasgow, Bialliesston G69 .120 A2
Hamilton ML3 .162 A3
Helensburgh G84 .16 C1
Howwood PA9 .130 C3
Johnstone PA5 .111 C2
Laurieston FK2 .42 C2
Motherwell ML1 .163 C2
Motherwell, New Stevenston
ML1 .143 A2
Paisley PA1 .113 B2
Stenhousemuir FK5 .23 B2
Stevenston KA20 .217 B4
George Street La G83 .27 C2
George Terr KA12 .219 B2
George Way 10 ML9 .185 A2
George's Ave KA8 .236 A2
Georgian Ct PA16 .45 C3
Gerald Terr FK5 .23 C2
Gerard Pl ML4 .142 A4
Germiston Cres G75 .180 A2
Germiston Ct G75 .180 A2
Gertrude Pl G78 .134 A1
Ghillies La ML1 .142 B1
Gibb Ct ML9 .198 C1
Gibb St Chapelhall ML6 .123 B1
Cleland ML1 .144 A1
Gibbdun Pl FK6 .39 C4
Gibbon Cres G74 .160 B2
Gibbshill Pl ML7 .127 B3
Gibshill Rd PA15 .46 C1
Gibson Ave G82 .50 A2
Gibson Cres PA5 .111 C1
Gibson La PA13 .69 B1
Gibson Quadrant ML1 .142 B1
Gibson Rd PA4 .94 A1
Gibson St Dumbarton G82 .50 A2
Glasgow G4 .241 C1
Glasgow, Kelvingrove G12 .96 C1
Greenock PA15 .46 C1
Kilmarnock KA1 .222 B1
Salsburgh ML7 .125 A1
Gibsongray St FK2 .42 A4
Giffen Rd KA21 .217 A4
Giffnock Park Ave G46 .136 B2
Giffnock Prim Sch G46 .136 B1
Giffnock Sta G46 .136 B2
Gifford Dr G52 .115 A3
Gifford Wynd PA2 .112 C1
Gigha Cres KA11 .220 A1
Gigha Gdns ML8 .202 A4
Gigha La KA11 .220 A1
Gigha Pl KA11 .220 A1
Gigha Quadrant ML2 .164 C1
Gigha Terr KA11 .220 A1
Gigha Wynd KA11 .220 A1
Gilbert St G3 .116 B4
Gilbertfield Path G33 .99 A1
Gilbertfield Pl
Glasgow G33 .99 A1
Irvine KA12 .219 B1
Gilbertfield Rd G72 .139 C2
Gilbertfield St G33 .99 A1
Gilburn Pl ML7 .146 C2
Gilchrist Dr FK1 .41 C2
Gilchrist St ML5 .122 A4
Gilchrist Way ML2 .165 B1
Gilderdale G74 .159 B1
Gilfillan Ave KA21 .206 A1
Gilfillan Pl Falkirk FK2 .24 B1
Overtown ML2 .186 B4
Gilfillan Way PA2 .132 C4
Gilhill St G20 .96 B4
Gill Pk FK6 .21 C1
Gill Rd ML2 .186 B3
Gillbank Ave ML8 .187 B1
Gillbank La 6 ML9 .185 B1
Gillburn Rd PA13 .89 B4
Gillburn St ML2 .186 B3
Gillespie Dr G84 .16 B2
Gillespie Pl FK7 .7 A1
Gillespie Terr FK7 .12 B1
Gillies Cres G74 .160 B3
Gillies Dr FK7 .7 B2
Gillies Hill FK7 .6 B3
Gillies La G69 .120 B2
Gillies St KA10 .229 C2
Gillsburn Gdns KA3 .223 A1
Gilmartin Rd PA3 .111 C3
Gilmerton St G32 .119 A2
Gilmour Ave
Clydebank G81 .74 A3
Thorntonhall G74 .158 A1
Gilmour Cres
Eaglesham G76 .178 C3
Rutherglen G73 .137 C4
Gilmour Dr ML3 .161 C1
Gilmour Pl Bellshill ML4 .141 C3
Coatbridge ML5 .121 C4
7 Glasgow G5 .117 B2
Gilmour St Alexandria G83 27 B3
Clydebank G81 .74 B2
Eaglesham G76 .178 C3
Greenock PA15 .46 B1
Kilmarnock KA1 .228 A4
Paisley PA1 .113 C3
Stewarton KA3 .195 C1
Gilmourton Cres G77 .156 B2
Gilroy Cl ML11 .215 B3
Gilsay Ct FK1 .42 B1
Gilshochill Sta G23 .96 C4
Gimmerscroft Cres ML6 123 C3
Girdle Gate KA11 .219 C3
Girdle Toll KA11 .220 A3
Girdons Way G71 .140 C3
Girthon St G32 .119 B2
Girvan Cres ML6 .123 B1
Girvan St G33 .118 B4
Glade The ML9 .185 A1
Gladney Ave G13 .94 C4
Gladsmuir Rd G52 .115 A3
Gladstone Ave
Barrhead G78 .134 A1
Johnstone PA5 .131 B4
Gladstone Ct ML3 .162 A3
Gladstone Pl FK8 .7 A3
Gladstone Rd
Saltcoats KA21 .217 A4
Stenhousemuir FK5 .23 B2
Gladstone St
Bellshill ML4 .142 A3
Clydebank G81 .73 C1
11 Glasgow G4 .97 A1
Glaive Ave FK7 .7 B2
Glaive Rd G13 .75 B1
Glamis Ave Carluke ML8 .187 C1
East Kilbride G74 .159 C2
Elderslie PA5 .112 A1
Newton Mearns G77 .156 C3
Glamis Ct ML1 .143 B1
Glamis Dr PA16 .45 A3
Glamis Gdns G64 .78 A2
Glamis Pl PA16 .45 A3
Glamis Rd G31 .118 B2
Glanderston Ave
Barrhead G78 .134 C1
Newton Mearns G77 .156 A3
Glanderston Ct G13 .95 A4
Glanderston Dr G13 .95 A4
Glanderston Gate G77 .156 A3
Glanderston Rd G77 .155 B3
Glasgow & Edinburgh Rd
Calderbank ML1,ML6 .123 A1
Coatbridge G69,ML5 .121 B2
Glasgow G69 .120 B3
Motherwell ML1 .144 A4
Glasgow Acad G12 .96 C2
Glasgow Bot Gdns★ G12 96 B2
Glasgow Caledonian Univ
G4 .241 A4
Glasgow Caledonian Univ
Park Campus G3 .96 C1
Glasgow Coll of Building &
Printing G5 .117 B3
Glasgow Coll of Building &
Printing (Annexe) G31 118 C3
Glasgow Coll of Building &
Printing (David Dale Bldg)
G40 .117 C3
Glasgow Coll of Printing
(Bridgeton Annexe)
G40 .117 C3
Glasgow Dental Hospl
G2 .240 B3
Glasgow Gaelic Sch G3 240 A4
Glasgow Homeopathic Hospl
G12 .96 A2
Glasgow La KA22 .205 B1
Glasgow Prestwick Int
Airport KA9 .233 C1
Glasgow Rd
Bannockburn FK7 .11 B4
Barrhead G53 .134 B2
Blantyre G72 .161 C4
Bonnybridge FK4 .39 B2
Cambuslang G72,G73 .138 C1
Cambuslang, Silverbank
G72 .138 C3
Clarkston G76 .157 B1
Clydebank G81 .94 B4
Clydebank, Hardgate G81 .74 B3
Coatbridge ML5 .121 B3
Cumbernauld G67 .82 B4
Cumbernauld, Kildrum G67 .62 A2
Denny FK6 .21 C1
Dumbarton G82 .50 B1
Eaglesham G76 .178 C4
East Kilbride G72,G74 .160 A4
Falkirk FK1 .41 B3
Glasgow G69 .120 A2
Kilmarnock KA3 .223 B3
Kilsyth G65 .60 A4
Kirkintilloch G66 .79 A4
Lanark ML11 .214 C2
Milngavie G62 .55 A1
Paisley PA1 .114 B2
Port Glasgow PA14 .47 C1
Renfrew PA4 .94 C1
Rutherglen G73 .117 C1
Stirling FK7 .7 A1
Strathblane G63 .31 A2

Glenmore Ave *continued*
Bellshill ML4 .... 142 A2
Glasgow G42 .... 137 C4
Glenmore Dr FK4 ...... 39 C3
Glenmore Rd ML1 ...... 143 B2
Glenmoss Ave PA8 ...... 72 C1
Glenmosston Rd PA13 ... 89 C4
Glenmount Pl KA7 ...... 238 A1
Glenmuir Ct KA8 ...... 236 B1
Glenmuir Dr G53 ...... 135 A3
Glenmuir Pl KA8 ...... 236 B1
Glenmuir Rd KA8 ...... 236 B1
Glenmuir Sq KA8 ...... 236 B1
Glenochil Pk FK10 ...... 4 C2
Glenochil Rd FK1 ...... 42 A2
Glenochil Terr FK10 ...... 4 C2
Glenoran La 1 ML9 ... 185 A2
Glenoran Rd G84 ...... 16 A2
Glenorchard Rd G64 ... 56 B1
Glenorrin Way G78 ... 154 B3
Glenpark ML6 .... 123 C3
Glenpark Ave
Glasgow G46 .... 136 A1
Prestwick KA9 .... 236 B3
Glenpark Dr PA14 ...... 47 A1
Glenpark Gdns G72 .... 138 C4
Glenpark Pl KA7 ...... 239 A2
Glenpark Rd PA12 ...... 129 B2
Glenpark St
Glasgow G31 .... 118 A3
Wishaw ML2 .... 165 A2
Glenpark Terr G72 .... 138 C4
Glenpath G82 .... 50 B2
Glenpatrick Bldgs PA5 .112 B1
Glenpatrick Rd PA5 ... 112 B1
Glenraith Path G33 .... 99 A2
Glenraith Rd G33 ...... 99 A1
Glenraith Sq G33 ...... 99 A2
Glenraith Wlk G33 ...... 99 B2
Glenriddel Rd KA7 .... 239 A3
Glenriddet Ave KA25 ... 170 A4
Glenshee Ct G31 ...... 118 B2
Glenshee Gdns G31 .... 118 C2
Glenshee St G31 ...... 118 B2
Glenshee Terr ML3 .... 183 A4
Glenshiel Ave PA2 .... 114 A1
Glenshira Ave PA2 .... 114 A1
Glenside Ave G53 ...... 115 A1
Glenside Cres KA23 .... 190 B3
Glenside Dr G73 ...... 138 C3
Glenside Gr KA23 ...... 190 B3
Glenside Rd
Dumbarton G82 .... 50 B3
Port Glasgow PA14 ...... 68 B4
Glenspean Pl ML5 ...... 122 B3
Glenspean St G43 ...... 136 B3
Glentanar Dr G69 ...... 81 A1
Glentanar Pl G22 ...... 97 A4
Glentanar Rd G22 ...... 97 A4
Glentarbert Rd G73 .... 138 B2
Glentore Quadrant ML6 103 A1
Glentrool Gdns
Glasgow G22 .... 97 B2
Moodiesburn G69 .... 81 A2
Glenturret St G32 ...... 119 A2
Glentyan Ave PA10 .... 111 A2
Glentyan Dr G53 ...... 135 A3
Glentye Gdns FK1 ...... 41 C1
Glentyan Pl G53 ...... 135 A4
Glenview Airdrie ML6 ... 123 B3
Denny FK6 .... 21 A2
2 Kirkintilloch G66 ...... 79 B4
Larkhall ML9 .... 184 C2
Menstrie FK11 .... 4 A3
West Kilbride KA23 ...... 190 B2
Glenview Ave
Banknock FK4 .... 38 C2
Caldercruix ML6 .... 105 A2
Glenview Cres G69 ...... 81 A2
Glenview Dr FK1 ...... 41 C1
Glenview Pl G72 ...... 140 B1
Glenview St ML6 ...... 102 C2
Glenview Terr PA15 .... 45 B2
Glenville Ave G46 ...... 136 A2
Glenville Gate G76 .... 158 A3
Glenville Terr G76 .... 158 A3
Glenward Ave G66 ...... 57 C4
Glenwell St ML6 ...... 102 C2
Glenwinnel Rd FK12 ...... 4 C4
Glenwood Ave ML6 .... 123 B2
Glenwood Bsns Ctr G45 137 C2
Glenwood Ct G66 ...... 79 A3
Glenwood Dr G46 ...... 135 C1
Glenwood Gdns G66 .... 79 A3
Glenwood Path G45 .... 137 C2
Glenwood Pl
Glasgow G45 .... 137 C2
Kirkintilloch G66 .... 79 A3
Glenwood Rd G66 ...... 79 A3
Glenyards Rd FK4 ...... 40 A1
Glidden Ct ML2 ...... 186 B4
Glorat Ave G66 ...... 57 C4
Gloucester Ave
Clarkston G76 .... 157 B4
Rutherglen G73 .... 138 B3
Gloucester St G5 ...... 117 A3
Glowrorum Dr FK6 ...... 39 C4
Glynwed Ct FK2 ...... 42 B4
Goatfell View KA10 ... 229 D4
Gockston Rd PA3 ...... 113 B4
Goddard Pl ML2 ...... 166 A3
Godfrey Ave FK6 ...... 21 B1
Godfrey Cres FK5 ...... 23 B1
Gogar Loan FK9 .... 3 B3
Gogar Pl Glasgow G33 ... 118 C4
Gogar Pl *continued*
Stirling FK7 .... 7 B1
Gogar St G33 .... 118 C4
Goil Ave ML4 .... 141 B3
Goil Way ML1 .... 143 A3
Goldberry Ave G14 ...... 95 A3
Goldcraig Ct KA11 .... 220 A3
Goldenacre Pl ML6 .... 103 C2
Goldenberry Ave KA23 .190 B2
Goldenhill Ct G81 ...... 74 A3
Goldenhill Prim Sch G81 74 A3
Goldenlee View PA6 ... 111 A4
Goldie Pl KA20 .... 206 B1
Goldie Rd G71 .... 141 A2
Golf Ave Bellshill ML4 ... 142 A2
Stevenston KA20 .... 217 C3
Golf Course Rd
Balmore G64 .... 77 C4
Bridge of W PA11 .... 110 B4
Golf Cres KA10 .... 229 C1
Golf Ct G44 .... 136 C1
Golf Dr Clydebank G15 ... 74 C1
Paisley PA1 .... 114 B2
Port Glasgow PA14 ...... 68 B4
Golf Gdns ML9 .... 185 B1
Golf Pl Bellshill ML4 ... 142 A2
Greenock PA16 .... 45 B4
Helensburgh G84 .... 17 A1
Irvine KA12 .... 219 A3
Troon KA10 .... 229 C1
Golf Rd Bishopton PA7 ... 72 A2
Clarkston G76 .... 157 B4
Gourock PA19 .... 44 B3
Rutherglen G73 .... 138 A2
Golf View G81 .... 73 C2
Golffields Rd KA12 .... 219 B1
Golfhill Dr Alexandria G83 .27 C3
Glasgow G31 .... 118 A4
Helensburgh G84 .... 16 C1
Golfhill Prim Sch
Airdrie ML6 .... 102 C1
Glasgow G31 .... 117 C4
Golfhill Quadrant ML6 .103 A1
Golfhill Rd ML2 ...... 164 C2
Golfloan KA3 .... 211 C4
Golfview G61 .... 75 B3
Golfview Dr ML5 ...... 121 B4
Golfview Pl ML5 ...... 121 B3
Golspie Ave ML6 ...... 122 C2
Golspie St G51 .... 116 A4
Good Shepherd Prim Sch
KA8 .... 236 B1
Goodview Gdns ML9 ... 185 B1
Goosecroft Rd FK8 ...... 7 A4
Goosedubbs G1 .... 241 A1
Gooseholm Cres G82 .... 50 A3
Gooseholm Rd G82 .... 50 A3
Gopher Ave G71 ...... 141 A4
Gorbals Cross
Glasgow G5 .... 117 B3
Larkhall ML9 .... 185 A2
Gorbals St G1,G5 ...... 117 B3
Gordon Ave Bishopton PA7 72 A2
Glasgow G69 .... 119 C3
Glasgow, Netherlee G44 .136 C1
Paisley G52 .... 114 C4
Gordon Cres
Bridge of A FK9 .... 2 A4
Newton Mearns G77 .... 156 C3
Stirling FK8 .... 1 C1
Gordon Ct ML6 .... 123 C4
Gordon Dr Alloa FK10 ... 10 B4
East Kilbride G74 ...... 160 A2
Glasgow G44 .... 136 C2
Gordon La G1 .... 240 C2
Gordon Pl Bellshill ML4 .141 C1
Falkirk FK1 .... 41 C3
Gordon Rd Glasgow G44 .136 C1
Hamilton ML3 .... 161 C2
Gordon Sq PA5 .... 111 C1
Gordon St Ayr KA8 .... 236 A2
Glasgow G1 .... 240 C2
Greenock PA15 .... 45 C2
Paisley PA1 .... 113 C2
Gordon Terr Ayr KA8 ... 239 A4
Blantyre G72 .... 140 B1
Hamilton ML3 .... 161 C2
Gorebridge St G32 .... 118 C4
Goremire Rd ML8 ...... 202 A4
Gorget Ave G13 .... 75 B1
Gorget Pl G13 .... 75 B1
Gorget Quadrant G13 ... 75 A1
Gorrie St FK6 .... 21 B1
Gorse Cres PA11 ...... 110 C4
Gorse Pk KA7 .... 239 B2
Gorse Pl G71 .... 141 A4
Gorsehall St ML1 ...... 144 A1
Gorsewood G64 .... 77 C1
Gorstan Pl G20 .... 96 B3
Gorstan St G23 .... 96 B4
Goschen Terr KA8 ...... 236 A1
Gosford La G14 .... 95 A2
Gotterbank PA11 ...... 89 C1
Gottries Pl KA12 ...... 219 A1
Gottries Rd KA12 ...... 219 A1
Goudie St PA3 .... 113 B4
Gough St G33 .... 118 B4
Goukscroft Pk KA7 .... 238 B2
Gould St KA8 .... 236 B1
Gourlay G74 .... 160 B3
Gourlay Dr G73 .... 186 B3
Gourlay St Glasgow G21 .97 B2
1 Glasgow, Springburn
G21 .... 97 C2
Gourock High Sch PA19 .44 B4
Gourock Prim Sch PA19 .44 C4
Gourock St G5 .... 117 A2
Gourock Sta PA19 .... 44 C4
Govan Dr G83 .... 27 B3
Govan High Sch G51 ... 115 C4
Govan Rd Glasgow G51 .115 C4
Glasgow, Plantation G51 .116 B3
Govan Underground Sta
G51 .... 116 A4
Govanhill St G42 ...... 117 A1
Gowan Ave FK2 .... 42 A3
Gowan Brae ML6 ...... 105 A3
Gowan La FK2 .... 42 A3
Gowanbank Gdns PA5 .111 C1
Gowanbank Prim Sch
G53 .... 135 A3
Gowanbank Rd KA7 .... 239 A1
Gowanbrae G66 .... 79 B3
Gowanhill Gdns FK8 ...... 1 C1
Gowanlea Ave G15 ...... 75 A1
Gowanlea Dr
Glasgow G46 .... 136 B2
Slamannan FK1 .... 86 A3
Gowanlea Terr G71 .... 141 A4
Gowanside Pl ML8 .... 187 B1
Gower Pl KA7 .... 239 A2
Gower St G41 .... 116 B2
Gower Terr G41 .... 116 B3
Gowkhall Ave ML1 .... 143 C2
Gowkhouse Rd PA13 .... 89 C4
Goyle Ave G15 .... 75 B2
Grace Ave G69 .... 120 C3
Grace St G3 .... 240 A2
Gracie Cres FK7 .... 8 B2
Gradlon Pl FK1 .... 42 A2
Graeme Ct ML1 .... 142 B1
Graeme High Sch FK1 ... 42 C2
Graeme Pl FK1 .... 41 C1
Graffham Ave G46 .... 136 C2
Grafton Pl G1 .... 241 A3
Graham Ave
Cambuslang G72 .... 139 B3
Clydebank G81 .... 74 A2
East Kilbride G74 ...... 159 C1
Hamilton ML3 .... 183 B4
Larbert FK5 .... 23 A2
Stirling FK9 .... 2 B2
Graham Cres G82 ...... 48 A4
Graham Ct KA1 .... 228 C3
Graham Dr G62 .... 54 C1
Graham Ho G67 .... 61 C1
Graham Pl Ashgill ML9 .. 185 C1
Helensburgh G84 .... 17 A1
Kilmarnock KA3 .... 223 B1
Kilsyth G65 .... 36 B1
Graham Rd
Crossford ML8 .... 201 A1
Dumbarton G82 .... 49 B2
Graham Sq G31 .... 117 C3
Graham St Airdrie ML6 .. 123 A4
Barrhead G78 .... 134 A2
Bridge of A FK9 .... 2 A4
Greenock PA16 .... 45 B3
Hamilton ML3 .... 162 C2
Johnstone PA5 .... 111 C1
Motherwell ML1 .... 143 A3
Wishaw ML2 .... 165 A1
Graham Terr Airth FK2 ... 14 B2
Bishopbriggs G64 .... 98 A4
Stewarton KA3 .... 195 B1
Graham Wlk KA3 ...... 223 B1
Grahamfield Pl KA15 ... 171 A4
Grahams Ave PA12 .... 129 B2
Grahams Rd FK1,FK2 .... 42 A3
Grahamsdyke Cres FK4 .40 A2
Grahamsdyke Rd
Bonnybridge FK4 .... 40 A2
Kirkintilloch G66 .... 58 C1
Grahamsdyke St FK2 ... 42 C2
Grahamshill Ave ML6 .. 123 B4
Grahamshill St ML6 .... 123 B4
Grahamston Ave KA14 .170 A4
Grahamston Cres PA2 .. 134 B4
Grahamston Ct PA2 .... 134 B4
Grahamston Pk G78 ... 134 A3
Grahamston Pl PA2 .... 134 B4
Grahamston Rd G78,
PA2 .... 134 B3
Grahamston Sta FK1 .... 42 A3
Graigleith View FK10 .... 4 B2
Graignestock Pl 8 G40 117 C3
Graignestock St G40 ... 117 C3
Graigside Pl G68 .... 81 C4
Grainger Rd G64 .... 78 B1
Grammar School Sq
ML3 .... 162 C2
Grampian Ave PA2 .... 133 B4
Grampian Cres
Chapelhall ML6 .... 123 C1
Glasgow G32 .... 119 A2
Grampian Ct KA11 .... 220 A2
Grampian Dr G75 ...... 180 A2
Grampian Pl G32 ...... 119 A2
Grampian Rd
Kilmarnock KA1 .... 228 A2
Port Glasgow PA14 ...... 69 A3
Stirling FK7 .... 6 C3
Wishaw ML2 .... 164 C2
Grampian St G32 ...... 119 A2
Grampian Way
Barrhead G78 .... 134 B1
Bearsden G61 .... 75 A4
Cumbernauld G68 .... 61 A1
Gran St G81 .... 94 C4
Granary Rd FK2 .... 42 A4
Granary Sq FK2 .... 42 A4
Granby La G12 .... 96 B2
Grandtuly Dr G12 ...... 96 B3
Grange Acad KA1 ...... 227 B4
Grange Ave Ayr KA7 .... 239 A1
Falkirk FK2 .... 42 B3
Grange Ave *continued*
Milngavie G62 .... 55 A1
Wishaw ML2 .... 164 C1
Grange Ct Lanark ML11 .. 214 C3
Stevenston KA20 .... 206 B1
Grange Dr FK2 .... 42 B3
Grange Gdns
Bothwell G71 .... 141 A1
Bridge of A FK9 .... 2 B4
Grange Pl Alexandria G83 .27 C3
Kilmarnock KA1 .... 227 C4
Grange Rd Alloa FK10 ..... 9 C3
Bearsden G61 .... 75 C3
Bridge of A FK9 .... 2 B3
Glasgow G42 .... 137 A4
Stevenston KA20 .... 206 B1
Grange St
Kilmarnock KA1 .... 227 C4
Motherwell ML1 .... 164 A2
Grange Terr KA1 ...... 227 B4
Grange The KA11 ...... 220 B3
Grange Twr ML1 ...... 164 A1
Grangemouth Rd FK2 ... 42 C3
Grangemuir Ct KA9 .... 236 A4
Grangemuir Rd KA9 .... 236 A4
Grangeneuk Gdns G68 .. 61 B1
Granger Rd Balloch G83 . 27 C4
Kilmarnock KA1 .... 227 C3
Grangeview FK5 .... 23 C1
Grannoch Pl ML5 ...... 122 B1
Grant Cres G82 .... 27 B1
Grant Ct Airdrie ML6 .... 123 C4
Hamilton ML3 .... 183 B4
Grant Pl Coatbridge ML5 .122 B2
Kilmarnock KA3 .... 223 B1
Stirling FK9 .... 2 A2
Grant St Alloa FK10 ...... 9 C3
Glasgow G3 .... 240 A4
Greenock PA15 .... 46 B2
Helensburgh G84 .... 16 B1
Grantholm Ave ML1 .... 143 A3
Grantlea Gr G32 ...... 119 B2
Grantlea Terr G32 .... 119 B2
Grantley Gdns G41 .... 136 B4
Grantley St G41 ...... 136 B4
Grantoften Path G75 ... 180 C3
Granton St G5 .... 117 C1
Grantown Ave ML6 .... 123 C3
Grantown Gdns ML6 ... 102 C3
Grants Ave PA2 .... 113 B1
Grants Cres PA2 ...... 133 B4
Grants Pl PA2 .... 133 B4
Grants Way PA2 .... 113 B1
Granville St
Clydebank G81 .... 74 A2
Glasgow G3 .... 240 A3
Helensburgh G84 .... 16 C1
Grasmere G75 .... 179 C3
Grasmere Ct ML3 ...... 183 B3
Grassyards Intc KA3 .... 223 B2
Grassyards Rd KA3 .... 223 B1
Grathellen Ct ML1 .... 164 A4
Gray Cres KA12 .... 224 C4
Gray Dr G61 .... 75 C2
Gray St Alexandria G83 ... 27 C3
Cleland ML1 .... 144 A1
Glasgow G3 .... 96 C1
Greenock PA15 .... 46 A2
Kirkintilloch G66 .... 80 A4
Larkhall ML9 .... 185 A2
Prestwick KA9 .... 236 B4
Shotts ML7 .... 147 A2
Gray's Cl ML11 .... 214 B2
Gray's Rd G71 .... 141 A3
Grayshill Rd G68 .... 81 C3
Graystale Rd FK7 .... 7 A2
Graystonelee Rd ML7 ... 146 B3
Graystones KA13 ...... 207 C3
Great Dovehill G1, G4 ... 241 B1
Great George La 6 G12 .96 B2
Great George St G12 .... 96 B2
Great Hamilton St PA2 .113 C1
Great Kelvin La G12 .... 96 C1
Great Western Rd
Clydebank G15,G81 ...... 74 B2
Glasgow G12,G20 .... 96 B2
Great Western Terr 33
G12 .... 96 B2
Great Western Terrace La 32
G12 .... 96 B2
Green Ave KA12 .... 219 B2
Green Bank KA24 ...... 191 B4
Green Bank Rd G68 .... 61 B1
Green Dale ML2 .... 165 B3
Green Gdns ML1 .... 144 B1
Green Loan ML1 .... 143 A2
Green Pl Bothwell G71 .. 141 A1
Calderbank ML6 .... 123 A1
Green Rd Paisley PA2 ... 113 A2
Rutherglen G73 .... 138 A4
Green St Ayr KA8 ...... 235 C1
Bothwell G71 .... 141 A1
Clydebank G81 .... 74 A2
Glasgow G40 .... 117 C3
Saltcoats KA21 .... 216 C4
Stonehouse ML9 .... 198 C1
Green Street La KA8 ... 235 C1
Green Street Lane Bsns Pk
KA8 .... 235 C1
Green The Alva FK12 ...... 5 A4
Glasgow G40 .... 117 C2
Greenacre Ct FK7 .... 7 C1
Greenacre Pl FK7 .... 7 C1
Greenacres
Ardrossan KA22 .... 205 C2
Motherwell ML1 .... 163 B3
Greenacres Ct G53 .... 135 B2
Greenacres Dr G53 .... 135 B2
Greenacres View ML1 .. 163 B3
Greenacres Way G53 ... 135 B2
Greenan Ave G42 ...... 137 C4
Greenan Gr KA7 ...... 238 A2
Greenan Pk KA7 ...... 238 A2
Greenan Pl KA7 ...... 238 B2
Greenan Rd Ayr KA7 .... 238 B2
Kilmarnock KA3 .... 228 A4
Greenan Terr KA9 .... 236 B4
Greenan Way KA7 .... 238 A2
Greenbank G72 .... 161 B4
Greenbank Ave G46 .... 157 A4
Greenbank Ct KA12 .... 219 B1
Greenbank Dr PA2 .... 133 B4
Greenbank Gdn* G76 ... 157 B3
Greenbank Pl FK1 ...... 41 B2
Greenbank Rd Falkirk FK1 41 B2
Irvine KA12 .... 219 B1
Wishaw ML2 .... 165 B2
Greenbank St 3 G73 ... 138 A4
Greenbank Terr ML8 ... 187 C1
Greencornhills Rdbt FK7 11 C4
Greencraig Ave FK1 .... 66 B3
Greendyke St G1 ...... 241 B1
Greenend Ave PA5 .... 111 B1
Greenend Pl G32 ...... 119 B4
Greenend View ML4 ... 141 C3
Greenfarm Rd
Linwood PA3 .... 112 A3
Newton Mearns G77 .... 156 A3
Greenfaulds Cres G67 ... 83 A4
Greenfaulds Rd
Cumbernauld G67 .... 83 A4
Cumbernauld, Greenfaulds
G67 .... 82 C4
Greenfaulds Sta G67 ... 82 C4
Greenfield Ave Ayr KA7 .238 B1
Glasgow G32 .... 119 A4
Greenfield Cres ML2 ... 165 B2
Greenfield Dr
Irvine KA12 .... 219 B1
Wishaw ML2 .... 165 B2
Greenfield Pl G32 .... 119 A3
Greenfield Prim Sch
G51 .... 115 C4
Greenfield Quadrant
ML1 .... 143 C2
Greenfield Rd
Carluke ML8 .... 187 C2
Clarkston G76 .... 157 C3
Glasgow G32 .... 119 B3
Hamilton ML3 .... 162 A3
Greenfield St Alloa FK10 .. 10 A4
Bonnybridge FK4 .... 40 A3
Glasgow G51 .... 115 C4
Wishaw ML2 .... 165 B2
Greenfields High Sch
G67 .... 82 B4
Greenfoot KA13 .... 207 C2
Greengairs Ave G51 .... 115 B4
Greengairs Prim Sch
ML6 .... 83 C1
Greengairs Rd ML6 ...... 83 C1
Greenhall Pl G72 ...... 161 B3
Greenhead FK12 .... 5 A3
Greenhead Ave
Dumbarton G82 .... 50 A2
Stevenston KA20 .... 206 C1
Greenhead Gdns G82 .... 50 A2
Greenhead Rd
Bearsden G61 .... 75 C2
Dumbarton G82 .... 50 B2
Inchinnan PA4 .... 93 B3
Lennoxtown G66 .... 57 C4
Wishaw ML2 .... 165 B1
Greenhead St G40 .... 117 C2
Greenhill G64 .... 98 B4
Greenhill Ave
Gartcosh G69 .... 100 C4
Glasgow G46 .... 136 B1
Greenhill Bsns Ctr ML5 .102 A1
Greenhill Bsns Pk PA3 .113 B3
Greenhill Cres
Elderslie PA3,PA5 ...... 112 B1
Linwood PA3,PA5 ...... 112 B3
Greenhill Ct Irvine KA11 .220 A3
Rutherglen G73 .... 138 A4
Greenhill Dr PA3 ...... 112 B3
Greenhill Ind Est ML5 .. 102 A1
Greenhill Prim Sch ML5 122 A4
Greenhill Rd
Blackridge EH48 .... 107 C2
Bonnybridge FK4 .... 40 A2
Cleland ML1 .... 144 C2
Paisley PA3 .... 113 B3
Rutherglen G73 .... 138 A4
Greenhill Smallholdings
KA2 .... 222 A1
Greenhill St G73 ...... 138 A4
Greenhill Terr KA2 .... 221 C2
Greenhills KA15 ...... 172 A1
Greenhills Cres G75 ... 180 A3
Greenhills Prim Sch
G75 .... 180 B3
Greenhills Rd G75 .... 180 B3
Greenhills Sq G75 .... 180 A3
Greenholm Ave
Clarkston G76 .... 157 C4
Uddingston G71 .... 140 C4
Greenholm St KA1 .... 227 C3
Greenholme Ct G44 ... 137 A3
Greenholme St G44 ... 137 A3
Greenhorn's Well Ave
FK1 .... 41 C2
Greenhorn's Well Cres
FK1 .... 41 C2
Greenhorn's Well Dr FK1 41 C2
Greenknowe Dr ML8 ... 186 C3

Greenknowe Pk KA9 ...233 B2
Greenknowe Rd G43 ...136 A3
Greenknowe St ML2 ...186 A3
Greenlady Wlk ML11 ...215 B2
Greenlaw Ave
Paisley PA1 ...114 A3
Wishaw ML2 ...165 B3
Greenlaw Cres PA1 ...114 A3
Greenlaw Dr
Newton Mearns G77 ...156 B3
Paisley PA1 ...114 A3
Greenlaw Ho PA1 ...114 A3
Greenlaw Ind Est PA3 ...113 C3
Greenlaw Rd Glasgow G14 94 C3
Newton Mearns G77 ...156 B3
Greenlea Rd G69 ...100 A4
Greenlea St G13 ...95 C3
Greenlees Ct KA24 ...191 A4
Greenlees Gdns G72 ...138 C2
Greenlees Gr ML5 ...122 B3
Greenlees Pk G72 ...139 A2
Greenlees Rd G72 ...139 A2
Greenloan Ave G51 ...115 B4
Greenloan View ML9 ...185 A1
Greenmoss Pl ML4 ...142 B3
Greenmount G22 ...97 A4
Greenmount Dr FK1 ...66 B3
Greenock Acad PA16 ...45 B4
Greenock Ave G44 ...137 A3
Greenock Central Sta
PA15 ...46 A2
Greenock High Sch PA16 44 B1
Greenock Rd
Bishopton PA7 ...71 B3
Greenock PA15 ...46 C1
Inchinnan PA4 ...93 B3
Langbank PA14 ...70 B4
Paisley PA3 ...113 B4
Port Glasgow PA14 ...47 B1
Greenock West Sta PA15 45 C3
Greenrig G71 ...140 C3
Greenrig Rd ML11 ...214 A1
Greenrig St G33 ...98 B2
Greenrigg Cotts ML7 ...127 C3
Greenrigg Prim Sch
ML7 ...127 C3
Greenrigg Rd G67 ...62 A1
Greenrigg St G71 ...140 C3
Greens Ave G66 ...79 B4
Greens Cres G66 ...79 B4
Greens Rd G67 ...82 C3
Greenshields Rd G69 ...120 A3
Greenside
Carmunnock G76 ...158 C4
Irvine KA11 ...220 A2
Greenside Ave
Kilbirnie KA25 ...170 A4
Prestwick KA9 ...236 B4
Springside KA11 ...221 A1
Greenside Cl ML11 ...215 A2
Greenside Cres G33 ...98 C2
Greenside La ML11 ...215 A2
Greenside Pl G61 ...75 B4
Greenside Rd
Clydebank G81 ...74 A4
Motherwell ML1 ...143 B4
Wishaw ML2 ...165 B1
Greenside St Alloa FK10 ...10 A3
Glasgow G33 ...98 C2
Motherwell ML1 ...143 C2
Greenside Terr KA11 ...221 A1
Greenside Way KA11 ...220 A2
Greentowers Rd ML11 ...214 C4
Greentree Dr G69 ...119 C2
Greentree Pk KA7 ...239 B2
Greenview St G43 ...136 B4
Greenway La G72 ...161 B3
Greenways Ave PA2 ...113 A1
Greenways Ct PA2 ...113 A1
Greenwood Acad KA11 .220 A1
Greenwood Ave
Cambuslang G72 ...139 C3
Chryston G69 ...80 C1
Stirling FK8 ...7 A4
Greenwood Cres ML5 ...122 B3
Greenwood Ct G76 ...157 C3
Greenwood Dr
Bearsden G61 ...76 A2
Johnstone PA5 ...131 C4
Greenwood Intc KA11 ...224 D4
Greenwood Quadrant
G81 ...74 B1
Greenwood Rd
Clarkston G76 ...157 B4
Irvine KA11 ...220 B1
Greenwood St ML7 ...146 C3
Greenyards Intc G67 ...62 B1
Greer Quadrant G81 ...74 A2
Grenada Pl G75 ...159 A1
Grenadier Gdns ML1 ...163 B2
Grendon Ct FK8 ...7 A3
Grendon Gdns FK8 ...7 A3
Grenville Ct FK1 ...41 C2
Grenville Dr G72 ...138 C2
Grenville Rd PA19 ...44 C3
Gresham View ML1 ...164 A1
Greta Meek La G66 ...58 B3
Gretna St G40 ...118 A2
Grey Pl PA15 ...45 C3
Greyfriars Ct ML11 ...214 C2
Greyfriars Rd G71 ...140 B4
Greyfriars St G32 ...118 C4
Greygoran FK10 ...5 B1
Greystone Ave G73 ...138 B3
Greystone Bauks ML11 .214 C2
Greywood St G13 ...95 C4
Grier Pl ML9 ...184 C1
Griers Wlk KA11 ...225 B3
Grierson Cres FK7 ...6 B3
Grierson La G33 ...118 B4
Grierson St G33 ...118 B4
Grieve Croft G72 ...140 C1
Grieve Rd
Cumbernauld G67 ...62 A2
Greenock PA16 ...45 A3
Griffen Ave PA1 ...112 C3
Griffin Dock Rd KA8 ...235 C1
Griffin Pl ML4 ...142 A4
Griffiths St FK1 ...42 A2
Griffiths Way ML8 ...186 C2
Griqua Terr G71 ...141 A1
Grodwell Dr FK12 ...4 C4
Grogarry Rd G15 ...75 A2
Grosvenor Cres 10 G12 ...96 B2
Grosvenor Crescent La 12
G12 ...96 B2
Grosvenor La
Glasgow G12 ...96 B2
Greenock PA15 ...46 B2
Grosvenor Rd PA15 ...46 B2
Grosvenor Terr 13 G12 ...96 B2
Grougar Dr KA3 ...223 A2
Grougar Gdns KA3 ...223 A2
Grougar Rd KA3 ...228 B4
Grove Cres Falkirk FK2 ...24 A1
Larkhall ML9 ...185 B1
Grove Park Gdns G20 ...97 A1
Grove Pk G66 ...79 B2
Grove St FK6 ...21 B1
Grove The Bishopton PA7 ...72 A2
Bridge of W PA11 ...110 C3
Kilbarchan PA10 ...111 A2
Neilston G78 ...154 B3
Rutherglen G46 ...157 A4
Grove Way ML4 ...141 C2
Grove Wood G71 ...121 B1
Grove Wynd ML1 ...143 A2
Groveburn Ave G46 ...136 A2
Grovepark Ct G20 ...97 A1
Grovepark Pl G20 ...97 A1
Grovepark St G20 ...97 A2
Groves The G64 ...98 B4
Grovewood Bsns Ctr
ML4 ...141 C4
Grudie St G34 ...120 A4
Gryfe Rd
Bridge of W PA11 ...110 B4
Port Glasgow PA14 ...68 C4
Gryfe St PA15 ...46 A1
Gryfebank Ave PA6 ...91 C1
Gryfebank Cl PA6 ...91 C1
Gryfebank Cres PA6 ...91 C1
Gryfebank Way PA6 ...91 C1
Gryfewood Cres PA6 ...91 C1
Gryfewood Way PA6 ...91 C1
Gryffe Ave PA11 ...90 B1
Gryffe Cres PA2 ...112 C1
Gryffe Gr PA11 ...110 B4
Gryffe High Sch PA6 ...91 A1
Gryffe Rd PA13 ...89 B4
Gryffe St G44 ...137 A4
Guildford St G33 ...99 B1
Guiltreehill KA7 ...239 A1
Gullane Cres G68 ...61 C3
Gullane Ct Hamilton ML3 183 A4
Irvine KA11 ...224 C4
Gullane Pl KA13 ...207 A2
Gullane St G11 ...96 A1
Gulliland Ave KA2 ...225 C1
Gulliland Pl KA12 ...219 B1
Gullin Dr KA9 ...236 C3
Gunn Quadrant ML4 ...141 C2
Gushet Ho ML6 ...122 C4
Guthrie Ct ML1 ...163 B3
Guthrie Dr G71 ...121 A1
Guthrie Pl
East Kilbride G74 ...159 C1
Rhu G84 ...15 B2
Torrance G64 ...57 B1
Guthrie Rd KA21 ...217 A4
Guthrie St Glasgow G20 ...96 B3
Hamilton ML3 ...162 B2
Guy Mannering Rd G84 ...25 B4
Gyle Pl ML2 ...165 C2

H

Habbieauld Rd KA3 ...222 A4
Haberlea Ave G53 ...135 B2
Haberlea Gdns G53 ...135 B1
Haddington Gdns KA11 .220 A3
Haddington Way ML5 ...121 C2
Haddow Gr 6 G71 ...141 A4
Haddow St ML3 ...162 C2
Hadrian Terr ML1 ...163 B4
Hagart Rd PA6 ...91 A1
Hagen Dr ML1 ...143 C1
Hagg Cres PA5 ...111 C2
Hagg Pl PA5 ...111 C2
Hagg Rd PA5 ...111 C1
Haggs Castle★ G41 ...116 B1
Haggs La G41 ...116 B1
Haggs Rd G41 ...116 B1
Haggswood Ave G41 ...116 B1
Haghill Prim Sch G31 ...118 A4
Haghill Rd G31 ...118 B4
Hagholm Rd ML11 ...215 C4
Hagmill Cres ML5 ...122 B1
Hagmill Rd ML5 ...122 A1
Hagthorn Ave KA25 ...170 A4
Haig Ave FK8 ...2 A1
Haig Dr G69 ...119 C2
Haig St Glasgow G21 ...98 A2
Greenock PA15 ...45 C3
Hailes Ave G32 ...119 B3
Haining Ave KA1 ...228 A3
Haining Rd PA4 ...94 B2
Haining The PA4 ...94 B1
Hairmyres Dr G75 ...179 C4
Hairmyres Hospl G75 ...179 C4
Hairmyres Pk G75 ...179 C4
Hairmyres Rdbt G75 ...158 C1
Hairmyres St G42 ...117 B1
Hairmyres Sta G75 ...158 C1
Hairst St PA4 ...94 B2
Halbeath Ave G15 ...74 C2
Halbert St G41 ...116 C1
Halberts Cres FK7 ...7 A1
Haldane Ave FK9 ...2 A3
Haldane Ct G83 ...27 C4
Haldane La 29 G14 ...95 B2
Haldane Pl G75 ...180 C4
Haldane Prim Sch G83 ...27 C4
Haldane St G14 ...95 B2
Haldane Terr G83 ...19 C1
Halfmerk N G74 ...160 A1
Halfmerk S G74 ...160 A1
Halfmerke Prim Sch
G74 ...160 A2
Halfway St KA3 ...190 B3
Halgreen Ave G15 ...74 C2
Halifax Way 7 PA4 ...94 B1
Halket Cres FK2 ...24 B1
Halkett Cres G83 ...27 C4
Hall Bar Gdns ML8 ...201 C2
Hall La KA10 ...230 A2
Hall Pl Lanark ML11 ...215 A2
Stepps G33 ...99 C3
Hall Rd Nemphlar ML11 ...214 A3
Rhu G84 ...15 B3
Hall St Alexandria G83 ...27 C2
Clydebank G81 ...74 A1
Hamilton ML3 ...162 B1
Motherwell ML1 ...143 A2
Renton G82 ...49 B4
Hallbrae St G33 ...98 C1
Hallcraig St ML6 ...123 A4
Halley Dr G13 ...94 C4
Halley Pl G13 ...94 C4
Halley Sq G13 ...94 C4
Halley St G13 ...94 C4
Hallforest St G33 ...99 A1
Hallglen Prim Sch FK1 ...42 A1
Hallglen Rd FK1 ...42 A1
Hallglen Terr FK1 ...42 A1
Hallgraig Pl ML8 ...187 B1
Hallhill Cres G33 ...119 C3
Hallhill Rd Glasgow G32 .119 A3
Glasgow, Barlanark G33 ...119 C3
Glasgow, Garrowhill G69 ...120 A3
Johnstone PA5 ...131 B4
Halliburton Cres G34 ...119 C4
Halliburton Terr G34 ...120 A4
Hallidale Cres PA4 ...94 C1
Hallinan Gdns ML2 ...164 C1
Hallpark FK10 ...10 B4
Hallrule Dr G52 ...115 B3
Halls Vennal 3 KA8 ...235 C1
Hallside Ave G72 ...139 C3
Hallside Bvd G72 ...139 C2
Hallside Cres G72 ...139 C3
Hallside Dr G72 ...139 C3
Hallside Gdns ML2 ...165 C2
Hallside Pl G5 ...117 B2
Hallside Prim Sch G72 .139 C2
Hallside Rd G72 ...139 C2
Hallside St PA9 ...130 C3
Hallydown Dr G13 ...95 B3
Halpin Cl ML4 ...141 B3
Halton Gdns G69 ...119 C2
Hamersley Pl G75 ...180 A4
Hamilcomb Rd ML4 ...142 A2
Hamill Dr G65 ...60 C4
Hamilton Ave
Glasgow G41 ...116 B2
Stenhousemuir FK5 ...23 C2
Hamilton Bsns Pk ML3 .162 B3
Hamilton Coll ML3 ...162 B3
Hamilton Cres Ayr KA7 ...239 A4
Bearsden G61 ...75 C4
Bishopton PA7 ...71 C2
Cambuslang G72 ...139 B3
Coatbridge ML5 ...122 A3
Renfrew PA4 ...94 B3
Stevenston KA20 ...206 C1
Hamilton Ct KA3 ...222 A4
Hamilton Dr Airdrie ML6 103 A1
Blantyre G72 ...161 A3
Bothwell G71 ...141 A1
Cambuslang G72 ...139 A3
Erskine PA8 ...72 C2
Falkirk FK1 ...42 A2
Glasgow G12 ...96 C2
Glasgow, Giffnock G46 ...136 B1
Motherwell ML1 ...163 C2
Stirling FK9 ...2 B2
Hamilton Gate PA15 ...45 C3
Hamilton Gdns KA3 ...195 C1
Hamilton Gram Sch
ML3 ...162 B2
Hamilton Int Tech Pk
G72 ...161 B3
Hamilton Mauoleum★
ML3 ...162 C3
Hamilton Mus★ ML3 ...162 C2
Hamilton Park Ave G12 ...96 C2
Hamilton Park N ML3 ...162 B3
Hamilton Park S ML3 ...162 B3
Hamilton Pl
East Kilbride G75 ...180 C4
Hamilton ML3 ...183 B3
Motherwell ML1 ...143 A2
Hamilton Pl *continued*
Motherwell, Whittagreen
ML1 ...143 B2
Hamilton Rd
Bellshill ML4 ...141 C2
Blantyre G72 ...161 A3
Bothwell G71 ...141 A1
Cambuslang G72 ...139 B2
East Kilbride G72,G74 ...160 B3
Glasgow G32 ...119 B1
Larkhall ML9 ...184 C3
Motherwell ML1 ...163 B3
Rutherglen G73 ...138 B4
Stenhousemuir FK2,FK5 ...23 B3
Hamilton Sch for the Deaf
ML3 ...162 A1
Hamilton St Carluke ML8 187 C1
Clydebank G81 ...94 B4
Dumbarton G82 ...50 A2
Falkirk FK1 ...41 B3
Glasgow G42 ...117 B1
Kilwinning KA13 ...207 C2
Larkhall ML9 ...185 A2
Paisley PA3 ...113 C3
Saltcoats KA21 ...216 C4
Hamilton Terr G81 ...94 B4
Hamilton View G71 ...141 A4
Hamilton Way
Greenock PA15 ...45 C3
Prestwick KA9 ...233 B1
Stonehouse ML9 ...198 C1
Hamiltonhill Cres G22 ...97 A2
Hamiltonhill Rd G22 ...97 A2
Hamlet G74 ...160 A3
Hampden Dr G42 ...137 A4
Hampden La G42 ...137 A4
Hampden Park Visitors Ctr★
G42 ...137 A4
Hampden Pk (Queen's Park
FC)★ G42 ...137 A4
Hampden Terr G42 ...137 A4
Hampden Way 11 PA4 ...94 B1
Handel Pl 3 G5 ...117 B2
Hangingshaw Pl G42 ...137 B4
Hannah Pl G82 ...27 C1
Hanover Cl G42 ...137 A4
Hanover Ct Glasgow G1 .241 A3
Paisley PA1 ...114 A3
Hanover Gdns
Bishopbriggs G64 ...78 A1
Paisley PA1 ...113 B2
Hanover St Glasgow G1 .241 A2
Helensburgh G84 ...25 A4
Hanson St G31 ...117 C4
Hapland Ave G53 ...115 B1
Hapland Rd G53 ...115 B1
Happyhills KA23 ...190 B3
Haran Rd G83 ...19 C1
Harbour Ind Est KA22 ...205 B1
Harbour La PA3 ...113 C3
Harbour Pl KA22 ...205 A1
Harbour Rd
Ardrossan KA22 ...216 A4
Irvine KA12 ...219 A1
Paisley PA3 ...113 C3
Troon KA10 ...229 B2
Harbour St
Ardrossan KA22 ...216 A4
Irvine KA12 ...219 A1
Saltcoats KA21 ...216 C4
Harburn Pl G23 ...76 C1
Harbury Pl G14 ...94 C3
Harcourt Dr G31 ...118 A4
Hardacres ML11 ...215 A3
Hardgate Dr G51 ...115 B4
Hardgate Gdns G51 ...115 B4
Hardgate Pl G51 ...115 B4
Hardgate Rd G51 ...115 B4
Hardie Ave G73 ...138 B4
Hardie Cres FK7 ...8 B2
Hardie Ct FK7 ...7 B2
Hardie St Alexandria G83 ...27 B4
Blantyre G72 ...161 B4
Hamilton ML3 ...162 A1
Motherwell ML1 ...163 C4
Hardmuir Gdns 1 G66 ...58 C1
Hardmuir Rd G66 ...58 C1
Hardridge Ave G52 ...115 C1
Hardridge Pl G52 ...115 C1
Hardridge Rd G52 ...115 C1
Hardy Hill G84 ...17 A1
Harebell Pl KA7 ...239 A2
Harefield Dr G14 ...95 A3
Harelaw Ave
Barrhead G78 ...134 B1
Glasgow G44 ...136 C2
Neilston G78 ...154 B3
Port Glasgow PA14 ...68 B4
Harelaw Cres PA2 ...133 B4
Hareleeshill Prim Sch
ML9 ...185 B1
Hareleeshill Rd ML9 ...185 B1
Hareshaw Dr KA3 ...223 A3
Hareshaw Gdns KA3 ...223 A3
Hareshaw Rd ML1 ...144 B2
Harestanes Gdns G66 ...59 A1
Harestanes Ind Est ML8 201 C3
Harestanes Prim Sch
G66 ...59 A1
Harestanes Rd ML8 ...201 C2
Harestone Cres ML2 ...165 B1
Harestone Rd ML2 ...165 B1
Harfield Dr G33 ...119 C3
Harfield Gdns G33 ...119 C3
Harhill St G51 ...116 A4
Harkins Ave G72 ...161 B4
Harkness Ave G66 ...58 A3
Harland Cotts G14 ...95 B2
Harland St G14 ...95 B2
Harlands The FK10 ...9 C4
Harlaw Gdns G64 ...78 B1
Harley Ct FK2 ...42 A4
Harley Pl KA21 ...205 C1
Harley St G51 ...116 B3
Harling Dr KA10 ...229 C1
Harmetray St G22 ...97 B3
Harmony Ct G51 ...116 A4
Harmony Pl G51 ...116 A4
Harmony Row 1 G51 ...116 A4
Harmony Sq G51 ...116 A4
Harmsworth St G11 ...95 C1
Harper Cres ML2 ...165 C2
Harperland Dr KA1 ...227 B4
Harport St G46 ...135 C2
Harrier Wynd PA16 ...45 A2
Harriet Pl G43 ...136 A3
Harriet Rd KA3 ...223 A1
Harriet St G73 ...138 A4
Harrington Rd G74 ...159 C1
Harris Cl G77 ...156 A3
Harris Cres G60 ...73 A3
Harris Ct Alloa FK10 ...10 A3
Irvine KA11 ...225 B4
Harris Dr G60 ...73 A3
Harris Gdns G60 ...73 B3
Harris Pl Airdrie ML6 ...123 B3
Kilmarnock KA3 ...223 A3
Harris Quadrant ML2 ...165 C3
Harris Rd Glasgow G23 ...76 C1
Old Kilpatrick G60 ...73 B3
Port Glasgow PA14 ...69 A4
Harris Terr KA11 ...225 B4
Harrison Dr G51 ...116 A3
Harrison Pl Falkirk FK1 ...41 C3
Renton G82 ...27 B1
Harrow Ct G15 ...74 C2
Harrow Pl G15 ...74 C2
Hart St Clydebank G81 ...74 B4
Glasgow G31 ...118 C3
Linwood PA3 ...112 B3
Hart Wynd FK7 ...7 C1
Hartfield Cres G78 ...154 C4
Hartfield Ct G82 ...50 A2
Hartfield Gdns G82 ...50 A2
Hartfield Rd KA7 ...238 C3
Hartfield Terr
Paisley PA2 ...114 A1
Shotts ML7 ...167 A4
Harthall KA8 ...236 C1
Harthill Ind Est ML7 ...127 B3
Harthill Prim Sch ML7 .127 C3
Harthill Rd EH48 ...107 B1
Hartlaw Cres G52 ...115 A3
Hartree Ave G13 ...94 C4
Hartstone Pl G53 ...135 A4
Hartstone Rd G53 ...135 A4
Hartstone Terr G53 ...135 A4
Hartwood Gdns
Hartwood ML7 ...146 A1
Newton Mearns G77 ...156 B1
Hartwood Hospl ML7 ...145 C2
Hartwood Rd ML7 ...145 C1
Hartwood Sta ML7 ...145 C2
Hartwoodhill Hospl
ML7 ...146 A2
Harvest Dr ML1 ...163 B2
Harvest St FK9 ...2 A2
Harvey Cotts PA12 ...129 B1
Harvey Ct PA12 ...129 B1
Harvey Gdns KA22 ...205 B2
Harvey Sq PA12 ...129 B1
Harvey St
Ardrossan KA22 ...205 B2
Glasgow G4 ...97 B1
Harvey Terr PA12 ...129 B1
Harvey Way ML4 ...142 B4
Harvey Wynd FK8 ...2 A1
Harvie Ave G77 ...156 B3
Harvie St G51 ...116 B3
Harvies L Ctr★ KA21 ...217 A4
Harwood Gdns G69 ...81 A2
Harwood St G32 ...118 C4
Hastie St G3 ...96 B1
Hastings G75 ...180 A4
Hatfield Ct PA13 ...89 B4
Hatfield Dr G12 ...96 A3
Hathaway Dr G46 ...136 A1
Hathaway La G20 ...96 C3
Hathaway St G20 ...96 C3
Hathersage Ave G69 ...120 A3
Hathersage Dr G69 ...120 A3
Hathersage Gdns 15
G69 ...120 A3
Hatton Gdns G52 ...115 A2
Hatton Pl ML1 ...143 B1
Hatton Terr ML1 ...143 B1
Hattonhill ML1 ...143 B1
Hattonrigg Rd ML4 ...142 A4
Haugh Gdns FK2 ...24 A1
Haugh Pl ML3 ...162 C1
Haugh Rd Glasgow G3 ...116 B4
Kilsyth G65 ...60 B4
Stirling FK9 ...2 A1
Haugh St FK2 ...24 A1
Haughburn Pl G53 ...135 A4
Haughburn Rd G53 ...135 A4
Haughburn Terr G53 ...135 B4
Haughs Way FK6 ...21 C1
Haughton Ave G65 ...60 C4
Haughview Rd ML1 ...163 A3
Haupland Rd KA22 ...205 A3
Havelock La G11 ...96 B1
Havelock Pk G75 ...159 A1

Havelock Pl G84 16 C1
Havelock St Glasgow G11 96 B1
Helensburgh G84 16 C1
Haven Pk G75 179 C3
Haven The FK7 9 C2
Havoc Rd G82 49 B2
Hawbank Rd G74 159 A2
Hawbank Rdbt G75 159 A1
Hawick Ave PA2 113 A1
Hawick Cres ML9 185 A1
Hawick Dr ML5 122 B2
Hawick St Glasgow G13 94 C4
Wishaw ML2 165 B3
Hawkhead Ave PA2 114 A1
Hawkhead Hospl PA2 114 B1
Hawkhead Rd PA1,PA2 114 A2
Hawkhead Sta PA1 114 A2
Hawkhill Ave KA8 236 A1
Hawkhill Avenue La
KA8 236 A1
Hawkhill Dr KA20 206 C1
Hawkhill Pl KA20 206 C1
Hawkhill Rd FK10 10 B3
Hawkhill Ret Pk KA20 206 C1
Hawksland Wlk ML3 162 C1
Hawkwood G75 180 C3
Hawkwood Rd ML6 102 C2
Hawley Rd FK1 42 B2
Hawthorn Ave
Bearsden G61 76 A4
Bishopbriggs G64 98 A4
Dumbarton G82 49 A3
Erskine PA8 93 C4
Johnstone PA5 112 A1
Kirkintilloch G66 79 B3
Prestwick KA9 236 B4
Wishaw ML2 166 B3
Hawthorn Cres
Beith KA15 171 A4
Erskine PA8 93 C4
Fallin FK7 8 B2
Stirling FK8 1 C1
Hawthorn Ct
Clarkston G76 157 C3
Kilwinning KA13 207 C1
Hawthorn Dr Airdrie ML6 123 B3
Ayr KA7 239 B2
Banknock FK4 38 C1
Barrhead G78 155 B4
Coatbridge ML5 122 B3
Denny FK6 21 B2
Falkirk FK1 41 C2
Fallin FK7 8 B2
Harthill ML7 127 C3
Motherwell ML1 143 A2
Shotts ML7 147 B2
Stevenston KA20 206 C2
Wishaw ML2 165 B2
Hawthorn Gdns
Bellshill ML4 142 B2
Cambuslang G72 139 C2
Clarkston G76 157 C3
33 Larkhall ML9 185 B1
Prestwick KA9 236 B4
Hawthorn Gr ML8 186 C3
Hawthorn Hill ML3 162 C1
Hawthorn Pl
Blantyre G72 161 C4
Shotts ML7 167 A4
Troon KA10 229 C2
Hawthorn Prim Sch G22 97 B2
Hawthorn Quadrant G22 97 B3
Hawthorn Rd
Clarkston G76 157 C3
Cumbernauld G67 62 C2
Erskine PA8 93 C4
Hawthorn Sq KA1 227 B4
Hawthorn St
Clydebank G81 74 A2
Glasgow G22 97 B3
Torrance G64 57 B1
Hawthorn Terr
East Kilbride G75 180 A3
Uddingston G71 141 A4
Hawthorn Way
Dumbarton G82 49 A2
Erskine PA8 93 C4
Hamilton ML3 183 C2
Milton of C G66 58 B3
Hawthorn Wlk G72 138 B3
Hawthornden Gdns G23 76 C1
Hawthorne Pl
Gourock PA19 44 A3
Stenhousemuir FK5 23 B1
Hawthornhill Rd G82 49 B3
Hay Ave PA7 72 B2
Hay Dr PA5 112 A2
Hay Hill KA8 236 C1
Hay St PA15 45 C2
Hayburn Cres G11 96 A2
Hayburn Gate G11 96 A1
Hayburn La G11 96 A2
Hayburn St G11 96 A1
Hayes Gr G83 27 C3
Hayfield FK2 42 B4
Hayfield Ct G5 117 B2
Hayfield Rd FK2 42 B4
Hayfield St G5 117 B2
Hayfield Terr FK6 39 C4
Hayford Mills FK7 6 B3
Hayford Pl FK7 6 B3
Hayhill Rd G74 179 B4
Hayle Gdns G69 80 C2
Haylnn St G14 95 C1
Haymarket St G32 118 C4
Hayocks Prim Sch KA20 206 C1
Hayocks Rd KA20 206 C1
Hayocks Rdbt KA20 206 C1
Haypark Rd FK6 39 B3
Haysholm Sch KA12 219 C2
Haystack Pl G66 79 C2
Hayston Cres G22 97 A3
Hayston Rd
Cumbernauld G68 61 C2
Kirkintilloch G66 79 A4
Hayston St G22 97 A3
Hayward Ave ML8 202 B4
Hayward Ct ML8 202 B4
Haywood St G22 97 B3
Hazel Ave
Ardrossan KA22 205 B2
Bearsden G61 76 A4
Dumbarton G82 49 A3
Glasgow G44 136 C2
Johnstone PA5 112 A1
Kilmarnock KA1 227 B4
Kirkintilloch G66 79 B3
Hazel Bank G66 58 A2
Hazel Cres FK6 21 B2
Hazel Dene G64 98 A4
Hazel Gdns ML1 163 C2
Hazel Gr Falkirk FK2 42 B4
Kirkintilloch G66 79 B3
Law ML8 186 C3
Shotts ML7 147 A2
Hazel Path ML1 144 A1
Hazel Pk ML3 162 C1
Hazel Rd Banknock FK4 38 C1
Cumbernauld G67 62 B2
Hazel Terr Gourock PA19 44 B3
Uddingston G71 141 A4
Hazel Wood ML2 165 B3
Hazelbank
Motherwell ML1 143 A3
Plains ML6 103 C2
Hazelbank Gdns FK8 2 A1
Hazelbank Wlk ML6 122 B4
Hazeldean Cres ML2 165 B3
Hazelden Pk G44 136 C2
Hazelden Rd G77 177 B4
Hazelden Sch of Equitation
G77 156 B1
Hazeldene La 12 ML9 185 B1
Hazeldene Pk KA13 207 C2
Hazelfield Gr ML6 123 C1
Hazelgrove KA13 208 A2
Hazelhead G74 160 A1
Hazellea Dr G46 136 C2
Hazelmere Rd PA13 89 A4
Hazelton ML1 163 B3
Hazelwood Ave
Bridge of W PA11 110 C4
Newton Mearns G77 156 C2
Paisley PA2 132 C4
Hazelwood Dr G72 161 B4
Hazelwood Gdns G73 138 B2
Hazelwood La PA11 110 B4
Hazelwood Rd Ayr KA7 238 C3
Bridge of W PA11 110 B3
Glasgow G41 116 B2
Hazlitt Gdns G22 97 A3
Hazlitt Pl G20 97 A3
Hazlitt St G20 97 A3
Head of Muir Prim Sch
FK6 39 B3
Head St KA15 171 B4
Headhouse Ct G75 180 B4
Headhouse Gn G75 180 C4
Headlands Gr KA15 171 B4
Headlesscross Rd EH47 147 C1
Headrigg Gdns KA23 190 B3
Headrigg Rd KA23 190 B3
Headsmuir Ave ML8 187 B1
Healthcare International
(HCI) G81 73 C1
Heath Ave
Bishopbriggs G64 98 A4
Kirkintilloch G66 79 B2
Heath Rd ML9 185 A2
Heathcliffe Ave G72 140 B1
Heathcot Ave G15 74 C1
Heathcot Pl G15 74 C1
Heather Ave
Alexandria G83 27 C3
Barrhead G78 134 A3
Bearsden G61 75 C4
Clydebank G81 74 A4
Motherwell ML1 143 A3
Shieldhill FK1 66 B3
Heather Dr G66 79 A2
Heather Gdns G66 79 A2
Heather Gr 16 G75 180 C4
Heather Pk KA7 239 B2
Heather Pl
Johnstone PA5 112 A1
Kilmarnock KA1 227 B4
Kirkintilloch G66 79 A2
Heather Rd ML11 214 A3
Heather Row ML8 187 C2
Heather St ML6 105 A3
Heather View G66 33 C1
Heather Way ML1 143 A2
Heatherbank Wlk ML6 122 B4
Heatherbrae G64 77 C1
Heatherdale Gdns FK6 39 C4
Heatherhouse Ind Est
KA12 224 B4
Heatherhouse Rd KA12 224 B4
Heatherstane Bank
KA11 220 B1
Heatherstane Way KA11 220 B1
Heatherstane Wlk KA11 220 B1
Heathery Knowe G75 180 C4
Heathery Knowe Prim Sch
G75 180 C4
Heathery Lea Ave ML5 122 B2
Heathery Rd ML2 164 C2
Heatheryknowe Rd
Coatbridge G69 120 C4
Glasgow G69 120 C4
Heathfield ML2 186 A4
Heathfield Ave G69 81 A1
Heathfield Dr G62 55 A2
Heathfield Ind Est KA8 236 B2
Heathfield Prim Sch
KA8 236 A3
Heathfield Rd KA8 236 B2
Heathfield St G33 119 B4
Heathpark KA8 236 B3
Heathside Rd G46 136 B2
Heathwood Dr G46 136 A2
Hecla Ave G15 74 C2
Hecla Pl G15 74 C2
Hecla Sq G15 74 C2
Hector Rd G41 136 B4
Hedges The FK1 41 C3
Heggies Ave PA14 69 A4
Heights Rd EH48 107 B2
Helen St G51 116 A3
Helen Way G83 27 C1
Helen Wynd ML9 185 A1
Helen's Terr KA13 207 C1
Helena Pl G76 157 C4
Helensburgh Central Sta
G84 16 B1
Helensburgh Dr G13 95 C3
Helensburgh Upper Sta
G84 16 B2
Helenslea G72 139 C2
Helenslea Pl ML4 141 C2
Helenslee Cres G82 49 B2
Helenslee Ct G82 49 B2
Helenslee Rd
Dumbarton G82 49 B2
Langbank PA14 70 B4
Helenvale Ct G31 118 B3
Helenvale St G31 118 B2
Helmsdale Ave G72 140 B2
Helmsdale Ct G72 139 B3
Helmsdale Dr PA2 112 C1
Hemlock St G13 95 C4
Hemmingen Ct ML8 187 C2
Hemphill View KA2 221 C2
Henderland Dr G61 75 C1
Henderland Rd G61 75 C1
Henderson Ave
Alloa FK10 10 A4
Cambuslang G72 139 C3
Henderson Pl FK12 5 A4
Henderson Rd KA10 229 C1
Henderson St
Airdrie ML6 123 A4
Bridge of A FK9 2 A4
Clydebank G81 94 C4
Coatbridge ML5 121 C3
Glasgow G20 96 C2
Paisley PA1 113 B3
Henderson Terr PA19 44 C3
Hendry St FK2 42 A4
Hennings The FK10 5 B1
Henrietta St G14 95 B2
Henry Bell Gn 8 G75 180 C4
Henry Bell St G84 16 C1
Henry St Alva FK12 5 A3
Barrhead G78 134 A2
Hepburn Hill ML3 183 B4
Hepburn Rd G52 115 A4
Hepburn Way KA11 220 B4
Herald Ave G13 75 B1
Herald Gr ML1 163 B2
Herald St KA22 216 A4
Herald Way 2 PA4 94 B1
Herbert St G20 96 C2
Herbertshire St FK6 21 C1
Herbertson Cres KA12 219 B2
Herbertson Gr G72 140 B1
Herbertson St
Blantyre G72 161 C4
4 Glasgow G5 117 A3
Herbison Ct ML9 185 A2
Herbson Ct ML9 185 A2
Hercules Way PA4 94 B1
Herdshill Ave FK1 66 B3
Heriot Ave PA2 132 C4
Heriot Cres G64 78 A2
Heriot Ct PA2 132 C4
Heriot Prim Sch PA2 132 C4
Heriot Rd G66 79 B2
Heriot Way PA2 132 C4
Heritage Ct G77 156 C3
Heritage Dr FK2 24 A2
Heritage View ML5 121 C4
Heritage Way ML5 121 C4
Herma St G23 96 C4
Hermes Way ML4 142 C3
Hermiston Ave G32 119 B3
Hermiston Pl
Glasgow G32 119 B3
Motherwell ML1 143 A3
Hermiston Rd G32 119 A3
Hermitage Acad G84 25 B4
Hermitage Ave G13 95 B3
Hermitage Cres ML5 122 A2
Hermitage Prim Sch G84 16 B1
Hermitage Rd FK9 2 C3
Herndon Ct G77 157 A3
Heron Ct G81 74 A3
Heron Pl PA5 131 B4
Heron Rd PA16 45 A2
Heron Way PA4 94 B1
Heronswood KA13 207 C3
Herries Rd G41 116 B1
Herriet St G41 116 C2
Herriot Ave KA25 149 A2
Herriot St ML5 121 C4
Herschell St G13 95 C3
Hertford Ave G12 96 A3
Hervey St FK10 10 A4
Hestan Pl KA3 223 A3
Heugh St FK1 42 A2
Hewett Cres PA6 91 B1
Hexham Gdns G41 116 B1
Heys St G78 134 B1
Hibernia St PA16 45 B2
Hickman St G42 117 B1
Hickman Terr G42 117 B1
Hickory Cres G71 141 B4
Hickory St G22 97 C3
High Avon St ML9 184 C2
High Banton Rd G65 37 B2
High Barholm PA10 111 A2
High Barrwood Rd G65 60 C4
High Beeches G76 158 C4
High Blantyre Prim Sch
G72 161 A4
High Blantyre Rd G72,
ML3 161 C3
High Burnside Ave ML5 121 C3
High Calside PA2 113 C2
High Carnegie Rd PA14 68 C4
High Coats ML5 122 A4
High Common Rd G74,
G75 181 A4
High Cotts G64 78 A3
High Craigends G65 60 C4
High Flender Rd G76 157 B3
High Glencairn St KA1 227 C4
High Graighall Rd G4 97 A1
High Kirk View PA5 111 C1
High Mains Ave G82 50 B2
High Mair PA4 94 B1
High Mdw ML8 188 B1
High Mill Rd ML8 188 A1
High Murray Gr G72 139 B3
High Overton St ML9 200 B2
High Parks Cres ML3 183 B3
High Parksail PA8 93 B4
High Patrick St ML3 162 C2
High Pleasance ML9 185 A2
High Rd Ayr KA8 236 C2
Motherwell ML1 163 C4
Paisley PA2 113 B2
Saltcoats KA20,KA21 206 A1
Stevenston KA20 206 B1
High Sch of Glasgow (Jun
Sch) G61 75 B2
High Sch of Glasgow The
G13 95 C3
High St Airdrie ML6 122 C4
Airth FK2 14 B2
Alloa FK10 10 A3
Ayr KA7 238 C4
Bonnybridge FK4 40 A3
Carluke ML8 187 C1
Clackmannan FK10 10 C2
Dumbarton G82 49 C2
Falkirk FK1 42 A2
Glasgow G1 241 B2
Greenock PA15 45 C3
Irvine KA12 219 B1
Johnstone PA5 111 C2
Kilbirnie KA25 149 A2
Kilmacolm PA13 69 B1
Kilmarnock KA3 223 A1
Lanark ML11 215 A2
Lochwinnoch PA12 129 B1
Motherwell ML1 143 C2
Neilston G78 154 C4
Paisley PA1 113 C2
Renfrew PA4 94 C2
Rutherglen G73 138 A4
Shotts ML7 146 C2
Slamannan FK1 86 A4
Stewarton KA3 195 C1
High Station Ct FK1 42 A2
High Station Rd FK1 42 A2
High Street Sta G1 241 B2
High View Gr FK1 66 B3
High Whitehills Rd G75 180 C3
High Wood Gdns ML4 141 C3
Highburgh Ave ML11 215 A2
Highburgh Ct ML11 215 A2
Highburgh Dr G73 138 B3
Highburgh Rd G12 96 B1
Highcraig Ave PA5 111 B1
Highcroft Ave G44 137 B3
Highcross Ave ML5 121 B2
Highdykes Prim Sch G83 28 A1
Higherness Way ML5 121 C2
Highet Gdns KA12 219 A2
Highet St KA3 222 C1
Highfield Ave
Kilmarnock KA3 223 A2
Kirkintilloch G66 58 C1
Paisley PA2 133 B4
Prestwick KA9 236 B4
Highfield Cres
Motherwell ML1 164 A4
Paisley PA2 133 B4
Highfield Ct G66 58 C1
Highfield Dr
Clarkston G76 157 B4
Glasgow G12 96 A3
Rutherglen G73 138 B2
Stevenston KA20 206 C1
Highfield Gr 5 G66 58 C1
Highfield Pl
East Kilbride G74 159 C2
Glasgow G12 96 A3
Highfield Pl *continued*
Irvine KA11 219 C3
Highfield Rd Ayr KA8 236 C2
Ayr, Belmont KA7 239 A2
Kirkintilloch G66 58 C1
Larkhall ML9 185 A2
Highfield St KA13 207 C2
Highholm Ave PA14 47 A1
Highholm Prim Sch PA14 47 B1
Highholm St PA14 47 A1
Highland Ave G72 161 B4
Highland Dr FK5 23 B2
Highland Dykes Cres
FK4 40 A3
Highland Dykes Dr FK4 40 A3
Highland La G51 116 B4
Highland Pk G65 36 B1
Highland Pl G65 36 B1
Highland Rd G62 55 A1
Highlanders' Acad Prim Sch
PA15 45 C2
Highlandman's Rd G84 15 C3
Highmill Prim Sch ML8 187 C1
Highstonehall Rd ML3 162 A1
Highthorne Cres KA23 190 C3
Hilary Cres KA7 239 A3
Hilary Dr G69 119 C3
Hilda Cres G33 98 C2
Hill Ave G77 156 B2
Hill Cres G76 157 C3
Hill Dr G76 178 C2
Hill House Rd FK6 39 C4
Hill House The* G84 16 C2
Hill Intc KA11 219 C3
Hill La KA22 205 B1
Hill Pk FK10 10 A4
Hill Pl Alloa FK10 10 A4
Ardrossan KA22 205 B1
Bellshill ML4 141 C2
Motherwell ML1 143 B1
Shotts ML7 146 C3
Hill Rd Cumbernauld G67 61 C1
Harthill ML7 127 B3
Howwood PA9 130 C3
Kilsyth G65 36 B1
Netherburn ML9 199 C3
Stonehouse ML9 198 C1
Hill St Alexandria G83 27 B3
Alloa FK10 10 A4
Ardrossan KA22 205 B1
Caldercruix ML6 104 C3
Chapelhall ML6 123 B1
Dumbarton G82 49 B2
Glasgow G3 240 B4
Greenock PA15 46 A2
Hamilton ML3 161 C2
Irvine KA12 219 B1
Kilmarnock KA3 222 C1
Larkhall ML9 185 A1
Saltcoats KA21 216 C4
Stirling FK7 7 A2
Wishaw ML2 165 A2
Hill Street Ind Est KA22 205 B1
Hill Terr ML1 143 B1
Hill View
East Kilbride G75 180 C4
Milton G82 50 C1
Hill View Rd ML11 214 A2
Hill's Trust Prim Sch
G51 116 A4
Hillary Ave G73 138 B3
Hillary Rd FK5 23 C1
Hillbank Rd KA3 222 C2
Hillbank St G83 27 C2
Hillcrest Carmunnock G76 158 B4
Chryston G69 100 B4
Stewarton KA3 211 C4
Hillcrest Ave
Clydebank G81 74 A4
Coatbridge ML5 122 B3
Cumbernauld G67 82 C4
Glasgow G44 136 C2
Glasgow, Carmyle G32 139 A4
Paisley PA2 133 B3
Wishaw ML2 164 C2
Hillcrest Ct G67 61 C1
Hillcrest Dr Alloa FK10 10 B3
Newton Mearns G77 157 A3
Stevenston KA20 206 C1
Hillcrest Pl Denny FK6 39 B4
Kilwinning KA13 207 C2
Hillcrest Rd Bearsden G61 75 C2
Falkirk FK1 41 C1
Glasgow G32 139 B4
Queenzieburn G65 59 C4
Uddingston G71 141 A4
Hillcrest St G62 55 A1
Hillcrest Terr G71 141 A2
Hillcrest View ML9 185 A2
Hillcroft Terr 6 G64 97 C4
Hillend Cres
Clarkston G76 157 B3
Clydebank G81 73 C4
Hillend Dr PA15 46 B2
Hillend Pl PA15 46 B2
Hillend Rd Clarkston G76 157 B3
Glasgow G22 97 A4
Rutherglen G73 138 A3
Hillfoot Houston PA6 111 C4
Renton G82 27 B1
Hillfoot Ave Bearsden G61 75 C3
Dumbarton G82 50 B2
Rutherglen G73 138 A4
Wishaw ML2 165 B4
Hillfoot Cres Ayr KA7 239 A3
Wishaw ML2 165 B4
Hillfoot Dr Bearsden G61 75 C3
Coatbridge ML5 121 B3

Hillfoot Dr *continued*
Howwood PA9 130 C3
Wishaw ML2 165 B4
Hillfoot Gdns
Uddingston G71 140 C4
Wishaw ML2 165 B4
Hillfoot Rd Airdrie ML6 123 A3
Ayr KA7 239 B3
Hillfoot St G31 118 A4
Hillfoot Sta G61 76 A3
Hillfoot Terr ML8 188 A1
Hillfoots Rd FK9 2 C2
Hillhead Ave
Banknock FK4 38 C2
Carluke ML8 188 A1
Chryston G69 80 C1
Motherwell ML1 143 A1
Rutherglen G73 138 A2
Hillhead Cres
Hamilton ML3 161 C2
Motherwell ML1 143 A1
Hillhead Dr Airdrie ML6 123 A3
Falkirk FK1 41 C1
Motherwell ML1 143 A1
Hillhead High Sch G12 96 C1
Hillhead Pl G73 138 A2
Hillhead Prim Sch
Glasgow G12 96 B2
Kilmarnock KA3 222 C2
Kirkintilloch G66 79 C4
Hillhead Rd Glasgow G21 98 B4
Kirkintilloch G66 58 C1
Stevenston KA20 206 C2
Hillhead Sq KA3 222 C2
Hillhead St Glasgow G12 96 B1
Milngavie G62 55 A1
Hillhead Terr ML3 161 C2
Hillhead Underground Sta
G12 96 B2
Hillhouse Cres ML3 161 C2
Hillhouse Farm Gate
ML11 214 C3
Hillhouse Farm Rd
ML11 214 C2
Hillhouse Gate ML8 202 B4
Hillhouse Gdns KA10 229 C3
Hillhouse Pk Ind Est
ML3 161 C2
Hillhouse Pl KA3 195 B1
Hillhouse Rd
Hamilton ML3 161 C2
Troon KA10 229 C3
Hillhouse St G21 98 A3
Hillhouse Terr ML3 161 C2
Hillhouseridge Rd ML7 146 B3
Hillington East Sta G52 115 A3
Hillington Gdns G52 115 B2
Hillington Ind Est
Glasgow G52 115 A4
Paisley PA3 114 C4
Hillington Park Cir G52 115 B3
Hillington Prim Sch
G52 115 A3
Hillington Quadrant
G52 115 A3
Hillington Rd
Glasgow G52 115 A4
Renfrew G52 94 C1
Hillington Rd S G52 115 A3
Hillington Terr G52 115 A3
Hillington West Sta
G52 114 C4
Hillkirk Pl G21 97 C2
Hillkirk St G21 97 C2
Hillmoss KA3 222 A4
Hillneuk Ave G61 76 A3
Hillneuk Dr G61 76 A3
Hillocks Pl KA10 229 D4
Hillpark KA6 237 C3
Hillpark Ave PA2 113 B1
Hillpark Cres FK7 7 B1
Hillpark Dr
Bannockburn FK7 7 B1
Glasgow G43 136 B3
Kilmarnock KA3 222 C1
Hillpark Rise KA13 207 A2
Hillpark Sec Sch G43 136 B3
Hillrigg ML6 83 B1
Hillrigg Ave ML6 123 B4
Hillsborough Rd G69 119 C3
Hillshaw Foot KA11 220 B1
Hillshaw Gn KA11 220 B1
Hillside Alloa FK10 5 B1
Croy G65 60 C2
Houston PA6 111 C4
West Kilbride KA23 190 B2
Hillside Ave
Alexandria G83 27 B2
Bearsden G61 75 C3
Clarkston G76 157 B4
Kilmacolm PA13 69 B1
Hillside Cotts
Dalry KA24 191 C4
Glenboig ML5 101 C3
Hillside Cres
Coatbridge ML5 121 C2
Hamilton ML3 162 B1
Motherwell ML1 143 B2
Neilston G78 154 B4
Prestwick KA9 236 B4
Hillside Ct Glasgow G46 135 C2
Stevenston KA20 217 B4
Hillside Dr Barrhead G78 134 A2
Bearsden G61 76 A3
Bishopbriggs G64 78 A1
Blackridge EH48 107 B2
Port Glasgow PA14 47 A1
Hillside Gardens La 6
G11 96 A2
Hillside Gr G78 134 A1
Hillside Pk G81 74 A3
Hillside Pl
Blackridge EH48 107 B2
Motherwell ML1 143 B2
Hillside Quadrant G43 136 A3
Hillside Rd Barrhead G78 134 A2
Cardross G82 26 A1
Glasgow G43 136 A3
Gourock PA19 44 B4
Greenock PA15 46 A1
Neilston G78 154 B4
Paisley PA2 114 A1
Hillside St KA20 217 B4
Hillside Terr Alloa FK10 10 A4
Hamilton ML3 162 B1
Milton of C G66 58 A3
Hillswick Cres G22 97 A4
Hilltop Ave ML4 142 A4
Hilltop Cres PA19 44 C3
Hilltop Pl KA7 239 B3
Hilltop Rd Chryston G69 80 C1
Gourock PA19 44 C3
Hillview Banton G65 37 B2
Greengairs ML6 83 C1
Hillview Ave Kilsyth G65 60 B4
Lennoxtown G66 57 C4
Hillview Cotts G65 59 C2
Hillview Cres
Bellshill ML4 142 A4
Larkhall ML9 185 A1
Uddingston G71 140 C4
Hillview Dr Blantyre G72 140 B1
Bridge of A FK9 2 A3
Clarkston G76 157 C4
Helensburgh G84 16 B2
Hillview Gdns G64 98 B4
Hillview Pl Clarkston G76 157 C4
Fallin FK7 8 B2
Newton Mearns G77 156 B2
Hillview Rd
Bridge of W PA11 110 C4
Elderslie PA5 112 B1
High Bonnybridge FK4 40 B2
Stenhousemuir FK5 23 B2
Hillview St G32 118 C3
Hillview Terr FK10 10 B3
Hilton FK7 12 C4
Hilton Cres FK10 10 B4
Hilton Ct Ardrossan KA21 205 C2
Bishopbriggs G64 78 A2
Hilton Gdns G13 95 C4
Hilton Pk G64 77 C2
Hilton Rd Alloa FK10 10 B4
Bishopbriggs G64 78 A2
Milngavie G62 54 C1
Hilton Terr
Bishopbriggs G64 77 C2
Cambuslang G72 138 C2
Fallin FK7 8 B2
Glasgow G13 95 C4
Hiltonbank St ML3 162 A2
Hindog Pl KA24 191 A4
Hindsland Rd ML9 185 A1
Hinshaw St G20 97 A2
Hinshelwood Dr G51 116 A3
Hinshelwood Pl G51 116 A3
Hirsel Pl G71 141 A1
Hirst Cres FK7 8 B2
Hirst Ct FK7 8 B2
Hirst Gdns ML7 146 B3
Hirst Rd ML7 126 B2
Hirstrigg Cotts ML7 126 A2
Hobart Cres G81 73 B3
Hobart Quadrant ML2 165 C2
Hobart Rd G75 180 B4
Hobart St G22 97 A2
Hobden St G21 98 A2
Hoddam Ave G45 138 A2
Hoddam Terr G45 138 A2
Hodge St FK1 42 A2
Hoey Dr ML2 186 B4
Hogan Ct G81 73 C3
Hogan Way ML1 143 C1
Hogarth Ave
Glasgow G32 118 B4
Saltcoats KA21 205 C1
Hogarth Cres G32 118 B4
Hogarth Ct G83 27 C3
Hogarth Dr G32 118 B4
Hogarth Gdns G32 118 B4
Hogg Ave PA5 111 C1
Hogg Rd ML6 123 B2
Hogg St ML6 123 A4
Hogganfield St G33 98 B1
Holbourne Pl FK11 4 A4
Hole Farm Rd PA15,PA16 45 B2
Holeburn La G43 136 B3
Holeburn Rd G43 136 B3
Holehills Dr ML6 103 A1
Holehills Pl ML6 103 A1
Holehouse Brae G78 154 B4
Holehouse Dr
Glasgow G13 95 A3
Kilbirnie KA25 149 A2
Holehouse Rd
Eaglesham G76 178 C3
East Kilbride G74 179 A4
Kilmarnock KA3 228 A4
Holehouse Terr G78 154 B4
Holland St G2 240 B3
Hollandbush Ave FK4 38 C2
Hollandbush Cres FK4 38 C2
Hollandbush Gr ML3 183 B4
Hollandhurst Rd ML5 101 C1
Hollinwell Rd G23 76 B1
Hollow Pk KA7 239 A1
Hollowglen Rd G32 119 A3
Hollows Ave PA2 132 C4
Hollows Cres PA2 132 C4
Hollows The G46 136 A1
Holly Ave Milton of C G66 58 A3
Stenhousemuir FK5 23 C2
Holly Bank KA7 239 B3
Holly Dr Dumbarton G82 49 A3
Glasgow G21 98 A2
Holly Gr Banknock FK4 38 C1
Bellshill ML4 142 C3
Holly Pl Johnstone PA5 132 A4
Kilmarnock KA1 222 B1
Holly St Airdrie ML6 123 B3
Clydebank G81 74 A2
Hollybank Pl G72 139 A2
Hollybank St G21 98 A1
Hollybrook Pl 6 G42 117 A1
Hollybrook Sch G42 117 A1
Hollybrook St G42 117 A1
Hollybush Ave PA2 133 A4
Hollybush Pl KA3 223 A3
Hollybush Rd G52 114 C3
Hollymount G61 75 C1
Hollytree Gdns G66 57 B4
Holm Ave Paisley PA2 113 C1
Uddingston G71 140 C4
Holm Cres KA3 213 A2
Holm Ct ML8 201 A1
Holm Gdns ML4 142 B2
Holm La G74 159 C1
Holm Pl Larkhall ML9 184 C1
Linwood PA3 112 A4
Holm Rd ML8 201 A1
Holm St Carluke ML8 187 C1
Glasgow G2 240 C2
Motherwell ML1 143 A2
Stewarton KA3 211 C4
Holmbank Ave G41 136 B4
Holmbrae Ave G71 140 C4
Holmbrae Rd G71 140 C4
Holmbyne Ct G45 137 A1
Holmbyre Rd G45 137 A1
Holmbyre Terr G45 137 B1
Holmcrest ML8 201 A1
Holmes Ave PA4 94 B1
Holmes Cres KA1 227 B3
Holmes Farm Rd KA1 227 B3
Holmes Park Ave KA1 227 B3
Holmes Park Cres KA1 227 B3
Holmes Park Gdns KA1 227 B3
Holmes Park View KA1 227 B3
Holmes Park Wynd KA1 227 B3
Holmes Quadrant ML4 142 A2
Holmes Rd KA1 227 B3
Holmes Village KA1 227 B3
Holmfauld Rd G51 95 C1
Holmfauldhead Dr G51 115 C4
Holmfauldhead Pl 3
G51 115 C4
Holmfield G66 79 C4
Holmhead KA25 170 A4
Holmhead Cres G44 137 A3
Holmhead Pl G44 137 A3
Holmhead Rd G44 137 A3
Holmhill Ave G72 139 A2
Holmhills Dr G72 138 C2
Holmhills Gdns G72 138 C2
Holmhills Gr G72 138 C2
Holmhills Pl G72 138 C2
Holmhills Rd G72 138 C2
Holmhills Terr G72 138 C2
Holmlands Pl KA1 227 B3
Holmlea Dr KA1 227 C3
Holmlea Pl KA1 227 C3
Holmlea Prim Sch G44 137 A3
Holmlea Rd G42,G44 137 A4
Holmpark PA7 72 A2
Holmquarry Rd KA1 227 C3
Holms Ave KA11 220 B1
Holms Cres PA8 72 C1
Holms Pl G69 100 C4
Holms Rd KA14 170 A3
Holmscroft Ave PA15 45 C2
Holmscroft St PA15 45 C3
Holmscroft Way PA15 45 C2
Holmston Cres KA7 239 B4
Holmston Dr KA7 239 B3
Holmston Prim Sch
KA7 239 A4
Holmston Rd KA7 239 B4
Holmston Rdbt KA7 239 C4
Holmswood Ave G72 140 B1
Holmwood Ave G71 140 C4
Holmwood Gdns G71 140 C3
Holmwood Ho★ G44 137 A2
Holton Cres FK10 5 B1
Holton Sq FK10 5 B1
Holy Cross High Sch
ML3 162 C2
Holy Cross Prim RC Sch
G42 117 A1
Holy Cross Prim Sch G65 60 C2
Holy Cross RC Prim Sch
PA16 45 A3
Holy Family Prim Sch
Kirkintilloch G66 79 A3
Port Glasgow PA14 69 A4
Holy Family RC Prim Sch
ML4 142 B3
Holy Trinity Episcopal Prim
Sch FK8 7 A4
Holy Trinity Prim Sch FK8 7 A4
Holyknowe Cres G66 57 C4
Holyknowe Rd G66 57 C4
Holyoake Ct KA1 228 C4
Holyrood Cres G20 96 C1
Holyrood Pl FK5 23 C2
Holyrood Quadrant 9
G20 96 C1
Holyrood Sec RC Sch
G42 117 B1
Holyrood St ML3 162 A3
Holytown Prim Sch
ML1 143 A3
Holytown Rd ML1,ML4 142 C3
Holytown Sta ML1 143 A2
Holywell St G31 118 A3
Home Farm Cotts FK6 39 C3
Home Farm Rd Ayr KA7 239 A1
Hartwood ML7 145 C2
Home St ML11 215 B2
Homeglen Ho G46 136 B1
Homer Pl ML4 142 C3
Homesteads The FK8 6 B4
Homeston Ave G71 141 A2
Honeybank Cres ML8 188 A2
Honeybog Rd G52 114 C3
Honeycomb Pl ML9 200 B2
Honeyman Cres ML11 215 B2
Honeysuckle La G83 27 C4
Honeysuckle Pk KA7 239 A1
Honeywell Cres ML6 123 C1
Hood Ct G84 16 A1
Hood St Clydebank G81 74 B1
Greenock PA15 45 C3
Hookney Terr FK6 21 B1
Hooper Pl ML4 142 A3
Hope Ave PA11 89 C1
Hope Cres ML9 185 A2
Hope St Ayr KA7 238 C4
Bellshill ML4 142 B3
Carluke ML8 188 A1
Falkirk FK1 42 A3
Glasgow G2 240 C3
Greenock PA15 45 C2
Hamilton ML3 162 C2
Helensburgh G84 25 A4
Lanark ML11 215 A2
Motherwell ML1 163 C4
Stirling FK8 1 C1
Wishaw ML2 166 A2
Hopefield Ave G12 96 B3
Hopehill Gdns G20 97 A2
Hopehill Rd G20 97 A2
Hopeman PA8 73 A2
Hopeman Ave G46 135 C2
Hopeman Dr G46 135 C2
Hopeman Path G46 135 C3
Hopeman Rd G46 135 C2
Hopeman St G46 135 C2
Hopepark Terr FK4 39 C3
Hopeton St PA19 44 C4
Hopetoun Bank KA11 220 B1
Hopetoun Dr FK9 2 A4
Hopetoun Pl G23 76 C1
Hopetoun Terr G21 98 A2
Hopkin's Brae 7 G66 58 B1
Horatius St ML1 142 A1
Hornal Rd G71 140 C2
Hornbeam Dr G81 74 A2
Hornbeam Rd
Cumbernauld G67 62 C3
Uddingston G71 141 A4
Horndean Ct G64 78 A2
Horne St G22 97 C3
Hornock Rd ML5 101 C1
Hornshill Dr ML1 144 A1
Hornshill Farm Rd G33 99 C3
Hornshill St G21 98 A2
Horsbrugh Ave G65 36 B1
Horsburgh St G33 99 B1
Horse Isle View KA22 205 A2
Horse Shoe KA23 190 B3
Horse Shoe Rd G61 75 C2
Horsewood Rd PA11 110 B4
Horslet St ML5 121 B2
Horslethill Rd G12 96 B2
Horsley Brae ML2 186 A2
Horton Pl G84 17 A2
Hospital Rd Wishaw ML2 186 A4
Wishaw ML2 165 B1
Hospital St ML5 122 A2
Hospitland Dr ML11 215 B2
Hotspur St G20 96 C2
Houldsworth Cres ML7 167 A4
Houldsworth La 7 G3 116 C4
Houldsworth St G3 240 A3
House O' Muir Rd ML7 126 A2
Househillmuir Cres G53 135 B4
Househillmuir La G53 135 B4
Househillmuir Pl G53 135 B4
Househillmuir Rd G53 135 A3
Househillmuir Sch G53 135 A3
Househillwood Cres
G53 135 A4
Househillwood Rd G53 135 A3
Housel Ave G13 95 A4
Houston Cres KA24 191 A4
Houston Ct
Kilbirnie KA25 149 A1
Renfrew PA4 94 B2
Houston Pl Elderslie PA5 112 B1
Glasgow G5 116 C3
Houston Prim Sch PA6 91 A1
Houston Rd
Bridge of W PA11 90 B1
Houston PA6 91 A1
Inchinnan PA3,PA4,PA6 92 B2
Kilmacolm PA13 89 C4
Houston St Glasgow G5 116 C3
Greenock PA16 45 C3
Hamilton ML3 162 B1
Renfrew PA4 94 B2
Wishaw ML2 165 B1
Houston Terr G74 159 B1
Houstonfield Quadrant
PA6 91 A1
Houstonfield Rd PA6 91 A1
Houstoun Ct PA5 111 C2
Houstoun Sq PA5 111 C2
Howacre ML11 214 C3
Howard Ave G74 160 A3
Howard Ct
East Kilbride G74 160 A3
Kilmarnock KA1 227 C4
Howard Park Dr KA1 227 C4
Howard St Falkirk FK1 41 C2
Glasgow G1 241 A1
Kilmarnock KA1 227 C4
Larkhall ML9 185 B1
Paisley PA1 114 A2
Howat Cres KA12 219 C2
Howat St G51 116 A4
Howatshaws Rd G82 50 A3
Howburn Cres ML7 127 C3
Howburn Rd ML7 127 B3
Howden Ave
Kilwinning KA13 207 C2
Motherwell ML1 143 B4
Howden Dr PA3 112 A3
Howden Pl ML1 143 A3
Howe Gdns G71 141 A4
Howe Rd G65 60 B4
Howe St PA1 112 C2
Howes St ML5 122 A2
Howetown FK10 5 B2
Howford Rd G52 115 A2
Howford Sch G53 115 A1
Howgate KA13 207 B2
Howgate Ave G15 74 C2
Howgate Rd ML3 183 B4
Howgate Sh Ctr 7 FK1 42 A2
Howie Bldgs G76 157 C4
Howie Cres G84 15 A2
Howie St ML9 185 A1
Howie's Pl FK1 41 A2
Howieshill Ave G72 139 A3
Howieshill Rd G72 139 A3
Howlands Rd FK7 7 A2
Howlet Pl ML3 162 C1
Howletnest Rd ML6 123 B3
Howson Lea ML1 164 A2
Howson View ML1 163 A4
Howth Dr G13 95 C4
Howth Terr G13 95 C4
Howwood Prim Sch
PA9 131 A3
Howwood Sta PA9 130 C3
Hoylake Pk G72 140 C1
Hoylake Pl G23 76 C1
Hoylake Sq KA13 207 B2
Hozier Cres G71 140 C4
Hozier Loan 8 ML9 185 A2
Hozier Pl 16 G71 141 A2
Hozier St Carluke ML8 187 C1
Coatbridge ML5 122 A2
Hudson Pl KA9 233 B1
Hudson Terr G75 180 B4
Hudson Way G75 180 B4
Hudspeth Ct G83 27 B4
Hugh Watt Pl KA3 222 A4
Hughenden Ct G12 96 A2
Hughenden Dr G12 96 A2
Hughenden Gdns G12 96 A2
Hughenden La G12 96 A2
Hughenden Rd G12 96 A2
Hugo St G20 96 C3
Hulks Rd G67,ML6 83 B2
Humbie Ct G77 156 C1
Humbie Gate G77 156 C1
Humbie Gr G77 156 C2
Humbie Lawns G77 156 C1
Humbie Rd
Eaglesham G76 178 B4
Newton Mearns G77 156 C1
Hume Cres FK9 2 A3
Hume Ct FK9 2 A3
Hume Dr Bothwell G71 141 A2
Uddingston G71 140 C4
Hume Pl G75 180 B4
Hume Rd G67 62 A2
Hume St G81 74 A1
Hunt Hill G68 60 B1
Hunt Hill Rdbt G68 60 B1
Hunter Ave KA22 205 B1
Hunter Cres KA10 230 A1
Hunter Dr Irvine KA12 219 A3
Newton Mearns G77 156 A2
Hunter Gdns
Bonnybridge FK4 40 A3
Denny FK6 21 B1
Hunter High Sch G74 160 B1
Hunter House Mus★
G74 160 B2
Hunter Pl
Kilbarchan PA10 111 A1
Kilwinning KA13 208 A2
Milngavie G62 54 C1
Shotts ML7 146 C3
Stenhousemuir FK2 24 A2
Hunter Prim Sch G74 160 B1
Hunter Rd
Crosshouse KA2 221 C1
Hamilton ML3 162 A3
Milngavie G62 54 C1
Rutherglen G73 118 B1
Hunter St Airdrie ML6 103 A1
Bellshill ML4 142 A3
East Kilbride G74 159 C1

John McEwan Way G64 78 A4
John Murray Ct ML1 163 C2
John Murray Dr FK9 2 A4
John Ogilvie High Sch ML3 161 C2
John Paul Acad G23 76 B1
John Rushforth Pl FK8 1 C1
John Smith Ct ML6 122 C4
John Smith Gate G78 134 B2
John Smith Gdns ML5 122 B3
John Smith Way ML7 146 B3
John St Ayr KA8 239 A4
Barrhead G78 134 A2
Bellshill ML4 142 A3
Blantyre G72 161 C4
Carluke ML8 187 C1
Falkirk FK2 42 A4
Glasgow G1 241 A2
Gourock PA19 44 C4
Greenock PA15 46 A2
Haggs FK4 39 A2
Hamilton ML3 162 C2
Helensburgh G84 16 B1
Kirkintilloch G66 58 B1
Larkhall ML9 185 A1
Renton G82 49 B4
Wishaw ML2 164 B2
John Street La G84 16 B1
John Wheatley Coll G32 119 A3
John Wheatley Coll (Easterhouse Campus) G34 120 A4
John Wilson Dr G65 36 A1
John Wilson St PA15 46 B1
John Wood St PA14 47 B1
John Wright Sports Ctr The G74 160 A1
Johnsburn Dr G53 135 A3
Johnsburn Rd G53 135 A3
Johnshaven PA8 73 A1
Johnshaven St G43 136 B4
Johnshill PA12 129 B2
Johnson Ct G84 16 C1
Johnson Dr G72 139 A3
Johnston Ave
Clydebank G81 94 B4
Kilsyth G65 60 B4
Stenhousemuir FK5 23 C2
Stirling FK9 2 A2
Johnston Dr KA10 229 C3
Johnston Pl FK6 21 B1
Johnston Rd G69 101 A3
Johnston St Airdrie ML6 123 A4
Bannockburn FK7 7 B1
Greenock PA16 45 B4
Paisley PA1 113 C2
Johnston Terr PA16 45 B4
Johnstone Ave G52 115 A4
Johnstone Ct FK12 5 A3
Johnstone Dr
Lochwinnoch PA12 129 B1
Rutherglen G73 138 A4
Johnstone High Sch PA5 131 B4
Johnstone Hospl PA5 111 C2
Johnstone La ML8 188 A1
Johnstone Rd ML3 162 C1
Johnstone St Alva FK12 5 A3
Bellshill ML4 142 B3
Menstrie FK11 3 C3
Johnstone Sta PA5 112 A1
Johnstone Terr G65 59 C1
Joiners La KA3 195 A4
Jones Ave FK5 41 B4
Jones Wynd ML1 143 C1
Jonquil Way ML8 201 C4
Joppa St G33 118 C4
Jordan St G14 95 B1
Jordanhill Cres G13 95 B3
Jordanhill Dr G13 95 B3
Jordanhill La G13 95 C3
Jordanhill Sch G13 95 B3
Jordanhill Sta G11 95 C2
Jordanvale Ave G14 95 B1
Jowitt Ave G81 74 B1
Jubilee Bank G66 79 B2
Jubilee Ct G52 114 C4
Jubilee Dr KA3 195 C1
Jubilee Gdns G61 75 C2
Jubilee Pl KA3 195 C1
Jubilee Rd FK6 21 C2
Jubilee Terr PA5 111 B1
Julian Ave G12 96 B2
Julian La G12 96 B2
Juniper Ave G75 180 B3
Juniper Ct G66 79 A3
Juniper Dr G66 58 A2
Juniper Gn KA7 239 B3
Juniper Gr ML3 162 C1
Juniper Pl Glasgow G32 119 C2
Johnstone PA5 132 A4
Uddingston G71 141 B4
Juniper Rd G71 141 B4
Juniper Terr G32 119 C2
Juniper Wynd ML1 143 A3
Juno La PA16 44 B2
Juno St ML1 142 B1
Juno Terr PA16 44 B2
Jupiter La PA16 44 B2
Jupiter Pl G84 15 B3
Jupiter St ML1 142 B1
Jupiter Terr PA16 44 B2
Jura G74 181 A4
Jura Ave PA4 94 B1
Jura Ct Glasgow G52 115 C3
Irvine KA11 225 B4
Jura Dr Blantyre G72 140 B2
Jura Dr *continued*
Kirkintilloch G66 80 A4
Newton Mearns G77 156 A3
Old Kilpatrick G60 73 B3
Jura Gdns Carluke ML8 202 A4
Hamilton ML3 162 A1
Larkhall ML9 185 B2
Old Kilpatrick G60 73 B3
Jura Pl Old Kilpatrick G60 73 B3
Troon KA10 229 D4
Jura Quadrant ML2 164 C1
Jura Rd Old Kilpatrick G60 73 B3
Paisley PA2 133 B4
Jura St Glasgow G52 115 C3
Greenock PA16 45 B2
Jura Wynd ML5 101 B3
Jutland Ct G84 16 A2

K

Kaim Dr G53 135 B3
Kairnhill Ct ML11 214 C2
Kames Ct KA11 220 A3
Kames Rd ML7 146 C3
Kane Pl ML9 198 C1
Kane St G82 27 B1
Karadale Gdns ML9 185 A2
Karol Path G4 97 A1
Karries Ct FK6 39 B4
Katewell Ave G15 74 C2
Katewell Pl G15 74 C2
Katherine Pl G82 27 C1
Katherine St ML6 123 C4
Kathleen Pk G84 16 A2
Katrine Ave
Bishopbriggs G64 78 A1
Uddingston ML4 141 B3
Katrine Cres ML6 102 C1
Katrine Ct Alloa FK10 10 B3
Kilmarnock KA1 228 A3
Katrine Dr
Newton Mearns G77 157 A2
Paisley PA2 113 A1
Katrine Pl
Cambuslang G72 139 A3
Coatbridge ML5 101 B1
Denny FK6 39 B3
Irvine KA12 219 B3
Katrine Rd Greenock PA15 46 A2
Shotts ML7 146 C3
Katrine Way 6 G71 141 A2
Katrine Wynd ML1 143 A3
Katriona Path 21 ML9 185 B1
Kay Gdns ML1 163 A3
Kay Park Cres KA3 223 A1
Kay Park Gr KA3 223 A1
Kay Park Terr KA3 223 A1
Kay St G21 97 C2
Kaystone Rd G15 75 A1
Keal Ave G15 95 A4
Keal Cres G15 95 A4
Keal Dr G15 95 A4
Keal Pl G15 95 A4
Keane Path ML1 164 A2
Kearn Ave G15 75 A1
Kearn Pl G15 75 A1
Keats Pk G71 141 A2
Keil Cres G82 49 B2
Keil Sch G82 49 B2
Keilarsbrae FK10 5 B1
Keir Ave FK8 2 A1
Keir Cres ML2 165 A2
Keir Dr G64 77 C1
Keir Gdns FK9 2 A4
Keir Hardie Ave
Laurieston FK2 42 C2
Motherwell ML1 143 A3
Keir Hardie Cres KA13 208 A2
Keir Hardie Ct G64 78 A1
Keir Hardie Dr
Ardrossan KA22 205 A2
Bellshill ML4 141 C2
Kilbirnie KA25 149 A1
13 Kilsyth G65 60 B4
Keir Hardie Meml Prim Sch ML1 143 B2
Keir Hardie Pl
Bellshill ML4 141 C2
Saltcoats KA21 206 A1
Keir Hardie Rd Alva FK12 5 B4
Larkhall ML9 185 B1
Stevenston KA20 206 C1
Keir Hardie St PA15 46 C1
Keir St Bridge of A FK9 2 A4
Glasgow G41 116 C2
Keir's Wlk G72 139 A3
Keith Ave Glasgow G46 136 B2
Stirling FK7 7 B2
Keith Ct G11 96 B1
Keith Pl KA3 223 B1
Keith Quadrant ML2 165 A3
Keith St Bellshill ML4 142 A3
Glasgow G11 96 B1
Hamilton ML3 162 C2
Kelbourne Cres ML4 141 C3
Kelbourne Sch G20 96 C2
Kelbourne St G20 96 C2
Kelburn Cres KA1 227 C2
Kelburn St G78 134 A1
Kelburn Terr PA14 48 A1
Kelburne KA13 207 B1
Kelburne Dr PA1 114 A3
Kelburne Gdns
Glasgow G69 120 A2
Paisley PA1 114 A3
Kelburne Oval PA1 114 A3
Kelhead Ave G52 114 C3
Kelhead Dr G52 114 C3
Kelhead Path G52 114 C3
Kelhead Pl G52 114 C3
Kellas St G51 116 A4
Kellie Gr G74 159 B2
Kellie Pl FK10 10 A4
Kelliebank FK10 9 C3
Kells Pl G15 74 C2
Kelly Ct FK8 7 A4
Kelly Dr FK6 21 C2
Kelly St PA16 45 B3
Kelly's La ML8 188 A1
Kelso Ave
Bridge of W PA11 110 B4
Paisley PA2 113 A1
Rutherglen G73 138 A4
Kelso Cres ML2 165 A3
Kelso Dr Carluke ML8 188 B1
East Kilbride G74 160 A2
Kelso Gdns G69 80 C2
Kelso Pl Glasgow G14 94 C3
Renton G82 27 C1
Kelso Quadrant ML5 121 C4
Kelso St G13 94 C4
Kelt Rd FK4 38 C2
Kelton St G32 119 A2
Kelvin Ave Glasgow G52 115 A4
Kilwinning KA13 207 C1
Paisley G52 114 C4
Kelvin Cres G61 75 C1
Kelvin Ct Glasgow G12 96 A3
2 Kirkintilloch G66 58 B1
Kelvin Dr Airdrie ML6 103 A1
Barrhead G78 134 B1
Bishopbriggs G64 78 A1
Chryston G69 80 C1
East Kilbride G75 180 C4
Glasgow G20 96 B2
Kirkintilloch G66 79 A4
Shotts ML7 147 A2
Kelvin Gdns
Hamilton ML3 161 C2
Kilsyth G65 60 B4
Kelvin Hall Transport Mus* G3 96 B1
Kelvin Park S G75 181 A2
Kelvin Pl G75 181 A4
Kelvin Rd Bellshill ML4 142 A4
Cumbernauld G67 83 A4
East Kilbride G75 181 A4
Milngavie G62 54 C2
Uddingston G71 140 C4
Kelvin Rd N G67 83 A4
Kelvin Sch G3 96 B1
Kelvin South Bsns Pk G75 180 C2
Kelvin St ML5 122 B3
Kelvin Terr G65 59 C2
Kelvin View Torrance G64 78 B4
Twechar G65 59 C2
Kelvin Way
1 Bothwell G71 141 A2
Glasgow G3,G12 96 C1
Kilsyth G65 36 B1
Kirkintilloch G66 79 A4
Kelvinbridge Rdbt G64 78 A4
Kelvinbridge Underground Sta G4 96 C1
Kelvindale G64 57 B1
Kelvindale Gdns G20 96 B3
Kelvindale Pl 11 G20 96 B3
Kelvindale Prim Sch G12 96 A3
Kelvindale Rd G12 96 B3
Kelvingrove Mus & Art Gall* G3 96 B1
Kelvingrove St G3 116 C4
Kelvinhall Underground Sta G11 96 B1
Kelvinhaugh Gate G3 116 B4
Kelvinhaugh Pl G3 116 B4
Kelvinhaugh Prim Sch G3 116 B4
Kelvinhaugh St G3 116 B4
Kelvinhead Rd G65 37 C1
Kelvinside Acad G12 96 B2
Kelvinside Ave G20 96 C2
Kelvinside Cres G65 37 C2
Kelvinside Dr G20 96 C2
Kelvinside Gardens La 7 G20 96 C2
Kelvinside Gdns G20 96 C2
Kelvinside Gdns E G20 96 C2
Kelvinside Terr S 9 G20 96 C2
Kelvinside Terr W 8 G20 96 C2
Kelvinvale G66 58 B1
Kelvinview Ave FK4 38 C1
Kemp Ave PA3 94 A1
Kemp Ct Ardrossan KA21 205 C2
Hamilton ML3 162 C2
Kemp St 8 Glasgow G21 97 C2
Hamilton ML3 162 C2
Kemper Ave FK1 42 B2
Kempock Pl PA19 44 C4
Kempock St
Glasgow G40 118 B2
Gourock PA19 44 C4
Kempsthorn Cres G53 115 A1
Kempsthorn Rd G53 115 A1
Ken Rd KA1 228 A3
Kenbank Cres PA11 110 B4
Kenbank Rd PA11 110 B4
Kendal Ave Glasgow G12 96 A3
Glasgow, Giffnock G46 136 B2
Kendal Dr G12 96 A3
Kendal Rd G75 179 C3
Kendoon Ave G15 74 C2
Kenilburn Ave ML6 103 A1
Kenilburn Cres ML6 103 A1
Kenilworth G74 160 C2
Kenilworth Ave
Glasgow G41 136 B4
Helensburgh G84 25 B4
Paisley PA2 132 C4
Wishaw ML2 165 A2
Kenilworth Cres
Bearsden G61 75 B3
Bellshill ML4 142 A3
Greenock PA16 45 B2
Hamilton ML3 161 C2
Kenilworth Ct
Bridge of A FK9 2 A4
Carluke ML8 187 C1
Cumbernauld G67 82 C4
Motherwell ML1 143 A3
Kenilworth Dr
Airdrie ML6 123 B4
Laurieston FK2 42 C2
Saltcoats KA21 206 A1
Kenilworth Rd
Bridge of A FK9 2 A4
Kirkintilloch G66 79 C4
Lanark ML11 215 A2
Kenilworth Way PA2 112 C1
Kenmar Gdns G71 140 C4
Kenmar Rd ML3 162 A3
Kenmar Terr ML3 162 A3
Kenmore KA10 229 C2
Kenmore Ave KA9 236 B3
Kenmore Dr PA16 45 A2
Kenmore Gdns G61 76 A3
Kenmore Pl
Greenock PA16 45 A2
Troon KA10 229 C2
Kenmore Rd
Cumbernauld G67 62 A1
Kilmacolm PA13 89 B4
Kenmore St G32 119 A3
Kenmore Way
Carluke ML8 187 C2
Coatbridge ML5 122 B2
Kenmuir Ave G32 119 C2
Kenmuir Rd G32 139 B4
Kenmuir St
Coatbridge ML5 121 B2
Falkirk FK1 41 A3
Kenmuiraid Pl ML4 141 C2
Kenmuirhill Gate G32 119 B1
Kenmuirhill Gdns G32 119 B1
Kenmuirhill Rd G32 119 B1
Kenmure Ave G64 77 C1
Kenmure Cres G64 77 C1
Kenmure Dr G64 77 C1
Kenmure Gdns G64 77 C1
Kenmure La G64 77 C1
Kenmure Pl FK5 23 C2
Kenmure Rd G46 157 A3
Kenmure St G41 116 C2
Kenmure View PA9 130 C3
Kenmure Way G73 138 A2
Kennard St FK2 42 B3
Kennedar Dr G51 115 C4
Kennedy Ave G65 60 A2
Kennedy Ct Glasgow G46 136 B2
Kilmarnock KA3 223 B2
Kennedy Dr Airdrie ML6 122 C4
Helensburgh G84 16 B2
Kilmarnock KA3 223 B2
Kennedy Gdns ML2 186 A4
Kennedy Path G4 241 B3
Kennedy Rd
Saltcoats KA21 205 C1
Troon KA10 229 B1
Kennedy St Glasgow G4 241 B3
Kilmarnock KA1 227 C3
Wishaw ML2 165 B2
Kennedy Way FK2 14 C2
Kennedy's La PA15 46 A2
Kennelburn Rd ML6 123 B1
Kenneth Rd ML1 163 B3
Kennihill ML6 103 A1
Kennihill Quadrant ML6 103 A1
Kenningknowes Rd FK7 6 C3
Kennishead Ave G46 135 C3
Kennishead Path G46 135 C3
Kennishead Pl G46 135 C3
Kennishead Rd G53 135 B3
Kennishead Sta G46 135 C3
Kennisholm Ave G46 135 C3
Kennisholm Path G46 135 C3
Kennisholm Pl G46 135 C3
Kennoway Dr G11 95 C1
Kennyhill Sch G31 118 B4
Kennyhill Sq G31 118 A4
Kenshaw Ave ML9 199 A4
Kenshaw Pl ML9 199 A4
Kensington Dr G46 136 B1
Kensington Gate 21 G12 96 B2
Kensington Gate La 22 G12 96 B2
Kensington Rd G12 96 B2
Kent Ct G84 17 A2
Kent Dr Helensburgh G84 17 A2
Rutherglen G73 138 B3
Kent Pl G75 179 C3
Kent Rd Alloa FK10 9 C4
Glasgow G3 240 A3
Stirling FK7 7 A3
Kent St G40 241 C1
Kentallen Rd G33 119 C3
Kentigern Terr G64 98 A4
Kentmere Cl G75 180 A3
Kentmere Dr G75 180 A3
Kentmere Pl G75 180 A3
Keppel Dr G44 137 C3
Keppoch St G21 97 B2
Keppochhill Dr G21 97 B2
Keppochhill Pl G21 97 B1
Keppochhill Rd G21 97 B2
Keppochhill Way G21 97 B1
Keppock Pl FK1 41 C1
Ker Rd G62 54 C2
Ker St PA15 45 C3
Kerelaw Ave KA20 206 C1
Kerelaw Rd KA20 206 B1
Kerelaw Sch KA20 206 B1
Kerfield Pl G15 74 C2
Kerr Ave KA21 217 A4
Kerr Cres Haggs FK4 39 A2
Hamilton ML3 162 B1
Kerr Dr Glasgow G40 117 C3
Irvine KA12 219 B1
Motherwell ML1 163 B3
Kerr Gdns G71 141 A4
Kerr Grieve Ct 8 ML1 163 C3
Kerr Pl Denny FK6 21 B1
Glasgow G40 117 C3
Irvine KA12 219 B1
Kerr Rd KA3 223 B1
Kerr St Barrhead G78 134 A1
Blantyre G72 161 C4
Glasgow G40 117 C3
Kirkintilloch G66 79 B4
Paisley PA3 113 B3
Kerrera Pl G33 119 B3
Kerrera Rd G33 119 B3
Kerrix Rd KA1 231 A1
Kerrmuir Ave KA1 228 C3
Kerrs La KA21 216 C4
Kerry Pl G15 74 C2
Kerrycroy Ave G42 137 B4
Kerrycroy Pl G42 137 B4
Kerrycroy St G42 137 B4
Kerrydale St G40 118 A2
Kerrylamont Ave G42 137 C4
Kerse Ave KA24 191 C4
Kerse Gdns FK2 42 C3
Kerse Gn Rd FK10 10 C3
Kerse La FK1 42 B3
Kerse Pl FK1 42 B3
Kerse Rd FK7 7 B3
Kersebonny Rd FK8 6 B4
Kersehill Cres FK2 42 B4
Kersepark KA7 239 A1
Kershaw St ML2 186 B4
Kersie Rd FK7 9 A2
Kersie Terr FK7 9 C2
Kersland Cres KA1 228 C3
Kersland Dr G62 55 A1
Kersland Foot KA11 219 C3
Kersland Gait KA3 211 C4
Kersland La
1 Glasgow G12 96 B2
Milngavie G62 55 A1
Kersland Rd KA14 170 B3
Kersland Sch PA2 114 B1
Kersland St G12 96 B2
Kerswinning Ave KA25 170 A4
Kessington Dr G61 76 A2
Kessington Rd G61 76 A2
Kessington Sq G61 76 A2
Kessock Dr G22 97 A2
Kessock Pl G22 97 A2
Kestrel Cres PA16 45 A3
Kestrel Ct G81 74 A3
Kestrel Pl Greenock PA16 45 A3
Johnstone PA5 131 B4
Kestrel Rd G13 95 B3
Kestrel View
Bellshill ML4 141 C4
Coatbridge ML4 121 C1
Keswick Dr ML3 183 B3
Keswick Rd G75 179 C3
Kethers La ML1 163 B4
Kethers St ML1 163 B3
Keverkae FK10 9 C3
Kevoc Cotts KA6 237 A3
Kew Gdns G71 141 A4
Kew La G12 96 B2
Kew Terr G12 96 B2
Keynes Sq ML4 142 B2
Keystone Ave G62 76 A4
Keystone Quadrant G62 76 A4
Keystone Rd G62 76 A4
Kibble Sch The PA3 113 B4
Kibbleston Rd PA10 130 C4
Kidsneuk KA12 219 A3
Kidsneuk Gdns KA12 219 A3
Kidston Dr G84 16 A1
Kidston Pl 5 G5 117 B2
Kidston Terr 4 G5 117 B2
Kier Ct FK9 2 A4
Kier Hardie Ct KA15 171 A4
Kierhill Rd G68 61 B1
Kilallan Ave PA11 90 B1
Kilallan Rd PA6 90 B3
Kilbarchan Prim Sch PA10 111 A2
Kilbarchan Rd
Bridge of W PA11 110 C3
Johnstone PA5,PA10 111 B1
Kilbarchan St 2 G5 117 A3
Kilbean Dr FK1 41 C1
Kilbeg Terr G46 135 B2
Kilberry St G21 98 A1
Kilbirnie Pl G5 117 A2
Kilbirnie St G5 117 A2
Kilbirnie Terr FK6 21 B2
Kilblain St PA15 45 C3
Kilbowie Pl ML6 123 B3
Kilbowie Prim Sch G81 74 A2

272 Kil – Kir

Kilbowie Rd
Clydebank G81 74 A2
Cumbernauld G67 62 A1
Kilbrandon Cres KA7 238 A1
Kilbrandon Way KA7 238 A1
Kilbrannan Ave KA21 205 C1
Kilbrannan Dr PA16 45 A2
Kilbreck Gdns G61 75 B4
Kilbreck La ML1 143 B2
Kilbrennan Dr Falkirk FK1 41 A2
Motherwell ML1 163 A4
Kilbrennan Rd PA3 112 A3
Kilbride Dr G84 16 C2
Kilbride Rd KA3 195 B1
Kilbride St G5 117 B1
Kilbride View G71 141 A4
Kilburn Gr G72 140 B1
Kilburn Pl G13 95 A3
Kilchattan Dr G44 137 B4
Kilchoan Rd G33 99 B1
Kilcloy Ave G15 75 A2
Kilcreggan View PA15 46 B1
Kildale Rd PA12 129 A1
Kildale Way G73 137 C4
Kildare Dr ML11 215 A2
Kildare Pl ML11 215 A2
Kildare Rd ML11 215 A2
Kildary Ave G44 137 A3
Kildary Rd G44 137 A3
Kildean Hospl FK8 1 C1
Kildean Sch FK8 1 C1
Kildermorie Rd G34 120 A4
Kildonan Ct ML2 165 C4
Kildonan Dr Glasgow G11 96 A1
Helensburgh G84 16 C1
Kildonan Ho KA9 236 A3
Kildonan Pl
Motherwell ML1 163 B4
Saltcoats KA21 205 C1
Kildonan St ML5 122 A4
Kildrostan St G41 116 C1
Kildrum Prim Sch G67 62 B2
Kildrum Rd G67 62 B2
Kildrum South Rdbt G67 62 A1
Kildrummy Ave FK5 23 C2
Kildrummy Pl G74 159 B2
Kilearn Rd PA3 114 A4
Kilearn Sq PA3 114 A4
Kilearn Way PA3 114 A4
Kilfinan Rd ML7 146 B3
Kilfinan St G22 97 A4
Kilgarth St ML5 121 B2
Kilgraston Rd PA11 110 B3
Kilkerran KA13 207 A2
Kilkerran Ct G77 156 A2
Kilkerran Dr Glasgow G33 98 C3
Troon KA10 229 C4
Kilkerran Pk G77 156 A2
Kilkerran Way G77 156 A2
Killearn Dr PA1 114 C2
Killearn Rd PA15 46 A1
Killearn St G22 97 B2
Killermont Ave G61 76 A1
Killermont Ct G61 76 A2
Killermont Mdws G72 140 C1
Killermont Pl KA13 207 A2
Killermont Prim Sch G61 76 A2
Killermont Rd G61 76 A1
Killermont St G1 241 A3
Killermont View G20 76 A1
Killiegrew Rd G41 116 B1
Killin Ct ML5 122 A2
Killin Dr PA3 111 C3
Killin Pl Greenock PA16 45 A2
Troon KA10 229 D2
Killin St G32 119 A2
Killoch Ave PA3 113 A3
Killoch Dr Barrhead G78 134 B1
Glasgow G13 95 A3
Killoch La PA3 113 A3
Killoch Pl Ayr KA7 238 C4
Irvine KA11 219 C2
Killoch Rd PA3 113 A3
Killoch Way Irvine KA11 219 C2
Paisley PA3 113 A3
Killochend Dr PA15 45 C2
Kilmacolm Pl PA15 46 B1
Kilmacolm Prim Sch PA13 89 B4
Kilmacolm Rd
Bridge of W PA11 90 A1
Greenock PA15 46 A1
Houston PA6 91 A2
Port Glasgow PA14 69 A3
Kilmahew Ave G82 26 A1
Kilmahew Ct
Ardrossan KA22 205 B1
Cardross G82 26 A1
Kilmahew Dr G82 26 A1
Kilmahew Gr G82 26 A1
Kilmahew St KA22 205 B1
Kilmailing Rd G44 137 A3
Kilmair Pl G20 96 B3
Kilmaluag Terr G46 135 B2
Kilmannan Gdns G62 54 C2
Kilmany Dr G32 118 C3
Kilmany Gdns G32 118 C3
Kilmardinny Ave G61 75 C3
Kilmardinny Cres G61 76 A3
Kilmardinny Dr G61 75 C3
Kilmardinny Gate G61 75 C3
Kilmardinny Gr G61 75 C3
Kilmari Gdns G15 74 C2
Kilmarnock Acad KA1 228 A4
Kilmarnock Coll KA3 228 A4
Kilmarnock Coll (Irvine Campus) KA12 219 B2
Kilmarnock Rd
Crosshouse KA2 222 A1
Dundonald KA2 225 C1
Glasgow G43 136 B4
Kilmaurs KA3 222 B3
Monkton KA9 233 C3
Springside KA11 221 A1
Symington KA1 231 B2
Troon KA10 229 D3
Kilmarnock Sta KA1 222 C1
Kilmartin La ML8 187 C2
Kilmartin Pl Airdrie ML6 123 B3
Glasgow G46 135 C2
Uddingston G71 121 A1
Kilmaurs Dr G46 136 C2
Kilmaurs Prim Sch KA3 222 A4
Kilmaurs Rd
Crosshouse KA2 221 C1
Fenwick KA3 212 C1
Kilmarnock KA3 222 C2
Kilmaurs St G51 115 C3
Kilmaurs Sta KA3 222 A4
Kilmeny Cres ML2 165 B3
Kilmeny Ct KA22 205 B1
Kilmeny Terr KA22 205 B1
Kilmichael Ave ML2 166 A3
Kilmore Cres G15 74 C2
Kilmorie Dr G73 137 C4
Kilmory Ave G71 141 A4
Kilmory Ct
East Kilbride G75 180 B2
Falkirk FK1 41 B2
Kilmory Dr G77 156 C3
Kilmory Gdns ML8 188 A2
Kilmory Pl
Kilmarnock KA3 222 C2
Troon KA10 229 D3
Kilmory Rd Carluke ML8 202 A4
Saltcoats KA21 205 C1
Kilmory Terr PA14 47 B1
Kilmory Wlk KA3 195 B1
Kilmuir Cres G46 135 B2
Kilmuir Dr G46 135 C2
Kilmuir Rd Glasgow G46 135 C2
Uddingston G71 120 C1
Kilmun Rd PA15 46 A2
Kilmun St G20 96 B4
Kiln Ct KA12 219 B1
Kilnbank Cres KA7 239 B4
Kilnburn Rd ML1 163 B4
Kilncadzow Rd ML8 202 C4
Kilncraigs Ct FK10 10 B3
Kilncraigs Rd FK10 10 B3
Kilnford Cres KA2 225 B1
Kilnford Dr KA2 225 C1
Kilnknowe Cotts PA9 131 A3
Kilns Pl FK2 41 C3
Kilns Rd FK1 42 A3
Kilnside Rd PA1 114 A2
Kilnwell Quadrant ML1 163 B4
Kiloran Gr G77 156 A2
Kiloran Pl G77 156 A2
Kiloran St G46 135 C2
Kilpatrick Ave PA2 113 A1
Kilpatrick Cres PA2 133 B4
Kilpatrick Ct Irvine KA11 220 A2
Old Kilpatrick G60 73 A3
Kilpatrick Dr
Bearsden G61 75 B4
East Kilbride G75 180 A2
Erskine PA8 73 A2
Renfrew PA4 114 A4
Stepps G33 99 C3
Kilpatrick Gdns G76 157 B4
Kilpatrick Pl KA11 220 A1
Kilpatrick Sta G60 73 A3
Kilpatrick View G82 50 A2
Kilpatrick Way 9 G71 141 A4
Kilrig Ave KA13 207 C2
Kilruskin Dr KA23 190 B2
Kilsyth Acad G65 36 B1
Kilsyth Cres KA11 220 A2
Kilsyth Gdns G75 180 A2
Kilsyth Prim Sch G65 60 B4
Kilsyth Rd Banknock FK4 38 A2
Kirkintilloch G66 58 C1
Queenzieburn G65 59 C4
Kilsyth Wlk KA11 220 A2
Kiltarie Cres ML6 123 C3
Kiltearn Rd G33 119 C4
Kiltongue Cotts ML6 122 B4
Kilvaxter Dr G46 135 C2
Kilwinning Abbey★ KA13 207 C2
Kilwinning Acad KA13 207 B2
Kilwinning Cres ML3 161 C1
Kilwinning Rd
Dalry KA24 191 A4
Irvine KA12 219 A3
Stevenston KA20 206 C1
Stewarton KA3 211 B4
Kilwinning Sta KA13 207 B2
Kilwynet Way PA3 114 A4
Kimberley Gdns G75 180 B4
Kimberley St
Clydebank G81 73 C3
Wishaw ML2 164 B2
Kinalty Rd G44 137 A3
Kinarvie Cres G53 134 C4
Kinarvie Pl G53 134 C4
Kinarvie Rd G53 134 C4
Kinarvie Terr G53 134 C4
Kinbuck St G22 97 B2
Kincaid Dr G66 33 B1
Kincaid Field G66 58 B3
Kincaid Gdns G72 139 A3
Kincaid St PA16 45 A4
Kincaid Way G66 58 B3
Kincaidston Dr KA7 239 B2
Kincaidston Prim Sch KA7 239 A2
Kincardine Dr G64 98 B4
Kincardine Pl
Bishopbriggs G64 98 B4
East Kilbride G74 160 B2
Kincardine Rd FK2 24 B2
Kincardine Sq G33 99 B1
Kincath Ave G73 138 B2
Kinclaven Ave G15 75 A2
Kincraig St G51 115 B3
Kinellan Rd G61 75 C1
Kinellar Dr G14 95 A3
Kinfauns Dr Glasgow G15 75 A2
Newton Mearns G77 156 C3
King Edward La 8 G13 95 C3
King Edward Rd G13 95 C3
King Edward St G83 27 C3
King George Ct PA4 94 C1
King George Gdns PA4 94 C1
King George Park Ave PA4 94 C1
King George Pl PA4 94 C1
King George Way PA4 94 C1
King James Dr FK10 4 B1
King O' Muirs Ave FK10 4 C2
King O' Muirs Rd FK10 4 C2
King Pl G69 121 A3
King Robert Ct FK8 1 C1
King St Ayr KA8 236 A1
Clydebank G81 94 B4
Coatbridge ML5 121 C3
Falkirk FK2 42 B3
Fallin FK7 8 B2
Glasgow G1 241 A1
Gourock PA19 44 C4
Greenock PA15 45 C3
Hamilton ML3 162 A2
Kilmarnock KA1 227 C4
4 Kilsyth G65 60 B4
Kilwinning KA13 207 C2
Larkhall ML9 185 A2
Paisley PA1 113 B3
Port Glasgow PA14 47 B1
Renton G82 27 B1
Rutherglen G73 138 A4
Shotts ML7 146 C2
Stenhousemuir FK5 23 C2
Stirling FK8 7 A4
Stonehouse ML9 198 C1
Wishaw ML2 165 A1
Wishaw, Newmains ML2 166 A3
King St E G84 16 C1
King Street La
3 Kilsyth G65 60 B4
5 Rutherglen G73 138 A4
King's Cres
Cambuslang G72 139 A3
Carluke ML8 188 A1
Helensburgh G84 16 C1
King's Ct KA15 150 A1
King's Dr Cumbernauld G68 61 C3
Glasgow G40 117 C2
Newton Mearns G77 157 A2
King's Gdns G77 157 A2
King's Glen Prim Sch PA15 46 B1
King's Inch Rd PA4 94 C2
King's Park Ave G44 137 B3
King's Park Prim Sch G44 137 B3
King's Park Rd
Glasgow G44 137 A4
Stirling FK8 7 A4
King's Park Sec Sch G44 137 B3
King's Park Sta G44 137 B3
King's Pk Rd FK8 6 C3
King's Pl G22 97 A3
King's Rd Beith KA15 150 A1
Elderslie PA5 112 A1
King's View G68 61 C3
King's Way G82 49 B3
Kingarth La G42 117 A1
Kingarth St Glasgow G42 117 A1
Hamilton ML3 183 B4
Kingcase Ave KA9 236 A3
Kingcase Prim Sch KA9 236 A3
Kingfisher Dr G13 94 C4
Kingfisher Gdns G13 95 A4
Kinghorn Dr G44 137 B4
Kinghorn La G44 137 B4
Kinglas Rd G61 75 B1
Kings Cres PA5 112 B2
Kings Ct Alloa FK10 10 A4
Ayr KA8 236 A1
8 Falkirk FK1 42 A2
Stenhousemuir FK5 23 B1
Kings Dr ML1 142 C2
Kings Inch Dr G51 95 A1
Kings Inch Pl PA4 95 A1
Kings Knot★ FK8 6 C4
Kings Myre ML11 215 B2
Kings Pk G64 57 B1
Kings View G73 137 C4
Kingsacre Rd G44 137 B4
Kingsbarns Dr G44 137 A4
Kingsborough Gate 4 G12 96 A2
Kingsborough Gdns G12 96 A2
Kingsborough La G12 96 A2
Kingsborough La E G12 96 A2
Kingsbrae Ave G44 137 B4
Kingsbridge Cres G44 137 B3
Kingsbridge Dr G44 137 C3
Kingsburgh Dr PA1 114 A3
Kingsburn Dr G73 138 A3
Kingsburn Gr G73 138 A3
Kingscliffe Ave G44 137 B3
Kingscourt Ave G44 137 B3
Kingscroft Rd KA9 236 A4
Kingsdale Ave G44 137 B4
Kingsdyke Ave G44 137 B4
Kingseat Pl FK1 41 C2
Kingsford Ave G44 136 C2
Kingsford Ct G77 156 B3
Kingsford Pl KA3 223 A3
Kingsgate Ret Pk G74 160 A3
Kingsheath Ave G73 137 C3
Kingshill Ave G68 60 C1
Kingshill Dr G44 137 B3
Kingshill Rd ML7 167 A4
Kingshill View ML8 187 A2
Kingshouse Ave G44 137 B3
Kingshurst Ave G44 137 B4
Kingsknowe Dr G73 137 C3
Kingsland Cres G52 115 A3
Kingsland Dr G52 115 B3
Kingsland La G52 115 B3
Kingslea Rd PA6 91 A1
Kingsley Ave
Glasgow G42 117 A1
Stenhousemuir FK5 23 C2
Kingsley Ct G71 141 A4
Kingslynn Dr G44 137 B3
Kingsmuir Dr G73 137 C3
Kingstables La FK8 7 A4
Kingston Ave
1 Airdrie ML6 123 B4
Neilston G78 154 B3
Uddingston G71 141 A4
Kingston Flats G65 36 B1
Kingston Gr PA7 72 A2
Kingston Ind Est G5 116 C3
Kingston Pl G81 73 B2
Kingston Rd
Bishopton PA7 72 A2
Kilsyth G65 36 B1
Neilston G78 154 B3
Kingston St G5 240 C1
Kingsway Dalry KA24 191 A4
East Kilbride G74 160 A2
Glasgow G14 95 A3
Gourock PA19 44 B3
Kilsyth G65 36 B1
Kirkintilloch G66 59 A1
Kingsway Ct G14 95 A3
Kingswell Ave KA3 223 A3
Kingswell Pk FK10 10 B4
Kingswood Dr G44 137 B4
Kingswood Rd PA7 71 C2
Kingussie Ave KA3 195 B1
Kingussie Dr G44 137 B3
Kiniver Dr G15 75 A1
Kinkell Gdns G66 59 A1
Kinloch Ave
Cambuslang G72 139 A2
Linwood PA3 112 A3
Stewarton KA3 195 B1
Kinloch Dr ML1 142 B1
Kinloch La PA16 44 C2
Kinloch Rd
Kilmarnock KA1 228 A3
Newton Mearns G77 156 B3
Renfrew PA4 94 A1
Kinloch St G40 118 B2
Kinloch Terr PA16 44 C2
Kinloss Pl G74 159 C1
Kinmount Ave G44 137 A4
Kinmount La G44 137 B4
Kinnaird Ave Falkirk FK2 24 A2
Newton Mearns G77 157 A3
Kinnaird Cres G61 76 A2
Kinnaird Dr Linwood PA3 112 A3
Stenhousemuir FK5 23 C2
Kinnaird Pl G64 98 A4
Kinnear Rd G40 118 A2
Kinneil Pl ML3 161 C1
Kinnell Ave G52 115 B2
Kinnell Cres G52 115 B2
Kinnell Path G52 115 B2
Kinnell Pl G52 115 B2
Kinnell Sq G52 115 B2
Kinnier Rd KA21 217 A4
Kinnin Brae KA23 190 B2
Kinning Park Ind Est G5 116 C3
Kinning Park Underground Sta G41 116 B3
Kinning St G5 117 A3
Kinnis Vennel KA13 207 B2
Kinnoul Gdns G61 75 B4
Kinnoull Pl G72 161 B4
Kinnoull Rd KA1 228 A2
Kinpurnie Rd PA1 114 B3
Kinross Ave
Glasgow G52 115 A2
Port Glasgow PA14 47 B1
Kinross Pk G74 160 B2
Kinsail Dr G52 114 C3
Kinstone Ave G14 95 A3
Kintail Gdns G66 59 A1
Kintessack Pl G64 78 B1
Kintillo Dr G13 95 A3
Kintore Pk ML3 183 A4
Kintore Rd G43 136 C3
Kintore Twr G72 138 C2
Kintra St G51 116 A4
Kintyre Ave PA5 112 A2
Kintyre Cres
Newton Mearns G77 156 B3
Plains ML6 104 A2
Kintyre Gdns G66 59 A1
Kintyre Pl FK1 41 B2
Kintyre Rd G72 161 B4
Kintyre St G21 98 A1
Kintyre Terr PA16 44 B2
Kintyre Wynd ML8 187 C2
Kipland Wlk ML5 122 B3
Kippen Dr G76 158 A3
Kippen St Airdrie ML6 122 C4
Glasgow G22 97 B3
Kipperoch Rd G82 49 A4
Kippford Pl ML6 123 C1
Kippford St G32 119 B2
Kipps Ave ML6 122 C4
Kirk Ave FK5 23 C1
Kirk Cl KA24 191 B4
Kirk Cres G60 73 A4
Kirk Ct ML9 198 C1
Kirk Glebe Neilston G78 154 C4
Stewarton KA3 211 B4
Kirk La Bearsden G61 75 C3
Glasgow G43 136 B4
Kirk O' Shotts Prim Sch ML7 125 B2
Kirk Path ML7 167 A4
Kirk Pl Bearsden G61 75 C3
Cumbernauld G67 82 A4
Uddingston G71 140 C3
Kirk Port KA7 238 C4
Kirk Rd Bearsden G61 75 C3
Beith KA15 171 A4
Carluke ML8 187 C1
Carmunnock G76 158 B4
Dalserf ML9 186 A1
Houston PA6 91 B1
Motherwell ML1 143 B4
Shotts ML7 146 C2
Wishaw ML2 165 B2
Kirk St Carluke ML8 187 C1
Coatbridge ML5 121 C3
Milngavie G62 54 C1
Motherwell ML1 163 C4
Prestwick KA9 233 B1
Stonehouse ML9 198 C1
Kirk Vennel KA12 219 B1
Kirk View KA15 171 A4
Kirk Wynd
7 East Kilbride G74 159 C1
2 Falkirk FK1 42 A2
Stirling FK7 7 A2
Kirkaig Ave PA4 94 C1
Kirkbean Ave G73 138 A2
Kirkbrae FK10 10 C2
Kirkbride Terr FK7 12 B2
Kirkbriggs Gdns G73 138 A3
Kirkbriggs Way G73 138 A3
Kirkburn FK1 86 A4
Kirkburn Ave G72 139 A2
Kirkburn Dr G63 31 B2
Kirkburn Rd G63 31 B2
Kirkcaldy Rd G41 116 B1
Kirkconnel Ave
Cumbernauld G68 60 C1
Glasgow G13 94 C3
Kirkconnel Dr G73 137 C3
Kirkcudbright Pl G74 160 B2
Kirkdale Dr G52 115 C2
Kirkdene Ave G77 157 A3
Kirkdene Bank G77 157 A3
Kirkdene Cres G77 157 A3
Kirkdene Gr G77 157 A2
Kirkdene Pl G77 157 A3
Kirkfield Bank Way ML3 162 A2
Kirkfield Rd
Bothwell G71 141 A2
Kirkfieldbank ML11 214 B2
Kirkfield Terr ML2 165 B2
Kirkfield Wynd PA9 130 C3
Kirkfieldbank Brae ML11 214 C2
Kirkfieldbank Prim Sch ML11 214 B2
Kirkford KA3 211 C4
Kirkford Rd G69 80 C1
Kirkgate Alloa FK10 10 A3
Irvine KA12 219 B1
Saltcoats KA21 216 C4
Wishaw ML2 165 C2
Kirkhall Gdns KA22 205 B1
Kirkhall Pl FK6 21 C1
Kirkhall Rd ML1 143 B2
Kirkhill KA13 207 B1
Kirkhill Ave G72 139 A2
Kirkhill Cres
Neilston G78 154 C4
Prestwick KA9 236 A3
Kirkhill Dr G20 96 B3
Kirkhill Gate G77 157 A2
Kirkhill Gdns G72 139 A2
Kirkhill Gr G72 139 A2
Kirkhill Pl 16 Glasgow G20 96 B3
Wishaw ML2 164 B1
Kirkhill Prim Sch G77 157 A3
Kirkhill Rd Gartcosh G69 100 C3
Newton Mearns G77 157 A3
Uddingston G71 140 C4
Wishaw ML2 164 B1
Kirkhill St ML2 164 B1
Kirkhill Sta G72 139 A2
Kirkhill Terr G72 139 A2
Kirkholm Ave KA8 236 A2
Kirkhope Dr G15 75 A1
Kirkhouse Ave G63 31 B2
Kirkhouse Cres G63 31 B2
Kirkhouse Rd G63 31 B2
Kirkinner Rd G32 119 B2
Kirkintilloch High Sch G66 80 A4

Kirkintilloch Ind Est G66 58 B1
Kirkintilloch Rd
Bishopbriggs G64 78 B3
Kirkintilloch G66 58 A1
Kirkintilloch, Waterside G66 80 B4
Kirkland Ave
Kilmarnock KA3 222 C2
Strathblane G63 31 B2
Kirkland Cres KA24 191 A4
Kirkland Dr FK6 21 A1
Kirkland Gdns KA3 222 B3
Kirkland Gr PA5 111 C2
Kirkland La G83 27 C2
Kirkland Rd Dunlop KA3 195 A4
Glengarnock KA14,KA25 170 A4
Kirkland St Glasgow G20 96 C2
Motherwell ML1 163 B4
Kirkland Terr KA11 220 C1
Kirklandholm KA9 236 B3
Kirklandneuk Cres PA4 94 A2
Kirklandneuk Prim Sch
PA4 94 A2
Kirklandneuk Rd PA4 94 A2
Kirklands Cres
Bothwell G71 141 A2
Kilsyth G65 60 B4
Kirklands Dr G77 156 B1
Kirklands Hospl G71 141 A2
Kirklands Pl G77 156 B1
Kirklands Rd
Lanark ML11 215 A2
Newton Mearns G77 156 B1
Kirklandside Hospl KA1 228 B3
Kirkle Dr G77 157 A3
Kirklea Gdns PA3 113 A2
Kirklee Cir G12 96 B2
Kirklee Gardens La G12 96 B2
Kirklee Gate G12 96 B2
Kirklee Gdns G12 96 B2
Kirklee Pl G12 96 B2
Kirklee Quadrant 42 G12 96 B2
Kirklee Quadrant La G12 96 B2
Kirklee Rd Glasgow G12 96 B2
Motherwell ML1,ML4 142 C2
Kirklee Terr G12 96 B2
Kirklee Terrace La G12 96 B2
Kirklee Terrace Rd 41
G12 96 B2
Kirkliston St G32 118 C3
Kirkmichael Ave 9 G11 96 A2
Kirkmichael Gdns 8
G11 96 A2
Kirkmichael Rd G84 16 C1
Kirkmuir Dr
Rutherglen G73 138 A2
Stewarton KA3 195 B1
Kirkness St ML6 123 A4
Kirknethan ML2 164 B1
Kirknewton St G32 119 A3
Kirkoswald G74 160 B2
Kirkoswald Dr G81 74 B2
Kirkoswald Rd
Glasgow G43 136 B3
Motherwell ML1 143 C2
Kirkpatrick Cres G83 27 B4
Kirkpatrick St G40 118 A3
Kirkriggs Ave G73 138 A3
Kirkriggs Prim Sch G45 138 A3
Kirkriggs View G73 138 A3
Kirkshaw Ct PA5 111 C2
Kirkshaws Ave ML5 121 C2
Kirkshaws Pl ML5 121 C2
Kirkshaws Prim Sch
ML5 121 C2
Kirkshaws Rd ML5 121 C2
Kirkside Cres FK7 7 A3
Kirkslap FK6 21 C1
Kirkstall Gdns G64 78 A2
Kirkstone G77 157 A3
Kirkstone Cl G75 179 C3
Kirkstyle Ave ML8 187 C1
Kirkstyle Cres
Airdrie ML6 102 C1
Neilston G78 154 B4
Kirkstyle Ct KA11 220 A3
Kirkstyle La G78 154 C4
Kirkstyle Pl ML6 102 B2
Kirkstyle Prim Sch KA1 228 A3
Kirksyde Ave G66 79 C4
Kirkton
Erskine, North Barr PA8 73 A2
Old Kilpatrick G60 73 A4
Kirkton Ave
Barrhead G78 134 A1
Blantyre G72 161 B3
Carluke ML8 187 C1
Glasgow G13 95 A3
West Kilbride KA23 190 B2
Kirkton Cres
Cardross G82 26 A1
Coatbridge ML5 122 B2
Glasgow G13 95 A3
Milton of C G66 58 B3
Kirkton Ct Carluke ML8 187 C1
Eaglesham G76 178 C2
Kirkton Dr G76 178 C3
Kirkton Gate G74 159 C1
Kirkton Moor Rd G76 178 A2
Kirkton Pk G74 159 C1
Kirkton Pl Blantyre G72 161 B3
Coatbridge ML5 122 B2
East Kilbride G74 159 C1
Falkirk FK2 24 B2
Fenwick KA3 213 A2
Kirkton Prim Sch ML8 187 C1
Kirkton Rd
Cambuslang G72 139 A3
Cardross G82 26 A1
Kirkton Rd *continued*
Dumbarton G82 49 B2
Fenwick KA3 213 A2
Kilmarnock KA3 222 C3
Kilmaurs KA3 222 B3
Neilston G78 154 C3
Kirkton St ML8 187 C1
Kirkton Terr G66 32 C2
Kirktonfield Dr G78 154 C4
Kirktonfield Pl G78 154 C4
Kirktonfield Rd G78 154 C4
Kirktonholm Pl 14 KA1 227 C4
Kirktonholm St 12 KA1 227 C4
Kirktonholme Cres G74 159 B1
Kirktonholme Prim Sch
G74 159 B1
Kirktonholme Rd G74 159 B1
Kirktonside G78 134 A1
Kirkvale Cres G77 157 A3
Kirkvale Ct G77 157 A3
Kirkvale Dr G77 157 A3
Kirkview G67 82 A3
Kirkview Ave ML7 125 B1
Kirkview Cres G77 156 C2
Kirkview Ct G67 82 A3
Kirkview Gdns G71 140 C4
Kirkville Pl G15 75 A1
Kirkwall G67 62 A3
Kirkwall Ave G72 140 B2
Kirkwall Pl KA3 223 A3
Kirkwall Rd PA16 44 C2
Kirkway FK2 14 B2
Kirkwell Rd G44 137 A3
Kirkwood Ave
Clydebank G81 74 C1
Stepps G33 100 A3
Kirkwood Pl ML5 121 C3
Kirkwood Quadrant G81 74 B1
Kirkwood Rd G71 140 C4
Kirkwood St
Coatbridge ML5 121 C3
Glasgow G51 116 B3
Rutherglen G73 138 A4
Kirkwood Sta ML5 121 B3
Kirn Dr PA19 44 B3
Kirn Rd KA3 222 C1
Kirn St G20 96 B4
Kirriemuir G74 160 B3
Kirriemuir Ave G52 115 B2
Kirriemuir Gdns G64 78 B1
Kirriemuir Pl G52 115 B2
Kirriemuir Rd G64 78 B1
Kirstie Pl G83 27 C1
Kirtle Dr PA4 94 C1
Kirtle Pl G75 179 C4
Kishorn Pl G33 99 B1
Kitchener St ML2 165 A2
Kittoch Pl 4 G74 159 C1
Kittoch Sch G75 180 B4
Kittoch St G74 159 C1
Kittochside Rd G76 158 C3
Kittyshaw Rd KA24 191 A4
Klondike Ct ML1 143 A2
Knapdale St G22 97 A4
Knights Gate G71 140 C3
Knights Way FK6 21 B1
Knightsbridge St G13 95 B4
Knightscliffe Ave G13 95 C4
Knightswood Ct G13 95 B3
Knightswood Prim Sch
G13 95 C4
Knightswood Rd G13 95 B4
Knightswood Sec Sch
G13 95 B3
Knightswood Sec Sch
(Annexe) G13 95 B4
Knightswood Terr G72 140 C1
Knivysbridge Pl ML4 141 C2
Knock Jargon Ct KA21 205 C2
Knock Way PA3 114 A4
Knockbuckle Ave PA13 69 A1
Knockbuckle Rd PA13 89 B4
Knockburn Prim Sch
G21 98 B4
Knockburnie Rd G71 141 A2
Knockentiber Rd KA11 221 A1
Knockhall St G33 99 B1
Knockhill Dr G44 137 A4
Knockhill Rd PA4 94 A1
Knockinlaw Mount KA3 222 C2
Knockinlaw Rd KA3 222 C2
Knockmarloch Dr KA1 227 C2
Knocknair St PA14 68 C4
Knockrivoch Gdns KA22 205 C2
Knockrivoch Pl KA22 205 C2
Knockrivoch Wynd
KA22 205 C2
Knockside Ave PA2 133 B4
Knoll Croft Rd ML7 147 A2
Knoll Pk KA7 238 C2
Knollpark Dr G76 157 B4
Knowe Cres ML1 143 B2
Knowe Rd Chryston G69 100 B4
Greenock PA15 46 A2
Paisley PA3 114 A4
Knowe St G62 54 C1
Knowe The Alloa FK10 5 B1
Troon KA10 229 D4
Knowefaulds Rd FK10 4 A2
Knowehead Dr G71 140 C3
Knowehead Gdns G71 140 C3
Knowehead Rd
Clachan of C G66 32 C2
Hurlford KA1 228 C3
Kilmarnock KA1 227 C2
Wishaw ML2 165 B1
Knoweholm KA7 238 B1
Knowenoble St ML1 144 A1
Knowes Ave G77 156 C3
Knowes Rd G77 156 C3
Knowetap St G20 96 C4
Knowetop Ave ML1 163 C2
Knowetop Cres G82 49 B3
Knowetop Prim Sch
ML1 163 C2
Knowhead Gdns 5 G41 116 C2
Knowhead Terr 4 G41 116 C2
Knox Ave PA11 110 B4
Knox Pl
Newton Mearns G77 156 A2
Saltcoats KA21 206 A1
Knox St Airdrie ML6 123 A4
Paisley PA1 113 B2
Knoxland Prim Sch G82 50 A2
Knoxland Sq G82 50 A1
Knoxland St G82 50 A1
Knoxville Rd KA25 149 A1
Kronborg Way G75 180 C3
Kyle Acad KA7 239 B4
Kyle Ave Cowie FK7 12 C4
Springside KA11 220 C1
Kyle Cres KA10 230 A2
Kyle Ct Ayr KA7 239 A4
Cambuslang G72 139 A3
Kyle Ctr KA7 238 C4
Kyle Dr Glasgow G46 136 C2
Troon KA10 229 C3
Kyle Gr ML1 143 A2
Kyle Quadrant
Motherwell ML1 143 B2
Wishaw ML2 164 C1
Kyle Rd Cumbernauld G67 62 A2
Irvine KA12 224 B4
Kyle Sq G73 137 C3
Kyle St Ayr KA7 238 C4
Glasgow G4 241 A4
Motherwell ML1 163 A4
Prestwick KA9 236 B4
Kyle Terr G82 49 A3
Kyleakin Dr G72 140 A1
Kyleakin Rd G46 135 B2
Kyleakin Terr G46 135 B2
Kylemore Cres ML1 142 B1
Kylemore La PA16 44 C2
Kylemore Terr PA16 44 C2
Kylepark Ave G71 140 B3
Kylepark Cres G71 140 B4
Kylepark Dr G71 140 B4
Kylerhea Rd G46 135 B2
Kyleshill KA21 216 C4
Kyleswell St KA13 207 C2

L

La Belle Allee 13 G3 96 C1
La Belle Pl 12 G3 96 C1
La Crosse Terr G12 96 C2
Laberge Gdns ML1 143 A2
Laburnum Ave
Beith KA15 171 A4
Cambuslang G72 139 C2
East Kilbride G75 180 B3
Laburnum Cres ML2 165 A3
Laburnum Ct G75 180 B3
Laburnum Dr G66 58 A3
Laburnum Gdns G66 79 A3
Laburnum Gr
Coatbridge ML5 122 A3
Kirkintilloch G66 79 A3
Stirling FK8 6 C3
Troon KA10 229 C2
Laburnum Lea ML3 162 C1
Laburnum Pl PA5 132 A4
Laburnum Rd Ayr KA7 239 B3
Banknock FK4 38 C1
Cumbernauld G67 62 B1
Glasgow G51 116 B2
Kilmarnock KA1 227 B4
Uddingston G71 141 B4
Laburnum St PA15 46 C1
Lachlan Cres PA8 72 C1
Lacy St PA1 114 A2
Ladder Ct G75 180 A2
Lade Ct PA12 129 B1
Lade Dr FK5 41 B4
Lade Mill FK7 7 B1
Lade Rd FK4 40 A3
Lade Terr G52 115 A2
Lade The G83 27 C3
Ladeside KA3 222 B4
Ladeside Cl G77 156 B3
Ladeside Cres FK5 23 C1
Ladeside Ct KA25 170 A4
Ladeside Dr
Johnstone PA5 111 B1
Kilsyth G65 36 C1
Ladeside Gdns KA3 222 B4
Ladeside Prim Sch FK5 41 B4
Ladeside Rd KA3 222 B4
Ladhope Pl G13 94 C4
Lady Alice Prim Sch
PA16 45 B2
Lady Ann Cres ML6 123 B3
Lady Anne St G14 94 C3
Lady Isle Cres G71 140 C3
Lady Jane Gate G71 140 C2
Lady La PA1 113 B2
Lady Margaret Dr KA10 230 A1
Lady Mary Wlk ML3 162 C1
Lady Watson Gdns ML3 162 A1
Lady Wilson St ML6 123 A4
Lady's Gate G83 27 C1
Ladyacre KA13 207 C2
Ladyacre Rd ML11 215 A2
Ladyacres PA4 93 B3
Ladyacres Way PA4 93 B3
Ladybank G68 61 C3
Ladybank Ct 12 G74 159 C1
Ladybank Dr G52 115 C2
Ladybank Gdns G74 159 C1
Ladybank Pl 11 G74 159 C1
Ladyburn Ct KA11 219 C3
Ladyburn St
Greenock PA15 46 B2
Paisley PA1 114 A2
Ladyford Ave KA13 207 C2
Ladyha Ct KA11 220 A3
Ladyhill Dr G69 120 A2
Ladykirk Cres
Glasgow G52 115 A3
Paisley PA2 113 C2
Ladykirk Dr G52 115 B3
Ladykirk Rd KA9 236 B4
Ladyland Dr KA25 149 A2
Ladyloan Ave G15 74 C2
Ladyloan Ct G15 74 C2
Ladyloan Gdns G15 74 C2
Ladymuir Circ PA8 72 C1
Ladymuir Cres G53 115 B1
Ladysgate Ct FK2 24 A2
Ladysmill FK2 42 B3
Ladysmill Ind Est FK1 42 B3
Ladysmith Ave PA10 111 B1
Ladysmith Dr G75 180 A2
Ladysmith Rd KA25 149 A1
Ladysmith St ML2 164 B2
Ladysneuk Rd FK9 2 B1
Ladyton G83 27 C2
Ladyton Prim Sch G83 28 A2
Ladywell Ct FK5 23 A2
Ladywell Dr FK10 4 A2
Ladywell Pl FK10 4 A2
Ladywell Prim Sch ML1 163 B4
Ladywell Rd ML1 163 B4
Ladywell St G4 241 C2
Ladywood G62 55 A1
Lagan Rd ML8 188 A1
Laggan Ave ML7 147 A2
Laggan Ho KA9 236 A3
Laggan Path ML7 146 C3
Laggan Quadrant ML6 102 C1
Laggan Rd Airdrie ML6 102 C1
Bishopbriggs G64 78 A1
Glasgow G43 136 C3
Newton Mearns G77 156 B4
Laggan Terr PA4 94 A2
Laggan Way ML2 165 C4
Laggary Pk G84 15 C3
Laggary Rd G84 15 C3
Laidlaw Ave ML1 142 C2
Laidlaw Gdns G71 120 C1
Laidlaw St G5 240 B1
Laidon Rd ML6 102 C1
Laidon Wlk 3 ML2 165 C3
Laigh Ct KA15 150 A1
Laigh Milton Viaduct★
KA2 226 B3
Laigh Mount KA7 238 C1
Laigh Rd Beith KA15 150 A1
Newton Mearns G77 157 B3
Laighcartside St PA5 112 A2
Laighdykes Rd KA21 205 C1
Laighland KA9 236 B3
Laighlands Rd G71 141 A1
Laighmuir St G71 140 C3
Laighpark Ave PA7 72 A2
Laighpark View PA3 113 C4
Laighstonehall Rd ML3 162 A1
Laightoun Ct G67 82 A3
Laightoun Dr G67 82 A3
Laightoun Gdns G67 82 A3
Lainshaw KA13 207 B1
Lainshaw Ave KA1 227 C2
Lainshaw Dr G45 137 A1
Lainshaw Prim Sch KA3 211 B4
Lainshaw St KA3 211 B4
Laird Gr G71 141 A4
Laird Pl G40 117 C2
Laird St Coatbridge ML5 122 A4
Greenock PA15 45 C3
Laird Weir KA22 205 B2
Laird's Hill Ct G65 60 A4
Laird's Hill Pl G65 60 A4
Lairds Gate G71 140 B3
Lairds Hill G67 61 C1
Lairdsland Prim Sch G66 79 B4
Lairg Dr G72 140 B1
Lairhills Rd G75 180 C4
Lake Ave ML11 215 B1
Lakefield Ct G72 161 B3
Lamb St Glasgow G22 97 A3
Hamilton ML3 162 C2
Lambert Terr FK10 10 B4
Lamberton Ave FK7 7 B2
Lamberton Dr G52 115 B3
Lamberton Gdns KA11 220 B3
Lamberton Rd KA3 195 B1
Lambhill Quadrant 5
G41 116 C3
Lambhill St G41 116 B3
Lambie Cres G77 156 B3
Lambie Ct KA21 216 C4
Lamerton Rd G67 62 B1
Lamford Dr KA7 238 B1
Lamington Rd G52 115 A3
Lamlash Cres G33 119 A4
Lamlash Pl
East Kilbride G75 180 A2
Glasgow G33 119 A4
Helensburgh G84 16 C1
Motherwell ML1 163 B4
Lamlash Prim Sch G33 119 A4
Lamlash Sq G33 119 B4
Lammer Wynd 16 ML9 185 B1
Lammerknowes Rd G65 37 C2
Lammermoor G74 160 C2
Lammermoor Ave G52 115 B2
Lammermoor Cres G66 79 C4
Lammermoor Dr G67 82 C4
Lammermoor Gdns G66 79 C4
Lammermoor Prim Sch
ML2 165 A3
Lammermoor Rd G66 79 C4
Lammermoor Terr ML2 165 A2
Lammermuir Ct KA11 220 A2
Lammermuir Dr PA2 133 C4
Lammermuir Gdns G61 75 B4
Lammermuir Pl ML1 143 A3
Lammermuir Rd KA1 228 A2
Lammermuir Way ML6 123 C1
Lammermuir Wynd
ML9 184 C3
Lamond View FK5 23 B1
Lamont Ave PA7 72 B2
Lamont Cres Fallin FK7 8 B3
Renton G82 27 B1
Lamont Dr KA12 224 C4
Lamont Pl KA12 224 C4
Lamont Rd G21 98 A3
Lanark Ave ML6 123 A2
Lanark Gram Sch ML11 215 A2
Lanark Ind Est ML11 215 C3
Lanark Moor Ctry Pk★
ML11 215 C2
Lanark Mus★ ML11 214 C2
Lanark Prim Sch ML11 215 A3
Lanark Rd
Carluke ML8,ML11 202 A2
Larkhall ML9 185 B3
Netherburn ML8 200 B4
Lanark St G1 241 B1
Lanark Sta ML11 215 A2
Lancaster Ave
Beith KA15 171 A4
Chapelhall ML6 143 C4
Lancaster Cres G12 96 B2
Lancaster Crescent La
G12 96 B2
Lancaster Rd G64 78 A2
Lancaster Terr 31 G12 96 B2
Lancaster Terrace La 30
G12 96 B2
Lancaster Way 4 PA4 94 B1
Lancefield Quay G3 240 A2
Lancefield St G3 240 A2
Landemer Dr G73 138 A3
Landressy Pl G40 117 C2
Landressy St G40 117 C2
Landsborough Ct KA21 205 C1
Landsborough Dr KA3 223 A2
Landsborough Pl KA20 206 C1
Landsdowne Gdns ML3 162 C2
Landsdowne Rd ML9 185 B1
Lane The G68 61 B3
Lanfine Rd PA1 114 B2
Lanfine Terr KA11 219 C3
Lanfine Way KA11 220 A3
Lang Ave Bishopton PA7 72 B2
Renfrew PA4 94 B1
Lang Pl PA5 111 C2
Lang Rd KA10 229 D4
Lang St PA1 114 A2
Langa St G20 96 C4
Langbank Dr PA13 69 C1
Langbank Prim Sch
PA14 70 A4
Langbank Rise PA13 69 C1
Langbank St 1 G5 117 A3
Langbank Sta PA14 70 B4
Langbar Cres G33 119 C4
Langbyres Rd ML1 144 B1
Langcraig Rd KA1 227 C1
Langcraigs Ct PA2 133 B4
Langcraigs Dr PA2 133 B3
Langcraigs Prim Sch
PA2 133 B4
Langcraigs Terr PA2 133 B3
Langcroft Ave KA9 233 C1
Langcroft Dr G72 139 B2
Langcroft Pl G51 115 B4
Langcroft Rd G51 115 B4
Langcroft Terr G51 115 B4
Langdale
East Kilbride G74 159 B2
Newton Mearns G77 157 A3
Langdale Ave G33 98 C2
Langdale Rd G69 80 C1
Langdale St G33 98 C2
Langdales Ave G68 61 B1
Langfaulds Cres G81 74 B3
Langfaulds Prim Sch
G15 74 C2
Langford Dr G53 135 A2
Langford Pl G53 135 A2
Langhaul Rd G53 114 C1
Langhill Dr G68 61 B2
Langhill Pl FK6 21 B1
Langholm G75 179 C3
Langholm Cres ML2 165 A3
Langholm Ct G69 81 A1
Langholm Dr PA3 112 B3
Langlands Ave
East Kilbride G75 180 C2
Glasgow G51 115 B4
Langlands Brae KA1 222 C1
Langlands Ct
East Kilbride G75 180 C2
Glasgow G51 115 C4

Lewis Rd Greenock PA16 45 B2
Port Glasgow PA14 69 A4
Lewis Rise KA11 220 A1
Lewis Terr KA11 220 A1
Lewis Wynd KA11 220 A1
Lewiston Dr 15 G23 76 B1
Lewiston Pl 16 G23 76 B1
Lewiston Rd G23 76 B1
Lexwell Ave PA5 112 B2
Leyden Ct G20 96 C3
Leyden Gdns G20 96 C3
Leyden St G20 96 C3
Leys Pk ML3 162 A2
Leys The G64 78 A1
Libary Gdns G72 138 C3
Libberton Way ML3 162 A2
Liberator Dr KA8 236 C2
Liberton St G33 118 C4
Liberty Ave G69 121 A3
Liberty Path G72 161 B4
Liberty Rd Bellshill ML4 142 A2
Caldercruix ML6 105 A3
Libo Ave Glasgow G53 115 B1
Uplawmoor G78 153 A2
Libo Pl PA8 72 C1
Library La G46 135 C2
Library Rd ML2 165 A2
Lichtenfels Gdns KA9 236 C4
Lickprivick Rd G75 180 A3
Liddel Rd G67 61 C1
Liddell Gr G75 180 B4
Liddell St G32 119 B1
Liddells Ct G64 98 A4
Liddesdale Pl G22 97 C4
Liddesdale Rd G22 97 B4
Liddesdale Sq G22 97 C4
Liddesdale Terr G22 97 C4
Liddlesdale Ave PA2 132 B4
Liddlesdale Pass G22 97 B4
Liddoch Way G73 137 C4
Liff Gdns G64 98 B4
Liff Pl G34 100 B1
Lifnock Ave KA1 228 C3
Lightburn Hospl G32 119 A4
Lightburn Pl G32 119 A4
Lightburn Rd G72 139 C2
Lilac Ave Clydebank G81 73 B3
Cumbernauld G67 62 C3
Lilac Cres G71 141 B4
Lilac Ct G67 62 C3
Lilac Gdns G64 98 A4
Lilac Hill Cumbernauld G67 62 C3
Hamilton ML3 162 C1
Lilac Pl Cumbernauld G67 62 C3
Kilmarnock KA1 227 C4
Lilac Way ML1 143 A3
Lilac Wynd G72 139 C2
Lillyburn Pl G15 74 C3
Lily St G40 118 A2
Lilybank Ave Airdrie ML6 103 A1
Cambuslang G72 139 B2
Muirhead G69 100 B4
Lilybank Ct FK10 5 B1
Lilybank Gardens La G12 96 B1
Lilybank Gdns G12 96 B1
Lilybank La G12 96 B1
Lilybank Rd
Port Glasgow PA14 47 A1
Prestwick KA9 236 A3
Lilybank Sch PA14 47 A1
Lilybank St ML3 162 B2
Lilybank Terr G12 96 B1
Lilybank Terrace La G12 96 B1
Lime Cres Airdrie ML6 123 B4
Cumbernauld G67 62 C2
Lime Gr Blantyre G72 140 B1
Kirkintilloch G66 79 B3
Motherwell ML1 163 C2
Stenhousemuir FK5 23 B1
Lime La 24 G14 95 B2
Lime Loan ML1 143 A2
Lime Pl KA1 227 B4
Lime Rd Dumbarton G82 49 C2
Falkirk FK1 41 A2
Lime St Glasgow G14 95 B2
Greenock PA15 45 C2
Limecraigs Ave PA2 133 B4
Limecraigs Cres PA2 133 B4
Limecraigs Rd PA2 133 B4
Limegrove St ML4 142 A4
Limekiln Rd Ayr KA8 236 A2
Stevenston KA20 217 C4
Limekilnburn Rd ML3 183 B2
Limekilns Rd G67 82 C3
Limekilns St G81 74 B4
Limelands Quadrant
ML6 104 C2
Limerigg Prim Sch FK1 86 B1
Limes The G44 137 A2
Limeside Ave G73 138 B4
Limeside Gdns G73 138 B4
Limetree Ave G71 141 B4
Limetree Cres G77 156 B2
Limetree Ct ML3 162 A3
Limetree Dr G81 74 A2
Limetree Quadrant G71 141 B4
Limetree Wlk G66 58 A2
Limeview Ave PA2 133 A4
Limeview Cres PA2 133 A4
Limeview Rd PA2 133 A4
Limeview Way PA2 133 A4
Limonds Ct KA8 236 A1
Limonds Wynd KA8 236 A1
Limpetlaw ML11 215 A3
Linacre Dr G32 119 B3
Linacre Gdns G32 119 B3
Linburn Pl G52 115 A3
Linburn Rd Erskine PA8 72 C1
Linburn Rd *continued*
Glasgow G52 114 C4
Linburn Sch G52 114 C3
Linclive Intc PA3 112 B3
Linclive Terr PA3 112 B3
Lincluden Path 3 G41 116 C2
Lincoln Ave Glasgow G13 95 B3
Uddingston G71 120 C1
Lincoln Rd PA16 44 B2
Lincuan Ave G46 157 B4
Lindams G71 140 C3
Linden Ave Denny FK6 21 B2
Stirling FK7 7 B3
Wishaw ML2 165 B3
Linden Dr Banknock FK4 38 C1
Clydebank G81 74 A3
Linden Lea Hamilton ML3 162 A2
Milton of C G66 58 A3
Linden Pl G13 95 C4
Linden St G13 95 C4
Linden Way G13 95 C4
Lindens The G71 141 A1
Lindores Ave G73 138 B4
Lindores Dr G74 159 B1
Lindores Pl G74 159 B1
Lindores St G42 137 A4
Lindrick Dr 4 G23 76 C1
Lindsay Ave
Kilbirnie KA25 149 A2
Saltcoats KA21 205 C1
Lindsay Dr Glasgow G12 96 A3
Kilmarnock KA3 223 B2
Stirling FK9 2 A2
Lindsay Gdns G83 27 C3
Lindsay Gr G74 159 C1
Lindsay Loan ML11 215 B3
Lindsay Pl
East Kilbride G74 160 A1
Glasgow G12 96 A3
Johnstone PA5 112 A2
Kirkintilloch G66 79 B2
Lindsay Quadrant G83 28 A4
Lindsay Rd G74 159 C1
Lindsay St Ayr KA8 236 B1
Kilmarnock KA1 227 C4
Lindsay Terr G66 57 C4
Lindsaybeg Ct G69 100 B4
Lindsaybeg Rd G69 80 A1
Lindsayfield Ave G75 180 B2
Lindsayfield Rd G75 180 A2
Lindston Pl KA7 239 A1
Lindum Cres ML1 163 A4
Lindum St ML1 163 A4
Lineside Wlk G84 15 C3
Linfern Ave KA1 228 B4
Linfern Ave E KA1 228 B4
Linfern Ave W KA1 228 B4
Linfern Pl KA7 239 A2
Linfern Rd G12 96 B2
Linghope Pl ML2 185 C4
Lingley Ave ML6 123 A3
Linhope Pl G75 179 C4
Linister Cres PA9 130 C3
Links Cres KA10 229 D3
Links Rd Glasgow G44 137 B2
Glasgow, Mount Vernon
G32 119 B2
Prestwick KA9 233 A1
Saltcoats KA21 205 C1
Links The G68 62 A3
Links View ML9 185 B1
Linksview Rd ML1 143 A1
Linkwood Ave G15 74 C2
Linkwood Cres G15 75 A2
Linkwood Ct KA11 220 A3
Linkwood Dr G15 75 A2
Linkwood Gdns G15 75 A2
Linkwood Pl
Clydebank G15 74 C2
Irvine KA11 220 A3
Linlithgow Gdns G32 119 B3
Linlithgow Pl FK5 23 C2
Linn Cres
Kirkfieldbank ML11 214 A2
Paisley PA2 133 B4
Linn Dr G44 136 C2
Linn Gdns G68 61 A1
Linn Glen G66 57 C4
Linn Park Gdns PA5 112 A1
Linn Park Ind Est G45 137 A1
Linn Park Nature Trail★
G44 136 C2
Linn Pl FK2 14 C2
Linn Rd KA22 205 B2
Linn Valley View G45 137 B2
Linnburn Terr KA22 205 A2
Linnet Ave PA5 131 B4
Linnet Pl G13 94 C4
Linnet Rd Bellshill ML4 142 A2
Greenock PA16 45 A2
Linnet Way ML4 141 C4
Linnhe Ave
Bishopbriggs G64 78 A1
Glasgow G44 137 A2
Hamilton ML3 162 A1
Linnhe Cres ML2 165 A1
Linnhe Ct ML9 184 C3
Linnhe Dr G78 134 A3
Linnhe Pl Blantyre G72 140 B1
Erskine PA8 72 C1
Linnhead Dr G53 135 B3
Linnhead Pl G14 95 A2
Linnpark Ave G44 136 C1
Linnpark Ct G44 136 C1
Linnvale Prim Sch G81 74 B1
Linnvale Way G68 61 B3
Linnwell Cres PA2 133 B4
Linrigg Rd ML1 144 B4
Linside Ave PA1 114 A2
Lint Brae KA3 195 C1
Lint Riggs FK1 42 A3
Lintfield Loan G71 141 A3
Linthaugh Rd G53 115 A2
Linthaugh Terr G53 115 B1
Linthill ML11 215 A3
Linthouse Bldgs 1 G51 115 C4
Linthouse Rd G51 95 C1
Linthouse Vennel KA12 219 A1
Lintie Rd ML1 143 B2
Lintlaw G72 140 B1
Lintlaw Dr G52 115 A3
Lintmill Terr G78 154 B3
Linton Pl ML5 121 C2
Linton St G33 118 C4
Lintview FK1 86 A3
Lintwhite Cres PA11 110 C4
Lintwhite Ct PA11 110 C4
Linwood Ave
Clarkston G76 157 C4
East Kilbride G74 159 A1
Linwood Ct G44 137 A3
Linwood High Sch PA3 111 C3
Linwood Ind Est PA3 112 A2
Linwood Rd PA1 112 C2
Linwood Terr ML3 162 A2
Lion Bank G66 58 B1
Lionthorn Rd FK1 41 C1
Lipney FK11 4 A3
Lisburn Rd KA8 236 A2
Lismore G74 181 B4
Lismore Ave
Motherwell ML1 163 A4
Port Glasgow PA14 69 A4
Renfrew PA4 94 B1
Lismore Ct FK1 42 A1
Lismore Dr
Coatbridge ML5 121 C2
Irvine KA11 225 A4
Linwood PA3 111 C3
Paisley PA2 133 B4
Lismore Gdns PA10 111 B1
Lismore Hill ML3 161 B2
Lismore Ho KA9 236 A3
Lismore Pl Airdrie ML6 123 B3
Moodiesburn G69 81 A2
Newton Mearns G77 156 A3
Lismore Rd G12 96 A3
Lismore Way KA11 225 B4
Lissens Wlk KA13 207 B3
Lister Ct FK9 2 A3
Lister Gdns G76 158 A3
Lister Pl 4 G52 115 A4
Lister Rd G52 115 A4
Lister St Crosshouse KA2 222 A1
Glasgow G4 241 B4
Lister Wlk ML4 142 B4
Lithgow Ave
Kirkintilloch G66 79 C4
Langbank PA14 70 A4
Lithgow Cres PA2 114 A1
Lithgow Dr ML1 144 A1
Lithgow Pl G74 159 A1
Little Bellsland Rd KA1 227 C3
Little Corseford PA10 131 B4
Little Denny Rd FK6 21 B1
Little Dovehill G1 241 B1
Little John Gdns ML2 165 C2
Little St G3 240 A2
Littlehill Prim Sch G33 98 B2
Littlehill St G21 98 A2
Littleholm Pl G81 73 C2
Littlemill Ave G68 60 C1
Littlemill Cres G53 135 A4
Littlemill Dr G53 135 A4
Littlemill Gdns 10 G53 135 A4
Littlemill La G60 72 B4
Littlemill Way ML1 143 A1
Littlestane Rd KA11 220 A3
Littlestane Rdbt KA11 220 A3
Littlestane Rise KA11 220 A3
Littleston Gdns PA8 72 C1
Littleton Dr 4 G23 76 B1
Littleton St G23 76 B1
Livilands Ct FK8 7 A3
Livilands Gate FK8 7 A3
Livilands La FK8 7 A3
Livingston Dr ML6 104 A2
Livingston La 4 G71 141 A2
Livingston Terr KA3 195 A4
Livingstone Ave G52 115 A4
Livingstone Bvd G72 161 B2
Livingstone Cres
Blantyre G72 140 B1
East Kilbride G75 180 B4
Falkirk FK2 42 C3
Livingstone Ct KA3 223 B2
Livingstone Dr
East Kilbride G75 180 C4
Laurieston FK2 42 C1
Livingstone Gdns ML9 185 A2
Livingstone Pk G65 36 B1
Livingstone Pl ML6 123 A4
Livingstone Quadrant
ML7 127 B2
Livingstone St
Clydebank G81 74 B1
Hamilton ML3 161 C2
Livingstone Terr KA12 219 A3
Lloyd Ave G32 119 A1
Lloyd Dr ML1 143 A1
Lloyd St Glasgow G31 118 A4
Motherwell ML1 143 A1
Rutherglen G73 118 A1
Lloyd Wlk KA3 211 B4
Lloyds St ML5 122 A2
Llynallan Rd ML7 127 A3
Loach Ave KA12 219 B1
Loadingbank KA25 170 A4
Loadingbank Ct KA25 170 A4
Loan Lea Cres ML9 185 A1
Loan Pl ML7 127 C3
Loan The G62 54 B2
Loanbank Pl G51 116 A4
Loanbank Quadrant
G51 115 C4
Loancroft Ave G69 120 B2
Loancroft Gate G71 140 C3
Loancroft Gdns G71 140 C3
Loancroft Pl G69 120 A2
Loanend Cotts G72 139 C1
Loanfoot Ave
Glasgow G13 95 A4
Kilmarnock KA1 222 B1
Neilston G78 154 B3
Loanfoot Gdns FK7 12 B2
Loanfoot Rd G72 161 B3
Loanhead Ave
Bonnybridge FK4 39 B3
Linwood PA3 112 A3
Motherwell ML1 143 B2
Renfrew PA4 94 B2
Loanhead Cres ML1 143 B2
Loanhead La PA3 112 A3
Loanhead Prim Sch
KA1 228 A4
Loanhead Rd
Ardrossan KA22 205 B1
Linwood PA3 112 A3
Motherwell ML1 143 B2
Loanhead St
Coatbridge ML5 121 C2
Glasgow G32 118 C4
Kilmarnock KA1 228 A4
Loaning 1 ML9 185 B1
Loaning The Ayr KA7 239 A1
Bearsden G61 75 C3
Kirkintilloch G66 79 B4
Motherwell ML1 163 B4
Rutherglen G46 157 A4
Loaninghead Dr G82 50 A3
Lobnitz Ave PA4 94 B2
Loccard Rd KA20 206 B1
Loch Achray Gdns G32 119 B2
Loch Achray St G32 119 B2
Loch Ardinning Nature
Reserve★ G63 55 B4
Loch Ardinning Nature
Trail★ G63 55 B4
Loch Assynt G74 181 A4
Loch Ave ML8 201 C2
Loch Awe G74 181 A4
Loch Awe Pl ML5 121 C3
Loch Brora Cres ML5 121 C3
Loch Dr G84 16 A1
Loch Goil G74 160 A1
Loch Laidon St G32 119 B2
Loch Laxford G74 181 A4
Loch Lea G66 58 C1
Loch Lomond Factory Outlets
G83 27 B3
Loch Lomond YH★ G83 18 C2
Loch Long G74 181 A4
Loch Loyal G74 181 A4
Loch Maree G74 181 A4
Loch Meadie G74 181 A4
Loch Naver G74 181 A4
Loch Park Ave ML8 201 C4
Loch Park Pl ML9 185 A1
Loch Pk ML2 165 B2
Loch Pl PA11 110 B4
Loch Prim Sch G73 138 B2
Loch Rd
Bridge of W PA11 110 B4
Chapelhall ML6 123 B1
Kirkintilloch G66 79 C4
Milngavie G62 55 A2
Stepps G33 99 B2
Loch Shin G74 181 A4
Loch St ML6 123 A1
Loch Striven G74 160 A1
Loch Torridon G74 181 A4
Loch View
Calderbank ML6 123 A1
Caldercruix ML6 105 A3
Kilmarnock KA3 223 B1
Loch Voil St G32 119 B2
Lochaber Cres ML7 147 A2
Lochaber Dr
Rutherglen G73 138 B2
Stenhousemuir FK5 23 C2
Lochaber Path G72 161 B4
Lochaber Pl G74 159 C2
Lochaber Rd G61 76 A1
Lochaber Wlk G66 58 B4
Lochaline Ave PA2 113 A1
Lochaline Dr G44 137 A2
Lochalsh Cres G66 58 B4
Lochalsh Dr PA2 113 A1
Lochalsh Pl G72 140 A1
Lochans The G84 15 A2
Lochar Cres G53 115 B1
Lochar Pl G75 179 C4
Lochard Dr PA2 113 A1
Lochay Pl KA10 229 D3
Lochay St G32 119 B2
Lochbrae FK10 5 B1
Lochbrae Dr G73 138 B2
Lochbridge Rd G34 120 A4
Lochbroom Ct G77 156 C3
Lochbroom Dr
Newton Mearns G77 156 C3
Paisley PA2 113 A1
Lochbuie La ML6 102 C2
Lochburn Cres G20 96 C4
Lochburn Pass G20 96 C4
Lochburn Rd G20 96 C4
Lochcraig Ct KA11 220 A2
Lochdochart Rd G34 120 B4
Lochearn Cres
Airdrie ML6 102 C1
Paisley PA2 113 A1
Lochearnhead Rd G33 99 B3
Lochend Ave G69 100 C4
Lochend Com High Sch
G34 120 B4
Lochend Cotts G83 20 C2
Lochend Cres G61 75 B2
Lochend Dr G61 75 C2
Lochend Pl KA10 229 D1
Lochend Rd Bearsden G61 75 C2
Coatbridge ML5 101 A1
Glasgow G34,G69 100 B1
Glengarnock KA14 170 B4
Troon KA10 229 C1
Gartcosh G69 100 C3
Lochend St ML1 163 C3
Locher Ave PA6 91 C1
Locher Cres PA6 111 C4
Locher Gait PA6 111 C4
Locher Gdns PA6 111 C4
Locher Pl ML5 122 B2
Locher Rd PA10 110 C2
Locher Way PA6 111 C4
Locherburn Ave PA6 111 B4
Locherburn Gr PA6 111 B4
Locherburn Pl PA6 111 B4
Lochfauld Rd G23 77 A1
Lochfield Cres PA2 113 C1
Lochfield Dr PA2 114 A1
Lochfield Prim Sch
PA2 113 C1
Lochfield Rd PA2 114 A1
Lochgarry Way ML5 121 C2
Lochgilp St G20 96 B4
Lochgoin Ave G15 74 C2
Lochgoin Prim Sch G15 74 C2
Lochgreen Ave KA10 229 D4
Lochgreen Pl
Coatbridge ML5 101 B1
Hamilton ML3 183 A4
Kilmarnock KA1 227 C2
Lochgreen Rd FK1 41 C1
Lochgreen St G33 98 B2
Lochhead Ave Denny FK6 21 C1
Linwood PA3 112 A3
Lochiel Dr G66 58 B3
Lochiel La G73 138 B2
Lochiel Rd G46 135 C2
Lochinch Pl G77 156 A3
Lochinvar Pl FK4 40 B2
Lochinvar Rd G67 82 C4
Lochinver Cres PA2 113 A1
Lochinver Dr G44 137 A3
Lochinver Gr G72 139 A3
Lochknowe St ML8 201 C3
Lochlands Ind Est FK5 41 A4
Lochlea G74 160 B2
Lochlea Ave
Clydebank G81 74 B2
Troon KA10 229 D2
Lochlea Dr KA7 239 A3
Lochlea Rd
Clarkston G76 157 C3
Cumbernauld G67 62 B2
Glasgow G43 136 B3
Rutherglen G73 137 C3
Saltcoats KA21 206 A2
Lochlea Way ML1 143 C2
Lochlee Loan 4 ML9 185 B1
Lochleven La G42 137 A4
Lochleven Rd G42 137 A4
Lochlibo Ave G13 94 C4
Lochlibo Cres G78 134 A1
Lochlibo Ct KA11 220 A3
Lochlibo Rd
Barrhead G78 134 A1
Burnhouse KA15 172 C2
Irvine KA11,KA13 209 B2
Lugton G78 152 C1
Neilston G78 154 B4
Lochlibo Terr G78 134 A1
Lochlie Pl KA20 206 C1
Lochlip Rd PA12 129 B1
Lochmaben Dr FK5 23 C2
Lochmaben Rd G52 114 C2
Lochmaben Wynd KA3 223 A3
Lochmaddy Ave G44 137 A2
Lochnagar Dr G61 75 A4
Lochnagar Rd KA1 228 A2
Lochnagar Way 29 ML9 185 B1
Lochore Ave PA3 114 A4
Lochpark KA7 238 B2
Lochpark Pl FK6 21 C1
Lochranza Ct KA3 223 A3
Lochranza Dr
East Kilbride G75 180 A2
Helensburgh G84 16 C1
Lochranza La G75 180 B2
Lochranza Pl KA21 206 A1
Lochranze Ct ML1 143 A1
Lochridge Pl FK6 21 B1
Lochshore East Ind Est
KA14 170 B4
Lochshore South Ind Est
KA25 170 A4
Lochside Bearsden G61 75 C2
Gartcosh G69 100 C3
Lochside Ct KA8 236 A1
Lochside Rd Ayr KA8 236 A1

Mitchell Dr *continued*
Milngavie G62 ...55 B1
Rutherglen G73 ...138 A3
Mitchell Gr G74 ...159 B1
Mitchell Hill Rd G45 ...137 C1
Mitchell La G1 ...240 C2
Mitchell Pl Falkirk FK1 ...41 C1
Saltcoats KA21 ...205 C1
Mitchell Rd G67 ...62 A2
Mitchell St Airdrie ML6 ...122 C4
Beith KA15 ...150 B1
Coatbridge ML5 ...121 B3
Glasgow G1 ...240 C2
Greenock PA15 ...46 C1
Mitchell Way G83 ...27 C3
Mitchison Rd G67 ...62 A2
Mitre Ct G11 ...95 C2
Mitre Gate G11 ...95 C2
Mitre La G14 ...95 C2
Mitre La W G14 ...95 B2
Mitre Rd G14,G11 ...95 C2
Moat Ave G13 ...95 B4
Mochrum Ct KA9 ...236 B3
Mochrum Rd G43 ...136 C3
Modan Rd FK7 ...7 A2
Moffat Ave FK2 ...24 B2
Moffat Ct G75 ...179 C4
Moffat Gdns G75 ...179 C4
Moffat Pl Blantyre G72 ...140 B1
Coatbridge ML5 ...122 C2
East Kilbride G75 ...179 C4
Moffat Rd Airdrie ML6 ...123 C4
Prestwick KA9 ...233 B2
Moffat St Glasgow G5 ...117 B2
Greenock PA15 ...46 B2
Moffat View ML6 ...104 A2
Moffat Wynd KA21 ...205 C2
Moffathill ML6 ...123 C3
Mogarth Ave PA2 ...132 C4
Moidart Ave PA4 ...94 A2
Moidart Cres G52 ...115 C3
Moidart Ct G78 ...134 A2
Moidart Gdns
Kirkintilloch G66 ...59 A1
Newton Mearns G77 ...156 C3
Moidart Pl G52 ...115 C3
Moidart Rd Glasgow G52 115 C3
Port Glasgow PA14 ...68 C4
Moir St Alloa FK10 ...10 A4
Glasgow G1 ...241 B1
Molendinar St G1 ...241 B1
Molendinar Terr G78 ...154 B3
Mollanbowie Rd G83 ...19 C1
Mollins Ct G68 ...81 B3
Mollins Rd G68 ...81 B3
Mollinsburn Rd
Annathill G67,ML5 ...81 C1
Glenmavis ML5,ML6 ...102 B3
Mollinsburn St G21 ...97 C2
Mollison Ave ML7 ...127 C3
Monach Gdns KA11 ...225 A4
Monach Rd Glasgow G33 119 B4
Port Glasgow PA14 ...69 A4
Monaebrook Pl G84 ...25 A4
Monar Dr G22 ...97 A2
Monar Pl G22 ...97 A2
Monar St G22 ...97 A2
Monar Way 5 ML2 ...165 C3
Monart Pl G20 ...96 C2
Moncks Rd FK1 ...42 B2
Moncreiff Gdns G66 ...79 B3
Moncrieff Ave G66 ...79 B3
Moncrieff St 2 PA3 ...113 C3
Moncrieffe Rd ML6 ...123 B2
Moncur Ct KA13 ...207 B3
Moncur Rd KA13 ...208 A2
Moncur St G40 ...241 C1
Moness Dr G52 ...115 C2
Money Gr ML1 ...164 A2
Moniebrugh Cres G65 ...36 C1
Moniebrugh Rd G65 ...36 C1
Monifieth Ave G52 ...115 B2
Monikie Gdns G64 ...78 B1
Monkcastle Dr G72 ...139 A3
Monkland Ave G66 ...79 B3
Monkland La ML5 ...121 C2
Monkland St ML6 ...123 A4
Monkland Terr ML5 ...101 B3
Monkland View
Calderbank ML6 ...123 A1
Uddingston G71 ...121 A1
Monkland View Cres
G69 ...121 A3
Monklands KA10 ...229 D4
Monklands District General
Hospl ML5 ...122 B4
Monklands Ind Est ML5 121 C1
Monkreddan Cres KA13 207 B3
Monks La ML8 ...201 C2
Monks Rd ML6 ...123 B2
Monksbridge Ave G13 ...75 B1
Monkscourt Ave ML6 ...122 C4
Monkscroft Ave 7 G11 ...96 A2
Monkscroft Ct G11 ...96 A1
Monkscroft Gdns G11 ...96 A1
Monkton Ct KA9 ...233 B1
Monkton Dr G15 ...75 B1
Monkton Gdns G77 ...157 A2
Monkton Pl PA14 ...68 C4
Monkton Prim Sch KA9 233 B2
Monkton Rd KA9 ...233 B1
Monktonhill Rd KA9 ...233 A4
Monktonhill Rdbt KA9 ...233 B3
Monkwood Pl KA7 ...239 A1
Monmouth Ave G12 ...96 A3
Monreith Ave G61 ...75 B1
Monreith Rd G43 ...136 C3
Monreith Rd E G44 ...137 A3
Monroe Dr G71 ...120 C1
Monroe Pl G71 ...120 C1
Montague La G12 ...96 A2
Montague St G4 ...96 C1
Montalto Ave ML1 ...143 A1
Montclair Pl PA3 ...112 A3
Montego Gn 2 G75 ...159 A1
Monteith Dr G76 ...158 A4
Monteith Gdns G76 ...157 C4
Monteith Pl Blantyre G72 161 C4
10 Glasgow G40 ...117 C3
Monteith Row G40 ...117 C3
Monteith Wlk ML7 ...146 C3
Montfode Ct KA22 ...205 B2
Montfode Dr KA22 ...205 A2
Montford Ave G44 ...137 C4
Montfort Pl FK1 ...42 A2
Montgomerie Cres
KA21 ...216 C4
Montgomerie Ct KA22 ...205 B1
Montgomerie Pier Rd
KA22 ...205 A1
Montgomerie Rd
Prestwick KA9 ...233 A1
Saltcoats KA21 ...216 C4
Montgomerie St
Ardrossan KA22 ...205 B1
Port Glasgow PA14 ...47 B1
Montgomerie Terr
Ayr KA7 ...235 C1
Kilwinning KA13 ...208 A2
Montgomerieston Pl 5
KA25 ...149 A1
Montgomerieston St 6
KA25 ...149 A1
Montgomery Ave
Beith KA15 ...171 B4
Coatbridge ML5 ...121 C4
Paisley PA3 ...114 A4
Montgomery Cres
Falkirk FK2 ...24 A1
Wishaw ML2 ...185 C4
Montgomery Ct
Eaglesham G76 ...178 C2
Kilbirnie KA25 ...149 A1
Paisley PA3 ...114 A4
Montgomery Dr
Falkirk FK2 ...24 A1
Glasgow G46 ...136 B1
Kilbarchan PA10 ...111 A2
Montgomery Pl
9 East Kilbride G74 ...159 C1
Falkirk FK2 ...24 A1
Irvine KA12 ...219 A1
Kilmarnock KA3 ...222 C1
Larkhall ML9 ...185 A1
Montgomery Rd PA3 ...114 A4
Montgomery Sq G76 ...178 C2
Montgomery St
Cambuslang G72 ...139 C3
Eaglesham G76 ...178 C2
6 East Kilbride G74 ...159 C1
Falkirk FK2 ...42 C3
Glasgow G40 ...118 A2
Irvine KA12 ...219 A1
Kilmarnock KA3 ...222 C1
Larkhall ML9 ...185 A2
Montgomery Terr G66 ...58 B3
Montgomery Way FK9 ...2 A2
Montgomery Well FK2 ...24 A1
Montgomery Wynd 5
G74 ...159 C1
Montgomeryfield KA11 ...225 A4
Montgreenan View
KA13 ...207 C2
Montraive St G73 ...118 B1
Montrave St G52 ...115 B2
Montreal Pk G75 ...159 B1
Montrose Ave
Glasgow G32 ...119 B1
Paisley G52 ...114 C4
Port Glasgow PA14 ...68 C3
Montrose Cres ML3 ...162 B2
Montrose Ct PA2 ...132 C4
Montrose Dr G61 ...75 C4
Montrose Gdns
Blantyre G72 ...140 B1
Kilsyth G65 ...36 B1
Milngavie G62 ...55 A2
Montrose La ML3 ...162 B2
Montrose Pl PA3 ...112 A3
Montrose Rd
Paisley PA2 ...132 C4
Stirling FK9 ...2 B2
Montrose St
Clydebank G81 ...74 B1
Glasgow G1 ...241 B2
Motherwell ML1 ...142 B1
Montrose Terr
Bishopbriggs G64 ...98 B4
Bridge of W PA11 ...110 B4
Montrose Way
Bonnybridge FK4 ...39 B3
Paisley PA2 ...132 C4
Monument Cres KA9 ...233 C1
Monument Rd KA7 ...238 C2
Monument View FK8 ...2 A1
Monymusk Gdns G64 ...78 B1
Monymusk Pl G15 ...74 C3
Moodie Ct KA1 ...227 C3
Moodiesburn St G33 ...98 C1
Moor Park Cres KA9 ...236 B3
Moor Park Pl KA9 ...236 B3
Moor Pk KA9 ...236 B3
Moor Pl KA8 ...236 B2
Moor Rd Ayr KA8 ...236 B2
Cartland ML8,ML11 ...202 C1
Eaglesham G76 ...178 B2
Milngavie G62 ...55 A1
Strathblane G63 ...31 B1
Moorburn Ave G46 ...136 A2
Moorburn Pl PA3 ...111 C3
Moorcroft Dr ML6 ...123 C4
Moorcroft Rd G77 ...156 B2
Moore Dr Bearsden G61 ...75 C2
Helensburgh G84 ...25 B4
Moore Gdns ML3 ...183 C4
Moore St Glasgow G31 ...117 C3
Motherwell ML1 ...143 A2
Moorend Workshops
KA11 ...224 D4
Moorfield Ave
Kilmarnock KA1 ...227 B3
Port Glasgow PA14 ...68 B4
Moorfield Cres ML6 ...123 C4
Moorfield Ind Est KA2 ...227 A4
Moorfield La PA19 ...44 B3
Moorfield Pl KA2 ...226 B3
Moorfield Rd
Blantyre G72 ...161 B3
Gourock PA19 ...44 B3
Prestwick KA9 ...236 B4
Moorfield Rdbt KA1 ...227 A4
Moorfoot G64 ...78 B1
Moorfoot Ave
Glasgow G46 ...136 A2
Paisley PA2 ...113 B1
Moorfoot Dr
Gourock PA19 ...44 B3
Wishaw ML2 ...164 C2
Moorfoot Gdns G75 ...180 A2
Moorfoot Path PA2 ...133 B4
Moorfoot Pl KA11 ...220 A2
Moorfoot Prim Sch PA19 44 B3
Moorfoot St G32 ...118 C3
Moorfoot Way
Bearsden G61 ...75 B4
Irvine KA11 ...220 A2
Moorhill Cres G77 ...156 B2
Moorhill Rd G77 ...156 B2
Moorhouse Ave
Glasgow G13 ...94 C3
Paisley PA2 ...113 A1
Moorhouse St G78 ...134 B1
Moorland Dr ML6 ...123 C4
Moorpark Ave
8 Airdrie ML6 ...123 C4
Muirhead G69 ...100 B4
Moorpark Dr G52 ...115 A3
Moorpark Ind Est KA20 ...217 B4
Moorpark Pl
Glasgow G52 ...114 C3
Stevenston KA20 ...217 B4
Moorpark Prim Sch
Kilbirnie KA25 ...149 A2
Renfrew PA4 ...94 A1
Moorpark Rd E KA20 ...217 B4
Moorpark Rd W KA20 ...217 B4
Moorpark Sq PA4 ...94 A1
Moorside St ML8 ...188 A1
Morag Ave G72 ...140 B1
Moraine Ave G15 ...75 A1
Moraine Cir G15 ...75 A1
Moraine Dr
Clarkston G76 ...157 B4
Glasgow G15 ...75 A1
Moraine Pl G15 ...75 A1
Morar Ave G81 ...74 A2
Morar Cres Airdrie ML6 ...102 C1
Bishopbriggs G64 ...77 C1
Bishopton PA7 ...72 B1
Clydebank G81 ...74 A2
Coatbridge ML5 ...101 B1
Morar Ct Clydebank G81 ...74 A2
Cumbernauld G67 ...82 A4
Hamilton ML3 ...162 A1
Morar Dr Bearsden G61 ...76 A2
Clydebank G81 ...74 A2
Cumbernauld G67 ...82 A4
Falkirk FK2 ...24 B1
Linwood PA3 ...112 A3
Paisley PA2 ...113 A1
Rutherglen G73 ...138 A2
Morar Pl
East Kilbride G74 ...159 C2
Irvine KA12 ...219 B3
Newton Mearns G77 ...156 B4
Renfrew PA4 ...94 A2
Morar Rd Clydebank G81 ...74 A2
Glasgow G52 ...115 C3
Port Glasgow PA14 ...68 C4
Morar St ML2 ...165 A1
Morar Terr
Rutherglen G73 ...138 B2
Uddingston G71 ...141 A4
Morar Way
Motherwell ML1 ...143 B2
Shotts ML7 ...147 A2
Moravia Ave G71 ...141 A2
Moray Ave ML6 ...123 A3
Moray Ct G73 ...138 A4
Moray Dr Clarkston G76 ...157 C4
Torrance G64 ...57 A1
Moray Gate G71 ...140 C2
Moray Gdns
Clarkston G76 ...157 C4
Cumbernauld G68 ...61 C3
Uddingston G71 ...140 C4
Moray Pl Bishopbriggs G64 78 B1
Blantyre G72 ...161 B3
Chryston G69 ...100 B4
Glasgow G41 ...116 C1
Kirkintilloch G66 ...59 A1
Moray Pl *continued*
Linwood PA3 ...112 A3
Moray Quadrant ML4 ...142 A3
Moray Rd PA14 ...47 B1
Moray Way ML1 ...143 A3
Mordaunt St G40 ...118 A2
Moredun Cres G32 ...119 B4
Moredun Dr PA2 ...113 A1
Moredun St G32 ...119 B4
Morefield Rd G51 ...115 B4
Morgan Ct FK7 ...7 B2
Morgan Mews 17 G42 ...117 A2
Morgan St Hamilton ML3 ...162 B1
Larkhall ML9 ...184 C2
Morina Gdns G53 ...135 B2
Morion Rd G13 ...95 B4
Moriston Ct ML2 ...165 C3
Morland G74 ...160 B2
Morley Cres FK7 ...7 A2
Morley St G42 ...137 A4
Morna La G14 ...95 C1
Mornay Way ML7 ...146 B3
Morningside Prim Sch
ML2 ...166 A2
Morningside Rd ML2 ...166 B2
Morningside St G33 ...118 C4
Morrin Path G21 ...97 C2
Morrin St G21 ...97 C2
Morris Cres Blantyre G72 161 B4
Hurlford KA1 ...228 C3
Motherwell ML1 ...143 C1
Morris La KA3 ...223 A1
Morris Moodie Ave
KA20 ...217 C4
Morris Rd KA9 ...233 B1
Morris St Greenock PA15 ...46 B2
Hamilton ML3 ...162 B1
Larkhall ML9 ...185 B1
Morris Terr FK8 ...7 A4
Morrishall Rd G74 ...160 B2
Morrishill Dr KA15 ...171 A4
Morrison Ave
Bonnybridge FK4 ...39 C3
Stevenston KA20 ...206 C1
Morrison Ct KA20 ...206 C1
Morrison Dr
Bannockburn FK7 ...7 B1
Lennoxtown G66 ...57 C4
Morrison Gdns Ayr KA8 ...239 A4
Torrance G64 ...78 B4
Morrison Pl KA3 ...223 B1
Morrison Quadrant G81 ...74 C1
Morrison Rd KA9 ...233 B2
Morrison St
Clydebank G81 ...73 C3
Glasgow G5 ...240 B1
Morriston Cres PA4 ...94 C1
Morriston Park Dr G72 ...139 A3
Morriston St G72 ...139 A3
Morten Gdns G41 ...116 B1
Morton Ave KA7 ...239 A3
Morton Pl KA1 ...222 C1
Morton Rd Ayr KA7 ...239 A3
Stewarton KA3 ...211 B4
Morton St ML1 ...163 C4
Morven Ave
Bishopbriggs G64 ...78 B1
Blantyre G72 ...140 B1
Kilmarnock KA3 ...222 C2
Paisley PA2 ...133 B4
Morven Cres KA10 ...229 C1
Morven Ct FK1 ...42 B1
Morven Dr Clarkston G76 157 B4
Linwood PA3 ...112 A3
Troon KA10 ...229 C2
Morven Gait PA8 ...93 C4
Morven Gdns G71 ...140 C4
Morven La G72 ...140 B1
Morven Rd Bearsden G61 ...75 C3
Cambuslang G72 ...138 C2
Morven St
Coatbridge ML5 ...122 A4
Glasgow G52 ...115 C3
Morven Way 3 G71 ...141 A2
Morville Cres KA13 ...207 C3
Mosesfield St G21 ...97 C3
Mosque Ave G5 ...117 B3
Moss Ave
Caldercruix ML6 ...105 A3
Linwood PA3 ...112 A3
Moss Dr Barrhead G78 ...134 A3
Erskine PA8 ...93 A4
Irvine KA11 ...224 D3
Moss Heights Ave G52 ...115 B3
Moss Knowe G67 ...62 B1
Moss Path G69 ...119 C2
Moss Rd Airdrie ML6 ...123 A3
Bridge of W PA11 ...110 C4
Cumbernauld G67 ...62 C2
East Kilbride G75 ...180 B2
Fallin FK7 ...8 B2
Glasgow G51 ...115 B4
Helensburgh G82 ...25 C2
Kilmacolm PA13 ...89 B4
Kirkintilloch G66 ...80 A4
Kirkintilloch, High Gallowhill
G66 ...79 A3
Linwood PA3 ...112 B4
Muirhead G69 ...100 B4
Port Glasgow PA14 ...68 C4
Wishaw ML2 ...165 C2
Moss Side Ave ML6 ...122 C4
Moss St PA1 ...113 C3
Moss-Side Ave ML8 ...187 B1
Moss-Side Rd G41 ...116 C1
Mossacre Rd ML2 ...165 B2
Mossband La ML7 ...146 C3
Mossbank Blantyre G72 ...161 B3
Mossbank *continued*
East Kilbride G75 ...179 C4
Prestwick KA9 ...236 C4
Mossbank Ave G33 ...98 C2
Mossbank Cres ML1 ...143 C2
Mossbank Dr G33 ...98 C2
Mossbank Rd ML2 ...165 B2
Mossbell Rd ML4 ...141 C3
Mossblown St ML9 ...184 C2
Mossburn Ave
Balloch G83 ...19 C1
Harthill ML7 ...127 B3
Mossburn Rd ML2 ...165 B2
Mossburn St ML2 ...165 B1
Mosscastle Rd
Glasgow G33 ...99 B1
Slamannan FK1 ...86 A4
Mossdale G74 ...159 B2
Mossdale Ct ML4 ...142 B3
Mossdale Gdns ML3 ...161 C1
Mossedge Ind Est PA3 ...112 B3
Mossend Ave
Helensburgh G84 ...16 C1
Kilbirnie KA25 ...170 A4
Mossend La G33 ...119 B4
Mossend Pl G84 ...16 C1
Mossend Prim Sch ML4 142 B2
Mossend St G33 ...119 B4
Mossgiel G75 ...180 A4
Mossgiel Ave Cowie FK7 ...12 B4
Kilmarnock KA3 ...228 B4
Rutherglen G73 ...138 A3
Stirling FK8 ...2 A1
Troon KA10 ...229 D2
Mossgiel Cres G76 ...157 C3
Mossgiel Dr
Clydebank G81 ...74 B2
Irvine KA12 ...219 B2
Mossgiel Gdns
Kirkintilloch G66 ...58 C1
Uddingston G71 ...140 C4
Mossgiel La 10 ML9 ...185 B1
Mossgiel Pl Ayr KA7 ...239 A3
Rutherglen G73 ...138 A3
Stevenston KA20 ...206 C1
Mossgiel Rd
Ardrossan KA22 ...205 B2
Ayr KA7 ...239 A3
Cumbernauld G67 ...62 A1
Glasgow G43 ...136 B3
Saltcoats KA21 ...206 A2
Mossgiel St FK1 ...41 A3
Mossgiel Terr G72 ...140 B1
Mossgiel Way ML1 ...143 B2
Mosshall Gr ML1 ...143 C2
Mosshall Rd ML1 ...143 B4
Mosshall St ML1 ...143 C2
Mosshead Prim Sch G61 75 C4
Mosshead Rd
Bearsden G61 ...76 A4
Kilmarnock KA1 ...228 A2
Mosshill Rd ML4 ...142 A4
Mosshouse FK7 ...6 C2
Mosside Pl KA3 ...222 C2
Mosside Rd KA8 ...236 B2
Mossland Dr ML2 ...165 B2
Mossland Rd G52 ...114 C4
Mosslands Rd PA3 ...113 C4
Mosslingal G75 ...180 C3
Mossmulloch G75 ...180 C3
Mossneuk Ave G75 ...179 C4
Mossneuk Cres ML2 ...165 B2
Mossneuk Dr
East Kilbride G75 ...179 C4
Paisley PA2 ...133 B4
Wishaw ML2 ...165 B2
Mossneuk Pk ML2 ...165 B2
Mossneuk Prim Sch
G75 ...179 C4
Mossneuk Rd G75 ...180 A4
Mossneuk St ML5 ...121 C2
Mosspark Ave
Glasgow G52 ...115 C2
Milngavie G62 ...55 A2
Mosspark Bvd G52 ...115 C2
Mosspark Dr G52 ...115 C2
Mosspark La G52 ...115 C2
Mosspark Oval G52 ...115 C2
Mosspark Prim Sch
G52 ...115 C2
Mosspark Rd
Coatbridge ML5 ...121 B4
Milngavie G62 ...55 A2
Mosspark Sq G52 ...115 C2
Mosspark Sta G52 ...115 B2
Mossvale Cres G33 ...99 B1
Mossvale La PA3 ...113 B3
Mossvale Rd G33 ...99 B1
Mossvale Sq Glasgow G33 99 A1
Paisley PA3 ...113 B4
Mossvale St PA3 ...113 B4
Mossvale Terr G69 ...81 A2
Mossvale Way G33 ...99 B1
Mossvale Wlk G33 ...99 B1
Mossview Cres ML6 ...123 A3
Mossview La G52 ...115 B3
Mossview Quadrant
G52 ...115 B3
Mossview Rd G33 ...99 C3
Mosswell Rd G62 ...55 A2
Mossyde Ave PA14 ...69 A4
Mossywood Ct G68 ...81 C4
Mossywood Pl G68 ...81 C4
Mossywood Rd G68 ...81 C4
Mote Hill ML3 ...162 C3
Mote View KA2 ...221 B1
Motehill Rd PA3 ...114 A4
Motherwell Coll ML1 ...163 C2

Netherhill Ave G44 ... 137 A1
Netherhill Cotts PA3 ... 114 A4
Netherhill Cres PA3 ... 114 A3
Netherhill Rd
Moodiesburn G69 ... 80 C1
Paisley PA3 ... 114 A4
Netherhill Way PA3 ... 114 A4
Netherhouse Ave
Coatbridge ML5 ... 121 C2
Kirkintilloch G66 ... 79 C2
Netherhouse Pl G34 ... 120 C4
Netherhouse Rd G69 ... 120 C4
Netherland Rd KA3 ... 211 C4
Netherlee Cres KA24 ... 169 A1
Netherlee Pl G44 ... 137 A2
Netherlee Prim Sch
G44 ... 136 C1
Netherlee Rd G44 ... 137 A2
Nethermains Prim Sch
FK6 ... 21 B1
Nethermains Rd
Denny FK6 ... 21 B1
Kilwinning KA13 ... 207 C1
Milngavie G62 ... 76 A4
Nethermiln Rd KA23 ... 190 B2
Netherpark Ave G44 ... 137 A1
Netherplace Cres
Glasgow G53 ... 135 A4
Newton Mearns G77 ... 156 B2
Netherplace Rd
Glasgow G53 ... 135 A4
Newton Mearns G77 ... 156 A2
Netherton Ave PA14 ... 69 A4
Netherton Ct
Glasgow G45 ... 137 C1
Newton Mearns G77 ... 157 A4
Netherton Dr G78 ... 134 C1
Netherton Hill G66 ... 57 A4
Netherton Ind Est ML2 ... 164 C1
Netherton Oval G66 ... 33 A1
Netherton Prim Sch
Glasgow G45 ... 137 B1
Wishaw ML2 ... 164 C1
Netherton Rd
East Kilbride G75 ... 180 A2
East Kilbride, The Murray
G75 ... 180 B4
Glasgow G13 ... 95 C4
Newton Mearns G77 ... 156 C3
Wishaw ML2 ... 164 C1
Netherton St
Harthill ML7 ... 127 B3
Wishaw ML2 ... 164 C1
Nethervale Ave G44 ... 136 C1
Netherview Rd G44 ... 137 A1
Netherway G44 ... 136 C1
Netherwood Ave G68 ... 81 C4
Netherwood Ct
Cumbernauld G68 ... 82 A4
Motherwell ML1 ... 164 A1
Netherwood Gr G68 ... 82 A4
Netherwood Pl G68 ... 81 C4
Netherwood Rd
Cumbernauld G68 ... 81 C4
Motherwell ML1 ... 164 B2
Netherwood Twr ML1 ... 164 A1
Netherwood Way G68 ... 82 A4
Nethy Way PA4 ... 94 C1
Neucks The FK1 ... 87 A3
Neuk Ave Houston PA6 ... 91 B1
Muirhead G69 ... 100 B4
Neuk Cres PA6 ... 91 B1
Neuk The ML2 ... 164 C2
Neuk Way G32 ... 139 B4
Neukfoot La G78 ... 153 A2
Nevan Rd KA10 ... 229 D3
Neville G74 ... 160 B2
Nevis Ave ML3 ... 162 A1
Nevis Cres FK10 ... 10 A4
Nevis Ct Barrhead G78 ... 134 B1
Coatbridge ML5 ... 122 B2
Motherwell ML1 ... 163 C2
Nevis Dr G64 ... 57 A1
Nevis Pl Falkirk FK1 ... 42 B1
Kilmarnock KA1 ... 228 A2
Shotts ML7 ... 147 A2
Nevis Rd Bearsden G61 ... 75 A4
Glasgow G43 ... 136 A3
Renfrew PA4 ... 94 A1
Nevis Way Irvine KA11 ... 220 A2
Renfrew PA3 ... 93 C1
Nevison St ML9 ... 185 A1
New Ashtree St ML2 ... 164 C2
New Ave PA9 ... 130 C3
New Bldgs ML11 ... 215 A1
New Bridge St KA7 ... 235 C1
New Carron Rd FK5 ... 24 A2
New Century Dr ML7 ... 146 C2
New City Rd Glasgow G4 240 B4
Glasgow G4 ... 240 C4
New City Row G63 ... 31 A2
New Cordale Rd G82 ... 27 B1
New Cross ML3 ... 162 C2
New Dock La PA15 ... 46 A3
New Edinburgh Rd G71,
ML4 ... 141 B3
New England Rd KA21 ... 206 A1
New Hallglen Rd FK1 ... 42 B1
New Hill Rd KA20 ... 218 B2
New Inchinnan Rd PA3 ... 113 C4
New Inchinnon Way
PA3 ... 113 C4
New Kirk Rd G61 ... 75 C3
New La ML6 ... 123 A2
New Lairdsland Rd G66 ... 79 B4
New Lanark (YH)★
ML11 ... 214 C1
New Lanark Heritage Trail★
ML11 ... 215 A1
New Lanark Prim Sch
ML11 ... 215 A1
New Lanark Rd ML11 ... 214 C1
New Lanark World Heritage
Village★ ML11 ... 215 A1
New Lime Pend 3 G74 ... 159 C1
New Line Rd FK7 ... 11 A4
New Luce Dr G32 ... 119 B2
New Mill Rd KA1 ... 228 A4
New Monkland Prim Sch
ML6 ... 102 C2
New Park St ML3 ... 162 B3
New Plymouth G75 ... 180 A4
New Rd Ayr KA8 ... 235 C1
Bannockburn FK7 ... 7 B1
Cambuslang G72 ... 139 C2
New Sneddon St PA3 ... 113 C3
New St Beith KA15 ... 171 A4
Blantyre G72 ... 161 B4
Bridge of A FK9 ... 1 C4
Clydebank G81 ... 74 A3
Dalry KA24 ... 191 B4
Irvine KA12 ... 219 A1
Kilbarchan PA10 ... 111 A2
Kilmarnock KA1 ... 227 C3
Lochwinnoch PA12 ... 129 B1
Paisley PA1 ... 113 C2
Slamannan FK1 ... 86 A4
Stevenston KA20 ... 217 B4
Stewarton KA3 ... 195 B1
Stonehouse ML9 ... 198 C1
New Stevenston Prim Sch
ML1 ... 142 C2
New Stevenston Rd
ML1 ... 143 A1
New View Cres ML4 ... 142 A2
New View Dr ML4 ... 142 A2
New View Pl ML4 ... 142 A2
New Wynd G1 ... 241 A1
Neward Cres KA9 ... 236 B3
Newark KA13 ... 207 B1
Newark Ave PA16 ... 45 B4
Newark Castle★ PA14 ... 47 B1
Newark Cres KA7 ... 238 A1
Newark Dr Glasgow G41 ... 116 C2
Paisley PA2 ... 133 B4
Wishaw ML2 ... 165 B3
Newark Pl
Port Glasgow PA14 ... 47 B1
Wishaw ML2 ... 165 B3
Newark St Greenock PA16 ... 45 B4
Port Glasgow PA14 ... 47 B1
Newark Terr KA9 ... 236 B4
Newarthill Prim Sch
ML1 ... 143 C2
Newarthill Rd ML1 ... 143 B1
Newbank Ct G31 ... 118 C2
Newbank Gdns G31 ... 118 B2
Newbank Rd G31 ... 118 C2
Newbarns St ML8 ... 187 C2
Newbattle Ave ML6 ... 123 A1
Newbattle Ct G32 ... 119 A1
Newbattle Gdns G32 ... 119 A1
Newbattle Pl G32 ... 119 A1
Newbattle Rd G32 ... 119 A1
Newbiggin Cres FK10 ... 4 B1
Newbold Ave 11 G21 ... 97 C4
Newburgh PA8 ... 73 A2
Newburgh St G43 ... 136 B4
Newcarron Ct FK2 ... 42 A4
Newcastleton Dr 9 G23 ... 76 C1
Newcraigs Dr G76 ... 158 B4
Newcroft Dr G44 ... 137 B3
Newdyke Ave G66 ... 79 C4
Newdyke Rd G66 ... 79 C4
Newdykes Rd KA9 ... 233 B1
Newfield Cres ML3 ... 162 A2
Newfield Dr KA2 ... 225 C1
Newfield La 15 G71 ... 141 A2
Newfield Pl
Dundonald KA2 ... 225 C1
Glasgow G46 ... 135 C1
Irvine KA11 ... 220 A3
Rutherglen G73 ... 137 C4
Newfield Rd ML9 ... 198 C1
Newfield Sq G53 ... 135 A3
Newford Gr G76 ... 157 C3
Newgrove Gdns G72 ... 139 A3
Newhall St G40 ... 117 C2
Newhaven Rd G33 ... 119 A4
Newhaven St G32 ... 119 A4
Newhills Rd G33 ... 119 C4
Newhouse FK8 ... 7 A3
Newhouse Dr Falkirk FK1 ... 41 C1
Kilbirnie KA25 ... 169 C4
Newhouse Ind Est ML1 ... 143 B4
Newhouse Intc KA11 ... 224 D3
Newhouse Way KA11 ... 220 A3
Newhousemill Cotts
G74 ... 181 B4
Newhousemill Rd
East Kilbride G74,G72 ... 181 B4
Hamilton G72,ML3 ... 161 B1
Newhouses Rd G68 ... 61 A2
Newhut Rd ML1 ... 142 B1
Newington La FK5 ... 22 B3
Newington St G32 ... 118 C3
Newlands Dr
Hamilton ML3 ... 183 B4
Kilmarnock KA3 ... 222 C3
Newlands Gdns PA5 ... 112 B1
Newlands Pl
East Kilbride G74 ... 159 C1
Kilmarnock KA3 ... 222 C2
Newlands Pl *continued*
Tullibody FK10 ... 4 B2
Newlands Rd
Bannockburn FK7 ... 11 B4
East Kilbride G75 ... 179 C3
East Kilbride, Newlandsmuir
G75 ... 180 A4
Glasgow G43 ... 136 C3
Uddingston G71 ... 140 C4
Newlands St
Coatbridge ML5 ... 122 A2
Lanark ML11 ... 215 B2
Newlands Terr
Carluke ML8 ... 187 C1
Milton of C G66 ... 58 B3
Newlandsfield Rd G43 ... 136 B4
Newlandsmuir Rd G75 ... 180 A3
Newmains Ave PA4 ... 93 A3
Newmains Prim Sch
Renfrew PA4 ... 94 B1
Wishaw ML2 ... 166 A2
Newmains Rd PA4 ... 94 B1
Newmarket FK7 ... 7 C1
Newmarket Ctr FK1 ... 42 A3
Newmarket St Ayr KA7 ... 238 C4
Falkirk FK1 ... 42 A3
Newmill & Canthill Rd
ML7 ... 146 A3
Newmill Gdns ML7 ... 145 C2
Newmill Rd Dunlop KA3 ... 195 B4
Glasgow G21 ... 98 B3
Newmills FK10 ... 4 A2
Newmilns Gdn KA3 ... 223 A3
Newmoor Intc KA11 ... 219 C1
Newnham Rd PA1 ... 114 C2
Newpark Cres
Cambuslang G72 ... 139 A4
Stirling FK7 ... 7 A1
Newpark Rd FK7 ... 7 A1
Newrose Ave ML4 ... 142 B4
Newshot Dr PA8 ... 73 B1
Newstead Gdns G23 ... 76 C1
Newton Ave
Cambuslang G72 ... 139 B3
Elderslie PA5 ... 112 C2
Skinflats FK2 ... 24 C2
Newton Brae G72 ... 139 C3
Newton Ct G77 ... 156 B2
Newton Dr Elderslie PA5 ... 112 C2
Uddingston G71 ... 141 A4
Wishaw ML2 ... 166 A3
Newton Farm Rd G72 ... 140 B3
Newton Gr G77 ... 156 C2
Newton Of Barr PA12 ... 129 A1
Newton on Ayr Sta KA8 236 A2
Newton Park Ct KA8 ... 236 A1
Newton Pl Glasgow G3 ... 240 A4
Newton Mearns G77 ... 156 C2
Newton Prim Sch KA8 ... 236 A1
Newton Rd Bishopton PA7 ... 72 A2
Kirkintilloch G66 ... 79 C2
Newton St
Coatbridge ML5 ... 121 C2
Glasgow G3 ... 240 B3
Greenock PA16 ... 45 B3
Kilbirnie KA25 ... 149 A1
Paisley PA1 ... 113 B2
Newton Sta G72 ... 139 C3
Newton Station Rd G72 139 C3
Newton Terr
Elderslie PA3 ... 112 C2
Glasgow G3 ... 240 A3
Greenock PA16 ... 45 B3
Newton Terrace La G3 ... 240 A3
Newton Trad Est KA8 ... 236 A1
Newton Way PA3 ... 114 A4
Newton Wlk KA1 ... 228 A4
Newtongrange Ave G32 119 A1
Newtongrange Gdns
G32 ... 119 A2
Newtonhead KA11 ... 220 A3
Newtonlea Ave G77 ... 156 C2
Newtonshaw FK10 ... 5 B1
Newtown St G65 ... 60 B4
Newtyle Dr G53 ... 114 C1
Newtyle Pl
Bishopbriggs G64 ... 78 B1
Glasgow G53 ... 114 C1
Newtyle Rd PA1 ... 114 B2
Nicholas St G1 ... 241 B2
Nicholson Pl FK1 ... 41 C1
Nicholson St G5 ... 117 A3
Nicklaus Way ML1 ... 143 C4
Nicol Dr PA16 ... 45 A3
Nicol St Airdrie ML6 ... 103 B1
Greenock PA16 ... 45 A2
Nicolson Ct G33 ... 99 C3
Nicolson St PA15 ... 45 C3
Niddrie Rd G42 ... 117 A1
Niddrie Sq 6 G42 ... 116 C1
Niddry St PA3 ... 113 C3
Nigel Gdns G41 ... 116 B1
Nigel St ML1 ... 163 B3
Nigg Pl G34 ... 120 A4
Nightingale Pl PA5 ... 131 B3
Nikitas Ave ML9 ... 199 A4
Nile Ct KA7 ... 238 C4
Nile St PA15 ... 45 C2
Nimmo Dr G51 ... 115 C4
Nimmo Pl Carluke ML8 ... 187 C2
Wishaw ML2 ... 165 B2
Nimmo Rd PA16 ... 45 B2
Nimmo St PA16 ... 45 B2
Nineyard St KA21 ... 216 C4
Ninian Ave PA6 ... 111 B4
Ninian Rd ML6 ... 123 B3
Ninian's Rise G66 ... 79 C4
Ninian's Terr KA13 ... 207 C1
Niph Ct PA4 ... 93 B4
Nisbet Dr Denny FK6 ... 21 B1
Prestwick KA9 ... 236 B3
Nisbet St G31 ... 118 B3
Nisbett Pl ML6 ... 123 C1
Nisbett St ML6 ... 123 C1
Nith Ave PA2 ... 112 C1
Nith Dr Hamilton ML3 ... 183 A4
Renfrew PA4 ... 94 C1
Nith La 24 ML2 ... 165 C3
Nith Path ML1 ... 144 B1
Nith Pl KA1 ... 228 A3
Nith Quadrant ML1 ... 143 B2
Nith St G33 ... 98 B1
Nithsdale G74 ... 160 B2
Nithsdale Cres G61 ... 75 B3
Nithsdale Cross G41 ... 116 B2
Nithsdale Dr G41 ... 116 C1
Nithsdale Pl G41 ... 116 C2
Nithsdale Rd
Ardrossan KA22 ... 205 B2
Glasgow G41 ... 116 B2
Nithsdale St
Glasgow G41 ... 116 C1
Shotts ML7 ... 146 B3
Nitshill Prim Sch G53 ... 135 A2
Nitshill Rd G53 ... 135 B2
Nitshill Sta G53 ... 135 A3
Niven Ct KA3 ... 223 B2
Niven St G20 ... 96 B3
Noble Prim Sch ML4 ... 142 A4
Noble Rd ML4 ... 142 A3
Nobles Pl ML4 ... 141 C2
Nobles View ML4 ... 141 C2
Nobleston G83 ... 27 C1
Noldrum Ave G32 ... 139 B4
Noldrum Gdns G32 ... 139 B4
Noltmire Rd KA8 ... 236 B2
Noran Cres KA10 ... 229 D3
Norbreck Dr G46 ... 136 B2
Norby Rd G11 ... 95 C2
Noremac Way ML4 ... 141 C4
Norfield Dr G44 ... 137 A4
Norfolk Cres G64 ... 77 C2
Norfolk Ct G5 ... 117 A3
Norfolk Ho 15 G74 ... 159 C1
Norfolk Rd PA16 ... 44 C2
Norfolk St G5 ... 117 A3
Norham St G41 ... 116 C1
Norman Cres KA12 ... 219 A3
Norman St G40 ... 117 C2
Norse La N G14 ... 95 B2
Norse La S 16 G14 ... 95 B2
Norse Pl G14 ... 95 B2
Norse Rd G14 ... 95 B2
North & South Rd ML1 ... 144 C1
North Ayrshire Mus★
KA21 ... 216 C4
North Ave
Cambuslang G72 ... 138 C3
Carluke ML8 ... 187 B1
Clydebank G81 ... 74 A1
Motherwell ML1 ... 143 A1
North Bank Pl G81 ... 94 B4
North Bank St G81 ... 94 B4
North Barr PA8 ... 73 A2
North Barr Ave PA8 ... 73 A1
North Berwick Ave G68 ... 61 C3
North Berwick Cres
G75 ... 180 A3
North Berwick Gdns G68 61 C2
North Biggar Rd ML6 ... 123 A4
North Birbiston Rd G66 ... 57 C4
North Bridge St ML6 ... 122 C4
North British Rd G71 ... 140 C3
North Broomagrge Rdbt
FK5 ... 23 A2
North Bute St ML5 ... 122 A2
North Caldeen Rd ML5 122 B3
North Calder Dr ML6 ... 123 B3
North Calder Gr G71 ... 120 A1
North Calder Pl G71 ... 120 A1
North Calder Rd G71 ... 121 B1
North Campbell Ave G62 54 C1
North Canal Bank G4 ... 97 B1
North Canal Bank St G4 ... 97 B1
North Carbrain Rd G67 ... 61 C1
North Castle St FK10 ... 10 A3
North Claremont La G62 ... 55 A1
North Claremont St 14
G3 ... 96 C1
North Corsebar Rd PA2 ... 113 B1
North Court La G1 ... 241 A2
North Crescent Ave
KA22 ... 205 B2
North Crescent Rd
KA22 ... 205 A2
North Croft St PA3 ... 113 C3
North Ct G1 ... 241 A2
North Dean Park Ave
G71 ... 141 A1
North Douglas St G81 ... 94 B4
North Dr Kilbirnie KA25 ... 170 A4
Linwood PA3 ... 112 A3
Troon KA10 ... 229 D2
North Dryburgh Rd ML2 165 A3
North Dumgoyne Ave
G62 ... 54 C2
North Elgin Pl G81 ... 94 B4
North Elgin St G81 ... 94 B4
North Erskine Pk G61 ... 75 B3
North Faulds Rd ML11 ... 215 C3
North Frederick St G1 ... 241 A3
North Gardner St G11 ... 96 A2
North Gargieston Rd
KA1 ... 227 B3
North Glasgow Coll
Glasgow G21 ... 98 B3
North Glasgow Coll *continued*
Glasgow, Springburn G21 ... 97 C2
North Gower St 2 G51 ... 116 B3
North Grange Rd G61 ... 75 C3
North Green Dr FK2 ... 14 B2
North Hamilton Pl KA1 ... 222 C1
North Hamilton St KA1 ... 222 C1
North Hanover St G1,
G4 ... 241 A3
North Harbour Ind Est
KA8 ... 235 C1
North Harbour St KA8 ... 235 C1
North Iverton Park Rd
PA5 ... 112 A2
North Kilmeny Cres
ML2 ... 165 B3
North La PA3 ... 112 B3
North Lodge Ave ML1 ... 163 C2
North Lodge Rd PA4 ... 94 B2
North Main St
Alexandria G83 ... 27 B3
Falkirk FK2 ... 24 B2
North Moraine La G15 ... 75 B1
North Neuk KA10 ... 229 D4
North Newmoor Ind Est
KA11 ... 219 C1
North Orchard St ML1 ... 163 B4
North Park Ave Ayr KA8 ... 236 A2
Barrhead G78 ... 134 A2
Glasgow G46 ... 135 C2
North Portland St G1,
G4 ... 241 B2
North Rd Bellshill ML4 ... 142 A4
Coatbridge ML5 ... 122 A1
Cumbernauld G68 ... 82 A4
Johnstone PA5 ... 111 C1
Port Glasgow PA14 ... 68 C4
West Kilbride KA23 ... 190 B3
North Ring Rd KA20 ... 218 A3
North Shore Rd KA10 ... 229 C2
North Sq ML5 ... 121 C4
North St Alexandria G83 ... 27 C3
Alloa FK10 ... 10 A4
Dalry KA24 ... 191 B4
Falkirk FK2 ... 42 A4
Glasgow G3 ... 240 A3
Greenock PA16 ... 45 B4
Houston PA6 ... 91 A2
Larkhall ML9 ... 185 A2
Motherwell ML1 ... 163 C4
Paisley PA3 ... 113 C3
Stirling FK9 ... 2 B1
North Street Ind Est G83 27 C3
North Vennel
Irvine KA11 ... 220 A2
Lanark ML11 ... 215 A2
North View G61 ... 75 B1
North View Rd PA11 ... 110 C3
North Wallace St G4 ... 241 B4
North Wood Rd FK10 ... 4 B1
North Woodside Rd G20 ... 96 C2
Northacre KA13 ... 207 C3
Northacre Gr KA13 ... 207 B3
Northall Quadrant ML1 ... 143 A1
Northampton Dr G12 ... 96 A3
Northampton La G12 ... 96 A3
Northbank Ave
Cambuslang G72 ... 139 B3
Kirkintilloch G66 ... 79 B4
Northbank Rd G66 ... 79 B4
Northbank St G72 ... 139 B3
Northbrae Pl G13 ... 95 A3
Northburn Ave ML6 ... 103 A1
Northburn Pl ML6 ... 103 A1
Northburn Rd ML5 ... 102 B1
Northburn St ML6 ... 104 A1
Northcraig Rd KA3 ... 223 A2
Northcroft Rd G69 ... 80 C1
Northdoon Pl KA7 ... 238 B2
Northend FK7 ... 6 B3
Northfield G75 ... 179 C4
Northfield Ave Ayr KA8 ... 236 A2
Port Glasgow PA14 ... 68 C4
Shotts ML7 ... 147 A1
Northfield Dr G83 ... 27 C3
Northfield Pl KA8 ... 236 A2
Northfield Rd
Alexandria G83 ... 28 A3
Denny FK6 ... 21 B2
Kilsyth G65 ... 36 A1
Northfield St ML1 ... 163 C4
Northflat Pl ML8 ... 202 B4
Northgate Quadrant G21 98 B3
Northgate Rd G21 ... 98 B4
Northinch Ct G14 ... 95 B1
Northinch St G14 ... 95 B1
Northland Ave G14 ... 95 B3
Northland Dr G14 ... 95 B3
Northland Gdns G14 ... 95 B3
Northland La G14 ... 95 B2
Northmuir Dr ML2 ... 165 B2
Northmuir Rd G15 ... 75 A2
Northpark St G20 ... 96 C2
Northumberland St G20 ... 96 C2
Northway G72 ... 140 B1
Northwood Dr ML2 ... 166 A3
Norton St FK12 ... 5 A4
Norval St G11 ... 96 A1
Norwich Dr G12 ... 96 A3
Norwood Ave Alloa FK10 ... 9 C4
Bonnybridge FK4 ... 40 A4
Kirkintilloch G66 ... 79 A4
Norwood Cres FK10 ... 9 C4
Norwood Ct FK4 ... 40 A4
Norwood Dr G46 ... 136 A1
Norwood Gr FK10 ... 9 C4
Norwood Pk G61 ... 75 C2
Norwood Pl FK4 ... 40 A4

Norwood Terr G71 ...141 A4
Notre Dame High RC Sch G12 ...96 B2
Notre Dame High Sch PA16 ...45 B2
Notre Dame Prim RC Sch G12 ...96 B2
Nottingham Ave G12 ...96 A3
Nottingham La G12 ...96 A3
Novar Dr G12 ...96 A2
Novar Gdns G64 ...77 C1
Novar St ML3 ...162 B1
Nuneaton St G40 ...118 A2
Nuneaton Street Ind Est G40 ...118 A2
Nurseries Rd G69 ...119 C3
Nursery Ave Erskine PA7 ...72 C2
Kilmarnock KA1 ...228 A4
Prestwick KA9 ...236 A3
Nursery Bldgs ML11 ...215 A1
Nursery Ct Carluke ML8 ...187 C2
Lanark ML11 ...214 C2
Nursery Dr ML9 ...200 A4
Nursery Gdns
Kilmarnock KA1 ...228 A4
Springside KA11 ...221 A1
Nursery Gr Ayr KA7 ...239 A3
Kilmacolm PA13 ...69 B1
Nursery La Glasgow G41 ...116 C1
Kilmacolm PA13 ...69 B1
Nursery Pk ML8 ...187 C1
Nursery Pl
Ardrossan KA22 ...205 B1
Blantyre G72 ...161 B3
Nursery Rd Ayr KA7 ...239 A3
Falkirk FK1 ...41 C2
Nursery St Glasgow G41 ...117 A2
Helensburgh G84 ...25 A4
Kilmarnock KA1 ...227 C4
Nursery Wynd KA7 ...239 A3
Nutberry Ct G42 ...117 A1

O

O'Connor Ct KA21 ...216 C4
O'Hanlon Way FK8 ...1 C1
O'Hare G83 ...28 A2
O'Neil Ave G64 ...98 A4
O'Neil Terr G83 ...27 C2
O'Wood Ave ML1 ...143 A3
Oak Ave Bearsden G62 ...75 C4
East Kilbride G75 ...180 A3
Oak Cres Glasgow G69 ...120 A2
Plean FK7 ...12 B2
Oak Dr Cambuslang G72 ...139 B2
Fallin FK7 ...8 B2
Kirkintilloch G66 ...79 A3
Stenhousemuir FK5 ...23 B1
Oak Fern Dr G74 ...159 B2
Oak Fern Gr G74 ...159 B2
Oak Gr ML6 ...123 C2
Oak Lea ML3 ...162 C1
Oak Mall The PA15 ...45 C3
Oak Path ML1 ...143 A3
Oak Pk Bishopbriggs G64 ...78 A1
Motherwell ML1 ...163 B2
Oak Pl Coatbridge ML5 ...122 B3
East Kilbride G75 ...180 A3
Kilmarnock KA1 ...227 B4
Uddingston G71 ...141 B4
Oak Rd Ardrossan KA22 ...205 B2
Clydebank G81 ...73 C3
Cumbernauld G67 ...62 C2
Paisley PA2 ...114 A1
Oak St Glasgow G2 ...240 B2
Stirling FK8 ...1 C1
Oak Wynd G72 ...139 C2
Oakbank Ave ML2 ...164 C1
Oakbank Dr G78 ...155 C4
Oakbank Ind Est G20 ...97 A2
Oakbank Rd PA14 ...68 C4
Oakbank St ML6 ...123 B4
Oakburn Ave G62 ...54 C1
Oakburn Cres G62 ...54 C1
Oakdene Ave
Bellshill ML4 ...142 A4
Uddingston G71 ...141 A4
Oakdene Cres ML1 ...143 B2
Oakfield Ave G12 ...96 C1
Oakfield Dr 2 ML1 ...163 C3
Oakfield La 2 G12 ...96 C1
Oakfield Prim Sch PA15 ...46 B2
Oakfield Rd ML1 ...163 C3
Oakgrove Prim Sch G4 ...97 A1
Oakhill Ave G69 ...119 C2
Oakland Dr KA20 ...206 C1
Oaklands Ave KA12 ...219 B2
Oaklea Cres G72 ...161 B4
Oakleigh Dr PA16 ...45 B4
Oakley Dr G44 ...136 C2
Oakley Terr 4 G31 ...117 C4
Oakridge Cres PA3 ...113 A3
Oakridge Rd G69 ...121 A3
Oaks The Glasgow G44 ...137 A2
Johnstone PA5 ...111 C1
Oakshaw Brae PA1 ...113 B3
Oakshaw St E PA1 ...113 C3
Oakshaw St W PA1 ...113 B3
Oakshawhead PA1 ...113 B3
Oakside Pl ML3 ...183 B4
Oaktree Gdns
Dumbarton G82 ...50 B1
Glasgow G45 ...137 C2
Oakwood Ave Ayr KA8 ...236 C1
Paisley PA2 ...113 A1
Oakwood Cres G34 ...100 B1
Oakwood Dr Beith KA15 ...171 A4
Oakwood Dr *continued*
Coatbridge ML5 ...121 B3
Glasgow G34 ...100 B1
Newton Mearns G77 ...156 C2
Oates Gdns ML1 ...164 A2
Oatfield St G21 ...98 A2
Oban Ct 5 G20 ...96 C2
Oban Dr G20 ...96 C2
Oban La G20 ...96 C2
Oban Terr PA16 ...44 C2
Oberon FK10 ...9 C4
Obiston Gdns G32 ...119 A3
Obree Ave KA9 ...236 C3
Observatory La 11 G12 ...96 B2
Observatory Rd G12 ...96 B2
Ochel Path ML6 ...123 C1
Ochil Cres FK8 ...2 A1
Ochil Ct East Kilbride G75 ...180 A2
Irvine KA11 ...220 A2
Tullibody FK10 ...4 B2
Ochil Dr Barrhead G78 ...134 B1
Paisley PA2 ...133 C4
Stenhousemuir FK5 ...23 C2
Ochil Pl Glasgow G32 ...119 A2
Kilmarnock KA1 ...228 A2
Ochil Rd Alva FK12 ...5 A4
Bearsden G61 ...75 A4
Bishopbriggs G64 ...78 B1
Menstrie FK11 ...4 A4
Renfrew PA4 ...94 A1
Stirling FK9 ...2 B2
Ochil St Alloa FK10 ...10 A4
Fallin FK7 ...8 B2
Glasgow G32 ...119 A2
Tullibody FK10 ...4 A2
Wishaw ML2 ...164 C2
Ochil Terr FK2 ...24 A1
Ochil View Denny FK6 ...39 B4
Shieldhill FK1 ...66 B4
8 Uddingston G71 ...141 A4
Ochil View Ct FK5 ...23 B3
Ochilmount FK7 ...7 C1
Ochiltree Ave G13 ...95 C4
Ochiltree Dr ML3 ...161 C1
Ochiltree Pl KA3 ...223 A3
Ochiltree Terr FK1 ...41 A3
Ochilvale Terr FK10 ...5 B2
Ochilview Alva FK12 ...5 A4
Cowie FK7 ...12 C3
Ochilview Pk (Stenhousemuir FC) FK5 ...23 B2
Ochre Cres FK7 ...12 B4
Octavia Terr PA16 ...45 B4
Odense Ct G75 ...180 C3
Ogilface Cres EH48 ...107 B1
Ogilvie Ct 2 ML6 ...123 C4
Ogilvie Pl Bridge of A FK9 ...2 A3
Glasgow G31 ...118 B2
Kilmarnock KA3 ...223 B1
Ogilvie Prim RC Sch G33 ...119 C4
Ogilvie Rd FK8 ...7 A3
Ogilvie St G31 ...118 B2
Old Airbles Rd ML1 ...163 B3
Old Aisle Rd G66 ...79 C4
Old Auchans View KA2 ...225 C1
Old Avon Rd ML3 ...163 A1
Old Balmore Rd G64 ...77 C4
Old Bellsdyke Rd FK5 ...23 A2
Old Biggar Rd ML6 ...83 A1
Old Bore Rd ML6 ...123 C4
Old Bothwell Rd G71 ...162 A4
Old Bridge of Weir Rd PA6 ...91 A1
Old Bridge Rd KA8 ...236 C2
Old Bridge St
9 Alloa FK10 ...10 A3
Ayr KA7 ...235 C1
Old Bridge Wynd FK9 ...2 A2
Old Bridgend ML8 ...187 C1
Old Caley Rd KA12 ...219 B2
Old Castle Gdns G44 ...137 A3
Old Castle Rd G44 ...137 A3
Old Church Gdns G69 ...121 A3
Old Coach Rd G74 ...159 C2
Old Cross 4 Airdrie ML6 ...123 A4
Hamilton ML3 ...162 C2
Old Dalmarnock Rd G40 ...117 C2
Old Dalnottar Rd G60 ...73 B3
Old Denny Rd FK5 ...23 A2
Old Drove Rd FK7 ...6 B3
Old Dulatur Rd G68 ...61 B3
Old Dumbarton Rd G3 ...96 B1
Old Eastfield St ML7 ...127 B3
Old Edinburgh Rd G71 ...141 B4
Old Farm Rd KA8 ...236 B2
Old Gartloch Rd G34 ...100 C3
Old Glasgow Rd
Cumbernauld G67 ...62 A2
Stewarton KA3 ...195 C1
Uddingston G71 ...140 C3
Uddingston, Kylepark G71 ...140 B4
Old Govan Rd PA4 ...94 C2
Old Greenock Rd
Bishopton PA7 ...71 B3
Bishopton, Kingston PA7, PA8 ...72 B1
Langbank PA14 ...70 B3
Old Hillfoot Rd KA7 ...239 A3
Old Humbie Rd G77 ...156 C1
Old Inns Int G67 ...62 B3
Old Inns Rdbt G68 ...62 A3
Old Inverkip Rd PA16 ...45 A2
Old Irvine Rd KA1 ...227 C4
Old Lanark Rd
Carluke ML8 ...202 A4
Old Lanark Rd *continued*
Carluke, Braidwood ML8, ML11 ...202 A2
Old Largs Rd PA16 ...45 C1
Old Loans Rd KA10 ...230 A2
Old Luss Rd Balloch G83 ...19 A1
Helensburgh G84 ...16 C1
Old Manse Gdns ML5 ...122 A4
Old Manse Rd
Glasgow G32 ...119 B3
Wishaw ML2 ...164 C1
Old McDonalds Clyde Valley Farm Pk★ ML9 ...186 A1
Old Military Rd G83 ...20 C4
Old Mill Ct G81 ...74 A3
Old Mill Gate G73 ...138 A3
Old Mill Park Ind Est G66 ...58 B1
Old Mill Rd Bothwell G71 ...141 A1
Cambuslang G72 ...139 B3
Clydebank G81 ...74 A3
East Kilbride G74 ...159 C1
Hartwood ML7 ...146 A1
Kilmarnock KA1 ...228 A4
Paisley PA2 ...113 A2
Uddingston G71 ...140 C3
Old Mill View G65 ...60 C2
Old Mill Wlk G83 ...27 C4
Old Monkland Prim Sch ML5 ...121 B2
Old Monkland Rd ML5 ...121 C2
Old Mugdock Rd G63 ...31 B1
Old Playfield Rd G76 ...158 B4
Old Quarry Rd
Cumbernauld G68 ...81 B3
Stevenston KA20 ...217 B4
Old Raise Rd KA21 ...206 A1
Old Rd PA5 ...112 B2
Old Redding Rd FK2 ...42 C2
Old Rome Way KA2 ...226 C3
Old School Ct FK10 ...4 A1
Old Schoolhouse La PA6 ...91 A2
Old Shettleston Rd G32 ...119 A3
Old Sneddon St PA3 ...113 C3
Old St Clydebank G81 ...73 C3
Kilmarnock KA1 ...227 C3
Old Stable Row ML5 ...122 A4
Old Station Ct G71 ...141 A1
Old Station Wynd KA10 ...229 D2
Old Town FK7 ...7 B1
Old Union St ML6 ...123 A4
Old Willowyard Rd KA15 ...171 A4
Old Wishaw Rd ML8 ...187 C2
Old Wood Rd G69 ...120 A2
Old Woodwynd Rd KA13 ...207 C2
Old Wynd G1 ...241 A1
Oldbarhills TP Site PA2 ...134 B4
Oldhall Dr PA13 ...69 B1
Oldhall Rd PA1 ...114 B3
Oldhall Rdbt KA11 ...224 D3
Oldhall West Ind Est KA11 ...224 D3
Olifard Ave G71 ...141 A2
Oliphant Cres
Clarkston G76 ...157 C3
Paisley PA2 ...132 C4
Oliphant Ct Paisley PA2 ...132 C4
Stirling FK8 ...2 A1
Oliphant Dr KA3 ...228 B4
Oliphant Oval PA2 ...132 C4
Olive Bank G71 ...121 B1
Olive Ct ML1 ...143 A3
Olive Rd KA1 ...228 A4
Olive St G33 ...98 B2
Oliver Rd FK1 ...42 B2
Olympia Arc 4 G74 ...180 C4
Olympia Ct G74 ...180 C4
Olympia St 5 G40 ...117 C3
Olympia The 3 G74 ...180 C4
Omoa Rd ML1 ...144 A1
Onich Pl ML7 ...147 A2
Onslow G75 ...180 B4
Onslow Dr G31 ...118 A4
Onslow Rd G81 ...74 B1
Onslow Sq G31 ...118 A4
Ontario Pk G75 ...159 A1
Ontario Pl G75 ...159 A1
Onthank Dr KA3 ...222 C2
Onthank Prim Sch KA3 ...222 C3
Onyx St ML4 ...142 A2
Open Shore PA15 ...46 A3
Oran Gate G20 ...96 C3
Oran Gdns G20 ...96 C3
Oran Pl G20 ...96 C2
Oran St G20 ...96 C2
Orangefield PA15 ...45 C3
Orangefield Dr KA9 ...233 B1
Orangefield Ind Est KA9 ...233 B1
Orangefield La PA15 ...45 C3
Orbiston Ct ML1 ...164 A3
Orbiston Dr Bellshill ML4 ...142 B2
Clydebank G81 ...74 B4
Orbiston Pl G81 ...74 B4
Orbiston Rd Bellshill ML4 ...141 C2
Bellshill ML4 ...142 A1
Orbiston Sq ML4 ...141 C2
Orbiston St ML1 ...163 C3
Orcades Dr G44 ...137 B2
Orchard Ave Ayr KA7 ...239 A3
Bothwell G71 ...141 A1
Orchard Brae
Hamilton ML3 ...162 B2
Kirkintilloch G66 ...79 C2
Orchard Ct Glasgow G32 ...139 A4
Glasgow, Orchard Pk G46 ...136 A2
Orchard Dr Blantyre G72 ...161 B4
Orchard Dr *continued*
Glasgow G46 ...136 A2
Rutherglen G73 ...137 C4
Orchard Field G66 ...79 C2
Orchard Gate ML9 ...185 A1
Orchard Gn G74 ...160 A2
Orchard Gr
Coatbridge ML5 ...122 A3
Glasgow G46 ...136 A2
Kilmacolm PA13 ...89 B4
Kilwinning KA13 ...207 C2
Orchard House Hospl FK8 ...2 A1
Orchard Park Ave G46 ...136 A2
Orchard Pk G46 ...136 B2
Orchard Pl Ayr KA7 ...239 A3
Bellshill ML4 ...141 C2
Hamilton ML3 ...162 B2
Kilwinning KA13 ...207 C2
Kirkintilloch G66 ...80 A4
Orchard Rd FK9 ...2 A3
Orchard St Carluke ML8 ...187 C1
Falkirk FK1 ...42 A3
Glasgow G69 ...119 C2
Greenock PA15 ...46 A2
Hamilton ML3 ...162 C2
Kilmarnock KA3 ...222 C1
Motherwell ML1 ...163 B4
Paisley PA1 ...113 C2
Renfrew PA4 ...94 B2
West Kilbride KA23 ...190 B3
Wishaw ML2 ...186 A3
Orchard The FK10 ...4 A1
Orchard View Dr ML11 ...214 A2
Orchardcroft FK8 ...7 A4
Orchardton Rd G68 ...81 B4
Orchardton Woods Ind Pk G68 ...81 B4
Orchid Pl G66 ...57 B4
Orchy Ave G76 ...136 C1
Orchy Cres Airdrie ML6 ...123 B2
Bearsden G61 ...75 B1
Paisley PA2 ...112 C1
Orchy Ct G81 ...74 B3
Orchy Dr G44 ...136 C1
Orchy Gdns G76 ...136 C1
Orchy St G44 ...137 A3
Orchy Terr G74 ...160 A1
Orefield Pl G74 ...159 C2
Oregon Pl G5 ...117 B2
Orion Pl ML4 ...142 C3
Orion Way
Cambuslang G72 ...139 A3
Carluke ML8 ...187 B1
Orkney Ct FK10 ...10 A3
Orkney Dr KA3 ...223 A3
Orkney Pl Falkirk FK1 ...42 A1
6 Glasgow G51 ...116 A4
Orkney Quadrant ML2 ...165 B2
Orkney St G51 ...116 A4
Orlando G74 ...160 B3
Orleans Ave G14 ...95 C2
Orleans La G14 ...95 C2
Orlington Ct ML5 ...121 C4
Ormiston Ave G14 ...95 B2
Ormiston Dr Alloa FK10 ...4 C1
Hamilton ML3 ...183 B4
Ormiston La 12 G14 ...95 B2
Ormiston La N 6 G14 ...95 B2
Ormiston La S 14 G14 ...95 B2
Ormiston Pl KA11 ...220 B4
Ormond Ct FK5 ...23 A2
Ormonde Ave G44 ...136 C2
Ormonde Cres G44 ...136 C2
Ormonde Ct G44 ...136 C2
Ormonde Dr G44 ...136 C2
Ornsay St G22 ...97 B4
Oronsay Ave PA14 ...69 A3
Oronsay Cres
Bearsden G61 ...76 A2
Old Kilpatrick G60 ...73 B3
Oronsay Ct G60 ...73 B3
Oronsay Gdns G60 ...73 B3
Oronsay Pl
Old Kilpatrick G60 ...73 B3
Wishaw ML2 ...165 A1
Oronsay Sq G60 ...73 B3
Orr Sq PA1 ...113 C3
Orr Square Church PA1 ...113 B3
Orr St Glasgow G40 ...117 C3
Paisley PA2 ...113 C2
Paisley, Castlehead PA1 ...113 C3
Orr Terr Harthill ML7 ...127 B2
Neilston G78 ...154 B3
Orton Pl G51 ...116 A3
Osborne Cres G74 ...158 A2
Osborne Gdns FK1 ...41 C2
Osborne St Clydebank G81 ...74 A2
Falkirk FK1 ...41 C2
Glasgow G1 ...241 A1
Oslie View KA3 ...195 C1
Osprey Cres ML2 ...165 A2
Osprey Dr
Kilmarnock KA1 ...228 B4
Uddingston G71 ...141 A4
Osprey Rd PA16 ...45 A2
Ossian Ave PA1 ...114 C3
Ossian Rd G43 ...136 C3
Oswald Ct KA8 ...236 A2
Oswald Dr KA9 ...233 B1
Oswald Gdns ML8 ...201 C2
Oswald La KA8 ...235 C1
Oswald Pl KA8 ...236 A3
Oswald Rd KA8 ...236 A2
Oswald St Falkirk FK1 ...42 A2
Glasgow G1 ...240 C2
Oswald Wlk G62 ...76 B4
Otago La G12 ...96 C1
Otago La N G12 ...96 C1
Otago Pk G75 ...159 A1
Otago Pl G82 ...50 B1
Otago St G12 ...96 C1
Othello G74 ...160 A3
Ottawa Cres G81 ...73 B2
Otterburn Ave KA3 ...223 A2
Otterburn Dr G46 ...136 B1
Otterswick Pl G33 ...99 B1
Ottoline Dr KA10 ...229 D1
Oudenarde Ct ML8 ...188 A1
Our Holy Redeemer's RC Prim Sch G81 ...94 B4
Our Lady & St Francis RC Prim Sch ML1 ...143 B1
Our Lady & St Patricks High Sch G82 ...49 B2
Our Lady of Loretto Prim Sch G81 ...73 C2
Our Lady of Lourdes RC Prim Sch G75 ...180 B4
Our Lady of Peace Prim Sch PA3 ...112 A3
Our Lady of the Annunciation Prim RC Sch G43 ...136 C3
Our Lady of the Assumption Prim RC Sch G20 ...97 A3
Our Lady of the Missions Prim Sch G46 ...136 A1
Our Lady of the Rosary Sch G52 ...115 B2
Our Lady's High Sch G67 ...61 B1
Our Lady's RC High Sch ML1 ...164 A2
Outdale Ave KA9 ...236 C4
Oval The Glasgow G76 ...136 C1
Glenboig ML5 ...101 B3
Overbrae Gdns G15 ...74 C3
Overbrae Pl G15 ...74 C3
Overburn Ave G82 ...49 C2
Overburn Cres G82 ...49 C3
Overburn Terr G82 ...50 A3
Overdale Ave G42 ...136 C4
Overdale Cres KA9 ...236 B3
Overdale Gdns G42 ...136 C4
Overdale Pl ML2 ...186 B3
Overdale St G42 ...136 C4
Overjohnstone Dr ML2 ...164 B2
Overlea Ave G73 ...138 B3
Overlee Ho G76 ...157 C4
Overlee Rd G76 ...157 C4
Overmills Cres KA7 ...239 B4
Overmills Rd KA7 ...239 B4
Overnewton Pl G3 ...116 B4
Overnewton Sq G3 ...96 B1
Overnewton St G3 ...96 B1
Overton Cres Denny FK6 ...21 B1
Greenock PA15 ...45 B2
Johnstone PA5 ...112 A2
West Kilbride KA23 ...190 B3
Overton Ct KA23 ...190 B3
Overton Dr KA23 ...190 B3
Overton Gdns PA13 ...69 C1
Overton Gr PA13 ...69 C1
Overton Pl KA11 ...220 A3
Overton Prim Sch PA16 ...45 B2
Overton Rd Alexandria G83 ...27 B2
Cambuslang G72 ...139 B2
Johnstone PA5 ...112 A1
Netherburn ML9 ...200 B3
Springside KA11 ...220 C2
Overton St Alexandria G83 ...27 C3
Cambuslang G72 ...139 B2
Overton Terr FK6 ...21 B1
Overtoun Ave G82 ...50 A2
Overtoun Ct KA11 ...221 A1
Overtoun Dr
Clydebank G81 ...73 C2
Rutherglen G73 ...138 A4
Overtoun Est★ G82 ...50 C3
Overtoun Rd G81 ...73 C2
Overtown Ave G53 ...135 A3
Overtown Prim Sch ML2 ...186 B4
Overtown Rd ML2 ...165 C1
Overtown St G31 ...118 A3
Overwood Dr
Dumbarton G82 ...50 A2
Glasgow G44 ...137 B3
Overwood Gr G82 ...50 A2
Owen Ave G75 ...180 B4
Owen Kelly Pl KA21 ...205 C1
Owen Pk G75 ...180 B4
Owen St ML1 ...163 C4
Owendale Ave ML4 ...142 A4
Oxford Ave PA19 ...45 A3
Oxford Dr PA3 ...112 A3
Oxford La Glasgow G5 ...117 A3
Renfrew PA4 ...94 B2
Oxford Rd Greenock PA16 ...44 B2
Renfrew PA4 ...94 B2
Oxford St Coatbridge ML5 ...121 C3
Glasgow G5 ...240 C1
Kirkintilloch G66 ...79 B4
Oxgang Pl G66 ...79 C4
Oxgang Prim Sch G66 ...79 C4
Oxgang Smallholdings G66 ...79 C4
Oxhill Pl G82 ...49 B2
Oxhill Rd G82 ...49 B2
Oxton Dr G52 ...115 A3

P

Pacemuir La PA13 ...89 A4

Pine Cres *continued*
East Kilbride G75 180 A3
Johnstone PA5 112 A1
Pine Ct Coatbridge ML5 121 C2
Cumbernauld G67 62 C2
East Kilbride G75 180 B3
Pine Gr Alloa FK10 10 B3
Calderbank ML6 123 A1
Cumbernauld G67 62 C2
Motherwell ML1 143 A3
Uddingston G71 141 A4
Pine Ho KA9 236 A3
Pine Lawn ML2 165 B3
Pine Pk ML3 162 C1
Pine Pl Cumbernauld G67 62 C2
Glasgow G5 117 B2
Pine Quadrant ML6 123 C2
Pine Rd Clydebank G81 73 B2
Cumbernauld G67 62 C2
Dumbarton G82 49 C2
Kilmarnock KA1 227 B4
Pine St Airdrie ML6 123 B4
Greenock PA15 45 C2
Lennoxtown G66 57 C4
Paisley PA2 114 A1
Pine Wlk FK5 23 B1
Pineapple The★ FK2 14 A3
Pinelands G64 78 A2
Pines The G44 137 A2
Pineview Ct G15 75 A2
Pinewood G61 75 C2
Pinewood Ave G66 79 A3
Pinewood Ct
Dumbarton G82 50 B3
Kirkintilloch G66 79 A3
Pinewood Pl G66 79 A3
Pinewood Prim Sch G15 75 B2
Pinkerton Ave G73 137 C4
Pinkerton La PA4 94 B1
Pinkston Dr G21 97 C1
Pinkston Rd G21, G4 241 B4
Pinmore KA13 207 B1
Pinmore Pl G53 134 C3
Pinmore St G53 134 C3
Pinwherry Dr G33 98 C3
Pinwherry Pl G71 141 A2
Pioneer Pk G82 50 A1
Piper Ave PA6 111 B4
Piper Rd Airdrie ML6 123 B3
Houston PA6 111 B4
Piperhill KA7 239 A1
Piping Ctr The G4 240 C4
Pirleyhill Dr FK1 66 B3
Pirleyhill Gdns FK1 42 A1
Pirnhall Rd FK7 11 B4
Pirnie Pl G65 60 B4
Pirnmill Ave
East Kilbride G75 180 A2
Motherwell ML1 163 A4
Pirnmill Pl G84 16 C1
Pirnmill Rd KA21 205 C1
Pit Rd Bellshill ML4 141 C3
Kirkintilloch G66 80 B4
Pitcairn Cres G75 179 C4
Pitcairn Gr G75 180 A4
Pitcairn Pl G75 179 C4
Pitcairn St G31 118 C2
Pitcairn Terr ML3 162 A2
Pitcaple Dr G43 136 A3
Pitfairn Rd FK10 5 C2
Pitlochry Dr
Glasgow G52 115 B2
Larkhall ML9 185 B1
Pitmedden Rd G64 78 B1
Pitmilly Rd G15 75 B2
Pitreavie Ct ML3 183 A4
Pitreavie Pl G33 99 B1
Pitt St G2 240 B3
Pitt Terr FK8 7 A3
Place Of Bonhill G82 27 B2
Place View KA25 149 A1
Pladda Ave Irvine KA11 220 A1
Port Glasgow PA14 69 A4
Pladda Cres KA11 220 A1
Pladda Ct KA11 220 A1
Pladda Dr KA9 236 B3
Pladda Rd Renfrew PA4 94 B1
Saltcoats KA21 205 C1
Pladda St ML1 163 A4
Pladda Terr KA11 220 A1
Pladda Way G84 16 C1
Pladda Wynd KA11 220 A1
Plains Prim Sch ML6 104 A1
Plaintrees Ct PA2 113 C1
Plan View KA25 149 A2
Plane Pl G71 121 B1
Planetree Pl PA5 112 A1
Planetree Rd G81 74 A3
Plann Ho KA2 221 C2
Plant St G31 118 B3
Plantation Ave ML1 143 A3
Plantation Park Gdns 5
G51 116 B3
Plantation Sq G51 116 C3
Plateau Dr KA10 229 D4
Platthorn Dr G74 159 C1
Platthorn Rd G74 159 C1
Players Rd FK7 7 B4
Playfair St G40 118 A2
Playingfield Cres KA2 221 C1
Playingfield Rd KA2 221 C1
Plaza The G74 159 C1
Pleaknowe Cres G69 80 C1
Pleamuir Pl G68 61 B1
Plean Ctry Pk★ FK7 12 A1
Plean Ind Est FK7 12 B1
Plean St G14 95 A3
Pleasance FK1 42 A2
Pleasance Ct 13 FK2 42 A2
Pleasance Gdns FK1 42 A2
Pleasance Rd FK2 42 A2
Pleasance Sq 12 FK1 42 A2
Pleasance St G43 136 B4
Pleasantfield Rd KA9 236 A3
Pleasantside Ave PA14 69 A4
Pleasures The FK10 9 C4
Plotcock Rd ML3 198 B4
Plover Dr G75 180 A3
Plover Pl PA5 131 B4
Plusgarten Loan ML2 165 C4
Plymouth Ave PA19 44 C3
Pochard Way ML4 141 C4
Poet's View G66 79 C4
Poindfauld Terr G82 50 A2
Pointhouse Rd G3 116 B4
Pokelly Pl KA3 195 C1
Polbae Cres G76 178 C3
Polden Ave G75 180 A2
Poles Rd KA3 213 A2
Polkemmet Dr ML7 127 C3
Polkemmet La ML7 127 C3
Polkemmet Rd ML7 127 C3
Pollick Ave G78 153 A2
Pollick Farm La G78 153 A1
Pollock Ave
Eaglesham G76 178 C3
Hamilton ML3 162 A2
Pollock Cres KA13 207 C1
Pollock Rd Bearsden G61 76 A2
Newton Mearns G77 156 B2
Pollock St Bellshill ML4 142 B3
Motherwell ML1 163 C4
Pollok Ave G43 136 A4
Pollok Country Pk★
G43 116 A1
Pollok Ctry Pk G43 116 A1
Pollok Dr G64 77 C1
Pollok Ho★ G43 135 C4
Pollok La G74 160 A2
Pollok Pl G74 160 A2
Pollokshaws East Sta
G43 136 B4
Pollokshaws Rd G41 117 A2
Pollokshaws West Sta
G43 136 A4
Pollokshield Sq G41 116 C1
Pollokshields East Sta
G41 117 A2
Pollokshields Prim Sch
G41 116 C2
Pollokshields Prim Sch
Annexe (Infs) G41 116 C2
Pollokshields West Sta
G41 116 C1
Polmadie Ave G5 117 B1
Polmadie Ind Est G5,
G73 117 C1
Polmadie Rd G42,G5 117 B1
Polmadie St G42 117 B1
Polmaise Ave FK7 7 A2
Polmaise Cres FK7 8 B3
Polmaise Ct FK7 7 A2
Polmaise Rd FK7,FK8 6 C2
Polnoon Ave G13 95 A3
Polnoon Dr G76 178 C3
Polnoon Mews G76 178 C3
Polnoon St G76 178 B2
Polo Ave KA10 229 D1
Polo Gdns KA10 229 D1
Polquhap Ct 4 G53 135 A4
Polquhap Gdns 6 G53 135 A4
Polquhap Pl 5 G53 135 A4
Polson Dr PA5 111 C1
Polsons Cres PA2 113 B1
Polwarth La G12 96 A2
Polwarth St G12 96 A2
Pomona Pl ML3 161 C1
Pompee Rd FK10 5 A1
Poplar Ave Bishopton PA7 72 A1
Glasgow G11 95 C2
Johnstone PA5 112 A1
Newton Mearns G77 156 C2
Poplar Cres
Bishopton PA7 72 A1
Hamilton ML3 183 C2
Poplar Ct ML5 121 C2
Poplar Dr Clydebank G81 73 C3
Kirkintilloch G66 79 A3
Milton of C G66 58 B3
Poplar Gdns G75 180 B3
Poplar Pl Blantyre G72 140 B1
Gourock PA19 44 B3
Motherwell ML1 143 A2
Uddingston G71 141 B4
Poplar Rd G82 49 C2
Poplar St Airdrie ML6 123 B4
Greenock PA15 46 C1
Poplar Way Ayr KA7 239 B3
Cambuslang G72 139 C2
Poplars The Bearsden G61 75 B4
Tullibody FK10 4 A1
Poplin St G40 118 A2
Porchester St G33 99 B1
Port Dundas Ind Est G4 97 B1
Port Dundas Pl G2 241 A3
Port Dundas Rd G4 241 A4
Port Glasgow High Sch
PA14 69 A3
Port Glasgow Ind Est
PA14 68 C4
Port Glasgow Rd
Greenock PA15 46 C2
Kilmacolm PA13 69 A1
Port Glasgow Sta PA14 47 B1
Port Ranald dr KA10 229 B2
Port St Glasgow G3 240 A2
Port St *continued*
Stirling FK8 7 A4
Portal Rd G13 95 B4
Portdownie FK1 41 B3
Portencross Rd KA23 190 B3
Porter Dr KA2 227 A3
Porter St 1 G51 116 B3
Porterfield Rd
Kilmacolm PA13 89 C4
Renfrew PA4 94 A2
Porters La ML6 123 B1
Porters Well G71 140 C3
Portessie PA8 73 A1
Porthlethen PA8 73 A1
Porting Cross Pl KA3 223 A3
Portland Ave KA12 224 B4
Portland Brae KA1 228 C3
Portland Ct KA1 228 C3
Portland Pk ML3 162 C1
Portland Pl
Hamilton ML3 162 C1
Irvine KA12 224 B4
Kilmarnock KA1 227 C4
Lanark ML11 215 A2
Stevenston KA20 217 B4
Portland Place Ind Est
KA20 217 B4
Portland Rd
Cumbernauld G68 61 C3
Irvine KA12 224 B4
Kilmarnock KA1 227 C4
Paisley PA2 114 A2
Portland Rdbt KA12 219 A1
Portland Sq ML3 162 C1
Portland St
Coatbridge ML5 122 A4
Kilmarnock KA1 222 C1
Troon KA10 229 C2
Portland Terr KA10 229 B1
Portland Wynd 4 ML9 185 A2
Portman St G41 116 C3
Portmark Ave KA7 238 B1
Portmarnock Dr G23 96 C4
Porton Pl PA7 72 A2
Portpatrick Rd G60 72 C4
Portreath Rd G69 80 C2
Portree Ave
Coatbridge ML5 121 C2
Kilmarnock KA3 223 A3
Portree Pl G15 74 C2
Portree Terr PA16 44 C2
Portsmouth Dr PA19 44 C3
Portsoy PA8 73 A1
Portsoy Ave G13 94 C4
Portsoy Pl G13 94 C4
Portugal St G5 117 A3
Portwell ML3 162 C2
Possil Cross G22 97 B2
Possil Rd G4 97 A2
Possilpark & Parkhouse Sta
G22 97 A3
Postgate ML3 162 C2
Posthill FK10 5 B1
Potassels Rd G69 100 B4
Potrail Pl ML3 162 A2
Potter Cl G32 118 C2
Potter Gr G32 118 C2
Potter Pl Glasgow G32 118 C2
Skinflats FK2 24 C2
Potter St G32 118 C2
Potterhill Ave PA2 133 C4
Potterhill Rd G53 115 A1
Potters Wynd ML11 215 B3
Pottery Pl KA3 222 C1
Pottery St PA15 46 C2
Pottis Rd FK7 7 B2
Potts Way ML1 142 B1
Powbrone G75 180 C3
Powburn Cres G71 140 B4
Power Plant Rd KA20 218 A3
Powfoot St G31 118 B3
Powforth Cl ML9 184 C2
Powgree Cres KA15 171 B3
Powmill Gdns KA9 233 B1
Powmill Rd KA9 233 B1
Powrie St G33 99 B2
Prentice La 5 G71 141 A4
Prentice Rd ML1 163 A3
President Kennedy Dr
FK7 12 B2
Preston Pl Glasgow G42 117 A1
Gourock PA19 44 B4
Preston St G42 117 A1
Prestonfield G62 54 C1
Prestonfield Ave KA13 207 A2
Prestwick Acad KA9 233 B1
Prestwick Ct G68 61 C2
Prestwick Int Airport Sta
KA9 233 A2
Prestwick Pl G77 157 A2
Prestwick Rd KA8 236 A2
Prestwick St G53 135 A3
Prestwick Sta KA9 233 A1
Pretoria Ct G75 180 A2
Pretoria Rd FK5 23 A1
Priestfield Ind Est G72 161 B3
Priestfield St G72 161 B3
Priesthill & Darnley Sta
G53 135 B3
Priesthill Ave G53 135 B3
Priesthill Cres G53 135 B3
Priesthill Rd G53 135 B3
Priestknowe Rdbt G74 159 C1
Priestland Cl KA3 223 A3
Prieston Rd PA11 110 B4
Primrose Ave
Bellshill ML4 142 A4
Larkhall ML9 199 A4
Primrose Cres ML1 163 C3
Primrose Ct 21 G14 95 B2
Primrose Pk KA7 239 B2
Primrose Pl Alloa FK10 10 A3
Cumbernauld G67 82 A3
Kilmarnock KA1 222 B1
Saltcoats KA21 206 A1
Uddingston G71 141 B4
Primrose St Alloa FK10 10 A4
Bonnybridge FK4 40 A3
Glasgow G14 95 B2
Primrose Way ML8 201 C4
Prince Albert Rd G12 96 B2
Prince Albert Terr G84 16 B1
Prince Edward St 2
G42 117 A1
Prince of Wales Gdns
G20 96 B4
Prince Pl ML2 166 A3
Prince's Gdns G12 96 A2
Prince's Pl 20 G12 96 B2
Prince's Terr G12 96 B2
Princes Ct KA8 236 A1
Princes Gardens La G12 96 A2
Princes Gate
Bothwell G71 140 C2
Hamilton ML3 162 C2
Rutherglen G73 138 A4
Princes Mall G74 159 C1
Princes Pk PA7 72 C2
Princes Pl KA22 205 A1
Princes Sq Barrhead G78 134 B2
14 East Kilbride G74 159 C1
Troon KA10 229 C2
Princes Square Shop Ctr
G1 241 A2
Princes St
Ardrossan KA22 205 A1
Caldercruix ML6 105 A3
California FK1 66 C3
Falkirk FK1 42 A3
Greenock PA15 45 C3
Kilmarnock KA1 227 C4
Motherwell ML1 163 C4
Port Glasgow PA14 47 B1
Rutherglen G73 138 A4
Stirling FK8 7 A4
Princess Anne Quadrant
ML1 142 C3
Princess Cres PA1 114 A3
Princess Ct
Helensburgh G84 16 B1
Kilmarnock KA1 228 A2
Princess Dr G69 121 A3
Princess Rd ML1 142 C2
Princess Sq 25 ML2 165 C3
Princess St FK4 40 A3
Princess Way G84 15 A2
Printers Land G76 158 A3
Printers Lea G66 57 B4
Priorwood Ct G13 95 B3
Priorwood Gate G77 156 A2
Priorwood Rd G77 156 A2
Priorwood Way G77 156 A2
Priory Ave PA3 114 A4
Priory Dr G71 140 B4
Priory Gate ML2 186 A4
Priory Pl Cumbernauld G68 60 C1
Glasgow G13 95 B4
Priory Rd G13 95 B4
Priory St G72 161 B4
Priory Terr ML2 164 B1
Priory Wynd KA13 207 B3
Procession Rd PA2 133 B3
Professors' Sq G12 96 B1
Progress Dr ML6 105 A3
Promenade KA8 236 A2
Propulsives Rd KA20 218 A2
Prosen St G32 118 C2
Prospect Ave
Cambuslang G72 138 C3
Uddingston G71 140 C4
Prospect Ct G72 161 B3
Prospect Dr ML9 199 C4
Prospect Rd Dullatur G68 61 B3
Glasgow G41 136 B4
Prospect St FK1 41 C3
Prospecthill Cir G42 117 B1
Prospecthill Cres G42 137 C4
Prospecthill Dr G42 137 B4
Prospecthill Pl
Glasgow G42 137 C4
Greenock PA15 45 C2
Prospecthill Rd
Falkirk FK1 42 A1
Glasgow G42 137 B4
Saltcoats KA21 206 A1
Prospecthill Sq G42 137 B4
Prospecthill St PA15 45 C2
Provan Hall★ G34 99 C1
Provan Rd G33 118 B4
Provand Hall Cres G69 120 A2
Provand's Lordship Ho★
G4 241 C3
Provanhall Prim Sch
G34 100 A1
Provanhill St G21 97 C1
Provanmill Rd G33 98 C1
Provost Cl PA5 111 C2
Provost Driver Ct PA4 94 C1
Provost Gate ML9 185 A2
Provost Hunter Ave FK12 5 B4
Pullar Ave FK9 2 A3
Pullar Ct FK9 2 A3
Pundeavon Ave KA25 149 A2
Purdie G74 160 B3
Purdie St ML3 162 A3
Purdon St G11 96 A1
Putyan Ave KA24 191 A4
Pyatshaw Rd ML9 185 A1

Q

Quadrant Rd G43 136 C3
Quadrant The G76 157 C4
Quail Rd KA8 236 A2
Quakerfield FK7 7 C1
Quantock Dr G75 180 A2
Quarrelton Rd PA5 111 C1
Quarrier St PA15 46 B2
Quarrolhall Cres FK2 24 A2
Quarry Ave G72 139 C2
Quarry Dr Kilmacolm PA13 69 B1
Kirkintilloch G66 79 C4
Quarry Knowe
Bannockburn FK7 11 C4
Dumbarton G82 49 B3
Rhu G84 15 C3
Quarry La Dumbarton G82 49 C2
Eaglesham G76 178 B2
Lennoxtown G66 33 B1
Quarry Pk G75 180 C4
Quarry Pl Alloa FK10 10 B4
Cambuslang G72 138 C3
Dumbarton G82 49 B3
Hamilton ML3 162 C2
Shotts ML7 146 B3
Quarry Rd Airdrie ML6 103 A1
Barrhead G78 134 A2
Cambusbarron FK7 6 B3
East Kilbride G75 180 B3
Irvine KA12 219 B2
Larkhall ML9 185 A1
Paisley PA2 113 C1
Port Glasgow PA14 68 C4
Shotts ML7 146 B3
Quarry St Coatbridge ML5 122 B4
Hamilton ML3 162 C2
Johnstone PA5 111 C1
Larkhall ML9 185 A1
Motherwell ML1 143 A2
Shotts ML7 146 B3
Wishaw ML2 165 A2
Quarrybank PA10 111 B1
Quarrybrae Ave G76 157 B4
Quarrybrae Gdns G71 141 B3
Quarrybrae Prim Sch
G31 118 B3
Quarrybrae St G31 118 C3
Quarryknowe
Lanark ML11 215 A2
Rutherglen G73 137 C4
Quarryknowe Pl ML4 141 C2
Quarryknowe St
Clydebank G81 74 C4
Glasgow G31 118 C3
Quarryside St ML6 102 C2
Quarrywood Ave G21 98 B2
Quarrywood Rd G21 98 B2
Quarter Prim Sch ML3 183 C2
Quay (Leisure Complex) The
G5 240 A1
Quay Pend G82 49 C2
Quay Rd G73 118 A1
Quay Road N G73 118 A1
Quay St Dumbarton G82 49 C2
Saltcoats KA21 216 C4
Quebec Dr G75 159 B1
Quebec Gn G75 159 B1
Quebec Wynd G32 139 B4
Queen Elizabeth Ave
G52 114 C4
Queen Elizabeth Ct
Clydebank G81 74 A2
Motherwell ML1 163 B4
Queen Elizabeth Gdns
G81 74 A2
Queen Elizabeth Sq 11
G5 117 B2
Queen Margaret Acad
KA7 239 B2
Queen Margaret Ct 6
G20 96 C2
Queen Margaret Dr G20 96 C2
Queen Margaret Rd G20 96 C2
Queen Mary Ave
Clydebank G81 74 B1
Glasgow G42 117 A1
Queen Mary Gdns G81 74 A2
Queen Mary St G40 118 A2
Queen Mother's Hospl The
G3 96 B1
Queen Rd KA12 219 B3
Queen Sq G41 116 C1
Queen St Alexandria G83 27 B2
Alloa FK10 10 A4
Alva FK12 5 A4
Ayr KA8 236 A1
Bannockburn FK7 7 B1
Falkirk FK2 42 B3
Fallin FK7 8 B2
Glasgow G1 241 A2
Hamilton ML3 162 A3
Helensburgh G84 16 B2
11 Kilmarnock KA1 227 C4
Kilwinning KA13 208 A2
Kirkintilloch G66 79 B4
Motherwell ML1 163 C4
Paisley PA1 113 B2
Port Glasgow PA14 47 B1
Renfrew PA4 94 B2
Rutherglen G73 138 A4

Ritchie St *continued*
West Kilbride KA23 190 B3
Wishaw ML2 164 B2
Ritchie's Cl ML11 215 A2
River Ct G76 157 C3
River Dr PA4 93 B2
River Pl KA25 149 A1
River Rd G32 139 A4
River St Ayr KA8 235 C1
Falkirk FK2 24 A1
River Terr KA8 235 C1
River View Cres G82 48 A4
River Wlk KA13 207 C3
Riverbank Dr ML4 142 B2
Riverbank Pl KA1 228 A4
Riverbank St G43 136 B4
Riverbank View FK8 7 B4
Riverdale Gdns ML3 162 C1
Riverford Rd
Glasgow G43 136 B4
Rutherglen G73 118 B1
Riversdale La G14 95 A2
Riverside Balloch G83 27 C4
Houston PA6 91 B1
Milngavie G62 55 A1
Riverside Bsns Pk KA11 224 D4
Riverside Ct G76 157 C1
Riverside Dr FK8 2 B1
Riverside Gdns
Balloch G83 27 C4
Clarkston G76 157 C3
Gourock PA19 44 C4
Riverside La G82 49 C2
Riverside Pk G44 137 A1
Riverside Pl Ayr KA8 239 A4
Cambuslang G72 139 C3
Irvine KA11 225 A4
Kilbirnie KA25 149 A1
Riverside Prim Sch FK8 2 A1
Riverside Rd
Eaglesham G76 178 C4
Glasgow G43 136 C4
Greenock PA15 46 A2
Irvine KA11 220 B1
Kilbirnie KA25 149 A1
Kirkfieldbank ML11 214 B2
Larkhall ML9 199 A4
Stewarton KA3 211 C4
Riverside Rdbt KA11 225 A4
Riverside Ret Pk KA12 219 A1
Riverside Terr G76 157 C3
Riverside View FK10 10 A2
Riverside Way KA11 224 D4
Riverside Wlk ML1 163 C4
Riverton Dr G75 180 A4
Riverview Dr G5 240 B1
Riverview Gdns G5 240 B1
Riverview Pl G5 240 B1
Riverway KA12 219 A1
Riverway Ret Pk KA12 219 A1
Roaden Ave PA2 132 C4
Roaden Rd PA2 132 C4
Roadhead PA12 150 C4
Roadmeetings Hospl
ML8 202 B4
Roadside G67 62 A3
Roadside Pl ML6 103 B4
Robb Terr G66 80 A3
Robert Bruce Ct FK5 23 A1
Robert Burns Ave
Clydebank G81 74 B2
Motherwell ML1 143 C2
Robert Burns Ct KA15 150 A1
Robert Burns Quadrant
ML4 141 C3
Robert Creighton Pl
KA3 222 C1
Robert Dick Ct FK10 4 B1
Robert Dr G51 116 A4
Robert Gilson Gdns
ML5 122 A3
Robert Hardie Ct FK5 23 B1
Robert Kinmond Ave FK10 4 B1
Robert Knox Ave FK10 4 B1
Robert Noble Pl KA1 222 B1
Robert Owen Meml Prim Sch
ML11 215 B2
Robert Smillie Cres
ML9 185 A1
Robert Smillie Meml Prim
Sch ML9 185 A1
Robert St Glasgow G51 116 A4
Port Glasgow PA14 47 C1
Shotts ML7 146 C2
Robert Stewart Pl KA1 222 C1
Robert Templeton Dr
G72 139 A3
Robert W Service Ct
KA13 207 C1
Robert Wynd ML2 166 A3
Robertland Rigg KA3 211 C2
Robertland Sq KA3 211 C4
Roberton Ave G41 116 B1
Roberton St ML6 123 C2
Roberts Quadrant ML4 142 A2
Roberts St Clydebank G81 73 C2
Wishaw ML2 165 A2
Robertson Ave
Bonnybridge FK4 40 A3
Renfrew PA4 94 A2
Robertson Cl PA4 94 B2
Robertson Cres Ayr KA8 236 B1
Neilston G78 154 B4
Saltcoats KA21 217 A4
Robertson Ct FK5 23 B1
Robertson Dr
Bellshill ML4 142 A2
East Kilbride G74 160 A1
Robertson Dr *continued*
Renfrew PA4 94 A2
Robertson La G2 240 C2
Robertson Pl
Kilmarnock KA1 228 A4
Stirling FK7 7 A2
Robertson Rd KA9 233 B2
Robertson St
Airdrie ML6 122 C4
Alva FK12 5 A4
Barrhead G78 134 A1
Glasgow G1, G2 240 C2
Greenock PA16 45 C3
Hamilton ML3 161 C3
Robertson Terr G69 120 B3
Robin Pl ML2 165 A2
Robin Rd PA16 45 A3
Robin Way G32 139 B4
Robroyston Ave G33 98 C2
Robroyston Rd
Bishopbriggs G64 78 C1
Glasgow, Barmulloch G33 98 B2
Glasgow, Blackhill G33 98 C2
Glasgow, Robroyston G33 98 C3
Kirkintilloch G66 79 A2
Robshill Ct G77 156 B2
Robsland Ave KA7 238 C3
Robslee Cres G46 136 A2
Robslee Dr G46 136 A2
Robslee Prim Sch G46 136 A1
Robslee Rd G46 136 A2
Robson Gr 16 G42 117 A2
Rocep Dr PA4 94 C1
Rochdale Pl 1 G66 79 B4
Roche Way KA24 191 B4
Rochsoles Cres ML6 103 A1
Rochsoles Dr ML6 103 A1
Rochsolloch Farm Cotts
ML6 122 C4
Rochsolloch Prim Sch
ML6 122 C3
Rochsolloch Rd ML6 122 B3
Rock Dr PA10 111 A1
Rock St G4 97 A2
Rockall Dr G44 137 B2
Rockbank Pl
Clydebank G81 74 B3
Glasgow G40 118 A3
Rockbank St G40 118 A3
Rockburn Cres ML4 142 A4
Rockburn Dr G76 157 B4
Rockcliffe St G40 117 C2
Rockfield Pl G21 98 B3
Rockfield Rd G21 98 B3
Rockhampton Ave G75 180 A4
Rockliffe Path ML6 123 C1
Rockmount Ave
Barrhead G78 134 B1
Glasgow G46 136 A2
Rockrose Pk KA7 239 A2
Rockwell Ave PA2 133 B4
Rodding The ML11 215 A3
Roddinghead Rd G46 157 A3
Rodger Ave G77 156 B3
Rodger Dr G73 138 A3
Rodger Pl G73 138 A3
Rodil Ave G44 137 B2
Rodney Pl G84 17 A1
Rodney Rd PA19 44 C3
Rodney St G4 97 A1
Roebank Dr G78 134 B1
Roebank Rd KA15 150 B1
Roebank St G31 118 A4
Roffey Park Rd PA1 114 B3
Rogart St G40 117 C3
Rogerfield Prim Sch
G34 120 B4
Rogerfield Rd G34 120 B4
Rogers Ct ML9 198 B1
Rokeby La G12 96 C2
Roland Cres G77 156 C2
Roman Ave Bearsden G61 75 C3
Glasgow G15 75 A1
Roman Cres
Old Kilpatrick G60 72 C4
Shotts ML7 147 A2
Roman Ct Bearsden G61 75 C3
Cleghorn ML11 215 C4
Clydebank G81 74 A3
Roman Dr Bearsden G61 75 C3
Bellshill ML4 142 A2
Falkirk FK1 41 B3
Roman Gdns G61 75 C3
Roman Hill Rd G81 74 A4
Roman Pl ML4 141 C2
Roman Rd Ayr KA7 239 B3
Bearsden G61 75 C3
Bonnybridge FK4 40 A2
Clydebank G81 74 A3
Kirkintilloch G66 79 A4
Motherwell ML1 163 C4
Roman Way G71 141 B3
Romney Ave G44 137 B3
Romulus Ct ML1 142 B1
Rona Ave PA14 69 A4
Rona Pl KA3 223 A3
Rona St G21 98 A1
Rona Terr G72 138 C2
Ronades Rd FK2 42 A4
Ronald Cres FK5 23 A1
Ronald Pl FK8 7 A4
Ronaldsay Ct KA11 225 A4
Ronaldsay Dr G64 78 B1
Ronaldsay Pl G67 82 B4
Ronaldsay St G22 97 B4
Ronaldshaw Pk KA7 238 C3
Ronay St Glasgow G22 97 B4
Wishaw ML2 165 C3
Rook Rd PA16 45 A3
Rooksdell Ave PA2 113 B1
Ropework La G1 241 A1
Rorison Pl ML9 185 C1
Rosa Burn Ave G75 180 A2
Rosa Pl KA21 206 A1
Rose Cres Gourock PA19 44 B3
Hamilton ML3 161 C2
Rose Dale G64 98 A4
Rose Knowe Rd G42 137 B4
Rose Mount Ct ML6 123 B4
Rose Pl G74 160 B2
Rose St Alloa FK10 4 C1
Bonnybridge FK4 40 A3
Cumbernauld G67 82 A3
Glasgow G3 240 C4
Greenock PA16 45 B2
Kirkintilloch G66 79 B4
Motherwell ML1 164 A3
Rose Terr Denny FK6 21 B1
Stenhousemuir FK5 23 C2
Rosebank FK10 5 B1
Rosebank Ave
Blantyre G72 140 C1
Falkirk FK1 41 C3
Kirkintilloch G66 79 C4
Rosebank Cres KA7 238 C3
Rosebank Dr
Cambuslang G72 139 B2
Uddingston G71 141 B4
Rosebank Gdns
Alloa FK10 10 B4
Glasgow G71 120 A1
Irvine KA11 219 C4
Rosebank La 10 G71 141 A2
Rosebank Pl Dullatur G68 61 B3
Falkirk FK1 41 C3
Glasgow G71 120 A1
Hamilton ML3 162 A2
Kilmarnock KA3 222 C1
Rosebank Rd
Bellshill ML4 142 A4
Wishaw ML2 186 B3
Rosebank Sch KA7 239 A3
Rosebank St ML6 123 C4
Rosebank Terr
Bargeddie G69 121 A2
Kilmacolm PA13 89 B4
Rosebay Pk KA7 239 A1
Roseberry La ML6 123 C2
Roseberry Pl ML3 162 A2
Roseberry Rd ML6 123 C2
Roseberry St G5 117 C1
Rosebery Ct KA25 149 A1
Rosebery Pl FK8 2 A1
Roseburn Ct G67 62 C3
Rosedale G74 159 B2
Rosedale Ave PA2 132 B4
Rosedale Dr G69 120 A2
Rosedale Gdns
Glasgow G20 96 B4
Helensburgh G84 16 C1
Rosedale St ML11 214 C1
Rosedene Terr ML4 142 A3
Rosefield Gdns G71 140 C4
Rosegreen Cres ML4 142 A4
Rosehall Ave ML5 122 A2
Rosehall High Sch ML5 121 C2
Rosehall Ind Est ML5 122 A2
Rosehall Rd Bellshill ML4 141 C3
Shotts ML7 146 B2
Rosehall Terr Falkirk FK1 42 A2
Wishaw ML2 164 C1
Rosehill Dr G67 82 A3
Rosehill Rd G64 78 B4
Roseholm Ave KA12 219 C1
Roselea ML6 104 C2
Roselea Dr G62 55 A2
Roselea Gdns G13 95 C4
Roselea Pl G72 140 B1
Roselea Rd G71 140 C4
Roselea St ML9 185 A2
Rosemary Cres G74 159 B2
Rosemary Ct FK6 21 B1
Rosemary Pl G74 159 B2
Rosemead Terr FK1 66 C3
Rosemount
Cumbernauld G68 61 C3
Kilwinning KA13 207 B1
Rosemount Ave G77 156 B1
Rosemount Ct G77 156 B1
Rosemount Dr KA10 229 C4
Rosemount Gdns
Prestwick KA9 236 B3
Shieldhill FK1 66 B3
Rosemount La
Bridge of W PA11 110 A3
13 Larkhall ML9 185 B1
Rosemount Mdws G72 140 C1
Rosemount Pl PA19 44 A3
Rosemount St G21 97 C1
Rosendale Way G72 161 C4
Roseneath Dr G84 16 A1
Roseneath Gate G74 159 B1
Roseneath Prim Sch G84 15 A2
Roseneath St PA16 45 B4
Roseness Pl G33 119 A4
Rosepark Ave G71 141 B3
Rosepark Cotts ML5 121 C2
Rosevale Cres
Bellshill ML4 142 B2
Hamilton ML3 162 A1
Rosevale Rd G61 75 C2
Rosevale Sch G22 97 B4
Rosevale St G11 96 A1
Rosewood Ave
Bellshill ML4 142 A4
Paisley PA2 113 A1
Rosewood Path ML4 141 C3
Rosewood St G13 95 C4
Roseyard Pl PA14 47 B1
Roslea Dr G31 118 A4
Roslin Ct PA13 89 B4
Roslin St PA15 45 C3
Roslin Twr G72 138 C2
Roslyn Dr G69 120 C3
Rosneath Rd
Port Glasgow PA14 68 B4
Rosneath G84 15 A1
Rosneath St G51 116 A4
Ross Ave Kirkintilloch G66 79 C4
Renfrew PA4 94 A1
Ross Cres Falkirk FK1 41 B3
Motherwell ML1 163 B3
Ross Ct FK7 7 A2
Ross Dr Airdrie ML6 122 C2
Motherwell ML1 163 B3
Uddingston G71 121 B1
Ross Gdns ML1 163 B3
Ross Hall Hospl G52 115 A2
Ross Hall Pl PA4 94 B2
Ross Pl G73 138 B2
Ross Rd KA21 205 C1
Ross St Ayr KA8 236 B1
Coatbridge ML5 122 A4
Glasgow G40 241 B1
Paisley PA1 114 A2
Ross Terr ML3 163 B1
Ross Wlk KA3 223 A1
Rossbank Rd PA14 47 A1
Rossendale Ct G43 136 B4
Rossendale Rd G43 136 B4
Rosshall Ave PA1 114 B2
Rosshall Sec Sch G52 115 A2
Rosshill Ave G52 114 C3
Rosshill Rd G52 114 C3
Rossie Cres G64 98 B4
Rossie Gr G77 156 A3
Rossland Cres PA7 72 A2
Rossland Pl PA7 72 A1
Rossland View PA7 72 A2
Rosslea Dr G46 136 B1
Rosslyn Ave
East Kilbride G74 160 A2
Rutherglen G73 138 B4
Rosslyn Ct ML3 162 A2
Rosslyn Pl KA8 236 A2
Rosslyn Rd Ashgill ML9 199 C4
Bearsden G61 75 A3
Rosslyn Terr 38 G12 96 B2
Rossvail Sch FK1 41 B3
Rostan Rd G43 136 B3
Rosyth Rd G5 117 C1
Rosyth St G5 117 C1
Rotherwick Dr PA1 114 C2
Rotherwood Ave
Glasgow G13 75 B1
Paisley PA2 132 C4
Rotherwood La G13 75 B1
Rotherwood Pl G13 95 B4
Rotherwood Way PA2 132 C4
Rothes Dr G23 96 B4
Rothes Pl 3 G23 76 B1
Rothesay Cres ML5 122 A2
Rothesay Pl
Coatbridge ML5 122 A2
East Kilbride G74 159 C1
Kilmarnock KA3 222 C2
Rothesay Rd PA16 44 C2
Rothesay St G74 180 C4
Rottenrow Glasgow G4 241 B3
Glasgow G4 241 C2
Rottenrow E G4 241 B2
Roughburn Rd FK9 2 A3
Roughcraig St ML6 103 A1
Roughlands Cres FK2 24 A2
Roughlands Dr FK2 24 A2
Roughlea Pl KA10 229 D3
Roughrigg Rd ML6 124 B3
Rouken Glen Pk★ G46 135 C1
Rouken Glen Rd G46 136 A1
Roukenburn St G46 135 C2
Round Riding Rd G82 50 A2
Roundel The Falkirk FK2 42 B4
Wishaw ML2 165 B1
Roundelwood FK10 5 A1
Roundhill Dr PA5 112 C2
Roundhouse FK7 12 B4
Roundknowe Rd G71 120 B1
Rousay Wynd KA3 223 A3
Rowallan KA13 207 B1
Rowallan Cres KA9 236 B4
Rowallan Ct 17 KA7 235 C1
Rowallan Dr
Bannockburn FK7 11 C4
Kilmarnock KA3 223 A2
Rowallan Gdns G11 96 A2
Rowallan La
Clarkston G76 157 C4
Glasgow G11 96 A2
Rowallan Rd G46 135 C1
Rowallan St G84 16 A2
Rowallan Terr G33 99 A2
Rowan Ave Beith KA15 171 B4
Milton of C G66 58 B3
Renfrew PA4 94 B2
Rowan Cres Ayr KA7 239 B3
Chapelhall ML6 123 C2
Falkirk FK1 41 A2
Kirkintilloch G66 79 B3
Rowan Ct Bannockburn FK7 7 C1
Cambuslang G72 139 C2
Wishaw ML2 164 B1
Rowan Dr Banknock FK4 38 C1
Bearsden G61 76 A4
Clydebank G81 73 C2
Rowan Dr *continued*
Dumbarton G82 49 A2
Rowan Gate PA2 113 C1
Rowan Gdns G41 116 A2
Rowan Gr ML3 183 C2
Rowan Ho KA9 236 A3
Rowan La ML1 143 A1
Rowan Pl Beith KA15 171 B4
Blantyre G72 161 B4
Cambuslang G72 139 B3
Coatbridge ML5 121 C2
Kilmarnock KA1 227 B4
Troon KA10 229 C2
Rowan Rd
Cumbernauld G67 62 B2
Glasgow G41 116 A2
Linwood PA3 111 C4
Rowan Rise ML3 162 C1
Rowan St Greenock PA16 45 B3
Paisley PA2 113 C1
Wishaw ML2 165 A3
Rowan Terr KA12 219 B2
Rowanbank Pl ML6 122 B4
Rowanbank Rd KA9 236 C4
Rowand Ave G46 136 B2
Rowandale Ave G69 120 A2
Rowanden Ave ML4 142 A3
Rowanhill Pl KA1 227 B4
Rowanlea ML6 103 C2
Rowanlea Ave PA2 132 C4
Rowanlea Dr G46 136 B2
Rowanpark Dr G78 134 A3
Rowans Gdns G71 141 A2
Rowans The Alloa FK10 5 B1
Bishopbriggs G64 77 C1
Rowanside Terr KA22 205 B2
Rowantree Ave
Motherwell ML1 143 B4
Rutherglen G73 138 A3
Uddingston G71 141 B4
Rowantree Gdns
Irvine KA11 220 A3
Rutherglen G73 138 A3
Rowantree Gr G83 27 C2
Rowantree Pl
Johnstone PA5 111 C1
Larkhall ML9 185 B1
Lennoxtown G66 57 C4
Rowantree Rd PA5 112 A1
Rowantree Terr
Lennoxtown G66 57 C4
Motherwell ML1 143 A3
Rowantree Wlk FK5 23 B2
Rowantreehill Rd PA13 89 C4
Rowanwood Cres ML5 121 B3
Rowena Ave G13 75 B1
Rowmore Quays G84 15 C2
Roxburgh Ave PA15 45 C2
Roxburgh Dr
Bearsden G61 75 C4
Coatbridge ML5 122 B2
Roxburgh Pk G74 159 C1
Roxburgh Pl
Blantyre G72 161 B4
Stenhousemuir FK5 23 C2
Roxburgh Rd
Hurlford KA1 228 C3
Paisley PA2 132 B4
Roxburgh St Glasgow G12 96 B2
Greenock PA15 45 C2
Roxburgh Way PA15 45 C2
Roy St G21 97 B2
Roy Young Ave G83 28 A4
Royal Alexandra Hospl
PA2 113 B1
Royal Bank Pl G1 241 A2
Royal Cres G3 116 C4
Royal Dr ML3 163 A1
Royal Exchange Ct G1 241 A2
Royal Exchange Sq G1 241 A2
Royal Gdns Bothwell G71 140 C1
Stirling FK8 7 A4
Royal Hospl (For Sick
Children) G3 96 B1
Royal Inch Cres PA4 94 B3
Royal Infmy G4 241 C3
Royal Scottish Acad of Music
& Drama G3 240 C3
Royal Scottish National Hospl
The FK5 22 C2
Royal St PA19 44 C4
Royal Terr Glasgow G3 96 C1
Wishaw ML2 165 B4
Royal Terrace La G3 96 C1
Royal Troon Golf Club★
KA10 232 B4
Royellen Ave ML3 161 C1
Royston Rd G21,G33 98 B2
Royston Sq G21 241 C4
Roystonhill G21 97 C1
Rozelle★ KA7 238 C1
Rozelle Ave Glasgow G15 75 A2
Newton Mearns G77 156 A2
Rozelle Dr G77 156 A2
Rozelle Pl G77 156 A2
Rozelle Terr KA7 239 A1
Rubie Cres KA12 219 B1
Rubislaw Dr G61 75 C2
Ruby St G40 118 A2
Ruchazie Pl G33 118 C4
Ruchazie Prim Sch G33 99 A1
Ruchazie Rd G32 118 C4
Ruchill Pl G20 96 C3
Ruchill Prim Sch G20 96 C3
Ruchill St G20 96 C3

Seafar Rd G67 61 C1
Seafield Ave G61 75 C4
Seafield Cottage La
PA16 45 B4
Seafield Cres Ayr KA7 238 C3
Cumbernauld G68 60 C1
Seafield Ct
Ardrossan KA22 205 A2
Falkirk FK1 41 C1
Seafield Dr
Ardrossan KA22 205 B2
Ayr KA7 238 B3
Rutherglen G73 138 B2
Seafield Rd KA7 238 C3
Seafield Sch KA22 205 A2
Seaford St KA1 227 C4
Seaforth Cres Ayr KA8 236 A2
Barrhead G78 134 A2
Seaforth La G69 81 A1
Seaforth Pl Bellshill ML4 141 C2
Stirling FK8 7 A4
Seaforth Rd Ayr KA8 236 A2
Clydebank G81 74 A1
Falkirk FK2 24 B1
3 Glasgow G52 115 A4
Seaforth Rd N G52 115 A4
Seaforth Rd S G52 115 A4
Seagate Irvine KA12 219 A2
Prestwick KA9 233 B1
Seagrove St G32 118 B3
Seamill Gdns G74 159 B1
Seamill Path G53 134 C3
Seamill St G53 134 C3
Seamore St 1 G20 97 A1
Seath Ave Airdrie ML6 122 C4
Langbank PA14 70 B3
Seath Rd G73 118 A1
Seath St G42 117 B1
Seaton Pl FK1 42 B2
Seaton Terr
Hamilton ML3 162 A2
Irvine KA12 219 B3
Seaview Rd KA21 216 C4
Seaview Terr KA10 230 A2
Seaward La G41 116 C3
Seaward St 6 G41 116 C3
Second Ave
Alexandria G83 27 C3
Bearsden G61 76 A2
Clydebank G81 74 A2
Dumbarton G82 50 B1
Glasgow G44 137 A3
Irvine KA12 224 C4
Kirkintilloch G66 79 B1
Millerston G33 99 A3
Renfrew PA4 94 B1
Uddingston G71 120 C1
Second Ave La G44 137 A4
Second Gdns G41 116 A2
Second Rd G72 161 C3
Second St G71 140 C4
Seedhill PA1 113 C2
Seedhill Rd PA1 114 A2
Seggielea La G13 95 B3
Seggielea Rd G13 95 B3
Segton Ave KA13 207 B2
Seil Dr G44 137 B2
Selborne Pl 5 G13 95 C3
Selborne Place La 4
G13 95 C3
Selborne Rd G13 95 C3
Selby Gdns G32 119 B3
Selby Pl ML5 101 B1
Selby St ML5 101 B1
Selkirk Ave Glasgow G52 115 B2
Paisley PA2 133 A4
Selkirk Dr G73 138 B4
Selkirk Pl
East Kilbride G74 160 B2
Hamilton ML3 162 C1
Selkirk Rd PA14 68 B4
Selkirk St Blantyre G72 161 B4
Hamilton ML3 162 B1
Wishaw ML2 165 B3
Selkirk Way Bellshill ML4 142 A4
Coatbridge ML5 122 C2
Sella Rd G64 78 B1
Selvieland Rd G52 114 C3
Semphill Gdns G74 160 A1
Sempie St ML3 161 C2
Sempill Ave PA8 72 C1
Semple Ave
Bishopton PA7 72 A2
Lochwinnoch PA12 129 B2
Semple Pl PA3 112 A4
Semple Rd KA9 236 B3
Semple View PA9 130 C3
Senate Pl ML1 142 B1
Senga Cres ML4 142 A4
Seres Rd G76 157 B4
Sergeant Law Rd
Paisley PA2,G78 132 C2
Uplawmoor G78 153 A4
Seright Cres KA3 228 B4
Seright Sq KA3 228 B4
Serpentine Wlk PA15 46 B2
Sersley Dr KA25 148 C1
Service St G66 33 B1
Seton Dr FK7 7 B2
Seton La KA22 205 B1
Seton St KA22 205 B1
Seton Terr 3 G31 117 C4
Settle Gdns G69 119 C2
Seven Sisters G66 79 C3
Seventh Ave G71 140 C4
Seventh Rd G72 161 C3
Severn Rd G75 179 C4
Seward Pl G41 116 C3
Seymour Ave KA13 207 C1
Seymour Gn G75 180 A4
Seyton Ave G46 136 B1
Seyton Ct G46 136 B1
Seyton La G74 159 C2
Shaftesbury St Alloa FK10 10 A4
Glasgow G3 240 A3
Shafton Pl G13 95 C4
Shafton Rd G13 95 C4
Shaftsbury Ave G81 73 C1
Shaftsbury Cres ML1 143 B2
Shakespeare Ave G81 73 C2
Shakespeare St G20 96 C3
Shalloch Pk KA7 238 B1
Shalloch Pl KA11 220 A1
Shamrock St
Glasgow G4 240 B4
Kirkintilloch G66 79 B4
Shand La ML8 187 C2
Shand St ML2 165 B1
Shandon Brae G83 27 C4
Shandon Cres Balloch G83 27 C4
Bellshill ML4 142 A4
Shandon Pl PA15 46 B1
Shandon Terr ML3 161 C2
Shandwick St G34 120 A4
Shangill Ct ML8 186 C2
Shankland Gr PA15 46 C1
Shankland Rd PA15 46 C1
Shanks Ave
Barrhead G78 134 B1
Denny FK6 39 C4
Shanks Cres PA5 111 C1
Shanks Ct KA3 222 C1
Shanks Ind Pk G78 134 B2
Shanks St Airdrie ML6 103 A1
Glasgow G20 96 C3
Shanks Way G78 134 B3
Shannon Dr FK1 41 C2
Shannon St G20 96 C3
Shanter Pl Ayr KA7 238 C1
Kilmarnock KA3 228 B4
Shanter Way KA7 238 C1
Shanter Wynd KA7 238 C1
Shantron Rd G83 27 C3
Shapinsay St G22 97 B4
Sharon St KA24 191 A4
Sharp Ave ML5 121 B2
Sharp St Gourock PA19 44 C4
Motherwell ML1 163 A4
Sharpe Ave KA11 220 B1
Sharphill Ind Est KA21 206 A2
Shavian Terr KA13 207 C1
Shavin Brae KA7 239 B3
Shaw Ave PA7 72 B2
Shaw Cres ML2 164 B1
Shaw Ct PA8 72 C2
Shaw Farm Ind Est KA9 233 C1
Shaw Pl Dalry KA24 191 A4
Greenock PA15 45 C3
Linwood PA3 112 A3
Saltcoats KA21 206 A1
Shaw Rd Milngavie G62 76 A4
Newton Mearns G77 156 C2
Prestwick KA9 233 C1
Shaw St Glasgow G51 116 A4
Larkhall ML9 199 A4
Shawbank Pl KA1 228 A4
Shawbridge Arc G43 136 B4
Shawbridge Ind Est
G43 136 A4
Shawbridge St G43 136 B4
Shawburn Cres ML3 162 A2
Shawburn St ML3 162 A2
Shawfarm Ct KA9 233 B1
Shawfarm Pl KA9 233 B1
Shawfield Ave KA7 239 A2
Shawfield Cres ML8 186 C3
Shawfield Dr G5 117 C1
Shawfield Ind Est G73 117 C1
Shawfield Rd G73 117 C1
Shawhead Ave ML5 122 A2
Shawhead Cotts ML5 122 A2
Shawhead Prim Sch
ML5 122 A2
Shawhill Cres G77 156 C2
Shawhill Rd G41 136 B4
Shawholm Cres G43 136 A4
Shawlands Acad G41 116 C1
Shawlands Arc G41 136 C4
Shawlands Cross 5
G41 116 C1
Shawlands Prim Sch
G41 136 B4
Shawlands Sta G41 136 B4
Shawmoss Rd G41 116 B1
Shawpark St G20 96 C3
Shawrigg Rd ML9 185 B1
Shaws Rd ML9 199 B4
Shawstonfoot Rd ML1 145 A1
Shawwood Cres G77 156 C2
Shearer Dr ML3 183 B4
Shearer Quadrant G83 28 A4
Sheddens Pl G32 118 C3
Sheena Dr G83 27 C1
Sheepburn Rd G71 140 C4
Sheila St G33 98 C2
Sheildhill 18 G75 180 C4
Sheiling Hill ML3 162 C2
Sheldaig Rd G22 97 A4
Sheldrake Pl PA5 131 B3
Shellbridge Way KA22 205 B1
Shelley Ct G12 96 A3
Shelley Dr Bothwell G71 141 A1
Clydebank G81 74 A2
Shelley Rd G12 96 A3
Shells Rd G66 58 C1
Sherbrooke Ave G41 116 B2
Sherbrooke Dr G41 116 B2
Sherbrooke Gdns G41 116 B2
Sherbrooke Pl G75 159 B1
Sherburn Gdns G69 119 C2
Sherdale Ave ML6 123 B1
Sheriff Park Ave G73 138 A4
Sheriffmuir Rd FK9 2 B4
Sheriffmuirlands FK9 2 B2
Sherriff La FK5 23 C2
Sherry Dr ML3 162 A1
Sherwood Ave
Paisley PA1 114 A3
Uddingston G71 141 A3
Sherwood Dr G46 136 A2
Sherwood Pl G15 75 A2
Sherwood Rd
Hurlford KA1 228 C3
Prestwick KA9 236 C4
Shetland Ct FK10 10 A3
Shetland Dr
Glasgow G44 137 B2
Kilmarnock KA3 223 A3
Shettleston Rd G32 119 A3
Shettleston Sheddings
G32 118 C3
Shettleston Sta G32 119 A3
Shewalton Dr KA11 225 B3
Shewalton Moss KA11 225 B3
Shewalton Pits (Nature
Reserve)★ KA11 224 C4
Shewalton Rd KA11 225 A3
Shewalton Rdbt KA11 225 A3
Shiel Ave G74 159 C2
Shiel Ct G78 134 A3
Shiel Dr ML9 184 C3
Shiel Gdns Falkirk FK2 24 B1
Shotts ML7 147 A2
Shiel Hill KA7 239 A1
Shiel Pl Coatbridge ML5 122 B3
East Kilbride G74 159 C2
Irvine KA12 219 B3
Shiel Rd G64 78 A1
Shiel Terr ML2 165 C3
Shielbridge Gdns G23 76 C1
Shieldaig Dr G73 138 A2
Shieldburn Rd G51 115 B4
Shieldhall Gdns G51 115 B4
Shieldhall Rd G51 115 B4
Shieldhill Prim Sch FK1 66 B3
Shieldhill Rd
Carluke ML8 201 C4
Shieldhill FK2 66 C4
Shieldmuir St ML2 164 B2
Shieldmuir Sta ML2 164 B2
Shields Ct ML1 164 A2
Shields Dr ML1 164 A2
Shields Loan ML11 214 C3
Shields Rd
East Kilbride G75 180 A2
Glasgow G41 116 C2
Motherwell ML1 164 A2
Shields Road Underground
Sta G5 116 C3
Shields Twr ML1 164 A2
Shielhope Ct KA11 220 A2
Shieling Pk KA7 238 C4
Shierlaw Gdns FK2 14 B2
Shilford Ave G13 95 A4
Shilford Rd G78 132 B1
Shillay St G22 97 C4
Shilliaw Dr KA9 236 B3
Shilliaw Pl KA9 236 B3
Shillinghill FK10 10 A3
Shillingworth Pl PA11 110 B3
Shilton Dr G53 135 B3
Shilton La PA7 72 C2
Shinwell Ave G81 74 B1
Shipbank La G1 241 A1
Shiphaugh Pl FK8 2 B1
Shira Terr G74 160 A1
Shire Way FK10 9 C3
Shirley Quadrant ML1 163 B2
Shirley's Ct ML11 215 A2
Shirra's Brae Rd FK7 7 A2
Shirrel Ave ML4 142 A4
Shirrel Rd ML1 143 A2
Shirva Lea G65 59 C2
Shiskine Dr Glasgow G20 96 B4
Kilmarnock KA3 222 C2
Shiskine Pl Glasgow G20 96 B4
Helensburgh G84 16 C1
Shiskine St G20 96 B4
Sholto Cres ML4 141 B4
Shore Rd Airth FK2 14 B2
Ayr KA8 235 C2
Stevenston KA20 217 B4
Stirling FK8 7 B4
Troon KA10 229 B1
Shore St Glasgow G40 118 A1
Gourock PA19 44 C4
Port Glasgow PA14 47 A1
Shore The FK10 10 A3
Shortlees Cres KA1 227 C2
Shortlees Prim Sch
KA1 227 C2
Shortlees Rd KA1 227 C1
Shortridge St G20 96 C3
Shortroods Ave PA3 113 C4
Shortroods Cres PA3 113 B4
Shortroods Rd PA3 113 B4
Shotts Rd ML7 126 C1
Shotts St G33 119 B4
Shotts Sta ML7 146 C2
Shottsburn Rd ML7 126 A2
Shottskirk Rd ML7 146 B3
Shuna Pl Glasgow G20 96 C3
Newton Mearns G77 156 A3
Shuna St G20 96 C3
Shuttle St Glasgow G1 241 B2
Kilbarchan PA10 111 A2
Kilsyth G65 60 B4
Paisley PA1 113 C2
Sidehead Rd
Harthill ML7 127 C3
Stonehouse ML9 198 C1
Sidland Rd G21 98 B3
Sidlaw Ave Barrhead G78 134 B1
Hamilton ML3 161 C1
Port Glasgow PA14 68 C3
Sidlaw Ct ML5 122 B2
Sidlaw Dr ML2 164 C2
Sidlaw Foot KA11 220 B1
Sidlaw Pl KA1 228 A2
Sidlaw Rd G61 75 A4
Sidlaw Way
Chapelhall ML6 123 C1
Larkhall ML9 184 C3
Sidney St KA21 216 C4
Sielga Pl G34 120 A4
Siemens Pl G21 98 A1
Siemens St G21 98 A1
Sievewright St G73 118 B1
Sighthill Loan 5 ML9 185 A2
Sighthill Prim Sch G21 97 B2
Sighthill Terr ML7 125 A1
Sikeside Pl ML5 122 B3
Sikeside Prim Sch ML5 122 B3
Sikeside St ML5 122 B3
Silk Ho FK1 42 A3
Silk St PA1 113 C3
Silkin Ave G81 74 B1
Sillars Mdw KA12 219 C1
Silvan Pl G76 158 A3
Silver Birch Dr G51 115 B4
Silver Birch Gdns G51 115 B4
Silver Firs ML1 143 B2
Silver Glade G52 115 A2
Silverbirch Gdns ML3 183 C2
Silverbirch Gr ML3 183 C2
Silverburn Cres ML1 143 B2
Silverburn Gdns FK12 5 B4
Silverburn St G33 118 C4
Silverdale G74 159 B2
Silverdale Cres ML11 214 C2
Silverdale Ct ML11 214 C2
Silverdale St G31 118 B2
Silverdale Terr ML6 103 C2
Silverfir St G5 117 B2
Silvergrove St G40 117 C3
Silvermuir Ave ML11 215 C4
Silverton Ave G82 50 A2
Silvertonhill Ave ML3 162 C1
Silvertonhill La G82 50 A2
Silvertonhill Pl ML3 183 B4
Silverwells G71 141 A1
Silverwells Cres G71 141 A1
Silverwood Ct G71 141 A1
Silverwood Prim Sch
KA3 223 B2
Silverwood Rd KA3 228 B4
Sim St KA3 211 B4
Simons Cres
Kilmarnock KA1 227 C2
Renfrew PA4 94 B3
Simonsburn Rd KA1 227 C2
Simpson Ct Clydebank G81 74 A1
Uddingston G71 140 C3
Simpson Dr
East Kilbride G75 180 B4
Saltcoats KA21 205 C2
Simpson Gdns G78 134 A1
Simpson Pl
East Kilbride G75 180 B4
Kilwinning KA13 207 C1
Simpson Quadrant G83 28 A4
Simpson St
Crosshouse KA2 222 A1
Falkirk FK1 41 C3
Glasgow G20 96 C2
Simpson Way ML4 142 B4
Simshill Prim Sch G44 137 A2
Simshill Rd G44 137 B2
Simson Ave KA23 190 C2
Sinclair Ave G61 75 C3
Sinclair Cres FK6 21 B1
Sinclair Ct Bannockburn FK7 7 C1
Kilmarnock KA3 223 B2
Sinclair Dr
Coatbridge ML5 121 B4
Fallin FK7 8 B2
Glasgow G42 136 C4
Helensburgh G84 16 C2
Sinclair Gdns G64 98 A4
Sinclair Gr ML4 141 C1
Sinclair La G84 16 C2
Sinclair Pk 6 G75 180 C4
Sinclair Pl
East Kilbride G75 180 C4
Falkirk FK2 24 A1
Sinclair St Clydebank G81 94 B4
Greenock PA15 46 B2
Helensburgh G84 16 B1
Milngavie G62 55 A1
Stevenston KA20 206 B1
Singer Rd Clydebank G81 73 C2
East Kilbride G75 181 A3
Singer St G81 74 A2
Singer Sta G81 74 A1
Sir John Graham Ct FK5 23 A1
Sir John Maxwell Prim Sch
G43 136 B4
Sir Michael Pl
Greenock PA15 45 C3
Sir Michael Pl *continued*
Paisley PA1 113 B2
Sir Michael St PA15 45 C3
Sir William Wallace Ct
FK5 23 A2
Sixth Ave PA4 94 B1
Sixth St G71 120 C1
Skaethorn Rd G20 96 A4
Skaithmuir Ave FK2 24 A2
Skaithmuir Cres FK2 24 A2
Skara Wlk ML2 165 C4
Skaterigg Dr G13 95 C3
Skaterigg Gdns G13 95 C3
Skaterigg La G13 95 C3
Skelbo Path G34 100 B1
Skelbo Pl G34 100 B1
Skellyton Cres ML9 185 A1
Skelmorlie Pl
Kilwinning KA13 207 B2
Stenhousemuir FK5 23 C2
Skene Rd Glasgow G51 116 A3
Kilmarnock KA3 223 B2
Skene St FK4 40 A3
Skerne Gr G75 179 C3
Skernieland Rd KA3 213 A2
Skerray Quadrant G22 97 B4
Skerray St G22 97 B4
Skerryvore Pl G33 119 A4
Skerryvore Rd G33 119 A4
Skibo La G46 135 C2
Skipness Ave ML8 202 A4
Skipness Dr G51 115 C4
Skirsa Ct G23 97 A4
Skirsa Pl G23 96 C4
Skirsa Sq G23 97 A4
Skirsa St G23 96 C4
Skirving St G41 136 C4
Skovlunde Way G75 180 C3
Skye G74 160 B1
Skye Ave PA4 94 B1
Skye Cres Gourock PA19 44 B3
Old Kilpatrick G60 73 B3
Paisley PA2 133 B4
Skye Ct Cumbernauld G67 82 B4
Irvine KA11 225 A4
Skye Dr Cumbernauld G67 82 B4
Old Kilpatrick G60 73 B3
Skye Gdns Bearsden G61 75 A3
Kilmarnock KA3 223 A3
Skye Pl Cumbernauld G67 82 B4
Stevenston KA20 206 C1
Skye Quadrant ML2 165 C3
Skye Rd Cumbernauld G67 82 B4
Port Glasgow PA14 69 A3
Prestwick KA9 233 C1
Rutherglen G73 138 B2
Skye St PA16 45 B2
Skye Wynd ML3 161 C1
Skythorn Way FK1 41 C1
Slaemuir Ave PA14 68 C3
Slaemuir Gdns PA14 68 C3
Slaemuir Prim Sch PA14 69 A3
Slakiewood Ave G69 100 C4
Slamannan Prim Sch
FK1 86 A4
Slamannan Rd
Avonbridge FK1 87 C3
Falkirk FK1 42 A1
Slamannan FK1 86 A1
Slatefield G66 57 B4
Slatefield Ct G31 118 A3
Slatefield St G31 118 A3
Sleaford Ave ML1 163 B2
Slenavon Ave G73 138 B2
Slessor Dr G75 180 C4
Slioch Sq ML1 143 B2
Sloan Ave KA12 219 B1
Sloan Pl KA8 236 B1
Sloan St KA8 236 B1
Sloy St Glasgow G22 97 B2
Wishaw ML2 165 A1
Small Cres G72 161 B4
Smeaton Ave G64 78 A4
Smeaton Dr G64 78 A2
Smeaton St G20 96 C3
Smiddy Ct
Kilwinning KA13 207 C2
Lanark ML11 215 A2
Smiddy Wynd FK12 5 A3
Smillie Pl KA2 227 B3
Smillie St PA15 46 C1
Smith Art Gallery & Mus★
FK8 7 A4
Smith Ave
Glengarnock KA14 170 B3
Irvine KA12 219 B2
Wishaw ML2 186 A4
Smith Cres Balloch G83 27 C4
Clydebank G81 74 A3
Kilwinning KA13 207 C1
Smith Dr KA21 217 A4
Smith Pl FK6 21 B1
Smith Quadrant ML5 122 B4
Smith St Ayr KA7 239 A4
Dalry KA24 191 B4
Falkirk FK2 42 A4
Glasgow G14 95 C1
Greenock PA15 45 C3
Prestwick KA9 236 B4
Smith Terr G73 118 A1
Smith's La PA3 113 C3
Smithfield Loan FK10 9 C3
Smithhills St PA1 113 C3
Smithston Cotts PA16 45 A2
Smithstone Cres G65 60 C3
Smithstone Ct KA11 219 C3
Smithstone Terr KA13 207 A4
Smithstone Way KA11 219 C3

Tweedmuir Pl ML5 .....122 B2
Tweedsmuir G64 ....78 B1
Tweedsmuir Cres G61 ...75 C4
Tweedsmuir Pk ML3 ...183 B4
Tweedsmuir Rd G52 ...115 A3
Tweedvale Ave G14 .....94 C3
Tweedvale Pl G14 ....94 C3
Twinlaw St G34 ....100 B1
Tygetshaugh Ct FK6 .....21 B2
Tylney Rd PA1 ....114 B3
Tyndrum Rd G61 ....76 A3
Tyndrum St G4 ....241 A4
Tyne Pl G75 ....179 C3
Tynecastle Cres G32 ...119 A4
Tynecastle Path G32 ...119 A4
Tynecastle Pl G32 .....119 A4
Tynecastle St G32 .....119 A4
Tynron Ct ML3 ....161 C1
Tynwald Ave G73 ....138 B2

U

Uddingston Gram Sch
G71 ....140 C3
Uddingston Rd G71 ....141 A2
Uddingston Sta G71 ...140 C3
Udston Hospl ML3 .....161 C2
Udston Prim Sch ML3 ..161 C2
Udston Rd ML3 ....161 C3
Udston Terr ML3 ......161 C3
Uig Pl G33 ....119 C3
Uist Ave PA14 ....69 A4
Uist Cres G33 ....99 C2
Uist Dr G66 ....80 A4
Uist Pl ML6 ....123 B3
Uist St G51 ....115 C4
Uist Way ML2 ....165 C3
Ulg Way ML7 ....147 A2
Ullswater G75 ....179 C3
Ulundi Rd PA5 ....111 C1
Ulva St G52 ....115 C3
Ulverston Terr ML3 ...183 B3
Umachan PA4 ....93 B4
Umberly Rd KA1 ....227 C2
Underwood KA13 ......207 B3
Underwood Cotts FK7 ....6 B3
Underwood Dr ML2 ....166 A4
Underwood La PA1 ....113 B3
Underwood Pl KA1 ....227 C2
Underwood Rd
Cambusbarron FK7 ....6 B3
Paisley PA3 ....113 B3
Prestwick KA9 ....236 B4
Rutherglen G73 ....138 B3
Underwood St G41 ....136 C4
Union Arc KA7 ....238 C4
Union Ave KA8 ....236 A2
Union Gdns FK1 ....41 B3
Union Pl Glasgow G1 ....240 C2
Larbert FK5 ....23 A1
Union Rd FK1 ....41 B3
Union St Alexandria G83 ..27 C2
6 Alloa FK10 ....10 A3
Bridge of A FK9 ....2 A4
Carluke ML8 ....187 C1
Falkirk FK2 ....42 A4
Glasgow G1 ....240 C2
Greenock PA16 ....45 C3
Hamilton ML3 ....162 B2
Hurlford KA1 ....228 C3
Kilmarnock KA3 ....222 C1
Kirkintilloch G66 ....79 B4
Larkhall ML9 ....185 A2
Motherwell ML1 ....143 A2
Paisley PA2 ....113 C1
Saltcoats KA21 ....216 C4
Shotts ML7 ....146 B3
Stenhousemuir FK5 ....23 C2
Stirling FK8 ....2 A1
Stonehouse ML9 ....198 C1
Troon KA10 ....229 B2
Union Street La G83 ....27 C2
Unitas Cres ML8 ....187 C1
Unitas Rd ML4 ....142 B3
Unity Pk ML7 ....146 B2
Unity Pl G4 ....97 A1
Univ of Glasgow (Kelvin
Campus) G20 ....76 A1
Univ of Glasgow (St Andrew's
Campus) G61 ....75 B4
Univ of Glasgow (Veterinary
Medicine) G61 ....96 A4
Univ of Paisley Ayr KA8 .239 B4
Paisley PA1 ....113 B2
Univ of Paisley (Thornly Park
Campus) PA2 ....133 C4
Univ of Stirling FK9 ......2 B3
Univ of Strathclyde G1,
G4 ....241 B3
Universal Rd FK2 ......42 C4
University Ave G12 ......96 B1
University Gdns G12 .....96 B1
University Pl G12 ....96 B1
University Rd W FK9 .....2 B3
Unsted Pl PA1 ....114 A2
Unthank Rd ML4 ....142 B3
UP La G65 ....60 B4
UP Rd G65 ....60 B4
Uphall Pl G33 ....118 C4
Upland La 2 G14 ....95 B2
Upland Rd G14 ....95 B2
Uplawmoor Prim Sch
G78 ....153 A2
Uplawmoor Rd G78 ....153 C2
Upper Adelaide St G84 ...16 C1
Upper Arthur St G83 ....27 B2
Upper Bourtree Ct G73 .138 B2
Upper Bourtree Dr G73 138 B2
Upper Bridge St
Alexandria G83 ....27 B2
Stirling FK8 ....2 A1
Upper Cartsburn St PA15 46 A2
Upper Castlehill FK8 .....7 A4
Upper Colquhoun St G84 16 B2
Upper Craigs FK8 ....7 A4
Upper Crofts KA7 ......238 C1
Upper Glenburn Rd G61 .75 B3
Upper Glenfinlas St G84 .16 C1
Upper Hall Rd G84 ....15 B3
Upper Loaning KA7 ....238 C1
Upper Mill St ML6 .....123 A4
Upper Mill St Ind Est
ML6 ....123 A4
Upper Newmarket St
FK1 ....42 A3
Upper Smollett St G83 ..27 B2
Upper Stoneymollan Rd
G83 ....27 A4
Upper Sutherland Cres
G84 ....16 A2
Upper Sutherland St G84 16 A2
Upper Torwoodhill Rd
G84 ....15 C2
Ure Cres FK4 ....40 A3
Urquhart Cres PA4 ......94 B1
Urquhart Dr
East Kilbride G74 ....160 A2
Gourock PA19 ....43 C3
Urquhart Pl G84 ....16 B2
Urquhart Rd KA3 ....223 B1
Urrdale Rd G41 ....116 A3
Usmore Pl G33 ....119 C3

V

Vaila Pl G23 ....97 A4
Vaila St G23 ....96 C4
Vale Gr FK9 ....1 C3
Vale of Leven Acad G83 .27 B2
Vale of Leven Hospl
(General) G83 ....27 B3
Vale of Leven Ind Est
Renton G82 ....27 C1
Renton G82 ....49 C4
Vale Pl FK6 ....21 C2
Valentine Cres G71 ....141 A4
Valerio Ct G72 ....161 B4
Valetta Pl G81 ....73 B2
Valeview FK5 ....23 B1
Valeview Terr
Dumbarton G82 ....50 A3
Glasgow G42 ....137 A4
Vallantine Cres G71 ...141 A4
Vallay St G22 ....97 B4
Valley Ct ML3 ....162 B1
Valley View
Cambuslang G72 ....139 B3
Motherwell ML1 ....164 A2
Valleybank G65 ....37 B2
Valleyfield
East Kilbride G75 ......159 B1
Milton of C G66 ....58 A3
Valleyfield Dr G68 ......60 C1
Valleyfield Pl FK7 ....7 B3
Valleyfield St 2 G21 ....97 C2
Valleyview Dr FK2 ......42 A4
Valleyview Pl FK2 ......42 A4
Vancouver Ct 9 G75 ...159 A1
Vancouver Dr G75 .....159 A1
Vancouver La
17 Glasgow G14 ....95 B2
8 Glasgow G14 ....95 B2
Vancouver Pl G81 ....73 B2
Vancouver Rd G14 ......95 B2
Vanguard St G81 ....74 B1
Vanguard Way PA4 ......94 B1
Vardar Ave G76 ....157 B4
Vardon Lea ML1 ....143 C1
Varna La G14 ....95 C2
Varna Rd G14 ....95 C2
Varnsdorf Way ML6 ....123 C3
Vasart Pl G20 ....96 C2
Vatersay Pl KA3 ....223 A3
Vaults La KA13 ....207 C2
Veir Terr G82 ....49 C2
Veitch Pl G66 ....57 B4
Veitches Ct G81 ....74 A3
Vennachar St ML7 .....146 C3
Vennacher Rd PA4 ......94 A2
Vennal St KA24 ....191 A4
Vennard Gdns G41 .....116 C1
Vennel La KA3 ....211 C4
Vennel St KA3 ....211 C4
Vennel The FK6 ....21 C1
Vermont Ave G73 ......138 A4
Vermont St G41 ....116 C3
Vernon Bank G74 ......159 C2
Vernon Dr PA3 ....112 A3
Vernon Pl KA2 ....225 C1
Vernon St KA21 ....216 C4
Verona Ave G14 ....95 B2
Verona Gdns 4 G14 .....95 B2
Verona La G14 ....95 B2
Verona Pl KA22 ....205 B1
Vesalius St G32 ....119 A3
Viaduct Circ KA13 .....207 C3
Viaduct Rd G76 ....157 C4
Vicar St FK1 ....42 A3
Vicarfield St G51 ......116 A4
Vicarland Pl G72 ......139 A2
Vicarland Rd G72 .....139 A3
Vicars Rd ML9 ....198 C1
Vicars Wlk G72 ....139 A3
Vickers St ML1 ....163 A4
Victor St ML6 ....104 A1
Victoria Ave
Barrhead G78 ....134 A2
Carluke ML8 ....187 C1
Victoria Cir G12 ....96 B2
Victoria Cres
Airdrie ML6 ....122 C3
Barrhead G78 ....134 A2
Clarkston G76 ....157 C4
Irvine KA12 ....219 A1
Kilsyth G65 ....60 A4
Wishaw ML2 ....164 B2
Victoria Crescent La G12 96 B2
Victoria Crescent Pl 16
G12 ....96 B2
Victoria Crescent Rd
G12 ....96 B2
Victoria Cross G42 ....117 A1
Victoria Ct Larkhall ML9 .185 A2
Newton Mearns G77 ....156 B1
Victoria Dr Barrhead G78 134 A2
Troon KA10 ....229 C1
Victoria Dr E PA4 ....94 B1
Victoria Dr W PA4 ......94 A2
Victoria East Rd KA1 ..228 A4
Victoria Gdns
Airdrie ML6 ....122 C4
Barrhead G78 ....134 A2
Kilmacolm PA13 ....69 B1
Paisley PA2 ....113 B1
Victoria Glade G68 .....61 B3
Victoria Gr G78 ....134 A2
Victoria Infmy
Glasgow G42 ....137 A4
Helensburgh G84 ....16 C1
Victoria La G77 ....156 B1
Victoria Meml Cottage Hospl
G65 ....60 A4
Victoria Park Cnr G14 ...95 B2
Victoria Park Dr N G14 ..95 C2
Victoria Park Dr S G14 ..95 C2
Victoria Park Gdns N
G11 ....95 C2
Victoria Park Gdns S
G11 ....95 C2
Victoria Park La N G14 ..95 B2
Victoria Park La S G14 ..95 B2
Victoria Park Sch ML8 .187 C1
Victoria Park St 27 G14 ..95 B2
Victoria Pk Ayr KA7 ...238 C3
Glasgow G14 ....95 C2
Kilsyth G65 ....60 A4
Victoria Pl Airdrie ML6 ..122 C3
Barrhead G78 ....134 B2
Bellshill ML4 ....141 C2
Kilsyth G65 ....60 B4
Milngavie G62 ....55 A1
4 Rutherglen G73 ......138 A4
Stirling FK8 ....7 A4
Victoria Prim Sch
Airdrie ML6 ....122 C4
Falkirk FK2 ....42 B3
Glasgow G42 ....117 A1
Victoria Quadrant ML1 .142 C3
Victoria Rd
Barrhead G78 ....134 A2
Brookfield PA5 ....111 B3
Dullatur G68 ....61 B3
Falkirk FK2 ....42 B3
Glasgow G42 ....117 A2
Gourock PA19 ....44 B4
Harthill ML7 ....127 C3
Helensburgh G84 ....16 C1
Kirkintilloch G66 ....79 B2
Larbert FK5 ....23 A1
Paisley PA2 ....113 B1
Rutherglen G73 ....138 A3
Saltcoats KA21 ....217 A4
Stepps G33 ....99 B3
Stirling FK8 ....7 A4
Victoria Rdbt KA12 ....219 A1
Victoria Sq
Newton Mearns G77 ....156 B1
Stirling FK8 ....7 A4
Victoria St Alexandria G83 27 C2
Alloa FK10 ....10 A4
Ayr KA8 ....236 A1
Blantyre G72 ....161 B4
Dumbarton G82 ....50 A2
Hamilton ML3 ....162 A3
Harthill ML7 ....127 C3
Kirkintilloch G66 ....79 B4
Larkhall ML9 ....185 A2
Rutherglen G73 ....138 A4
Wishaw ML2 ....166 A2
Victoria Terr Dullatur G68 .61 B3
Menstrie FK11 ....4 A4
Victoria Way KA3 .....195 C1
Victory Dr PA10 ......111 A2
Victory Way G69 ......120 A2
Viewbank G46 ....136 A2
Viewbank Ave ML6 ....123 A1
Viewbank St ML5 .....101 C3
Viewfield Airdrie ML6 ..122 C4
Moodiesburn G69 ....80 C2
Viewfield Ave
Bishopbriggs G64 ....97 C4
Blantyre G72 ....140 C1
Glasgow G69 ....119 C3
Kirkintilloch G66 ....79 B3
Lochwinnoch PA12 .....129 A1
Milton of C G66 ....58 A3
Viewfield Bsns Ctr KA8 .236 A1
Viewfield Dr Alva FK12 ...4 C3
Bishopbriggs G64 ....97 C4
Glasgow G69 ....119 C3
Viewfield La G12 ....96 C1
Viewfield Rd Ayr KA8 ..236 A1
Viewfield Rd *continued*
Banknock FK4 ....38 B2
Bellshill ML4 ....141 C2
Bishopbriggs G64 ....97 C4
Coatbridge ML5 ....121 B2
Viewfield St Harthill ML7 127 C3
Stirling FK8 ....7 A4
Viewforth FK8 ....7 A3
Viewglen Ct G45 ......137 B1
Viewmount Dr G20 .....96 B4
Viewpark Beith KA15 ..150 A1
Milngavie G62 ....55 A1
Viewpark Ave G31 ....118 A4
Viewpark Ct G73 ......138 B3
Viewpark Dr G73 ......138 A3
Viewpark Gdns PA4 ....94 A1
Viewpark Pl ML1 ......163 B3
Viewpark Rd ML1 .....163 B3
Viewpark Sh Ctr G71 ..141 B3
Viewpoint Pl G21 ....97 C3
Viewpoint Rd G21 ......97 C3
Viking Cres PA6 ....111 B4
Viking Rd ML6 ....123 A3
Viking Terr G75 ....180 C3
Viking Way Glasgow G46 135 C3
Renfrew PA4 ....94 B1
Villa Bank FK6 ....21 C1
Villafield Ave G64 ......78 A2
Villafield Dr G64 ....78 A2
Villafield Loan G64 .....78 A2
Village Gdns G72 .....140 C1
Village Rd G72 ....139 C2
Vincent Ct ML4 ....142 A2
Vine Park Ave KA3 ....222 A4
Vine Park Dr KA3 .....222 A4
Vine St G11 ....96 A1
Vineburgh Ave KA12 ..219 B2
Vineburgh Ct KA12 ....219 A2
Vinicombe La 3 G12 ....96 B2
Vinicombe St G12 ......96 B2
Vintner St G4 ....97 B1
Viola Pl G64 ....78 B4
Violet Gdns ML8 ......201 C4
Violet Pl ML1 ....143 A3
Violet St PA1 ....114 A2
Virginia Ct G1 ....241 A2
Virginia Gdns Ayr KA8 .236 A1
Milngavie G62 ....76 B4
Virginia Pl G1 ....241 A2
Virginia St Glasgow G1 .241 A2
Greenock PA15 ....46 A2
Viscount Ave PA4 ....94 B1
Viscount Gate G71 ....140 C3
Vivian Ave G62 ....54 C1
Voil Dr G44 ....137 A2
Voil Rd FK9 ....2 A2
Vorlich Ct G78 ....134 B1
Vorlich Dr FK1 ....66 C4
Vorlich Gdns G61 ......75 B4
Vorlich Pl
Kilmarnock KA1 ....228 A2
Stirling FK9 ....2 A2
Vorlich Wynd ML1 ....143 B2
Vrackie Pl KA1 ....228 A2
Vryburg Cres G75 .....180 A2
Vulcan St 5 Glasgow G21 97 C2
Motherwell ML1 ....163 C4

W

Waddell Ave ML6 .....102 B2
Waddell Ct Glasgow G5 .117 B3
Kilmarnock KA3 ....222 C2
Waddell St Airdrie ML6 .103 A1
Falkirk FK2 ....24 B1
Glasgow G5 ....117 B2
Waggon Rd Ayr KA8 ..235 C1
Falkirk FK2 ....42 A4
Waid Ave G77 ....156 B3
Waldemar Rd G13 ......95 B4
Walden Rd KA1 ....228 C3
Waldo St 3 G13 ....95 C4
Walk The FK10 ....10 A3
Walker Ave
Kilmarnock KA3 ....228 A4
Troon KA10 ....229 C3
Walker Ct Glasgow G11 ..96 A1
Hurlford KA1 ....228 C3
Walker Dr
Bonnybridge FK4 ....39 B3
Elderslie PA5 ....112 B1
Walker Path 2 G71 ....141 A4
Walker Rd KA8 ....236 A1
Walker St Glasgow G11 ..96 A1
Greenock PA16 ....45 B3
2 Kilbirnie KA25 ....149 A1
Paisley PA1 ....113 B2
Walkerburn Dr ML2 ...165 B3
Walkerburn Rd G52 ...115 A2
Walkinshaw Rd PA4 ....93 B2
Walkinshaw St
Glasgow G40 ....118 A2
Johnstone PA5 ....112 A2
Walkinshaw Way PA3 ..113 C4
Walkmill La G81 ....74 A3
Wall Gdns FK1 ....41 B3
Wall St FK1 ....41 B3
Wallace Ave
Bishopton PA7 ....72 A2
Dundonald KA2 ....225 C1
Elderslie PA5 ....112 B1
Stevenston KA20 ....206 B1
Troon KA10 ....229 C3
Wallace Cres Denny FK6 ..21 B1
Plean FK7 ....12 B2
Wallace Ct
Kilmarnock KA1 ....228 C3
Wallace Ct *continued*
Prestwick KA9 ....236 B4
Stirling FK8 ....2 A1
Wallace Dr ML9 ....185 B1
Wallace Gate FK8 ....7 A4
Wallace Gdns Stirling FK9 .2 B2
Torrance G64 ....57 A1
Wallace High Sch FK9 ...2 A2
Wallace Ho G67 ....61 C1
Wallace Monument* FK9 .2 C2
Wallace Pl Blantyre G72 .140 C1
Cambusbarron FK7 ....6 B3
Falkirk FK2 ....42 B3
Fallin FK7 ....8 B2
Greenock PA15 ....45 C3
Hamilton ML3 ....163 A1
Wallace Prim Sch PA5 .112 B1
Wallace Rd Irvine KA12 .219 B2
Motherwell ML1 ....143 A1
Renfrew PA4 ....94 A1
Wallace St Alloa FK10 ...10 B4
Bannockburn FK7 ....7 C1
Clydebank G81 ....74 A1
Coatbridge ML5 ....122 A3
Dumbarton G82 ....50 A2
Falkirk FK2 ....42 B3
Glasgow G5 ....117 A3
Greenock PA16 ....45 B2
Kilmarnock KA1 ....227 C4
Motherwell ML1 ....163 B4
Paisley PA3 ....113 C3
Plains ML6 ....104 A1
Port Glasgow PA14 ....47 C1
Rutherglen G73 ....138 A4
Stirling FK8 ....2 A1
Wallace View
Kilmarnock KA1 ....227 C3
Shieldhill FK1 ....66 B4
Tullibody FK10 ....4 B2
Wallace Way ML11 ....215 B2
Wallace Wynd ML8 ....187 A3
Wallacefield Rd KA10 .229 C2
Wallacehill Rd KA1 ...227 C2
Wallacetown Ave KA3 .223 A3
Wallacewell Cres G21 ...98 A3
Wallacewell Pl G21 .....98 A3
Wallacewell Quadrant
G21 ....98 B3
Wallacewell Rd G21 ....98 B3
Wallbrae Rd G67 ....83 A4
Wallneuk 11 PA1 ......113 C3
Wallneuk Rd PA3 .....113 C3
Walls St G1 ....241 B2
Wallstale Rd FK7 ....7 A2
Walmer Cres G51 .....116 B3
Walnut Cres Glasgow G22 .97 B3
Johnstone PA5 ....112 A1
Walnut Ct G66 ....58 A3
Walnut Dr G66 ....79 A3
Walnut Gate G72 .....139 C2
Walnut Pl Glasgow G22 ..97 B3
Uddingston G71 ....121 B1
Walnut Rd Glasgow G22 ..97 B3
Kilmarnock KA1 ....227 B4
Walpole Pl PA5 ....131 B4
Walter St Glasgow G31 .118 B4
Wishaw ML2 ....165 B2
Walton Ave G77 ......156 B3
Walton St Barrhead G78 .134 B2
Glasgow G41 ....136 C4
Wamba Ave G13 ....95 C4
Wamphray Pl G75 ....179 B4
Wandilla Ave G81 ......74 B1
Wanlock St G51 ......116 A4
Ward Ct KA8 ....236 A2
Ward Rd KA8 ....236 A2
Ward St FK10 ....10 A3
Warden Rd G13 ....95 B4
Wardend Rd G64 ....57 A1
Wardhill Rd G21 ....98 A3
Wardhouse Rd PA2 ...133 B4
Wardie Pl G33 ....119 C4
Wardie Rd G34 ....120 A4
Wardlaw Ave G73 ....138 A4
Wardlaw Cres
East Kilbride G75 ......181 A4
Troon KA10 ....230 A2
Wardlaw Dr 7 G73 ....138 A4
Wardlaw Gdns KA11 ..220 A4
Wardlaw Pl FK2 ....24 B1
Wardlaw Rd
Bearsden G61 ....75 C1
Kilmarnock KA3 ....223 C3
Wardneuk KA9 ....236 B3
Wardneuk Ct KA11 ...220 A3
Wardneuk Dr KA3 ....223 A2
Wardpark Ct G67 ....62 B3
Wardpark East Ind Est
G68 ....62 C4
Wardpark North Ind Est
G68 ....62 B4
Wardpark Pl G67 ....62 B3
Wardpark Rd G67 ......62 B3
Wardpark Rdbt G68 ....62 B4
Wardpark South Ind Est
G67 ....62 B3
Wardrop Pl G74 ......159 C2
Wardrop St Beith KA15 ..171 B4
2 Glasgow G51 ....116 A4
Paisley PA1 ....113 C2
Wardrop Terr KA15 ...171 B4
Wards Cres ML5 ......121 C3
Wards Pl KA1 ....227 C4
Ware Rd G34 ....120 A4
Warilda Ave G81 ....74 B1

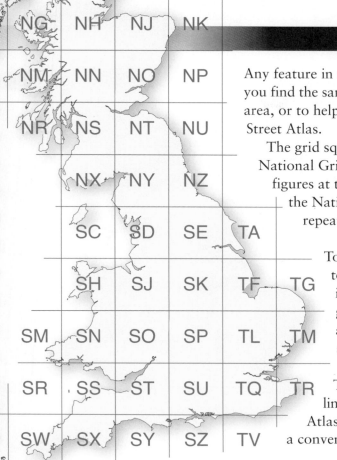

Any feature in this atlas can be given a unique reference to help you find the same feature on other Ordnance Survey maps of the area, or to help someone else locate you if they do not have a Street Atlas.

The grid squares in this atlas match the Ordnance Survey National Grid and are at 1 kilometre intervals. The small figures at the bottom and sides of every other grid line are the National Grid kilometre values (**00** to **99** km) and are repeated across the country every 100 km (see left).

To give a unique National Grid reference you need to locate where in the country you are. The country is divided into 100 km squares with each square given a unique two-letter reference. Use the administrative map to determine in which 100 km square a particular page of this atlas falls.

The bold letters and numbers between each grid line (**A** to **C**, **1** to **4**) are for use within a specific Street Atlas only, and when used with the page number, are a convenient way of referencing these grid squares.

Example   *The railway bridge over DARLEY GREEN RD in grid square A1*

Step 1: Identify the two-letter reference, in this example the page is in **SP**

Step 2: Identify the 1 km square in which the railway bridge falls. Use the figures in the southwest corner of this square: Eastings **17**, Northings **74**. This gives a unique reference: **SP 17 74**, accurate to 1 km.

Step 3: To give a more precise reference accurate to 100 m you need to estimate how many tenths along and how many tenths up this 1 km square the feature is. This makes the bridge about **8** tenths along and about **1** tenth up from the southwest corner.

This gives a unique reference: **SP 178 741**, accurate to 100 m.

Eastings (read from left to right along the bottom) come before Northings (read from bottom to top). If you have trouble remembering say to yourself "Along the hall, THEN up the stairs"!

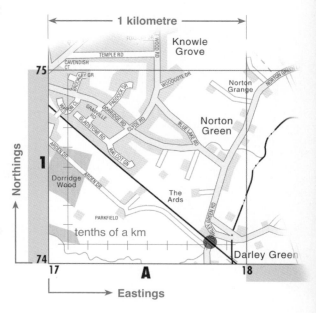

Addresses

Name and Address	Telephone	Page	Grid reference

Name and Address	Telephone	Page	Grid reference

Street Atlases from Philip's

Philip's publish an extensive range of regional and local street atlases which are ideal for motoring, business and leisure use. They are widely used by the emergency services and local authorities throughout Britain.

Key features include:

◆ Superb county-wide mapping at an extra-large scale of 3½ inches to 1 mile, or 2½ inches to 1 mile in pocket editions

◆ Complete urban and rural coverage, detailing every named street in town and country

◆ Each atlas available in two handy sizes – standard spiral and pocket paperback

1 Bedfordshire
2 Berkshire
3 Birmingham and West Midlands
4 Bristol and Bath
5 Buckinghamshire
6 Cambridgeshire
7 Cardiff, Swansea and The Valleys
8 Cheshire
9 Cornwall
10 Derbyshire
11 Devon
12 Dorset
13 County Durham and Teesside
14 Edinburgh and East Central Scotland
15 North Essex
16 South Essex
17 Glasgow and West Central Scotland
18 Gloucestershire
19 North Hampshire
20 South Hampshire
21 Hertfordshire
22 East Kent
23 West Kent
24 Lancashire
25 Leicestershire and Rutland
26 Lincolnshire
27 London
28 Greater Manchester
29 Merseyside
30 Norfolk
31 Northamptonshire
32 Nottinghamshire
33 Oxfordshire
34 Shropshire
35 Somerset
36 Staffordshire
37 Suffolk
38 Surrey
39 East Sussex
40 West Sussex
41 Tyne and Wear and Northumberland
42 Warwickshire
43 Worcestershire
44 Wiltshire and Swindon
45 East Yorkshire and Northern Lincolnshire
46 North Yorkshire
47 South Yorkshire
48 West Yorkshire

How to order

The Philip's range of street atlases is available from good retailers or directly from the publisher by phoning 01903 828503